The Handbook of High-Performance Virtual Teams

A TOOLKIT FOR COLLABORATING ACROSS BOUNDARIES

Jill Nemiro
Michael Beyerlein
Lori Bradley
Susan Beyerlein
Editors

JOSSEY-BASS
A Wiley Imprint
www.josseybass.com

Published by Jossey-Bass
A Wiley Imprint
989 Market Street, San Francisco, CA 94103-1741—www.josseybass.com

Jossey-Bass books and products are available through most bookstores. To contact Jossey-Bass directly call our Customer Care Department within the U.S. at 800-956-7739, outside the U.S. at 317-572-3986, or fax 317-572-4002.

Jossey-Bass also publishes its books in a variety of electronic formats. Some content that appears in print may not be available in electronic books.

Library of Congress Cataloging-in-Publication Data

The handbook of high-performance virtual teams : a toolkit for collaborating across boundaries / Jill Nemiro . . . [et al.].
    p.   cm.
Includes bibliographical references and indexes.
    ISBN-13: 978-0-470-17642-9 (cloth)
        1. Virtual work teams—Management—Handbooks, manuals, etc.   2. Teams in the workplace—Management—Handbooks, manuals, etc.   3. Performance—Management—Handbooks, manuals, etc.   I. Nemiro, Jill E., 1954-   II. Title: High-performance virtual teams.
    HD66.H36   2008
    658.4'022—dc22

                                                                        2007028792

Printed in the United States of America

FIRST EDITION

HB Printing   10 9 8 7 6 5 4 3 2 1

CONTENTS

WEB ANCILLARIES

Readers are invited to review and download the supplementary Web materials for *The Handbook of High-Performance Virtual Teams: A Toolkit for Collaborating Across Boundaries.* These materials include a variety of assessment surveys, practical tools, and additional chapters and references to assist in developing high-performing virtual teams. Related items on the Web have been listed at the end of relevant chapters in the handbook.

The supplementary Web materials are available FREE on-line at www.wiley .com/go/virtualteamshandbook.

For information concerning the Instructor's Manual, which includes chapter summaries, discussion questions, relevant reading lists, and suggestions for writing assignments and class activities, go to www.wiley.com/college.

Thank you,
Jill Nemiro, Michael Beyerlein, Lori Bradley, and Susan Beyerlein, Editors

FIGURES, TABLES, AND EXHIBITS

FIGURES

TABLES

EXHIBITS

ACKNOWLEDGMENTS

The editors and the nearly fifty chapter authors of this handbook were a virtual team, with 100 percent of the collaborative process of authoring and editing this project being done virtually. As an editorial virtual team, we offer our sincere appreciation and thanks to all the authors who contributed chapters. Not only have they offered through their contributions valuable wisdom and expertise for those undertaking the challenges of working virtually, but they have also shown themselves to be successful virtual collaborators themselves.

No virtual endeavor can sustain itself without a constant guiding force. We acknowledge and thank our senior editor at Jossey-Bass, Kathe Sweeney, who has been that guiding force for us. It was Kathe's initial excitement about our project that propelled this handbook into reality. And at every step through its development, Kathe has offered us enthusiasm, patience, flexibility, knowledge of the marketplace, and a keen editorial eye. For that, we are most grateful. We also express thanks to Beverly Miller for her careful manuscript editing, and to all the members of the Jossey-Bass team who collaborated with us in the creation of this handbook. We also acknowledge a friend and colleague who provided a wealth of both theoretical and practical knowledge on virtual teams, Susan G. Cohen. Her research contributed immensely to the understanding of new ways of working. Her presence in this field is and will continue to be sorely missed.

Working virtually stretches the balance between work and personal lives. To that end, Jill Nemiro wishes to thank David Foster, who has been her unwavering support system, offering love and encouragement all along the way. She also wishes to acknowledge the source of her creative energy: Sara, Rachel, and Mikey. Jill would also like to acknowledge Rabbi Carole L. Meyers, who inspired and taught so many through her wisdom, selflessness, warmth, and keen sense about what is truly important in life. Rabbi Meyers was the quintessential collaborator.

Every team that Michael and Susan Beyerlein have worked with to write books and grant proposals has taught them something useful about virtual collaboration. In addition to their coeditors on this book, they acknowledge the following people they have worked with virtually: Sue Freedman, Craig McGee, Linda Moran, Jerry Klein, Laurie Broedling, Frances Kennedy, Steve Jones, Yue Lin, Marty Bink, Barbara McCombs, and Anne Rinn. Hundreds of hours of teleconferences with these people have provided an excellent learning environment. Many lessons have been shared at our Center for Collaborative Organizations conferences about team effectiveness, but it takes the experience of working in relationships with diverse, talented people on challenging projects across time zones to make the lessons three-dimensional.

Lori Bradley also wishes to extend her deepest love and gratitude to Roger Duke, whose unwavering support and encouragement during the writing of this book meant the world to her.

Finally, we, as the editors of this handbook, wish to thank one another for not only advancing our own understanding of virtual collaboration, but also for demonstrating that being colocated is not necessary to display true friendship. As a team, we bonded at a level above and beyond the tasks of creating this handbook. We leave this project with respect and admiration for one another.

THE EDITORS

Jill Nemiro is an associate professor in the Psychology and Sociology Department at California State Polytechnic University, Pomona, and an adjunct professor in the Human Resources Design Master's Program at Claremont Graduate University. Her research interests are in the areas of organizational and team creativity and the virtual workplace. She has published numerous articles and book chapters and presented papers and workshops at professional conferences on the topics of creativity and virtual teams. She authored *Creativity in Virtual Teams: Key Components of Success* (2004) and coedited *The Collaborative Work Systems Fieldbook: Strategies, Tools, and Techniques* (2003). Nemiro consults and offers workshops to organizations on creativity in virtual teams. She also consults in the areas of creativity training, instructional design, and program evaluation. For many years, she worked in the entertainment industry as a film and videotape editor, specializing in management training and corporate videos, children's television programs, and documentaries. Nemiro received her Ph.D. in organizational psychology from Claremont Graduate University.

Michael Beyerlein is head of the Department of Leadership and Supervision at Purdue University. Formerly, he was director of the Center for Collaborative Organizations and professor of industrial/organizational psychology at the University of North Texas. His research interests include all aspects of collaborative work systems, organization transformation, creativity and innovation, knowledge management, and the learning organization. He has been a member of the editorial boards for *TEAM Magazine, Team Performance Management Journal,* and *Quality Management Journal* and senior editor of the Elsevier annual series Advances in Interdisciplinary Studies of Work Teams and the Jossey-Bass/Pfeiffer Collaborative Work Systems series. He has authored or edited nineteen books, including *Guiding the Journey to Collaborative Work Systems: A Strategic Design Workbook* (2004) and *Collaborative Capital* (2005). He received his Ph.D. in industrial-organizational psychology from Colorado State University.

Lori Bradley, executive director of Organizational Effectiveness for Wyeth Pharmaceuticals, recently completed doctoral course work in industrial/organizational psychology at the University of North Texas. Her research and practice areas include collaborative systems and technology, virtual teams and facilitation, organizational learning and executive development, and strategic talent management. As a consultant, she has designed virtual facilitator training programs for an international banking company. Based on emerging best practices in virtual meeting, these training programs help companies strengthen collaboration and increase meeting effectiveness by preparing facilitators to conduct multisite international meetings by video- or teleconference using collaborative software and group support systems. Bradley has worked in the defense, aerospace, medical, banking, real estate, and information services industries and has thirteen years of experience in designing and facilitating training programs and working with cross-functional teams in the aviation industry. She is a member of the International Association of Facilitators, the Academy of Management, and the Society for Industrial and Organizational Psychology.

Susan Beyerlein is a research associate with the Center for Collaborative Organizations at the University of North Texas. From 1995 to 2005, she was an instructor of business and psychology at Our Lady of the Lake University in Irving, Texas. She also has served as a research scientist–project manager with the Center for Collaborative Organizations at the University of North Texas and has been a recipient of research grant awards from the Association for Quality and Participation, the National Science Foundation, and corporate donors. Since 1995, she has coedited the Elsevier/JAI Imprint annual book series Advances in Interdisciplinary Studies of Work Teams and has served as a reviewer for the *Academy of Management Review*. She has been an editor of the Jossey-Bass/Pfeiffer Collaborative Work Systems series since its inception. Beyerlein has published book reviews on contemporary business offerings in *Business and the Contemporary World*, and her work has also appeared in *Structural Equation Modeling: A Multidisciplinary Journal, Journal of Management Education, Empirical Studies of the Arts,* and *Multiple Linear Regression Viewpoints*. She is a member of the Academy of Management, Beta Gamma Sigma (the honor society for collegiate schools of business), and Phi Kappa Phi National Honor Society. She received her Ph.D. in organization theory and policy with a minor in educational research from the University of North Texas.

THE CONTRIBUTORS

Arie Baan has his own independent consultancy company that provides consultancy, facilitation, and training in the area of virtual teamworking competence and supports organizations in creating and maintaining effective working environments for their virtual teams. He has worked most of his career in a large multinational oil company, in information science research and information technology management positions. Supporting the rapid globalization in the 1990s from the IT management perspective, he became interested in the topics of virtual teamworking and distant collaboration that are enabled by IT and designed and delivered learning programs for supporting team competency development in this area. He received his Ph.D. in information science from Eindhoven University in the Netherlands.

Dennis Bowyer has been supporting teaming and virtual team development since 1997. Presently he is promoting team effectiveness in the areas of knowledge discovery, capture, and reuse at Pratt and Whitney Rocketdyne. His activities include the development of collaborative processes in information life cycle management and institutionalizing innovation. He recently earned a master's in knowledge management at California State University at Northridge and holds an Ed.D. from Pepperdine University in organizational leadership.

Emanuel Brady is vice president of information technology for Raytheon Company's Space and Airborne Systems (SAS) and a member of the SAS leadership team. Previously he was vice president of information technology for Raytheon's Electronic Systems business, leading the development and implementation of enterprise-wide information systems fully aligned with Electronic Systems' business strategies. Brady received an M.B.A. from the University of Southern California.

David Braga is a program manager at the Boeing Company in charge of a multibillion-dollar fleet modernization project of a U.S. Air Force military transport, the C-17. In 1986, he joined Boeing and has held a variety of engineering management positions in both the military and commercial aircraft divisions. He is a frequent conference speaker on the subject of knowledge networks and global leadership. He received a doctorate in education, specializing in organizational leadership, from Pepperdine University.

Mal Conway is an IBM-certified business transformation managing consultant with IBM Global Business Services Public Sector Human Capital Management practice. His organization development specialization expertise is in improving and measuring organizational, team, and individual performance to achieve business results. He has worked with clients in both the public and private sectors.

Paul J. Erickson is a consultant with Downey Kates Associates, an organization design and development consulting firm in New York City. He works with organizations and leadership teams to help them assess their organizational capabilities, evaluate options, and improve effectiveness. A skilled writer, researcher, and course designer, he assists clients in distilling complex data into clear messages and actionable programs. In addition to management consulting, Erickson is an editor and consultant in the field of academic publishing, with a focus on the humanities and social sciences, particularly the field of international relations.

He is the editor of *Connections,* a journal published by the Partnership for Peace Consortium of Defense Academies.

Mehran Ferdowsian is the founder and general manager of Nur Management Solutions consulting firm. He has over twenty-four years of work experience at the national and international levels in engineering, manufacturing, and R&D communities and the development and implementation of programs dealing with people and effective business operations. He has worked for a Fortune 100 company, owned and managed a small business, and taught a number of business and engineering courses. He has led teams in developing mission-critical computer systems and value-added people programs in the areas of organization, workforce development, and business operations. He holds a doctoral degree in management and organizational leadership from the University of Phoenix.

Scott K. Filgo is senior research analyst for Harcourt Assessment's Talent Assessment team, pursuing product development projects, client-services research, and technical documentation. During the drafting of this chapter, he was the senior research associate for Profiles International. He was granted a master's of educational psychology (I/O concentration) by the University of Central Texas.

Kimball Fisher is the cofounder of the Fisher Group, a training and consulting firm that specializes in developing effective teams and leaders. Prior to becoming a consultant, he worked as a manager and staff specialist at Procter and Gamble and Tektronix. He is the author of *The Distance Manager: A Hands-On Guide to Managing Off-Site Employees and Virtual Teams* (with Mareen Fisher), *Leading Self-Directed Work Teams: A Guide to Developing New Team Leadership Skills, The Distributed Mind: Achieving High Performance Through the Collective Intelligence of Knowledge Work Teams* (with Mareen Fisher), and *Tips for Teams* (with others). He was the first recipient of the prestigious William G. Dyer Award for contributions to the field of organizational behavior. Fisher has a master's degree in organizational behavior from Brigham Young University.

Chris Francovich is an assistant professor in Gonzaga University's doctoral program in leadership studies and a senior research analyst for the Northwest Regional Faculty Development Center in Boise, Idaho. This work focuses postgraduate medical education in ambulatory medical clinics. His research group is working to identify and understand operational subcultures and the reciprocal effects of the clinic environment and the teaching mission on patient care. He also works with the Reina Trust Building Institute, which is devoted to building and sustaining trust in the workplace. His work has involved the design and management of Web-based technology to facilitate the development of trust in distributed teams. Francovich has an Ed.D. in curriculum and instruction from Boise State University. His specialty area is postgraduate medical education.

Sue Freedman is president and founder of Knowledge Work Global, a consulting firm specializing in the design and management of technology-based organizations, and adjunct professor at the University of Texas at Dallas, teaching in both the Executive Education Project Management Program and regular M.B.A. program. She is also codeveloper, with Lothar Katz, of the Managing Projects Across Borders Program. She has worked with a host of organizations, including Hitachi Data Systems, the 7–11 Corporation, AmeriCredit Corporation, AMR Services, American Airlines, and Lockheed Martin. Previously she was the manager of organizational effectiveness at Texas Instruments, serving the Defense Group and at the corporate level. She is coauthor of *Beyond Teams: Building the Collaboration Organization*. She is treasurer of the Dallas-Fort Worth Product Development Management Association and an active member of the University of North Texas Virtual Collaboration Research Group. She holds a Ph.D. in instructional design and personnel development from Florida State University.

Dipti Gupta is nearing completion of her doctoral program in industrial/ organizational psychology at the University of North Texas, Denton. She has been involved with various projects at the Center of Collaborative Organizations, including needs assessment, return on team investment, training and development, and facilitation. She is serving as the industrial/organizational Ph.D. intern at the BNSF Railway Company. She is heavily involved among other projects with moving the company from paper-and-pencil to online testing. Her research and practice areas include virtual collaboration, selection and assessment, online testing, and leadership development. She is a member of the Society for Industrial and Organizational Psychology and Dallas Area Industrial and Organizational Psychologists.

Laura A. Hambley is in the process of setting up a consulting company focusing on virtual leadership and teamwork. She has over seven years of experience providing organizational consulting to public and private organizations in Calgary, as well as internationally. Her work has included leadership development and selection assessments, team building, career planning, training, competency modeling, and organization surveys and studies. Her research focuses on virtual leadership and teamwork and telework. She is interested in how virtual leaders can more effectively lead teams through different communication media. Her publications include chapters in the forthcoming *Growing the Virtual Workplace: An Integrative Approach,* as well as forthcoming research papers in two journals: *Organizational Behavior and Human Decision Processes* and the *International Journal of e-Collaboration*'s special issue on virtual team leadership. She received her Ph.D. in industrial/organizational psychology from the University of Calgary.

Scott Hamilton is the senior vice president and director of research and development for Profiles International. He supervises a team of professional employees and consultants while coordinating research and development for the company to serve business, industry, government, and nonprofit organizations. He received his Ph.D. from the University of North Texas.

Gail Goodrich Harwood is a senior consultant affiliated with the Continuous Learning Group, specializing in organization design, large-scale change, and leadership strategies for high performance. She has supported performance and change efforts for a major food company and a major pharmaceutical firm. She also has extensive experience as an internal consultant at United Airlines, where she was manager of organizational development and lead consultant on a number of change, organization design, and start-up initiatives. She is listed in *Who's Who of American Women* and has served on the board of the Organization Design Forum (ODF), has cochaired the ODF global conference, and has presented at Organizational Design Forum, Organization Development Network, and Ecology of Work conferences. She received an M.B.A. from the University of Chicago and the certificate in organization design from the University of Southern California's Center for Effective Organizations.

Scott Hines is a research associate at Profiles International, where he conducts statistical projects for product development and develops white papers for products and services. He received his M.S. from Stephen F. Austin State University.

Gina Hinrichs is president of Hinrichs Consulting, an organizational development consulting firm. She works with organizations by applying strength-focused whole system approaches to continuously improve and deal with transformational change. Her focus has been working with leadership on strategic planning and translating it into global operations. This has involved extensive facilitation of face-to-face and virtual teams. Her clients include John Deere, Navistar—International Truck, Medical Associates Clinics, Schneider International, U.S. Cellular, and numerous social profit organizations. She is an adjunct professor for Capella University and Benedictine University, teaching organizational behavior and development courses. She earned a doctorate in organizational development from Benedictine University and an M.B.A. from the Kellogg School of Management at Northwestern University.

Trina Hoefling founder of GroupOne Solutions, LLC, is an organizational psychologist, executive coach, and business development consultant with over twenty-five years of experience in organization development, management consulting, coaching, and training. Her primary consulting work includes organizational assessments, organizational and team consulting, shadow consulting, individual coaching, implementation of virtual work initiatives and remote management, and speaking engagements. She has presented internationally on many subjects, including virtual work, creating and maintaining customers for life, developing bench strength, and virtual teaming. She is the author of *Working Virtually: Managing People for Successful Virtual Teams and Organizations*. She holds two M.A.s in industrial/organizational psychology and communication with a group and business emphasis.

Jack Jennings is an information technology (IT) operations manager with over twenty-five years of experience in technical and managerial roles within IT, including the last seventeen years at Sprint. Over the past eight years, he has led many virtual teams and extensively studied virtual teams. He is a member of the Virtual Collaboration Research Group Advisory Board and Collaborative Work Systems Consortium, associated with the Center for Collaborative Organizations at the University of North Texas.

Steve Jones is an associate professor at Middle Tennessee State University. He has twenty-five years of experience consulting in organizations as diverse as manufacturing plants, health care facilities, retail outlets, insurance companies, military installations, and universities. His areas of experience include team building, problem solving, business strategy development, training, performance measurement, and incentive plan design. He has published three books on work teams and speaks at national and international conferences. He holds a Ph.D. from the University of Houston in industrial/organizational psychology.

Anita Kamouri is a principal and cofounder of Iometrics, which provides consulting services that support organizational effectiveness through the design, implementation, and evaluation of work environments for mobile and distributed workforces. She brings over twenty years of consulting experience with Fortune 500 companies. Kamouri has assisted clients with global work environment initiatives using strategic decision frameworks, data-based planning, comprehensive employee profiling, measurement programs, and research evaluating the business-related impact of alternative workplace arrangements. Prior to joining Iometrics, Kamouri was managing principal at HRStrategies (now Aon Consulting). She was the practice leader in human resource outsourcing services and opened the firm's west coast office. She received her Ph.D. in industrial/organizational psychology from Bowling Green State University.

Amy Kates is a principal partner with Downey Kates Associates, an organization design and development consulting firm in New York City. She works with leaders and their teams around the world to assess organizational issues, reshape structures and processes, and build depth of management capability. Kates is coauthor, with Jay Galbraith, of the book *Designing Your Organization* (2007), and, with Jay Galbraith and Diane Downey, of *Designing Dynamic Organizations: A Hands-On Guide for Leaders at All Levels* (2002). Her article on *(Re)Designing the Human Resource Function* (2006) was awarded the Walker Prize by the Human Resource Planning Society.

Stan Lapidos is the manager of the Virtual Integrated Practice Project (VIP) at Rush University Medical Center in Chicago. He has authored or coauthored four articles on the project and has presented on the VIP model of team care at several national conferences and at academic and health care organizations in the United Kingdom and Israel. In addition, he is co-investigator and project coordinator for several other interdisciplinary team projects at Rush. He is a faculty member at Rush University and an adjunct faculty member at the Loyola University Chicago School of Social Work. Lapidos received a master's degree in aging and long-term care from the Center for Studies in Aging at the University of North Texas.

Rhys J. Lewis is completing the Ph.D. at the University of Western Ontario. Lewis is funded through a doctoral grant from the Social Sciences and Humanities Research Council and is conducting research on fairness in hiring decisions and performance evaluation.

Jessica Lipnack is CEO and cofounder of NetAge, www.netage.com, a consultancy based in Boston, Massachusetts. She is coauthor with Jeffrey Stamps of six books, including *Networking* (Doubleday), *The TeamNet Factor, The Age of the Network,* and *Virtual Teams* (all John Wiley & Sons), and many articles and book chapters. Their books have been translated around the world. An early online networker, Jessica maintains Endless Knots, www.netage.com/endlessknots, an active blog, and tends an informal global network of people interested in virtual teams, networks, and collaboration. A yoga practitioner and knitter, she also writes novels, short stories, and essays.

Dina M. Mansour-Cole is an associate professor of organizational leadership and supervision at Indiana University Purdue University Fort Wayne (IPFW). She has several publications in the areas of leadership, change, and team development. Her service to leadership and team development has been recognized locally for her outreach program, GLO: Girls Leading Others, a summer camp for middle school girls, and nationally, by the Girl Scouts of the United States of America. Her teaching innovations and course designs have been recognized by the Indiana University Faculty Colloquium on Excellence in Teaching, and she is currently a teaching fellow at IPFW. She received her Ph.D. in management of organizations from the University of Cincinnati.

Charles C. Manz is the Nirenberg Chaired Professor of Leadership in the Isenberg School of Management at the University of Massachusetts. Formerly a Marvin Bower Fellow at the Harvard Business School, he is a speaker, consultant, and best-selling author of over two hundred articles and scholarly papers and twenty books, including *Mastering Self-Leadership* (4th ed.); *Fit to Lead; The New Super-Leadership; The Power of Failure; Foreword* magazine best-book-of-the-year and Gold Award winner *Emotional Discipline;* and Stybel-Peabody National Book Prize-winning *SuperLeadership*. His clients have included 3M, Ford, Xerox, General Motors, Procter & Gamble, American Express, the Mayo Clinic, Banc One, the U.S. and Canadian governments, and many others. He received his Ph.D. from The Pennsylvania State University.

Martha Maznevski is professor of organizational behavior and international management at the International Institute for Management Development (IMD) in Lausanne, Switzerland. She is codirector of IMD's flagship Program for Executive Development and the new Strategic Leadership for Women program, as well as many company programs. Her research focuses on the dynamics of high-performing teams and networks in multinational organizations and managing people in global complexity. She teaches on topics spanning a broad range of organizational behavior topics, and she has presented and published widely on these subjects. She is the author of *The Blackwell Handbook of Global Management: A Guide to Managing Complexity* and a coauthor of a popular textbook, *International Management Behavior,* currently preparing the sixth edition. She has served as a consultant and advisor to public and private organizations in North America, Europe, and Asia on issues of managing people globally. She received her Ph.D. in organizational behavior from the University of Western Ontario.

Jodi Heintz Obradovich is a cognitive systems engineer at Intel Corporation, where she works in the User Centered Design Group. Her work includes understanding nurses' and physicians' work flow in acute health care settings, as well as exploring the challenges that virtual teams located around the world encounter as they try to collaborate with one another and coordinate their work. Her research interests include understanding how human and team cognition contributes to success and failure in complex, high-risk systems. She has explored collaborative virtual work as it occurs in the aviation domain between Federal Aviation Administration traffic managers and airline dispatchers, as well as in the U.S. Army between commanders and subordinates. She received her Ph.D. in industrial and systems engineering from the Ohio State University.

Jude G. Olson is a senior analyst in organization and leadership development with Lockheed Martin Aeronautics Company, where she consults on culture change and coaches high-potential executives. She has also taught at Texas Christian University and the University of Texas at Dallas. She presented at the 2003 Academy of Management on "Complex Collaboration: Building the Capabilities for Working Across Boundaries." Her publications include a chapter in *Complex Collaboration* (edited by Michael Beyerlein, Doug Johnson, and Susan Beyerlein) and an article on appreciative inquiry in *OD Practitioner Journal* (January 2005). She received a Ph.D. in human and organizational systems from Fielding Graduate University.

Thomas A. O'Neill is a Ph.D. candidate at the University of Western Ontario, Canada, where he is studying industrial/organizational psychology. His primary research focus is on using personality to predict team performance. In addition, he is exploring personality-based selection tools for colocated and virtual team members, as well as for teleworking arrangements. He has published several papers on virtual teamwork and leadership and has presented research at numerous conferences, including Interdisciplinary Network for Group Research, Academy of Management, Society for Industrial and Organizational Psychology, Canadian Psychological Association, and Administrative Sciences Association of Canada.

Kara L. Orvis is team leader for the leadership and collaboration consulting group at Aptima, with expertise in the areas of team leadership, dispersed team collaboration, dispersed leadership, and training technologies. Previously she worked as a postdoctoral research fellow for the Consortium of Universities at the Army Research Institute, where she conducted research projects involving teams, leadership, and training technologies. She has also worked as an independent consultant, helping organizations overcome cultural barriers in international training, and she taught at George Mason University. Orvis has coauthored or authored more than forty presentations and publications and is editing a book on the instructor's role in computer-supported collaborative learning environments. She is a member of the American Psychological Association, the Academy of Management, and the Society for Industrial and Organizational Psychology. She received her Ph.D. in industrial-organizational psychology from George Mason University.

Linda M. L. Peters is the Dean's Assistant Professor/Lecturer in the Isenberg School of Management at the University of Massachusetts. Following a career as a partner and executive in a national real estate investment firm, she has spent the past few years teaching several courses and literally hundreds of virtual students in the online Professional Masters in Business Administration program. Her primary research interest focuses on virtual teamwork, and she has published articles and made presentations at national and international conferences on the topic. She serves on several boards and advising committees, including the Entrepreneurship Initiatives, a college award program for young entrepreneurs sponsored by a charitable foundation, the Law and Business Center for Advancing Entrepreneurship at Western New England College, and the Innovator's Roundtable at Bay Path College. She received her Ph.D. from the University of Massachusetts Amherst.

Curt Raschke has over twenty-five years of experience in managing new product development projects for several high-technology companies in the Dallas/Fort

Worth area, most recently adapting new product development best practices to the global team environment. He has been active in various new product development professional associations and teaches a course on effective product life cycle management at the School of Management of the University of Texas at Dallas. He has spoken at conferences on portfolio and pipeline management and on managing codevelopment projects. He received his Ph.D. from Cornell University.

Michelle Reina and **Dennis Reina** cofounded the Reina Trust Building Institute, whose construct is an outgrowth of fifteen years of research and practice integrating trust-building behaviors into strategic organizational initiatives to achieve sustainable trust. Their work is supporting organizations such as American Express, Boeing, Children's Hospital, Dartmouth-Hitchcock Medical Center, Johnson & Johnson, Kimberly-Clark, Nokia, Harvard and Yale universities, U.S. Treasury, U.S. Army Corps of Engineers, U.S. Army Chaplaincy, and Walt Disney World and has been widely reported. They are the coauthors of *Trust and Betrayal in the Workplace: Building Effective Relationships in Your Organization* (2nd ed.). Both Michelle and Dennis Reina earned their Ph.D.s in human and organizational systems from the Fielding Graduate University.

Eric Richert is principal of 8 Corners Consulting, a consulting practice focused on the support of knowledge-based work. Previously he held a wide variety of management positions during eighteen years at Sun Microsystems, where in 1997 he cofounded and was vice president of Sun's Open Work Solutions Group. While at Sun, he also advised the European Commission on supporting collaborative work environments and provided testimony to the U.S. Congress on the support of contemporary workforces. Richert holds an M.B.A. from the University of California at Berkeley and a master of architecture degree from Syracuse University.

Steven K. Rothschild is an associate professor in the Departments of Family Medicine and Preventive Medicine at Rush University Medical Center in Chicago, where he is also the director of the Section of Community and Social Medicine. His academic activity is informed by his clinical practice at Rush University Family Physicians, which he established in 1988 and continues to serve as medical director. His research focuses on chronic disease management, with particular attention to reducing health disparities affecting minority groups and the medically underserved. He is the principal investigator for the Virtual Integrated Practice Project, as well as the Mexican-American Trial of Community Health Workers funded by the National Institutes of Health. He received his M.D. from the University of Michigan.

Jane Seiling is a writer, adjunct professor, and editor for the Taos Institute Publications Focus Book Series on social constructionism. She is the author of an award-winning book, *The Membership Organization: Achieving Top Performance in the New Workplace Community; The Meaning and Role of Organizational Advocacy: Responsibility and Accountability in the Workplace;* and coeditor of *Appreciative Inquiry and Organizational Transformation: Reports from the Field.* Her current writing project is a book, *Constructive Accountability: Moving Accountability into the Work of Working.* Most of her organizational consulting work is in South Africa in organizations struggling with dealing with their changing world. Her interests are in accountability, absorptive capability, combination capability, the psychology of working, and social constructionism. She received her Ph.D. in social science (managerial psychology) from the University of Tilburg, Netherlands.

Philip J. Smith is executive director of the Institute for Ergonomics at The Ohio State University and a professor in the industrial and systems engineering program. He teaches courses in cognitive systems engineering, artificial intelligence, human-computer interaction and the design of cooperative problem-solving systems, intelligent information retrieval systems, and intelligent tutoring systems. He has completed extensive research focusing on distributed work in air traffic management and military planning systems. Among other contributions, this research has led to the development of the Post-Operations Evaluation Tool, which is one of the major systems in use to evaluate performance in the National Airspace System, providing operational staff and analysts with access to graphical displays and data mining tools to evaluate performance. He received his Ph.D. from the University of Michigan.

Jeffrey Stamps is cofounder of NetAge, www.netage.com, a consultancy based in Boston, Massachusetts. He is coauthor with Jessica Lipnack of six books, including *Networking, The TeamNet Factor, The Age of the Network,* and *Virtual Teams,* and many articles and book chapters. He is also author of *Holonomy* and designer of complex processes and technologies for some of the world's largest enterprises. A competitive Alpine skier and a Fulbright scholar to Oxford, he rides his BMW motorcycle whenever he can. He received his Ph.D. from the Saybrook Institute.

Jackie Stavros is professor at Lawrence Technological University and editor for Taos Institute Publications. She coauthored *Dynamic Relationships: Unleashing the Power of Appreciative Inquiry in Daily Living* (2005) and *Appreciative Inquiry Handbook* (2003). She recently completed a book chapter for *The Change Handbook* (2007). Her clients include BAE Systems, ERIM International, Jefferson Wells, Tendercare, General Motors of Mexico, Girl Scouts USA, PriceWaterhouseCoopers' Advisory University, and many educational institutions and tier 1 and tier 2 automotive suppliers. She earned a doctorate in management at Case Western Reserve University and an M.B.A. in international business from Michigan State University.

Marilyn Sawyer Wesner is assistant professor of human and organizational learning at George Washington University in Washington, D.C. She is the director of the master's degree program in human resource development and teaches courses in organizational behavior, organizational diagnosis, and virtual teams.

Her continuing interest in team building, organizational effectiveness, and virtual work began at AT&T where, prior to joining GWU in 1999, she was the information services director in Basking Ridge, New Jersey. She holds an Ed.D. in adult and continuing education from Virginia Tech.

Mary B. Witort is a senior consultant with Verizon Business, a leading provider of advanced communications and information technology solutions. Her primary responsibilities are project development and management of sales campaigns for some of the company's newest products. During her more than twenty years in the telecommunications industry, she has developed and provided leadership and management expertise in engineering, product development, sales, and operations management. She has taught classes on project management for her employers and offered seminars to graduate students. She is a certified project manager and member of Project Management International (PMI), currently serving on the Dallas PMI Chapter's Education Committee. She earned her M.S. from the University of Texas, Dallas.

Terence Yeoh is a doctoral student in the industrial/organizational psychology program at the University of North Texas. His research interest areas focus on employee-related issues such as job attitudes, employee socialization, and turnover, as well as training and performance management issues. He is participating in research aimed at creating a new method of measurement for job satisfaction.

Stephen J. Zaccaro is a professor of psychology at George Mason University, Fairfax, Virginia. He has been studying, writing, teaching, and consulting about teams and leadership for over twenty-five years. He has directed funded research projects in the areas of team performance, shared mental models, leader-team interfaces, leadership training and development, leader adaptability, and executive leadership. He has written over a hundred articles, book chapters, and technical reports on group dynamics, team performance, leadership, and work attitudes. He is the author of *The Nature of Executive Leadership: A Conceptual and Empirical Analysis of Success* and coeditor of *Occupational Stress and Organizational Effectiveness, The Nature of Organizational Leadership: Understanding the Performance Imperatives Confronting Today's Leaders,* and *Leader Development for Transforming Organizations.* He received his Ph.D. from the University of Connecticut.

Jill Nemiro dedicates this book to the team members she collaborates with and loves daily: her daughters, Sara and Rachel.

Michael and Susan Beyerlein dedicate this book to the main source of their current joy and their most direct tie to the future: their daughter, Marisa.

For the opportunities that their love and support have made possible, Lori Bradley dedicates this book to her mother and father, Jeannie and Eddie Bradley.

The Challenges of Virtual Teaming

Jill Nemiro, Lori Bradley, Michael Beyerlein,
Susan Beyerlein

Collaboration, defined as "the collective work of two or more individuals where the work is undertaken with a sense of shared purpose and direction that is attentive, responsive, and adaptive to the environment" (Beyerlein & Harris, 2004, p. 18), is a robust tool for getting things done, creating change, and extending resources to their furthest imaginable limits. More and more, organizations are relying on collaborative work to integrate and align their human resources, better tap into the external environment, adapt a flexible stance, and ultimately achieve a competitive advantage in the fast-paced global marketplace.

We are witnessing a conscious transformation of the structures, values, and business practices that drive contemporary organizations to encourage and support collaboration on many levels. A *collaborative organization* supports both informal and formal forms of collaboration, uses teams to accomplish work when needed, and is designed to support collaboration. Broader still is what has been referred to as a *collaborative work system* (CWS), defined as systems "in which a conscious effort has been made to create structures and institutionalize values and practices that enable individuals and groups to effectively work together to achieve strategic goals and business results" (Beyerlein, McGee, Klein, Nemiro, & Broedling, 2003, p. 1). A CWS may range from a colocated team to a global, multiorganizational strategic alliance. Collaboration knows no boundaries. The terrain of the contemporary workplace is now characterized by independent knowledge workers who are collaborating together across the globe. Indeed, one of the major challenges facing organizations is how to connect these knowledge workers, regardless of distance, time zone, or national culture, to form temporary or permanent business alliances, formalized virtual corporations or virtual teams, or more informal virtual working relationships and knowledge exchange systems such as virtual communities.

By using a myriad of new technologies, companies have found ways for people to work together on essential tasks while staying put. Knowledge of virtual communication tools like e-mail, online chat, instant messaging, and Web conferencing is quickly becoming necessary for workers. Thus, the very meaning of collaboration has been extended, and such efforts are referred to as *virtual collaboration*. Virtual collaboration is about achieving the organization's desired results by focusing on goals and actions that could not be accomplished by working alone. Virtual collaboration occurs when people who are not colocated use communication technologies to work together and facilitate getting the job done. In sum, virtual collaboration is the process through which virtual teams get work done.

Like any conventional team, a virtual team consists of a group of people who interact to complete interdependent tasks and work toward a common goal. But instead of meeting in the same office, the team members work in different places, often at home, and in different time zones. They may never meet their coworkers face-to-face. Virtual teams are typically project- or task-focused groups. Team membership may be relatively stable (such as an established sales team) or may change on a regular basis (such as a project team). Members may be drawn from the same organization or several different organizations (for example, projects that involve external consultants or evaluators or strategic business pursuits sought by partnering organizations). Further distinctions can be made concerning physical proximity (whether the team members are colocated) and by work cycle synchronicity (whether the team members are in the same time zones).

In a virtual team, the task itself usually provides the initial motivation to work together across time and space. However, in order to keep working together successfully, more is often needed. A virtual team is more than a collection of individuals working in isolation. Virtual team members depend on one another to fulfill a common goal. As such, they need to be connected on both a task and interpersonal level (Nemiro, 2004) because challenges in working virtually emerge in both domains. Task-related demands such as the planning and scheduling of work need to be balanced against interpersonal aspects such as a shared social context, expressions of trust, and a genuinely human interest in one another in order to maximize the overall performance of the team. Virtual teams often tend to evolve incrementally over time rather than spring into existence intentionally and fully formed. However, whether one consciously chooses to be part of a virtual team or finds oneself joining in a more informal way, the team is likely to exist for one or more of the following purposes:

- To engage individuals on the team with the best skills and expertise for the work, regardless of where those individuals are physically located

- To ensure twenty-four-hour coverage on a service, problem, or task by team members working across time zones

- To reduce office overhead by having team members work from home

- To adapt an as-needed approach to scheduling human resources in order to save time or money, or both

Working on a virtual team may sound simple enough until one realizes that geographically dispersed members wholly dependent on technology make true collaboration, a difficult undertaking in any circumstance, all the more challenging. Many progressive companies have provided their workers with the technological capabilities to collaborate virtually, but they may not be aware of the training and support needed in areas such as decision making, communication skills, cultural awareness, and virtual meeting facilitation. Many have touted the upsurge of collaborative technologies that have made virtual collaboration possible around the globe—and with good reason: the business results of virtual collaboration can be dramatic. However, before face-to-face interpersonal interaction is abandoned altogether, it is crucial to consider the challenges in setting up and sustaining effective virtual teams. For every virtual team success story, there are doubtless other stories that convey feelings of discomfort or dissatisfaction and the belief that "this would have taken us half the time and turned out better if we had been together in the same room, face-to-face."

For over a decade, practitioners and academics alike have struggled with the realities of virtual teaming. O'Hara-Devereaux and Johansen's book, *Global Work* (1994), outlines the problems facing organizations that need to bridge distance, culture, and time in accomplishing their work and provides a set of "third-way strategies" to assist with these new challenges. Many others since then have offered suggestions and answers for those who work virtually (for example, Duarte & Snyder, 1999; Lipnack & Stamps, 2000; Gibson & Cohen, 2003; Mankin & Cohen, 2003; Nemiro, 2004; Jones, Oyung, & Pace, 2005; Garton & Wegryn, 2006).

From the work of these authors, six major challenges of virtual teams have been identified: distance, time, technology, culture, trust, and leadership. The first three—distance, time, and technology—are defining characteristics or givens of virtual teams. Distance and time represent discrete (measurable), bounded conditions that are dissolved through technology. The last three—culture, trust, and leadership—are created and sustained by the virtual team itself. Culture or cultural differences may impede or propel forward virtual team success and occur at many levels concurrently (such as nationally, at corporate headquarters, and within dispersed units of a particular organization). Trust and leadership, and their more negative derivatives, are present or absent in varying degrees and forms (for example, distrust) in brick-and-mortar and virtual organizations alike and can be considered dynamic, organizational, cultural realities. In virtual teams, distance, time, and technology are necessary but not sufficient for high performance. An awareness of cultural differences and potential connections among members, as well as commitment to development over time of member trust and leadership capability, are the real building blocks to high-performance virtual teams.

This handbook addresses the six challenges inherent in working virtually and provides practical strategies for leveraging the givens (distance, time, technology), through effective development of cultural and interpersonal competencies (culture, trust, leadership), to move toward the resulting promise of high-performance virtual teams. Figure I.1 presents a graphical representation of the path outlined to high-performance virtual teams.

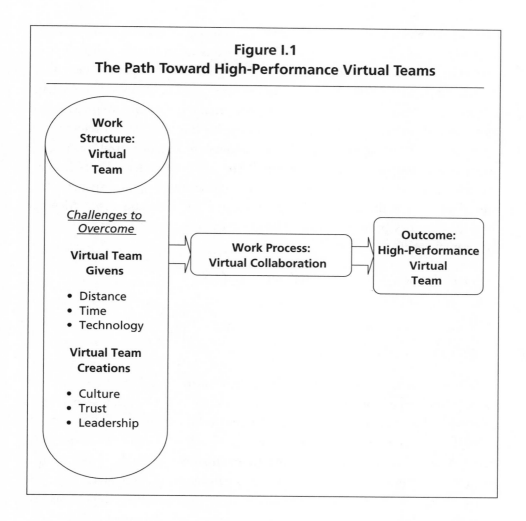

Figure I.1
The Path Toward High-Performance Virtual Teams

Work Structure: Virtual Team

Challenges to Overcome

Virtual Team Givens

- Distance
- Time
- Technology

Virtual Team Creations

- Culture
- Trust
- Leadership

Work Process: Virtual Collaboration

Outcome: High-Performance Virtual Team

ISSUES SURROUNDING THE SIX CHALLENGES

This section addresses some of the current issues surrounding each of the six challenges for virtual teaming.

Distance

Distance represents a challenge for virtual teams because it imposes limits on the face-to-face interaction that is important in building trust, monitoring performance, inspiring teamwork, maintaining cultural norms, and understanding cultural differences. That virtual teams do not share physical work space as traditional colocated teams do creates both obvious and subtle challenges. One of the main challenges is organization and team identification. Wiesenfeld, Raghuram, and Garud (1998) point out that over most of the past century, large corporations created mass production systems that required the congregation of employees at central places of work. Member identification, which refers to the strength of an individual's cognitive attachment to the organization, is constructed and supported by cues that pull employees together. These elements include shared language, dress code, organizational norms, and organizational identifiers such as the office building, coworkers, and company logos. Member identification has been linked to employees' feelings of trust characterized by (Wiesenfeld et al., 1998):

- Internalization of organizational norms and practices
- Desire to remain with the organization
- Willingness to cooperate with others
- Willingness to share knowledge

Information technology and the use of virtual teams enable a decentralization of work and make it possible for employees in some jobs to work together while being spatially and temporally separated. However, according to Wiesenfeld et al. (1998), this freedom to work any time and anywhere may also weaken the bond between organizational members and their employer, possibly resulting in a reduction in employee commitment to the organization and job satisfaction.

Nevertheless, some virtual teams have been able to achieve high levels of interpersonal bonding. This personal connection among team members has been described as a family-like feeling that goes beyond common goals and commitment to the work, resulting in knowing and appreciating that team members are also committed to and care for one another. This connection can be strengthened through a variety of techniques, including face-to-face get-togethers, electronically sharing humorous stories or incidents, creating playful games to build and maintain team identity, taking the time to show personal interest in one another (by electronically passing along information they thought other team members might be interested in), sharing personal issues and crises with other team members, and functioning as a support network for one another (Nemiro, 2004).

Members of virtual teams are also susceptible to the perils of not having member identification with each other (Workman, 2001). It is much more challenging to build rapport, trust, group norms, and work protocols when not working in a face-to-face setting (Knoll, 2001). Communication is more of a challenge, and team members must be more diligent and disciplined about keeping in touch and sharing information with the rest of the team, since it does not happen automatically as it often does in shared physical space.

On an individual level, there is also a concern that an employee working off-site on his or her own may begin to feel isolated. This may result in a loss of productivity, lower organizational commitment, loneliness, and feelings of vulnerability as a result of feeling out of the loop, although research results are only beginning to confirm these assertions.

Time

Virtual teams are simultaneously more and less bound than traditional face-to-face teams by the restrictions of time. Time differences create advantages and disadvantages. It is extremely challenging to schedule meetings and coordinate a globally dispersed team. However, one advantage of time differences is that a twenty-four-hour workday may be created as members of the team hand work off at the end of their day to members located around the globe who are just beginning their workday. In fact, teams can hand off work in progress literally around the clock among the three main economic centers—the United States, Europe, and Asia—which can shorten project time by having near around-the-clock progress (Kimble, Li, & Barlow, 2000).

For projects that require real-time collaboration, time differences can be problematic. As an example, consider a team made up of members from the United Kingdom and the Pacific Northwest in the United States. There is an eight-hour time difference between the two sites. In this example, just as the U.S. team members are arriving at work, the U.K. team members are wrapping up their workday. Therefore, in order to collaborate in a synchronous fashion, one group or the other must work outside normal work hours. Questions that require the other group's guidance may have to wait several hours to be answered. As a result, decisions may take longer to be made. The common solution to this problem is for the team to adopt a "call anytime" policy: every attempt is made not to contact a team member outside his or her working hours, but if an answer is vital to the project, contact at any time is allowed. This creates a twenty-four-hour workday in a different sense than was used earlier. In this version, an employee may struggle to maintain a good work/life balance where around-the-clock demands of work gradually erode the quality of both work and nonwork experience. Attitudes differ among cultures and individuals regarding work outside normal office hours and can create tension among members of a team. And even without drastic time differences, it can be difficult to coordinate schedules, tasks, and meeting times when a team is virtual.

Technology

The vast majority of virtual team communication is carried out with the assistance of technology, which creates its own set of challenges: employees must learn the technology before they can begin to use it for collaboration. Getting members comfortable with this type of interaction with coworkers can be difficult. There is also the additional challenge of getting team members up to needed skill levels in using communication technology, which includes both knowing how to operate the technology and also when it is appropriate to use different types of technology for different purposes. This is often referred to as matching technology and task (Wang, 2001).

Interorganizational virtual teams (virtual teams made up of members from different organizations) often have the added problem of incompatible technology platforms and communication tools. Technology incompatibilities can also contribute to trust and security issues that can arise on interorganizational teams (Rowe, 2001). These arrangements require team members to act outside their traditional comfort zones by trusting information to individuals who in other situations would be competitors.

Some, however, have suggested that collaborative technology enables both virtual team functioning and organizational learning: technology is less important than the techniques virtual teams have developed to interact, such as communication and group norms, appropriate virtual team leadership styles and structures, regularly scheduled meetings, and occasional face-to-face meetings (Gorelick, 2000).

Culture

The way a team functions is often directly related to the culture of the organization, but challenges in teams can also come about as a result of national cultural differences. For example, it has been shown that teams in the United States value the individual, whereas Japanese teams place more emphasis on the capabilities of a group as a whole (Hong, 1999). There may also be regional differences, generational differences, departmental or functional differences, and, in the case of interorganizational virtual teams, organizational differences. There may be differences in management styles across cultures and nations that affect members of the same virtual team in different ways. For example, a worker from one culture may find the management style of a team leader objectionable even though the members from other cultures are not bothered by the same behavior. Cultural differences increase with virtual work because more boundaries are crossed as a result of the team members' being embedded in different cultures. Adding to the complexity is the fact that the team creates its own additional culture, which can be deliberately developed to transcend the embedding problem.

Trust

Teamwork always depends on trust. When members are colocated, trust may be easier to develop because of the informal, spontaneous interactions that can occur between meetings to develop confidence in each other. Virtual teams depend on trust but find it more difficult to develop. Trust and identity, a basic familiarity with a person based on interaction or time spent together, are crucial elements for the effective formation and functioning of virtual teams. Identity plays a crucial role in communication because knowledge of those with whom one works and communicates is necessary for understanding and interpreting interaction styles. However, when people are separated by distance and time, identity tends to be ambiguous at best because many of the fundamental cues about personality and social roles are absent (Kimble et al., 2000). These cues are typically gained through experience, history, and face-to-face interaction with a person. Trust is based on knowing and being known by one another, and the absence of routine interaction, nonverbal indicators, and informal social time can result in a lack of trust and misperceptions that lead to less than successful project results (Creighton & Adams, 1998).

Trust may develop more slowly among virtual team members as compared to face-to-face team members. With less visual contact, it may simply take longer to identify and adjust to the habits, quirks, and skills of team members. Unfortunately, mistrust is likely, as employees from different locations, cultures, and technical backgrounds are likely to question how the information they offer will be used, whether their contribution will be recognized outside the team, and whether other team members will make an equal contribution to the work (Nemiro, 2004).

Teams possessing sufficient levels of trust can build strong relationships that make it possible to have disagreements over content or information and yet continue to work together successfully. When trust is absent, individuals are more prone to be tense and uncertain because the position they take may determine whether they are accepted by the group (Creighton & Adams, 1998). As a result, collaboration suffers.

Teams initially develop trust based on social communication (Kimble et al., 2000). Action-based trust emerges after the team has worked together for a while. Face-to-face meetings foster social-based trust, which can carry over into the electronic space. Once a team has started computer-mediated working, the role of action-based trust needs to be considered and maximized. Communication is a key element of trust. Regular and frequent communication fosters and sustains trust, while trust tends to deteriorate in relation to decreasing levels of communication (Alexander, 2000; Solomon, 2001). Trust is related to the frequency and quality of communication. Generally the more communication there is, the greater the trust (Jarvenpaa, Knoll, & Leidner, 1998; Nemiro, 2004). Teams that have high levels of trust among members tend not only to perform better but rate the working arrangement as a more positive and satisfying experience (Jarvenpaa et al., 1998).

Trust in virtual teams, while built slowly, can be developed from positive, ongoing experiences among members of the team; from members believing in the individual expertise of one another; and, perhaps most important, from a sense of accountability, that is, from seeing that others follow through on what they agree to do (Nemiro, 2004). This means that a key to virtual team success is members' keeping their commitments to each other and therefore making only commitments they can and will keep.

Leadership

Virtual team leaders operate in different conditions than leaders of traditional colocated teams. They are often called on to play both a team member and leader role simultaneously, and they may be part of more than one virtual team (Wilson, George, & Wellins, 1994), with a leadership role in one and a member role in another. When in the leader role, these virtual team leaders face special challenges: they need to ensure quality performance of team members and mentor and coach team members, all from afar. These new competencies include technological proficiency and appropriate use of technology, cross-cultural management skills, ability to coach distant team members, ability to build trust among dispersed team members, networking with others outside the team such as customers or other stakeholders, and remote project management skills.

Researchers have found that effective virtual team leaders need to perform multiple leadership roles simultaneously. Fisher and Fisher (2001) suggest that virtual team leaders need to assume six different roles, which are indicative of effective leadership in brick-and-mortar settings as well:

- *Living example:* Serve as a role model of effective virtual teaming
- *Coach:* Help team members develop their own potential and ensure accountability in others
- *Business analyzer:* Translate changes in the business environment into opportunities for the organization
- *Barrier buster:* Open doors and run interference for the team
- *Facilitator:* Bring together necessary tools, information, and resources for the team to get the job done
- *Results catalyst:* Help the team improve performance and achieve good results

Highly effective virtual team leaders are mentors and exhibit a high degree of understanding (empathy) toward their team members. At the same time, they are able to assert their authority without being perceived as overbearing or inflexible. Furthermore, they are adept at providing regular, detailed, and prompt communication with their peers and in articulating role relationships (responsibilities) among the virtual team members (Kayworth & Leidner, 2002).

Virtual team leaders do not control others; rather, they coach individuals in remote locations on how to control themselves (Fisher & Fisher, 2001). As a result, the leadership structures (different types of leadership forms) that they depend on may vary. Leadership structures that virtual teams use range from permanent leaders, to rotating leaders, to either a leaderless structure or one assisted by a facilitator or coordinator. Leadership structures may not remain constant throughout the team's life cycle (Nemiro, 2004). Virtual team leaders need to be able to function in all of these different types of structures.

ORGANIZATION OF THE HANDBOOK

In this chapter, we set forth six crucial challenges faced by those working in virtual teams and striving to get work done through the process of virtual collaboration: distance, time, technology, culture, trust, and leadership. To overcome these challenges, this handbook has been assembled to provide readers with an understanding of the principles necessary for establishing and designing successful and high-performing virtual teams. Those principles represent the content of Parts One through Six:

PRINCIPLES OF HIGH-PERFORMANCE VIRTUAL TEAMS

- Part One: Working Collaboratively
- Part Two: Building a Collaborative Culture
- Part Three: Leading Collaboratively

DESIGNING HIGH-PERFORMANCE VIRTUAL TEAMS

- Part Four: Setting Up a Collaborative Team
- Part Five: Working on a Collaborative Team
- Part Six: Tools and Assessments for Collaboration

Part Seven, Case Studies, offers real-world examples of high-performance virtual teams. Included in this part are four case stories of successful virtual teams and collaboration in health care, computing, banking, and aerospace. The practices, tools, processes, and strategies shared in these stories include patient care, business-focused decision making, matrix relationships, and knowledge transfer and learning systems.

Part Eight, Conclusion, offers one chapter that provides readers with a summary of the key principles from the book and another that prods readers into active thinking about the future of virtual teams and collaboration.

There are at least two ways to tackle reading the chapters in this book. The most obvious and comprehensive is to read through from start to finish in linear order. This method will give readers a thorough understanding of the requirements and ingredients necessary for high-performance virtual teams. The next section briefly describes the chapters. Another way to read this book that readers may find useful is to review specific chapters by the challenges of virtual teaming they discuss: distance, time, technology, leadership, culture, and trust. For that purpose, Table I.1 links the chapters to specific virtual team challenges.

SUMMARY OF CHAPTERS

Part One is concerned with the principles for working collaboratively in high-performance virtual teams. Certain enabling conditions build the context for excellence within virtual teams. Chapters One and Two outline key design conditions and principles for working collaboratively in virtual teams. In Chapter One, Michael Beyerlein, Jill Nemiro, and Susan Beyerlein address the issue of working across boundaries. Every virtual team crosses boundaries of time, location, and culture, and most have to cross multiple other boundaries to connect well enough for the open sharing of information that can generate new knowledge and effective decisions. The authors put forth five principles needed to manage boundaries successfully: (1) mapping out appropriate organizational and team structures and work processes for collaboration, (2) crafting a culture supportive of collaboration, (3) developing continuously evolving knowledge sharing and management systems, (4) defining new roles for leaders, and (5) ensuring alignment of support systems. Without conscious effort to develop and maintain these principles, team and organizational performance will remain mediocre.

In Chapter Two, Gail Goodrich Harwood offers nine principles for successful virtual team collaboration. These principles guide the reader in understanding how to (1) select and set up leaders for success, (2) establish a common vision among team members, (3) create the context for energy and understanding, (4) develop common operating principles and standards, (5) develop ways to document work processes, (6) establish clear boundaries around when autonomy is needed and when collaboration is needed, (7) set up goals and measures, (8) establish mechanisms for debriefing, problem solving, and celebration, and (9) create a plan to swing the net wider. The chapter concludes with a final design checklist, a valuable tool for readers who are beginning to design a virtual team.

Virtual teams do not exist in isolation; they are embedded in a context and culture that can or cannot be supportive of collaboration and high performance. In Part Two, Chapters Three to Six deal with how to build a collaborative culture in virtual teams. For Trina Hoefling, the path to prepare for virtual work includes

Table I.1

Handbook Chapters Relating to Each Virtual Team Challenge

	1	2	3	4	5	6	7	8	9	10	11	12	13	14	15	16	17	18	19	20	21	22	23	24	25	26	27	28
Distance	X	X								X						X									X			X
Time	X													X					X						X			X
Technology											X		X	X					X			X			X			
Leadership	X	X					X	X	X			X						X		X			X	X		X	X	
Culture	X			X	X								X	X		X					X		X				X	X
Trust			X	X	X	X				X		X			X		X	X	X		X		X					X

the development of what she refers to in Chapter Three as emotional bandwidth or emotional connection needed between virtual team members. Hoefling lays out three paths that lead to an increase in emotional bandwidth: creating a cohesive team culture, supporting the team community, and producing successful outcomes. Useful discussion questions are provided to help virtual teams traverse each of these paths. Hoefling also outlines several processes that assist in the journey along each path: team development and planning, virtual team maintenance, perpetuating synergy, and dealing with the rolling and fluid membership of virtual teams.

In Chapter Four, Linda M. L. Peters and Charles C. Manz suggest three powerful ingredients for promoting a supportive culture for virtual teams: trust, shared understanding, and depth of relationships. Each of these (and the interactions between them as well) is explained in detail, with theoretical and real-life examples as support. The authors conclude with a list of specific actions and recommendations for building high levels of each of these ingredients into one's virtual team and organization.

Gina Hinrichs, Jane Seiling, and Jackie Stavros present in Chapter Five an innovative application of sensemaking theory (Weick, 1995) to virtual teams for the purpose of increasing the effectiveness of conversations and relationships in virtual teams, and therefore the decision outcomes that result. A practical tool based on sensemaking theory is also offered for virtual team use; it includes the five C's of conversations and relationships: clarity, connection, candor, co-creation, and commitment. Finally, the authors propose creating a new role within virtual teams, a sensemanager, to ensure effective application of the five C's within the team.

Trust is a key ingredient in preparing to work virtually. Chris Francovich, Michelle Reina, Dennis Reina, and Christopher Dilts clearly recognize and assert in Chapter Six that trust is an essential ingredient for virtual teams and collaboration. They note the lack of strategies or models that seek to systematically and measurably improve trust and trust-related behaviors within a virtual environment. Their chapter describes one such model, the Reina Trust and Betrayal Model, and details the authors' efforts and research on how trust is built and broken in relationships, teams, and organizations. The authors also describe an innovative tool they designed to build and support trust in virtual teams.

Leaders of virtual teams face unique challenges and require additional competencies beyond those needed by leaders of more traditional colocated teams. Part Three offers practical advice on how to lead collaboratively in virtual teams. In Chapter Seven, David Braga addresses the difficult question, "What types of leadership attributes are needed for leaders of virtual teams?" After an initial look at the history of leadership theory, Braga focuses on transformational leadership as an effective framework for leading virtual teams. A transformational leader is described as a holistic leader, more concerned with people than processes, whose focus is on raising the level of performance and behavior for both the leader and his or her followers. After a thorough review of the characteristics of transformational leaders, Braga details a case study on transformational leadership in virtual teams in a Fortune 500 company. He contrasts the characteristics of the ideal transformational virtual team leader and those of actual leaders in this case investigation.

Most leadership prescriptions for virtual teams have understandably looked at how to manage a myriad of complexities and boundary issues. Not well addressed is the fact that virtual teams are subject to many changes as well. As our knowledge of virtual collaboration and teaming matures, there is a clear need to prepare leaders for uncertain situations that call for a change in roles, strategies, policies and procedures, technology, work processes, and plans. In Chapter Eight, Dina M. Mansour-Cole proposes a model that provides a framework for what leaders should attend to during change. Three broad categories are identified: taking action that is primarily focused on furthering the organization's interests, taking action to further other followers' needs or interests, and taking action to protect the individual leader's self-interests. The model provides explicit advice on when the attention should be given to each of these three areas and how to justify moving from one category to another.

Thomas A. O'Neill, Rhys J. Lewis, and Laura A. Hambley examine in Chapter Nine the major barriers virtual team leaders encounter in motivating, coordinating, and developing their teams. Along with each barrier is a list of suggestions to help virtual team leaders overcome these obstacles. Suggestions are categorized according to a team's life cycle: start-up, midpoints, and endings. Readers will be able to identify and take away specific strategies for leading their virtual teams from start-up to maturity through the entire team life cycle.

Starting any team endeavor has its own set of requirements, challenges, and resource needs, and virtual teams are no different. Becoming part of a virtual team requires preparation that goes beyond mastering technology. The chapters in Part Four offer strategies to set up a collaborative, virtual team.

In Chapter Ten, Kara L. Orvis and Stephen J. Zaccaro devote attention to an aspect of virtual teaming that has largely been ignored: team member selection and composition. They propose a team-staffing framework to support the selection of team members that considers the criticality of both expertise and teamwork. Four processes make up the framework: (1) identifying the mission and task requirements and skill markers, (2) selecting potential candidates for team members based on their status on task and team generic skill markers, (3) identifying the specific task work skills needed, and (4) determining the appropriate mix of team skills.

Emanuel Brady and Lori Bradley examine in Chapter Eleven the different needs of multigenerational members working together on a virtual team. Four generations exist in many companies today (legacy, baby boomer, Generation X, and Generation Y). The authors acknowledge that each of these generations is marked by the collaboration technologies of its day and, as a result, its own relative comfort zone with respect to technology. Brady and Bradley provide an overview of the most common types of technological adoption challenges as they relate to the generational makeup of the workforce and propose an approach for deployment planning that is informed in the light of generational differences and therefore useful to today's managers.

Chapter Twelve by Marilyn Sawyer Wesner outlines the types of needs assessment required to prepare for virtual teams and the types of questions to ask in completing these analyses. Wesner suggests a series of competencies that are necessary for those involved in virtual collaboration. Finally, she addresses general assumptions about adult learners, individual learning styles, and generational characteristics that may be important to consider and apply in virtual teaming and collaboration training.

In Chapter Thirteen, Jodi Heintz Obradovich and Philip J. Smith examine a series of design concepts that need to be addressed in setting up the work, technology use, and shared commitment necessary for effective virtual teams. These design concepts have emerged from the authors' examination of several case studies representing a variety of organizations and disciplines, including health care, aviation, and the military. The design concepts address task decomposition; nonverbal and verbal coordination and communication; the use of video, and auditory-mediating technologies; synchronous and asynchronous problem solving; and procedures for building common ground and sharing data and knowledge. For each design concept, they provide a series of recommendations to assist readers in achieving an optimum performance with respect to each concept.

Part Five outlines technological and interpersonal competencies needed to work collaboratively in a virtual team: knowledge of available technology, cross-cultural competence, communication skills, and problem-solving and decision-making skills. In Chapter Fourteen, Lori Bradley offers a good overview of the types of collaborative technology available to those working and collaborating virtually. She segments the tools she describes into three categories: electronic message systems, audio and video systems, and collaboration supporting systems. The chapter concludes with a valuable table that readers may use to determine when each collaborative tool is best used and what it has to offer.

Arie Baan and Martha Maznevski present in Chapter Fifteen three key challenges of working virtually: complexity, invisibility, and restricted communication. Then they relate these challenges to three critical success factors for virtual teams: shared understanding, communication, and trust. The authors argue that virtual teams that build shared understanding through effective communication, with continuous awareness of the importance of building trust, can achieve high levels of performance. In addition, because the authors believe training plays a critical role in achieving high performance, they describe the structure and content of a modularized training program for helping virtual teams develop the necessary critical success factors.

Chapter Sixteen, by Sue Freedman, addresses the challenges and misconceptions that virtual teams face when membership bridges cross-cultural borders. First, Freedman outlines five common misconceptions frequently held by American business leaders that suggest that cross-cultural teaming is not really that hard after all. Each one of these misconceptions is then peeled apart to reveal the challenges in working across borders. Colorful and useful examples are shared to illustrate each misconception. In the second half of the chapter, Freedman reviews a series of cultural dimensions well documented in the research literature that affect cross-cultural virtual team performance. The chapter concludes with a practical outline of the characteristics of high-performing project teams, linked with the unique challenges cross-border teams face, and a series of strategies useful in meeting those challenges.

Problem solving is a group process that can be exceedingly difficult when workers are dispersed. David Braga, Steve Jones, and Dennis Bowyer offer guidelines in Chapter Seventeen on how virtual teams can prepare themselves for the problem-solving process. As a part of this initial preparation, the authors offer a problem-solving checklist. Consistent with the literature, they then make the distinction between simple (or well-defined) problems and complex (or wicked) problems and illustrate both types with case examples. In addressing simple problems, the authors offer a six-step process with the activities needed to perform successfully at each step. The chapter concludes with a discussion of complex problems and a list of recommendations for addressing them.

With nearly thirty years of experience in the corporate world, Mehran Ferdowsian writes in Chapter Eighteen about many of the key decision-making problems readers may have experienced in teams and organizations without even realizing them. He skillfully brings to the forefront those "silent or unspoken micromessages" that erode effective decision making and collaboration and offers valuable antidotes to these deterrents. The major solution is to use a new thirteen-step decision-making model that Ferdowsian presents in flowchart form. He thus outlines a series of principles for highly effective virtual collaboration and decision making and a new set of roles, responsibilities, and expectations that effective virtual decision makers and collaborators should consider adopting.

Chapters Nineteen to Twenty-Four in Part Six examine the tools needed for effective and creative virtual teams to do their work and the assessment strategies that can be used to both predict and build a case for virtual team success. In Chapter Nineteen, Kimball Fisher provides a set of perspectives and tools specific to the needs of virtual team start-ups. These tools focus on the essentials of creating a team charter, role clarification, operating guidelines, and setting technology protocols. Kimball also addresses the personal system, an important addition to the social, technical, and environmental systems considered in traditional team and organizational design. Finally, he offers a list of valuable suggestions on how members of virtual teams can achieve balance between work and home life.

Dipti Gupta, Lori Bradley, and Terence Yeoh provide new insight and tools in Chapter Twenty to address an age-old problem: dysfunctional and ineffective team meetings. After an initial discussion of when meetings should be held virtually or face-to-face, the chapter authors stress the importance of using a virtual team facilitator or cofacilitators, or both, to ensure the effectiveness of the team's meeting. They provide a series of tools and actions for facilitators and team leaders to use during a virtual team's initial face-to-face meeting, and prior to, during, and after a team's virtual meeting in order to ensure meeting effectiveness and success.

Suggestions for how to run effective virtual team meetings are also found in Chapter Twenty-One by Mal Conway, Jack Jennings, Curt Raschke, Mary B. Witort, and Michael Beyerlein. A major premise is that collaboration is a key driver of business performance. It occurs when a team culture encourages sharing and open interaction—what the authors term VEtiquette (which stands for *virtual etiquette*). By VEtiquette, the authors are referring to a subset of norms and behaviors necessary for effective, high-quality virtual interaction and communication. This chapter provides a rich and valuable list of VEtiquette practices, procedures, and lessons learned to assist both newcomers and those with experience in planning and facilitating virtual team meetings.

In Chapter Twenty-Two, Jill Nemiro reviews a variety of well-known techniques that individual members of virtual teams and virtual teams themselves can use to boost their creativity. These techniques are categorized according to whether they facilitate a linear/rational or intuitive/instinctive approach to creativity and idea generation. For each technique, Nemiro offers a set of tips specific to their use in virtual teams. The chapter concludes with a set of criteria to assist virtual teams in determining which creativity technique is most appropriate for a particular situation.

Scott K. Filgo, Scott Hines, and Scott Hamilton address in Chapter Twenty-Three the essential requirement for selecting appropriate virtual team members: using assessments to predict successful virtual team performance. They begin by reviewing a series of traits and abilities that the literature shows as somewhat universal to virtual team members. They then take a different direction in stating that all assessments should take into consideration the traits and abilities that are not only job specific but company specific as well. Filgo, Hines, and Hamilton, consultants in the assessment field, share their expertise by describing a suggested process of assessment for both universal and job- and company-specific traits and abilities that virtual team members need. Central to this process is the concept of benchmarking to create valid and reliable instruments for assessment.

Top management must assess and make decisions about how best to use resources to generate valued outcomes. One proven method for generating support from the top is the business case. In Chapter Twenty-Four, Michael Beyerlein and Susan Beyerlein present a step-by-step procedure for building and making the business case for virtual teams and illustrate it with a variety of useful virtual team examples.

The chapters in Part Seven share real-life applications of virtual teams and collaboration. Chapter Twenty-Five, by Steven K. Rothschild and Stan Lapidos, starts with an intriguing application of virtual teams in the health care industry. They outline what they term the virtual integrated practice (VIP) model, currently being implemented at Rush University Medical Center in Chicago. The model uses virtual interdisciplinary teams comprising health care professionals from various disciplines (for example, pharmacists, dieticians, social workers, occupational therapists, physicians, and others) who join together to fully meet patient needs. The four elements of the model—standardized processes, communication protocols, patient self-management tools, and group visits (patients with the same diagnosis meet with physicians in small group appointments)—are described. The authors illustrate the application of the VIP model through the sharing of a case story of one patient and how the virtual team members on this patient's "VIP team" pulled together to supply the patient with a well-rounded set of actions to assist in making her well.

Anita Kamouri and Eric Richert discuss in Chapter Twenty-Six the process through which organizations make decisions on whether to and to what degree to use distributed versus proximate work. The general practice of many organizations is to make these decisions and move into related investment decisions based on insufficient data or analyses. More specifically, these types of decisions are often made without directly linking the decisions back to the organization's business goals or objectives. Kamouri and Richert describe an approach they have developed for distributed work initiatives at Sun Microsystems, a network computing company. Their strategy involves making distributed work decisions that are data driven and linked to the company's business objectives. Five data perspectives are offered to assist readers in making informed decisions about distributed work process. The chapter includes a list of practical recommendations for implementation of the business-focused decisions to ensure distributed work implementation success.

The information technology group in a large U.S. bank is the setting in Chapter Twenty-Seven for an illustration of an old form of organizational structure, the matrix, in a new context involving virtual relationships. Amy Kates and Paul J. Erickson begin with a description of traditional matrix structures and their benefits and pitfalls. They present two major principles and a series of related actions and tools that assist in designing a matrix for successful virtual collaboration. The first principle deals with ways to build social capital, and the second principle is to instill disciplined work and management processes.

The aerospace industry provides the context for Chapter Twenty-Eight. Jude G. Olson describes how the Joint Strike Fighter (JSF) program, a triservice, multinational transformational weapon system awarded to Lockheed Martin Aeronautics Company in Fort Worth, Texas, relied on virtual integrated product teams as the coordinating structure to link a disparate group of engineers, many of whom had previously been competitors, for the purpose of new product development. A major focus of the chapter is the vertical and horizontal coordination mechanisms that strengthened these links between the multiple parties during simultaneous design activities on the new product start-up. Barriers to innovation and information sharing across organizational boundaries are also identified. Through the sharing of the actual words of the participants on these teams, examples of virtual collaborative work provide an illustration of the complex challenges in aligning a large, distributed, globally integrated product team.

The two chapters in Part Eight synthesize the handbook's previous chapters and offer new insight into the future of virtual teaming and collaboration. In Chapter Twenty-Nine, the book editors pull together the knowledge shared in this book into an integrative list of key principles for high-performance virtual teams. Also shared are the benefits that contemporary organizations can expect to gain from pursuing the path of toward high-performance virtual teams.

In Chapter Thirty, Jeffrey Stamps and Jessica Lipnack, pioneers in the virtual teams literature, bring the handbook to a close by sharing a real-life account of the birth of one virtual organization, spread across four countries, that became transparent and seamless. Although this story documents only one case, it encompasses what the future holds for organizations. To achieve transparency in virtual organizations, Stamps and Lipnack advocate the use of formal networked hierarchies, drawing new maps so individuals can see where they are and who they are connected to, and organizational shapes resembling diamonds (distribution of positions by level) rather than traditional pyramid-shaped organizational charts.

To enhance application of the principles outlined in the handbook, most chapters conclude with a set of reminders, crafted to provide readers with useful suggestions and recommendations. Readers also have Web access (www.wiley.com\go\virtualteamshandbook) to a variety of assessment surveys, practical tools, and additional chapters and references to assist in developing high-performing virtual teams. Related items on the Web have been listed at the end of relevant chapters in this handbook.

FINAL THOUGHTS

One need only acknowledge the diversity of the contributors to this handbook, the organizations represented, and the disciplines from which the insights are drawn to understand the complexity and richness of virtual teams and collaboration and the pervasive need for effective practices. Working with this group of talented practitioners and researchers has been both humbling and inspiring. It is humbling to realize that we are still early in the process of establishing the best practices that will guide new ways of working and organizing. And it is inspiring to witness the individuals and organizations that are stepping up and bringing their best thinking to the challenges that virtual teams face. Technologies will continue to change shape and leapfrog current offerings, but one thing will remain reassuringly constant: the need for individuals to come together to ponder and find answers in concert, in whatever human configurations that work, including those perhaps not yet anticipated or designed, in order to create the breakthrough solutions for advancing toward the future.

References

Alexander, S. (2000, November 13). Virtual teams going global: Communication and culture are issues for distant team members. *InfoWorld 22*(46), 55.

Beyerlein, M., & Harris, C. (2004). *Guiding the journey to collaborative work systems: A strategic design workbook.* San Francisco: Jossey-Bass/Pfeiffer.

Beyerlein, M., McGee, C., Klein, G., Nemiro, J., & Broedling, L. (Eds.). (2003). *The collaborative work systems fieldbook: Strategies, tools and techniques.* San Francisco: Jossey-Bass/Pfeiffer.

Creighton, J. L., & Adams, J. W. (1998). *Cyber meeting: How to link people and technology in your organization.* New York: AMACOM.

Duarte, D. L., & Snyder, N. T. (1999). *Mastering virtual teams: Strategies, tools, and techniques that succeed.* San Francisco: Jossey-Bass.

Fisher, K., & Fisher, M. D. (2001). *The distance manager: A hands-on guide to managing off-site employees and virtual teams.* New York: McGraw-Hill.

Garton, C., & Wegryn, K. (2006). *Managing without walls: Maximize success with virtual, global, and cross-cultural teams.* Double Oak, TX: MC Press, LLC.

Gibson, C., & Cohen, S. (2003). *Virtual teams that work: Creating conditions for virtual team effectiveness.* San Francisco: Jossey-Bass.

Gorelick, C. K. (2000). Toward an understanding of organizational learning and collaborative technology: A case study of structuration and sensemaking in a virtual project team. *Dissertation Abstracts International, 61*(05), 1806A. (UMI No. 9973090)

Hong, I. (1999). Information technology to support any-time, any-place team meetings in Korean organizations. *Industrial Management and Data Systems, 99*(1), 18–24.

Jarvenpaa, S. L., Knoll, K., & Leidner, D. E. (1998). Is anybody out there? Antecedents of trust in global virtual teams. *Journal of Management Information Systems, 14,* 29–64.

Jones, R., Oyung, R., & Pace, L. (2005). *Working virtually: Challenges of virtual teams.* Hershey, PA: Cybertech Publishing.

Kayworth, T., & Leidner, D. (2002). Leadership effectiveness in global virtual teams. *Journal of Management Information Systems, 18*(3), 7–40.

Kimble, C., Li, F., & Barlow, A. (2000). *Effective virtual teams through communities of practice.* Research paper No. 2000/9. Glasgow: Strathclyde Business School. Retrieved December 15, 2001, from http://www.mansci.strath.ac.uk/papers.html.

Knoll, K. E. (2001). Communication and cohesiveness in global virtual teams. *Dissertation Abstracts International, 61*(08), 4251B. (UMI No. 9983268)

Lipnack, J., & Stamps, J. (2000). *Virtual teams: People working across boundaries with technology.* Hoboken, NJ: Wiley.

Mankin, D., & Cohen, S. (2003). *Business without boundaries: An action framework for collaborating across time, distance, organization, and culture.* San Francisco: Jossey-Bass.

Nemiro, J. (2004). *Creativity in virtual teams: Key components for success.* San Francisco: Jossey-Bass/Pfeiffer.

O'Hara-Devereaux, M., & Johansen, R. (1994). *Global work: Bridging distance, culture, and time.* San Francisco: Jossey-Bass.

Rowe, B. J. (2001). Group task structure, rewards, and virtual teams: A study of computer-mediated collaboration. *Dissertation Abstracts International, 61*(11), 4449A. (UMI No. 999322)

Solomon, C. M. (2001). Managing virtual teams. *Workforce, 80*(6), 1–5.

Wang, P. (2001). Media choice in virtual teams: Linking task requirement and communication technology to enhance task effectiveness. *Dissertation Abstracts International, 62*(04), 1255A. (UMI No. 3011885)

Weick, K. (1995). *Sensemaking in organizations.* Thousand Oaks, CA: Sage.

Wilson, J., George, J., & Wellins, R. (1994). *Leadership trapeze: Strategies for leadership in team-based organizations.* San Francisco: Jossey-Bass.

Wiesenfeld, B., Raghuram, S., & Garud, R. (1998). Communication patterns as determinants of organizational identification in a virtual organization. *Journal of Computer-Mediated Communication, 3*(4). Retrieved September 7, 2007, from http://jcmc.indiana.edu/vol3/issue4/wiesenfeld.html.

Workman, M. D. (2001). The effects of cognitive style and communications media on commitment to telework and virtual team innovations among information systems teleworkers. *Dissertation Abstracts International, 61*(10), 5592B. (UMI No. 9989532)

PRINCIPLES OF HIGH-PERFORMANCE VIRTUAL TEAMS

PART ONE

Working Collaboratively

To begin the path toward high-performance virtual teams requires an understanding and appreciation of the fundamental principles of effective virtual teams and collaboration and the environments that enable it. The chapters on the topic of working collaboratively describe the how and why of organizing, creativity, trust, sensemaking, culture, leadership, and other facets related to working virtually. Chapter One looks at the fundamental problem of virtual teams, crossing boundaries, and discusses a wide array of boundaries that create barriers separating team members, including geography, time, discipline, company, and culture. The creative potential of a virtual team depends on how well members can share their knowledge across those boundaries. When well done, the sharing creates opportunities for leveraging the knowledge of individuals and creating new perspectives and solutions. Chapter Two extends the theme of achieving synergies across boundaries by presenting ten fundamental principles for enabling the team to achieve high levels of performance over time. The principles are accompanied by practical steps that can be taken to create the conditions for excellence.

A Framework for Working Across Boundaries

Michael Beyerlein, Jill Nemiro, Susan Beyerlein

90% of team failures are caused by support system problems.

S. Mohrman, S. Cohen, and A. Mohrman (1995)

80% of the value of using teams comes from between the teams.

S. D. Jones and D. J. Schilling (2000)

Mohrman, Cohen, and Mohrman (1995) and Jones and Schilling (2000) independently claim that individuals who collaborate in teams do not always achieve their goals. In fact, there are many causes of poor performance (Jones & Schilling, 2000). Often mediocrity is taken for granted, as many teams have little awareness or understanding of what constitutes optimal performance. Consequently there is no investment in improving the effectiveness of the commonly agreed on critical success factors needed for team success—elements such as team structure and process, team skills, shared understanding, and the varied support systems that provide facilitative organization contexts for team activities.

This handbook addresses a number of these requirements; however, this chapter focuses specifically on those that are crucial for virtual teams that operate by necessity across the boundaries of time, space, and culture without the benefits of real-time face-to-face interaction. This chapter provides a framework of key principles that addresses the challenges in working and collaborating successfully across boundaries. Practical suggestions and tools are included to assist virtual teams in assessing their current level of effectiveness on each of these dimensions and developing strategies for using this information to improve their boundary-spanning efforts.

THREE CHARACTERISTICS OF COLLABORATION

Before discussing this framework specific to virtual teams, it is important to examine the nature of collaboration in general and provide a rationale for investing in it. Collaboration, as formally defined, has three main characteristics. Katzenbach and Smith (1993) in their popular book, *The Wisdom of Teams*, provided six necessary ingredients to effective teamwork, including urgency of purpose and shared goals. By extension, collaboration (an operationalization of the popular understanding of teamwork ushered into our consciousness by Katzenbach and Smith and others) occurs when individuals work together toward a shared goal, completing the work is dependent on relationships with a purpose, and individuals working together in purposeful ways toward a shared goal are committed to one another's success.

Achieving each of these characteristics of collaboration takes sustained commitment on the part of team members. First, ownership of shared goals does not happen without intentional and effortful communication among members. In other words, absence of or lukewarm efforts toward mutual understanding for whatever reasons may leave members grappling individually with different work goals and, as a result, experiencing loss of that concerted power to act that comes with consensus decision making and a shared and energizing vision of what can be achieved. Instead team members may unwittingly find themselves with competing frames of reference, differing purposes, confusion about what needs to be done and how it can best be accomplished, interpersonal misunderstandings, and ultimately performance decrements that belie why they came together in the first place. Thus, there is a clear business case for doing the hard work of communicating from the outset in order to reach shared understanding and agreement on process and outcome goals, as well as strategies and tactics for accomplishing them before getting too mired in the work of the team.

In a somewhat different vein, in the mid- to late twentieth century, before widespread engagement in virtual teaming, work in teams (or groups, as they were called then) often focused on leveraging social relationships among members as a success factor rather than simply attending to the stated purposes of the work (that is, the task case for working together). Paying attention to group dynamics in addition to performance targets, without the advantage of the rich body of knowledge on team effectiveness available today, tended to dilute team efforts toward product quality (team success) rather than strengthen them. However, by definition, *relationships with a purpose* in team settings refers to members who are highly committed to working together to achieve outcomes they believe they cannot achieve alone. This idea, of course, goes back to the cave dwellers, and it can be argued in numerous epochs and echelons since then that there is tangible value in this belief because it promotes survival and in team settings contributes to cohesion (that is, "we are all in this together and for a good reason") and thus momentum toward purposeful, collaborative (and, ideally, financially rewarding) action.

Third, a by-product of working together for a shared purpose is often a commitment to one another's success rather than a singular focus on taking care of oneself at the expense of others—the latter a sure-fire formula for poor team performance. Commitment to others' success tends to be a function not only of familiarity (that is, time spent on task and in informal gatherings outside work, which tend to break down cultural barriers and increase interpersonal comfort levels; see Chapter Twenty-Eight), but also of awareness among team members that "another's success is my success," captured in the now somewhat trite TEAM acronym found on posters: "Together We Achieve More." Taken together, these three characteristics of collaboration send the message that no on can go it alone, as in traditional Western approaches to work and life; rather, one's success (or lack thereof) is intimately tied to the efforts of one's fellow teammates and perhaps soberly captured by the notion from the midcentury European Gestalt tradition that we perceive the whole as different from the sum of its parts (Wulf, 1996). We would prefer to say *greater* as the phrase has been restated in popular lore in that, indeed, collaborative efforts represent a significant investment of time and energy and should therefore pay significant dividends, but this is not always the case. Furthermore, in virtual team settings, distance complicates the equation with cultural differences and other constraints that potentially separate members, making the investment of all members all the more critical.

CROSSING BOUNDARIES

Attempting collaborative work arrangements in today's world is an incredibly complex and challenging endeavor. Team members are often distributed across company sites around the globe. The geographical spread of facilities and people brings with it enormous diversity, cultural and otherwise, including a host of different perspectives, languages, goals, doctrines for getting the work done ("this is how we do things around here"), trade and governmental sanctions, permitting venues, management styles, natural resource and supply chain infrastructures, legal channels to effective business practice, attitudes toward worker board participation, and many other potentially divisive features, including perhaps too frequent political upheavals and terrorist acts in host countries. Virtual teams may have the advantage of avoiding the ground skirmishes, but nonetheless, like their brick-and-mortar cohorts, face many of the same challenges at a relentless twenty-four-hour-workday pace.

Taking an organizational perspective, Mankin and Cohen (2004) have captured the complexity of these contexts for doing business collaboratively with six continua:

From	To
Simple	Complex problems
Well defined	High task uncertainty
Two people	Multiple people
Lots in common	Diverse perspectives

Common goals   Different goals

Face-to-face   Virtual

Moving from left to right on each of these dimensions creates circumstances that generally make collaboration more difficult. This handbook addresses the complexity of the face-to-face/virtual continuum, which, by virtue of its nature, holds or contains the tensions of the other five. Thus, problems such as the following are likely to emerge in both traditional face-to-face and virtual work settings:

- Product development that is too slow
- Reinventing the wheel from one situation to another
- Stifled creativity
- Stress that takes its toll
- Team performance that falls below expectations

Therefore, why is collaboration so difficult? In virtual settings, the answer seems to be a function of the boundaries that need to be spanned in order for effective sharing, idea generation, and use of knowledge to take place. A boundary is, by definition, a delimiter, a condition that defines and identifies who is in and who is out. Boundaries separate the system from its surroundings, control in-flow and out-flow, protect the team (or seem to), require management (for example, specifying who owns the boundary and has the ability to manage it), create a division between units, and represent limits of known or recognizable quantity, area, and scope. The term *boundary spanner* in management circles refers to the legitimate and necessary role of the manager in communicating beyond the unit borders with upper management or other outside policy holders and stakeholders for the purpose of ensuring the unit's survival through positive press, brokering needed resources, and involvement in a host of other activities on the unit's behalf.

Throughout history, a boundary has been considered an organization design tool; a fence to keep members and nonmembers (nonhuman intruders as well) in or out in all levels and types of organizations; a social construction of class warfare, entitlement, or good breeding; fodder for turf battles all the way from neighborhoods to nation-states; unspoken rules for staying in one's place or politely circumventing uncomfortable or politically incorrect topics of discourse or conversation; uniforms and other visible signs of authority; government and corporate regimes that prohibit free access and management of its citizens' rightful inheritance (for example, the airwaves); the center aisle in Washington and other great capitals of the world where elected officials strive to reach across in bipartisan fashion; and finally, the delimiters in one's own mind that keep individuals from stretching themselves and achieving more. These are all boundary conditions of enormous scope and significance that have an impact on human life, sometimes without our awareness and often without our consent. This is not an exhaustive list but perhaps an interesting one concerning how individuals may bounce up against any subset of these boundary conditions in their daily lives as others not mentioned. Some are of one's own making, and others are thrust on individuals as members of the societies (defined very broadly) they inhabit.

In transgressing boundaries, one (or one's behavior) is sometimes labeled out-of-bounds. In traditional organizational societies, including the family, this often results in sanctions of varying severity or duration, for example, docking of pay, grounding (as in teenagers), or a disapproving look. However, by its very nature, collaboration always involves crossing boundaries. This first requires recognizing the various delimiters as borders, borderlands, walls, membership requirements, or limitations. Boundaries limit the flow of essential inputs and outputs such as people, information, materials, ideas, and energy. Individuals who exist on the boundary (that is, at the margins of the organization or society) are usually those best suited in temperament and interest to comment on the status quo, often a high-risk activity in itself, or take the practical actions necessary to step into foreign territory and create something new. In other words, for teams to leverage local resources, boundaries have to be opened up so flow is permitted, valued, and supported. It takes courageous individuals to do this.

In recent decades, crossing disciplinary boundaries has created new sciences such as biochemistry and information genomics; traversing boundaries between product and service groups has created integrated solutions for taking care of customers, thus expanding customer bases worldwide; crossing company boundaries has created rich opportunities for knowledge and technology transfer as well as more formal collaborations such as joint ventures and strategic alliances. Each of these boundary crossings has likely involved individuals who are fully committed to doing the hard work of communicating with one another other, risking venturing into uncharted territory and all the ambiguity this entails, sharing their tangible product and process knowledge and skill as well as the very human desire to be involved in creative work for the sake of new possibilities, and turning these assets into successful shared outcomes that can later provide the impetus for further innovation.

On a more practical note, members of virtual teams can benefit by identifying the boundaries that may limit their progress toward successful boundary crossings. The following boundary conditions may impede the attempts of virtual team members to collaborate on projects:

Individual Boundaries

- Gender
- Age
- Discipline
- Identity (who are we?)
- Ethnic background
- Personal (differing tastes or preferences)
- Native language
- Preverbal (unable to articulate hunches)
- Theoretical framework
- Ethical
- Historical (differing experience with virtual teams)
- Individual (assumptions, values, biases, goals, styles, and so on)

Technical Boundaries

- Differing technological systems (such as differing computer systems)
- Technical language

Spatial/Geographic/Environmental Boundaries

- Time (different time zones)
- Geography (distance, political environment)
- Country (such as restrictions in sharing technical knowledge with defense implications)

- Economic
- Culture (differing country value systems)

Task-related Boundaries
- Task (different understanding of what is to be done)
- Skills (consider differing skill levels)
- Project (such as assignment to multiple projects that compete for one's time)
- Resources (for example, some members have plentiful and some have scarce support and resources)

Organizational Boundaries
- Culture (differing company value systems)
- Departmental (differing local politics)
- Company (restrictions in sharing proprietary knowledge)
- Control or authority (who is leading what?)
- Hierarchical (status differences)
- Institutional (competitors, regulators, supply chain)
- Political (whom do I trust?), organizational (vertical and horizontal)

Although this list is somewhat exhaustive, it is not intended to be overwhelming. Rather, treat the items as a checklist to identify the top three, four, or five boundaries that one's virtual team needs to explicitly address. Questions to facilitate team member discussion include the following:

- How is this boundary affecting the team's ability to work together to achieve its goals?
- Is something extra needed to make crossing each of these boundaries easier?
- What can be done to reduce the barriers represented by this boundary condition?

Figure 1.1 illustrates boundary permeability as a reality that affects the ability of virtual teams (and brick-and-mortar units) to span boundary limits and form new configurations. *Permeability* is defined as the degree to which matter (using the biological paradigm at the cell level) can pass through the cell (or unit) walls

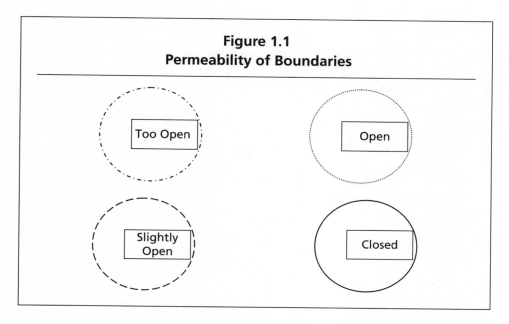

Figure 1.1
Permeability of Boundaries

Too Open

Open

Slightly
Open

Closed

and is represented as a continuum of four conditions: too open, open, slightly open, or closed. For example, an organization can control membership by adding or deleting requirements that applicants must meet—minimal requirements may allow too many to join whereas excessive requirements may prevent good candidates from joining.

It is important to note that there is no optimal condition. Boundaries ideally fluctuate in degree of openness depending on the level of permeability needed by particular task requirements. In fact, it is useful to think of permeability as a condition that can be actively managed for success rather than a stable constraint. Figure 1.2 illustrates the early stages of a four-member team that is embedded in separate discipline, department, and country silos but is beginning to build a shared culture through learning about the members' differing work contexts.

Managing boundaries is an inherently complex process with a number of discrete operations. One can recognize, maintain, close, open, cross, reform, change, destroy, or merge boundaries. The choice of operation and the effectiveness of action determine whether the boundary will be managed in a way that promotes excellence or mediocre performance. The most suppressive boundaries are those that are not recognized, are invisible, or are taken for granted. There is a tendency to assume that one's own local conditions apply to all other members on the team

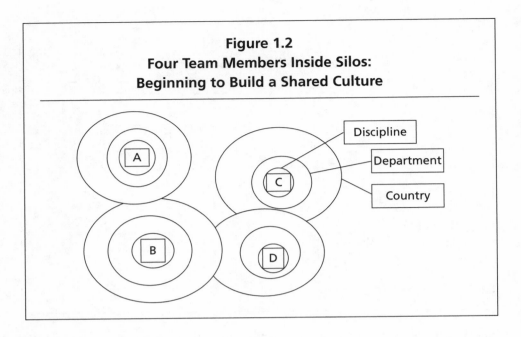

Figure 1.2
Four Team Members Inside Silos:
Beginning to Build a Shared Culture

and therefore that there are no boundaries that need attention. This tendency, known as silo thinking, is in fact another boundary.

Traditional functional organizations tend to encourage silo thinking. Individuals are placed in separate departments with discrete tasks that require little cross-boundary communication. Silo thinking is also characterized by the attitude that one's department or team (one's silo) is superior to other units. Silo thinking tightens boundaries that restrict teamwork and productivity, thereby placing unnecessary restrictions on work and resources flow and knowledge sharing. Silo thinking leads to mistrust and conflict between teams, and as a result, opportunities for creativity, learning, and collaboration are missed.

A FRAMEWORK FOR EDUCATING TEAM MEMBERS

One way that virtual teams can get past silo thinking is to create a framework for educating team members in working across boundaries based on the following principles:

Principle 1: Map out collaborative work structures and processes.

Principle 2: Craft a supportive culture.

Principle 3: Develop continuously evolving knowledge-sharing and management systems.

Principle 4: Define new roles for leaders.

Principle 5: Align and sustain support systems.

Each of these principles is discussed in detail in the sections that follow.

Principle 1: Map Out Collaborative Work Structures and Processes

Changing business conditions due to the impact of globalization have stimulated the invention of new forms of organization. Forms appearing in the past two decades include the team-based, flat, empowering, entirely virtual (no physical facilities), entirely outsourced, shamrock, networked, and old standbys such as joint venture, matrix, hybrid, and decentralized designs. Each of these and other forms are actually experiments in organizing that are being conducted on the business playing field around the world. Some of these experiments succeed, and some fail. When they succeed, copycats rush in to duplicate what the pioneers have created—for example, Dell's tailored assembly, Wal-Mart's supply chain management, and Nike's networked organization. The goal in each case is to create a sustainable competitive advantage through organizing elements of the business for high performance. Each of the forms of organization possesses some common features, including the need to span boundaries of one kind or another to create added value.

Organizational design options vary on at least four continua:

- Formal versus informal, which determines paths of communication
- Centralized versus decentralized, which determines the influence of local members
- Control versus autonomy, which determines the degree of empowerment among employees
- Silos versus links, which determines how work is handed off as task domains move downstream toward the end user

Within any of these organizational forms, the core characteristics of collaborative work design are the same: people have to depend on each other, share information freely, and coordinate their efforts toward common goals. Organizing these collaborative units often means focusing on the factors that affect performance from within the team. However, performance in the larger work unit depends on integration across teams and work groups. In this process, the area between teams is often ignored. Mechanisms for integration across teams include:

1. Starpoints: members with specific responsibility for management tasks (such as safety)

2. Boundary workers: members with responsibility for linking across teams

3. Integration teams: groups of members from diverse teams who meet to coordinate cross-team activities

4. Liaisons: nonmembers who work to link a variety of teams or levels in the organization

Each of the four deliberately functions as a transboundary mechanism. Thus, the potential for information flow is enhanced across units, and with it the likelihood of decision making and implementation improvements to the overall linked system.

There are a variety of ways to organize members directly involved in boundary-spanning activities. Collaborative structures include different types of teams (for example, work, project, management, or parallel), communities of practice, and learning networks. Teams vary on a number of dimensions including:

- Temporary or permanent
- Single function or multifunctional
- Inside one organization or across several work units
- Colocated or distributed membership

For example, one team may be relatively permanent, representing a single function inside the factory floor with colocated members in daily attendance, whereas another team may be temporary, with multifunctional members spread across several organizations and distributed around the globe (thus inhabiting various time zones). Many of the structural and process principles of effectiveness for these two examples are the same. However, the sheer number and comparative intractability of the boundaries in the second virtual team example suggest quantum differences in barriers to high performance.

Geographically dispersed virtual teams must rely on technology improvements in electronic communication. The members may never meet each other face-to-face in spite of the obvious value of such experience. Being in far-flung locations means members report to their own local managers, have a different set of colocated peers, dine at their own preferred eating establishments without their coworkers, and often have to deal with the frustrations of asynchronous communication.

Virtual teams can accomplish their tasks through two different types of work processes: the modular and iterative work design approaches (Nemiro, 1997, 2004). These are not mutually exclusive. In fact, many virtual teams frequently use the compartmentalized or modular approach to accomplish work, but in order to avoid isolation and the loss of human exchange, they also rely on the iterative process as well.

In the modular process, team members meet initially to decide on the need, task, or project to be pursued. Then the work is parceled out or distributed among team members, usually based on an individual team member's expertise or interest. Team members then go off to work on their pieces of the pie, sometimes by themselves, sometimes with one or two other members of the team. After the work is completed, the efforts are presented to the team for feedback before finalization and implementation. Revisions are done as needed. The entire team then assesses the work outcomes, which in reality represent a compilation of all the individual pieces.

In the iterative process, virtual team members engage in back-and-forth development cycles. Members work a little, present those results to the team, get feedback, work a little more, present those results, get more feedback, and so on until the project is finished. Electronic communication allows team members to exchange ideas and different versions of the work in a comfortable fashion. Elements of the work are bounced back and forth and built on one another with ease.

Two questions provide discussion starters for virtual teams to assess their level of understanding and application of Principle 1: Mapping Out Collaborative Work Structures and Processes:

- Does the organization's design support collaboration?
- Is the team's current design optimal for guiding the team toward successful collaborative results?

For each question, team members should realistically answer yes or no. If the answer is yes, team members need to brainstorm, considering and recording actions that would lead to further growth. If the answer is no, discussion among the team members should consider and record actions that would lead to further improvement in this area.

Principle 2: Craft a Supportive Culture

Each member of the organization is unique in important ways and similar to coworkers in others. A key uniqueness is the perspective he or she brings to the team. Each looks at the job and the organization through a particular lens consisting of ways of seeing, thinking, deciding, relating, and so forth that have been learned and absorbed over many years of life. Much of one's perspective and behavior patterns develops from exposure to surrounding cultures, including the ways of thinking and working in one's native country, one's training including the assumptions and polarities of the chosen field of study, formative experiences, and the accepted ways of getting things done in one's places of employment.

These differences are well represented metaphorically in John Godfrey Saxe's (1878) poem concerning the six blind men and the elephant. Each blind member of the group bumped into a different part of the elephant and in attempting to figure out what he had encountered formed a different impression, for example, the tusk experienced by one man as a spear, the leg by another as a tree, and the tail by a third as a rope. None of the men knew from prior experience what an elephant really was, and thus they failed to integrate their disparate views into a whole picture that would have been a better map of reality. Local cultures within an organization easily duplicate the blind men's problem with trying to make sense of the unknown. There are significant gaps between management, engineering, and production cultures. The members' backgrounds, languages, and goals differ to such an extent that Schein (1996) describes them as coming from different countries. Cross-functional teams must pay attention to such gaps in understanding and practice across functions, resulting from often unstated, dramatic differences in assumptions about what is important, in order to have any chance of high performance.

Culture is usually defined as a shared set of values, beliefs, and norms—in short, a shared language (unspoken) and perspective that helps diverse individuals within that environment work together in harmony. The identical people working under different cultures, including units of the same organization, can act in very different ways. The differences can be useful when they are made explicit and part of the team's larger picture of the job; left unarticulated, they present barriers to concerted action. There are a number of ways for dealing with cultural barriers.

First, members must recognize the differences that cultures create in their approach to work and then talk about them. This is a common challenge for virtual teams and is discussed in more detail in other chapters in this book. The initial step is choosing an attitude of genuine interest and openness concerning differences and approaching the learning about one another's cultures with respect.

Second, changing the culture changes the way people act. In other words, a change in culture is a major change in work context that influences behavior. For example, changing from a culture of blame to one of collaboration gradually shifts most behaviors from finger pointing and self-protection toward seeking partnering opportunities and sharing openly.

Third, the team can take the steps to create its own culture. Team chartering, which is described in Chapter Nineteen, is a process for quickly creating a culture that involves all members, so that a shared approach to all aspects of the work exists. The new culture or subculture represents a set of agreements developed through formal activities and evolves through informal social experiments yielding ways to get along and get things done. It creates an informal infrastructure—a web of joint assumptions, beliefs, and values that support a dynamic social and intellectual network

A variety of traditional and contemporary work cultures that are found in today's organizations are outlined in Beyerlein and Harris (2004): collaborative, entrepreneurial, innovation, empowerment, command and control, laissez-faire, involvement, learning, and quality. These and other types of cultures either tend to evolve rather accidentally or their development is formally facilitated through major change initiatives. A large organization probably has pockets of subcultures that represent every variety. Some of these cultural options facilitate work on complex projects and virtual work, and some do not. The choice to deliberately build a facilitative and shared culture for the virtual team is an important one. It provides bridges across the cultural boundaries that separate the members and inhibit their ability to collaborate. Shared patterns of action aligned with beliefs and assumptions enable the team to achieve higher levels of performance.

Table 1.1
Cultures for High and Low Creativity

Culture Promoting High Creativity	Culture Promoting Low Creativity
Ideas/input valued	Ideas dismissed
Trust; high level of honesty	Mistrust
Constructive tension	Unconstructive tension
High level of challenge	Lack of challenge
Collaboration	Competition
Freedom	Lack of freedom
Supportive management	Status quo
Sufficient resources	Insufficient resources and time
Understand work styles	

Source: Adapted from Nemiro (2004).

Every member of the organization works daily across cultural boundaries with the team's goals in mind. Building bridges reduces the barriers and provides ways to truly capitalize on the diversity of the group.

One of the major goals of most virtual teams is the discovery of new methods, processes, and devices. Creativity is an important ingredient in making this happen. Table 1.1 contrasts the cultures that promote and inhibit creativity. In other words, when the team maps out the ideal culture for its work environment, it needs to emphasize the culture that best promotes creativity. Table 1.1 can be used as a checklist when the team works to create its own internal culture or as a diagnostic tool when creativity falls short of expectations.

The team and the organization can take a number of steps to create a shared culture so there is a uniform work environment of expectations and values (Trice & Beyer, 1993):

• Find or create common symbols, language, and rituals to co-create a new culture.

• Emphasize trust, nonjudgment, support of new ideas, integrity, and personal contribution as a measure of effectiveness.

- Establish shared processes for protecting the vitality and viability of the social network the group depends on.

- Share stories as examples of success and failure.

- Hold face-to-face meetings so interpersonal bonds can develop.

- Practice cultural immersion to get deeply involved with another point of view. These can range from informally visiting restaurants representing the ethnicity of team members to more formal job rotation assignments.

- Conduct formal team chartering. If it is for the whole organization, cascade it down from the top.

- Work patiently. Understand resistance to culture change because one's culture is part of one's identity.

- Change many elements, but maintain some continuity, respecting history and preserving the useful parts.

- Recognize the importance of implementation. Buy-in and change come only through involvement.

- Build the cultural competence of the members so that more sensitive and appreciative behaviors occur when engaging with new collaborators from other cultures.

Leaders have a role in making the cultural change work succeed. They can establish the formal conditions for a set of congruent behaviors, attitudes, and policies that enable effective interactions in a cross-cultural framework. Leaders should also remember that cultural differences have value as a source of unique points of view.

Here are two discussion questions for initial assessment of a virtual team's application of Principle 2: Crafting a Supportive Culture:

- Does the culture within your team or organization support collaboration?

- Does the culture within your team or organization support creativity?

For each question, team members should realistically answer yes or no. If the answer is yes, team members should brainstorm and record actions leading to further growth. If the answer is no, team members need to consider and record actions leading to further improvement in this area.

Principle 3: Develop Continuously Evolving Knowledge-Sharing and Management Systems

Sustainability of organizations in the twenty-first century depends on the development and use of knowledge as much as the human body depends on the flow of blood. Virtual teams and their environments should be designed to facilitate knowledge processes. Human, technical, and organizational factors need attention to optimize them.

Knowledge Sharing   Nearly every virtual team is focused on the problem of effective knowledge sharing. Creating the team of geographically distributed members is often driven by the need to connect people with diverse knowledge sets. The same difficulties in sharing occur in face-to-face groups as well, but the virtual setting that relies heavily and sometimes exclusively on electronic communications faces more extreme challenges in this regard.

The most valuable resources in the team and in the organization for generating, sharing, and using knowledge are expertise and knowledge, innovation and creativity, time and speed, and trust. What exactly does one trust in? Trusting in other members' abilities, intentions, and dependability makes it possible to move forward with a complex knowledge-based project quickly. Without trust, resources are wasted, including the shared leadership capability on the team; the ideas, hunches, questions, and concerns that could be voiced; and the spin-off ideas that may seem irrelevant to dominant members on the team or to managers outside the team who do not grasp the broader context of the ideas.

One of the boundaries that impedes knowledge sharing is pride (also referred to as hubris or narcissism). Pride is often justified within a silo but not outside the local situation. For example, most people experience being the local expert on some topic, but as soon as they change environments, they find their mastery is only at a modest level. Few have won Nobel Prizes or other recognition of world-level mastery. Stepping across boundaries in sharing knowledge depends on some humility, and that is a precondition to learning from others. A story from Zen literature illustrates the problem.

A U.S. businessman went to Japan to meet with a Zen master to learn how to become more successful. They sat on opposite sides of a table with a tea service between them. The master picked up a cup and began to fill it with tea for the visitor. When the cup was full to the brim, the master continued to pour tea and the cup ran over. The visitor said, "The cup is full. You can't get any more in." The Zen master said, "Yes, so is your mind. Until you empty it, I can add nothing more." Humility is a prerequisite to learning across boundaries.

This expertise scale (Wiig, 1994) can assist in self-assessment to determine where one stands on this dimension in relationship to others on the team:

Level 0: Totally unaware

Level 1: Amateurish (Beginner)

Level 2: Aware but relatively unskilled (Novice)

Level 3: Deeper understanding but narrowly skilled (Apprentice)

Level 4: Experienced and reliable (Proficient)

Level 5: Master of a particular area (Expert)

Level 6: Leader in the knowledge area: teacher or proficient and expert

Level 7: World-class expert, broad expertise, wide recognition

Each member of the team brings significant expertise in some areas but noticeably less knowledge in others. For example, on a cross-functional team with members from marketing, engineering, and manufacturing, the marketing member knows far more than the other members about how to generate public interest in a product but probably knows little about the engineering requirements and manufacturing processes compared to other members. Coordination of the diverse types of knowledge requires that team leadership be driven by expertise in a particular domain, not by voice volume and speaking frequency—a too common occurrence. The dominant member may not be the expert on needed content. Effective team process requires norms and practices that allow appropriate expertise to be shared and absorbed by the other members.

Knowledge Management   The management of knowledge-intensive work begins with a conscious or unconscious decision about what knowledge means. The equating of knowledge with information seems to dominate popular conversations and publications but is considered a serious oversimplification by a growing number of experts. Knowledge as information that has a purpose or use is an improvement (Postman, 1999). Knowledge as the meaning that individuals and groups give to information is a richer construction. The key to the third definition is that it depends on people, their interpretations, and their conversations, not on computers and paper forms of information storage. It is socially driven, not technology driven. Technology merely facilitates the storage and sharing of knowledge.

Quinn and Anderson (1996) have created four categories of knowledge: know-what, know-how, know-why, and care-why. There are other terms for the first two types of knowledge, but the important piece is how they differ. *Know-what* is information and can be stored fairly easily, whereas *know-how* is knowledge of procedures and processes that is context dependent and difficult to share. The former is explicit (easily made visible), and the latter is tacit (mostly invisible). Tacit knowledge is typically learned from experience and from following the example of others. The problem for virtual teams is that observing examples and models is far more difficult at a distance.

The value of knowledge increases with such things as its accessibility (Harrison, 1995), how frequently it is shared (Davenport & Prusak, 1998), the degree of dissemination (Dirksen, Huizing, & Smit, 2005), and wider accessibility and use (Antoniou, Reeve, & Stenning, 2000). Open sharing attaches added value to knowledge, which is often characterized as intellectual capital—the intangible assets of the organization. There is a growing understanding of the strategic importance of intellectual capital among practitioners in global industry. Whether deliberately or accidentally engineered, virtual teams are assembled to increase that capital and find ways to convert it to financial capital (Saint-Onge, 1996; Saint-Onge & Wallace, 2003).

Knowledge sharing is difficult under the best conditions, with time pressure, complexity, and social issues increasing the challenges on a daily basis. Knowledge management has emerged as one of the disciplines that attempts to manage these situations. In the broadest sense of the term, knowledge management involves building tacit knowledge into communities, building explicit knowledge into artifacts, and providing infrastructure to make both tacit and explicit knowledge readily available to those that depend on it.

This description of knowledge management means that the chief knowledge officer (CKO) should be paying attention to the processes and support systems that the organization's virtual teams rely on. The CKO can also work with other executives, such as those responsible for learning and organization development, research and development, and operations, to establish an environment where knowledge sharing is rewarded, political self-interest is discouraged, technical barriers to the sharing process are minimized, face-to-face meetings are funded, and training is provided for increasing cultural competence.

One question can be used to begin assessment of a virtual team's competence with respect to Principle 3: Developing Continuously Evolving Knowledge-Sharing and Management Systems:

- Does the team have the necessary resources and tools to ensure successful collaborative results in terms of:

    Expertise and knowledge

    Communication tools

    Creative thinkers

    Time

Team members should realistically answer yes or no. If the answer is yes, they need to brainstorm and then consider and record actions that could lead to further growth. If the answer is no, team members should consider and record actions that would lead to still further improvement in this area.

Principle 4: Define New Roles for Leaders

The leaders of the past controlled and commanded their followers. Communication flowed one way, from management down. Employees were motivated by fear and punishment. For virtual collaboration, or any other collaborative effort for that matter, the old way of leading no longer works. Virtual team leaders need to become "side-by-side" leaders (Romig, 2003) who encourage two-way communication and shared decision making. Accountability based on mutual respect and honest and caring feedback replaces fear as a form of motivation.

Collaborative leaders empower those they lead. Leadership is viewed as a process or system rather than a position, and it is shared and distributed throughout a collaborative work structure. Beyerlein and Harris (2004) offer a series of characteristics for collaborative leaders:

- Develop organizational context.
- Build teams or groups.

- Support individual development.
- Set direction.
- Actively support and model collaboration.
- Provide resources.
- Integrate the organization.
- Interface with the environment.
- Counsel and coach others.
- Communicate and provide information.
- Lead performance management.

Although there is no one best way to lead a virtual team, research (Nemiro, 1997, 2004) indicates five leadership structures that virtual teams use:

1. Permanent team leaders
2. Rotating team leaders (every team member is a leader at some point)
3. Managing partners who govern the overall operation of the team, combined with rotating project leaders who supervise specific projects or tasks
4. Facilitators or coordinators used by self-managed teams that need additional support in a specific area
5. Leaderless or self-led teams

Table 1.2 indicates when each of the leadership structures is most appropriate for use.

Virtual teams can ask themselves two questions to assess their application of Principle 4: Defining New Roles for Leaders:

- Are virtual team leaders and team members being supported in terms of developing the required characteristics for leading collaborative efforts?
- Is the team's chosen leadership structure optimal for guiding the team in its path toward successful collaborative results?

If yes is the answer, consider and record actions that could lead to further growth. If no is the answer, continue the discussion with searching for ways to further improve in this area.

Table 1.2
When to Use Different Types of Virtual Team Leadership Structures

Leadership Structure	When to Use
Permanent leader	High degree of role differentiation among members
	Members with different areas of expertise/knowledge
	Different areas of work task integrated by leader
	High level of interaction between leader and individual members
Rotating team leader	Members perform similar tasks
	Projects divided up based on client preference and type of projects members enjoy
	All members are equally able to lead
	All members know ins and outs of the business
	Meetings formally established
	High level of trust
	Some stable staff and procedures
Managing partners combined with rotating project leaders	Diverse business; multiple projects for different companies
	Members with different areas of expertise but can also support others
	High level of trust
	Comfortable with being leader or member
Facilitator or coordinator	Self-managing teams that need additional support
	Open and constant communication and information exchange
	Facilitators possess technical, interpersonal, and project and task management skills
Leaderless or self-led	Members with similar or equal status or rank
	Members with similar backgrounds and expertise levels
	Members choose to be part of a team that benefits them in some way and all are equally invested in the team's outcomes
	High level of trust

Source: Nemiro (2004).

Principle 5: Align and Sustain Support Systems

Team support systems provide the hard and soft infrastructure that is intended to support high levels of performance. This intention often fails. For successful support to occur, managers need to pay attention to alignment of the support systems and teams' needs. For example, if information is stored on computers but team members are not authorized to access it or do not have adequate equipment for access, the information cannot be used to enhance performance. Beyerlein and Harris (2004) have identified a set of support systems where lack of alignment can harm team performance. Leadership is a key support system and includes executive and senior managers whose decision making provides resources for the teams, direct supervisors and team facilitators who have frequent contact with the team, and formal team leaders and members who may temporarily assume leadership as an informal role. Individuals in each of these roles make decisions and model behaviors on a daily basis that either promote or inhibit team effectiveness. As a further complication facing virtual teams, members often report to multiple supervisors and managers—one for on-site work and one for virtual work—who issue conflicting orders. This is reminiscent of the traditional matrix structure with dual reporting to line and project bosses.

Performance can be managed in a number of ways. The systems that have emerged that appear to be best practices solutions include a number of approaches to guiding and rewarding behavior: participative goal setting, measurement and feedback of performance to allow opportunities for correcting processes, and reward and recognition of appropriate behaviors. These components of performance management must align with each other. However, in virtual teams, there is even greater challenge because the behaviors are typically invisible or intangible—thoughts, conversations, and cyberspace exchanges—so extra attention should be paid to these components and their alignment.

An array of team designs can be used to create tailored organizational responses to work challenges. For example, a temporary, multidisciplinary virtual team may be appropriate for dealing with an emergency when expertise is scattered across the company's sites, whereas a more permanent single function team may be a better fit for developing the design of an electronic subcomponent for a new product. The choice of organizing one way or another and the development work that needs to be invested represent support functions.

Financial tracking drives most high-level resource allocation decisions. However, the quality of the information provided by the tracking system to decision makers may not suffice for high performance (Chenhall, 2003). Thus, when the intangibles surrounding the performance of virtual teams are not captured by the tracking system, decisions about resources tend to provide less support, and teams may become malnourished.

The learning system includes formal training, job rotation, mentoring, coaching, workshops, conferences, and modeling. Formal classroom training is not enough. For virtual teams, online training systems are most convenient but not necessarily most effective. Learning is essential for creative knowledge work, as well as for developing the team's processes. Chief knowledge officers and chief learning officers are new executive roles for individuals who oversee the whole learning system. They need to be educated about the special needs of virtual teams.

Other support systems include work space and equipment. Without adequate and compatible hardware and software, team members cannot communicate well. Incompatible platforms create artificial handicaps to the team's process.

Change is constant, but decisions to introduce new change initiatives are not. Such initiatives may range from removing one member from a team and adding another (perhaps with the simplistic rationale that change is good) to reconfiguring the whole project or program or undergoing a merger that affects everyone. Treating change as a support system shifts the perspective on change decisions so that support of performance is emphasized. The executive role of the organizational development vice president is commonly associated with change systems, but all decision makers need a basic education in how to manage the process, as well as seek ways of aligning change initiatives with their existing virtual teams. One final major problem with virtual teams is inconsistency of support across sites. Alignment of those systems becomes a major source of performance improvement or decrement.

As a way to jump-start assessment of a virtual team's application of Principle 5: Aligning and Sustaining Support Systems, team members may examine each of their relevant support systems with the following questions in mind:

- What does the support system look like in the organization?
- How does the support system enhance collaboration?
- How does the support system undermine collaboration?

Using the Framework

Emerging from the above discussion, a series of themes can be generated around characteristics that do and do not support collaboration, for each relevant support system. From these themes, team members can brainstorm ideas for actions to improve each support system with regard to sustaining virtual team collaboration.

FINAL THOUGHTS

Virtual teams work across boundaries, sometimes a multitude of boundaries. The members connect through electronic means. Hurdles to high performance are multiplied by these conditions. Support for the teams is essential if the goal is high performance. The support requires continuous investment: investment in equipment, training, and leadership, for example. Without attention to a variety of methods for reducing hurdles and enhancing capabilities and competencies for crossing boundaries, the team will be stuck in silos and performance will suffer, especially when creative solutions to complex problems are the target.

REMINDERS

- Recognize that boundary crossing is a challenge that must be managed for virtual teams to achieve high performance levels.
- Recognize that team members have to learn how to connect with other members across the boundaries, and new competencies may need to be developed to facilitate this linking.
- Provide training that builds cultural competencies so the team processes will enable all members to feel ownership for the project and have a voice for sharing expertise.
- Recognize that the more complex the project is, the more the boundaries must be effectively navigated.
- Create integration mechanisms to link members with each other and with other parts of the organization so flow of information and decisions is facilitated.

- Match team design with the project so that the right people are involved in the right process.

- Align support systems with the team's needs, especially leadership, learning, and measurement.

- Model cultural competence at each opportunity so that the whole organization can build boundary-crossing capability.

References

Antoniou, I., Reeve, M., & Stenning, J. (2000). The information society as a complex system. *Journal of Universal Computer Science, 6*(3), 272–288.

Beyerlein, M., & Harris, C. L. (2004). *Guiding the journey to collaborative work systems: A strategic design workbook.* San Francisco: Jossey-Bass/Pfeiffer.

Chenhall, R. H. (2003). Management control systems design within its organizational context: Findings from contingency-based research and directions for the future. *Accounting, Organizations and Society, 28,* 127–168.

Davenport, T. H., & Prusak, L. (1998). *Working knowledge: How organizations manage what they know.* Boston: Harvard Business School Press.

Dirksen, V., Huizing, A., & Smit, B. (2005). *A cultural critique of organizational change: Getting in touch with reality stream: Social networks.* Paper presented at the Fourth International Critical Management Studies Conference, Judge Institute of Management, University of Cambridge, Cambridge, UK. Retrieved March 11, 2007, from http://www.mngt.waikato.ac.nz/ejrot/cmsconference/2005/proceedings/socialnetworks/Dirksen.pdf.

Harrison, S. (1995, October). Anthropological perspectives: On the management of knowledge. *Anthropology Today, 11*(5), 10–14.

Jones, S. D., & Schilling, D. J. (2000). *Measuring team performance.* San Francisco: Jossey-Bass.

Katzenbach J., & Smith, D. (1993). *The wisdom of teams: Creating the high-performance organization.* Boston: Harvard Business School Press.

Mankin, D., & Cohen, S. (2004). *Business without boundaries.* San Francisco: Jossey-Bass.

Mohrman, S., Cohen, S., & Mohrman, A. (1995). *Designing team-based organizations: New forms of knowledge work.* San Francisco: Jossey-Bass.

Nemiro, J. (1997). *Creativity in virtual teams.* Unpublished doctoral dissertation, Claremont Graduate University.

Nemiro, J. (2004). *Creativity in virtual teams: Key components for success.* San Francisco: Jossey-Bass/Pfeiffer.

Postman, N. (1999). *Building a bridge to the enlightenment: How the past can improve our future.* New York: Knopf.

Quinn, J. B., & Anderson, P. (1996). Leveraging intellect. *Academy of Management Executive, 10*(3), 21–28.

Romig, D. (2003). Side-by-side leadership. In M. Beyerlein, C. McGee, G. Klein, J. Nemiro, & L. Broedling (Eds.), *The collaborative work systems fieldbook: Strategies, tools and techniques.* San Francisco: Jossey-Bass/Pfeiffer.

Saint-Onge, H. (1996). Tacit knowledge: The key to the strategic alignment of intellectual capital. *Strategy & Leadership, 24*(2), 10–14.

Saint-Onge, H., & Wallace, D. (2003). *Leveraging communities of practice for strategic advantage.* Boston: Butterworth-Heinemann.

Saxe, J. G. (1878). "The blind men and the elephant." Retrieved March 6, 2007, from http://www.noogenesis.com/pineapple/blind_men_elephant.html.

Schein, E. H. (1996). Three cultures of management: The key to organizational learning. *Sloan Management Review, 38*(1), 9–20.

Trice, H. M., & Beyer, J. M. (1993). *The culture of work organizations.* Upper Saddle River, NJ: Prentice Hall.

Wiig, K. (1994). *Knowledge management: The central management focus for intelligent-acting organizations.* Arlington, TX: Schema Press.

Wulf, R. (1996, November). *Gestalt dialogues: Newsletter for the Integrative Gestalt Centre.* Christchurch. Retrieved March 14, 2007, from http://www.gestalt.org/wulf.htm.

Design Principles for Successful Virtual Teams

Gail Goodrich Harwood

Virtual collaboration is assumed to present particular organizational challenges. It can be argued, however, that "virtual" actually sets up the conditions for *more effective* collaboration. Any collaborative effort requires good design, clear vision and goals, boundary setting, and explicit work agreements. When collaborators are not seen or perhaps not even known, the requirement for good design intensifies. The very nature of virtual work requires more thought and greater design specificity than face-to-face work. If virtual collaboration is designed and led well, the conditions for success are explicitly defined, and the probability of success expands.

Virtual collaboration has the best chance of success when:

• The consequences of not collaborating are clear.

• Organizational success also matters to individuals.

I thank and acknowledge the Continuous Learning Group; the University of Southern California Center for Effective Organizations; Deborah Bethea Berkley; Kathie Dannemiller; Jay Galbraith; James Hartigan; Chuck Raben; Julie Smith; and Paul Tolchinsky.

- The results are heavily dependent on collaboration.
- The conditions (for example, time zones and cultures) are sufficiently challenging to cause people to raise their individual creativity and performance levels.
- Leaders are specially selected and supported to be effective in managing the virtual collaborative work situation.

The typical corporate organization has not set up the natural conditions for collaborative success. Corporations have historically organized for efficiency. Early twentieth-century theories strongly influenced how corporations organized: division and specialization of labor, hierarchy, central control, and decision making at the top. While many companies tried decentralized models and empowered team models in the 1980s and 1990s, lack of education and faulty designs often led to inefficiency, confusion, and a return to the control model.

The "efficient organization" is typically characterized by:

- Internal competition
- "Tall walls"—a silo mentality
- Lack of trust and a tendency to place blame
- An overriding need to "win" and take credit, especially when bonus structures are tied to hitting results targets

Contrast this with the requirements for effective virtual collaboration:

- Cooperation internally to compete externally
- Partnering across boundaries
- Trust, learning, and transparency
- A mentality that says, "We all win together"

Rosabeth Moss Kanter (1997) wrote in the *Frontiers of Management,* "Boundaries are sometimes a mental imposition—a decision to divide the world a certain way. They become real when social patterns come to enforce the imaginary walls and when once deliberate choices become mindless habits. . . . But history teaches us not to assume their permanence. . . . What matters most today is the ability to think *together,* not alone. To think imaginatively about matters of substance, incorporating many perspectives and reaching beyond conventional categories. To create new concepts that make new connections . . ." (p. 120).

While traditional organizations by design promote noncollaborative behavior, this circumstance can be overcome. Purposeful design, led by enlightened leaders, can reshape behavior and unleash a collaborative win-win spirit. This chapter breaks down the design process for virtual collaboration into ten principles, defining why the principle is important and giving practical advice on how to design for success. A summary design checklist concludes the chapter.

PRINCIPLE 1: SELECT AND POSITION LEADERS FOR SUCCESS

Why It Matters

Effective leadership is central to all aspects of designing and managing virtual collaborative work. Today's organizations look much different from yesterday's. Boundaries are blurred across geographies, countries and cultures, markets, supplier networks, and alliances. Today's leaders must embrace, teach, coach, and encourage collaboration as the norm. Communication is the critical competency for leaders of virtual collaboration work—"the capacity to create a compelling vision that takes people to a new place, and to translate that vision into action" (Bennis & Goldsmith, 1997, p. 4).

How to Do It

Select for Key Competencies and Attributes   Leaders charged with managing virtual collaboration work will face challenging circumstances such as managing across time zones and cultures. They are more likely to be successful if they possess the following skills and attributes:

- Curious learners by nature. They should possess an attitude that says, "What can we learn here?" versus "What's wrong here, and who's to blame?"

- Relationship focused. They demonstrate an orientation toward "people" versus "things" and a genuine interest in others' success.

- Experienced and credible in the business but not stuck in their ways. Their track record is one of results and innovation.

- Emotionally intelligent. They display a mature, even-handed approach in their dealings with others.

- Process and outcome focused. They have shown their ability to keep self and team on track and motivated.

- Able to give positive and constructive feedback. They are good observers and use objective data to encourage positive behaviors and address behaviors that need work.

- Able to teach and coach others to perform their best. They have supported and involved teams and individuals in problem solving.

- Adept at giving recognition. They have provided recognition formally and informally in a way that is appreciated and motivates continued success.

- Exceptional communicators and listeners. They have demonstrated skill in communicating face-to-face as well as virtually and to groups as well as one-to-one.

Use a Comprehensive Selection Process   To increase predictability and the probability of leader success in virtual collaboration, consider these elements in the selection process. Post or advertise leader positions with a realistic job preview that makes clear the limitations and challenges of virtual collaboration and the degree of skill required. A realistic preview will draw the right candidates and encourage less competitive candidates to opt out.

Create a structured interview process that places the candidate "in the role" of virtual collaboration leader. Use multiple raters and behaviorally anchored rating scales to create an objective assessment. Be ready to probe with additional questions to gain more insight into how the candidate would think and act in situations where members are dispersed across geographies, time zones, and cultures.

Use real situations to assess candidates; for example, test their abilities to organize and communicate information by giving them a work sample. Create an in-box exercise where data must be sorted and distilled and then communicated to virtual team members to create the context for collaboration and performance. Check with the human resource (HR) professionals to consider using standard validated tests to determine work style and work preferences. As a final check, invite the top candidates to meet knowledgeable senior leaders who can talk with them about expectations and the challenges of collaborative virtual work.

Leverage Executive Leadership   The role of an executive leader responsible for virtual collaborative work is to:

- Create the business case, vision, and corporate outcomes.
- Be an ambassador, able to represent the work to senior executives and the board, if necessary.
- Ensure goal alignment with corporate direction and other organizations.
- Invest time and energy as an educator and communicator.
- Select the right leaders to manage virtual collaborative work.
- Approve or veto decisions that require executive-level involvement.
- Encourage learning from mistakes and continuous improvement.
- Ensure that the right recognition and rewards systems are in place, including bonuses.
- Lead by example in coaching, positive encouragement, and celebration.

Virtual collaboration is not a state or way of working that can be dictated from on high. Ideally it begins with people who have a stake in the outcome designing their future together. When people are personally invested in success, their level of commitment and discretionary effort rises. Face-to-face design sessions enable relationships to be built and differences to be aired and worked out before being cast in a virtual mode. Enlightened executives justify the expense of design and learning sessions, considering them an investment rather than an expense. They know that when team members are truly engaged, their level of commitment and effort expands. In a virtual project, face-to-face design increases the probability of success and therefore has a positive impact on the bottom line. Consider the following firsthand experience.

An Executive Point of View   James Hartigan is CEO of Integres, a transportation logistics solutions company based near Sacramento, California. While a vice president at United Airlines, Hartigan was charged with developing an airline within the airline, operating initially over nine locations and ultimately twenty. He was also head of the Cargo Division and spearheaded the launch of a global freighter operation. On an industry basis, he worked with executive counterparts in the global Star Alliance to oversee development of seamless service for customers across carriers and led the development of industry-wide cargo standards for the twenty-first century. Here he speaks to his significant experience as executive sponsor of virtual operation design efforts.

> The work of executive sponsor is "real work." The success or failure of a design effort falls squarely in the sponsor's court. Spending time with the team is critical, both as an educator and as a link with stakeholders and would-be detractors and critics. Having experienced the sponsor role on numerous initiatives where people would be operating in a virtual team effort, sometimes around the world, here is my advice:
>
> - Don't assume that people know the big picture. Err on the side of providing more information and perspective than might seem necessary.
>
> - When an idea seems wacky, trust that there is good thought behind it. Don't shoot down the idea until you've asked a lot of questions to understand.
>
> - Support in-person design and checkpoint sessions. Take a leap of faith that the investment will pay off when it counts. Be prepared to be amazed at the initiative, creativity, and forged commitment of people who may never have met and who may not even speak the same language.

Position Leaders for Success   To position leaders for success in managing virtual collaborative work, design an interactive high-energy work session to explore roles and responsibilities in the context of corporate objectives. Use senior executives as educators to enroll leaders in the vision and corporate outcome targets. Set high-level expectations and boundaries. Involve leaders in fleshing out the details of their own roles. Work with leaders to create and align goals and objectives. Prepare leaders for design meetings and taking a leadership role by involving them in the creation of team launch and work sessions.

A critical part of positioning leaders for success is to set expectations for how leaders will get results. Figure 2.1 can be a helpful guide for setting expectations and analyzing "how" leaders can get results in the right way to create a culture of "want to do" versus "have to do."

The quadrant 1 leader does not demonstrate either a strong results focus or positive, reinforcing leadership. This leader gets poor business results, instability,

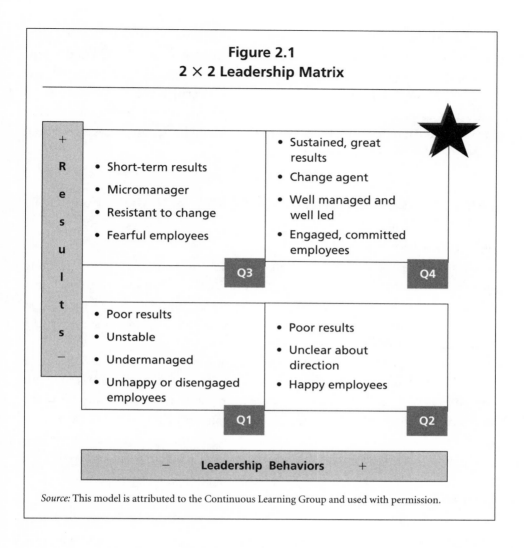

Figure 2.1
2 × 2 Leadership Matrix

Results +	
• Short-term results • Micromanager • Resistant to change • Fearful employees	• Sustained, great results • Change agent • Well managed and well led • Engaged, committed employees
	Q3 Q4
• Poor results • Unstable • Undermanaged • Unhappy or disengaged employees	• Poor results • Unclear about direction • Happy employees
Results −	Q1 Q2

−   Leadership Behaviors   +

Source: This model is attributed to the Continuous Learning Group and used with permission.

and unhappy or disengaged team members. The quadrant 2 leader demonstrates excellent reinforcing leadership skills but lacks focus and direction. This leader also gets poor results but often has happy employees who are not necessarily engaged in the success of the enterprise. The quadrant 3 leader is totally focused on getting results but uses negative leadership behaviors. This leader may get results in the short run, but creates fear and therefore unsustainable results. The quadrant 4 leader has a balanced focus on results and on getting those results through involvement, positive reinforcement, and constructive feedback and coaching.

The Q4 leader represents the leadership balance to strive for to create sustainable results and highly engaged, committed team members. "Q4 leadership" is desirable in any work situation, but it is critical in a virtual collaboration setting. The leader must find ways to "observe" and give positive and constructive feedback and coaching in a timely way and, more often than not, without being face-to-face. Thinking through these implications in the design process is essential to position leaders and teams for success.

PRINCIPLE 2: ENGAGE ALL IN A COMMON VISION, PURPOSE, AND DESTINY

Why It Matters

A sense of "destiny" is important in unleashing discretionary effort. Helping people become part of the vision is the essential building block in the design process. All other design elements flow from this foundational element. It is impossible, for example, to set up work processes and measures of success if the vision and purpose are unclear.

Everyone wants to be part of something meaningful. In *Competing for the Future,* Hamel and Prahalad (1994) punctuate their discussion of destiny with this employee quote: "I have worked here for eight years. The pressure for profit improvement, quality improvement and cost containment never goes away. But I never had any sense of being part of a worldwide team, fighting a worldwide war. And I never really understood the consequences of winning or losing" (p. 147).

How to Do It

If appropriate for the organization, a vision statement can be drafted first with the leadership team and then presented and worked through with a design team or representative sample of the whole. Using this draft as a sort of "straw model" helps the leadership team get to common ground. By then opening up the debate to the larger team, they give a visible and tangible signal about the way in which leaders are expected to lead.

To contribute to vision work, people first need context. Ask executive leaders to help educate and enroll people in vision and purpose. Executives can paint the picture by answering the following questions: What is the industry landscape? Who are our competitors? What makes them formidable? How do we compare?

What are our customer requirements? How do we know? What product or service will we deliver? What is our strategy? How do we want to be known? When we are successful, what will that mean to our customers, our employees, and our shareholders? How would we describe our vision and purpose—our destiny?

Getting people "enrolled" in the vision requires involvement. Once executive leaders have painted the picture, consider the following activities to involve everyone and create shared ownership:

- *Explore the context.* Use a senior leader "panel" to discuss the above points. Have people at table groups that mix functional expertise and experience discuss what they thought they heard and identify key questions for the panel. Moderate a panel discussion asking questions from the tables.

- *Imagine the future.* Present a draft vision. Ask people to imagine what it would be like to be wildly successful three to five years into the future. What would they see? What would they hear? What would customers be saying? What would it look and feel like to work on a wildly successful team? Add to the vision to make it even more compelling.

- *Have fun.* Write "headlines" for industry news publications or business magazines. Create individual or group "paintings" depicting the vision.

PRINCIPLE 3: CREATE THE CONTEXT FOR ENERGY AND UNDERSTANDING

Why It Matters

The average design team member will have had little exposure to the reasoning behind corporate strategy. Their work may be so far removed from the marketplace and the customer that they have weak lines of sight between what they do every day and what difference it makes. Even if they are close to strategy and have a strong line of sight to results, their perspective may be narrow. A virtual setting can add yet another measure of distance between the work and its impact. To focus the design process on "what" and "how" may result in an efficient model, but one that lacks heart. Virtual collaboration takes energy and imagination that go beyond the normal working environment. Grounding design team members and work team members in the "why" can pay big dividends. Engaged employees consistently perform at a heightened level of effort, which translates positively to bottom-line results. Towers Perrin's global data show a significant link between engagement, employee behavior, and customer behavior—and, ultimately, revenue growth and profitability (Towers Perrin, 2004).

How to Do It

To create energy and build understanding, consider these sorts of activities:

- Invite customers to address the group and describe their business challenges. Ask what they think the organization does well or not so well, and recommend three things that could be done better to meet their needs. Provide an opportunity to ask questions.

- Invite suppliers or partners to address the group and describe their business challenges and what it is like to be a partner. Ask what they think the organization does well, and what they need from the organization so that *they* can be more successful. Similar panels could be set up with internal partners, customers, or suppliers.

- Divide the group into teams, and assign each a competitor to research. Have the group describe the competitor, what it promises the customer, and what its vision and competitive edge are. Present the research to the whole group and explore distinctions between "us" and "them."

- Find a way to experience what it is like to be the organization's customer or supplier. Observe a customer operation using a checklist to record observations. Debrief insights as a group to inform the development of operating principles and standards.

PRINCIPLE 4: CREATE A UNIVERSAL LANGUAGE IN OPERATING PRINCIPLES

Why It Matters

Clear expectations are essential to good organizational functioning and take on heightened significance in virtual collaborative work. Trust, confidence, and outcomes are stronger when all people in the system are operating under the same principles and to the same standards. When people representing the whole system have participated in creating those principles and standards, there is greater ownership and effort to uphold what has been created. The operating principles become a universal language and provide common focus that transcends time zones and cultures.

How to Do It

To involve people in the creation of operating principles, use a structured process that includes steps similar to these:

1. Give people a sample of design principles to jump-start their thinking.

2. Have people work in small groups, assigning or asking groups to choose a subject—for example, financial outcomes, customer satisfaction, employee experience, or product or service quality. Give the groups time to brainstorm ideas and then draft operating principles or standards.

3. Post all drafts, and set up a "gallery walk" for all participants to give feedback and add suggestions.

4. Reconvene the small groups to review feedback and fine-tune their drafts.

5. Recruit an "editor group" that will edit the final drafts and bring them back to the whole group. Have people signal their endorsement using a win-win consensus method (adapted from Brooke, 1984). Each person should be at least 70 percent comfortable with the team's decision but 100 percent committed to uphold it. Use thumbs up, thumbs down, or a sideways thumb (questions/not sure) as a quick way to review each statement and work to consensus.

Here is a sample list of operating principles from a virtual network:

Sample Operating Principles for a Virtual Network

- We think globally and act locally.

- Our processes and efforts on a daily basis are focused on meeting the customer's expectations, both internal and external.

- Our work process is designed to promote open, full sharing of information within and across teams.

- We work to eliminate artificial boundaries between people and work units in pursuit of our common goals.

- We know exactly how our work contributes to company success and what our customers value most.

- We are clear about latitude for local decision making and the process for escalating decisions and issues.
- Measurements are owned by teams to promote accountability and continuous improvement.
- We are all working to the same standards:
  - Customer inquiries answered within the hour; if complex, within four hours, letting the customer know interim status
  - Colleague calls and e-mails answered within the hour
  - Zero defects in packing and shipping
  - Measures updated to share drive by close of business on Wednesdays

PRINCIPLE 5: DOCUMENT RELIABLE, REPEATABLE WORK PROCESSES

Why It Matters

Creating work process is the heart of the design. Designing understandable processes that can be easily followed increases the probability that desired outcomes will be met consistently. Documented processes are also important to facilitate periodic review of results to identify process improvement opportunities.

How to Do It

Creating a valid work process is best accomplished in small working groups. Leaders, as part of their preparatory work, should review and determine what the logical groups should be and which leaders will work with each design team group. The use of templates will help organize work process and flow, help the process move along, and ensure that all teams use a similar approach. Leaders should decide in advance such issues as level of detail and format for output. If process flow symbols and process are not typically used, conduct a brief lesson. Borrowing from the world of sports, some successful virtual teams have created "playbooks"—handy reference guidebooks that spell out vision and goals, process, and critical performer behaviors. A playbook that everyone in the network follows forms the basis for measures and continuous improvement.

Work design groups should comprise people from different business units, divisions, or functions to mirror the groups that will need to collaborate.

The design work should proceed in intense detail within each team, punctuated by report-outs and check-ins with the whole group to review progress and get feedback. Work with the lead team to map out blocks of time for design work and reviews. If the design work is spread out over several weeks, design a check-in process so that team members can get input from people back home. Keep a visible record of open issues to ensure that questions that surface in team reviews, typically cross-team and boundary issues, are resolved and communicated.

PRINCIPLE 6: ESTABLISH ROLES AND ACCOUNTABILITY FOR DECISION MAKING

Why It Matters

In most virtual situations, some activities and tasks do not require collaboration across teams, functions, or units. Finding the right balance of collaborative and autonomous tasks is essential to avoid confusion. Identifying roles and responsibilities in decision making is important in any work design, and especially in virtual collaborative work where real-time face-to-face discussions are not always possible.

How to Do It

Once work processes have been designed, gather teams across functions, units, and locations to create a full picture of decision making. Job descriptions, training, and standards go a long way toward assisting people in understanding their roles and responsibilities. The matrix tool in Table 2.1 takes responsibility to the task level. It shows the key tasks in a sales process to achieve consistent process across regions. Moreover, it links different jobs or functions together so that accountability for a whole process can be seen and understood. Use the following steps to guide this process:

1. For a given process, assemble the people involved (or representatives of business units or functions). This tool is easily self-facilitated. Replicate the matrix on a large board or on a wall. Sticky notes or index cards work well.

2. Working as a group, identify all the functions, units, and locations involved in the process. Record those individuals or groups across the top of the matrix.

3. Identify the essential tasks or decisions where clarity is desired. Record those down the left side of the matrix. Examine the sample role codes. Agree on

Table 2.1
Example of a Roles and Decision Accountability Matrix

Key Decisions or Tasks	Regional Sales Manager	Regional Marketing Manager	Regional Sales Associates	Senior Vice President, Sales and Marketing	Executive Vice President, Customer Experience
Define customer target population	R	C	C/I	A/V	C
Define selling methodology	C/I	C/I	C/I	R/A	C
Design sales collateral materials	C/I	R	C/I	A	C/V
Create quarterly sales plan	A	I	R	I	I
Determine success measures	C/I	C/I	C/I	R/A	C

Note: R = responsibility and authority to make the decision. A = may not make the decision but will be held accountable. Often a more senior role. V = veto. Not just hierarchy; refers to a role that can block a specific decision. C = consult. May be consulted and give input before a decision is made. I = informed. Needs to be informed about the decision after it is made. Other labels can be used. (Tool adapted from Galbraith, Downey, and Kates, 2002.)

which ones will be used, and add or delete as desired. Discuss the meaning of each action code to be sure everyone has the same meaning in mind.

4. Work through each task and decision, determining each role. Debate and negotiation are the keys to a well-thought-out result.

5. Review the results with the whole group, and determine whether there are other stakeholders who need to review and approve the completed matrix.

6. Use the matrix for a periodic review to check how the process is going and make any necessary adjustments to improve it.

PRINCIPLE 7: CREATE GOALS AND MEASURES ACCESSIBLE TO ALL

Why It Matters

Creating goals that can be held in common across the network is an essential anchor for effective virtual organizations. "The organizations of the future will be networks, clusters, cross-functional teams, temporary systems, ad hoc task forces, lattices, modules, matrices—almost anything but pyramids. We don't even know yet what to call these new configurations, but we do know that the ones that succeed will be less hierarchical and have more linkages based on common goals rather than traditional reporting relationships" (Bennis, 2000, p. 29).

Identifying measures that can be easily accessed through technology is also crucial. Line of sight and destiny are reinforced if people and teams can readily see the results of their efforts. The opportunity for early correction to create better outcomes is also enhanced. Measures are important in any endeavor, and even more so in a virtual collaborative effort, as they serve to bind teams in pursuit of common goals that transcend differences.

How to Do It

The leadership team should do some preliminary work to bring to the larger team. This starts with the executive leader identifying goals for the organization, which align vertically with corporate goals and horizontally with peer organizations, using the "SMART" model:

Specific	Clear statement of what is to be accomplished or delivered, in concrete terms that can be easily observed and mutually understood
Measurable	Define how success will be measured in quantitative and qualitative terms, stating the outcomes and benefits
Attainable	Challenging and stretching but achievable
Relevant	Tied to the overall direction of the company or business unit
Time bound	Time frame for the goal is stated, including stages

This model gives virtual teams a common framework for fine-tuning, challenging, and aligning goals and measures. Using a common organizing model helps overcome the disadvantages of not being able to work on goals face to face. (See the www.wiley.com/go/virtualteamshandbook Web site for a SMART Goals Worksheet and Example.)

The leadership team should develop goals that cascade from and align with the executive leader's goals. This then becomes the starting point for the larger group. Many organizations use too many measures. The trick is to isolate the critical few. To get to "the critical few" measures, work through the following steps (adapted from Covey, 2004):

1. Consider the framework created, which includes vision and purpose, operating principles and standards, work process, roles and key decision points, and draft goals created by the leaders.

2. Consider and define the different types of measures, including lagging, leading, and real-time indicators. Examples of each are shown in Table 2.2.

3. Given your virtual operating framework, time zones, and other differences, brainstorm all the current and possible measures that could indicate success and progress toward goals. For each, identify whether it is a lagging, leading, or real-time indicator. Evaluate measures against these criteria.

Table 2.2
Types of Measures

Lagging Indicators	Leading Indicators	Real-Time Indicators
Provide a historical look at past performance.	Can be predictors of future results; data can be analyzed and action taken to affect outcomes.	Provide a snapshot of where things stand right now. Corrective action can be taken immediately to improve future results.
Examples: quarterly earnings, employee turnover	*Examples:* quality audits, employee survey results	*Examples:* inventory levels, sales and order volumes

Can activities and outcomes be tracked? How and by whom? Will the value of the measure exceed the cost of measuring? Do we have a way to make the measure readily accessible to everyone? Will the measure drive the right behaviors with no unintended consequences?

4. Based on discussion and debate of brainstormed measures, identify the critical few that will be practical, timely, accessible to everyone in the virtual network, and be actionable (leading and real time). Finally, identify who will be responsible for setting up and collecting measures and communicating results.

PRINCIPLE 8: SET UP MECHANISMS FOR FEEDBACK AND CELEBRATION

Why It Matters

Connecting across functions, units, time zones, and cultures is essential to reinforce the notion that "we're in this together." If the connections are managed to focus on learning and positive encouragement, people will look forward to the opportunity to participate and will be inclined to look for opportunities to improve.

How to Do It

A robust design process will be managed so that people become familiar with and value feedback. The process of going deep in small groups and airing results in broader groups becomes an operational norm that can be extended into the regular work environment.

Working in virtual collaboration mode requires a review both within the immediate team and across the larger network of teams, functions, or locations. Review within the immediate team can be facilitated by a checklist, or "scorecard," that contains key activities and tasks that reflect the agreed principles and standards and also features the key measures. Checklists will be most effective if they are large and posted in work areas. For example, use laminated chart-sized checklists that can be written on with erasable markers. This creates a natural way for teams to focus and debrief. (See the Sample Review Plan on the www.wiley .com/go/virtualteamshandbook Web site.)

Leaders Play a Critical Feedback Role   Checklists and scorecards can go a long way to promote self-management, focus, and commitment, but nothing substitutes for leadership. A Corporate Leadership Council study (2004) that examined 106 performance management strategies found that "fair and accurate informal feedback from a knowledgeable source is the single most effective performance management lever available to the organization. Feedback should be voluntary, immediate and positive" (p. 4).

To use feedback most effectively, leaders should strive for a four-to-one ratio of positive feedback to negative or constructive feedback (Braksick, 2007). Encouraging positive behaviors has a huge payoff in commitment and discretionary effort. Recognizing positive behaviors and celebrating "what is going right" needs to be part of the organization's day-to-day operations. Involve people in establishing those norms so that it feels right for the organization. As part of the design process, you will want to create a performance tracking plan. (See the www.wiley.com/go/virtualteamshandbook Web site for a Performance and Recognition Tracking Log Template.)

Issue Management Is a Critical Part of Effective Virtual Collaboration   The overall review plan should contain methods for identifying and addressing issues, including the escalation of concerns to senior leaders in cases where resolution is beyond the control of the group. To manage issues and opportunities effectively, consider these steps:

- Determine how people and teams will raise issues and make suggestions for improvement. Consider an online method that everyone can view.

- Establish a process for review, daily in the beginning and perhaps less frequently as time goes on. Team leaders across locations could have a standing agenda item for their daily or weekly calls, for example.

- Involve people beyond the leadership team and from different teams.

- Establish standards for resolution, for example, same-day resolution on clarification of process or policies, and three- to fourteen-day resolution for more complex issues or new opportunities.

- Ensure that when issues and opportunities are resolved, there is a method for communicating outcomes.

- Avoid blame by encouraging the team to adopt a "curious learner" mentality, as in, "What can we learn from this?"

(See the www.wiley.com/go/virtualteamshandbook Web site for an Issues and Opportunities Tracking template.)

PRINCIPLE 9: CREATE A PLAN TO "CAST" THE NET WIDER

Why It Matters

Working with a design team or representative sample of the whole is an important ingredient in successful design, but it is not enough. If people and teams beyond the design team can also be enrolled in the vision and involved in creating work processes and measures, the whole system can be set up for success. The transition from design to implementation requires a strategy of involvement. As Confucius shared, "I hear and I forget, I see and I remember, I do and I understand."

How to Do It

The transfer of energy, information, knowledge, and commitment from a representative sample design team to the broader population can be tricky. Ideally there will be some communication and involvement during the design process, especially around the design of work process. Good stakeholder analysis at the start will ensure that all relevant parties are included as the net is cast wider. Leaders must help design team members prepare to educate and support their peers. There can be a fine line between sharing enthusiasm and communicating as a know-it-all, which can create resentment. Designing the communication and education process should involve both leaders and design team members and for authenticity should include people who have not been directly involved in the design process. Together, they can explore and create ways to "cast the net wider."

Working in virtual mode heightens the need to have a consistent approach so that all people in the network experience the same education process. Education that works at the emotional level will be most effective. Ideally the process will link head and heart. Holding work sessions that are interactive and involve people from different local teams is essential. A memo or a briefing is insufficient. Following are some transition session activities (based on Bridges, 1991) that work to connect head and heart:

- Use informal taped messages from executive leaders to help people get the context, strategy, corporate goal connection, and importance of delivering the product or service well. Help people understand what is ending. Assuming the design requires letting go of some old ways of doing business, help people through the transition from ending what was to exploring what will be. If possible, create a videoconference or Webcast so that there can be an opportunity for interaction and questions.

- Tape interviews with local customers so that everyone can experience the same sort of "Aha!" moment as the design team does.

- Beyond presenting the operating principles and standards, help people take ownership by exploring the statements further to identify what they need to stop, start, or change to live up to the principles and standards.

- Help people "see" the new work process by presenting a "day in the life," where design team members tell the story as a panel or in a skit. Include in it issues faced, measures taken, and decisions made. Follow with discussions where table groups relate what they heard or saw, what they would like to know more about, and their top three questions.

- Moderate a whole room discussion. Table questions are posed and discussed by the process experts. If people work in subteams, move from mixed tables to subteam tables to discuss work process more fully and explore the implications of operating in the way that has been described.

- Identify issues and opportunities as part of the introduction and learning process, and work them as designed.

- Anticipate obstacles. Write down challenges and worries. Ask tables (or individuals) to swap lists and develop suggested solutions. Then swap back, review, and discuss insights.

PRINCIPLE 10: DESIGN FOR SUSTAINABILITY
Why It Matters
Marketplaces change, technology leaps, customer and consumer preferences shift, and corporate strategy evolves. As the saying goes, "Nothing is constant but change." Design for successful virtual collaboration must therefore be dynamic. By building plans for checks after implementation, the design can evolve to align with changing landscapes. To succeed, the design must also be aligned with other

corporate systems. For example, a virtual collaboration design will typically rely on technology for connection. If existing technology cannot support the process designed, results will not be optimal.

How to Do It

Hold Periodic Checkpoints Considering the cycles and dynamics of your business, establish points in the future where "checkpoints" would make sense. To continue to cast the net wider, involve original design team members as well as those who are living the design but were not involved at the start. To ensure corporate alignment, include partners such as human resources and information technology.

Set up virtual checkpoints by teleconference, Webcast, or videoconference at intervals that work for the business, for example, quarterly or semiannually. Also set up face-to-face checkpoints when significant shifts have occurred in the marketplace or corporate strategic direction.

A typical checkpoint agenda may include these items:

- Reinforcement and celebration of results achieved
- Briefings and Q&A about "changes in the landscape"
- Active work on issues and opportunities, including systems alignment
- Review and revision of goals and measures
- Follow-up actions agreed

Conduct Periodic Surveys In addition to design checkpoints, use leadership and employee surveys to check how the system is working. Design is, above all, a process that creates the environment in which people can succeed. Periodic checks will ensure that the design is working optimally and will enable participants to make course correction ahead of crisis points. Check effectiveness using the DCOM Model, testing the four dimensions that can be thought of as cornerstones of high performance. DCOM is based on more than a decade of research on what actions distinguish sustained high-performance organizations from others.

DCOM is attributed to CLG and used with permission.

Direction	The extent to which goals, tasks, and boundaries are clear
Competence	The extent to which teams have the technical and team skills to perform well
Opportunity	The extent to which people have the latitude to take initiative
Motivation	The extent to which people are positively reinforced

Think of these dimensions as a framework that must be balanced to create high performance. If any one element is lacking, true high performance is not possible. (See the www.wiley.com/go/virtualteamshandbook Web site for Assessing Virtual Collaboration Effectiveness Through DCOM.)

FINAL THOUGHTS

Good design anchors virtual collaboration in a way that allows energy and initiative to be unleashed. If managed well, the design process and those who lead it become the "glue" that links units, geographies, and cultures in pursuit of common goals. To be successful, design must be thought of as providing a dynamic framework for success that must be owned and embraced by those who live it.

Virtual collaboration requires visionary leadership, inspired design work, and a mind-set of "the curious learner." Executed well, a dynamic design process can overcome natural and historic boundaries to create new and better ways to function than traditional organizational models would allow. People want to be successful. The ten principles outlined in this chapter are underpinned by the belief that good design connects heart and head, and good design enables people to be successful in the system. (See the www.wiley.com/go/virtualteamshandbook Web site for the Virtual Collaboration Design Worksheet.)

VIRTUAL COLLABORATION DESIGN REMINDERS

Principle 1: Select and position leaders for success

• Identify key competencies and attributes, and design a comprehensive selection process.

- Leverage executive leadership to support the design process and remove barriers.
- Formally orient selected leaders to create ownership and set expectations for leading by driving for results and involving, reinforcing, and coaching employees.

Principle 2: Engage all in a common vision, purpose, and destiny

- Use executive leaders to describe the industry landscape and the vision. Explore the strategy framework and pose questions to a leader panel.
- Imagine what the future could be and add to the vision to make it even more compelling. Have fun creating visions of the future such as imagined headlines.

Principle 3: Create the context for energy and understanding

- Invite customers and/or suppliers to tell their stories.
- Research the competition to discover competitive advantage.
- Experience what it is like to be our customer or supplier.

Principle 4: Create a universal language in operating principles

- Begin with samples and output of vision and customer experiences.
- Use small groups to work various aspects of operating principles: financial/shareholder, customer and employee outcomes, product or service quality.
- Work to conclusion using a win-win consensus model.

Principle 5: Document reliable, repeatable work processes

- Work in small groups focused on a particular aspect of work process.
- Work iteratively to refine processes and work issues and linkages.

Principle 6: Establish roles and accountability for decision making

- Create a matrix chart to aid the discussion.
- Identify roles and accountability for activities and decisions. Work to consensus in an iterative fashion, reviewing the matrix and logic with the larger group.

Principle 7: Create goals and measures accessible to all

- Use the SMART model to create a common goal framework across units.
- Leaders create draft goals to create the framework for setting next-level goals.
- Identify the critical few measures and how they will be maintained and accessed.

Principle 8: Set up mechanisms for feedback and celebration

- Agree on scorecards or other mechanisms.
- Create the process for review and continuous improvement, including leader feedback.
- Create the process and standards for resolution of issues.

Principle 9: Create a plan to "cast" the net wider

- Identify all stakeholders who will be touched by the design.
- Develop transition activities that create understanding and ownership, for example, taped customer interviews.

Principle 10: Design for sustainability

- Create a plan to hold virtual and face-to-face checkpoints to adjust the design.
- Create a plan to survey leaders and employees to check system effectiveness and make course corrections.

RELATED ITEMS ON THE WEB

- SMART Goal Worksheet
- Sample Review Plan
- Performance and Recognition Tracking Log Template
- Issues and Opportunities Tracking Template
- Assessing Virtual Collaboration Effectiveness Through DCOM
- Virtual Collaboration Design Worksheet: Principles and Process Points

References

Bennis, W. (2000). *Managing the dream.* New York: Perseus Books.

Bennis, W., & Goldsmith, J. (1997). *Learning to lead.* New York: Perseus Books.

Braksick, L. (2007). *Unlock behavior, unleash profits* (2nd ed.). New York: McGraw-Hill.

Bridges, W. (1991). *Managing transitions: Making the most of change.* New York: Perseus Books.

Brooke, K. A. (1984). *Facilitator tools: Conflict resolution model.*

Corporate Leadership Council. (2004). *2002 Performance Management Survey.* Washington, DC: Corporate Executive Board.

Covey, S. R. (2004). *The four disciplines of execution.* New York: Simon and Schuster.

Galbraith, J., Downey, D., & Kates, A. (2002). *Designing dynamic organizations.* New York: AMACOM.

Hamel, G., & Prahalad, C. K. (1994). *Competing for the future.* Boston: Harvard Business School Press.

Kanter, R. M. (1997). *Frontiers of management.* Boston: Harvard Business School Press.

Towers Perrin. (2004). *Talent Survey: Reconnecting with employees and attracting, retaining and engaging your workforce.* New York: Towers Perrin.

PART TWO

Building a Collaborative Culture

The four chapters addressing how to build a collaborative culture focus on the soft infrastructure of organizational and team culture. Although organizational culture has always had an impact on performance, its intelligent management has never been more critical than with virtual teams. The support, guidance, shaping, and identification that flow from the culture help focus the attention, effort, and expertise of the team's members more quickly and with more stability, especially when teams are dissolving and reforming rapidly.

Chapter Three focuses on people-centric virtual networks and the emotional bandwidth they depend on to enable members to feel connected and cared for. Where some managers may consider the social nature of virtual teamwork to be a handicap, in this chapter it is viewed as an opportunity and a tool to create an atmosphere of support and community. Use of a variety of methods to communicate support leads to the achievement of the team's performance goal.

The work of virtual teams is more complex and dynamic than that of traditional teams. Excellence takes more planning and support. It also depends on trust. In Chapter Four, the authors show that collaboration in a virtual team context requires trust, shared understanding, and constructive relationships among team members. As management control becomes more difficult in work situations, trust must be relied on to fill the gap so resources are used well to achieve objectives. The first rule of trust is for team members to keep the commitments and promises they make to each other. Then the foundation is in place for dealing with conflict and for effective collaboration.

Chapter Five focuses on a problem that affects all virtual teams: making sense of fragmented information flowing in from multiple sources. This is a key competence that virtual teams must master. Meetings are important milestones in the team dynamic, but the conversations that take place between meetings are even more important. An intentional approach to the design of conversations helps build the relationships among the team members. This chapter describes five methods for making those conversations effective: clarity, connection, candor, co-creation, and commitment.

This topic concludes with an example of methods for building trust in the virtual team in Chapter Six. Trust has three facets: contractual, communication, and competence. A tool designed to build and support trust in virtual teams is described. The authors build a strong case that the effectiveness of virtual collaboration is contingent not on technology but on the trust-based relationships that the technology supports.

The Three-Fold Path
of Expanding Emotional
Bandwidth in Virtual Teams

Trina Hoefling

The *American Heritage Dictionary* defines *virtual* as "existing or resulting in essence or effect though not in actual fact, form, or name." *Virtual reality* suggests a simulation that is so lifelike as to feel real but is not in fact real. *Virtual teaming* and *virtual work* can take on that same feeling of "essential closeness but not realness." In fact, however, they *are* real. Virtual work is not a close approximation of work but a viable alternative way of working. It is not second best based on circumstances, and it is not compromise, mirage, or simulation. Neither is it overlay, replication, or poor substitute. Leaders and organizations need to begin thinking of virtual work as distributed work, not a compromised situation.

Increasingly organizations are challenged by employees, contractors, and clients to redefine work as deliverable results created through a process of relationship building among a host of stakeholders, both inside and outside the formal walls of the organization. A new sociology is being born using teams and virtual work as a way of organizing the workplace. Communities are creating and building on the Internet daily. The number of host sites that enable virtual communities on any interest to instant message, chat, schedule, and store knowledge and communication streams expands daily. Many of us open our e-mail each day to several virtual community messages from people we talk to frequently but have never met. In cyberspace, romantic matches are made, friendships deepen, and knowledge is shared among strangers based on a simple request for help, all proving that the old-fashioned handshake networking strategy is alive and well in cyberspace.

Nevertheless, the overriding perception in most companies continues to be that a virtual team is a poor substitute for colocated work based on unfortunate circumstances. Many managers charged with implementing virtual teams attempt to have the group meet in person as much as possible and then make do with inferior communication strategies between what are sometimes referred to as "real meetings." Group dynamics, ground rules, and meeting guidelines are rolled over to a virtual environment with little regard to the effectiveness of the fit. Not every dynamic, rule, or guideline needs to change in a virtual environment, nor should they. Yet some should. With collaborative software, huge opportunities to enhance group process are being missed because of people's tendency to stick with the familiar.

WHAT IS WORK, AND WHERE DOES IT HAPPEN?

The capabilities of technology change the way we think not only of basic work processes, but also of the way organizations and teams are built and managed. DSL, broadband cable, interactive and on-demand TV, intranets and extranets, virtual private networks, integrated supply chains, online communities, smart cards and devices, wireless devices integrated with the Internet: all expand what is possible. What also needs to expand along with the technical tools and toys, however, is the way people think about work itself. The first step in the path to greater emotional bandwidth is the acceptance of three mind shifts about work itself.

Mind Shift 1: Work Is Becoming People-Centric, Not Place-Centric

Networks are the workplace, not a building. It is no longer necessary to go to a place to perform basic functions: buy, sell, work, research, share information, and communicate. Virtual work can draw talent quickly from different functions, locations, and organizations. The goal is to leverage intellectual capital and apply it as quickly as possible. This gives organizations the agility to increase speed, expand expertise, and access strategic alliances to meet customer demands better.

Mind Shift 2: Connecting Through Networks Is the Process of Work

Organizations can distribute organizational learning faster through knowledge-sharing networks such as functional areas, professional associations, or client or product teams. Technically, global networking options proliferate. The Internet transforms how people find and communicate with one another. Two relationships matter: the relationship between people and the relationship between people and technology. The relationships between people are built and maintained face-to-face and across the wires. Work relationships are more accessible as geographical and technical boundaries fall. The second relationship, however, decides the limits. People and technology have relationships as well. As long as e-mail is second choice in all cases, work is accommodating unfortunate distance. What if, rather, e-mail connects to GroupWise, a crossplatform collaborative software product offering e-mail, calendaring, instant messaging, and document management? What if it also downloads automatically into team BlackBerries, so that team schedules, documents, and intelligence are immediately available to every team member without fail? This redefines work and how work gets done. E-mail is no longer a quick note-messaging service and courier; it is a vehicle for team scheduling, project management, time management, electronic administrative support, tracking critical success factors, and calendaring. It still couriers messages too. The BlackBerry is a phone, a GPS, a Gameboy, a camera, an MP3 player, and a remote e-mailing device.

Networks, human and electronic, have traditionally been valued as vehicles leading to a specific result, such as comparison shopping or online directories. It becomes fundamentally more powerful to think of networks as the process itself: how work gets done, teams get built, knowledge gets shared, and complexity gets managed. Today's organization is literally and figuratively built around the interconnection of virtual, human, and electronic networks with very high bandwidth, and not the workplace per se. In other words, the technical and emotional bandwidth among organization members fundamentally affects the quality of work being done.

Mind Shift 3: Commitment Beyond "Doing My Job"

Since the industrial age, organizational leaders and management consultants have been trying to recreate a sense of camaraderie through engaging employees' commitment and connection to more than their job description. Without pursuing the effectiveness of these efforts, it is relevant to say that in an increasingly virtual work world, organization members are more geographically and physically isolated, not only from their team members but from their organizations and sometimes their customers. At the same time, many people require a greater sense of meaning and purpose from their work and seek belonging to something greater than themselves.

On a practical level, if distributed team members do not have a clear sense of commitment and how their work connects with the overall plan, individual efforts run a greater risk of being misaligned with the strategic priorities and organizational mission. Virtual work mutually demands individual and organizational commitment beyond a job description to ensure connection, purpose, meaning, and focus. The commitment has to come not just from the work itself, but also from the way the group members find, interact, and depend on the team and each other. Individually and collectively, the virtual job is about outputs *and* relationship management, about process *and* a way of working.

Employees, even contractors, increasingly seek connection to the workplace community as part of their identity. Many workers today are knowledge workers, not producers on a mechanical assembly line. Labor's contribution is primarily mental, not muscle. These same employees and contractors expect to have a voice in defining the quality of their work lives, a self-definition that goes beyond being merely resources to use or discard at will. Cross-functional teams are expected to practice boundary crossing. In order for this collection of individuals to begin functioning as a team, the barriers are, or need to be, dissolving between people and functions.

EXPANDING EMOTIONAL BANDWIDTH

The electronic handshake moves people into connection. How much more powerful can collaboration be in a work team that is connected to one another personally as well as electronically? Just as productivity dramatically increases when an Internet user moves from dial-up to broadband, so does a virtual team's productivity increase when the group has emotional as well as electronic connection. Emotional bandwidth is the personal and sustainable connection created among virtual team members who are working together for a common purpose toward a goal. It also reflects increased organizational commitment.

What makes an organization an entity that takes on a consciousness, a life of its own? It is a collective of the thinking and feeling that is held in common by its members, a co-creation. It is not, as is commonly believed, an entity that preexists and to which people merely contribute outputs. It is an organism, ever changing, based on the collective beliefs of its members, focused together on aligning with mission, vision, and goals. Members give the organization life, and more life is given by committed organizational members.

Whether colocated or distributed, organization members are more committed to an organization when they see how they contribute to the mission. Commitment can be hard enough to create in a colocated workplace. The virtual environment appears to run the risk of increased disconnection and isolation, and it may—if the organization's leaders do not shift toward a more holistic, systemic view of individual members' relationships to the collective whole. The community—the collective itself—takes on power, precedence, and focus; it is not a corporate machine that uses people and financial resources to achieve goals. The strength of this connection to the workplace and team is measured by emotional bandwidth. The more people know and feel connected to one another (that is, the wider the emotional bandwidth), the greater the commitment to the work is.

Workplace community building has been viewed by most as an organizational ideal, but it does not need to be a utopian dream. If the interaction among people is the actual process of work, it is the promise of virtual teams to redefine interaction, which makes boundary crossing and network development truly powerful. Virtual teams are part of larger virtual organizations and are deeply embedded within the larger whole. Rather than creating more distance, virtual teams make expanded emotional bandwidth possible by using relationship rather than geography as the connecting point.

The virtual manager's work is to see the network as the workplace, to work with other organizational members who also work there to connect people interpersonally and organizationally, lead the team to success, and watch as emotional bandwidth widens with full attention to quality.

This chapter is a road map for expanded emotional bandwidth, enabling every organizational member to share responsibility in building highly committed virtual teams and producing successful outcomes (Figure 3.1). The reader will travel the threefold path for creating and maintaining systems, protocols, and processes that support expanded emotional bandwidth in distributed teams without geographical or functional limitations. Virtual teaming bypasses silos while systemically

Figure 3.1
Road Map to Expanded Emotional Bandwidth

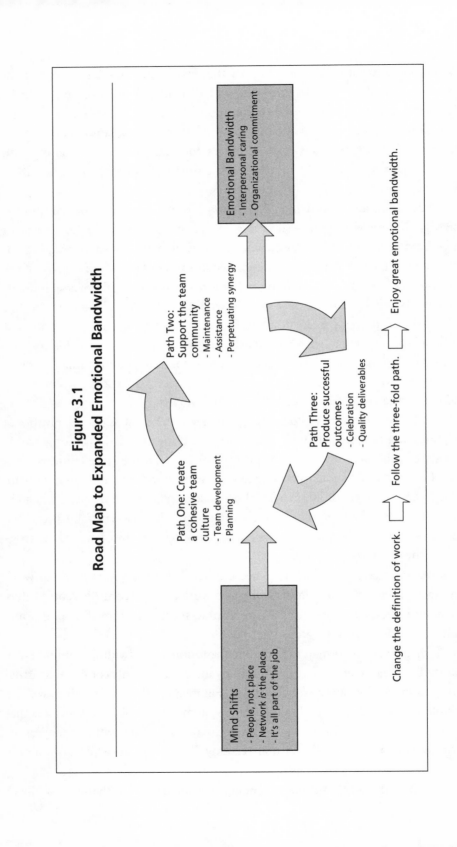

supporting access and commitment to organizational membership that is more than merely functional responsibility.

THE TAO OF VIRTUAL TEAM FUNCTIONING: THE THREE-FOLD PATH

When every virtual team member and leader commits to sharing responsibility for fulfilling three fundamental responsibilities, virtual teams can create and maintain a smooth pathway.

Path 1: Create a Cohesive Team Culture

The work of team managers is to engage people in their work, their projects, and their teams through collaboration. Collaboration is about more than good communication. Communication is only the medium by which conversations occur. Virtual groups sometimes fail to become synergistic teams because they do not recognize the deep truth that most work gets done through relationship, not task. The first of the three-fold path is to create a cohesive team culture through relationship building and establishing agreed-on ways of working together.

Teamwork is fundamentally social. Virtual team members need special care. Despite becoming more commonplace, despite distributed employees being more accepted, despite organizations' strategic commitments to becoming truly global internally as well as externally, working as part of a team that one seldom sees can feel isolating.

Cohesion is critical to team functioning in colocated *and* virtual environments. Although the technology that supports virtual teams gets most of the attention, it is really the change in the nature of teams, not the use of technology, that creates new connection opportunities for team leaders and members. Simple team discussions should occur early in the team formation to determine communication infrastructure, protocols, and process flow. Decisions should be revisited as often as needed to ensure continual emotional bandwidth. When the electronic network goes down, work is interrupted. When the emotional bandwidth is strained, work is also interrupted. Planning and preventive maintenance are small investments if work flows easily among people.

A virtual team has more difficulty seeing itself as a whole that is moving together toward a common goal. The communication infrastructure and ground rules help, but it is also important to help each member know every part of this whole team so that everyone sees how individual actions contribute to forward movement and how individuals contribute to the collective.

Team Atmosphere   Establishing infrastructure does not mean that strict rules and regulations must be created and stringently enforced, but it is important to decide as a group what kind of atmosphere the team wants to create and sustain. They can place priority on being personally supportive or work focused only. They can prioritize deep dialogue or not. They can be fast moving or reflective, risk taking or conservative. They can exchange e-mail jokes or ban them. The nature of the team mission will drive some preferences, but the individuals on the team have a lot to say about the atmosphere itself.

A literal team room or space seems to hold the energy of the group, forming a sort of container, just as a glass holds water or a pocket holds personal effects. Virtual teams can experience a sort of energy leak, like the glass having a leak, if sacred virtual space is not created and nurtured. Energy cannot be at full throttle all the time, or the team would burn out. If the ebb and flow is not managed, the risk of a virtual environment is too much dissipation, resulting in lagging commitment or focus.

Learning and Information Sharing   Learning occurs to a large degree through conversation. A person hanging around talking online or off-line is not a distraction; it is instead the work of collaboration. If it is not happening, the virtual manager's job is to stir things up, getting tongues wagging and fingers smoking on the keyboards. The manager must build relationships as well as schedule meetings. Most team members ask for help and make appropriate demands from one another when they know each other, and that freedom to ask and expect is necessary for highly effective work teams. Different tools and forums are best suited for different outcomes, so match tools, forums, people, and goals effectively. Time will not be wasted, people will be well supported, and work will get done.

Self-Image and Team Identity   As a team leader, think about what kind of mood to set for the team. What metaphors and symbols guide how people interact with one another? How will they think about their team purpose? A team is primarily social, and team members use that social relationship to get the work done. Managers must support relationships, not just production. The team's self-image should be a reflection of relationship as much as output. For example, a well-oiled machine conveys a different essence than a more organic koi pond or a spun web does. Help the team define itself through metaphor or analogy, and continue to work with that metaphor by using phrases and references that remind the team of how they see themselves.

Personalities and Habits The team manager should talk about what styles, behaviors, and technical tools will support creating the desired atmosphere. What does interaction look like? What role, if any, will power and politics play in this team and between this team and the larger organization? How public does the team want to make its accomplishments? How involved will stakeholders be?

There is no right answer as long as the focus is on individual and team well-being as well as team purpose. Whether this is a short-term project team or an ongoing team, there need to be routinized, scheduled time and negotiated agreements, whether virtual or face-to-face, for the team to come together to strengthen and deepen the team's commitment.

Practical Tools Watercooler talk—those casual conversations that spontaneously occur in offices—disappears in a virtual environment. This is the kind of talking that is often a critical success factor for team synergy, and it must be encouraged virtually. Simple mechanisms might include intranet team home pages, instant messaging, open and ongoing chatrooms, electronic bulletin boards, and virtual and face-to-face team meetings. Post pictures of team members at work stations or as screen savers. Create metaphors to anchor the work, the team's connection to one another, and value drivers. The team leader should attend vigilantly to the team's need to be connected to one another through both the work and the relationships.

Regardless of the tools, what matters most is to remember that the team exists, even when it is not electronically or personally connected. Team members hold the space with the group between connections, ensuring that the sacred space continues even when people are not talking every day.

Team Development and Planning Process A team development process is a highly effective way to get a virtual team started right. If possible, bring the team together in person, especially if team members do not know each other or are unfamiliar with virtual teaming. If that is not possible, plan and get acquainted virtually through listservs, chatrooms, and virtual conferences. With a team of virtual veterans, let the team decide the setting. Include support functions and key stakeholders as appropriate to build relationships. Build clarity about project expectations, communication infrastructure, and work flow.

Develop as few or many group process guidelines as the team and organization require, and commit to using them. Define common language, methodologies, and processes. Make sure all team members understand them. Decide how decisions will be made and conflicts resolved. Identify criteria for both project decisions and team process needs. Create and commit to the way the team will inform and involve one another and its stakeholders. Aim for fair division of team caretaking labor. Agree also on not only what, when, and how information will be shared, but also on how team members will respond. Share responsibility for getting the team back on track if virtuality gets in the way. Meet support functions and people, and link with them as often as needed. Make all in-person meetings strategic and relational rather than strictly informational.

 The agenda template in Exhibit 3.1 can be used as is. Many guidelines may be standardized by the organization, or at least templated, simplifying the team development process. (A Sample Team Development Process Checklist is included on the www.wiley.com/go/virtualteamshandbook Web site.) Each team manager can customize the complete checklist to fit the team's needs.

Path 2: Support the Team Community

The energy is built, the space is set, and now the team needs to keep the fires burning. Team support comes in many forms. Although it is sometimes created spontaneously based on need, much team support can be anticipated and planned. Minimally the following types of support matter to every team.

Celebrations   When two team members have their heads together and hit a "Eureka!" moment, they need to run virtually to the whole group and share the excitement. And they need to do this immediately, not later. When a team member receives a special award, find ways to feature her or him in a video clip or e-mail press release. Develop a habit of posting fun and exciting news to a team bulletin board or team Web page. Celebrate accomplishments together as a team, even when members are dispersed. And celebrate again when everyone comes together. No team can be too spirited, whether virtual or colocated. Do a virtual jig. Send e-cards. Send songs. Have fun. Meet face-to-face, and take a team picture.

Exhibit 3.1
Session Agenda Template

---

1. Getting Acquainted

2. Team Charter, Vision, Values

3. Team and Project Planning [Project planning is the time for establishing project goals, identifying resources, setting milestone and deliverable deadlines, as well as delineating roles, responsibilities, and authority. This is the time to decide how to share and embed learning, operating norms, and self-evaluation.]

4. Team Process Planning [Process planning is the time for determining how to ensure that the team functions effectively as a collective.]

5. Communication Infrastructure [Who needs to communicate with whom about what, how often, through what means, and who else needs to be informed?]

6. Membership and Maintenance [Plan for new member orientation over time, reports and updating, document sharing, and so on.]

Post pictures and personal biographies to the team home page. Post a map with everyone's locations. All of these habits expand emotional bandwidth.

Touching Base   Frequent check-ins should be the norm. Simple conversation among individuals is how much work gets done. As a committed team member and leader, keep the conversations going. Much of Path Two is sustained informally in addition to the negotiated protocols and communication infrastructure.

Trusting Actions   In virtual teams, team members are expected to trust one another and become interdependent, sometimes sight unseen. Trust is given to another based on the professional reputation and integrity of the team members. When it is tentatively given, it is not guaranteed to continue. Trust is tentative until experience proves it is deserved. Research shows that virtual teams that maintain high trust produce higher-quality work. Social communication is interwoven throughout task-based interactions to build and maintain confidence in the relationship.

Integrity can be simply defined as doing what one says one will and following through on commitments or renegotiating with enough lead time when a deadline will be missed. Consistent reliability is the greatest trust builder, and actions speak much louder than words when it comes to work trust.

Creating Stories Together In a virtual environment, taking extra time to give everyone a sense of place and to reconnect when the team comes together is critical to maintain emotional bandwidth. Culture is a product of shared stories, norms, shared rituals, repeated interactions, and shared experiences. Provide opportunities to create shared history together beyond the team development process—both face-to-face and electronically.

Helping Out Support is more than trust and interpersonal connection. Practical helping hands are extended virtually. Who has not had a day when everything seems to go wrong? The project is off track and behind schedule, the children are sick, the customer is cranky, no one mentioned that casual day this week was actually a client-on-premises-wear-your-business-best day, and the network has gone down twice. These are the days when teammates become friends, when the extra support or cup of coffee is highly appreciated. How does that day change in a virtual home office? Network is still down, so no e-mail whining allowed. Kids are running temperatures and cannot be in school, so they are whining in the next room. Clothing does not matter, but the client is still cranky, making it difficult to juggle with sick children.

These are the days when the strength of the team's emotional bandwidth is tested. Decide together before the need arises how to relieve uncontrollable difficulties. It may be difficult for people to call a team member they barely know and ask for help. Is it acceptable to call a colleague and simply blow some steam? Discuss ahead of time and implement team-created protocols for inevitable challenges like technical issues and dependent-care surprises.

A connected team supports one another. Assuming professional integrity, it is not only acceptable, it should be expected that occasionally the team has to flex and help out. Part of maintaining emotional bandwidth is taking the time, before a crisis, to develop relationships, to get to know one another, to identify together what attending to the well-being of one another looks like.

Negotiating Style Differences   Personal work habits must also be negotiated. Some people like to be more fully informed, while others prefer to have information on a need-to-know basis. It gets more complicated when one person's need-to-know looks fundamentally different from another's. The potential negative results of not getting clear with one another about interpersonal needs and preferences are violating inclusion and exclusion issues and boundaries and undermining trust.

Jack, for example, comes from a highly bureaucratic corporation where he learned to copy ten people on every correspondence, load every version of a document to the intranet, keep hard copies of every memo that crosses his desk, and ask his manager for "permission" about many things. Jill, Jack's teammate, grew up professionally in a fast-growth, entrepreneurial environment where everyone learned to act now and fix later. Both Jill and Jack are highly dedicated, competent, and creative. Jack's modus operandi feels to Jill like information obesity (too much to bother with) and reeks of self-protection. Jill's modus operandi is that unless her actions have an immediate or direct impact on a teammate's work, she will provide an update at the team's weekly conference call—in executive briefing fashion, very high level. Jack likes documentation and tracking; Jill prefers oral reports with work production serving as the tracking device.

If both Jack and Jill continue to operate in their preferred ways without discussing with one another or the team, personal liking, trust, and respect will suffer. Jill will begin to think of Jack as a verbose and defensive bureaucrat or offensive braggart. Jack will begin to think of Jill as a prima donna or loose cannon, needing to be watched closely because few controls are in place. Loyalty and commitment to one another cannot automatically happen in this relationship. Jill may even feel her boundaries are being violated when Jack constantly asks to be kept in the loop.

Let's complicate the story even further. Jill works closely with Nell because their responsibilities are closely aligned and interdependent. Their work and their relationship are more fluidly interactive, so Jill naturally keeps Nell more fully informed. Now Jack feels even more excluded. What begins as simple style differences and habits may develop into a perception of power and political game playing and intentional exclusion, and soon the focus of work becomes the interpersonal dynamics rather than the project or the customer. Place this in a virtual environment, and Jack very likely may drop out, going unnoticed for too long. In fact, if Jack does overdo the e-mail communications, his communication dearth may feel like relief rather than be noticed as an early warning sign of team dysfunction.

Preventing Problems   Most of us know that liking, loyalty, commitment, and willingness to participate with a group are desirable but not automatic. In order to avoid strained relationships like Jack and Jill's, decisions should be consensually made regarding:

- Who needs to participate in what decisions, actions, and commitments.
- Who needs to be included, informed, and asked about what.
- What participation with this team looks like. Does it mean daily telephone contact with every team member? Does it include a sacred commitment to meet with the team in person monthly?
- How much information sharing is too much or not enough.
- What agreements are made as a collective about pushing information and posting information.
- When someone is struggling, what help looks like for this group. What is appropriate to ask, to offer, to leave private?

In other words, what does full support look like for this team? The rightness of the answers depends on organizational culture and norms to some degree, but more important, the interpersonal needs and preferences of the team members themselves. Discussions up front can go a long way to support team members and maintain emotional bandwidth.

Virtual Team Maintenance   A successful team development planning process will serve the team well, but is not in itself enough. As frequently as seems appropriate, the team should review the norms and agreements, the systems, processes, and protocols, adjusting to fit the team and project needs better. As groupware tools are introduced, technical and user problems are common. Ask the team where the information exchange is working well or not, what technical challenges are common to many or all, and what additional training or support is needed. Frequently revisit the communication infrastructure and its use, effectiveness, and any modifications or recommitments needed.

Perpetuating Team Synergy   Synergy is more easily created by being together in the same place at the same time. It happens virtually, but in a different way. The team has to build it in if it matters to them. This may include virtual high-fives, conference calls, groupware, a more active use of e-mail and other electronic communication. If geographically possible, encourage scheduling lunches with team members that are informal and celebratory, or joining the same gym. Schedule more social time than normally would occur in a colocated environment.

The Rolling Present: Entry and Reentry   A benefit of virtual work is removing geography as a limitation for team membership, although the challenge remains in how to bring new or renewing members of a formed team up to speed quickly, especially if the team is moving at a fast pace. Virtual teams do have a distinct advantage: much work is done asynchronously and groupware provides a history that can be sorted by time, topic, and other threads. Nevertheless, the sheer volume can be overwhelming. The team manager needs to help enrolling team members sort through the history for fast assimilation. These questions can guide late-joining team members:

- What reference documents, history, strategic planning documents, progress reports, and deliverables do joining team members need to review?
- Who do joining team members need to talk to, and about what?
- Who will serve as orientation coach and mentor?
- How will new team members learn the operating norms of the team?
- How will new team members be introduced to the existing team?

The informal aspect of entry is more social. Minimally, virtual conferencing and other orientation strategies are necessary to introduce new team members to the group and the group's culture, metaphors, routines, norms, infrastructure, and etiquette. Maintaining a team Web page or electronic yearbook that includes social aspects are increasingly used tools to maintain team relationships electronically and allow asynchronous orientation. They can never, however, fully replace the rich human energy that comes with live conversation. Virtual work does not mean face-to-face disappears.

Path 3: Produce Successful Outcomes

While team maintenance and support matter, mission accomplishment is still the goal, and all else serves this purpose. The trust developed within any team is fragile, and even more so in a virtual team if it is not reinforced by performance that can be seen. Milestones and joint achievements provide the fuel to stay focused on mission accomplishment and the oil to lubricate trust.

Success begins with a clear and shared purpose, a vision of how that purpose will look when accomplished, and identified outcomes to accomplish that purpose. An effective team achieves concrete, complete results.

In order to accomplish the mission in a virtual environment, more structure and planning are required. Emergency gatherings and on-the-fly planning are exhilarating and can be done virtually, but only as the exception rather than the rule. They cannot be the standard operating norm because chaos and frustration will result, and virtual team members will see through the exhilaration to the disorganization lying beneath the surface.

If everybody starts with the same vision and work plan, then virtual team members are more inclined to progress collectively. If there is not an agreed-on plan or a clear structure for communication and feedback, it is easy for virtual members to work hard but get four degrees to the left of where the team originally meant to go. If it goes undetected, people are getting more off track without knowing it. Nothing is more frustrating than working hard only to discover that rework is required because the focus was slightly off. Everyone needs to take an active role in making sure that everyone remains aligned to purpose.

Paradoxically less structure is also required. Command-and-control management models do not work in a distributed work team environment. Managers cannot possibly micromanage in a virtual environment without slowing team production. Frequently managers new to the virtual environment ask for more reports in more detail than they would when colocated. This attempt to stay fully informed is understandable, but production slows when too much emphasis is placed on structuring reports instead of milestones and outcomes. Emotional bandwidth and a production plan, not controlling oversight, should drive accountability.

As a team, discuss and decide together:

- What does task accomplishment look like?
- How real are deadlines?
- How does the group want to individually and collectively approach problem solving and decision making?
- What authority levels need definition?
- Who has what project responsibility?

FINAL THOUGHTS

Consistent and integrated processes, delivery systems, and communication infrastructure yield great results for virtual teams. A commitment to follow the three-fold path smoothes the journey and engages team members' minds and hearts. Rough spots will be recognized and remedied with little disturbance to the overall efficiency and functioning of the virtual team. Following the pathways provided in this chapter increases any virtual team's chance of being the winning team every time.

REMINDERS

- In organizational environments built on electronic networks, work is becoming people-centric, not place-centric; connecting through networks is the process of work; and commitment goes beyond "doing my job."
- Emotional bandwidth is the personal and sustainable connection and caring created among virtual team members.
- Path 1 is to create a cohesive team culture. It encompasses relationship building and establishing agreed-on ways of working together. It is fundamentally social. A highly effective way to get a virtual team started is the team development process.
- Path 2 is to support the team community. This support, which can be anticipated and planned, encompasses celebrations, check-ins, trust building, story creating, helping others, negotiating differences, and preventing problems.

- Path 3 is to produce successful outcomes. Here, mission accomplishment is the goal, and all else serves this purpose. An effective team achieves concrete, complete results.

- The three-fold path engages team members' minds and hearts.

RELATED ITEM ON THE WEB

- Sample Team Development Process Checklist

Getting Virtual Teams Right the First Time

Keys to Successful Collaboration in the Virtual World

Linda M. L. Peters, Charles C. Manz

The virtual world, enabled by technology, has opened doors that were once unimaginable outside of science fiction movies. Organizations today are using these new opportunities to gain a competitive advantage over other companies in their industries by forming project teams, made up of experts from around the country and globe, in order to accomplish their strategic goals. However, jumping head first into virtual collaborative arrangements without establishing a solid foundation for success may not be the best approach. Many employees who collaborate beyond their immediate physical location are being asked to participate on teams with others they have never met and may never meet. According to numerous testimonies from employees, developing an understanding as to how to work virtually has typically been an afterthought, done only when failure has occurred at one or more levels of the project.

This chapter is intended to educate upper managers, project managers, and team members alike by identifying and examining some key foundational factors that affect a virtual team's ability to collaborate successfully, including trust, shared understanding, and depth of relationships. A model outlining these key antecedents for effective collaboration is provided, along with support in the form of both theory and real-life examples. The first part of the chapter elaborates fully on the concepts included in the model, followed by a how-to section intended to provide organizations and team members with the knowledge and skills necessary to implement the model.

KEY INGREDIENTS FOR EFFECTIVE VIRTUAL COLLABORATION: A RECIPE FOR SUCCESS

Two primary keys to working in a collaborative way are the empowerment of employees and team-based work, which are both well documented in organizational practice. Prominent examples are often centered on creating employee teams that are assigned responsibilities that previously were part of the role of external managers (Lawler, Mohrman, & Ledford, 1995; Kirkman & Rosen, 1999; Uhl-Bien & Graen, 1998). Frequently referred to as self-managing teams (SMTs), these worker units are provided with increased discretion for making decisions and taking action (Hackman, 1986; Manz & Sims, 1986), and rely less on traditional authority figures (Cummings, 1978; Manz & Sims, 1987; Pearce & Conger, 2003; Sims & Manz, 1996).

Making the evolution from the traditional visual team structure to the virtual team structure has required that several components of organizations be transformed. In order for organizations to benefit from virtual collaboration, they first need to understand how to adapt their work processes and behaviors to the challenges of working virtually. While there are many potentially important factors (or ingredients, as we refer to them), we believe three are particularly notable and must be considered in order to achieve an optimum level of virtual collaboration: trust, shared understanding, and depth of relationships.

Trust can be conceived as a combination of two separate definitions: "a state involving confident positive expectations about another's motives with respect to one's self in situations entailing risk" (Boon & Holmes, 1991), and the extent to which a person is "willing to act on the basis of the words, actions, and decisions of another" (McAllister, 1995). Many researchers believe that underlying this decision to trust is an increased vulnerability to opportunistic behavior on the part of trusted others (Jarvenpaa, Knoll, & Leidner, 1998; Mayer, Davis, & Schoorman, 1995). Trust is an ingredient needed in almost any significant relationship, and it becomes even more important when face-to-face interaction is not possible. Before technology enabled the recent rise of virtual teamwork, many employees within organizations were controlled through the use of authority systems in which managers or supervisors would oversee them directly while they worked (Jarvenpaa et al., 1998). This kind of close supervision is almost impossible in a virtual team context since managers have no real direct control over the virtual worker. In this more loosely managed context, trust serves as the aligning mechanism for team members who work from dispersed locations (Kirkman, Rosen, Gibson, Tesluk, & McPherson, 2002).

A shared understanding, defined as a clear sense of strategic direction for all team members (Liedtka, 1996), is the second ingredient for creating virtual collaboration. By encouraging members to care about the ultimate goal of the team and not just their specific contributions, they become motivated to cooperate and collaborate in order to make the virtual team relationship work.

The depth of relationships that exists among team members is the third important ingredient. This term is intended to encompass not just the amount of face-to-face communication that takes place between team members during the project, but also all previous and current experience and communication with, or knowledge of, other members that gives them a sense of who they are. Since many members work from different geographical locations, sometimes crossing several time zones, communicating using technology often supplants face-to-face meetings. Nevertheless, it is important for team members to develop relationships with the other members in order to work collaboratively. Often these relationships are the foundation for developing trust among the members and a shared understanding of the ultimate goal of the team.

As suggested by the model we propose in Figure 4.1, the anticipated result of having strong relationships, trust, and a shared understanding among the team members is a high level of collaboration. But what constitutes collaboration? In a team context, we define it simply as the interaction of members in such a way as to develop positive synergy where the team's performance is greater than the sum of individual members' performances. It is a win-win situation. No member is

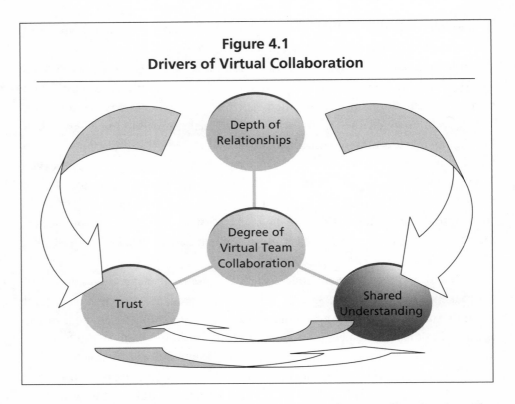

Figure 4.1
Drivers of Virtual Collaboration

Depth of Relationships

Degree of Virtual Team Collaboration

Trust

Shared Understanding

asked to compromise on quality or innovativeness, and no member gives in to the demands of another. Rather, the team uses conflict as a way of enhancing creativity and innovation.

In the following discussion, we first explore the notion of virtual collaboration as a win-win effort and then examine each of the three ingredients needed for it to occur in greater detail. In order to support our analysis, more than forty individuals who are part of a university's professional M.B.A. program were surveyed and asked to share experiences that they have had with virtual team projects and offer their views on the strengths and weaknesses of these teams based on their own firsthand knowledge. These students are from a variety of organizations and industries.

VIRTUAL COLLABORATION: A WIN-WIN EFFORT

In general, collaboration is stimulated by a desire or need that exists to solve a problem, create, or discover something (Schrage, 1990). For collaboration to occur, team members must work interdependently, assuming joint ownership for decisions and collective responsibility for results. This interdependence and collective responsibility suggests that collaboration has the potential to be a far richer process than routine communication or straightforward teamwork. Although many resources may be limited, such as expertise, time, or money, the innovative aspect of collaboration helps teams create value beyond that found in standard teamwork (Schrage, 1990). To illustrate, consider the following comment from a member of a thirty-three-person virtual team in the banking industry who was responsible for relocating operations out of the path of natural disasters:

> Our team was able to collaborate very effectively and exceeded leadership expectations in terms of delivery. . . . The team even won an internal recognition award. While it was difficult to get the team going because of the different locations of the members, once everyone got started with the work, being virtual was not a problem.

Before collaboration can begin, team members must come to the realization that they are not alone, even if their expertise and contribution are expected to be different from those of the other members. It is only when they begin to accept and respect the insights, questions, and ideas of others that collaboration begins to occur. According to Schrage (1990), the success of collaborative effort can be measured by its results. In other words, collaboration is successful when it produces results superior to those in which compromises are made or when conflict is allowed to permeate and affect the team negatively, creating a form of separateness among the members. The positive synergy needed for effective collaboration occurs when team members have an open mind, are willing to listen to and trust in their teammates, deal with conflict productively, and support the team's goals. One virtual member of a cross-functional, international team in the software and telecommunications industry put it this way:

> After the team became familiar with one another, the collaboration among the team was excellent. The new product release was actually delivered ahead of schedule. . . . The different cultures involved impacted the team's collaboration abilities initially, but being able to spend time to get to know those that I was working with made a big difference. This same team has gone on to complete additional projects without struggling through some of the trust issues that accompanied the first project.

TRUST: BELIEVING IN YOUR TEAM MEMBERS

In order to trust in a team context, a member needs to believe that other members will act for the benefit of the team rather than in a selfish manner. This means that each team member needs to be open to being vulnerable to opportunistic behavior on the part of those they have chosen to trust. Commitments and promises must translate into actions that clearly demonstrate their intentions to follow through and remain committed to the timeliness, quality, and quantity of their work. One team member whose project involved implementing customer service improvements for a telecommunications company emphasized the importance of seeing that these commitments are honored: "I have a guarded sense of trust. Very often individuals may not possess the commitment to complete tasks, or individuals may be strained for time to complete tasks. . . . I try to circumvent these issues by being the squeaky wheel and by following up and sending reminders."

Self-managed teams serve as a prime example of the need for a solid foundation of trust. With SMTs, workers are significantly empowered to manage themselves, and organizational management assumes less control over team members. This makes trust between the workers and management, as well as each other, a critical basis for ensuring that teams will perform as expected given the goals of the team. In a virtual team, monitoring members' actions is difficult given the geographical dispersion of the membership. Consequently, trust becomes a substitute for control: the less control there is, the greater the need is for trust (Leifer & Mills, 1996). In other words, where traditional control mechanisms are minimal at best, trust becomes a vital component for team effectiveness (Kasper-Fuehrer & Ashkanasy, 2001) in terms of both collaboration and performance.

There are at least three forms of trust: cognitive based, institution based, and personality based. Cognitive-based trust is manifested through logic and derived rationally: the benefits of trusting outweigh the possible costs of not trusting (Lewicki & Bunker, 1995; Sarker, Valacich, & Sarker, 2003). With this form of trust, if we view other team members as having the technical competency and ability to perform, we are likely to trust them in the short term by mentally placing them in categories (Sarker et al., 2003). More specifically, as we learn something about the behavior and dependability of others, we use cognitive schema to stereotype them so that we can better predict their behaviors. To highlight the importance of knowing something about other team members and how this information can subsequently affect the level of trust placed in them, consider the following views of two virtual team members, the first an engineer for a computer hardware manufacturing firm and the second a public policy advocate for an international telecommunications firm:

> I had very little trust in the beginning of the project. I did not know any of these people and am one to trust only after it is earned. As I got to know the other team members and how they worked, I built up a level of trust in those who followed through on their promises (or at least e-mailed me to let me know there would be a delay in fulfilling them). The key was that communication had to be very open and timely in order for each team member to trust the others.

> I didn't find it as easy to trust members of the team if I didn't previously know them. Sad to say, I didn't develop a trust for others until they gave me a reason to trust them. If they followed up on promises or showed knowledge or expertise on the subject, it was easier to develop trust in that individual.

It is really the other forms of trust, however, that help explain how we are able to trust those with whom we have never had any prior experience or knowledge. Institutional-based trust reflects an individual's trust in the organization with which the other members are affiliated (Scott, 1987). If members believe that the norms and rules of the organization will help control opportunistic behavior, they will gain confidence that other members will not act in their own self-interest. One team member from the aerospace industry, who worked on an interorganizational virtual team, succinctly described this trust development process:

> I had no basis as to whom I could trust so instead relied heavily on the opinions of the people I worked for to form my initial opinions. As tasks within the project came together, I learned to refine these initial impressions and have my own set of "go to" members on the team whom I had a good rapport with and I knew would help out.

Personality-based trust is derived from each individual's disposition to trust. It represents a form of trust that reflects a person's willingness to depend on others

(Mayer et al., 1995). This may account for the apparently unexplainable trust that some people have in others. This tendency is reflected in the following statement made by a virtual team member from a prestigious academic institution who worked on an interorganizational curriculum project involving several other colleges:

> I trusted everyone completely from day one. Yes, I'm basically a trusting person. There was a member who might not have pulled his weight on the project, but that didn't change my level of trust in him. I just lowered my expectations and realized that others would have to do more—or live without his potential contributions.

In virtual team environments, team members must be willing to create dependencies and trust that these dependencies will not be exploited by their team members (Brown, Poole, & Rodgers, 2004). Communication, particularly meaningful dialogue among the members, may be the most effective tool that organizations can rely on to build trust in virtual teams (Holton, 2001). Although some individuals are born with a natural disposition to trust, organizations can enhance the cognitive-based and institutional-based trust that their employees experience on virtual teams by providing opportunities for meaningful dialogue. In turn, this meaningful dialogue can create the foundation for shared understandings. Two examples illustrate this, the first from a virtual team member who lives in Saudi Arabia and works in the medical field and the second from a member of a five-person virtual team at a state university who was responsible for developing an educational Web site:

> Trust in the rest of the team members happened toward the middle of the work period. Those who contributed to the discussion with valuable substance were trusted the most. Those who were weak with contributions that didn't make sense were not trusted.

> Some of the cues that I took for developing trust in the early stages of the project came from how the virtual team members interacted with the larger team during our teleconference calls. In particular, I paid attention to how the members I didn't know interacted with each other. If one person either didn't say much or brought up too many objections,

I think I probably interpreted this to mean that they would be a more challenging team player to work with. In the absence of any physical cues, like facial expressions, these behaviors take on greater importance.

SHARED UNDERSTANDING: THE BIG PICTURE

Shared understanding is more than a common goal recognized by all the members of the team. It involves a comprehensive understanding of the team's capacities and objectives, including knowledge of the expertise each member possesses and how they plan to interact in order to realize the team's overall strategic goal (Liedtka, 1996). This means that negotiating the responsibilities and accountabilities that each member of the team will assume is critical at an early stage of the team formation process. A telecommuter for a telecommunications company who worked on a virtual team project to reduce companywide standard intervals illustrates this point very clearly: "When a member sees the bigger picture, and they see how important their piece is in the overall success of the project, they become more accountable. They understand that even if their piece is small, all progress may stop if they do not perform as required."

Virtual teams in general, and especially virtual project teams, often bring together individuals from many different disciplines, functions, and geographies to work on a goal. The heterogeneity in all of these areas can create the potential for significant conflict and inherent uncertainties, which both need to be reduced in order for members to discover ways to work together. Developing a shared understanding is the first step in this process as it promotes team members' looking to each other in decision-making situations, helping to enhance the collaborative abilities of the team.

Accomplishing this is not easy in a virtual environment given the reduced likelihood of previous contact with other team members. Similar to developing trust, communication becomes a key organization tool in developing a shared understanding. It can serve as the means for helping team members to understand the tasks and responsibilities being assumed, the specific expertise being contributed, and the needs and expectations of each individual member of the team. As illustrated by the following statement from a member of a cross-functional virtual team in the medical industry responsible for developing solutions to marketing problems, communication can enable the team to create its own identity and promote collaboration toward mutual goals:

> It has always amazed me that we all read the same thing but have different views and understanding of the problem. Achieving a common understanding of the problem and what was needed usually took a couple of weeks of back-and-forth correspondence. Once this was agreed on by the whole team, the flow of the project was much smoother.

DEPTH OF RELATIONSHIPS: GETTING TO KNOW ONE ANOTHER

One of the major obstacles members of virtual teams need to overcome is the lack of personal interaction. Without face-to-face meetings, facial expressions and body language are lost, making communications between team members difficult to interpret and understand. This is especially likely when cultural differences exist among members of the team. Consider the following example offered by a member of a thirty-five-person team in the software development industry whose goals included developing solutions to hardware and software products, concerning relationships between members of a team in the United States with a team in China:

> The team in the United States felt threatened by the team in China. These feelings made it challenging to build trust among the team members. Eventually the key members of the China team visited the United States. Putting a face with the name and voice really helped to build trust as it helps you realize that the person is actually a human being just like you. Completing the project on time and on budget would have been extremely difficult without this critical face-to-face time.

Although it is clearly advantageous to bring team members together face-to-face early in the formation of a virtual team, this is not always possible given time and money constraints. As organizations expand their use of virtual teams across country borders, they will need to identify alternatives to face-to-face contact that offer many of the same benefits and help avoid misunderstanding and miscommunication. The following example offered by a student participating in a virtual team project as part of the requirements for an M.B.A. course describes the use of one technology that enabled a team to enjoy some of these benefits without direct face-to-face communication:

> The team members had little knowledge/familiarity and/or previous experience working together. Once we were able to connect and interact using VOIP [voice over Internet protocol], I started feeling a connection. This feeling was stronger with one of the members, who not only discussed the project at hand but also discussed his personal life. In contrast, the discussion with the other member was brief and impersonal. . . . Genuine sharing of personal information that is interesting and somewhat relevant to others definitely facilitates the feeling of being connected.

In addition to face-to-face interaction when it is feasible, relationships are often developed based on reputation or familiarity. If a team member has had previous experience working with another member and found him or her to be committed and responsible, fewer face-to-face meetings are necessary since a basis for the formation of trust and shared understanding has already been established. One person on a five-member virtual team, brought together to test a collaborative software product for an academic institution, described this kind of relationship development process:

> We were somewhat familiar with each other because we had worked on a previous project but never met face-to-face. We talked through the computer and chatted through instant messaging, swapping stories of our professions, how the weather was, and about the traffic (we were all in different parts of the country). . . . This communication helped us become even more familiar, especially on a personal basis. Because our team had worked together before, a high level of trust already existed. We knew that each of us would do our part of the project and get it done on time. We expected that each member would be online at the designated time in order to collaborate, and if we could not make it at the proposed time, we would let the others know. Working virtually required trust.

Familiarity can also occur if a person's reputation supersedes him or her. If a team member whom you have never met or worked with before has a reputation for working successfully on virtual teams, you are likely to trust this person more easily than someone you have never met or heard of prior to the current experience. An M.B.A. student who was part of a six-member market development virtual team to fulfill a course requirement put it this way: "Initially I didn't know any of the team members. I also didn't trust any of them unless I felt their technical ability was up to par. This would be determined based on their reputation on previous projects that I had heard about." Our viewpoint is that face-to-face interaction and familiarity together contribute to the depth of the relationship that members have with each other.

Some experts believe that building solid relationships within teams, often through team empowerment, can act as a substitute for face-to-face interaction (Kirkman, Rosen, Tesluk, & Gibson, 2004; Montoya-Weiss, Massey, & Song, 2001). Comments by two individuals, one who worked on an eight-member cross-functional team and the other who worked on a virtual team in the investments industry responsible for a high-tech communications product, emphasized that promoting deeper relationships can help equalize the playing field for virtual teams:

> We were involved in this project for approximately two months. Even though I never had a chance to meet the other team members face-to-face or even on videoconferencing, I had the feeling that I knew them personally as I associated each name with an imaginary face. . . . We would even send e-mails not related to the project as we got to know each other more.

> Individual calls to team members allowed me to get to know each of them and to keep on top of daily work without inundating people with meetings and e-mails. Remembering that it's a person on the other end of the phone and replicating what one might do with in-person coworkers (i.e., asking about their weekend, how the family is, getting to know each other, etc.) were also key.

Strengthened relationships enable team members to effectively work with each other from afar (Kirkman et al., 2004), which can support important team requirements such as collaboration and conflict resolution. Better relationships can also help resolve problems such as ambiguity, conflicting interests, and scarcity of resources, which can be amplified in a virtual, asynchronous environment. This point can be best exemplified by the following comments from two members of very different virtual teams. The first comment is made by an M.B.A. student working on a marketing project with other individuals located in various parts of the world; the second is by an officer in the military in regard to a virtual project he worked on that involved resourcing equipment for overseas operations:

> In my opinion, we had very good communication even though it was strictly through e-mail. None of my teammates had negative things to say. On the contrary, they were really supportive and only gave constructive comments. This made me feel more comfortable and willing to share my ideas with the team.

> I had never met the other four members of this group. Everything was done via e-mail, and I didn't feel any real connection to them—it was all very direct and impersonal. Then about five weeks into the project, we began weekly video-teleconferences. Being able to watch others' body language and hear their voices helped me feel more comfortable in sharing some thoughts I didn't want to write via e-mail earlier for fear that someone may misinterpret a comment. The video-teleconferences ended after about a month, but our e-mail dialogue continued to be more relaxed and informal (one member actually interjected some humor, which opened the door for others to submit less formal e-mails). . . . There seemed to be a real connection. This was really the turning point in terms of trust. In addition to improved comfort levels and trust, video-teleconferencing helped improve our structure in that we were now able to ask each other questions about roles and responsibilities that we weren't comfortable asking before.

MIXING THE INGREDIENTS TOGETHER

Understanding the interconnectedness of all the pieces necessary to affect virtual collaboration is important to the overall model. For example, not only can the depth of team members' relationships affect their ability to collaborate, it can also affect their level of trust and shared understanding. In a team context, trust and a shared understanding develop through frequent and meaningful interaction. As a result, a comfort level among team members is established, making them feel relatively secure in sharing insights and concerns, including conflicting opinions, without fear of repercussion (Holton, 2001). Developing trust and a shared understanding requires relatively rich personal relationships. In fact, as the comment of an employee working on a six-member virtual team responsible for identifying process and procedure improvements in the financial markets industry suggests, the more virtual a team becomes, the more its members need to get to know each other in order to perform well together: "After developing relationships and becoming familiar with each other, we were able to trust each other and develop a strong team performance."

Furthermore, the amount of trust and the amount of shared understanding team members experience are usually closely related. In other words, the more there is of one, the more there will be of the other. When team members develop a shared understanding of their roles and what they expect to contribute based on their expertise, as well as assume responsibility for following through on commitments, trust is likely to increase as well. One person on a cross-functional virtual team in an electronics device company put it this way:

> I think the components of our success built over a span of a couple of meetings. We began to understand the task more clearly, and simultaneously we gained confidence in each other as we witnessed each other's competencies and commitments. The result was that we got into a rhythm and started to get truly productive. Once we were synchronized, our level of focus on the task at hand was heightened.

Similarly, as an individual in the computer software development industry who was on a virtual team made up of members from other countries pointed out, when team members trust each other, they are able to open up to a greater extent and communicate in developing a shared understanding:

> The team understood the goals of the project immediately, but understanding everyone's contribution took some time to develop. Typically in projects with many people and involving a few different functional areas, it can take a little time for the team to learn the capabilities of the other members. In this virtual project, ascertaining the capabilities of a counterpart thousands of miles away, who speaks English as a second language, only made this more difficult. It requires a great deal of trust to build this understanding.

Currently, organizations often resort to face-to-face meetings and social gatherings when trying to develop relationships, shared understandings, or trust among virtual team members. Although this may be feasible for some types of teams whose members are relatively close geographically and the cost of bringing members together can be easily offset by the benefits of doing so, there are many virtual teams for which this is not feasible. Fortunately for members of teams that have a history of working together or have substantial knowledge (personal or by reputation) of other members, there may be less of a need for substantial face-to-face interaction since the foundation for a shared understanding and trust may already exist. One team member from a cross-functional project responsible for comparing software at an academic institution described how members' previous experience with each other can be a key consideration:

> Working previously in a virtual setting helped us tremendously as we were already familiar with each other so trust and a shared understanding were already established before we started the project. I think it becomes easier to collaborate in a virtual team after members have worked together for a bit. It allows for norms to form in the team.

In other words, deeper relationships with team members may lead to increased levels of collaboration by making it easier to trust or form a shared understanding in relation to the team's goals. This is especially important, and often critical, for virtual teams.

ACHIEVING VIRTUAL COLLABORATION

The model we have introduced has important implications for practice. As organizations continually update and expand their use of technology, virtual teamwork will become more commonplace. However, diving into the virtual world without enough preparation to establish a foundation for collaborative efforts can potentially leave you wondering where you went wrong. One former team member working in the airline industry described his own virtual team nightmare that resulted from an organization's poor implementation of virtual collaboration involving the merging of processes for several acquisitions that needed to be consolidated:

> I had an experience with a virtual team that did not have good results. There was no clear definition of the scope of work for the team and no support from upper management of either company involved in the project. As a trusting person, I initially trusted the other team

members, but this faded quickly as the resistance to work together increased. Distrust of other team members and upper management became abundant. After two months of weekly conference calls and working the issues, it was obvious to members from both companies that we could not work together. Eventually the project was cancelled. The entire experience was unpleasant and was part of the reason for my decision to leave the company.

Instead, we have suggested that promoting the development of relationships, shared understanding, and trust will lead to effective virtual collaboration. This may promote subsequent innovation and performance. Contributions from both the organization and from individual team members are important for putting these things in place. (Table 4.1 summarizes this information.)

How Organizations Can Promote Successful Virtual Collaboration

To reap the potential benefits of virtual collaboration, it is important that organizations create a context for team members to achieve increased levels of the three key ingredients.

In order to develop deeper relationships among the team members:

• *Provide opportunity for face-to-face meeting.* Organizations should bring team members together face-to-face at the early stages of team formation in order to develop relationships and trust. Being physically in the same room will enable them to get to know each other more quickly than they would if all interaction was virtual.

• *Share biographical information electronically.* If a face-to-face meeting is not possible, organizations should encourage all team members to e-mail a brief biography (including personal information if they feel comfortable sharing this) to the other members. Follow up with an opportunity for continued dialogue related to these biographies (for example, facilitate video or telephone conferencing or group e-mails, or provide a collaborative software tool). Even sharing information as seemingly unimportant as which college or professional football team they cheer for can open up the type of communication that more easily leads to trust at the onset of a relationship. It is important that the initial meeting

Table 4.1

Summary of Actions to Promote Successful Virtual Collaboration

	Actions for Organizations	Actions for Individual Team Members
Trust	Be responsive to team members and routinely acknowledge their work and efforts in order to promote institutional trust.	Be proactive in creating a trusting relationship by talking to others who have worked with various team members in order to verify their competency and intentions.
	Establish deadlines for various benchmarks and periodic progress reports depending on the length and complexity of the project.	Fulfill all commitments and deadlines that are established and expected throughout the project.
	In order to reinforce the organization's commitment to making virtual teams work, institute a training program for employees that simulates the virtual team experience.	Communicate regularly and respond to all inquiries in a timely fashion.
Shared Understanding	Create a forum for communication to occur in order to familiarize team members with the overall goals of the project as well as the individual roles and responsibilities each will fulfill.	Assume ownership for team goals instead of only goals that apply to one's expertise or expected contribution.
	Develop procedures for dealing with problems outside the scope of the team's capabilities, should any arise.	Take responsibility for understanding the role that every team member will play and how each fits into the overall project goal.
	Ensure that team members understand the benefits of collaboration.	Look to other team members as resources for resolving issues that arise related to the project.
Depth of Relationships	Bring team members together face-to-face or use computer-mediated communication in order to facilitate the development of comfortable relationships that will form a basis for trust and shared understanding to occur.	Take responsibility for getting to know the other team members as much as possible.
	Encourage communication (both professional and personal) throughout the project to promote relationships that deepen trust.	Keep lines of communication open in order to deal more effectively with intrateam conflict that occurs.
	Capitalize on existing relationships by keeping team membership as constant as possible from one project to another.	

be more focused on developing deeper relationships among the members rather than task-related communication.

• *Capitalize on existing relationships.* Whenever possible, organizations should keep team membership constant in order to benefit from the relationships that have already been formed.

In order to create a shared understanding among the team members:

• *Create a forum for open dialogue regarding team goals.* Once team members appear comfortable with each other, organizations should establish a forum in which they can discuss the responsibilities of the project team as a whole, what role they see themselves fulfilling on the team based on their expertise, and how this fits into the big picture, including the other team members' roles.

• *Determine accessibility of external expertise.* A discussion of how questions or problems that are beyond the scope of the team's expertise will be handled should be agreed on at the organizational level. By providing a channel to help resolve these issues, the team is less likely to become stagnant and unable to move forward.

• *Educate team members on the benefits of collaboration.* All team members should be reminded by the organization that they are working as a single unit and together are responsible and accountable for the success of the project. Part of the challenge is that in many highly competitive organizational contexts, the focus may predominantly emphasize the task at hand for each individual separately rather than the importance of relationship building. In a traditional team, where direct management and visual cues are present, this may work reasonably well. However, in a virtual team, focusing only on one's individual task connections and avoiding or resisting collaboration can promote distrust and miscommunication.

In order to develop trust among the team members:

• *Be responsive to virtual team members.* Organizations should establish a culture of responsiveness in dealing with virtual team members. Often these members feel like a name without a face, and by consciously remembering to acknowledge their work and efforts, organizations can enjoy an increased sense of loyalty among virtual employees or contractors. It is also important that organizations adopt communication and responsiveness as part of their corporate culture.

In order to promote institutional trust, all members of the company need to understand that communicating consistently and responsively with virtual employees is expected.

• *Establish good meeting management practices.* Identifying and agreeing on periodic progress reporting deadlines serves to keep everyone on track and management aware of the ongoing work-in-progress status. It also serves to create a sense of urgency among the team members who may not be as committed to the project as other members, a condition that hurts rather than helps trust within the team.

• *Develop a training program.* Organizations should formulate a training program for the purpose of educating employees and managers on working in a virtual environment. This program will vary depending on the diversity (functional, cultural, national, gender) expected based on the scope of the company's operations. But in all cases, it needs to communicate the organization's commitment to virtual teams and teach them how to work successfully in this context, with full consideration given to the foundational ingredients discussed in this chapter.

How Individual Team Members Can Promote Successful Virtual Collaboration

Members of the team also have responsibilities and contributions to make in regard to establishing effective virtual collaboration.

In order to develop deeper relationships with other members:

• *Assume responsibility for developing and maintaining relationships.* Share as much information and experiences with other team members as you feel comfortable doing in order to allow others to understand who you are. Understanding the lens one uses to view the world can make it much easier to accept differences in opinion.

• *Keep the lines of communication open to deal with conflict effectively.* Usually conflicts related to the team's tasks can be resolved more easily and with less dysfunctional behavior than those that arise of a personal nature. However, it is the formation of a personal relationship that drives the ability to trust in another even though these relationships usually have some level of conflict. Balancing the more impersonal focus on task with the personal focus on relationships can be difficult but is an essential group process skill in achieving effective collaboration.

In order to develop a shared understanding among the members:

• *Assume ownership for team goals.* It is important that every member assume responsibility for the goals of the team as a whole and not just for their own contribution. In order to do this, a shared understanding of the ultimate team goals and how each member is expected to achieve them is essential.

• *Problem-solve internally when possible.* Team members should look initially to the team when trying to resolve issues rather than try to handle them alone or seek assistance outside the team. Because the majority of virtual teams in existence today are project based and composed of members from different functional backgrounds (that is, R&D, marketing, sales, and finance), a tendency may emerge to discard problems in an area of expertise outside one's own as "not my problem." When this occurs, the team's ability to collaborate is negatively affected, which could create an undesirable domino effect for performance and innovation.

• *Understand team member roles.* All members should take responsibility for knowing what role every other member of the team is to assume and the expertise they possess that will help them accomplish their goals as well as ways in which each can support the other members of the team.

In order to achieve a trusting relationship among all members of the team:

• *Be proactive in seeking a trusting relationship.* A team member who does not have enough information to develop trust with the other team members should talk to others who may have worked with them previously or are at least aware of their work habits and level of competency.

• *Keep promises.* Team members can help build and maintain others' trust by fulfilling all commitments and promises made to the team and by meeting all deadlines imposed by the organization.

• *Check in regularly.* Team members can be responsive to the others by communicating on a regular basis, even if just to check in. Knowing you are there to support them will help to give you credibility as a team member. In addition, everyone should respond to requests and inquiries from other team members in a timely fashion. Avoid ignoring communications or assuming that the other party will know you received, read, and understood it. Be responsive.

A CASE EXAMPLE

The following case provides an experience shared by a particularly reflective team member that integrates the components of the model we have proposed. It highlights the manner in which organizations and team members can effectively work virtually. The situation described concerns a nine-member cross-functional sales technology project team in the specialty metals distribution and service industry. The team was responsible for evaluating the needs of the outside sales force and making recommendations for technological improvements in order to increase overall effectiveness:

> During the six months of this project, there was never an occasion when the entire team was assembled together in person. . . . Only some of the team members had ever actually met face-to-face.
>
> From the beginning, expectations were high, and it was clear that everyone was required to participate and to perform. The project sponsors attended the kick-off conference call and emphasized the strategic importance of this project. One of the team members did not have a very good reputation as a team player; however, his functional area of expertise was [essential to the project]. Both of the co-leaders were aware of this and kept an eye on it throughout. The level of trust improved as the project progressed, particularly when team members met their commitments and deadlines.
>
> Prior to the kick-off, there were several discussions between the project sponsors and co-leaders. A concise PowerPoint presentation was prepared to identify the team members, the objectives, project scope, critical success factors (that is, team availability/commitment and urgency required), and the first steps. On the initial conference call, there was ample time allowed for the presentation as well as for the brainstorming of ideas and input from all team members. Specific tasks were assigned with achievable due dates. Comprehensive meeting minutes were distributed immediately, outlining many of the key comments made during the call and the assigned tasks and due dates.
>
> I believe that this team was successful for several reasons. First of all, there was clear direction from the top. Everyone on the team understood the importance, the urgency, and the goals of this project

from day one. Next, the exceptional individual effort and the close collaboration between the co-leaders and several team members pushed this project forward expeditiously. The virtual setting was more of a benefit than a hindrance to this project. The convenience of communications significantly improved our abilities to accomplish tasks. Many ideas and written drafts were exchanged via e-mail. Regular communications of meeting summaries, data collection, requests for proposals, and so on were all done electronically. It was more efficient.

FINAL THOUGHTS

Our model is intended as an initial source of guidance for organizations and virtual team members to better understand the efforts that must be made on each party's behalf in order to achieve effective virtual collaboration. The primary ingredients outlined in this chapter can serve as a source for designing organizational training that fosters the development of conditions needed for this desired collaboration to occur. Based on what we know thus far, it appears that establishing effective virtual collaboration requires considerable patience, learning, and experience. Organizations need to recognize the importance of providing the support necessary to fulfill the strategic goals of the team. It is essential to provide an opportunity, in person or using computer-mediated communication, for members to get to know each other. By fostering effective communication and providing training that helps establish a solid foundation of trust, shared understanding, and strong relationships between team members, effective virtual collaboration can be achieved.

REMINDERS

- Virtual teams are more dynamic and complex than more traditional teams. They require members to be more adept at working with individuals from cultures other than their own.

- The understanding of individual behavior and work processes within organizations must evolve in order to adapt to the challenges of working virtually.

- Collaboration is a result of positive synergy that encourages a win-win relationship among the members.

- Collaboration in a virtual team context requires trust, shared understanding, and constructive relationships to form among team members.

- Team members are more likely to collaborate if they care about the ultimate goal of the team and not just their own expected contributions.

- Trust may be a substitute for control in virtual teams: the less control there is, the greater is the need for trust.

- In order for trust to occur, team members need to follow through on commitments and promises to each other.

- Shared understanding means that team members are aware of the team's capacities and objectives, the expertise offered by each member, and how they will interact to achieve the ultimate team goal.

- Virtual team members must work interdependently, assuming collective responsibility for results and developing a positive synergy, in order for collaboration to occur.

- Making team members comfortable in their communications with each other promotes creativity and innovation in the collaboration process.

- Open communication may be the most effective means of building trust, developing a shared understanding, and forming deeper relationships among team members.

- Organizations need to identify alternatives to face-to-face contact using various technologies that are available.

- Familiarity or previous experience with other members can enable teams to develop trust and shared understanding more quickly as a foundation already exists.

- Better relationships among virtual team members will help resolve conflicts that may arise and increase the opportunity for collaboration to occur.

References

Boon, S. D., & Holmes, J. G. (1991). The dynamics of interpersonal trust: Resolving uncertainty in the face of risk. In R. A. Hinde & J. Groebel (Eds.), *Cooperation and prosocial behavior* (pp. 190–211). Cambridge: Cambridge University Press.

Brown, H. G., Poole, M. S., & Rodgers, T. L. (2004). Interpersonal traits, complementarity, and trust in virtual collaboration. *Journal of Management Information, 20,* 115–128.

Cummings, T. G. (1978). Self-regulating work groups: A socio-technical synthesis. *Academy of Management Review, 3*, 625–634.

Hackman, J. R. (1986). The psychology of self-management in organizations. In M. S. Pollack & R. O. Perloff (Eds.), *Psychology and work: Productivity, change, and employment* (pp. 85–136). Washington, DC: American Psychological Association.

Holton, J. A. (2001). Building trust and collaboration in a virtual team. *Team Performance Management, 7*, 36–47.

Jarvenpaa, S. L., Knoll, K., & Leidner, D. E. (1998). Is anybody out there? Antecedents of trust in global virtual teams. *Journal of Management Information Systems, 14*, 29–64.

Kasper-Fuehrer, E. C., & Ashkanasy, N. M. (2001). Communicating trustworthiness and building trust in interorganizational virtual organizations. *Journal of Management, 27*, 235–254.

Kirkman, B. L., & Rosen, B. (1999). Beyond self-management: Antecedents and consequences of team empowerment. *Academy of Management Journal, 42*, 58–74.

Kirkman, B. L., Rosen, B., Gibson, C. B., Tesluk, P. E., & McPherson, S. O. (2002). Five challenges to virtual team success: Lessons from Sabre, Inc. *Academy of Management Executive, 16*, 67–79.

Kirkman, B. L., Rosen, B., Tesluk, P. E., & Gibson, C. B. (2004). The impact of team empowerment on virtual team performance: The moderating role of face-to-face interaction. *Academy of Management Journal, 47*, 175–192.

Lawler, E.E.I., Mohrman, S. A., & Ledford, G. E., Jr. (1995). *Creating high performance organizations: Practices and results of employee involvement and total quality management in Fortune 1000 companies.* San Francisco: Jossey-Bass.

Leifer, R., & Mills, P. K. (1996). An information processing approach for deciding upon control strategies and reducing control loss in emerging organizations. *Journal of Management, 22*, 113–137.

Lewicki, R. J., & Bunker, B. B. (1995). Trust in relationships: A model of trust development and decline. In B. B. Bunker & J. Z. Rubin (Eds.), *Conflict, cooperation and justice* (pp. 133–173). San Francisco: Jossey-Bass.

Liedtka, J. M. (1996). Collaborating across lines of business for competitive advantage. *Academy of Management Executive, 10*, 20–34.

Manz, C. C., & Sims, H. P., Jr. (1986). Leading self-managed groups: A conceptual analysis of paradox. *Economic and Industrial Democracy, 7*, 141–165.

Manz, C. C., & Sims, H. P., Jr. (1987). Leading workers to lead themselves: The external leadership of self-managing work teams. *Administrative Science Quarterly, 32*, 106–128.

Mayer, R. C., Davis, J. H., & Schoorman, F. D. (1995). An integrative model of organizational trust. *Academy of Management Review, 20*, 709–734.

McAllister, D. J. (1995). Affect- and cognition-based trust as foundations for interpersonal cooperation in organizations. *Academy of Management Journal, 38*, 24–59.

Montoya-Weiss, M. M., Massey, A. P., & Song, M. (2001). Getting it together: Temporal coordination and conflict management in global virtual teams. *Academy of Management Journal, 44*, 1251–1262.

Pearce, C. L., & Conger, J. A. (2003). *Shared leadership: Reframing the hows and whys of leadership.* Thousand Oaks, CA: Sage.

Sarker, S., Valacich, J. S., & Sarker, S. (2003). Virtual team trust: Instrument development and validation in an IS educational environment. *Information Resources Management Journal, 16,* 35–55.

Schrage, M. (1990). *Shared minds: The new technologies of collaboration.* New York: Random House.

Scott, W. R. (1987). The adolescence of institutional theory. *Administrative Science Quarterly, 32,* 493–511.

Sims, H. P., Jr., & Manz, C. C. (1996). *Company of heroes: Unleashing the power of self-leadership.* Hoboken, NJ: Wiley.

Uhl-Bien, M., & Graen, G. B. (1998). Individual self-management: Analysis of professionals' self-managing activities in functional and cross-functional work teams. *Academy of Management Journal, 41,* 340–350.

Sensemaking to Create High-Performing Virtual Teams

Gina Hinrichs, Jane Seiling, Jackie Stavros

In organizations, teams are formed to determine a course of action based on a choice among alternatives, usually under conditions of risk. Decision making has been a central process for teams and supported action and progress for years. The importance of decision making is reflected in the focus our society places on it. Currently, based on an Amazon.com search, there are over 125,000 books and countless articles published on decision making. As greater innovation in a context of accelerating change, complexity, and uncertainty is demanded, a more robust decision-making process is called for. Decision making must shift to a more holistic, inclusive, and relational process so organizational members can live with uncertainty yet act with confidence. Sensemaking is that more robust, innovative process. In its simplest form, sensemaking is making sense of the world by noticing that something has changed, challenging existing thinking, applying relevant information, making a decision, taking action, learning from the action, and repeating the cycle until the risk of the uncertainty is at an acceptable level. A new normal is created. Sensemaking is a continuous cycle of learning and action.

In this chapter, we provide an expanded definition and theory of sensemaking as it applies to virtual teams. A nonlinear sensemaking process model is offered that results in greater innovation and higher performance in virtual teams. Significant to this approach to sensemaking is the recognition that conversations and relationships are vital to understanding situations and making decisions based on good collective sense (Hinrichs, Stavros, & Seiling, 2005). The conversations and relationships need to be dynamic so that assumptions are challenged, decisions are made, and accountability becomes constructive. With the foundation of dynamic relationships and constructive accountability, effective sensemaking can occur. Each of these two critical elements of sensemaking—constructive accountability and dynamic relationships—is described. Finally, a practical approach for virtual teams using sensemaking is proposed. This approach includes using the five C's of conversations and relationships—clarity, connection, candor, co-creation, and commitment—and a sensemanager to ensure effective application of the five C's. *Sensemanager* is a new term for a role that is many times unrecognized or missing in teamwork. The sensemanager focuses on the context and process of sensemaking. It goes beyond a facilitation role to adding the responsibility for being the catalyst for sensemaking. (Tools and a large group intervention case study in a nonprofit organization are provided on the www.wiley.com/go/virtual-teamshandbook Web site.)

A SENSEMAKING PROCESS MODEL FOR VIRTUAL TEAMS

Sensemaking is a continuous cycle of learning and action, and decision making is a critical phase of it. The power of sensemaking is adding holistic understanding prior to decision making and learning from the decision to take iterative action. The power of sensemaking is realized when stakeholders are involved in the understanding phase and thus become engaged early in the process. In addition, by seeing sensemaking as more iterative than decision making, participants are more willing to take smaller actions that test the complexity of situations. Virtual teams contribute to sensemaking by making it possible for more stakeholders to be involved in the understanding and the learning from action phases. Robust sensemaking occurs when the voices and vision of potentially global participants are added.

Sensemaking is a challenge for virtual teams because it depends on conversations that bring to the table all relevant ideas and information to be considered. It also depends on relationships among people most interested in or affected by the outcome of sensemaking. These conversations occur with limited time, social cues, or shared language (actual words and their definitions), yet they need to create shared understanding and committed, coordinated action. Since sensemaking is a collaborative, conversational process, it requires the appropriate voices to be heard and understood. This requires a more intentional level of managing conversations, language, and relationships. When sensemaking is explicitly available, the greater challenges of virtual teams produce better outcomes by virtue of greater diversity of thinking, language, and global coverage.

Virtual teams can achieve effective sensemaking and high levels of innovation and performance through this nonlinear process model, which can be applied to face-to-face teams as well (Weick, 1995; Paul, 1993; Nadler & Hibino, 1999):

1. *Focus on purpose and criteria.* Gaining clarity and commitment to a shared (higher) purpose, values, and a successful outcome is critical at the beginning of the sensemaking process. This identifies the conversation that the participants are in and provides the motivation to contribute fully. Sensemaking is a creative process that requires energy to be highly effective. Energy is created when the participants are aware that they share a purpose that is worth the investment of their best thinking and imagination. The criteria are created by values that bind the process and the vision of a worthy outcome. The greater the clarity and commitment, the greater the effectiveness and innovation of the sensemaking process.

2. *Clarify the question or issue.* Creating greater clarity requires focused thinking. There are many paths to achieve a purpose and desired outcomes. The group needs to spend sufficient time identifying and understanding the question or issue that is their path to the purpose and outcome. Too often this step is assumed, which results in a lack of focus of collective thinking and efforts. An answer flows more easily when the question or issue has collective meaning and bounds.

3. *Expose existing perspectives.* Acknowledging that each participant has an initial perspective allows all participants' perspectives to be exposed and used for creating new perspectives. This is another step that is often missed because participants traditionally are encouraged to reserve judgment until they have fully considered facts. This should be a nonjudgmental step that serves to access intuition. Another important aspect of perspectives is self-perception. Perspectives are in the context of self-perception. Each participant has a perception of his or her role in the group that enlarges other perspectives and the willingness to contribute.

4. *Identify and challenge assumptions.* Going deeper into perspectives uncovers assumptions, which are generally invisible and a key to sensemaking. Since sensemaking requires awareness and mindfulness, anything that contributes to awareness must be used. Greater understanding and innovation can be achieved when assumptions are identified and challenged. Members must help each other uncover and challenge assumptions. Access to assumptions comes with questions such as, "In order for you to have that perspective, what are you assuming?" or "If I believe that, what am I assuming?"

5. *Generate purposeful alternatives.* Generating purposeful alternatives follows from clarity and exposure of assumptions. This can be accomplished in myriad ways, including brainstorming and inquiry. Since creativity is not encouraged in many organizations, it may be necessary to provide an environment where creativity is encouraged. It is important to get as many alternatives on the table as possible.

6. *Gather and apply relevant information.* Traditionally data gathering has been accomplished at the beginning of the process. This may result in unfocused data gathering, poor resource use, and even analysis paralysis if the process is not bounded. Gathering relevant information requires clarity of purpose, outcomes, the question to be answered, and potential solutions.

7. *Make decisions.* Making decisions involves reducing or prioritizing the purposeful alternatives. Many methods can be employed to make good choices. It will be important for the team to be intentional about its method of decision making since there are so many valid approaches. The decision must have clear alignment to the purpose and criteria. Good decisions should be made that balance the risk and reward. However, perfection or the one right answer is not the goal. Finding an 80 percent good decision and then iterating should be the goal.

8. *Enact and learn.* Enacting and learning requires testing or piloting solutions and noticing the impact. This step leads to additional cycles of sensemaking. Enacting an 80 percent or better solution provides information that in an environment of complexity and accelerating change cannot be fully anticipated. The solution is then improved in subsequent cycles.

All of these steps are accomplished in conversations, which are based in and create relationships. The quality of sensemaking is dependent on the quality of conversations and relationships. The more trust, safety, and candor are present in conversations and relationships, the higher the quality of each step in the sense-making process.

At the core of appropriate response to situations and circumstances of uncertainty is the activity of making sense. Uncertainty triggers sensemaking when changes in the environment or the existence of a perceived need become evident (Weick, 1995). As shown in Figure 5.1, it occurs in a somewhat linear process.

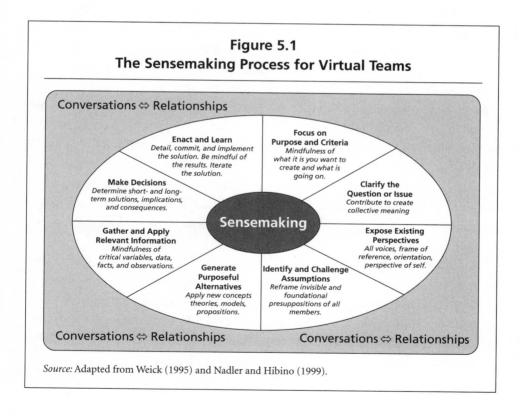

Figure 5.1
The Sensemaking Process for Virtual Teams

Conversations ⇔ Relationships

Enact and Learn
Detail, commit, and implement the solution. Be mindful of the results. Iterate the solution.

Focus on Purpose and Criteria
Mindfulness of what it is you want to create and what is going on.

Make Decisions
Determine short- and long-term solutions, implications, and consequences.

Clarify the Question or Issue
Contribute to create collective meaning

Sensemaking

Gather and Apply Relevant Information
Mindfulness of critical variables, data, facts, and observations.

Expose Existing Perspectives
All voices, frame of reference, orientation, perspective of self.

Generate Purposeful Alternatives
Apply new concepts theories, models, propositions.

Identify and Challenge Assumptions
Reframe invisible and foundational presuppositions of all members.

Conversations ⇔ Relationships   Conversations ⇔ Relationships

Source: Adapted from Weick (1995) and Nadler and Hibino (1999).

The wheel is meant also to depict cycles and the potential to move freely among the steps. Decision making does not go away; it remains an important step in sensemaking. Decision making provides a linear or rational aspect within the complex, nonlinear, collaborative, intuitive, and iterative cognitive process of sensemaking.

Weick (1979) defined and focused on the importance of sensemaking in uncertain environments. According to Weick, sensemaking refers to sizing up a situation: trying to discover what you have while simultaneously acting and having some effect on what you discover. It is not a passive diagnosis. Acts of sensemaking are accomplishing reality while discovering it. Sensemaking sets the frame from which decisions are made. At the time Weick was formulating sensemaking as a theory, the general environment was more stable. His focus and contribution were in highly uncertain environments or crisis. This led to conceptualizing a more robust decision making that was proactive before, during, and after the decision to act. Stavros and Torres (2005) suggest that practicing reflection and action can develop greater awareness of self, others, and the interplay between self and others as meaning is generated together. Engaging in reflection, sense seeking, and sense sharing prior to deciding is accomplished after quick identification of the challenge and purpose of the solution (Seiling, 2005).

Weick (1995) provides seven properties of sensemaking (see Table 5.1). These properties gain increased relevancy for today's uncertain environment and for virtual teams. Weick's emphasis is not only on the cognitive process of sensemaking but on the social process as well. This is especially important with virtual teams since the social processes require more intention and attention than face-to-face teams do. Thus, reframing Weick's seven properties for virtual teams adds seven challenges in a virtual environment. Table 5.1 lists Weick's original seven properties of sensemaking and the proposed accompanying challenges for those working in virtual teams.

In addition to Weick's seven properties (1995), the element of perceived member control in virtual teams is a factor of personal involvement and contribution. Skinner (1995) suggests that one's belief in having adequate control over work performance contributes to and strengthens trust in other members of the group. Sensemaking and accountability practices that are constructive contribute to the perception of control. People have been shaped to derive psychological benefits

Table 5.1
Weick's Seven Properties of Sensemaking and Related Challenges for Virtual Teams

Weick's Original Sensemaking Property	Definition of Weick's Sensemaking Property	Related Challenge for Virtual Teams
Social context	Meanings created from conversations and relationships	Temporal coordination and effective synchronous and asynchronous conversations must be designed and facilitated to create meaning from relationships.
Personal identity	Each member's perception of his or her role in the group	Cultural diversity is important to the sense of role and group interpretation of roles. Membership takes on greater significance. The need for definition regarding one's role and identity is more significant to the virtual team member.
Retrospect	How the group interprets what has occurred	Access to information and each person's native language understandings affect how information creates and sustains shared understanding and meaning.
Salient cues	The group's taking cues and expanding them into explanations	Interpretation of cues and the conversations needed to expand them into explanations is affected by diversity, native language, and the ability to have conversations (temporal coordination and asynchronous systems).

(Continued)

Table 5.1 (Continued)

Weick's Original Sensemaking Property	Definition of Weick's Sensemaking Property	Related Challenge for Virtual Teams
Ongoing events	Dealing with the reality that members must act and respond as things continue to change	Both face-to-face and virtual teams are affected by the flow of ongoing events. The presence of demands in the physical workplace is more evident than in the virtual workplace. The overlap of physical and virtual workplace demands on time and effort can be confusing (Roberts, Smith, & Pollock, 2002).
Plausibility	The credible sense (stories) the group makes of salient cues and ongoing events within the social context	Since plausibility builds on social context, retrospect, and salient cues, virtual teams are affected by the challenges of temporal coordination, the quality of synchronous and asynchronous conversations, cultural diversity, and different native languages (Powell, Piccoli, & Ives, 2004).
Enactment	Action and learning to inform further action	Like ongoing events, once the challenges of virtual teams are resolved, enactment is similar for face-to-face and virtual teams.

from a sense of control. The level of perceived control is related to the amount of constructive accountability activity there is. In virtual teams, meeting the need for perceived control is a challenge that is significant to prompting the members to take action and actively seeking solutions to problems.

Constructive Accountability

Within the context of virtual teams, shared knowledge and resources, open communication, relationships, collaborative ways of working together, and collective responsibility are vital to success. Constructive accountability is the element in sensemaking that encourages the above behaviors. *Constructive accountability* (CA) is defined as an ongoing process of conversations during the accomplishment of work that creates the relationships and context for making sense and being collectively responsible for outcomes (Seiling, 2005).

Foundational to sensemaking and critical to any team is accountability. Just as decision making requires a shift to sensemaking, accountability requires a shift to an ongoing concept of constructive accountability (Seiling & Hinrichs, 2005). Traditional accountability has an individual focus rather than a focus on collective responsibility. As part of efforts to organize and perform in the workplace, people must take responsibility and be accountable to and for the work, themselves, and others. When a staff member is assigned something to do, it is often one person's job to do it and he or she is accountable for accomplishment. Sometimes a situation does not appear to encourage group responsibility, yet an individual sense of accountability to the group remains. Being assigned suggests that the person knows how to do what he or she is responsible and accountable for or how to find out how to do it. If the assignment is not accomplished, there may be consequences for the person or the team, or both.

Since virtual collaborative work must be accomplished outside team meeting time, it requires commitment and accountability to build trust and achieve the performance objectives beyond the limited meeting times. In a face-to-face team, work can be accomplished during the time the team meets. Traditional accountability is important but insufficient for virtual teams, where team time is minimized. Accomplishing work outside the team requires commitment to accomplishing the goals. Constructive accountability is the social process that allows cooperative work in either synchronous or asynchronous virtual projects.

When activities of accountability are constructive, they are moved into the everyday activities of working with others. Within CA, no one person is responsible or accountable for an activity. All team members contribute and are significant to what occurs. Individual team member commitment still underlies CA behaviors. Accountability that is experienced and practiced as collaborative contributes to broadening relationships, performances, strengths, and learnings of the members in the organization. With an understood intention of CA as positive, contributive, integrated behaviors, arguing becomes a productive activity leading to better sensemaking. Examples of the practice of CA as an ongoing process of accomplishment in virtual teams include the following planned and unplanned activities:

- Participating and contributing fully in meetings and conversations, in both physical and virtual space, that are directly and at times indirectly connected to the team.

- Being mindful by noticing and hearing "something different" or "something the same" and asking questions to clarify or challenge assumptions.

- Providing personal resources and seeking or applying external resources, both sought (such as seminars, conferences, journals, magazines, or Web sites) and unexpected (accidental learnings), that help to question assumptions and expand thinking.

- Discussing what could be done to make better sense of a past or current situation and how to best move forward.

- Sharing knowledge (through calling, e-mail, and so on) regarding challenging issues and to cyberbrainstorm ways to approach the issue. Cyberbrainstorming is activated by offering a brainstorming question and asking all team members to individually offer their own thoughts without boundaries about what can be done to address an issue. These thoughts are offered to a collecting agent, who combines them for offering back to the group for discussion. Cyberbrainstorming has proven to be more effective than face-to-face brainstorming by invoking stronger individual brainstorming first (Wallace, 1999).

- Advocating for the team, team members, and its decisions as reliable and productive (Seiling, 2001).

- Committing to "I: X by Y": Each team member (I) personally commits to what he or she will do (X) by when (Y). If at any time, the team member becomes aware that he or she cannot deliver X by Y, he or she commits to informing the relevant teammates immediately. Timely delivery is important to the work of others and the team's outcomes (Furst, Reeves, Rosen, & Blackburn, 2004).

- Organizing additional virtual meetings to discuss, update, or plan around a specific emerging issue.

- Creating deeper relationships. This can be done through casually exchanging relevant stories, metaphors, and humorous anecdotes.

- Contacting key stakeholders to solicit feedback and collaboration on potential impacts of anticipated activities or new thinking.

Effective teams are constructed by their members. Member activities, contributions, and relationships determine the success or failure of the team. Recognizing the role of constructive accountability in everyday work contributes to the opportunity and ability of the team to reach the project and team goals. Progress on projects depends on CA.

Dynamic Relationships

Conversations and relationships are the foundation of effective sensemaking and teamwork. For any team, and especially virtual teams, relationships need to shift to being dynamic relationships. Dynamic relationships (DR), along with CA, are critical elements in sensemaking. The concept of dynamic relationships has been explained by Stavros and Torres (2005):

> *Dynamic:* characterized by continuous change, activity, or progress; characterized by vigor and energy. *Dynamics* (plural) has a subtle shift in its definition: the physical, virtual, intellectual or moral forces that provide motion, activity, and change in a given sphere; the conduct of an interpersonal relationship. Hence, *Dynamic Relationships* (DR): communities where members are self-reflectively aware of their relationship with and to others. Their awareness extends to understanding that relationships are dynamic; any action taken on the part of any member will result in changes for other members and potentially for the community as a whole [p. 42].

Especially significant to virtual teams is that DRs do not emphasize strong ties. They instead emphasize change, reflection, action, and progress. Thus, ongoing physical presence is not vital for sustaining dynamic relationships. Stavros and Torres's principle of awareness (2005) links to constructive accountability and making sense of the world. This principle reminds individuals to be mindful of the relational dynamics in interactions with others in the team environment. This applies to both how individuals should act and the moment of action. Every action is a change in the team's environment. When constructive accountability is the mind-set, virtual teams make progress and generate elevated feelings, processes, outcomes, and accountability. The dynamic nature of a relationship can be affected greatly by activities of cooperation, collaboration, and shared involvement in daily work activities—all important to virtual teams. The team's collective experience today determines what tomorrow will look like. That is change in action.

Dynamic relationships are not confined to the current relationships of the virtual team. Since *dynamic* suggests something is ever changing and ongoing, the previous relationships (networks) of virtual team members may also be used for the project. Relationships are the main tool for creating opportunities to access information from other resources, and this is especially true for virtual teams. According to recent research, the location of where information can best be developed and maintained is often different from where it can best be used (Lenox & King, 2004). It is vital to identify team members who have networks to access pertinent information or can scan for information. Team members' networks are the easiest and at times the best resources for moving projects forward.

Sensemaking is a holistic learning and action process that represents a shift from the root of decision making. To be effective, it requires dynamic relationships and the evidence of constructive accountability. Sensemaking is especially appropriate to virtual teams. The mindful, holistic, inclusive nature of sensemaking is enhanced by the spatially dispersed (global) nature of virtual teams. Virtual teams are enhanced by sensemaking's approach to culture, assumptions, constructive accountability, and dynamic relationships.

The next section illustrates how to practice effective sensemaking that includes constructive accountability and dynamic relationships through the application of the five C model.

THE FIVE C'S AND THE ROLE OF A SENSEMANAGER

The confluence of need, technological capability, and social learning has provided the ability for virtual teams to greatly improve how organizations anticipate and respond effectively to change. In corporate and educational settings, virtual teams have become viable, efficient, and effective (Powell et al., 2004). Based on our experience with corporate organizations, we offer some practical approaches and tools to create high-performing virtual teams by employing sensemaking.

This approach was gleaned from work with both face-to-face teams and virtual teams within corporations. The tools are conversation designs, applicable to both types of teams. The conversation designs use the five C's as criteria to actualize the sensemaking process model. The differences in application between face-to-face and virtual teams are in the intentionality. In a face-to-face team, it is possible to provide less attention to one of the design elements of the model and recover as a result of ongoing, rich face-to-face interaction. For application in virtual teams, having well-thought-out, well-prepared, and well-executed conversations that create relationships, learning, and coordinated action is essential. To this end, we propose five critical elements of conversations and relationships and a new role, that of sensemanager, to ensure that each of these elements is effectively used.

Conversations are the basic element for dynamic relationships, constructive accountability, and sensemaking that lead to positive outcomes. Conversations can be likened to air: conversation is always present, mostly taken for granted, and critical to living and working. That it is difficult to step back and be intentional about conversations is surprising in that all progress, team projects, and relationships are dependent on the quality of conversations. For high-performing virtual teams, the challenge of having conversations brings an additional level of awareness that may be missing for face-to-face teams. As a result, more intention (commitment) and attention (rigor) should be placed on this basic element: the conversation that creates relationship.

Many types of conversations occur within a team: conversations to inform, understand, engage, make a decision, solve a problem, support, and innovate. These types are the elements of and direct sensemaking. The outcome of any project is a result of the quality of the conversations. From a practical application standpoint, the design of a virtual team to produce results lies in the design of each personal conversation at a microlevel and a project at the macrolevel.

These five C's for effective sensemaking provide a thinking tool for designing and facilitating conversations that create the relationships in virtual teams (see Figure 5.2):

- *Clarity:* What is the purpose of the conversation or project? What are we committed to producing? How will we operate? What is my role?

- *Connection (Coordination):* What is our relationship that makes it possible for this conversation or project to take place and have meaning? How do we coordinate so we can connect and have the conversation or carry out the project?

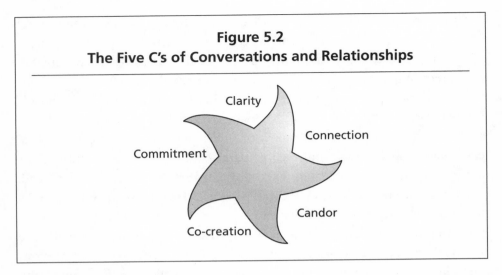

Figure 5.2
The Five C's of Conversations and Relationships

Clarity

Connection

Commitment

Candor

Co-creation

- *Candor:* How do we access and make available all the applicable information so we can make sense of that information? How can I feel safe in sharing knowledge, assumptions, or new thinking openly?

- *Co-creation:* How do we collectively make sense of the situation and issues and decide on the appropriate action?

- *Commitment:* What action will we commit to as a result of our conversation? What is our commitment to each other? How are we practicing constructive accountability?

The proposed role of a sensemanager is to ensure the criteria for the five C's are designed into conversations at all levels. The sensemanager manages the collective sense of the team by using the five C's. A sensemanager is the conversation designer and context leader. This role allows the team leader and members to stay focused on the purpose, content, and outcome of the team's project. Virtual meetings are conversations that need careful design and set up. (See the www.wiley .com/go/virtualteamshandbook Web site for a meeting set-up checklist: Checklist for Virtual Team Sensemanagers.)

Clarity

Clarity is needed for the project, how members are to operate, and each member's perception of his or her role. Understanding and alignment of purpose and outcome is the first step in any conversation or project. It becomes more critical and difficult as the members in a conversation are spatially dispersed, culturally diverse, and increase in number. The sensemanager's role is to ensure that the purpose and outcome of a conversation or project are collectively understood. What often happens is that team members have different interpretations of the purpose and outcome. The purpose needs to be clear and aligned to the team and organization's mission and vision. Members become disconnected or frustrated when the purpose, outcome, or time frame is different from their expectations.

The sensemanager's role in assisting virtual teams and virtual team members is especially critical in the early stages of team development. The sensemanager must orchestrate and insist on clarity. This person works with the team leader to gain initial clarity on the purpose, goals, deliverables, time frame, scope, and membership of the project team. This can be facilitated by using a charter as a tool to gain clarity. (See the www.wiley.com/go/virtualteamshandbook Web site for the charter tool: Initiate: Charter for Clarity.) The sensemanager assists the team in working through the charter early in the project for mutual discovery of the purpose. The members must find common ground and alignment. Awareness of management's support provides the willingness to negotiate difficult task and role activities.

Once the charter is complete, it should be visible and readily available in a team knowledge-sharing system. The charter can and must be modified as needed throughout the project to reflect new understanding. Paying attention to scope creep (the movement away from, adding to, or changing of direction) is significant to knowing when to make changes to the charter.

Another key aspect of clarity is in how the team operates. Some refer to this as ground rules, rules of engagement, or operating agreements. It cannot be emphasized enough how vitally important clarity of ground rules is for a virtual team. The sensemanager should facilitate a robust conversation that discovers and honors cultural differences (both geographical and functional), creates time zone coordination, and provides the basis for the creation of trust and commitment. (In face-to-face teams, ground rules are often posted without discussion or only minimal discussion, or are ignored completely, a practice that is often disruptive.) It must also be clear that the role of all members is to pay attention to when the rules are being violated and call it to the attention of the team immediately. There is little opportunity for a virtual team to become high performing without co-created ground rules that deal with the specific challenges of a virtual team. This conversation must also occur at the initiation of a virtual team. (See the www.wiley.com/go/virtualteamshandbook Web site for the ground rules tool: Connect: Team-Building Ground Rules Tool.)

Part of the ground rules conversation should deal with principles of membership (Seiling, 1997). Once defined, those principles remain the same even as new members enter or existing members leave. (An example is provided on the www .wiley.com/go/virtualteamshandbook Web site: Connection: Membership Principles Tool.) Membership clarity leads to role clarity. Since virtual teams depend on a minimum amount of team time, the majority of the work is done outside team time. Understanding one's role is critical for constructive accountability. Virtual team members must understand what they are doing, why they are doing it, and when the work is due.

Connection (Coordination)

Team members must be able to connect on professional, personal, and technical levels. Since work is accomplished through meaningful conversation, it is important to create and nurture relationships that make meaningful conversations possible. Conversely, if there are no conversations, there is no relationship.

Connections and relationships take time and intention to develop. A sensemanager facilitates the development of connections (cognitive and technological) and relationships that transcend cultures and create a new culture. An initial face-to-face meeting benefits virtual teams by accelerating connections and relationships. A sensemanager must handle the challenge of lack of physical proximity yet achieve emotional proximity. As trust, honesty, and openness are established, team members feel safe in the relationship and contribute fully to the project.

There are many ways relationships can be built in a team. (See the www.wiley .com/go/virtualteamshandbook Web site for a virtual relationship-building tool: Connection: Membership Principles.) For virtual teams, one of the most critical aspects of connection is coordinating technologically and temporally (time zones). Fortunately, collaborative technology has made great strides since the early 1990s.

Despite the vast improvement, it is still incumbent on the sensemanager to ensure before the initial meeting that the technology is reliable, available, and, above all, simple to use. Despite virtual team members' becoming more technologically savvy, the technology should be invisible to the process. Complexity may be required in the background to create simplicity (user friendliness) in the foreground. Team members should focus energy and effort on sensemaking as it relates to the project or situation, not making sense of the technological tools. The sensemanager has a key role in identifying the right platforms and testing prior to the first virtual team meeting.

In connection, considering the team member's time zones is important. The initial meeting should accommodate those in all time zones so all members can be present. In the initial meetings, a ground rule regarding meeting times can then be established. Another time-related challenge in a virtual team is the amount of time for team meetings, which in face-to-face meetings ranges from forty-five minutes to two hours. Because of the lure of multitasking and attention challenges, virtual team meetings must be well designed and well executed so that team members stay focused. A useful suggestion is to schedule one hour and design the virtual meeting for forty-five minutes. Again, the sensemanager has a key role to work with the team leader to influence time availability and, in the case of meetings, provide clear agendas and accountabilities before meetings and to provide a time management role. Materials and updates should be sent out ahead of the meeting so meeting time can be used to create shared understanding and committed action. (See the www.wiley.com/go/virtualteamshandbook Web site: Agenda Tool and the Stand-Up Meetings as Accountability-Generating Exchange Tool.) To move the virtual team to the next step, follow-up minutes and tasks agreed on should be sent out to members within a reasonable amount of time.

Candor

Candor is basic to sensemaking so that knowledge, assumptions, and new thinking can be processed within the group, thus leading to good decision making and committed action.

To operate effectively and make sound decisions, participants must have good information. This means that each member must be willing to provide and receive information. The development of communication strategies that encourage members to be honest with the group and themselves on how they interpret the information is important to membership satisfaction and individual and team performance. In order for candor to occur, perceptions and understandings must be open to examination. Members must feel safe in getting all relevant information out on the table and visible.

The sensemanager employs a variety of tools to help the virtual team move around the sense-making process through the encouragement of candor (refer to Figure 5.1). At each stage in the process, there is a series of conversations needed for the team to create collective sense for that phase. Also, the sensemanager must operate on a context level while the members operate at a content level. In this way, the sensemanager can listen for unproductive and damaging conflict that may occur as a result of differing assumptions, perceptions, or levels of discussion. Differing members' assumptions provide access to innovation, so being attuned to conflict as an opportunity for new thinking facilitates valued outcomes (Furst et al., 2004). In contrast, if there is too much agreement, the sensemanager might need to provide challenges to assumptions so the team does not fall prey to groupthink. In a virtual team, the opportunities for assumption or perception differences are much greater due to the potential for cultural diversity. The benefit of diversity requires the sensemanager be especially attuned to listening to what is said and not said and to be aware of the potential need for intervention. Virtual teams must be supported in balancing relational issues and competitive behaviors in the team (Furst et al., 2004).

Co-creation

Co-creation is the new thinking and specific plans that result from the journey around the sensemaking process of learning and acting. The term *co-creation* suggests that nothing is accomplished completely alone; this is especially true in virtual teams. The desired outcomes need to have been co-created. Mindfulness, as a key element of sensemaking (Seiling & Hinrichs, 2005), suggests that the team as a whole must be mindful of the needs and opportunities for what is needed to succeed; it suggests the continual creation and re-creation of meaning and sense through paying attention (Langer, 1989). Each member must feel that he or she had an important role in producing the outcome. And each member knows that it takes the whole team to produce the desired outcomes. Ultimately co-creation produces member satisfaction for being a part of the team. The solutions and the enactment of the solutions have an opportunity for higher quality due to the diversity inherent in a virtual team.

There is sensitivity to the operation and collective performance of the team that members of the team share. There is also the challenge of colocated members taking on more of the project work because it is easier not to manage virtually. The sensemanager must be aware of different levels of membership and the appropriate contribution to the conversations, solutions, and tangible outcomes. Since much of a virtual team's work must be accomplished outside teamwork time, the sensemanager must stay connected and available to support the team leader in coordination of tasks and responsibilities so that each virtual team member is participating and contributing.

Commitment

Commitment demonstrates how members are constructively accountable outside the team meetings to accomplish the work and produce the tangible outcomes. It is the outcome that is expected from the conversations and to the project work. What is the team committed to producing as a result of conversations regarding the virtual team? Just like the clarity element of the conversation, alignment of the purpose and outcome is needed for each action. The sensemanager facilitates the demonstration of commitment by explicitly asking for I: X by Y. Who will take responsibility for which action item and by when? If a project plan is needed, the sensemanager ensures each task has a team member responsible. In a virtual team, the minutes with explicit I: X by Y must be published. The sensemanager works with the team leader to ensure that the commitments are met on a timely basis.

Virtual teams depend on each member to represent the team positively to others. Commitment refers to the goals of the project and the relationship of team members. Commitment to each other has another aspect besides relational: it is the role of each member to acquire the resources the team needs. Often the investment of resources is adjusted by the perception of the potential provider regarding the team. Resources are limited and will be invested in teams seen as providing the best return on the resource investment.

At times, virtual team members may appear to be "freeloading"—that is, they are part of the team but unwilling to do a fair share of the work. Although it may seem that the potential for freeloading is greater in virtual than face-to-face teams, the opposite seems to be the case when the virtual team is well designed. Detection of those not fully contributing can be more apparent in virtual teams since there are fewer verbal exchanges and more digital exchanges like e-mail, which provides automatic documentation. With the efforts of the sensemanager, the team leader, and team members, issues of motivation, team advocacy, or not making or living up to commitments early are addressed. Ground rules to address these issues should have been established in ways that are constructive and contributive, so when there is an appearance of lack of commitment or contribution, there are grounds for addressing the issue with the person.

FINAL THOUGHTS

According to Fineman, Sims, and Gabriel (2005), "Some of the effects of virtualization on working life are still only beginning to emerge" (p. 233). They also state, "Virtuality is everywhere—and nowhere" (p. 224), suggesting that the promise virtual teams hold in the future are yet to be experienced by many organizations that have not taken advantage of this virtual working world. There is great interest in the potential of working and contributing virtually. The perceived need for existing together in a physical place (same location) remains a barrier to the idea of technology being able to perform equally to face-to-face presence. The flexibility offered by being virtual addresses some of the issues presented by distance and globalization, motivating experimental use of virtual teams. Thus, virtual teams hold the promise of greater responsiveness in the face of accelerating change and the need for the escalation of innovation activities essential to remaining competitive in the global environment.

In an effort to combine remote resources, companies are using virtual teams to reduce costs, identify issues, create new products and services, and share learning. This promise can be realized as virtual teams become high-performance teams through the application of sensemaking. Meeting the potential of the virtual team requires sense-making efforts in meeting the challenges of virtual teams: temporal coordination, cultural diversity, and less evident social cues. Sensemaking theory (Weick, 1995; Weick & Roberts, 1993) has been provided in a process model and translated into practical application using the design criteria of five C's: clarity, connection, candor, co-creation, and commitment. In addition, the organizational role of sensemanager is suggested to facilitate sensemaking. The execution of the five C model designs the intention and attention needed for effective sensemaking, dynamic relationships, and constructive accountability. All of these are offered to face-to-face teams that are now being informed by virtual teams.

REMINDERS

- Move from decision making to sensemaking by applying the sensemaking process.

- Use a sensemanager to facilitate the sensemaking process.

- Understand how dynamic relationships and constructive accountability are needed to make progress on the team project between virtual team meetings.

- Focus on the intentional design of conversations to build relationships as the foundation of any team, especially virtual teams.

- To design conversations, use the five C's: clarity, connection, candor, co-creation, and commitment.

RELATED ITEMS ON THE WEB

- Checklist for Virtual Team Sensemanagers
- Large Group Interventions Project: Taking Large Groups Virtual—A Case Study
- Initiate: Charter for Clarity Tool
- Connect: Team-Building Ground Rules Tool
- Connection: Membership Principles Tool
- Agenda Tool
- Standup Meetings as Accountability-Generating Exchange

References

Fineman, S., Sims, D., & Gabriel, Y. (2005). *Organizing and organizations.* Thousand Oaks, CA: Sage.

Furst, S. A., Reeves, M., Rosen, B., & Blackburn, R. S. (2004). Managing the life cycle of virtual teams. *Academy of Management Executive, 18*(2), 6–20.

Hinrichs, G., Stavros, J. M., & Seiling, J. G. (2005). *Sensemanaging as the soul of improvisation.* Presentation at the Midwest Academy of Management 48th Annual Conference, Chicago.

Langer, E. J. (1989). *Mindfulness.* Reading, MA: Addison-Wesley.

Lenox, M., & King, A. (2004). Prospects for developing absorptive capacity through internal information provision. *Strategic Management Journal, 25,* 331–345.

Nadler, G., & Hibino, S. (1999). *Creative solution finding: The triumph of breakthrough thinking over conventional problem solving.* n.p.: Prima Publishing.

Paul, R. W. (1993). *Critical thinking: What every person needs to survive in a rapidly changing world.* Sonoma, CA: Foundation for Critical Thinking.

Powell, A., Piccoli, G., & Ives, B. (2004). Virtual teams: A review of current literature and directions for future research. *ACM SIGMIS Database, 35*(1), 6–36.

Roberts, L. D., Smith, L. M., & Pollock, C. (2002). Mooing till the cows come home. In A. T. Fisher, S. C. Sonn, & B. J. Brishop (Eds.), *The psychological sense of community: Research, applications, and implications.* New York: Kluwer Academic/Plenum.

Seiling, J. G. (1997). *The membership organization: Achieving top performance through the new workplace community.* Palo Alto, CA: Davies-Black.

Seiling, J. G. (2001). *The meaning and role of organizational advocacy: Responsibility and accountability in the workplace.* Westport, CT: Greenwood Press.

Seiling, J. G. (2005). *Moving from individual to constructive accountability.* Tilburg, Netherlands: University of Tilburg.

Seiling, J. G., & Hinrichs, G. (2005). Mindfulness and constructive accountability as critical elements of effective sensemaking: A new imperative for leaders as senseman-agers. *OD Journal, 23*(3), 82–88.

Skinner, E. A. (1995). *Perceived control, motivation, and coping.* Thousand Oaks, CA: Sage.

Stavros, J. M., & Torres, C. B. (2005). *Dynamic relationships: Unleashing the power of appreciative inquiry in daily living.* Chagrin Falls, OH: Taos Institute Publishing.

Wallace, P. (1999). *The psychology of the Internet.* Cambridge: Cambridge University Press.

Weick, K. (1979). *The social psychology of organizing.* Reading, MA: Addison-Wesley.

Weick, K. (1995). *Sensemaking in organizations.* Thousand Oaks, CA: Sage.

Weick, K. E., & Roberts, K. H. (1993). Collective mind in organizations: Heedful interre-lating on flight decks. *Administrative Science Quarterly, 38,* 357–381.

Trust Building Online

Virtual Collaboration and the Development of Trust

Chris Francovich, Michelle Reina, Dennis Reina, Christopher Dilts

It is no secret that trust is an essential ingredient in an organization's ability to collaborate, drive business results, and achieve overall effectiveness. The business case for trust is easy to make. A Watson Wyatt Worldwide (2002) study found that organizations where frontline employees trusted senior leadership posted a 42 percent higher return on shareholder investment over firms where distrust was the norm. In a recent University of British Columbia report, economists found that trust in management is the most valued determinant of job satisfaction (Heliwell & Huang, 2005). The report suggests that a small increase in trust of management is similar to receiving a 36 percent pay increase. Conversely, if the same amount of trust is lost, the decline in employee job satisfaction is similar to taking a 36 percent pay cut. One of the obvious consequences of working in a high-trust organization is that these organizations do not experience the high cost of turnover. Their employees stay. There is also ample evidence supporting the claim that people who trust one another work more effectively together (Reina & Reina, 2006; Shaw, 1997). Individuals who trust one another are more inclined to collaborate freely, create, innovate, take risks, and openly communicate (Reina & Reina, 2006; Solomon & Flores, 2003). Strategic initiatives and change processes such as increased speed to market, decreased cycle time, research and development, and mergers and acquisitions all necessitate higher levels of shared responsibility and accountability, which are fostered by high levels of trust.

One of the most challenging and exciting aspects of this era is the incredible progress made in technologies and ideas about relating, connecting, and developing relationships. Communication technology, globalization, and an across-the-board awareness of the need to both tolerate and respect the "other" has given leaders and designers opportunities and tools that they have never had before.

What is surprising is that there are few strategies or models that seek to systematically and measurably improve trust and trust-related behaviors. This chapter reviews research findings about how trust is built and broken in relationships, teams, and organizations and focuses on how distributed teams and cohorts have engaged in learning about trust using a virtual environment. The chapter presents a rigorous model of trust at work, describes a tool that was designed to build and support trust in virtual teams, and presents a series of behavioral examples of transactional trust.

TRUST IN THE VIRTUAL ENVIRONMENT

Developing technologies and methods to facilitate trust and the skill of virtual collaboration is probably one of the most important tasks facing theorists and managers (Dourish, 2001; Duarte & Tennant-Snyder, 1999; Khan, 2005). The increasing complexity of relationships at global and local levels requires deep, effective, and sustained collaboration built on a foundation of mutual trust.

Information technology has broadened the scope of connectedness in terms of geography as well as increased the density and number of social connections that form relationships; for example, almost 71 percent of Americans currently use e-mail (Center for the Digital Future, 2006). The simultaneous development of personal social networks and work-related connectivity has resulted in a complex landscape of relationships and some confusion about how these relationships are formed and sustained. Research into the dynamics of relationship building in both colocated and virtual teams continues with mixed results. Some theorists are finding that proximity is the key factor in the development of teams and that social characteristics play a much more important role in team or group solidarity than either race or gender (Yuan & Gay, 2006).

The recognition that proximity is a key element in virtual communication has resulted in an increasing emphasis on the quality of the virtual experience as it relates to social presence and the development of social networks and ultimately interpersonal relationships. Many consider that any technology that brings us closer to face-to-face work is worth investing in (Sanders, 2006). Consequently many designers are tending to focus less on asynchronous methods and instead emphasize synchronous elements using technologies such as video, audio, chats and instant messaging, and conferencing. The technology discussed in this chapter is solely concerned with asynchronous communications and draws on trust-building behaviors to support collaboration using only this medium. Findings show that the effectiveness of virtual collaboration is not contingent on the technology or the possibilities of synchronous communication but on the underlying relationships and foundation of trust that the technology supports (Kimble, Li, & Barlow, 2000).

Consequently, the deeper question is, What is responsible for the development of robust trusting relationships in the first place? Is proximity the limiting factor? How exactly do people come to know one another? Literature on communities of practice (Wenger, McDermott, & Snyder, 2002; Wenger, 1998) and apprenticeship learning (Lave, 1988; Lave & Wenger, 1991) supports the idea that proximity and colocated presence are essential ingredients to effective team performance. In this view, shared meanings emerge from shared work, experience, and participation. The implications of this thinking at the very least point toward a climate of sustained engagement and familiarity at a local level. The key here is that the engagement is behavioral and communication based. People's relationships are based on talk and behavior. This talk is amenable to asynchronous talk, which also influences behavior.

What local means in the context of virtual teams is an interesting and important question. Our interpretation is that local is based on the key elements of engagement and participation and a basic realization that relationships and trust are at the heart of the matter. In other words, local is related more to thought and conversation (and the relationships that result) than to space and time. For example, even when we are colocated, we can extend the quantity, if not the quality, of our communications by using e-mail and the telephone. Extensive research shows that trust is built behaviorally (Brothers, 1995; Reina & Reina, 2006). These behaviors are as real in a virtual mode as they are in a face-to-face mode. In short, the behaviors that build trust in face-to-face relationships also build trust in virtual relationships. Moreover, the practice of these behaviors creates conditions that enhance collaboration in face-to-face or virtual mode. Our conclusion is that high trust tends to make both communication and collaboration easier. Our experience of building and field testing an online trust-building program, discussed later in the chapter, suggests that trust is as vital in virtual relationships as it is in local relationships.

THE REINA TRUST AND BETRAYAL MODEL

The model of trust and betrayal presented in this section is the outgrowth of unfolding research on trust at work over the past decade in over one hundred organizations. The model is based on some foundational principles. First, business is conducted through relationships, and trust is the foundation of effective relationships. People who are expected to work together successfully have to trust one another: that is, they have to respect each other and confirm the other's worth and value as a person.

Most leaders, managers, supervisors, and employees strive to build trusting relationships. They recognize that trust is central to healthy work environments and performance, and the need that people have to be trusted and to trust others. In order to sustain trust, these core truths must be recognized: although trust may be held as a value, it is actually built by behavior, and it will be both built and broken in all workplace relationships. Both building trust and breaking trust are natural elements of relationships. Broken trust causes pain, doubt, and confusion, but it may also be used to strengthen relationships and provide significant lessons when people recognize it and choose to work through it.

The purpose of building trust at work using the Reina Trust and Betrayal Model is illustrated in Figure 6.1. The ultimate goal is to increase awareness of trust dynamics between individuals in teams and organizations.

The problem of understanding the relationship between the dynamics of trust and specific trust behaviors has been addressed by the model. The three elements described in the model help simplify the complexity of trust.

Transactional trust describes trust as reciprocal in nature (you have to give it to get it) and created incrementally (step by step over time). There are three facets of transactional trust: contractual, communication, and competence trust. Each has essential behaviors that are associated with building that type. Figure 6.2 illustrates transactional trust and the sixteen specific behaviors that built it.

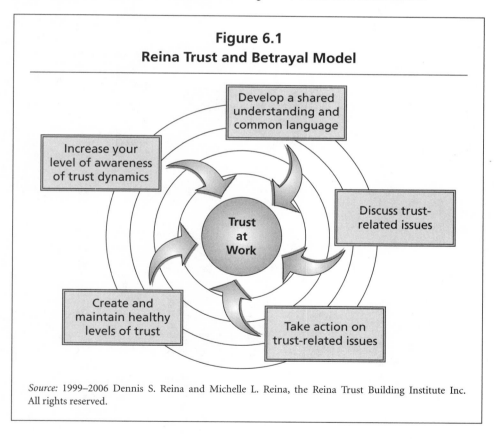

Figure 6.1
Reina Trust and Betrayal Model

Source: 1999–2006 Dennis S. Reina and Michelle L. Reina, the Reina Trust Building Institute Inc. All rights reserved.

Figure 6.2
Transactional Trust

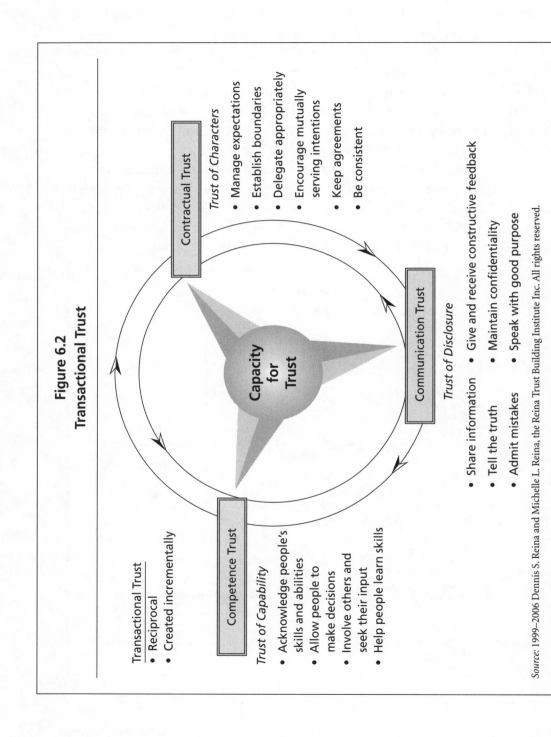

Transactional Trust
- Reciprocal
- Created incrementally

Contractual Trust

Trust of Characters
- Manage expectations
- Establish boundaries
- Delegate appropriately
- Encourage mutually serving intentions
- Keep agreements
- Be consistent

Capacity for Trust

Communication Trust

Trust of Disclosure
- Share information
- Tell the truth
- Admit mistakes
- Give and receive constructive feedback
- Maintain confidentiality
- Speak with good purpose

Competence Trust

Trust of Capability
- Acknowledge people's skills and abilities
- Allow people to make decisions
- Involve others and seek their input
- Help people learn skills

Source: 1999–2006 Dennis S. Reina and Michelle L. Reina, the Reina Trust Building Institute Inc. All rights reserved.

Contractual Trust

Contractual trust involves mutual understanding between people (both will do what they say they will do). Managing expectations, encouraging mutually serving intentions, and keeping agreements are examples of behaviors that build contractual trust. When this trust is practiced, people understand what is expected of them, roles and responsibilities are clear, and commitments are kept or renegotiated. People collaborate freely, depend on each other, and deliver results.

Communication Trust

Trust influences communication, and communication influences trust: the two are closely related. Sharing information, telling the truth, and speaking with good purpose are examples of behaviors that create communication trust. In an environment with strong communication trust, people feel safe to ask questions, honestly speak their minds, challenge assumptions, raise issues, give and receive feedback, or acknowledge that they do not understand and ask for help.

Competence Trust

Competence trust influences the ability to perform job responsibilities. Involving others, seeking input, and helping people to learn new skills are behaviors that build competence trust. Feelings of self-worth and value are directly tied to the presence or absence of competence trust. Of course self-trust and trustworthiness are fundamental issues, but they are not addressed using the transactional trust model.

TRANSACTIONAL TRUST AS THE FOUNDATION FOR VIRTUAL COLLABORATION

Interpreting and evaluating behavior through the lens of transactional trust can serve as the foundation for collaboration in a virtual environment. Each facet plays a particular role. Contractual trust sets the tone and direction, shapes roles and responsibilities, and helps make expectations clear. Communication trust helps establish norms for information flow and standards for how people talk with one another, share information, provide feedback, and work with mistakes that have been made. Competence trust allows individuals to leverage and further develop skills, abilities, and knowledge, particularly those required for virtual collaboration.

Development of Trust Building Online

Trust Building Online is a Web-based computer application developed to support building a foundation of trust using virtual collaboration. The primary goal was to engage participants in a meaningful conversation about trust. In the face-to-face environment, learners become aware of trust-related dynamics by engaging in content that defines trust and specific behaviors that build it. They derive meaning from the content by engaging in reflection on their experiences, brought to life through dialogue with others in the learning environment. Insight gained and meaning derived are guided by facilitation. Individuals and groups report that reflection and dialogue support a deeper understanding of trust and cultivate conscious choices to practice trust-building behaviors. A central design goal was to mirror the sequence of learning experienced during face-to-face trust building. Our goal was to create an asynchronous Internet-based communication platform that would exemplify the best of face-to-face facilitation and enhance the reflection time that is so powerfully effective in the workshop or seminar environment.

Confidence and passion about the utility of Trust Building Online came from material changes in participant behavior as evidenced by changes in trust-building scores shown by the Organizational Trust Scale (OTS), a self-report Likert-type scale survey that is research based, valid, and reliable. The instrument contains fifty-four quantitative questions and three open-ended questions. Pre- and postscores were tracked in pilot study organizations, and significant changes were shown in all three facets of transactional trust after people experienced Trust Building Online.

The progress of Trust Building Online spans a four-year period involving the development of a platform for delivering the trust content, methods for building trust, and tools to practically link those methods to team and organizational needs. It was a collaborative effort that involved the authors and a team of technical specialists. The application was created using PHP, Flash, and HTML protocols. A third-party discussion platform (a bulletin board) was incorporated to support dialogue among participants. The application consists of a set of features and functions designed to engage participants in trust content through reflection, introspection, dialogue, and action planning:

- Flexible and scalable content management system. Multiple cohorts can be deployed from one URL and managed on one integrated interface.
- Flexible and scalable discussion and query functionality, which allows multiple groups and discussion under one organizational umbrella.

- Interactive queries independent of the trust content and the discussion center to foster further collaboration.

- Discussion center (bulletin board system) for holding, categorizing, and tracking parallel discussions and dialogues related to the trust content, participant trust-related issues, and moderator-led discussions.

- Moderator-enabled design and architecture to enable a consistent thread of communication and a model for collaboration.

- Trust quizzes, help and FAQ functionality, a trust memory game, and progress tracking function to monitor engagement and commitments. (See the www .wiley.com/go/virtualteamshandbook Web site for a copy of The Reina Team Trust Quiz.)

- Trust platform design that accommodates the integration of trust-measuring surveys to provide a baseline of the level of trust, support action planning, and monitor progress through postmeasurements.

Two key features of Trust Building Online are the Query Space and the Discussion Center.

The Query Space   A major goal of this design was to optimize interaction and awareness. The Query Space was designed to heighten participants' awareness of how they practice or fail to practice trust-building behaviors through a simple and public question-and-answer format. It was our assumption that participants would, in reading their own and others' responses to questions, both reflect on and share their insights into trust-building and trust-breaking behaviors. Our hope was that participants would develop a heightened awareness of the choices they make to practice trust-building behaviors. Figure 6.3 shows a screen shot of the Query Space. Participants are invited to engage in exploration of trust-building content through their own experiences and to gain insight from one another through a sharing of those experiences.

A query is a reflection question asked of all participants with an option to respond in a time frame of the participant's choosing. The reflection question is asked within the context of a particular aspect of trust. For instance, after an introduction to communication trust behaviors, a query question may be, "Have you experienced gossip or unfair criticism about fellow employees going on behind their backs? If so, how do you tend to respond?"

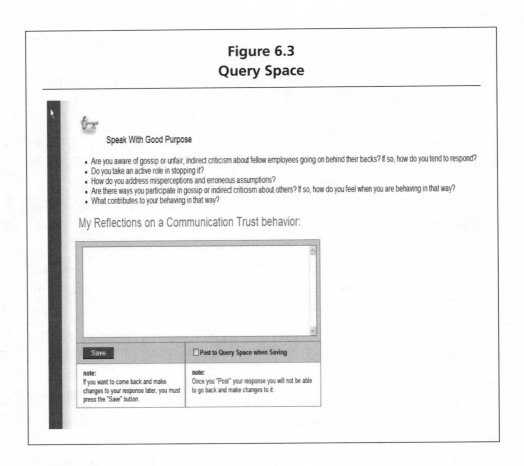

Figure 6.3
Query Space

Speak With Good Purpose

- Are you aware of gossip or unfair, indirect criticism about fellow employees going on behind their backs? If so, how do you tend to respond?
- Do you take an active role in stopping it?
- How do you address misperceptions and erroneous assumptions?
- Are there ways you participate in gossip or indirect criticism about others? If so, how do you feel when you are behaving in that way?
- What contributes to your behaving in that way?

My Reflections on a Communication Trust behavior:

Save   ☐ Post to Query Space when Saving

note:
If you want to come back and make changes to your response later, you must press the "Save" button.

note:
Once you "Post" your response you will not be able to go back and make changes to it.

Rather than include this function in the Discussion Center, it was designed within the content portion of the interface, allowing moderators or designers to add or change questions or queries within the content itself. Participants could then respond to the query and, when ready, post it to the Query Space, where they could read and reflect on their own responses and the responses of cohort members. Figure 6.4 illustrates the group view of the Query Space.

This proved to be one of the most powerful design elements of Trust Building Online. The depth of participants' responses and the threads of meaning woven through multiple responses were surprising. This process of engagement with the content and reflection on both participants' own and others' responses contributed to a significant improvement in team culture. Furthermore, a level

Figure 6.4
Group View of the Query Space

Building Trust in the Workplace Online

My Home | Resume | My Progress | Query Space | Discussion Center | Help & FAQs | Memory Game

Select Group | Group G | Group Progress

Choose a Cycle

Cycle 2:
The Model – Part 1

Beliefs & Challenges About Trust

Query – Beliefs & Challenges about Trust

Beliefs & Challenges About Betrayal & Healing

Query – Beliefs & Challenges about Betrayal & Heal

Transactional Trust

Query – Understanding Transactional Trust
Reflecting on Contractual Trust
Reflecting on Communication Trust
Reflecting on Competence Trust

Transactional Trust

Reflecting on Communication Trust

on 11-15-04 9pm

Like I said earlier I think the most important concept is speaking with good purpose. It is often difficult to do this and at times I have to actively remember to speak always well. Its easy to get caught up in the mess of other people gossiping. When that happens sometimes I try to divert attention away from the subject matter and other times I just shy away from it, or on my not so nice days, listen to it. I think its important to always try to remind people to only speak with good purpose but it is difficult to know how to tell others in a nice way.

on 12-08-04 11pm

Speak with Good Purpose–I feel this communication trust behavior could actually sum up all of them. Always speak with good purpose should be our motto! I don't think it just pertains to gossip...but overall being positive, saying and doing things to better our work environment—I think most people would agree they want to work somewhere where everyone looks out for eachother, respects differences, is open-minded, works as a team, and learns from eachother.

12-15-04 9pm

Speak with good purpose– I think this is very important in everything we do, everyday wherever we are. The saying goes. "Think before you speak" and I believe that if everyone did this more, communication could be improved.

12-17-04 4pm

One needs to be aware and try to avoid negative behaviors that would betray anothers trust.

12-28-04 6pm

On maintaining confidentiality, this is an area I feel very strongly about. Someone should not need to request that you keep a personal conversation confidential, common courtesy should tell you it's what you do! Have I ever broken someones confidence? Yes, there was a particular incident that could have been harmful to a number of other people, had I not spoken up. Sometimes it's a judgement call. That's the hard part.

01-19-05 03am

I feel it is hard to focus on one key behavior because they all are so closely related, part of each other. Being honest as well as maintaining confidentiality are very important to me. If you are honest you are truthful. Sometimes truth can be difficult to deal with; it can be positive or negative it allows us feedback which can be difficult. It allows us/me to grow and be a better and stronger person.

of frankness and disclosure that is typically not present even in face-to-face encounters was observed. In addition, in later follow-up, it was shared that face-to-face discussions were enriched by the opening up of difficult areas online.

The Discussion Center   The Discussion Center, a bulletin board, was a significant feature in an early pilot of Trust Building Online. Figure 6.5 provides a sample screen shot of the Discussion Center. This feature, in conjunction with the Query Space, was effective for sustaining meaningful conversations.

The blending of a structured query with the open-ended Discussion Center posts was an effective combination. The queries allowed participants who required a bit more direction and context to engage in a safe, bounded, and well-defined activity. Others more familiar with computer-mediated technology were able to

Figure 6.5
The Discussion Center

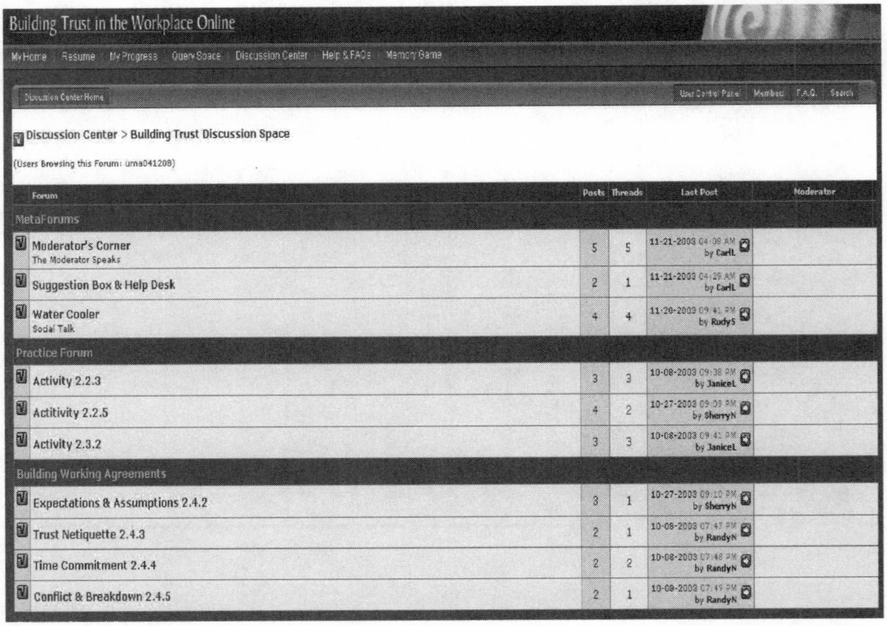

use the query as a means of stepping into a more open-ended, and in many cases deeper, conversation in the discussion center.

Learning from the Initial Design

Initial preparations to go live with the system required us to assess and determine a base level of readiness of participants to engage in the program. An important design element was to be sure that when participants logged in for the first time, they would quickly become engaged with both the technology and the material. We required the development of an attractive, simple-to-use, and compelling interface. Also important was the orientation of the trust-building content in a manner that was meaningful to the participants' work. We wanted to make it easy to engage in and comprehend.

One of the most difficult issues facing contemporary distance learning designers is the issue of participant motivation. Completion rates for standard e-learning applications are notoriously low (Cross & Hamilton, 2002). Our position has been that people have to be motivated to engage in the material in the first place and then gradually develop skills at working asynchronously through a Web-based and Web-moderated medium. Once these barriers are overcome, the disconnect becomes less and less relevant.

One of the issues that initial deployments struggled with was the degree to which participation was mandated. Experience confirms that some degree of "required-ness" is essential to get people on board and further that this "required-ness" is most effective when linked to business needs and desired outcomes. Participation is sustained when the technology is used to enable or develop performance competencies. "Requiredness" is most necessary when launching an engagement with a cohort or team. After engagement has been achieved, participants tend to take responsibility for their own pacing and set their own rate. Business, team, and individual goals influence the rate set. Leaders set the tone by clarifying expectations, and participants set the rate. In other words, participants determine how frequently they need to engage with the technology in order to accomplish what is expected of them. In any case, flexibility is needed.

Asynchronous feedback proved to be a critical element of the design and one that strengthened communication trust. Through asynchronous feedback, participants learned that their words were being heard and that they mattered.

Initially, designs of Trust Building Online required trained moderators whose chief task was to provide this feedback. As the program developed, it became apparent that feedback was also coming from the participants themselves, which is a core element of the construct being used (for example, the behavior of giving and receiving constructive feedback builds communication trust).

Initial designs also had the facilitator drawing the team's attention to the dynamics of its process and key insights that emerged. Feedback took the form of a synthesis of themes, categories, and questions. This feedback required the facilitator's time to analyze and evaluate the responses from the Query Space and the Discussion Center.

The feedback that participants received was intended to build a sense of ownership, shared responsibility, and involvement on the part of individual participants across their cohort's range of responses. The posted feedback became the catalyst for unmoderated or semimoderated communication through the Discussion Center and further building of communication trust. This type of iterative feedback process uses metacognitive and second-order reflection skills and can become a standard part of the cohort's toolkit.

The most important of these feedback opportunities was the creation and maintenance of the team's story line. As participants reflected and commented on the growing body of text, it was obvious that their trust in one another was growing. This observation was supported by increased scores on the trust instruments over three years of survey data analysis.

APPLICATION OF TRUST BUILDING ONLINE: TRANSACTIONAL TRUST AND VIRTUAL COLLABORATION

This section presents a series of posts written by participants in the initial launch of Trust Building Online. Their comments illustrate a sampling of the sixteen behaviors that contribute to the three types of trust composing transactional trust: contractual trust, competence trust, and communication trust.

Virtual Contractual Trust

The posts demonstrated a clear link to the behaviors that support contractual trust. "Managing expectations," a primary behavior of contractual trust, is essential for effective leadership and fundamental to peer relationships. It means being clear about what you expect of others. When people learn what is expected of them solely by hearing what they have done wrong, it breaks trust and leads to feelings of betrayal. Trust Building Online illustrated this behavior as people's expectations of others immediately surfaced in their desire for clarity around posting expectations, how frequently to log in and participate, and the scope and breadth of response expectations. The following post from a nurse in regional pediatric hospital illustrates this point: "I agree with all the expectations that were summarized by you [the moderator]. I just want the group to recognize that there are different styles of participation reflecting individual communication styles."

As both the moderator and participants engaged in dialogue, connections with the contractual trust content, and managing expectations became obvious and relevant. Participants were both reading about this aspect of trust and experiencing its place in their work simultaneously.

Another contractual trust behavior is "keeping agreements." When you keep your agreements, you do what you say you are going to do, or you renegotiate if you are unable to keep the initial agreement. Honoring agreements speaks to an individual's dependability in carrying out commitments. This behavior also surfaced as a fundamental issue during the trust-building process. One human resource employee wrote, "Keeping agreements is something that is very important in building trust in a relationship. It's hard to rely or trust someone if they routinely 'forget' to keep an agreement. It's important to be true your word, do what you say you will, and renegotiate if things change."

This type of explicit dialogue around critical trust-related issues links the key elements of the model to everyday concerns and topics. Developing the ability to talk plainly, directly, and honestly about these issues is fundamental to virtual or face-to-face team coherence. When people are able to articulate and then reference their expectations and understandings of boundaries and agreements, they are able to openly communicate as they continue to negotiate more difficult issues. The following extract from a lengthy post talks about the issue of boundaries: "When establishing boundaries, I feel consistency is the key. Boundaries in our unit mean change and clarifying that change is good and encourages others' positive attitudes." Members of this organization experienced a revelation in learning that issues of change, particularly the introduction of new technologies, affected the feeling of trust around boundaries.

Virtual Communication Trust

Communication is the very fabric of an organization. Some say that an organization is nothing more than a network of communicative structures (Armstrong & Hagel, 2000) and that the coherence of communication is the most important element to organizational effectiveness. Developing communication trust will significantly enhance collaboration and an organization's effectiveness.

An intriguing query posted by a participant who works in a large hospital system illustrates a reflection on a key communication trust behavior: "admitting mistakes." This post opened up a conversation with the participant's online cohort that goes to the very heart of what medical institutions are trying to develop in terms of transparency and the reduction of medical errors:

> I am going to reflect on making and admitting mistakes. This weekend I was asked to go to ER to get labs on a little girl that they already poked twice. When I got down there I didn't see any nurses around and I could hear a trauma in the next room so I just decided to do the lab alone. Well I really needed another hand with pulling the syringe back to get the blood and it ended up not working out. My mistake was thinking that my two little hands could do it by themselves and not going to go find someone to help me. . . . Admitting mistakes is risky because people might think you are not as competent as they thought you were, and then they will not trust you with doing things.

The response to this posting resulted in dialogue about how and why admitting mistakes is hard and what the consequences of not doing so are. Participants were able, once the issue was articulated, to go deeper into the topic and then begin to identify issues like this in day-to-day work. To a great extent, the ability to practice these skills online facilitated the eventual integration of these practices in daily work.

One of the most persistent breaches of trust is the practice of malicious gossip. Speaking with good purpose is the communication trust behavior that is the opposite of gossip. One team member said:

> I think one of the greatest challenges our group has regarding communication trust is "speaking with good purpose." It appears that it is

acceptable in our culture to speak without regard for the impact of one's words on others. I'm not talking about a person who is trying to give constructive feedback to another person who is hurt by the feedback. I have heard many examples of people apparently getting enjoyment out of sharing embarrassing or hurtful information (usually quite embellished from original form) about others to others.

This post resulted in a lively conversation both online and off-line that had the overall effect of making all the members of this team more conscious and aware of the type of speech they were using and its effect on the team. Giving and receiving feedback is a behavior that is vital to people in learning organizations. If there is a lack of basic trust in comments on the intentions of others, it is very difficult to learn from feedback. The following post offered by a nurse on a patient care team illustrates a degree of honesty and introspection:

> When constructive feedback is given to me, I definitely take it to heart and look at whether I need to change behavior/management of patients. Even when it is given appropriately, I sometimes still internalize it and think of it negatively and I need to work on that. When I am giving constructive feedback, at times I think I sugar-coat things too much and then I'm not sure I really made the point that I wanted to. I need to work more on that also.

Communication trust is vital for effective collaboration. Experience with Trust Building Online indicates that focused opportunities to think and write about these behaviors benefit both individuals and teams.

Virtual Competence Trust

Competence trust is fundamental to the performance of work and the collaboration needed within and between teams. Those who feel valued and esteemed for their competence exhibit a greater degree of competence in their work (Eraut, 1994) and tend also to confer on others their esteem. The development of skills in both identifying and articulating competence trust is critical. When people's skills and abilities are acknowledged, when they are involved in decision making, and when they are supported to learn new skills, competence trust is built. Dialogue in

Trust Building Online around the behaviors that support competence trust (refer back to Figure 6.2) were rich and varied. One nurse participant said:

> Almost every time I work, I ask for the advice or input of my coworkers because I am new at my job. The only time I don't feel comfortable or I feel a little hesitant to ask people is when I work with people who are "know-it-alls." Everybody knows these kinds of people. But in this setting, you cannot be a know-it-all because you will never know it all. I do not feel that I can trust what these people tell me or any nursing advice that they give me. In that case, I tend to research the question myself or try and find someone else to ask.

This comment served to open up a number of conversations related to competence trust. This person's status as a new employee, his effort at gaining new knowledge, and the clear roadblocks to learning posed by others stimulated the team to talk about and take responsibility for their actions in mentoring employees. Similar dynamics could be expected in a virtual environment where people are confronted with one or two individuals who write most of the shared text. Opening up the discussion and recognizing that people new to the space may be intimidated could foster an even greater sense of team coherence.

Another key behavior, and one particularly needed for collaboration, is involving others and seeking their input, as illustrated in the following post:

> In every group I have been in, it is important (for me) to be included in the change. It feels horrible when big things change and you weren't part of the discussion process and yet, you are profoundly affected by the change. It is also important to realize that things may not always go the way you would have chosen, but if people can at least feel that they were heard and had a voice in the decision making, I think things tend to be easier to accept.

Competence trust goes to the heart of people's feelings of self-worth and identity. People often measure their sense of personal worth and identity by the competence in their jobs. Most people want and need to be included in decisions that affect their jobs and their lives. They need to know they make a difference and contribute to the overall of the organization.

TRANSFORMATIVE TRUST

A key assumption of the Trust and Betrayal Model is that if people consciously and consistently practice behaviors that build transactional trust, the level of trust within the organization (or community) and among the individuals within the community transforms. This transformation from a personal perspective involves significant changes in how people interact with one another. People tend to be clear about their convictions, courageous in their willingness to raise issues, and compassionate and understanding toward one another, realizing they are all part of the same community. From an organizational perspective, an increase in trust will result in more transparent, equitable, and synergistic practices throughout the organization. This transformation is a reciprocal process. As the community changes, so do the individuals and therefore the community.

The following excerpt reflects the seeds of this transformative potential. This participant from a small pediatric hospital was reflecting on the query prompt, "When do you feel trustworthy?" She openly shared her deeply held convictions regarding what it feels like to be trustworthy. She also shared deep concerns and feelings of vulnerability regarding the breakdown of flexibility in her work environment:

> For me feeling trustworthy is something that comes from within. I know that I am an honest person and that I try hard to respect the feelings of others and to acknowledge when I may have a differing opinion, that the other person's opinion is also worthy of my respect. I don't have to agree with them, and at times for safety issues, I may need to point out the reasons that I disagree with them. Hopefully, I handle the situation in a manner that still supports their feelings yet justifies why they may need to "go along" with my plan, or way of thinking. Within our unit I feel a sense of respect from my coworkers and that they also value me as an individual. It makes the environment a comfortable place to practice in. I would however have to agree with previous statements that others have brought up about the change in the flexibility allowed by management. I feel very few if any people ever took advantage of this flexibility. As a whole I feel we have consistently demonstrated a very high level of accountability to our patients and their families. Patient safety, safe coverage was always

a priority. Now that the policies have become so strict in regards to having someone come in early or cover for you so you can get to school on time to pick your kids up, etc., etc. I think this has significantly harmed our sense of trustworthiness not among each other but from management. I think it also has diminished the strong drive that we felt to help out in times of high census. People were much more willing to make sacrifices in their home/personal schedules to accommodate, but now knowing the same accommodations can't be made for them in their time of need they are less likely to do so. It makes me sad that our environment has been changed in this way!

This post reveals a significant aspect of trust building in a reflective and contemplative virtual environment. Here the participant is voicing a link between her deepest sense of self and the impact that changes in her environment have had on her perceived trustworthiness. This post, and others like it, opened up conversations in the organization between management and employees that led to the development of a transformed community.

FINAL THOUGHTS

The depth and breadth of engagement related to meaningful and sometimes challenging topics increase with participants' comfort and familiarity with the trust content and the asynchronous Web-based tool. Distance learning educators have noted for some time the depth and quality of "postings" and discussions online (Collison, Elbaum, Haavind, & Tinker, 2000). This phenomenon is particularly evident in the Trust Building Online experience. It is clear that people respond naturally to issues of trust and betrayal. Once a safe climate for the exploration of trust is established, authentic dialogue opens up.

The Reina Trust and Betrayal Model and the Trust Building Online tool presented in this chapter provide an example of ways to create structure and form for the process of raising awareness and engaging in introspection, reflection, and dialogue; all are central to achieving sustainable levels of trust. Participants come to understand both trust and trust-related behaviors. More important, they begin to consistently practice these behaviors and consciously appreciate the benefits of this practice. They are able to articulate in a thoughtful and respectful way the linkages they experience in the workplace between their understanding of trust and the often technical, administrative, and system-driven issues they must respond to. It is through this kind of dialogue that individuals, teams, and organizations are transformed: communication opens up, collaboration develops, people share responsibility and accountability, and business results are achieved.

The Trust Building Online experience affirmed the possibilities for virtual collaboration, specifically for building trust within an organization. While the barriers to developing collaborative skills in virtual teams may be significant, Trust Building Online demonstrates that the effort can be advanced by focusing on trust as a foundation using a high-quality, scalable Internet-based learning tool. Once adequate levels of trust have been reached in a team or organization, the possibilities of leveraging groupware and Internet-based technology, supporting collaboration and coordination of work, are enormous.

REMINDERS

- Trust makes organizations work. It drives performance and business results. It also increases communication and collaboration, innovation, and risk taking; raises shared responsibility and accountability; increases employee satisfaction and retention; and enhances effective social networks and team relationships.

- The Reina Trust and Betrayal Model and approach systemically and measurably improve trust with organizations, particularly virtual environments.

- Behaviors that build trust face-to-face also build trust in virtual relationships.

- Transactional trust, a foundational element of the model, has three facets: contractual, communication, and competence trust.

- Trust and relationships are at the heart of engagement and participation in virtual environments.

- The effectiveness of virtual collaboration is contingent not on technology but on relationships based on trust, which the technology supports.

- Trust Building Online is a tool designed to build and support trust building in virtual teams. The platform engages participants with content in a meaningful, easy-to-navigate manner and supports conversation among team members about trust and its relationship to business goals. The process mirrors the sequence of learning experienced during face-to-face trust building.

- Asynchronous communication draws on trust-building behaviors to support communication and collaboration; proximity of team members is not important.
- Trust Building Online contributed to significant improvement in the teams' culture.
  - The Reina Organizational Trust Scale pre- and posttest scores demonstrated significant changes in all three types of trust.
  - High participant engagement with content and depth of responses to each other indicates deep reflection and introspection and openness and honesty not typical of face-to-face encounters. It later contributed to enriched face-to-face discussion when they did occur.
  - Blending of structured query with open dialogue and asynchronous feedback at the Discussion Center was a highly effective combination in sustaining participation and enabling performance.
  - Participants' motivation was linked to business needs and desired outcomes; participants took responsibility for their own pacing; business goals influenced the rate that was set.
  - The facilitator drew the team's attention to interpersonal dynamics and process; synthesized themes, categories, and questions; and analyzed and evaluated responses. Participants gained key insights.
  - Participants learned online about different aspects of trust and experienced those behaviors in their workplace simultaneously.
  - The depth and breadth of engagement relative to meaningful dialogue increased with participants' comfort and familiarity with the trust content and this asynchronous tool. Authentic dialogue between participants opens up as a result.
- The Reina Trust and Betrayal Model and the highly scalable Trust Building Online tool provided structure for raising awareness and engaging in introspection and dialogue among participants, which may enable them to link their understanding of trust to behavioral results in the workplace.

 RELATED ITEM ON THE WEB
- Reina Team Trust Quiz

References

Armstrong, A., & Hagel, J. I. (2000). *The real value of online communities.* In E. L. Lesser, M. A. Fontaine, & J. A. Slusher (Eds.), *Knowledge and communities.* Boston: Butterworth Heinemann.

Brothers, D. (1995). *Falling backwards: An exploration of trust and self-experience.* New York: Norton.

Center for the Digital Future. (2006). *USC Annenberg School for Communication: 2005 digital future report.* Retrieved August 20, 2006, from http://www.digitalcenter.org/pdf/Center-for-the-Digital-Future-2005-Highlights.pdf.

Collison, G., Elbaum, B., Haavind, S., & Tinker, R. (2000). *Facilitating online learning: Effective strategies for moderators.* Madison, WI: Atwood Publishing.

Cross, J., & Hamilton, I. (2002). *The DNA of elearning.* Retrieved September 20, 2006, from http://www.internettime.com/Learning/articles/DNA.pdf.

Dourish, P. (2001). *Where the action is: The foundations of embodied interaction.* Cambridge, MA: MIT Press.

Duarte, D. L., & Tennant-Snyder, N. (1999). *Mastering virtual teams.* San Francisco: Jossey-Bass.

Eraut, M. (1994). *Developing professional knowledge and competence.* Philadelphia: Falmer Press.

Heliwell, J. F., & Huang, H. (2005). *How's the job? Well-being and social capital in the* workplace. Working paper no. 11759, National Bureau of Economic Research, Cambridge, MA. Retrieved September 16, 2006, from http://www.nber.org/papers/w11759.

Khan, B. (2005). *Managing e-learning strategies: Design, delivery, implementation and evaluation.* Hershey, PA: Information Science Publishing.

Kimble, C., Li, F., & Barlow, A. (2000). *Effective virtual teams through communities of practice* (Research Paper No. 2000/9). Glasgow, Scotland: University of Strathclyde.

Lave, J. (1988). *Cognition in practice.* Cambridge: Cambridge University Press.

Lave, J., & Wenger, E. (1991). *Situated learning: Legitimate peripheral participation.* Cambridge: Cambridge University Press.

Reina, D., & Reina, M. (2006). *Trust and betrayal in the workplace: Building effective relationships in your organization.* San Francisco: Berrett-Koehler.

Sanders, R. (2006). The "imponderable bloom": Reconsidering the role of technology in education. *Innovate, 2*(6). Retrieved September 11, 2006, from http://www.innovateonline.info/index.php?view=article&id=232.

Shaw, R. B. (1997). *Trust in the balance: Building successful organizations on results, integrity, and concern.* San Francisco: Jossey-Bass.

Solomon, R. C., & Flores, F. (2003). *Building trust in business, politics, relationships, and life.* New York: Oxford University Press

Watson Wyatt Worldwide. (2002). WorkUSA 2002: *Weathering the storm: A study of employee attitudes and opinions.* Retrieved October 15, 2006, from http://www.watsonwyatt.com/research/resrender.asp?id=W-557&page=3.

Wenger, E. (1998*). Communities of practice: Learning, meaning, and identity.* Cambridge: Cambridge University Press.

Wenger, E., McDermott, R., & Snyder, W. M. (2002). *Cultivating communities of practice.* Cambridge, MA: Harvard Business School Press.

Yuan, Y. C., & Gay, G. (2006). Homophily of network ties and bonding and bridging social capital in computer-mediated distributed teams. *Journal of Computer-Mediated Communication, 11*(4). Retrieved October 12, 2006, from http://jcmc.indiana.edu/vol11/ issue4/yuan.html.

PART THREE

Leading Collaboratively

Chapter Seven focuses on transformational leadership. The author's extensive experience with globally dispersed teams in aerospace leads him to an understanding of the role of leadership and some practical process steps. For example, he suggests that virtual meetings not be held during peak work times, so more members can participate. In a survey, virtual team members said that the key characteristics they wanted in a leader were integrity, genuine concern for others, and self-confidence.

An argument for an additional leadership characteristic, the ability to manage change, is made in Chapter Eight. One challenge for leaders during times of change is balancing the trade-offs among taking care of the organization, their team members, and themselves. Careful decisions can be perceived by team members as unfair, so careful listening and an explicit attempt to achieve three kinds of justice is required for managing potential dissatisfaction and motivating members to embrace change rather than simply cope with it.

Chapter Nine looks at simple solutions for the problems that virtual team leaders encounter. The first problem of the virtual leader is the need to rely on electronic communications. The solution depends on using all the tools available and making an effort to convey courtesy and respect in communiqués since brief e-mails are easily viewed as rude. Another issue is how confident team members feel, both individually and as part of the team. A positive approach helps build confidence, and that reaps big dividends. This chapter shares a number of practical tips for generating team effectiveness in virtual settings.

Transformational Leadership Attributes for Virtual Team Leaders

David Braga

Virtual teams are an increasingly prevalent organizational form that promises to change the way business is conducted within and between organizations. The best employees, who can be located anywhere in the world, expect personal flexibility in a global workday that extends over twenty-four rather than the traditional eight hours. Virtual teams, characterized by horizontally structured and geographically distributed human resources, offer important challenges as well as opportunities for leaders.

Although the benefits of virtual teams have been documented, there has been an absence of an understanding of the leader's role and effectiveness in this type of environment. Therefore, a study (Braga, 2003) was conducted individuals of virtual teams to identify attributes that they consider the most important for leaders to have. The attributes are those common to transformational leadership, which starts with the development of a view of the future that will excite and convert potential followers. This vision may be developed by the leader or by members of a virtual team itself. This chapter reviews transformational leadership theory and its applicability to virtual teams.

Although the impetus for studying virtual teams came from advances in information technology, the implications for leaders are vitally important. A lack of leadership can create substantial obstacles to effective teamwork. In a virtual environment, a leader's position is compounded by the fact that team members work across different cultures and time zones with a lack of daily face-to-face contact.

Virtual team members in the aerospace industry were surveyed to find out what transformational leadership attributes they thought were important in a leader (Braga, 2003). The results of the survey led to a ranking of the most important qualities of a leader of a virtual team. In many cases, the perceived differences between the ideal perception of leadership behaviors and actual leader's behavior are significant. Nevertheless, many of the leaders far exceeded the ideal behaviors as perceived by members of the virtual teams surveyed.

LEADERSHIP OVERVIEW

New technology, whether it is faster computer chip processors, wireless communication, new forms of data storage and retrieval, or new software, creates inherent problems in teaching and leading people and getting them to accept and use new methods for acquiring and sharing knowledge. For example, when use of blogs and wikis involves a company's computing resources or information owned by or entrusted to that company, such use is subject to company rules. When used improperly, blogs and wikis present a significant risk for information loss. Virtual teams must be careful to use the appropriate technology for various tasks. For example, text messaging among virtual teams may be interpreted differently among team members due to cultural differences. And because of working in different time zones or on different schedules, team members may have difficulty contacting each other by any means of communication.

Virtual teams must learn and adapt within this turbulent environment. In all types of knowledge work, even where technology is helpful, people require conversation, experimentation, and shared experiences with others who do what they do. As the pace of change in business increases, it becomes imperative for organizations to increase their ability to capture, organize, and disseminate their collective knowledge in order to maintain or add to their competitive advantage.

The virtual team concept can be applied to the acquisition of new business, problem solving, and the improvement of procedures. The understanding of leadership has had a strong influence on the quest of knowledge (Wren, 1995). If the leader sets the example of new learning, others will follow by his or her example. The leader sets the example and creates positive conditions within the organization to create the possibilities for new learning opportunities.

Leaders can turn to many of the leadership models developed over the past several decades to understand not only their own organizations but also themselves as leaders. It is important to note that there are no right or wrong or all-encompassing theories.

The study of leadership historically has centered on the formation of leadership principles: what leaders do and why. Early studies attempted to identify inherent traits of leaders that set them apart from the general public. These attempts resulted in lists of "essential" leadership traits. However, the traits that were considered essential varied considerably from list to list, and there were exceptions to most of these traits.

By the 1940s, general dissatisfaction with the effort to isolate essential leadership traits led researchers to change their focus from the leader to the situation in which leadership occurred. The researchers realized that different people emerge as leaders in different situations and that a person who is successful in one leadership situation might not be successful in another.

More recently, a shift in emphasis has occurred in the importance of followers to leadership, to the extent that leadership is now often defined as the process of leaders and followers in a mutual exchange of influence on each other (Rosenbach & Taylor, 1993). The emergence of what was referred to as the new leadership approach (Bryman, 1992) in the 1980s represented a paradigm shift from transactional methods such as the situational and contingency models of Fiedler (1967), Vroom and Yetton (1973), and Yukl (1989) to the visionary (Sashkin, 1988), charismatic (Conger & Kanungo, 1987; House, 1977), and transformational models (Bass, 1985, 1998a, 1998b; Bass & Avolio, 1994). The literature during this period focused primarily on the personal traits of effective leaders.

FOUNDATION OF TRANSFORMATIONAL LEADERSHIP

Within the large body of literature on leadership, transformational leadership has attracted more empirical scrutiny than any other theory (Bass, 1985, 1998b). Research has shown that positive results continue to emerge on the results of transformational leadership. Transformational leadership enhances subordinate satisfaction (Hater & Bass, 1998) and trust in leadership (Barling, 2000; Pillani & Williams, 1999; Padsokoff, MacKenzie, & Bommer, 1996), and it is associated with increased business unit performance (Barling, Weber, & Kelloway, 1996; Geyer & Steyrer, 1998; Howell & Avolio, 1993). The theory suggests that transformational leadership can be distinguished from other leadership theories because it defines priorities, shared values, perceived common goals, and meaningful purposes. Bass defined transformational leadership in terms of how the leader affects followers, who are intended to trust, admire, and respect the transformational leader. He identified three ways in which leaders transform followers:

- Increasing their awareness of task importance and value
- Getting them to focus first on team or organizational goals rather than their own interests
- Activating their higher-order needs

In-depth qualitative analyses of transformational leadership attributes have been carried out in many studies. Transformational leadership attributes are seen by many modern leadership theorists as contributing to outstanding leadership (Northouse, 1997). Truly transformational leaders seek the greatest good for the greatest number without violating individual rights (Bass, 1998a).

The idea of transformational leadership was first described by Burns (1978) and later extended by Bass (1985), as well as others. According to Burns, transformational leadership "occurs when one or more persons engage with others in such a way that leaders and followers raise one another to higher levels of motivation and morality" (p. 20) and results in a transforming effect on both leaders and followers. Bass defined a transformational leader as one who motivates followers to do more than they were originally expected to do. Bass (1985), Conger and Kanungo (1987), House (1977), and Yagil (1998) view leadership as a function of the relationship between a leader and followers. Bass (1985), Berlew (1974), and Hollander and Offermann (1990) suggest models where transformational leadership is an extension to transactional leadership. Transformational leadership augments the effectiveness of transactional leadership; it does not replace transactional leadership (Waldman, Bass, & Yammarino, 1990).

In contrast, transactional leadership consists of a social system that works with a clear chain of command. People in teams led by transactional leaders are motivated by reward and punishment. The primary purpose of subordinates on the team is to do what the leader tells them to do. Transactional leadership is based in contingency, in that the person's reward or punishment is contingent on performance. Transactional leadership remains a prevalent and popular approach in many of today's organizations. The differences in characteristics are shown in Table 7.1.

The basic theoretical differences in transformational leadership theory between Burns and Bass come from the contexts in which they studied leadership. Burns's theory was developed with social movements and politics as the basis. Bass dealt with leadership from a management goal perspective (institutional), where organizational goals set the expectations of exceeding past accomplishments. Bass identified a serious problem in the work of Burns, who considered transactional (managerial) and transformational leadership to be the end points of a continuum.

Table 7.1
Transformational Versus Transactional Characteristics

Transformational	Transactional
Builds on the need for meaning	Builds on the need to get the job done and make a living
Focuses on purposes, values, morals, and ethics	Focuses on power, position, politics, and perks
Transcends daily affairs	Overcome by daily affairs
Oriented toward long-term goals without compromising human values and principles	Oriented to short-terms goals and hard data
Focuses more on missions and strategies for achieving them	Focuses on tactical issues
Makes full use of available resources (human)	Relies on human relations to oil human interactions
Designs and redesigns jobs to make them meaningful and challenging; realizes human potential	Follows and fulfills role expectations by striving to work effectively within current systems
Aligns internal structures and systems to reinforce overarching values and goals	Supports structures and systems that reinforce the bottom line

Bass found that they were really two independent dimensions: a person could exhibit one, the other, both, or neither (Coad & Berry, 1998).

The transformational leader is a holistic leader, more concerned with people than with processes. Transformational leadership raises the level of human conduct of both leader and follower. In addition, transformational leaders may increase their followers' confidence and expectations of success (Wren, 1995). Bennis and Nanus (1985) conceptualize transformational leadership as a process that changes the organization by focusing on action, converting followers to leaders and leaders to agents of change. A transformational leader's main function is to serve as a catalyst of change, but never as a controller of change (Avolio, 1994). This leader strives to achieve a true consensus by aligning individual and organization interests.

Transformational leadership consists of four factors: charismatic leadership or idealized influence, inspirational leadership or motivation, intellectual stimulation, and individualized consideration. Its inspirational motivation provides followers with challenges and meaning for engaging in shared goals and undertakings. Its intellectual stimulation helps followers to question assumptions and generate more creative solutions to problems. Its individualized consideration treats each follower as an individual and provides coaching, mentoring, and growth opportunities (Bass, 1985).

CHARACTERISTICS OF TRANSFORMATIONAL LEADERS IN A VIRTUAL ENVIRONMENT

Burns (1978) saw transformational leadership as moving followers and leaders to a higher moral level. Avolio (1994) hypothesizes that transformational leaders may be at a higher stage of moral development as a result of life experiences that allows the leader to put personal interests aside in favor of satisfying the needs of the followers. This section examines the common characteristics of transformational leaders.

A Genuine Concern for Others

Transformational leaders show a genuine interest in individuals and develop their followers' strengths. Transformational leadership raises the level of human contact of both the leader and the follower. This is especially important in virtual teams.

Because of the lack of personal contact within these teams, leaders must be especially sensitive to interpersonal, communication, and cultural factors. Studies have found significant and positive relationships between transformational leadership and the amount of effort followers are willing to exert, satisfaction with the leader, ratings of job performance, and perceived effectiveness (Bass, 1998b).

Politically Sensitive and Skillful

Krishman (2001) suggests that transformational leaders have better relations with superiors and make more of a contribution to the organization than those who are only transactional. Shamir and Howell (1999) found transformational leaders to be generally effective across a variety of situations. These leaders, sensitive to the political pressures and cultural differences that virtual teams face, understand the political and cultural dynamics of leading a group and can work with team members to achieve results.

Decisive, Determined, and Self-Confident

Ross and Offermann (1997) found that transformational leadership was positively related to self-confidence. Transformational leaders rate themselves high in personal effectiveness, interpersonal control, and social self-confidence (Sosik & Megerian, 1999). They are decisive when required and are prepared to make difficult decisions and be resilient to setbacks. They must exhibit competence and meet high performance expectations. They need to model behaviors that are required in a virtual environment, such as working across boundaries, time zones, and using technology effectively.

Trustworthy, Honest, and Open

For virtual teams to succeed, openness and trust are required. Trust is a fundamental relationship building block of any team (Vlosky, Fontenot, & Blalock, 2000). Followers decide whether to join a particular network according to what it stands for, what it is seeking to do, and the opportunities it provides for their own growth and development. A consideration of transformational leadership indicates the importance of subordinates' belief in their leader's words, and their consequent trust, if that leader is to play the role of a transformational leader. Due to the lack of personal interaction, many researchers identify trust among virtual team members to be the binding force in any network.

Developer of Potential in Others

Transformational leaders work to develop relationships with members of the virtual team, who feel elevated by the relationship itself. Human resource policies, reward and recognition systems, and career paths must fit the virtual workplace in order to meet the needs of virtual team members. In turn, followers become more active themselves, thereby creating other potential leaders. Transformational leaders look for potential in followers and help them develop into leaders.

Networkers, Promoters, and Communicators

Transformational leaders become role models for their virtual team members. They show great persistence and determination in the pursuit of objectives, show high standards of ethical and moral conduct, sacrifice self-gain for the gain of others, and share the success and the limelight. As a result, the leaders are admired, respected, and trusted, and followers identify with them and want to emulate them (Avolio & Bass, 1991).

Encouraging

Transformational leaders provide a flow of ideas, questions, and assumptions. They create a broad imaginative picture and encourage followers to come up with their own structures and solutions to problems. Richardson (1995) suggests that the task of transformational leaders is to support the creation of new ideas and follow them through into successful new products and services. This creative task is one that thrives on the interaction of the leader and the virtual members themselves. The key to transformational leadership is to enable creativity to thrive and redirect organizational practices and performance.

Accessible and Approachable

Transformational leaders give personal attention to team members, building a relationship with each individual and focusing on each person's needs. The leader provides challenges and learning opportunities and delegates to raise skill and confidence levels. In the process, the leader exhibits trust, respect, and appropriate tolerance for mistakes that occur as learning proceeds. The result is that virtual team members are more likely to develop competence and take initiative (Alimo-Metcalfe & Alban-Metcalfe, 1999). Furthermore, they feel trust and respect for the leader.

Visionary of the Future

Working on a project over the virtual work space can lead to a lack of project visibility, so the transformational leader must paint a clear picture of the future that is both optimistic and attainable. Leaders set high expectations, use symbolism to focus efforts, and communicate a vision to followers in simple language. Followers react by willingly increasing their efforts to attain the vision.

Sensitive and Relationship Oriented

A leader with strong transformational attributes on a virtual team provides opportunity for people to be themselves. These leaders put a high value on relationship skills and qualities such as sensitivity and humanity (Coulson-Thomas, 1998).

ACTUAL AND IDEAL TRANSFORMATIONAL LEADERSHIP ATTRIBUTES

In 2002, I conducted a study to examine to what extent transformational leadership attributes are practiced by leaders in various virtual teams in an aerospace Fortune 500 company (Braga, 2003). The questions from the survey are presented in Exhibit 7.1. The purpose of the study was to identify to what extent transformational leadership attributes were present in their current leader versus what attributes should ideally be practiced by a leader in a virtual team.

The study found that the perceptions of virtual team members indicated that their existing leaders often exhibited transformational leadership qualities. In all cases, however, the ideal leadership attribute mean was significantly higher than the actual mean. The perception of the virtual team members indicates that transformational leadership attributes are desired traits in leaders. The exception to this was a leader who is accessible to staff at all levels and keeps in touch using face-to-face communications. This would seem to indicate that although actual leaders exhibit a certain level of transformational leadership qualities, there is a perception by the virtual team members that there is a desire for improvement.

The survey suggests that command-and-control types of leadership and hierarchical organizational structures get in the way of rapid knowledge flow and information within virtual teams. Trustworthiness is clearly valued highly in the leader of a virtual team. Trustworthiness as an attribute was important in the rating

Exhibit 7.1
Survey Matrix of Questions

The leader:

- Shows a genuine interest in me as an individual.
- Develops my strengths.
- Understands the political dynamics of the leading the group.
- Works with the group to achieve results.
- Is decisive when required.
- Is prepared to make difficult decisions.
- Is self-confident.
- Is resilient to setback.
- Makes it easy for me to admit mistakes.
- Is trustworthy.
- Makes decisions based on moral and ethical principles.
- Trusts me to take decision/initiatives on important issues.
- Delegates effectively.
- Enables me to use my potential.
- Has a wide network of links to the external environment.
- Effectively promotes the work/achievements of the department/ organization to the outside world.
- Is able to communicate the vision of the group effectively.
- Is accessible to staff at all levels.
- Keeps in touch using face-to-face communications.
- Involves others in decisions.
- Involves the group when making decisions.
- Keeps people informed of what is going on.
- Encourages the questioning of traditional approaches to the job.

of both ideal and actual leaders. In addition, the results of the survey indicated that the ideal leader should have the ability to communicate effectively the vision for the group and work with the group to achieve results.

Virtual team members believe the ideal leaders should base their decisions on moral and ethical principles. It was important to these members that their leader be decisive when required and be prepared to make difficult decisions. They felt strongly that ideal leaders should use employees to their fullest potential. Respondents to the survey want an ideal leader who is self-confident and understands the political dynamics of leading the group. Finally, many of the participants felt that an ideal leader should trust them to make decisions and take the initiative on important issues.

The respondents who participated in the ranking portion of the survey identified integrity as the most important leadership attribute. The top-ranked attribute for a virtual leader was to exhibit a genuine concern for others. Ranked second was a leader who develops potential, empowers, and defines boundaries of responsibility. The third-ranked transformation attribute is that the leader exhibit self-confidence.

The virtual teams surveyed felt that there were some attributes that they did not consider important. For example, they felt the ideal leader did not particularly require a personal network of individuals. Virtual team members also felt it was not important for leaders to make it easy for them to admit mistakes and did not think leaders need to show a genuine interest in followers. The attributes that respondents identified as least important were a leader who involves them in determining the direction of the group and encourages the questioning of traditional approaches to the job.

When virtual member team members were asked what other attributes they would like in a leader, the most common response was regular and clear communication from the leader. This was followed by leadership attributes of honesty, trustworthiness, and fairness. Members of virtual teams felt that it was important for the leader to be responsible for their own personal wellness and development. The survey revealed that the leader should be sensitive to human relations and have the ability to handle and resolve conflicts. (See the www.wiley .com/go/virtualteamshandbook Web site for a tool to assess how virtual team leaders rate on each of these characteristics: Ideal Virtual Transformational Leader Attributes Tool.)

WEAKNESSES IN TRANSFORMATIONAL LEADERSHIP

One weakness of transformational leadership is that it lacks conceptual clarity (Northouse, 1997). Because transformational leadership covers a range of attributes, including creating a vision, motivating, being a change agent, building trust, empowering, and developing potential in people, it is difficult to clearly define its boundaries. In addition, many of the attributes of transformational leadership theory are contained within the definition of other leadership definitions.

Another limitation of transformational leadership is that it is often interpreted as an all-or-nothing approach instead of a matter of degree. There is a tendency to look at transformational leadership as something very few leaders can achieve instead of using the transformational attributes as a continuum that incorporates various components of leadership (Northouse, 1997).

According to Bryman (1992) a third limitation is the manner in which transformational leadership treats leadership as a personality rather than a behavior in which people can be trained. Bass and Avolio (1994) suggest that transformational leadership can be taught to individuals. Individuals can take the Multifactor Leadership Questionnaire, developed by Bass and Avolio, that determines strengths and weaknesses in relation to the degree of transformational leadership characteristics. Training programs can be developed to enhance leaders' transformational behaviors, although Northouse (1997) argues that this can take up to five years in some cases.

Another limitation of transformational leadership is that it is seen as elitist and antidemocratic (Bass & Avolio, 1993). Transformational leaders are viewed as playing an important role in advocating change, creating a vision, and advocating new directions. This can be interpreted as leaders' putting themselves above the needs of the followers or acting independently of them (Northouse, 1997). Bass and Avolio refute this limitation and contend that transformational leaders can be participative as well as democratic.

Keeley (1995) faults transformational leadership for lacking the checks and balances of transactional leadership. False transformational leadership or pseudo-transformational leadership may lend itself to unchecked abuses of power (Bass & Steidlmeier, 1998). Organizations must be aware of the potential risk of a pseudo-transformational leader. Whereas true transformational leaders are concerned about developing their followers into leaders, pseudo-transformational leaders are more concerned about maintaining the dependence of their followers. False transformational leaders set and control their agenda to manipulate the values of importance to followers, often at the expense of others or even harm to them. They can set up fictitious obstacles, imaginary enemies, and false visions and endorse diluted values, such as favoritism, victimization, racial superiority, and submission (Carey, 1992; Solomon, 1996).

Many find moral fault with transformational leadership when a leader motivates followers to go beyond their self-interests for the good of the group or organization. The followers of transformational leaders can be coerced or unknowingly seduced into adopting the values of the leadership. To the extent that transformational leadership moves members to sacrifice their own life plans for the sake of the organization, it is seen as immoral (Fairholm, 1991).

FINAL THOUGHTS

The virtual workplace poses unique concerns and challenges, and a greater understanding of leadership attributes that are important to members of a virtual team can have a profound impact on the learning processes that affect knowledge transfer and the team's success. The study examined in this chapter found that the most important attributes of leaders in virtual teams are trust, integrity, ethical decision making, decisiveness, and regular and clear communication.

REMINDERS

- Virtual teams can be composed of the best employees located anywhere in the world operating on a global workday.

- The lack of face-to-face interaction within virtual team can create substantial obstacles to effective teamwork. A survey of virtual teams identified the following attributes as the most important for team leaders: integrity, a genuine concern for others, and self-confidence.

- The survey identified the least important transformational leadership attributes of a leader: a wide network of link to the external environment, making it easy for team members to admit mistakes, involving them in the direction of the group, and encouraging the questioning of traditional approaches to the job.

- Virtual teams should decide for themselves what leadership attributes are best suited for their team.

RELATED ITEM ON THE WEB

- Ideal Virtual Transformational Leader Attributes Tool

References

Alimo-Metcalfe, B., & Alban-Metcalfe, R. J. (1999). The transformational leadership questionnaire (TLQ-LGV): A convergent and discriminate validation study. *Leadership and Organization Development Journal, 21*(6), 280–296.

Avolio, B. J. (1994). The alliance of total quality and the full range of leadership. In B. M. Bass & B. J. Aviolo (Eds.), *Improving organizational effectiveness through transformational leadership* (pp. 121–145). Thousand Oaks, CA: Sage.

Avolio, B. J., & Bass, B. M. (1991). *Full-range training of leadership. Manual.* Binghamton, NY: Bass/Avolio & Associates.

Barling, J. (2000). Editorial. *Journal of Occupational Health Psychology, 5*, 1–2.

Barling, J., Weber, T., & Kelloway, E. K. (1996). Effects of transformational leadership training on attitudinal and financial outcomes: A field experiment. *Journal of Applied Psychology, 81*, 827–832.

Bass, B. M. (1985). *Leadership and performance beyond expectations.* New York: Free Press.

Bass, B. M. (1986). *Transformational leadership: Charisma and beyond.* (Tech. Rep. No. 85—90). Binghamton: State University of New York, School of Management.

Bass, B. M. (1998a). The ethics of transformational leadership. In J. Ciulia (Ed.), *Ethics, the heart of leadership.* Westport, CT: Praeger.

Bass, B. M. (1998b). *Transformational leadership: Industrial, military, and educational impact.* Mahwah, NJ: Erlbaum.

Bass, B. M., & Avolio, B. J. (1993). Transformational leadership: A response to critiques. In M. M. Chemers & R. Ayman (Eds.), *Leadership theory and research: Perspectives and directions.* New York: Free Press.

Bass, B., & Avolio, B. J. (1994). Introduction. In B. Bass and B. Avolio (Eds.), *Improving organizational effectiveness through transformational leadership.* Thousands Oaks, CA: Sage.

Bass, B. M., & Steidlmeier, P. (1998). *Ethics, character, and authentic transformational leadership.* Escondido, CA: Center for Leadership Studies.

Bennis, W. G., & Nanus, B. (1985). *Leaders: The strategies for taking charge.* New York: HarperCollins.

Berlew, D. E. (1974). Leadership and organizational excitement. *California Management Review, 17*, 21–30.

Braga, D. (2003). *Transformational leadership attributes as perceived by team members of knowledge networks.* Doctoral dissertation. Pepperdine University.

Bryman, A. (1992). *Charisma and leadership in organizations.* Thousand Oaks, CA: Sage.

Burns, J. M. (1978). *Leadership.* New York: HarperCollins.

Coad, A. F., & Berry, A. J. (1998). Transformational leadership and learning orientation. *Leadership and Organization Development Journal, 19*(3), 164–172.

Carey, M. R. (1992). Transformational leadership and the fundamental option for self-transcendence. *Leadership Quarterly, 3,* 217–236.

Conger, J. A., & Kanungo, R. N. (1987, October). Toward a behavioral theory of charismatic leadership in organizational settings. *Academy of Management Review,* 637–647.

Coulson-Thomas, C. J. (1998). Career, development and the future of the organization. *Career Development International, 3,* 13–17.

Cross, K. P. (1981). *Adults as learners: Increasing participation and facilitating learning.* San Francisco: Jossey-Bass.

Fairholm, G. W. (1991). *Values leadership: Towards a new philosophy of leadership.* Westport, CT: Praeger.

Fiedler, F. E. (1967). *A theory of leadership effectiveness.* New York: McGraw-Hill.

Geyer, A.L.J., & Steyrer, J. M. (1998). Transformational leadership and objective performance in banks. *Applied Psychology: An International Review, 47,* 397–420.

Hater, J. J., & Bass, B. M. (1998). Superiors' evaluations and subordinates' perceptions of transformational and transactional leadership. *Journal of Applied Psychology, 73,* 695–702.

Hollander, E. P., & Offermann, L. R. (1990). Power and leadership in organizations: Relationships in transition. *American Psychologist, 45,* 179–189.

House, R. J. (1977). A 1976 theory of charismatic leadership. In J. Hunt & L. Larson (Eds.), *Leadership: The cutting edge* (pp. 189–207). Carbondale: Southern Illinois University Press.

Howell, J. M., & Avolio, B. J. (1992). The ethics of charismatic leadership: Submission or liberation? *Academy of Management Executive, 6*(2), 43–54.

Howell, J. M., & Avolio, B. J. (1993). Transformational leadership, transactional leadership, locus of control and support for innovation: Key predictors of consolidated-business-unit performance. *Journal of Applied Psychology, 78,* 891–902.

Keeley, M. (1995). The trouble with transformational leadership: Toward a federalist ethic for organizations. *Business Ethics Quarterly, 5,* 67–95.

Krishman, V. R. (2001). Value systems of transformational leaders. *Leadership and Organizational Development Journal, 22*(3), 126–131.

Northouse, P. G. (1997). *Leadership: Theory and practice.* Thousand Oaks, CA: Sage.

Padsokoff, P. M., MacKenzie, S. B., & Bommer, W. H. (1996). Transformational leader behaviors and substitutes for leadership as determinants of employee satisfaction, commitment, trust, and organizational citizenship behaviors. *Journal of Management, 22,* 259–298.

Pillani, P. M., & Williams, E. S. (1999). Fairness perception and trust as mediators for transformational and transactional leadership: A two-sample study. *Journal of Management, 25,* 649–661.

Richardson, B. (1995). Learning contexts and roles for the leaning organization leader. *Learning Organization, 2,* 15–33.

Rosenbach, W. E., & Taylor, R. L. (1993). *Contemporary issues in leadership* (3rd ed.). Boulder, CO: Westview Press.

Ross, S. M. & Offermann, L. R. (1997). Transformational leadership: Measurement of Personality attributes and work group performance. *Personality and Social Psychology Bulletin, 23*(10), 1078–1086.

Sashkin, M. (1988). *The organizational culture assessment questionnaire.* Seabrook, MD: Ducochon Press.

Shamir, B., & Howell, J. M. (1999). Organizational and contextual influences on the emergence and effectiveness of charismatic leadership. *Leadership Quarterly, 10*(2), 19–47.

Solomon, R. (1996). *Ethical leadership, emotions and trust: Beyond charisma.* College Park, MD: Kellogg Leadership Studies Project, Center for Political Leadership and Participation, University of Maryland.

Sosik, J. J., & Megerian, L. E. (1999). Understanding leader emotional intelligence and performance. *Group and Organization Management, 24*(3), 367–390.

Vlosky, R., Fontenot, R., & Blalock, L. (2000). Extranets: Impacts on business practices and relationships. *Journal of Business and Industrial Marketing, 15*(6), 438–457.

Vroom, V. H., & Yetton, P. W. (1973). *Leadership and decision-making.* Pittsburgh, PA: University of Pittsburgh Press.

Waldman, D. A., Bass, B. M., & Yammarino, F. J. (1990). Adding to contingent-reward behavior: The augmenting effect of charismatic leadership. *Group and Organizational Studies, 15,* 381–394.

Wren, J. T. (1995). *The leader's companion.* New York: Free Press.

Yagil, D. (1998). Charismatic leadership and organizational hierarchy: Attribution of charisma to close and distant leaders. *Leadership Quarterly, 9*(2), 161–176.

Yukl, G. (1989). Managerial leadership: A review of theory and research. *Journal of Management, 15*(2), 251–289.

Going Beyond Leadership Style

When and How Do We Lead Change?

Dina M. Mansour-Cole

One of the best-known statements about the role of leaders and managers comes from Kotter (1990), who said that managers deal with complexity, while leaders deal with change. Most prescriptions for leaders of virtual collaborations have understandably looked at how to manage the variety of complexities and boundary issues (Bell & Kozlowski, 2002; Lipnack & Stamps, 1999). Not addressed is the fact that virtual collaborations are subject to many changes as well. After all, technology upgrades and changes in personnel as members drop out or move to other teams are prevalent. Some team projects are completed, while others evolve. Strategic goals are realigned and operational goals and objectives reworked. Policies change, and, particularly in hybrid organizations where there are both virtual and colocated teams, there may be differential program benefits that accrue to one type of team or another. Team members' reactions to change are determined also by the timing of and justification for change. Sometimes change is a result of deep trouble, sometimes it is initiated because someone has the foresight to see change coming, and sometimes healthy organizations and teams undertake change to create a new vision or direction. Team members who feel they have been treated unfairly during changes engage in more conflict or withdrawal behaviors and fewer extra-role behaviors and supportive attitudes. Regardless of the impetus and type of change, the role of the leader needs to become more prominent as our knowledge of virtual collaboration effectiveness matures.

The rate and depth of changes throughout the business world should be causing managers to rethink how to prepare virtual team leaders. Increasingly managers are asking collaborative organizational members to take on complex leadership roles. Virtual leadership is discussed as being both internal and external to the team. Shared leadership within the virtual collaboration becomes a key talking point. Expectations for members include taking charge of sections of work that are in their area of expertise: taking responsibility for making that section of a project as effective as it can be, and ensuring a smooth transition from one part of a project to the next.

How, then, are real change leaders developed in the virtual environment? Much of the collaborative leadership development training is based on understanding individual strengths, comparing preferred cognitive styles or refining each leader's personal behavioral style. Although these are good tools for a member's personal development and insight, more than twenty-five years of leadership research show they do not predict much about leader emergence or effectiveness in face-to-face organizations. Leadership styles are unlikely to be the best predictors in collaborative organizations either. Real leadership requires a process focus, where characteristics of the leaders and followers, their relationships, and the organizational context are explicitly considered. Because of the popularity of leadership-style programs, one of the biggest hurdles will be switching from self-based leader development to a development process that is primarily (but not exclusively) others based.

Ironically, a more sophisticated look at the topic of virtual collaboration leadership may simplify the demands of the position. At the heart of leadership is the idea of change, and many researchers and authors contend that the real difference between managing and leading is in the outcomes sought (Katz & Kahn, 1978; Kotter, 1990; Rost, 1991; Schein, 1992). Leaders seek to make changes to the status quo, and effective leadership can be seen most clearly in the way decisions are made under conditions of uncertainty. This view of leadership is attractive in a collaborative organizational setting since it does not require position-based power.

A LEADERSHIP ACTION MODEL FOR FAIR CHANGE

When an organizational justice approach is added to change, the emerging model of leadership development naturally emphasizes areas for action. Prescriptions in this model are based on a well-researched literature of organizational justice that has been connected with change (Adams, 1965; Bies, 1987; Greenberg, 1987, 1990; Colquitt, 2001). The proposed model (see Figure 8.1) takes a change-based definition of leadership and provides a framework for what to attend to during change. Three broad categories are identified: (1) taking action that is primarily focused on furthering the organization's interests, (2) taking action to further other followers' needs or interests, and (3) taking action to protect the individual leader's self-interests. The model explicitly addresses when to focus on which category and how to justify moving from one interest category to another.

If full attention could be paid to all three requirements, then the change would be perceived as fair and the likelihood of success is high. Practically, leaders have limited amounts of time and resources and need some guidance about where to focus their attention. Processing the types of comments made by team members can provide cues to the amount of member dissatisfaction and their readiness for change. Understanding where potential violations of fair processes or outcomes are brewing can provide guidance on the most immediate areas or problems to address.

When change is initiated or implemented, the role of fairness perceptions should be considered. Previous research shows that creating a climate of fairness is an important precondition to a successful change program. Novelli, Kirkman, and Shapiro (1995) suggest that "effective change requires more than clearly articulating an energizing vision and getting people to buy in to the desired outcome of the change: it is crucial to focus on the justice aspects of the change

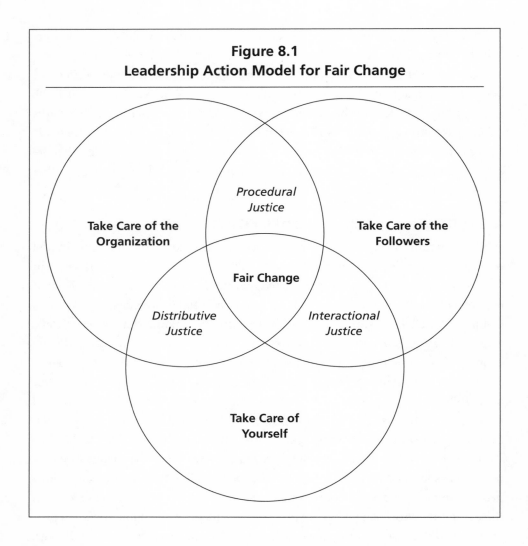

Figure 8.1
Leadership Action Model for Fair Change

Procedural Justice

Take Care of the Organization

Take Care of the Followers

Fair Change

Distributive Justice

Interactional Justice

Take Care of Yourself

process" (p. 16). When team members feel an injustice, they may use tactics to block the change process or at least be less committed to it.

Fairness is one of the more robust fundamental assumptions and motivations we humans have demonstrated across national cultures. In collaborations that actively span cultural boundaries, any action model must also work across these boundaries.

Behavioral economists have a game that they use to demonstrate how pervasive fairness concerns are. The allocating subject (A) is given ten one-dollar bills and told he or she may keep any dollars not given to the receiving subject (R) but must give some of it away. The receiver R is told these directions and advised that A will make only one offer. If both subjects were behaving in a perfectly rational or hedonistic manner, then A would offer the minimum one dollar and R would accept because something is better than nothing. Instead, R is usually offered more than one dollar, presumably out of a sense of fair play. When only one dollar is actually offered, the offer is usually rejected: R prefers to make a statement about justice than to take any small sum (Guth, Schmittberger, & Schwartze, 1982). Related research is ongoing and has been replicated with samples in many organizational and national cultures. Even when not prompted to think about justice, most humans want to be seen as fair and treated fairly (Guth et al., 1982; Hoffman, McCabe, Shachat, & Smith, 1994; Kravitz & Gunto, 1992).

Although there are still disagreements about the measurement of organizational justice, most agree that it is useful to think about justice in three ways (Colquitt, 2001). Organizational justice initially focused on two areas: outcome fairness, or *distributive justice* (Adams, 1965; Deutsch, 1985), and the processes that lead to outcomes, termed *procedural justice* (Levanthal, 1980; Thibaut & Walker, 1975). Greenberg (1993) suggested that a final factor, termed *interactional justice,* has two important aspects that are not as confounded as others: it focuses on the respect and sensitivity aspects of the interpersonal treatment people receive as procedures are enacted (Bies & Moag, 1986).

RELATING THE ORGANIZATIONAL JUSTICE TYPES TO TEAM LEADERSHIP

Distributive justice, or fairness of the decision outcomes received, is a central concern for team members. Of particular importance is whether the outcomes received match their perceptions of their contributions to the team or organization. Most research has focused on equity allocation rules, such as whether outcomes of rewards are proportional to members' inputs or contributions. Other allocation rules, such as basing fairness on whether members have been treated equally or according to what they need, are also important. Team members who perceive that they have gotten a "bad deal" have been shown to engage in more conflict or withdrawal behaviors. Members who feel they have been treated to fair outcomes are more likely to engage in extra-role behaviors and have supportive attitudes toward change.

One of the most important early discoveries in organizational justice is that members make relatively independent judgments of outcome fairness and the fairness of the procedures used to arrive at those outcomes. In fact, even when individuals receive unfavorable outcomes, they evaluate the change more favorably if they think that the process by which it was determined was fair. Criteria for procedural justice include the presence of formal procedures that ensure decisions are based on accurate and up-to-date information and are free from the personal bias of the decision makers. A person concerned with procedural justice also judges decisions for their consistent application across time and across people and whether they are made in a moral and ethical manner. Finally, it is important to procedural justice perceptions that members have an opportunity to voice their opinion during decision making and allow for their appeal of what they consider bad decisions. When any of these conditions is not present, a sense of injustice is processed. People hold fast to their desire for fair procedures because they believe that over time, fair procedures will lead to favorable outcomes for them. They may also apply a group values perspective, telling themselves that fair procedures signal that organization officials view them as important and respected members, and their own self-esteem and identity are enhanced.

Interactional justice shows that people react to their perceptions of the social sensitivity of the interpersonal treatment they receive. Most researchers now acknowledge that the distinction between procedural and interactional justice makes theoretical and analytical sense (Greenberg, 1996). We humans have an almost universal need to maintain a politeness as we express our needs for autonomy, fellowship, and competency. Team members expect to be treated with respect and provided with adequate explanations so that they are not insulted or demeaned. When actions or decisions violate the norm of politeness, members feel they have been treated in a disrespectful and more unfair manner than they deserve or expect. They perceive or report low interactional justice.

TRIGGERS FOR WHEN TO LEAD CHANGE

Justice researchers have shown that it is critical for leaders to manage team members' fairness perceptions. It is important that leaders of change initiatives routinely scan the communication and reaction of their employees. But scan for what? And what good can come to individuals or organizations from such cautious monitoring of communication? Leaders need a more concrete set of suggestions, grounded in theory, that can help them focus and then formulate their actions.

The first step in operationalizing the proposed model requires refocusing the listening skills of virtual collaboration members. This is done by providing a way to code comments made about the work of the members. The perceptual triggers presented in Table 8.1 correspond to the three types of justice. By recognizing the type of fairness concerns team members are articulating, any leader at any level can make judgments about what part of the model they are currently in and where they should next put their effort and attention.

The theory-based trigger questions are located where the circles overlap in the model in Figure 8.1. If, for example, there is a lot of communication about rules violations or wanting to be asked for input, the leader knows that procedural justice is an area to review since it may be at the heart of change acceptance or implementation problems.

A focus on the organization or the whole team may be in order when members begin to question the match between actual decision outcomes and perceived effort or need. The distributive justice column in Table 8.1 gives some examples of the types of questions and comments members may make. Similarly, if there are many concerns that the team or organization is not following its own policies and procedures, there is an opening for less committed members or stakeholders to charge the organization with capricious or discriminatory practices. The leader's job in these cases is to protect the entire team or organization—and members are signaling that they expect attention and energy to go into those protective actions.

When concerns seem to be over interpersonal treatment and rules violations, it is clear that the leadership focus should be on the followers. This is essential, particularly when members also voice frustration over not being asked for their thoughts or not having any recourse to change or even comment on decisions. Silence should not be interpreted as approval or dissent. A representative sample of individual members should be carefully encouraged to provide private feedback about the changes. A good change leader is expected to understand both the expectations and the opportunities for the team they lead.

Most popular change models assume that members will have a negative reaction to change and that leaders can minimize the negative if they convince employees to change their attitudes or learn how to cope with the new reality.

Table 8.1

Communicative Indicators: Questions and Comments Made by Team Members That Signal Their Justice Concerns

Distributive Justice (Outcome Fairness)	Procedural Justice	Interactional Justice
What happened to our leader? To us? Who is still on our team?	When are they going to let us have some input into these decisions?	We are not being treated very nicely. I'd appreciate a little more politeness and dignity.
Is this outcome consistent with our mission? Will we still be able to achieve our goals?	The procedures they are using are not fair. They are not our usual way of doing business—not in the policy manual, previous statements.	The way the decision was made showed disrespect for those of us on the team.
With all of the good work they say we've done, how are they justifying this outcome?	Has anyone contacted human resources to see if this is okay to do?	Did you notice the condescending tone of that last e-mail message? Any disparaging or disheartening remarks?
At least our outcome reflects the amount of contribution we've made to the organization.	It doesn't seem that they are treating the teams consistently.	If they treat [a peer, the leader] that way, imagine what they will do to us.
Let's take stock of our members and leaders. Who is for this initiative, and who is against it?	I thought decisions were supposed to be based on seniority [or merit or project] need.	The explanations and justifications they are giving do [or don't] seem reasonable to me.
Wait. Who is going to lead this initiative? Why does the leader have to change too?	There must be other things going on that we don't know about.	At least they seem to be answering my questions and meeting my needs.
If our leader(s) can't take care of themselves, we certainly aren't safe!	There is no way we can influence these decisions.	Communication with us seems to be timely and candid.
Given our performance, our outcome seems fair.	Management is doing a good job getting all the necessary information before they make decisions.	They have announced some difficult changes, but no one is being demeaned, insulted, or treated poorly.

In fact, changes rarely happen one at a time and rarely have equal outcomes for all members. Changes may result in some members' losing jobs, status, budgets, or other support, while others may benefit from related changes (and feel guilty for gaining new responsibilities or influence at a time when others experience loss). When team members are making comments such as those in the second and third columns of Table 8.1, it is time for leaders to take action to preserve the support and development of their employees. Although the answer is not as simple as convincing them to change their attitude or "get over it," it is not so complex that we are without suggestions for leader action.

A focus on self as leader also has an appropriate time and place during change. When it appears that actions will lead to unwanted change for the leader (loss of some power, increased responsibility, or job loss, for example), individual team members will signal their fairness concern by talking about outcome fairness or distributive justice. When the focus of member reaction to change is about disrespectful treatment or unfair outcomes, the team members may be worried that the leader is not being taken care of properly. One of the underappreciated prescriptions from this model is that leaders should take care of themselves during an organizational transition. Much popular discussion casts leaders as servants and leadership as service, but that literature does not discuss what happens when the leader takes self-sacrifice too far. Leaders are human and subject to stress and its outcomes, including burnout and feelings of being underappreciated and undervalued.

There is a significant research stream that shows that observing an injustice within an organization has a great deal of influence on individual employees' perceptions of organizational justice (Brockner & Wiesenfeld, 1996). Any informal or formal leader is in a position to be watched, and any policy or procedure that may result in an unfavorable outcome for the leader is likely to be observed by others. This is especially true when there are high-quality relationships between leaders and followers (Mansour-Cole & Scott, 1998). This link between leader treatment and perceived fairness can also be observed in training sessions about organizational change and fairness. In a simulation, participants are asked to play the role of employees of a small inner-city hospital that is merging with a larger university hospital (McDonald & Mansour-Cole, 2000). Each CEO communicates only in writing, and shortly after the merger announcement, their well-liked CEO is not heard from again. Within the first ten minutes of the simulation, participants have always voiced concerns about the fate of their leader. They form much of their opinions of the corporate changes from the observed and perceived treatment of their leader.

SUGGESTED ACTIONS FOR HOW TO LEAD CHANGE

If the first step toward leading a fair change is evaluating the communication surrounding it, the second step is to use these evaluations to determine where to put energy. Determining that the most vocal concern is in the area of procedural justice, for example, tells us that actions should be taken to communicate with followers about how much they are and will be valued in the newly changing team and how the team or organization itself will be better off because of the change. In this section, we take a closer look at the three sets of actions (see Table 8.2). Each action area has a set of responses that are either written or verbal or a combination of both. The arguments for their use will provide further guidance for action by change leaders.

Taking care of the unit or the organization requires taking a systemic view toward change. The goal is not to prevent all team or organizational failures, but to make sure there are no fatal failures or undiscussable gaffes in safety, laws, finances, or communication with stakeholders. Center for Creative Leadership author Robert C. Dorn (in Guthrie & King, 2004) often championed the idea that the leader's task is to envision and help bring about change in the organization—change that has positive long-term consequences for single parts of the organization and for the organization as a whole or the society it operates within. The importance of communicating a vision and mission for the team is also a theme in the virtual teams literature. This part of the model presented honors these prescriptions.

Leaders may choose to respond more directly to team members' concerns by giving a written or verbal response that reveals more about the reason or cause of a decision. Rather than simply providing an overarching vision, leaders who communicate a compelling rationale increase team members' perceptions of fair change. The rationale may be in the form of an excuse, which includes an explanation for what leaders admit might be an unfavorable or inappropriate action, or a justification, where responsibility for the act is admitted, but the behavior is deemed appropriate or necessary (Shaw, Wild, & Colquitt, 2003).

Table 8.2
Justice Indicators for Leadership Action

Area of Needed Leader Focus	How to Do It
Take care of the organization	Communicate vision and mission.
	Carefully compose decision announcements and justifications.
	Make decisions after gathering all necessary information.
	Consistently apply policies and procedures across time and people.
	Check that new decision outcomes are consistent with the mission.
Take care of the followers	Advocate for team members.
	Increase follower input.
	Be patient, candid, and empathetic.
	Treat all followers with respect and dignity, regardless of their expressed level of frustration with decision processes and outcomes.
	Retrieve justifications for decisions.
	Acknowledge violations to formal procedures.
	Check to see if there is a chance to reapply procedures or redress wrong outcomes.
	Issue an apology when the risks to self and organization associated with admitting fallibility are low. This restores belief in fairness even if it does not provide redress.
Take care of individual leaders (self)	Ask for justification of decisions that are unfavorable to you.
	Do not volunteer to take less than you deserve.
	Insist on respectful treatment, and do not share lapses with followers.
	Actively work to prevent your own burnout.
	Develop and nurture your own support system.
	Remember that your goal is to embrace change rather than cope with it.

Finally, when confronted by a predicament of injustice, some leaders may be tempted to engage in a level of strategic ambiguity. They may offer a social account that denies the injustice or simply fails to respond to the accusation. These may benefit the organization by decreasing liability or further damage to the unit's reputation than if the leader were seen to agree with a particular subordinate's concerns about fair outcomes or procedures. This inaction cannot be maintained for too long, however, and acts such as visioning or justification will create and sustain more positive fairness perceptions.

To take care of the followers, leaders need to do more than simply "be there for them"; they need to advocate for the other team members. If there are opportunities to increase follower input or retrieve justifications for decisions from higher administrators, effective change leaders take that action. They acknowledge violations to formal procedures and attempt to get justifications (for example, not enough time to follow procedure) or secure promises to do better in the future. Members also need a change leader to redress any disrespectful or improper remarks made during the change process. To increase fairness perceptions, leader contacts with followers need to be more personal, and richer media, such as the telephone or videoconferencing, are appropriate.

Many traditional change models focus almost exclusively on the coping skills of team members or followers. Those give leaders some good advice, including a need to be supportive, patient, and candid and to use good listening skills—but keep in mind that any two followers do not experience a particular change in the same way. A leader who is concerned with creating fair change will make additions to the traditional advice, including helping members conduct brainstorming sessions, decision-making sessions, and closure sessions. Team members need to know that their leader believes in equifinality—the idea that there is often more than one way to get to the same outcome. Sometimes team members need a leader to champion change, and sometimes they need an effective manager to take care of the details, making connections in order to get projects completed and members satisfied.

The leader who is not taking care of self may not be available to help the followers or the organization enjoy a fair and successful change. It may be in everyone's best interest to ask for reconsideration or redress of policies and procedures that put an effective leader at risk. Leaders need to keep involved in change initiatives to ensure they have both an opportunity to shape change and an opportunity or voice in subsequent decisions. Sometimes it is appropriate to ask for justification of decisions before someone else asks the same of you. The stress of being totally selfless and yet significantly responsible for others can result in outcomes that are not favorable for anyone.

An additional set of suggestions for leader self-care is found in the facilitation literature. Authors who write about organizational culture remind change agents that they will often need to go into organizations that may be toxic environments, filled with negative emotions and behavior motivated by fear, self-loathing, or worse (Schein, 1992). Although they were primarily writing for outside consultants and facilitators, leaders inside an organization need to take the facilitator role at some point during change. Leaders must take care of themselves to prevent their own burnout. They need to build and nurture a social support system for themselves. They need to listen to their own spoken and unspoken messages about the change. And they need to keep up behaviors that will allow them to embrace change rather than simply cope with it.

FINAL THOUGHTS

This chapter provides a model and recommendations for virtual collaboration professionals to use to prepare themselves for the future. What are the responsibilities of a leader of healthy, growing, maturing followers? What skills should leaders cultivate in order to maximize the benefits of change programs? Where do leaders keep their focus during transitions? There is much research on the issue of managing change: much of it defines the leader as the one who has a top management position or decision-making authority. Other models recommend paying attention to any number of variables simultaneously, without prescriptions of which is the most important variable at what time. The model in this chapter is explicitly designed for vertical and horizontal leaderships: those who have position power or informal leaders who share leadership with others. The model recognizes that those who hope to influence change within a team have three responsibilities: to take care of the organizational or unit (team), to take care of the team members and other followers, and to take care of themselves. These three core responsibilities form the three main circles, while concerns about specific types of fairness violations help leaders decide on their course of action.

This model is potentially more powerful in virtual collaborations because the use of new collaborative technologies provides more opportunities for the capture and review of comments than casual or formal face-to-face conversation would. Martins, Gilson, and Maynard (2004) note that "since the communication tools used for virtual interaction allow for records to be retained ... VTs [virtual teams] have a means for monitoring team activities that are not available to face-to-face teams" (p. 814). The potential of even a limited longitudinal record would provide an easy scanning interval, so fewer needs for change would be missed. It would also be easier to track trends in members' communications or perceptions through simple e-mails, discussion threads, and other tools. When it is easier for a leader to engage in a perception check with another organization member, the validity of any model-based actions is increased. This perception check may take time, but the increased effectiveness of communication and actions, coupled with the avoidance of time-consuming errors, can significantly increase the efficiency of leadership during change.

This model, like leadership, is all about making change. There can and should be change leaders at many levels in an organization. Although not all change leaders will have position power to wield, all can use the prescriptions from this model. This model is not a substitute for routine management or process facilitation skills, but it is appropriate under conditions of large or small changes, planned or unplanned transitions, and widespread or small pockets of employee uncertainty. In today's environment, that represents most of the time.

Yukl (2006) reminds us that those who think leadership is a "shared, diffuse process" are more likely to "pay attention to the complex influence processes that occur among members, the context and conditions that determine when and how they occur, and the consequences for the group or organization" (p. 4). As experience with virtual collaborations increases, the need to implement leadership action models will also increase. This chapter provides leaders with a tool to interpret and act on changes in context and conditions.

As leaders become more comfortable with virtual collaborations, the need for more sophisticated leader prescriptions will grow. In this handbook are many good suggestions for facilitating team processes. Although these are necessary for effective project management, they are not sufficient for effective leadership. Leaders at all levels must be ready to deal with change issues effectively, and the first step is to understand when and where to redirect their focus and energy. This model should provide enough information for that first important step.

REMINDERS

- The task of an effective virtual team leader goes beyond setting and meeting goals: it must include initiating or implementing change (or both).

- During times of change, leaders are charged with taking care of the organization, their team members, and themselves. It is not always evident when or how each of these three responsibilities should take top priority.

- All change situations have the potential to create feelings of unfairness since roles and rules are renegotiated and expectations are violated. If team members perceive a change as unfair, they are less likely to put effort and commitment into the implementation, less likely to be satisfied with outcomes, and more likely to resist the change.

- The types of comments team members make can provide clues to the amount of current member dissatisfaction and their readiness for change.

- Informal and formal feedback by team members provides a set of perceptual triggers to identify when leaders need to change their focus. The key is to listen carefully, and then code the feedback according to one of the three justice types. The type of justice expressed in this feedback can provide information about how best to approach issues.

- Encouraging virtual team members to discuss their feelings about impending or ongoing changes helps the leader seem caring and supportive. As important, the leader is gaining valuable information to guide their actions.

- While the lean communication afforded by e-mail, discussion forums, and other written forms of communication popular within virtual teams may seem a barrier to effective change, it may actually provide the key to accurate and timely appraisals of that feedback.

- Expect that some groups or individuals will have different perceptions of the change. Monitoring feedback should be an ongoing process. Some priorities and actions will need to shift to meet the new realities.

- Resistance to change is strongest when there are a lot of varied types of negative justice perceptions. As justice issues are addressed, team members are more likely to put positive effort into change initiatives.

- The goal for all virtual team members at all levels is to embrace change rather than simply cope with it.

References

Adams, J. S. (1965). Inequity in social exchange. In L. Berkowitz (Ed.), *Advances in experimental social psychology* (Vol. 2, pp. 267–299). New York: Academic Press.

Bell, B. S., & Kozlowski, S. W. (2002). A typology of virtual teams. *Group and Organization Management, 27,* 14–49.

Bies, R. J. (1987). The predicament of injustice: The management of moral outrage. *Research in Organizational Behavior, 9,* 289–319.

Bies, R. J., & Moag, J. S. (1986). Interactional justice: Communication criteria of fairness. In R. J. Lewicki, B. H. Sheppard, & M. H. Bazerman (Eds.), *Research on negotiation in organizations* (pp. 43–55). Greenwich, CT: JAI Press.

Brockner, J., & Wiesenfeld, B. (1996). An integrative framework for explaining reactions to decisions: Interactive effects of outcomes and procedures. *Psychological Bulletin, 120,* 189–208.

Colquitt, J. A. (2001). On the dimensionality of organizational justice: A construct validation of a measure. *Journal of Applied Psychology, 86,* 386–400.

Deutsch, M. (1985). *Distributive justice: A social-psychological perspective.* New Haven, CT: Yale University Press.

Greenberg, J. (1987). A taxonomy of organizational justice theories. *Academy of Management Review, 12,* 9–22.

Greenberg, J. (1990). Organizational justice: Yesterday, today and tomorrow. *Journal of Management, 16,* 399–432.

Greenberg, J. (1993). Justice and organizational citizenship: A commentary on the state of the science. *Employee Responsibilities and Rights Journal, 6*(3), 249–256.

Greenberg, J. (1996). *The quest for justice on the job: Essays and experiments.* Thousand Oaks, CA: Sage.

Guth, W., Schmittberger, R., & Schwartze, B. (1982). An experimental analysis of ultimatum bargaining. *Journal of Economic Behavior and Organization, 3*(4), 367–388.

Guthrie, V. A., & King, S. N. (2004). Feedback-intensive programs. In C. D. McCauley & E. Van Velsor (Eds.), *The Center for Creative Leadership handbook of leadership development* (2nd ed.). San Francisco: Jossey-Bass.

Hoffman, E., McCabe, K., Shachat, K., & Smith, V. (1994). Preferences, property rights and anonymity in bargaining games. *Games and Economic Behavior, 7*(3), 346–380.

Katz, D., & Kahn, R. L. (1978). *The social psychology of organizations* (2nd ed.). Hoboken, NJ: Wiley.

Kotter, J. P. (1990). *A force for change: How leadership differs from management.* New York: Free Press.

Kravitz, D. A., & Gunto, S. (1992). Decisions and perceptions of recipients in ultimatum bargaining games. *Journal of Socio-Economics, 21,* 65–84.

Levanthal, G. S. (1980). What should be done with equity theory? New approaches to the study of fairness in social relationships. In K. Gergen, M. Greenberg, & R. Willis (Eds.), *Social exchange: New advances in theory and research* (pp. 27–55). New York: Plenum.

Lipnack, J., & Stamps, J. (1999). Virtual teams: The new way to work. *Strategy and Leadership, 27,* 14–18.

Mansour-Cole, D., & Scott, S. (1998). Hearing it through the grapevine: The influence of source of layoff information and leader-member-relations on survivors' justice perceptions. *Personnel Psychology, 51,* 25–54.

Martins, L. L., Gilson, L. L., & Maynard, M. T. (2004). Virtual teams: What do we know and where do we go from here? *Journal of Management, 30*(6), 805–835.

McDonald, K., & Mansour-Cole, D. (2000). Change requires intensive care: An experiential exercise for learners in university and corporate settings. *Journal of Management Education, 24*(1), 127–149.

Novelli, L., Kirkman, B. L., & Shapiro, D. L. (1995). Effective implementation of organizational change: An organizational justice perspective. In C. L. Cooper & D. M. Rousseau (Eds.), *Trends in organizational behavior* (Vol. 2, pp. 15–36). Chichester, UK: Wiley.

Rost, J. C. (1991). *Leadership for the twenty-first century.* Westport, CT: Greenwood Press.

Schein, E. H. (1992). *Organizational culture and leadership* (2nd ed.). San Francisco: Jossey-Bass.

Shaw, J. C., Wild, E., & Colquitt, J. A. (2003). To justify or excuse? A meta-analytic review of the effects of explanations. *Journal of Applied Psychology, 88,* 444–458.

Thibaut, J., & Walker, L. (1975). *Procedural justice: A psychological analysis.* Mahwah, NJ: Erlbaum.

Yukl, G. A. (2006). *Leadership in organizations* (6th ed.). Upper Saddle River, NJ: Pearson Education.

Leading Virtual Teams
Potential Problems and Simple Solutions

Thomas A. O'Neill, Rhys J. Lewis, Laura A. Hambley

It is difficult to overemphasize the importance of good leadership. Leaders fulfill several key roles, including motivating people, coordinating efforts, and developing potential. This chapter explores these leadership roles in the context of virtual teams. Specifically, barriers to motivating, coordinating, and developing virtual teams are identified, along with suggestions for how leaders might overcome them.

Such issues in virtual team leadership will likely grow in importance over time. Combine the prevalent use of teams in organizations and an increasingly globalized and technology-dependent workplace, and the result is inevitably more teams relying on technology for communication. These virtual teams address challenges over and above those that traditional face-to-face ones deal with. Although many leadership skills and responsibilities apply to virtual teams, leading these teams is different from leading a face-to-face one (Hambley, O'Neill, & Kline, 2007). Good leaders will recognize these differences and adjust their behavior accordingly.

Many publications describe differences between face-to-face and virtual teams. Although identifying differences is an important first step, it is not likely to be helpful to someone (like a virtual team leader) trying to determine what he or she needs to do. In short, listing differences is easy; determining what should be done about those differences is another matter altogether. Despite the numerous reviews of virtual teamwork (for example, Driskell, Radtke, & Salas, 2003; Hertel, Geister, & Konradt, 2005; Kirkman & Mathieu, 2005; Martins, Gilson, & Maynard, 2004; Qureshi & Vogel, 2001), only recently has there been a focus on the potential of leaders to influence virtual teams (aside from this handbook, see reviews by Avolio, Kahai, & Dodge, 2001; Bell & Kozlowski, 2002; Connaughton & Daly, 2004a, 2004b; Gibson & Cohen, 2003; Hambley et al., 2007; Zaccaro, Ardison, & Orvis, 2004).

Using this body of knowledge, we identify the difficulties unique to virtual teams and, more important, provide specific suggestions for how leaders of virtual teams might overcome these challenges. This is done separately for each key leadership function: what leaders need to do to motivate, coordinate, and develop a virtual team (see Figure 9.1). As much as possible, we illustrate each suggestion with relevant studies of virtual team leadership. Besides providing strong evidence for the suggestions, these studies also serve as excellent sources of ideas for what can be done by leaders in a virtual team environment. Finally, all the suggestions are organized by when they are most applicable in a team's life span. The result is a checklist summarizing what leaders need to do and when they need to do it.

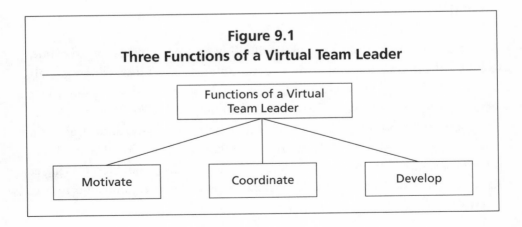

Figure 9.1
Three Functions of a Virtual Team Leader

MOTIVATION

Virtual team leaders face substantial challenges when it comes to motivating from a distance. At least three motivational challenges become more difficult when a team depends on technology for communication: providing a compelling message, managing conflicting goals, and establishing team identity.

Providing a Compelling Vision

In the words of Jack Welch, CEO of General Electric from 1981 to 2001, "Good business leaders create a vision, articulate the vision, passionately own the vision, and relentlessly drive it to completion" (Tichy & Charan, 1989, p. 3). In this case, both researchers and practitioners agree. Inspiring motivation by providing a compelling vision is central to leadership and consequently plays a prominent role in dominant theories (for charismatic leadership, see Conger & Kanungo, 1987, and House, 1977; for tranformational leadership, see Bass, 1985, and Burns, 1978). Effective leadership involves unapologetically and authoritatively setting a clear and engaging direction for the team (Hackman, 2002). In other words, the overall mission or purpose for the team is not open to debate; instead, the team's leader must vividly convey the team's ultimate purpose so that it inspires motivation in its members.

A problem for virtual team leaders is that inspiration may be difficult to convey using certain communication media. In transcribing a passionate speech into e-mail, a lot may be lost in translation. This difference between what can be conveyed through a speech versus by e-mail is due to a communication medium's richness, that is, the capacity of a medium to provide immediate feedback, convey cues (such as facial cues or intonation), personalize messages, and capitalize on language variety (Daft & Lengel, 1984, 1986). Richer media like videoconferencing better simulate face-to-face interactions compared to leaner, more text-based media such as e-mail. Given that humans evolved in face-to-face social situations, nonverbal cues may be irreplaceable sources of motivation. It is little wonder that an emoticon smile is simply not as contagious as a real one. Nor would an emoticon for motivation (if one existed) be nearly as effective as its face-to-face or voice-to-voice counterpart.

Many experts argue that richer communication technology is indeed better. For example, the establishment of motivation, particularly at early points in the team's life span, is affected by the medium used to convey the opening message

(Maruping & Agarwal, 2004). An obvious implication for leadership is that virtual team leaders should convey the team's mission and ultimate purpose through the richest media possible, such as videoconference or teleconference. As Wageman (2003) noted, it is unrealistic to expect inspiration to result from "a list of measurable objectives for a project sent to individuals via e-mail" (p. 78). Virtual team leaders should use rich media to convey a vivid and compelling vision.

Managing Conflicting Goals

Goal setting is an excellent way to motivate a team. Typically the leader's role is to develop the ultimate team goal, convey that goal vividly to the team, and then help each team member set goals tied to the team's mission. A tremendous amount of research shows that goal setting works when goals are clear, challenging, and consequential and when regular feedback is provided (see Locke & Latham, 2002). Interestingly, studies have also found that teams using goal setting in a computer-mediated situation reported higher team commitment, better cohesion, and a stronger collaboration climate than teams without goal setting (Huang, Wei, Watson, & Tan, 2001). In other words, goal setting is clearly important in both face-to-face and virtual teams. That said, there are again several aspects unique to virtual teams that will influence how leaders should form and introduce goals.

Compared to face-to-face teams, virtual team members are more likely to be involved in multiple projects and multiple teams. That places them in the precarious position of balancing several potentially competing commitments. The unfortunate result may be role ambiguity, stress, and decreases in performance in one or more work domains (Konradt, Hertel, & Schmook, 2003). For leaders, the implication is that individualized consideration in goal setting becomes even more critical within the context of virtual teams.

Individualized consideration means taking the time to appreciate each person's responsibilities outside the team. This will likely involve making individual appointments with each team member at start-up and at regular intervals thereafter. A primary consideration when setting goals in virtual teams is to avoid conflicts with other aspects of the individual's work and family life (Furst, Reeves, Rosen, & Blackburn, 2004).

Providing Feedback

Feedback is critical to motivation and goal setting in at least two ways. First, it allows an employee to adjust his or her behavior to better accomplish goals.

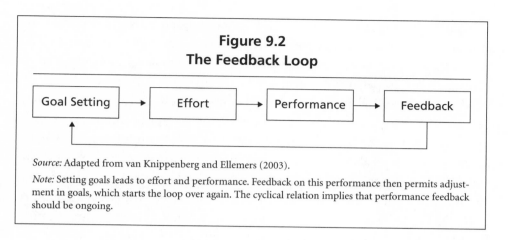

Figure 9.2
The Feedback Loop

Goal Setting → Effort → Performance → Feedback

Source: Adapted from van Knippenberg and Ellemers (2003).

Note: Setting goals leads to effort and performance. Feedback on this performance then permits adjustment in goals, which starts the loop over again. The cyclical relation implies that performance feedback should be ongoing.

Second, it is an essential tool for establishing goals in that it helps to set specific criteria for challenging yet realistic objectives. This relationship among feedback, goal setting, effort, and performance is depicted in Figure 9.2.

Once again the virtual environment poses several unique barriers: it is more difficult to gather and provide performance information. A lot of performance information comes from observing people at the office (for example, whether someone is late) or running into them in the hallway and chatting about work. Spontaneous face-to-face encounters also provide opportunities for conveying unofficial feedback. These unplanned opportunities to observe and interact are often lacking in virtual working arrangements and may be sorely missed.

With fewer unplanned opportunities to observe performance and provide feedback, additional planned ones must be put in place. For example, the virtual leader may need to schedule periodic meetings with each individual team member in order to monitor progress and provide feedback (Hambley et al., 2007).

Unfortunately research provides little guidance on how virtual leaders should convey feedback information. One apparently successful approach is to make each individual's achievements known to the team. For example, publicizing a graphical feedback report about each team member may lead to higher performance in electronic brainstorming groups (Shepherd, Briggs, Reinig, Yen, & Nunamaker, 1996). Providing ongoing feedback can make each team member's contributions clear, thereby creating a sense of duty to the other team members. Other suggestions include involving team members when setting performance standards (Scott & Tiessen, 1999) and establishing an open and trustworthy atmosphere at the beginning of feedback sessions. For example, the session could start with a brief nonwork-related discussion, followed by acknowledging the positive aspects of the person's performance before giving constructive feedback.

Media richness will likely be a crucial consideration in delivering feedback. Fewer cues mean greater ambiguity. In e-mail, for example, comments are often interpreted as rude or confrontational simply because the reader cannot see the expression of the speaker and mistakenly assumes the worst (Walther & Burgoon, 1992). The communication medium can therefore have a bearing on whether comments are perceived as criticism or constructive feedback (Connaughton & Daly, 2004b). Using rich media is strongly recommended when communicating feedback. Rich media are also more likely to allow immediate responses to the leader's statements, enhancing mutual understanding and perceptions of fairness (Dineen, Noe, & Wang, 2004; Maruping & Agarwal, 2004).

Establishing a Team Identity

When team members identify strongly with their team, they are less driven by personal considerations. Instead, they internalize the needs, goals, and expectations of the team and are energized to accomplish the team's mission. Research has shown that teams with a strong sense of collective identity engage in less social loafing (the tendency for individuals to exert less effort when part of a group; Ellemers, 2001; Karau & Williams, 1993), report higher levels of social cohesion (Hogg, Abrams, Otten, & Hinkle, 2004), conform more to local group norms (Hogg et al., 2004), receive higher supervisor ratings of effectiveness (Geister, 2004), and take more initiative to accomplish the team's mission (Dutton, Dukerich, & Harquail, 1994). Clearly leaders stand to benefit by tapping into the powerful motivational potential conveyed by a strong team identity.

Despite the advantages of promoting a team identity, there are challenges to fostering a collective orientation in virtual teams. Most obviously, being separated by vast geographical space is not a good way to cultivate feelings of closeness. Geographical separation makes it difficult for team members to identify with the collective and its mission, primarily because benefits of face-to-face communication cannot be realized. Exacerbating the communication woes, if team members are located in different countries, there may be cultural or language differences that hinder basic exchanges of information and highlight diversities rather than similarities. Helping a team get past these barriers may be one of the greatest contributions of a virtual team leader.

One particularly powerful way to build a team identity is to design work that is interdependent. Interdependent teamwork designs are characterized by conditions that require active collaboration to complete work. They have been related to increases in quality of social processes, mutual learning, and collective responsibility for accomplishing performance objectives (Wageman, 1995). In the virtual realm, interdependent team tasks make people feel indispensable to the team, thereby increasing team identity, motivation, and virtual team effectiveness (Hertel, Konradt, & Orlikowski, 2004). In short, working as a team helps make people feel as if they are part of that team. This sense of identity translates into motivation and performance. The implication is that leaders should capitalize as much as possible on opportunities to design interdependent tasks.

Another way to create a common team identity is to increase team members' confidence in each other and the team as a whole (van Knippenberg & Ellemers, 2003; van Knippenberg, van Knippenberg, De Cremer, & Hogg, 2004). People like to associate with groups they think are (or will be) successful and to dissociate from groups they think will fail. Of course, one has to know a person's abilities to have confidence in those abilities. Hence, familiarizing team members with each other will be essential to developing confidence in the team. The problem is that virtual teams might never meet in person and tend to communicate less personal information through virtual media. This makes it particularly difficult to learn about each other's knowledge, skills, and abilities and, consequently, difficult to develop team confidence.

Virtual team leaders can help to overcome this unfamiliarity barrier. A simple but effective solution is to outline each team member's expertise and make those strengths known early on in the team's formation. It would also be helpful to encourage non-work-related discussions whenever possible to foster the development of trust and cooperative exchanges.

Many tried-and-true face-to-face methods of confidence building still apply. Face-to-face kick-offs can be an effective way to establish a strong team identity early on, though are not always feasible (Hambley et al., 2007). In addition, regardless of whether one is face-to-face or far away, a leader should express, and demonstrate whenever possible, a belief that team members are capable of doing good work. Groups with confident leaders tend to have high confidence in themselves

(Watson, Chemers, & Preiser, 2001). Celebrating team victories whenever they happen is another way to bring everyone together.

The best way to establish confidence is through success. Small, early successes are great confidence builders. Experience ultimately informs team members as to whether the team is successful and whether confidence is justified. It is therefore essential to ensure that teams have the necessary backdrop for success. More specifically, a team should not fail because of a leader's inability to obtain the necessary resources. A good question to ask is, "Does the team have all of the resources necessary to complete its work?" If it does not, failures may cause feelings of helplessness rather than confidence.

The bottom line is that confident people do better work and that people identify more with teams they have confidence in. A leader who instills confidence reaps both rewards.

Leadership Behaviors That Motivate

Motivational leaders must overcome several challenges exacerbated by the virtual environment. Leaders can provide a compelling message, manage conflicting goals, and establish team identity by using these solutions:

- Use rich communication technologies such as videoconferencing and teleconferencing to convey the team's vision and inspire motivation.

- Make time to provide feedback by scheduling regular one-on-one conversations with each team member.

- Explore other creative ways to provide feedback, such as publicizing a report of each team member's performance.

- Acknowledge team members' responsibilities external to the virtual team, and avoid setting goals that conflict with their other work.

- Build a team identity by structuring tasks interdependently and building team confidence.

- Augment team confidence by displaying self-confidence, meeting face-to-face with the team, celebrating early successes, demonstrating optimism, helping the team surmount obstacles, and ensuring that adequate tools and resources are at the team's disposal.

COORDINATION

Virtual teams may take longer to perform their work compared to their face-to-face counterparts. Some estimates suggest that computer-mediated groups take up to four to five times longer than face-to-face groups to complete similar tasks (Dubrovsky, Kiesler, & Sethna, 1991; Hollingshead, 1996; Weisband, 1992). More recently, it has been suggested that the harmful effects of time pressure may also be worse in a virtual environment (Thompson & Coovert, 2006; Walther, 2002). A likely explanation is that working virtually places restrictions on communication, making coordination more difficult. It is therefore not surprising that recent models of virtual team leadership place great emphasis on building effective coordination (such as Zaccaro et al., 2004).

Working with others adds a layer of complexity that requires coordination among team members if task objectives are to be realized. Given that team members may cross functional, organizational, or national boundaries and are often temporally distributed, it is easy to imagine how working virtually poses several challenges to coordination.

Relationship Building

In a recent interview, Susan Turner, director of diversity and workplace programs at IBM Canada, stated, "We are in a world today where we cannot assume that the only way to build relationships is in a face-to-face environment" (Marron, 2005, p. C1). Indeed, relationships can and do develop online, but it takes more time (Walther, 1992, 2002; Walther, Loh, & Granka, 2005). Nevertheless, given sufficient time, it appears as though virtual team members attain equally positive interpersonal relationships as face-to-face teams do (Wilson, Straus, & McEvily, 2006). Besides increases in productivity, relationships help build trust, cohesion, commitment, and other interpersonal processes that are beneficial for coordination (Jarvenpaa, Knoll, & Leidner, 1998; Paris, Salas, & Cannon Bowers, 2000; Saphiere, 1996).

There is no shortage of impediments to building virtual relationships: decreased team member visibility, lack of normal social interaction and noticeable performance patterns, less inhibition of negative comments, and an absence of spontaneous nonwork-related exchanges, to name just a few. Virtual team leaders can offset these difficulties by building a culture based on frequent and open communication. As much as possible, leaders should promote the exchange of relational information in order to personalize messages and socialize team members. Including as many face-to-face cues as possible is also a great idea. Either one can promote the use of rich media (in which the cues are already built in) or encourage people to include substitutes for these cues. Such contextual additions can include the use of emoticons, capitalization of certain words, and the use of sounds to accentuate a particular point (Hollingshead, 2004; Walther & D'Addario, 2001). The idea is that embedding additional cues within messages helps make lean media richer.

Equally important in building team relationships is avoiding feelings of isolation. In fact, the challenges discussed—diminished social interaction, less inhibition of negative thoughts, and reduced humanizing—all contribute to and are fueled by isolation. Combating such feelings may be one of the virtual team leader's biggest challenges (Connaughton & Daly, 2004b). As Denis Chamberland, chief legal counsel for the global consulting firm Accenture, noted, the virtual environment can be cold and distant (Marron, 2005).

The question of how to overcome tendencies toward isolation has been addressed by several authors. For instance, Connaughton and Daly (2004a) found that the best strategy leaders can use to avert the negative feelings of remoteness and geographical separation is to promote a culture of overcommunication. Indeed, the survival of virtual teams depends on active and effective communication despite the differing time zone and location of each team member (Nemiro, 2003). This means encouraging and actively seeking out participation from individuals at remote sites, allowing each person an opportunity to share his or her perspective during team meetings, and enforcing small but important communication rules, such as confirming that a message or document was successfully received. These simple habits help to establish and maintain social presence, create increased feelings of connectedness, and consequently, improve performance (Armstrong & Cole, 2002; Short, Williams, & Christie, 1976; Griffith & Meader, 2004; Steuer, 1992; Weisband, 2002).

Choice of Communication Medium

Just as choice of communication medium is critical to instilling motivation early in a team's life cycle, it is central to the day-to-day operations of the virtual team. There is no one ideal communication medium. Each has its strengths and weaknesses.

Straus and McGrath (1994) showed that complex tasks requiring higher levels of coordination were performed better by groups interacting through richer communication media. More recently, Rico and Cohen (2005) found that teams performed a simple task most effectively using asynchronous media (media that do not permit real-time collaboration, like e-mail), while teams carrying out a complex task required synchronous media (media that allow individuals to work on the same task at the same time, such as teleconferencing). That similar results have been reported elsewhere (Daly, 1993; Farmer & Hyatt, 1994; Hollingshead, McGrath, & O'Connor, 1993) suggests that virtual team leaders' choice of communication medium should depend on the complexity of the message to be delivered or task to be completed.

As focal tasks often shift throughout the team's life cycle, so too will the ideal communication medium. Rich media such as videoconferencing help to develop interpersonal and task-related working patterns of team members, so those media may be particularly beneficial in the early stages of the team coordination. As the team develops a shared understanding of its resources (for example, members' knowledge, skills, and experience), the need for richer media may diminish. The leader may then wish to capitalize on the benefits of less rich technologies like e-mail. With less rich media, one domineering person is less likely to control the entire conversation, and emotions can be more easily regulated if individuals can take time to calm themselves before responding (Rhoades & O'Connor, 1996). Thus, as the team becomes more familiar with one another, rich media have diminishing returns, making the benefits of less rich media that much more attractive.

The choice of communication medium depends on the complexity of the team's task and the stage of the team's life cycle. The challenge facing a team leader is to find and promote the right balance.

Applying Face-to-Face Coordination Techniques to Virtual Teams

Coordination problems are not limited to virtual teams. Much time, money, and research have been devoted to developing strategies that maximize coordination in face-to-face teams. Many of these techniques are just as applicable in a virtual context.

Assigning tasks and deadlines to each team member during team formation is an effective strategy for achieving a swift start-up and avoiding procrastination.

This may be particularly relevant in a virtual context, because virtual teams are inherently slower to develop and show an even greater tendency to procrastinate at the beginning of projects (Walther & Bunz, 2005).

Another tried-and-true coordination mechanism is the use of weekly team meetings. The catch for virtual teams is that members tend to let out their emotions more, sometimes sparking unnecessary conflict (Reicher, Spears, & Postmes, 1995). People are less concerned with upsetting someone when that person is far away. This tendency toward interpersonal conflict makes the virtual team leader's role as a conflict moderator that much more important. As a moderator, leaders should make members aware that sharing conflicting viewpoints is beneficial but that the discussion should stay focused on the issue at hand instead of becoming interpersonally threatening. Leaders might also emphasize team identity, because in situations involving strong team identity, members tend to be more cohesive and committed to the team's (as opposed to individuals') goals.

Another challenge facing virtual teams is that introverted and less socially confident people can hide behind the technology. Leaders who are aware of this tendency can mediate meetings in such a way that each team member is appropriately included in the discussion. One suggestion given in a recent field study is for the leader to track who has spoken during a teleconference and provide opportunities for those who have not contributed to do so (Hambley et al., 2007). For example, leaders in that study prepared lists of team members prior to meetings and noted who participated in the discussion and when. In this way, they were able to call on team members who had not been given a fair opportunity to participate.

It is also worth noting that several collaboration tools are available to aid in the coordination of virtual teams, among them instant messaging, data-sharing applications, e-rooms, collaborative space, and project forums. For example, e-rooms provide team members with a place to store documents, post group members' schedules, plan projects, read and contribute to threaded discussions, and so on. Such tools are often critical to virtual team functioning but can also serve as barriers if they are not used effectively. Research suggests that successful use of these technologies largely depends on employees' experience. As one might expect, those who are more experienced with the technology adapt better to their use (Bajwa, Lewis, Pervan, & Lai, 2005). Similarly, employee expectations make a difference. If people expect a technology to help, it usually does; when they instead see it as a hassle, it often is (Davis, 1989; Davis, Bagozzi, & Warshaw, 1989; Townsend, Demarie, & Hendrickson, 2001). Taken together, it appears that when it comes to communication technology, the right experience and a positive attitude are important for teams.

Summary

A variety of leadership strategies can promote coordination:

- Facilitate the development of relationships between team members by building a culture based on frequent communication and exchanges of non-work-related information and promoting contextual additions to messages like emoticons.

- Combat feelings of isolation by overcommunicating.

- Align the complexity of the task or message with the richness of the communication medium such that complex tasks are handled with rich media and simple tasks with lean media.

- Gradually shift to less rich (or lean) communication methods as team members become accustomed to working with each other and familiar with their tasks.

- Establish tasks and deadlines early to avoid procrastination.

- Have weekly team meetings to update team members about work and nonwork-related issues.

- Ensure that everyone is given the opportunity to participate in team meetings by explicitly asking each member for his or her thoughts.

- Watch for and mitigate withdrawal behaviors within and outside regularly scheduled meetings.

- Choose familiar collaborative technologies that the team is comfortable using.

Many of the recommendations are examples of what have been termed standard operating procedures (Bell & Kozlowski, 2002). These norms specify appropriate and inappropriate behaviors and keep teams coordinated toward accomplishing their common goals.

DEVELOPMENT

Developing the virtual team into a mature and capable work unit does not occur instantaneously; instead, team development should be viewed as a process. What is known about training and development for virtual team leaders has been spearheaded by Rosen, Blackburn, Kirkman, and colleagues (see Blackburn, Furst, & Rosen, 2003; Furst et al., 2004; Kirkman, Rosen, Gibson, Tesluk, & McPherson, 2002; Rosen, Furst, & Blackburn, 2006). We review three relevant activities in this literature: team building, team coaching, and gathering performance information for feedback purposes.

Team Building

In Rosen et al.'s survey of training and development professionals (2006), 57 percent of 440 respondents reported that training on team-building skills is valuable. Although online team building is in its infancy, researchers have recommended social activities that involve eating and drinking. Surprisingly, such activities can be conducted electronically. Amusing as it may sound, some authors recommend sending video captions of members having bagels and coffee or champagne and cookies (Armstrong & Cole, 2002; Thompson & Coovert, 2006). Leaders can also facilitate team-building activities that are amenable to online interactions, such as discussing a relevant movie or book, completing survival exercises (like *Stranded in the Desert,* Johnson & Johnson, 1987) or personality questionnaires (such as the Myers-Briggs Type Indicator; Briggs & Myers, 1987), and facilitating other activities available in conventional team-building books (for examples, see Dyer, 1995; Johnson & Johnson, 2000; Miller, 2004; Phillips & Elledge, 1989).

Jarvenpaa and others (1998) provided an example of how team building can create the conditions that establish trust in virtual teams. They invited graduate students from around the globe to work on course projects in geographically distributed teams. The authors introduced a team-building intervention that involved exchanging information about project-related skills, motivations for contributing to the team effort, and work and study habits. When team members posted this personal information on a Web site accessible only to team members and administrators (in other words, when they participated in the team-building exercise), conditions that lead to trust were more likely to be present. So although virtual team building has been largely overlooked, clearly it can be accomplished, with benefits likely similar to those of traditional teams.

Team Coaching

Team coaching has been defined as "direct interaction with a team intended to help members make coordinated and task-appropriate use of their collective resources in accomplishing the team's work" (Hackman & Wageman, 2005, p. 269). Coaching has been shown to increase satisfaction and performance (Ellinger, Ellinger, & Keller, 2003) and is theorized to have roles in trust formation, conflict resolution, and team commitment (Kets de Vries, 2005). In short, it promotes many of the desired outcomes articulated throughout this chapter and, not surprising, involves many of the same activities, among them monitoring performance, providing feedback, promoting self-efficacy, and team building.

Several recent articles have highlighted the importance of coaching skills for virtual team leaders (Furst et al., 2004; Wageman, 2003). Despite this proposed importance, leaders report that they do not spend much time coaching the team as a whole (Wageman, Hackman, & Lehman, 2004), which may be especially true in virtual teams because the teams tend to be more autonomous.

Rather than eliminate the need for coaching, it may be that increased autonomy simply changes which coaching activities are likely to be most beneficial. For instance, it makes sense that effective self-management will be particularly important when teams are highly autonomous. Consequently, helping team members to be better at self-management is likely to be an important coaching activity for virtual team leaders.

Any strategy for the effective coaching of self-managed work teams will almost certainly include empowerment. Empowerment involves increasing team members' beliefs in their capability to perform (in other words, their self-confidence), experienced meaningfulness of their work, autonomy, and perceived extent to which their work contributes to the team and organization. Empowerment has been demonstrated to be associated with increased team effectiveness in both face-to-face (Wageman, 2001) and virtual contexts (Kirkman, Rosen, Tesluk, & Gibson, 2004).

The implications for virtual team coaches are straightforward: coaches may be best advised to shift from a directive and authoritative standpoint to more of a nondirective role that focuses on defining, facilitating, and encouraging performance. This does not mean that the team sets its own direction; rather, the team's purpose must be set and communicated by the leader. However, he or she should let the team decide how that objective is reached. Hackman (2002) wrote, "Those who create work teams should be insistent and unapologetic about exercising their authority to specify end states, but equally insistent about not specifying the details about the means by which the team is to pursue those ends" (p. 73). In this sense, the ideal role of coaches may be a consultative one characterized by empowering the team to manage its own work processes (Manz & Sims, 1987).

Gathering Performance Information for Feedback

Feedback is central to several leadership roles. Not only is it indispensable in setting goals and coordinating team progress, it is a key to personal and team development. All of the same difficulties still apply: fewer opportunities for monitoring performance and providing feedback still present challenges to virtual team leaders. The previous discussion regarding feedback focused on suggesting how leaders might communicate this feedback to employees. In this section, the focus shifts to the issues in obtaining accurate performance data.

To make up for the lack of unplanned face-to-face encounters, virtual team leaders often turn to more objective performance indicators (like completing assignments on time) compared to the visible cues (such as tardiness) available in face-to-face settings (Connell, 2002; Thompson & Coovert, 2003). Interestingly, this reliance on objective metrics rather than subjective cues (like random observations) may actually make performance appraisals in virtual teams more fair than ones conducted in face-to-face contexts. Weisband and Atwater (1999), for example, found that ratings of others' contributions were not confounded by team member liking in virtual teams, although they were in face-to-face teams. Similarly, Hedlund, Ilgen, and Hollenbeck (1998) found that leaders of computer-mediated groups were better able to differentiate the quality of group members' decisions compared to leaders of face-to-face groups. In other words, fewer observational opportunities may at first seem like a barrier, but they may ultimately result in fair and valid performance ratings.

Unfortunately, use of objective metrics is not a panacea for performance appraisal. While they typically aid accuracy, objective measures are prone to contamination by variables outside the team's control (like economic downturns) and may not capture beneficial acts not directly written into job descriptions (such as helping a coworker). Because of these limitations, the importance of obtaining multiple indexes of performance, such as one-on-one interviews, team discussions, and 360-degree feedback, has been emphasized (Wageman, 2003). Gathering more information offers a more holistic perspective of a person's work performance.

One promising way to compensate for shortcomings in objective metrics is to provide regular status reports through e-mail or telephone meetings (Connell, 2002). Such reports have the benefit of giving the subordinate a chance to contribute to his or her own performance appraisal (in other words, providing voice). When combined with objective data, these indirect approaches to gathering performance information should lead to fair performance appraisals.

Another related (and controversial) issue that warrants consideration is the use of electronic performance monitoring. Several authors have documented how electronic performance monitoring (for example, monitoring e-mail communication, number of keyboard presses per hour) is related to increases in subordinate stress, decreased physical health, and withdrawal from the monitored communication tools (Aiello & Kolb, 1995; Markus, 1983; Olson & Olson, 1999; Smith, Carayon, Sanders, Lim, & LeGrande, 1992). Due to these negative consequences, electronic monitoring should be avoided if possible, and done openly and sensitively if required.

One final consideration when developing virtual teams is to reflect on the teamwork experience before disbanding. Facilitating at least one group session for the sole purpose of reviewing the teamwork process may help members recall how they overcame certain challenges and how they can improve in the future (Wageman, 2003). Without an intervention aimed at reflecting on the team's experience, team members are unlikely to take steps at the end of their work to learn from the experience. However, the novelty of virtual teams implies that most team members will not have much prior experience with these work arrangements. Missing out on opportunities to discuss the experience and explore the lessons learned would be unfortunate.

Summary

The challenges to developing virtual teams toward their maximum potential were identified in this section. The following list provides a summary of the key leadership behaviors in performing these activities virtually:

- Engage in online team-building activities such as "eating" and "drinking" virtually, exploring the team members' diverse personality types (by feeding back questionnaire results), or completing a survival exercise.
- Coach the team toward self-management by empowering team members.

- Use a variety of objective (such as sales, meeting deadlines) as well as subjective techniques (like one-on-one interviews) to assess each team member's performance.
- Ask team members to provide regular status reports to the leader.
- If at all possible, avoid electronic performance monitoring.
- Prior to disbanding, call a team meeting to reflect on the teamwork process in general, reminisce about how certain challenges were overcome, celebrate successes and acknowledge failures, and review key lessons learned.

LEADER FUNCTIONS ACROSS THE VIRTUAL TEAM LIFE CYCLE

The checklist in Exhibit 9.1 pulls together the suggestions regarding motivating, coordinating, and developing according to when they need to be performed within the team's life cycle (start-up, midpoints, and endings). Because the leadership functions tend to be more or less important at various stages of the team's life cycle, the checklist shows not only what leaders need to do but when they need to do it. Thus, leaders can use the checklist to help direct their efforts at effectively managing a virtual team.

FINAL THOUGHTS

If there is a guiding principle to this chapter, it is that virtual team leaders have a dual challenge: they face all the normal difficulties of leading a team, plus the added complication of doing so virtually. The challenges associated with the latter have been reviewed, and suggestions for how leaders might overcome them have been offered. Thus, the main contribution of this chapter has been to go beyond identifying the potential problems involved in leading virtual teams by providing simple solutions that leaders can readily implement.

Of course, what is simple is a matter of perspective. It is a lot easier to identify a solution than to carry it out. We hope that the suggestions and examples in this chapter will assist virtual team leaders in doing both. (For additional references on leading virtual teams, see the reference list compiled by Dan Novak on the www.wiley.com/go/virtualteamshandbook Web site.)

Exhibit 9.1

What Virtual Team Leaders Need to Do and When They Need to Do It

	Virtual Team Leader Function		
Stage of Virtual Team Life Cycle	Motivate	Coordinate	Develop
Start-up	☑ Convey the team's purpose in a vivid and compelling way through rich media	☑ Encourage the exchange of personal and nonwork-related information	☑ Facilitate team-building activities
	☑ Manage conflicting goals	☑ Promote a culture of overcommunication	☑ Coach the team toward self-management by empowering team members
	☑ Give the team and team members feedback concerning their progress	☑ Establish tasks and deadlines early to avoid procrastination	
	☑ Build a team identity		
Midpoints		☑ Ensure conflict is directed at the task and intervene if directed at the team or a team member	☑ Monitor the team's performance by using multiple performance indicators
		☑ Use only collaboration tools that satisfy important team needs	
		☑ Use rich media for complex tasks and lean media for simple ones	
		☑ Gradually shift from relying more on richer to leaner media	
Endings			☑ Review lessons learned from the teamwork experience

REMINDERS

- Virtual team leaders should use rich media to convey a vivid and compelling vision.

- For leaders, individualized consideration in goal setting becomes even more critical within the context of virtual teams.

- Comments communicated through e-mail are often interpreted as ruder or more confrontational than intended because the reader cannot see the expression of the speaker and mistakenly assumes the worst.

- Confident people do better work, and people identify more with teams they have confidence in. A virtual team leader who instills confidence reaps both rewards.

- The survival of virtual teams depends on active and effective communication despite the location and potential time zone differences between members.

- As virtual team members become more familiar with one another, rich media have diminishing returns, making the benefits of less rich media that much more attractive.

- If people expect a technology to help, it usually does; if they perceive a technology as a hassle, it often is.

- Although virtual team building has been largely overlooked, clearly it can be accomplished, with benefits likely similar to those of traditional teams.

- Virtual team coaches may be best advised to shift from a directive and authoritative standpoint to more of a nondirect role that focuses on defining, facilitating, and encouraging performance.

- Feedback is central to leadership. Not only is it indispensable in setting goals and coordinating team progress, it is a key to personal and team development.

- Although fewer observational opportunities may at first seem like a barrier, they may result in fair and valid performance ratings because objective (as opposed to subjective) performance metrics must be used.

- Facilitating at least one group session for the sole purposes of reviewing the teamwork process may help members recall how they overcame certain challenges, and how they can improve in the future.

RELATED ITEM ON THE WEB

• Reference List on Leading Virtual Teams

References

Aiello, J. R., & Kolb, K. J. (1995). Electronic performance monitoring and social context: Impact on productivity and stress. *Journal of Applied Psychology, 80,* 339–353.

Armstrong, D. J., & Cole, P. (2002). Managing distances and differences in geographically distributed work groups. In P. Hinds & S. Kiesler (Eds.), *Distributed work* (pp. 167–186). Cambridge, MA: MIT Press.

Avolio, B. J., Kahai, S. S., & Dodge, G. E. (2001). E-leadership: Implications of theory, research, and practice. *Leadership Quarterly, 11,* 615–668.

Bajwa, D. S., Lewis, F. L., Pervan, G., & Lai, V. S. (2005). The adoption and use of collaboration information technologies: International comparisons. *Journal of Information Technology, 20,* 130–140.

Bass, B. M. (1985). *Leadership and performance beyond expectations.* New York: Free Press.

Bell, B. S., & Kozlowski, S. W. (2002). A typology of virtual teams: Implications for effective leadership. *Group and Organizational Management, 27,* 14–36.

Blackburn, R., Furst, S., & Rosen, B. (2003). Building a winning virtual team: KSAs, selection, training, and evaluation. In C. B. Gibson & S. Cohen (Eds.), *Virtual teams that work: Creating the conditions for virtual team effectiveness* (pp. 95–120). San Francisco: Jossey-Bass.

Briggs, K., & Myers, I. (1987). *Myers-Briggs Type Indicator: Form G.* Palo Alto, CA: Consulting Psychology.

Burns, J. M. (1978). *Leadership.* New York: HarperCollins.

Conger, J. A., & Kanungo, R. N. (1987). Towards a behavioral theory of charismatic leadership in organizational settings. *Academy of Management Review, 12,* 637–647.

Connaughton, S. L., & Daly, J. A. (2004a). Leading from afar: Strategies for effectively leading virtual teams. In S. H. Godar & S. P. Ferris (Eds.), *Virtual and collaborative teams: Process, technologies, and practice* (pp. 49–75). Hershey, PA: Idea Group Publishing.

Connaughton, S. L., & Daly, J. A. (2004b). Long distance relationships: Communicative strategies for leading virtual teams. In D. J. Pauleen (Ed.), *Virtual teams: Projects, protocols, and processes* (pp. 116–144). Hershey, PA: Idea Group Publishing.

Connell, J. B. (2002). Organizational consulting to virtual teams. In R. L. Lowman (Ed.), *Handbook of organizational consulting psychology: A comprehensive guide to theory, skills, and techniques* (pp. 285–312). San Francisco: Jossey-Bass.

Daft, R. L., & Lengel, R. H. (1984). Information richness: A new approach to manager information processing and organizational design. In B. Staw & L. L. Cummings (Eds.), *Research in organizational behavior* (pp. 191–233). Greenwich, CT: JAI Press.

Daft, R. L., & Lengel, R. H. (1986). Organizational information requirements, media richness and structural design. *Management Science, 32,* 554–571.

Daly, B. L. (1993). The influence of face-to-face versus computer-mediated communication channels on collective induction. *Accounting, Management, and Information Technologies, 3,* 1–22.

Davis, F. D. (1989). Perceived usefulness, perceived ease of use, and end user acceptance of information technology. *Management Information Systems Quarterly, 13,* 319–340.

Davis, F. D., Bagozzi, R. P., & Warshaw, P. R. (1989). User acceptance of computer technology: A comparison of two theoretical models. *Management Science, 35,* 982–1003.

Dineen, B. R., Noe, R. A., & Wang, C. (2004). Perceived fairness of Web-based applicant screening procedures: Weighing the rules of justice and the role of individual differences. *Human Resource Management, 43*(2, 3), 127–145.

Driskell, J. E., Radtke, P. H., & Salas, E. (2003). Virtual teams: Effects of technology mediation on team performance. *Group Dynamics: Theory, Research, and Practice, 4,* 297–323.

Dubrovsky, V. J., Kiesler, S., & Sethna, B. N. (1991). The equalization phenomenon: Status effects in computer-mediated and face-to-face decision-making groups. *Human-Computer Interaction, 6,* 119–146.

Dutton, J. E., Dukerich, J. M., & Harquail, C. V. (1994). Organizational images and member identification. *Administrative Sciences Quarterly, 39,* 239–263.

Dyer, W. (1995). *Team building: Current issues and new alternatives* (3rd ed.). Reading, MA: Addison-Wesley.

Ellemers, N. (2001). Social identity, commitment, and work behavior. In M. A. Hogg & D. J. Terry (Eds.), *Social identity processes in organizational contexts* (pp. 101–114). London: Psychology Press.

Ellinger, A. D., Ellinger, A. E., & Keller, S. B. (2003). Supervisory coaching behavior, employee satisfaction, and warehouse employee performance: A dyadic perspective on the distribution industry. *Human Resource Development Quarterly, 14*(4), 435–458.

Farmer, S. M., & Hyatt, C. W. (1994). Effects of task language demands and task complexity on computer-mediated work groups. *Small Group Research, 25,* 331–366.

Furst, S. A., Reeves, M., Rosen, B., & Blackburn, R. S. (2004). Managing the lifecycle of virtual teams. *Academy of Management Executive, 18*(2), 6–21.

Geister, S. (2004). *Development and evaluation of an online-feedback-system for virtual teams.* Unpublished dissertation. Kiel University, Kiel, Germany.

Gibson, C. B., & Cohen, S. G. (2003). *Virtual teams that work.* San Francisco: Jossey-Bass.

Griffith, T. L., & Meader, D. K. (2004). Prelude to virtual groups: Leadership and technology in semivirtual groups. In D. J. Pauleen (Ed.), *Virtual teams: Projects, protocols, and processes* (pp. 231–254). Hershey, PA: Idea Group Publishing.

Hackman, J. R. (2002). *Leading teams: Setting the stage for great performances.* Boston: Harvard Business School Press.

Hackman, J. R., & Wageman, R. (2005). A theory of team coaching. *Academy of Management Review, 30,* 269–287.

Hambley, L. A., O'Neill, T. A., & Kline, T.J.B. (2007). Virtual team leadership: Perspectives from the field. *International Journal of e-Collaboration, 3*(1), 40–64.

Hedlund, J., Ilgen, D. R., & Hollenbeck, J. R. (1998). Decision accuracy in computer-mediated versus face-to-face decision-making teams. *Organizational Behavior and Human Decision Processes, 76,* 30–47.

Hertel, G., Geister, S., & Konradt, U. (2005). Managing virtual teams: A review of current empirical research. *Human Resource Management Review, 15,* 69–95.

Hertel, G., Konradt, U., & Orlikowski, B. (2004). Managing distance by interdependence: Goal setting, task interdependence, and team-based rewards in virtual teams. *European Journal of Work and Organizational Psychology, 13,* 1–28.

Hogg, M. A., Abrams, D., Otten, S., & Hinkle, S. (2004). The social identity perspective: Intergroup relations, self-conception, and small groups. *Small Group Research, 35*(3), 246–276.

Hollingshead, A. B. (1996). Information suppression and status persistence in group decision making. *Human Communication Research, 23,* 193–219.

Hollingshead, A. B. (2004). Communication technologies, the Internet, and group research. In M. B. Brewer & M. Hewstone (Eds.), *Applied social psychology* (pp. 301–317). Malden, MA: Blackwell Publishing.

Hollingshead, A. B., McGrath, J. E., & O'Connor, K. M. (1993). Group task performance and communication technology: A longitudinal study of computer-mediated versus face-to-face work groups. *Small Group Research, 24*(3), 307–333.

House, R. J. (1977). A 1976 theory of charismatic leadership. In J. G. Hunt & L. L. Larson (Eds.), *Leadership: The cutting edge* (pp. 189–207). Carbondale: Southern Illinois University Press.

Huang, W. W., Wei, K., Watson, R. T., & Tan, B.C.Y. (2001). Supporting virtual team-building with a GSS: An empirical investigation. *Decision Support Systems, 34,* 359–367.

Jarvenpaa, S. L., Knoll, K., & Leidner, D. E. (1998). Is anybody out there? Antecedents of trust in global virtual teams. *Journal of Management and Information Systems, 14*(4), 29–64.

Johnson, D. W., & Johnson, F. P. (1987). *Joining together: Group theory and group skills* (3rd ed). Upper Saddle River, NJ: Prentice Hall.

Johnson, D. W., & Johnson, F. P. (2000). *Joining together: Group theory and group skills* (7th ed.). Needham Heights, MA: Allyn & Bacon.

Karau, S. J., & Williams, K. D. (1993). Social loafing: Research findings, implications, and future directions. *Current Directions in Psychological Science, 4,* 134–140.

Kets de Vries, M.F.K. (2005). Leadership group coaching in action: The zen of creating high performance teams. *Academy of Management Executive, 19*(1), 61–76.

Kirkman, B. L., & Mathieu, J. E. (2005). The dimensions and antecedents of team virtuality. *Journal of Management, 31*(5), 2005.

Kirkman, B. L., Rosen, B., Tesluk, P. E., & Gibson, C. B. (2004). The impact of team empowerment on virtual team performance: The moderating role of face-to-face interaction. *Academy of Management Journal, 47,* 175–192.

Kirkman, B. L., Rosen, B., Gibson, C. B., Tesluk, P. E., & McPherson, S. O. (2002). Five challenges to virtual team success: Lessons from Sabre, Inc. *Academy of Management Executive, 16*(3), 67–80.

Konradt, U., Hertel, G., & Schmook, R. (2003). Quality of management by objectives, task-related stressors, and non-task-related stressors as predictors of stress and job satisfaction among teleworkers. *European Journal of Work and Organizational Psychology, 12*(1), 61–79.

Locke, E. A., & Latham, G. P. (2002). Building a practically useful theory of goal setting and task motivation: A 35-year odyssey. *American Psychologist, 57,* 705–717.

Manz, C., & Sims, H. (1987). Leading workers to lead themselves: The external leadership of self-managing work teams. *Administrative Science Quarterly, 32,* 106–128.

Markus, M. L. (1983). *Systems in organization: Bugs and features.* San Jose, CA: Pitman.

Marron, K. (2005, February 9). Close encounters of the faceless kind. *Globe and Mail,* C1.

Martins, L. L., Gilson, L. L., & Maynard, M. T. (2004). Virtual teams: What do we know and where do we go from here? *Journal of Management, 30,* 805–835.

Maruping, L. M., & Agarwal, R. (2004). Managing team interpersonal processes through technology: A task-technology fit perspective. *Journal of Applied Psychology, 89,* 975–990.

Miller, B. C. (2004). *Quick team-building activities for busy managers.* New York: American Management Association.

Nemiro, J. E. (2003). How to effectively communicate virtually: Lessons from case studies of virtual teams. In M. M. Beyerlein, C. McGee, G. D. Klein, & J. E. Nemiro (Eds.), *The collaborative work systems fieldbook: Strategies, tools, and techniques.* San Francisco: Jossey-Bass.

Olson, J. S., & Olson, G. M. (1999). Computer supported cooperative work. In F. T. Durson, R. S. Nickerson, R. W. Schvaneveldt, S. T. Dumais, D. S. Lindsay, & M.T.H. Chi (Eds.), *Handbook of applied cognition* (pp. 409–442). Hoboken, NJ: Wiley.

Paris, C. R., Salas, E., & Cannon-Bowers, J. A. (2000). Teamwork in multi-person systems: A review and analysis. *Ergonomics, 43,* 1052–1075.

Phillips, S. L., & Elledge, R. L. (1989). *The team-building source book.* San Diego, CA: University Associates.

Qureshi, S., & Vogel, D. (2001). Adaptiveness in virtual teams: Organisational challenges and research directions. *Group Decision and Negotiation, 10,* 27–46.

Reicher, S. D., Spears, R., & Postmes, T. (1995). A social identity model of deindividuation phenomena. *European Review of Social Psychology, 6,* 161–198.

Rico, R., & Cohen, S. G. (2005). Effects of task interdependence and type of communication on performance in virtual teams. *Journal of Managerial Psychology, 20,* 261–274.

Rhoades, J. A., & O'Connor, K. M. (1996). Affect in computer-mediated and face-to-face work groups: The construction and testing of a general model. *Computer Supported Cooperative Work, 4*, 203–228.

Rosen, B., Furst, S., & Blackburn, R. (2006). Training for virtual teams: An investigation of current practices and future trends. *Human Resource Management, 45*(2), 229–247.

Saphiere, D.M.H. (1996). Productive behaviors of global business teams. *International Journal of Intercultural Relations, 20*, 227–259.

Scott, T. W., & Tiessen, P. (1999). Performance measurement and managerial teams. *Accounting, Organizations, and Society, 24*, 263–285.

Shepherd, M. M., Briggs, R. O., Reinig, B. A., Yen, J., & Nunamaker, J. F. (1996). Social comparison to improve electronic brainstorming. *Journal of MIS, 12*(3), 155–170.

Short, J., Williams, E., & Christie, B. (1976). *The social psychology of telecommunication.* Hoboken, NJ: Wiley.

Smith, M. J., Carayon, P., Sanders, K. J., Lim, S. Y., & LeGrande, D. (1992). Employee stress and health complaints in jobs with and without electronic performance monitoring. *Applied Ergonomics, 23*, 17–27.

Steuer, J. (1992). Defining virtual reality: Dimensions determining telepresence. *Journal of Communication, 42*(4), 73–93.

Straus, S. G., & McGrath, J. E. (1994). Does the medium matter? The interaction of task type and technology on group performance and member relations. *Journal of Applied Psychology, 79*, 87–97.

Thompson, L. F., & Coovert, M. D. (2003). Teamwork online: The effects of computer conferencing on perceived confusion, satisfaction, and postdiscussion accuracy. *Group Dynamics: Theory, Research, and Practice, 7*(2), 135–151.

Thompson, L. F., & Coovert, M. D. (2006). Understanding and developing virtual computer-supported cooperative work teams. In C. Bowers, E. Salas, & F. Jentsch (Eds.), *Creating high-tech teams* (pp. 213–241). Washington, DC: American Psychological Association.

Tichy, N., & Charan, R. (1989). Speed, simplicity, self-confidence: An interview with Jack Welch. *Harvard Business Review, 67*, 2–9.

Townsend, A. M., Demarie, S. M., & Hendrickson, A. R. (2001). Desktop video conferencing in virtual workgroups: Anticipation, system evaluation and performance. *Information Systems Journal, 11*, 213–227.

Van Knippenberg, D., & Ellemers, N. (2003). Social identity and group performance: Identification as the key to group-oriented effort. In S. A. Haslam, D. van Knippenberg, M. J. Platow, & N. Ellemers (Eds.), *Social identity at work: Developing theory for organizational practice* (pp. 29–42). New York: Psychology Press.

Van Knippenberg, D., van Knippenberg, B., De Cremer, D., & Hogg, M. A. (2004). Leadership, self, and identity: A review and research agenda. *Leadership Quarterly, 15*, 825–856.

Wageman, R. (1995). Interdependence and group effectiveness. *Administrative Sciences Quarterly, 40*(1), 145–180.

Wageman, R. (2001). How leaders foster self-managing team effectiveness: Design choices versus hands-on coaching. *Organizational Science, 12,* 559–577.

Wageman, R. (2003). Virtual processes: Implications for coaching the virtual team. In R. S. Peterson & E. A. Mannix (Eds.), *Leading and managing people in the dynamic organization* (pp. 65–87). Mahwah, NJ: Elrbaum.

Wageman, R., Hackman, J. R., & Lehman, E. (2004). Team Diagnostic Survey: Development of an instrument. *Journal of Applied Behavioral Science, 41*(4), 373–398.

Walther, J. B. (1992). Interpersonal effects in computer-mediated interaction: A relational perspective. *Communication Research, 19,* 52–90.

Walther, J. B. (2002). Time effects in computer-mediated groups: Past, present, and future. In P. Hinds & S. Kiesler (Eds.), *Distributed work* (pp. 235–257). Cambridge, MA: MIT Press.

Walther, J. B., & Bunz, U. (2005). The rules of virtual groups: Trust, liking, and performance in computer-mediated communication. *Journal of Communication,* 828–846.

Walther, J. B., & Burgoon, J. K. (1992). Relational communication in computer-mediated interaction. *Human Communication Research, 19,* 50–88.

Walther, J. B., & D'Addario, K. P. (2001). The impacts of emoticons on message interpretation in computer-mediated communication. *Social Science Computer Review, 19*(3), 324–347.

Walther, J. B., Loh, T., & Granka, L. (2005). Let me count the ways: The interchange of verbal and nonverbal cues in computer-mediated and face-to-face affinity. *Journal of Language and Social Psychology, 24*(1), 36–65.

Watson, C. B., Chemers, M. M., & Preiser, N. (2001). Collective efficacy: A multilevel analysis. *Personality and Social Psychology Bulletin, 27*(8), 1057–1068.

Weisband, S. P. (1992). Group discussion and first advocacy effects in computer-mediated and face-to-face decision making groups. *Organizational Behavior and Human Decision Processes, 53,* 352–380.

Weisband, S. P. (2002). Maintaining awareness in distributed team collaboration: Implications for leadership and performance. In P. Hinds & S. Kiesler (Eds.), *Distributed work* (pp. 311–333). Cambridge, MA: MIT Press.

Weisband, S. P., & Atwater, L. (1999). Evaluating self and others in electronic and face-to-face groups. *Journal of Applied Psychology, 84,* 632–639.

Wilson, M. J., Straus, S. G., & McEvily, B. (2006). All in due time: The development of trust in computer-mediated and face-to-face teams. *Organizational Behavior and Human Decision Processes, 99,* 16–33.

Zaccaro, S. J., Ardison, S. D., & Orvis, K. L. (2004). Leadership in virtual teams. In D. V. Day, S. J. Zaccaro, & S. M. Halpin (Eds.), *Leader development for transforming organizations: Growing leaders for tomorrow* (pp. 267–292). Mahwah, NJ: Erlbaum.

DESIGNING HIGH-PERFORMANCE VIRTUAL TEAMS

PART FOUR

Setting Up a Collaborative Team

High performance in virtual teams does not magically occur. Taking the time at the outset to build excellence into virtual team design and process is a crucial first step. The chapters that address setting up collaborative teams cover a range of topics: starting a virtual team, virtual meetings, generational differences among team members, decision making, and creativity within the team. Chapter Ten focuses on team composition and begins with a look at selecting members. Team membership assignments are driven by the search for expertise across the global face of the organization and often as needs arise, so systematic planning about selection may be difficult. The emphasis on content expertise means that the equally important focus on team process expertise is often overlooked—a competency of equal importance in finding members for a team where the highest levels of performance are desired.

Chapter Eleven adds another dimension to the membership challenge by pointing out that the newest generation has grown up in the high-tech world and so relates to technology in a different way than older generations do. Clients also differ by generation. This important demographic differentiator needs to be included in planning effective virtual work.

Selection of team members must be supplemented by their ongoing development. Training may be essential in building the capability of the team, but a systematic process is required to determine who needs what training. Chapter Twelve describes how that process begins with a needs assessment that can lead to alignment of training needs and training resources. An effective needs analysis depends on the expertise of the analyst and includes an assessment of the learners' characteristics.

Finally, Chapter Thirteen addresses the matching of team members to their assignments and supporting them with technology. Division of labor within the team is most effective when it maximizes task independence, so work can be done off-line and matches each team member's access to knowledge, data, and authority. The effectiveness of the team depends on the effectiveness of each member, and that begins with matching capability to assignments.

Team Composition and Member Selection

Optimizing Teams for Virtual Collaboration

Kara L. Orvis, Stephen J. Zaccaro

Teams are important in almost every organization and have been of particular interest to organizational psychologists over the past few decades. The use of teams allows consideration of expertise in multiple areas (Rouse, Cannon-Bowers, & Salas, 1992) as team members are often brought together with diverse knowledge, skills, and abilities. The greater wealth of information found in teams in comparison to any one individual member has prompted a plethora of research dedicated to understanding teams (see Kozlowski & Ilgen, 2006, for a review). Traditionally the study of teams has focused on teams whose members are located in the same place. With technological advancements in communication, greater attention has been paid to virtual teams, a configuration that allows organizations to build teams across barriers of time and space as project requirements arise.

Virtual teams have obvious benefits for organizations and their employees (Cascio, 1999; Horvath & Tobin, 2001). The most visible benefit to the organization is the accessibility of knowledgeable employees. Virtual team arrangements offer boundary-free access to information and expertise and remote participation from group members. The potential labor market is expanded as organizations are able to hire the best people regardless of where they live. Organizations achieve better use of human resources and can use outside consultants without spending large amounts of money on travel, lodging, and downtime. Dispersed teams can reduce costs and office space. In short, dispersed teams can save an organization time and travel expense and enable better access to experts.

Employees also benefit from the use of dispersed teams. Organizations are better able to accommodate personal and professional lives. Dynamic team membership allows people to move from one project to another over time and space without having to relocate their families. It is also easier for employees to participate in multiple coexisting teams. Finally, individual employees can have increased job flexibility and independence. Accordingly, virtual and dispersed teams have become a popular way of getting work accomplished in organizations. In response, researchers in several fields have become particularly interested in the processes and performance of these types of teams.

The majority of the research on virtual teams has focused on the effectiveness of virtual team processes and performance (see, for example, Baltes, Dickson, Sherman, Bauer, & LaGanke, 2002; Benbasat & Lim, 1993; Hwang, 1998; McLeod, 1992; Webber, 2002). Research has compared virtual and face-to-face teams on several process and outcome criteria, including performance, time to complete tasks, team member satisfaction, and communication. Research examining the performance discrepancies between these two types of teams has produced mixed results. Several studies have found no performance discrepancies between virtual and face-to-face teams (Chidambaram & Jones, 1993; Gallupe & McKeen, 1990; Hiltz, Johnson, & Turoff, 1986; Hollingshead, 1996b), and other studies have found that virtual teams perform less effectively than their colocated counterparts (Baltes et al., 2002; Dennis & Wixom, 2002; Hollingshead, 1996a; Webber, 2002).

Virtual teams differ from colocated teams on several other important outcomes. Specifically, researchers have reported that members of virtual teams communicate less frequently (Hiltz et al., 1986; Kiesler, Zubrow, Moses, & Geller, 1985; McGuire, Kiesler, & Siegel, 1987; Siegel, Dubrovsky, Kiesler, & McGuire,

1986; Webber, 2002), exhibit lower-quality communication (Webber, 2002), take longer to complete tasks (Baltes et al., 2002; Benbasat & Lim, 1993; Gallupe & McKeen, 1990; Hiltz et al., 1986; Kiesler, Siegel, & McGuire, 1984; McGuire et al., 1987; Siegel et al., 1986; Webber, 2002; Weisband, 1992), and report less satisfaction (Baltes et al., 2002; Benbasat & Lim, 1993; Hwang, 1998; McLeod, 1992) than face-to-face teams.

Researchers have also explored several moderators of virtual team outcomes, including anonymity, familiarity, synchronicity of communication, time limits, group size, and task type (Baltes et al., 2002; Benbasat & Lim, 1993; Chidambaram, 1996; Dennis & Wixom, 2002; Gallupe et al., 1988; Hwang, 1998; Mennecke, Valacich, & Wheeler, 2000; Siegel et al., 1986; Webber, 2002). However, researchers have largely ignored the key variable of member composition as an important driver of virtual team performance. Indeed, as we noted, the ability to construct teams from a geographically wider pool of potential members rapidly represents a particular strength of such teams over colocated teams. As such, the process and products of composing virtual teams should be especially influential in determining their degree of effectiveness.

Traditionally teams have been staffed by matching individual demographic characteristics (training, rank, experience) to generically functional roles and known project requirements (Klimoski & Jones, 1995; Klimoski & Zukin, 1999). However, little research or practical attention has been directed at evaluating the efficacy of particular staffing strategies or determining how well team members selected under certain strategies actually work together effectively as a team on given projects and within specific mission parameters. Team composition should reflect the full range of performance requirements posed by both the team task itself and the collaborative quality of teamwork (task work and teamwork skills; Cannon-Bowers, Tannenbaum, Salas, & Volpe, 1995; Klimoski & Zukin, 1999; Morgan & Lassiter, 1992; Salas, Burke, & Cannon-Bowers, 2002). A team staffing strategy should also reflect the most effective means of matching available human capital with the full range of requisite task work and teamwork skills demanded by the team's mission. While traditional staffing strategies have considered task work requirements, few, if any, have similarly acknowledged teamwork needs (Klimoski & Jones, 1995; Klimoski & Zukin, 1999).

At the core of any team are individuals who "interact independently in order to accomplish mission goals" (Morgan, Glickman, Woodard, Blaiwes, & Salas,

1986, p. 3). Each individual brings characteristics that influence the ability of the team to reach its task-related goal, in addition to characteristics that can both enhance and detract from the team's internal states and processes—in other words, characteristics that influence how the individuals will work together as a team. In line with other researchers (Klimoski & Jones, 1995; Klimoski & Zukin, 1999; Morgan & Lassiter, 1992), we propose that team staffing strategies should consider two critical questions:

1. Are the skills required for the team's task represented in those members selected?

2. Are the skills necessary for effective collaboration and interaction represented in those members selected?

As we have noted, many team designs fulfill the first requirement but not the second, especially for virtual teams whose members are often brought together because the relevant task-related expertise is not available locally. As such, the emphasis in staffing such teams tends to be much more on identifying task experts rather than individuals who can also work together well as a team. Such a limited staffing strategy represents a significant mistake, especially for virtual teams, where geographical dispersion can increase the challenge of engaging effectively in collaboration (Webber, 2002).

This chapter offers a team-staffing framework to support the selection of effective members of virtual and dispersed teams by considering the criticality of both expertise and teamwork.

TEAM STAFFING STRATEGY

The criterion for a successful team staffing strategy would be if an individual in charge of staffing a team for emergent projects and tasks builds one whose members have the right expertise and are likely to work together well. Athans (1982) refers to such an aggregation as an "expert team of experts." We propose a team staffing strategy that, when a project arises and requires the formation of a new team, directs managers to consider both the expertise needed for task attainment and skills needed for proper team functioning. The team staffing strategy has four steps: (1) identify the mission requirements and skill requirements; (2) select potential candidates for team members based on their status on task and team generic skill markers; (3) identify the specific task work skills needed; and (4) determine the appropriate mix of members based on their specific team skills (Cannon-Bowers et al., 1995; Klimoski & Jones, 1995; Klimoksi & Zukin, 1999).

A Framework for Team Staffing and Team Performance

The team staffing strategy we propose emerged from a conceptual framework that adheres to a basic input-process-output model of team effectiveness (Hackman & Morris, 1975; McGrath, 1964) (Figure 10.1), which asserts that team states (such as cohesion and trust) and team processes (such as how team members back each other up and deal with conflict) directly influence team performance. Furthermore, these team states and processes are directly dependent on staffing decisions, particularly with regard to the selection of individuals having what Cannon-Bowers et al. (1995) call task and teamwork skills that are either generic across most team tasks or specific to particular tasks and missions assigned to the team (see also Morgan & Lassiter, 1992). We discuss these different categories of skills in more detail below. Finally, our model specifies the importance of contextual mission and team variables such as team life span, team size, and interdependency of individual tasks that moderate the need for various individual-level skills such as specific task work skills and team-level attributes such as requirements for cohesion.

According to Hackman and Morris (1975), team performance is dependent on the individual capabilities of team members and how those members interact with each other. Their input-process-outcome framework, which ours is based on, proposes that processes and states are the mediating means linking team input variables (for example, characteristics of team members) to team performance outcomes. They argue that inputs brought to the team include individual, team, and organizational and environmental characteristics. Processes include team members' interaction, communication, and coordination behaviors. Marks, Mathieu, and Zaccaro (2001) identified three superordinate categories of team processes: transition processes, action processes, and interpersonal processes. Transition processes include mission analysis, goal specification, and strategy formulation and planning. Such processes are relevant to reflecting on past performance and preparing for future action. Action processes include systems analysis, monitoring progress toward goals,

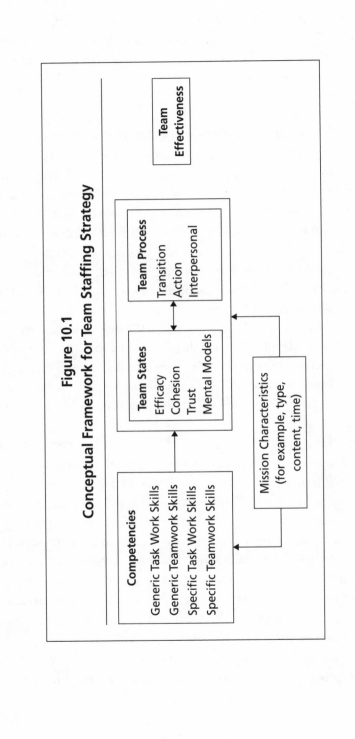

Figure 10.1
Conceptual Framework for Team Staffing Strategy

backup behaviors, and team coordination. They are more likely to occur when teams are acting in ways that contribute directly to goal accomplishment. Interpersonal processes include conflict management, motivating/confidence building, and affect management.

In addition to describing the nature of member interaction, Marks et al. (2001) described team emergent states, which reflect crucial proximal products and precursors of team interactions. Emergent states are defined as "properties of the team that are typically dynamic in nature and vary as a function of team context, inputs, processes, and outcomes" (Marks et al., 2001, p. 357). Accordingly they represent shared cognitive, motivational, and affective properties of teams. Team states include constructs such as mental models, trust, cohesion, and collective efficacy, all influenced by individual attributes of team members, particularly early in the team's life span. We would argue that these emergent states can represent markers of effective team staffing strategies.

Mental Models   Mental models are cognitive representations of the ways people structure and organize their knowledge to help with information processing (Rouse & Morris, 1986). Researchers have identified many different types of mental models. Most vary with regard to the content of the model (Klimoski & Mohammed, 1994). In a team environment, these models may include knowledge about the purpose of the team, member characteristics, linkages among team members, collective actions, and roles of team members (Cannon-Bowers, Salas, & Converse, 1993; Klimoski & Mohammed, 1994). These mental models can be very different or very similar among team members. Similarity between members' mental models represents sharedness or common understanding of the team and its members, the purpose of the team and its missions, and coordination requirements among members (Cannon-Bowers et al., 1993). Such sharedness represents an important determinant of team performance: when knowledge is shared, team members are able to anticipate the behavior of other team members and improve the communication and processing required for successful team performance and coordination (Klimoski & Mohammed, 1994; Kraiger and Wenzel, 1997; Cannon-Bowers et al., 1993; Rentsch, Heffner, & Duffy, 1994; Volpe, Cannon-Bowers, & Duffy, 1996; Koles, 2001). Accordingly, one index of a successful team staffing strategy should be the degree and rapidity with which members subsequently form shared accurate mental models.

Trust *Trust* is a theoretical construct in psychology most commonly viewed as "an expression of confidence between the parties in an exchange of some kind—confidence that they will not be harmed or put at risk by the actions of the other party" (Jones & George, 1998, p. 531). Basically trust means that people have expectations of others' behaviors and use these expectations to manage uncertainty or risk and allow themselves to interact cooperatively (Jones & George, 1998). Trust has been linked to cooperative behavior among individuals, groups, and organizations (Jones & George, 1998; Mayer, Davis, & Shoorman, 1995; McAllister, 1995) and is directly influenced by the values, attitudes, and moods and emotions of people (Jones & George, 1998). The opinions people form about team members are likely to influence their trust in those members.

The importance of trust for effective team processes and performance makes it another important criterion for the effectiveness of team staffing strategies, especially for distributed or virtual teams. Indeed, many researchers have noted the problems with developing trust in dispersed environments without any face-to-face contact (Handy, 1995; Nohria & Eccles, 1992; O'Hara-Devereaux & Johansen, 1994). For example, Daft and Lengel (1986) suggested that the lack of richness in communicating through technology inhibits the development of trust. In addition, social information sharing, an important ingredient for trust development, is often limited in dispersed teams, which tend to focus more on task information, especially when they have limited time (Lebie, Rhoades, & McGrath 1996). Thus, in dispersed teams, where tenure is short and people are dispersed, certain forms of trust are difficult to achieve; accordingly greater attention should be directed to initial team staffing, with the success of such staffing defined by how rapidly trust forms among selected members.

Cohesion In the past, cohesion has most commonly been defined as "member attraction to the group" (Evans & Jarvis, 1980, p. 360). Cohesion has been shown to be positively related to group performance (Vinokur-Kaplan, 1995; Mullen, Anthony, Salas, & Driskell, 1993; Evans & Dion, 1991; Mullen & Copper, 1994), especially for groups with high interdependence and when constructs were measured at the group level of analysis (Gully, Devine, & Whitney, 1995). Researchers have made a distinction between interpersonal (social) cohesion and task cohesion. Task cohesion is defined as a group's shared commitment or attraction to the group task or goal (Hackman, 1976). Interpersonal cohesion is defined as the group members' attraction to or liking of the group (Evans & Jarvis, 1980).

Researchers have speculated that geographical dispersion of the members influences the formation of social cohesion (Orvis, 2004). There is very little sharing of personal information in dispersed team environments, and teams have a tendency to focus primarily on the task in their interactions. Dispersed teams are less likely to know and feel positive toward their teammates (Weisband & Atwater, 1999). In addition, there is likely to be more diversity between teammates and therefore more personal information to be shared (Cramton & Orvis, 2003). Unfortunately, sharing of information is even more important in these teams, and dispersed team members are even less likely to share information than colocated team members (Cramton & Orvis, 2003). In addition, people do not have a chance to observe information from what someone looks like or how they behave. Therefore, social cohesion will likely be low in these types of teams. Team staffing strategies that emphasize teamwork skills may promote greater or faster development of social cohesion. If this is so, then the strength of such cohesion among selected members can serve as another indicator of the effectiveness of these strategies.

Collective Efficacy *Collective efficacy* reflects team members' beliefs that together they can accomplish the specific tasks necessary for successful team performance (Bandura, 1986). Because our focus is on staffing for particular team missions, we have chosen to focus here on the team efficacy beliefs rather than on the more generic collective competency beliefs defined as group potency (Guzzo, 1986; Shea & Guzzo, 1987). However, as teams are staffed in anticipation of multiple and qualitatively different missions, these more general beliefs may become more important. Few studies have examined the influence of team member dispersion on collective efficacy or group potency. However, studies have demonstrated that collective efficacy is predictive of both team performance (Koles, 2001; Marks, 1999; Mulvey & Klein, 1998) and team processes (Marks, 1999). Accordingly, the effectiveness of team staffing strategies may be seen in the level of collective competency beliefs among selected members. Indeed, we would argue that such efficacy beliefs may be the most immediate emergent state from initial interactions among members, as they become aware of each other's competencies relative to task and teamwork requirements.

STEPS IN A TEAM STAFFING STRATEGY

We defined four fundamental steps in team staffing. This model is similar to other team staffing models (Klimoski & Zukin, 1999) in that member selection is grounded first in identifying task and teamwork requirements and then in matching member skills to those requirements. However, we also argue that staffing should focus initially on selecting a potential membership pool based first on generic task skills and then on generic teamwork skills. Then we argue that the best mix of members should be identified using specific task work skills, followed by specific teamwork skills.

Step 1: Identify Mission and Skill Requirements

When choosing individuals to staff a team, the goal is to promote appropriate levels of team states and processes. Task parameters associated with the emerging projects are likely to influence the need for various personnel capabilities in teams; for example, virtual teamwork may require greater emphasis on certain communication skills, or a short time frame for mission completion may require greater familiarity among team members. Contextual mission and team variables such as team life span, team size, and interdependency of individual tasks will also moderate the need for various individual-level skills such as specific task work skills and team-level attributes such as requirements for cohesion. Therefore, project parameters that are likely to influence staffing and composition decisions must be identified before choosing individual members (Klimoski & Zukin, 1999).

Many aspects of the team task may influence the need for various team states, team processes, and individual skills. The purpose of this chapter is not to list all of those or to describe the steps in a team task analysis (for more information, see Bowers, Baker, & Salas, 1994; Klimoski & Zukin, 1999; Salas et al., 2002), but rather to stress the importance of considering task and team requirements before selecting team members. Such consideration includes identifying factors that influence the selection of both the expertise and individuals who are likely to have the needed team states and processes. The specification of skills for team staffing requirements needs to be grounded in the type of task assigned to the team (Klimoski & Zukin, 1999). At one level, this process refers to the obvious task and knowledge requirements. However, at another level, consideration of such parameters as task interdependence would place more (or less) weight on certain teamwork skills. Team decision tasks may also require more skills in decision making, conflict resolution, and communication than team tasks requiring psychomotor coordination. Other tasks that concern particularly sensitive issues may require certain homogeneous attitudes and values among team members (Klimoski & Jones, 1995). Thus, the specification of skills, particularly task-specific and team-specific competencies, need, to be driven clearly by the qualitative nature of the task.

At the completion of this step, the hiring manager should have a list of task parameters important for making team staffing decisions.

Step 2: Select Members Based on Task and Team Generic Skill Markers

After the missions and parameters have been identified, the next step is for the staffing manager to identify the specific and generic task work and teamwork competencies to consider in team composition. The competencies needed come directly from the team task analysis conducted in step one. The goal of step two is to identify a possible pool of team members based on the generic skills needed for team effectiveness. *Generic task work skills* refer to the individual capabilities that enhance one's ability to act effectively in broadly defined performance task domains (Cannon-Bowers et al., 1995). Accordingly, such skills are "transportable" (Cannon-Bowers et al., 1995, p. 337) across teams and performance domains. For example, when an applied research consulting organization staffs a proposal team, all team members would be required to possess a similar set of basic skills, such as writing skills, some statistical and mathematical background, and general research methods training. Furthermore, these skills are likely to apply to most tasks assigned to teams in this organization. Generic task work skills, then, are the set of skills that need to be held by most, if not all, of the members of a team. Thus, on these skills, team composition needs to reflect a relative homogeneity.

Typically the manager who is staffing a team will be able to pull from a pool of human resources. Therefore, the first cutoff for consideration of team membership should be whether potential team members have the appropriate level of generic task work skills as driven by the task requirements.

Generic teamwork skills refer to the capabilities to work effectively in any generic team environment, regardless of the task (Cannon-Bowers et al., 1995).

The possession of such skills should be a second factor to weigh when considering individuals for team membership. Teamwork skills reflect fundamental requirements for collaboration and integrated action on team tasks. Accordingly, they are also transportable across most, if not all, team performance domains. For example when staffing a scientific proposal team, all team members should possess basic communication skills, collaboration and coordination skills, generic leadership expertise, a preference for working in teams, dependability, trustworthiness, team performance regulation, knowledge of organizational climate and politics, and boundary-spanning skills. Thus, as with generic task work skills, generic teamwork skills should be distributed homogeneously among selected team members.

Step 3: Identify Specific Task Work Skills

Once steps one and two have been completed, the hiring manager should be left with a pool of people who have the skills for completing most generic team task requirements and doing so collaboratively. Steps three and four refer to identifying the optimal mix of those individuals. Our proposed team staffing strategy suggests that the hiring manager should first find the right mix of individuals based on the expertise needed for the task.

Specific task work skills refer to task capabilities necessary to complete all of the performance requirements for a particular task or project (Cannon-Bowers et al., 1995). For example, a team writing a proposal for a computer-based training project might require a number of specific skills and knowledge sets, such as mathematics, software programming, organizational and human factors psychology, and computer interface design. Thus, in our proposal example, team members share skills in research and writing (generic task work skills), and each individual would need to bring a separate set of specific areas of expertise to the overall project, dictated by mission requirements. Different team members have different levels of different skills, but the team as a whole would possess all required task work skills. For another example, a surgical team may need an anesthesiologist, a nurse, and a surgeon. Everyone on the team does not need to be a surgeon, but each team member should contribute unique valuable skills to team task accomplishment. Unlike generic skills, heterogeneity of variance is likely the preferred selection team staffing criterion for specific task skills. At the end of this step, the hiring manager should have a list of potential candidate teams based on specific task-related expertise.

Step 4: Determine Appropriate Mix of Team Skills

Once the potential mix of experts has been identified for each team, the final step is to optimize those teams by considering members' teamwork skills and other attributes that will contribute to appropriate team states and functioning (Klimoski & Jones, 1995; Klimoski & Zukin, 1999). *Specific teamwork skills* refer to the mix of attitudes, personality, and values that would optimize teamwork effectiveness and group cohesion among a particular set of individuals working within particular contexts (Cannon-Bowers et al., 1995). Klimoski and Jones (1995) note that "creating the right mix can also mean controlling for those factors that count for interpersonal compatibility. Thus, establishing team requirements . . . would involve the issue of just what personality, style, or values congruence would be necessary" (p. 312). Cannon-Bowers et al. (1995) suggest that these skills refer to knowledge of specific team members and their preferences and characteristics, and team cohesion, which can be interpreted as the strength of the unique bonds or connections among individuals. Examples include knowledge of potential team members, positive experiences with potential team members, particular leadership skills, team-building skills, collective information processing and idea generation skills, and conflict management skills.

For example, in the case of constructing a scientific proposal team, the person in charge of staffing may want to choose members who have the required generic teamwork and task work skills, the right mix of specific task work skills, and strong bonds of familiarity (perhaps by having worked together in the past). If the personnel pool does not allow choice of members who are familiar with one another, then the goal would be to select the right mix of individual characteristics that would predict efficient teamwork. For example, unfamiliar team members would require a leader who could build functionally diverse teams. Or individuals could be matched according to their personality variables or outside interests.

FINAL THOUGHTS

This chapter suggests a team staffing framework that can be used to staff teams that have the right expertise to do the job and that maximizes the likelihood that those experts will work together well as a team. We have outlined four steps in a framework that is based on first selecting generic task and teamwork requirements, followed by more specific task and teamwork competencies. Table 10.1 summarizes these levels of competencies and illustrates them in an applied social

Table 10.1
Example Knowledge and Skills Matrix

Levels of Competencies	Consulting Organization Example
Generic task knowledge and skills: These pertain to the task capabilities to act effectively in the prototypical broad missions of the team or its organization. These are competencies that are relevant for the full range of all possible missions assigned to the team. Most, if not all, of the team members need to possess these competencies. They are transportable across most, if not all, team and organizational missions.	Measurement skills Evaluation and analysis skills Basic technology skills Knowledge of military performance domains Problem-solving skills Project management skills
Generic teamwork knowledge and skills: These refer to the capabilities shared by all team members to work effectively together. The knowledge and skills reflect require-ments for collaboration and integrated action on team tasks. They are transportable across most, if not all, the teams the members might work on within the organization.	Communication skills Collaboration and coordination skills Generic leadership expertise Preference for working in teams Dependability, trustworthiness Team performance regulation Knowledge of organizational climate and politics Boundary-spanning skills
Specific task work knowledge and skills: These skills refer to the particular task capabilities necessary to complete all of the performance requirements for a specific task or project. These skills would be derived from particular mission requirements. Different team members would likely have different levels of different skills, but the team as a whole would possess all required task work skills.	Functional expertise Specific research and methodological expertise Specific technology expertise Knowledge of client context
Specific teamwork knowledge and skills: These skills refer to the mix of attitudes, personality, and values that would optimize teamwork effectiveness and group cohesion among a particular set of individuals working within particular contexts.	Knowledge of potential team members; positive experiences with potential team members Particular leadership skill Team-building skills Collective information processing and idea generation skills Conflict management skills

Source: Levels of confidence adapted from Cannon-Bowers et al. (1995).

science research organization. Also, the importance of these competencies is likely to vary according to a range of team and task parameters. Table 10.2 summarizes some of these parameters with suggestions about which competencies would likely gain or lose weight in each context.

Table 10.2
Example of Need for Skills Based on Mission Parameters

Team Parameter	Level of Parameter	
	High	Low
Geographical dispersion	Communication skills	Preference for working in teams
	Collaboration and coordination skills	
	Dependability and trustworthiness	
	Leaderships skills in direction setting and structuring	
Functional diversity	Conflict management skills	Boundary-spanning skills
	Collective information-processing and idea generation skills	
	Knowledge of and positive experiences with potential team members	
	Leaderships skills in direction setting and structuring	
Prior history of collaboration	Participative management skills	Team-building skills
		Team performance regulation
		Leaderships skills in direction setting and structuring

A team staffing strategy such as the one outlined here represents a particularly important requirement for virtual teams because they are usually composed quickly with a focus on leveraging expertise across barriers of time and space. People staffing these teams may have a tendency to focus more on task-related expertise and less on whether those experts will work together well. A simple process such as the one outlined here should help ensure that managers make the most of their virtual team staffing decisions, creating teams that can hit the ground running.

REMINDERS

- Virtual teams are often formed to respond to emerging tasks that require special expertise outside the organization.

- Virtual staffing decisions are often focused on finding the right experts, not on finding experts who are likely to work together well as a team.

- When staffing teams, it is good to analyze the task for requirements at both the individual and team levels.

- Selecting team members based on their generic and specific task work and teamwork skills is more likely to lead to high performance.

References

Athans, M. (1982). The expert team of experts approach to command-and-control (C2) organizations. *IEEE Control Systems Magazine, 2*(3), 30–38.

Baltes, B. B., Dickson, M. W., Sherman, M. P., Bauer, C. C., & LaGanke, J. S. (2002). Computer-mediated communication and group decision making: A meta-analysis. *Organizational Behavior and Human Decision Processes, 87*(1), 156–179.

Bandura, A. (1986). *Social foundations of through and action: A cognitive theory.* Englewood Cliffs, NJ: Prentice-Hall.

Benbasat, I., & Lim, L. H. (1993). The effects of group, task, context, and technology variables on the usefulness of group support systems: A meta-analysis of experimental studies. *Small Group Research, 24*(4), 430–462.

Bowers, C. A., Baker, D. P., & Salas, E. (1994). Measuring the importance of teamwork: The reliability and validity of job/task analysis indices for team-training design. *Military Psychology, 6,* 205–214.

Cannon-Bowers, J. A., Salas E., & Converse, S. (1993). Shared mental models in expert team decision making. In N. J. Castellan Jr. (Ed.), *Current issues in individual and group decision making* (pp. 221–246). Hillsdale, NJ: Lawrence Erlbaum.

Cannon-Bowers, J. A., Tannenbaum, S. I., Salas, E., & Volpe, C. E. (1995). Defining competencies and establishing team training requirements. In R. A. Guzzo & E. Salas (Eds.), *Team effectiveness and decision making in organizations* (pp. 333–380). San Francisco: Jossey-Bass.

Cascio, W. F. (1999). Virtual workplaces: Implications for organizational behavior. In C.L. Cooper & D. M. Rousseau (Eds.), *Trends in organizational behavior* (Vol. 6, pp. 1–14). Chichester, UK: John Wiley & Sons.

Chidambaram, L. (1996). Relational development in computer-supported groups. *MIS Quarterly, 20*(2), 143–163.

Chidambaram, L., & Jones, B. (1993). Impact of communication medium and computer support on group perceptions and performance: A comparison of face-to-face and dispersed meetings. *MIS Quarterly, 17*(4), 465–491.

Cramton, C. D., & Orvis, K. L. (2003). Overcoming barriers to information sharing in virtual teams. In C. Gibson & S. Cohen (Eds.), *Creating conditions for effective virtual teams* (pp. 214–230). San Francisco: Jossey-Bass.

Daft, R., & Lengel, R. (1986). Organizational information requirements, media richness, and structural design. *Management Science, 32*, 554–572.

Dennis, A. R., & Wixom, B. H. (2002). Investigating the moderators of the group support systems use with meta-analysis. *Journal of Management Information Systems, 18*(3), 235–257.

Evans, C. R., & Dion, K. L. (1991). Group cohesion and performance: A meta-analysis. *Small Group Research, 22*, 175–186.

Evans, C. R., & Jarvis, P. A. (1980). Group cohesion: A review and re-evaluation. *Small Group Behavior, 11*, 359–370.

Gallupe, R. B., & McKeen, J. D. (1990). Enhancing computer-mediated communication: An experimental investigation into the use of a group decision support system for face-to-face versus remote meetings. *Information and Management, 18*, 1–13.

Gully, S. M., Devine, D. S., & Whitney, D. J. (1995). A meta-analysis of cohesion and performance: Effects of level of analysis and task interdependence. *Small Group Research, 26*(4), 497–520.

Guzzo, R. A. (1986). Group decision making and group effectiveness in organizations. In P. Goodman (Ed.), *Designing effective work groups* (pp. 34–71). San Francisco: Jossey-Bass.

Hackman, J. R. (1976). Group influences on individuals. In M. Dunnette (Ed.), *Handbook of industrial organizational psychology* (pp. 1455–1526). Chicago: Rand McNally.

Hackman, J. R., & Morris, C. G. (1975). Group tasks, group interaction processes, and group performance effectiveness: A review and proposed integration. In L. Berkowitz (Ed.), *Advances in experimental social psychology* (Vol. 8). Orlando, FL: Academic Press.

Handy, C. (1995). Trust and the virtual organization. *Harvard Business Review, 73*(3), 40–50.

Hiltz, S. R., Johnson, K., & Turoff, M. (1986). Experiments in group decision making: Communication process and outcome in face-to-face versus computerized conferences. *Human Communication Research, 13*, 225–252.

Hollingshead, A. B. (1996a). Information suppression and status persistence in group decision making: The effects of communication media. *Human Communication Research, 23*(2), 193–219.

Hollingshead, A. B. (1996b). The rank-order effect in group decision making. *Organizational Behavior and Human Decision Processes, 68*(3), 181–193.

Horvath, L., & Tobin, T. J. (2001). Twenty-first century teamwork: Defining competencies for virtual teams. In M. M. Beyerlein & D. A. Johnson (Eds.), *Virtual teams: Advances in interdisciplinary studies of work teams* (pp. 239–258). New York: Elsevier Science/JAI Press.

Hwang, M. (1998). Did task type matter in the use of decision room GSS? A critical review and a meta-analysis. *Omega, 26*(1), 1–15.

Jones, G. R., & George, J. M. (1998). The experience and evolution of trust: Implications for cooperation and teamwork. *Academy of Management Review, 23*, 531–546.

Kiesler, S., Siegel, J., & McGuire, T. W. (1984). Social psychological-aspects of computer-mediated communication. *American Psychologist, 39*(10), 1123–1134.

Kiesler, S., Zubrow, D., Moses, A. M., & Geller, V. (1985). Affect in computer-mediated communication: An experiment in synchronous terminal-to-terminal discussion. *Human Computer Interaction, 1*(1), 77–104.

Klimoski, R., & Jones, R. G. (1995). Staffing for effective group decision making: Key issues in matching people and task. In R. A. Guzzo & E. Salas (Eds.), *Team effectiveness and decision making in organizations* (pp. 292–332). San Francisco: Jossey-Bass.

Klimoski, R., & Mohammed, S. (1994). Team mental model: Construct or metaphor? *Journal of Management, 20*(2), 403–437.

Klimoski, R., & Zukin, L. (1999). Selection and staffing for team effectiveness. In E. Sundstrom & Associates (Eds.), *Supporting work team effectiveness: Best management practices for fostering high performance.* San Francisco: Jossey-Bass.

Koles, K. L. (2001). *The impact of feedback induced self-attention on antecedents of team performance.* (Doctoral dissertation, George Mason University). Dissertation Abstracts International: Section B: the Sciences & Engineering, Vol. 62(2-B), 1127, US: Univ. Microfilms International.

Kozlowski, S.W.J., & Ilgen, D. R. (2006). Enhancing the effectiveness of work groups and teams. *Psychological Science in the Public Interest, 7*, 77–124.

Kraiger, K., & Wenzel, L. H. (1997). Conceptual development and empirical evaluation of measures of shared mental models as indicators of team effectiveness. In M. T. Brannick, E. Salas, & C. Prince (Eds.), *Team performance assessment and measurement* (pp. 63–84). Mahwah, NJ: Lawrence Erlbaum.

Lebie, L., Rhoades, J. A., & McGrath, J. E. (1996). Interaction process in computer-mediated and face-to-face groups. *Computer Supported Cooperative Work, 4*, 127–152.

Marks, M. A. (1999). A test of the impact of collective efficacy in routine and novel performance environments. *Human Performance, 12*(3–4), 295–309.

Marks, M. A., Mathieu, J., & Zaccaro, S. J. (2001). A temporally based framework and taxonomy of team processes. *Academy of Management Review, 26,* 356–376.

Mayer, R. C., Davis, J. H., & Schoorman, F. D. (1995). An integrative model of organizational trust. *Academy of Management Review, 20*(3), 709–734.

McAllister, D. J. (1995). Affect- and cognition-based trust as foundations for interpersonal cooperation in organizations. *Academy of Management Journal, 38*(1), 24–59.

McGrath, J. E. (1964). *Social psychology: A brief introduction.* New York: Holt.

McGuire, T. W., Kiesler, S., & Siegel, J. (1987). Group and computer-mediated discussion effects in risk decision making. *Journal of Personality and Social Psychology, 52*(5), 917–930.

McLeod, P. L. (1992). An assessment of the experimental literature on electronic group work: Results of a meta-analysis. *Human-Computer Interaction, 7,* 257–280.

Mennecke, J. S., Valacich, J. S., & Wheeler, B. C. (2000). The effects of media and task on user performance: A test of the task-media fit hypotheses. *Group Decision and Negotiation, 9*(6), 507–529.

Morgan, B. B., Glickman, A. S., Woodard, E. A., Blaiwes, A. S., & Salas, E. (1986). *Measurement of team behaviors in a Navy environment* (Tech. Report No. NTSC TR-86–014). Orlando, FL: Naval Training Systems Center.

Morgan, B. B., & Lassiter, D. L. (1992). Team composition and staffing. In R. Sweezy & E. Salas (Ed.), *Teams: Their training and performance* (pp. 75–100). Norwood, MA: Kluwer.

Mullen, B., Anthony, T., Salas, E., & Driskell, J. E. (1993). Group cohesiveness and quality of decision making: An integration of test of the groupthink hypothesis. *Small Group Research, 25*(2), 189–204.

Mullen, B., & Copper, C. (1994). The relation between group cohesiveness and performance: An integration. *Psychological Bulletin, 115,* 210–227.

Mulvey, P. W., & Klein, H. J. (1998). The impact of perceived loafing and collective efficacy in group goal processes and group performance. *Organizational Behavior & Human Decision Processes, 74*(1), 62–87.

Nohria, N., & Eccles, R. G. (1992). Face-to-face: Managing network organizations work. In N. Nohria and R. G. Eccles (Eds.), *Networks and organizations* (pp. 288–308). Boston: Harvard Business School Press.

O'Hara-Devereaux, M., & Johansen, R. (1994). *Global work: Bridging distance, culture, and time.* San Francisco: Jossey-Bass.

Orvis, K. L. (2004). *Leadership and team performance in collocated and distributed teams.* Doctoral dissertation, George Mason University. Dissertations Abstracts International.

Rentsch, J. R., Heffner, T. S., & Duffy, L. T. (1994). What you know is what you get from experience. *Group and Organization Management, 19*(4), 450–474.

Rouse, W. B., Cannon-Bowers, J. A., & Salas, E. (1992). The role of mental models in team performance in complex systems. *IEEE: Transactions on Systems, Man, and Cybernetics, 22,* 1296–1308.

Rouse, W. B., & Morris, N. M. (1986). On looking into the black box: Prospects and limits in the search for mental models. *Psychological Bulletin, 100,* 350–363.

Salas, E., Burke, C. S., & Cannon-Bowers, J. A. (2002). What we know about designing and delivering team training. In K. Kraiger (Ed.), *Creating, implementing, and managing effective training and development: State-of-the-art lessons for practice* (pp. 234–259). San Francisco: Jossey-Bass.

Shea, G. P., & Guzzo, R. A. (1987). Group effectiveness: What really matters? *Sloan Management Review, 3,* 25–31.

Siegel, J., Dubrovsky, V., Kiesler, S., & McGuire, T. W. (1986). Group processes in computer-mediated communication. *Organizational Behavior and Human Decision Processes, 37*(2), 157–187.

Vinokur-Kaplan, D. (1995). Treatment teams that work (and those that don't): An application of Hackman's group effectiveness models to interdisciplinary teams in psychiatric hospitals. *Journal of Applied Behavioral Science, 31*(3), 303–327.

Volpe, C. E., Cannon-Bowers, J. A., & Spector, P. E. (1996). The impact of cross-training on team functioning: An empirical analysis of the group mind. In B. Mullen & G. R. Goethals (Eds.), *Theories of group behavior* (pp. 185–208). New York: Springer-Verlag.

Webber, S. S. (2002). *Virtual teams: A meta-analysis.* Paper presented at the Academy of Management Conference, Denver, CO.

Weisband, S. (1992). Group discussion and first advocacy effects in computer-mediated and face-to-face decision making groups. *Organizational Behavior and Human Decision Processes, 53,* 352–380.

Weisband, S., & Atwater, L. (1999). Evaluating self and others in electronic and face-to-face groups. *Journal of Applied Psychology 84*(4), 632–639.

Generational Differences in Virtual Teams

Emanuel Brady, Lori Bradley

Developments in computer and information technologies are occurring at an unprecedented rate, and technology has become a fundamental component of most people's work. At the same time that we are experiencing explosive developments in technology, the U.S. population is aging. In 2003, 35 million people in the United States, or approximately 13 percent of the population, were over the age of sixty-five. This number is expected to increase to approximately 71 million by the year 2030 and will represent 20 percent of the U.S. population. For those over age eighty-five, there will also be a dramatic increase—from about 4 million in 2000 to nearly 21 million by 2050 (Czaja, 2006).

For the first time in our history, as many as four different generations are working side by side in companies across America. This mixing of generations can become a huge competitive advantage and add valuable diversity to our organizations. It can also be a source of potential conflict, complication, and challenge as workers from different generations work together (Burke, 2004).

This chapter provides an overview of some of the most common types of technology adoption challenges as they relate to the generational makeup of the workforce. It then proposes an approach for deployment planning that is better informed and therefore more useful to technology deployment managers and those supporting virtual collaboration in a generationally diverse workplace. The chapter describes various aspects of generational differences as they relate to the workplace and uses *generation* as a proxy for *group* to assess, in a systemic way, the opportunity for change.

FOUR GENERATIONS AT WORK

Generations are grouped into four categories or cohorts based on experiences and values common to each. There is only general agreement among theorists on the appropriate definition (including the years that establish the boundaries) of each generation. In general, and for the purposes of this discussion, the generations will be defined in the following way.

- The veterans, or World War II generation, were born before 1945. They came of age during the Great Depression and the war—experiences that had a lasting impact on their development and worldviews.

- The baby boomers (born between 1946 and 1964) grew up in a time of much more prosperity. The formative events for baby boomers included the Vietnam War and Watergate.

- Generation X refers to those born between 1965 and 1980. This group was raised on technology. Everything from televisions, video games, microwave ovens, and videocassette recorders to personal computers became commonplace early in their lifetime.

- The Nexters (sometimes referred to as Generation Y or millennials) were born between 1980 and 2000 and are starting their professional lives. They are just beginning to emerge with another unique generational personality (Burke, 2004).

According to a survey conducted by the Society for Human Resource Management (SHRM), the U.S. workforce as of 2004 consisted of approximately 10 percent veterans, 44 percent baby boomers, 34 percent Gen-Xers and 12 percent Nexters (Burke, 2004). It is important to remember that in addition to possessing age differences, individuals in each of these generational groups are at different stages in their life cycles. Some are nearing retirement and are empty nesters, some are beginning their professional careers and starting families, and some are already busy raising families. This observation may seem intuitive, but it is important to note because in addition to differences stemming from formative experiences, people at different life stages value things such as training and development, retirement benefits, and child care assistance very differently based on their current needs.

It is also important to note that a discussion of generational cohorts is not meant to reinforce stereotypes but rather to foster a better understanding of the differences and relationships commonly observed in the workplace across the different generations. Table 11.1 provides some additional characteristics of the various generational groups.

GENERATIONAL DIFFERENCES IN APPROACHES TO TECHNOLOGY

Different generations adopt technology and processes differently. While baby boomers may see the Internet as something to connect to in order to carry out a specific activity—sending an e-mail, perhaps, or buying a product—a millennial may see the Internet as a resource for doing everything from research to buying groceries, to making a restaurant reservation, to buying movie tickets, to downloading movies and music CDs. Cannell (2006) stated it simply: "One generation's technology is another generation's appliance."

Each generation is marked by the collaboration technologies its members grew up with: telegraph, telephone, fax, personal computer, e-mail, cell phone. As each technology came into existence, it helped to define how that generation would come to communicate and collaborate, thus establishing established their relative technological comfort zone The notions of a younger cybergeneration and an older generation for which Internet technology is somewhat episodic, if not producing a mild case of technophobia, is accurate in many cases (Shelley & Thrane, 2007).

Shelly and Thrane (2007) reported a study that investigated the impact of generational and socioeconomic differences on information technology (IT) literacy and political participation. The study found that as age declined, respondents reported more support for IT (beta = $-.33$) and fewer technological disadvantages (beta = $-.34$). Younger persons showed more desire for public IT

Table 11.1
Generational Group Affiliations and General Characteristics

Generation	Veterans 1922–1964	Baby Boomers 1946–1964	Generation X 1965–1980	Generation Y/Millennials 1981–2000
Communication media	Rotary phones, face-to-face	Touch-tone phones	Cell phones	Internet, camera phones, text messaging, instant messaging, e-mail
Core values	Respect for authority	Optimism, involvement	Skepticism, fun, informality	Realism, confidence, extreme fun, social
Family structures	Traditional, nuclear	Fracturing	Latchkey kids	Merged families
Work ethic	Hard work, sacrifice	Workaholics, personal fulfillment, desire for quality, question authority	Self-reliance, desire for structure and direction, skepticism	Multi-tasking, entrepreneurial, tolerant
Leadership style	Directive, command and control	Consensual, collegial	Challenge others, equality, ask why	Too early in most of their careers to know
Motivation	"Your experience is respected"	"You are valued and needed"	"Do it your way"; "The rules are just guides"	"You will work with other bright, creative people"; "You will learn from your coworkers"

availability (beta = $-.26$). Older respondents had a pronounced preference for traditional, face-to-face interaction. Higher levels of education led to stronger support for IT. Personal characteristics carried great weight in shaping access to innovation and receptivity to exploring technological advances. Older citizens and the less educated may face unique challenges that influence their desire to become fluent with information technology.

Recent data for the United States also indicate that although the use of technology such as computers and the Internet among older adults is increasing, there is still an age-based division. Not having access to and knowing how to use technology may put older people at a disadvantage. This can play out in terms of their ability to live independently but also in a competitive work environment. Technology offers the potential to improve the quality of life for older people by enhancing their ability to perform various tasks and access important information, but systems designers should make sure that their strategies include the needs of older people. As in other things, the research and design community needs to know the user to better understand his or her needs and preferences (Czaja, 2006).

In most research being done so far on the multigenerational workforce, the most frequently observed outcome is that workers from different generations work surprisingly effectively together. A consistent theme throughout the SHRM survey responses was that the advantages of an intergenerational workforce far outweigh any disadvantages. The most commonly occurring negative effect of an intergenerational workforce involved conflicts between workers of different generations regarding acceptable work hours. Most human resource professionals were not aware of intergenerational conflict among employees at their organization. When the researchers were aware of such conflict, it was most commonly cited in areas of ethics, organizational hierarchy, dealing with change, and technology issues (Burke, 2004).

CONSIDERING GENERATIONS IN APPROACHES TO CHANGE MANAGEMENT

It is imperative that change efforts begin to take generations into account when planning and communicating change. The problem is not solved when baby boomers retire or when all employees are taught how to use instant messaging or the newest technology: boomers may not retire as they have in the past, as many are choosing to continue working well past the traditional retirement age and companies are getting more aggressive about retaining retirement-eligible employees in the interest of retaining key knowledge, or at least buying time to enact a knowledge transfer plan. Also, new technologies will continue to be announced at a brisk pace. The multigenerational workforce is here to stay, and if businesses are to produce wider participation and get the most out of their workers, they need more informed methods of designing change with respect to virtual collaboration.

A well-thought-out change management plan should be informed relative to the customers it serves and tailored to address them. A one-size-fits-all change management approach assumes that the client base has essentially identical needs. This approach, if followed, will fail to seize the greatest opportunity and quite possibly leave many customers behind or ill prepared to participate in the broader community, while others may struggle needlessly because the approach taken did not consider their learning needs.

Although it may be easy and even entertaining to consider generational differences as the source of technology adoption, it might be a more useful characterization to use generation as a proxy for planning for change.

IMPACT ON VIRTUAL COLLABORATION

Any organizational change, whether in structure or processes, requires a change management plan. So too does the introduction of new technology. Elements that should be considered in a change management plan include organizational readiness, needed support systems, how the change will be communicated, and the stakeholders and groups likely to be affected by the change. For the last category, an astute change manager will ensure an understanding of how the change is likely to be received and an understanding of the skills, needs, and characteristics of the individuals and groups who will experience the change.

One of the key characteristics that can have a marked effect on receptivity and ability to accommodate or tolerate change is the generational group to which an individual belongs. This characteristic is frequently overlooked when planning effective change strategies. In the case of change related to the introduction of technology to support virtual collaboration, generational group affiliation is one of the most relevant characteristics to consider.

RECOMMENDATIONS

This section provides an overview of recommendations to ensure success in this area:

• *Understand your audience.* The human resources department should be able to provide accurate data such as ages and birthdates in an aggregate fashion across groups. Make sure that you clearly understand what percentage of the affected employee population falls in each of the generational groups and look for high concentrations of one generational group or another in certain groups. This will inform your decisions around training and technology and may illuminate current issues. It also is important information to have when hiring to ensure that you have a diverse group that ensures diversity of thought.

• *Educate leaders on generational differences.* Make sure that organizational leaders both understand and can help educate others on the advantages and challenges of a diverse generational workforce. Ensure also that leaders understand the change management strategy and are equipped to provide the appropriate level and type of support to the various groups. Be careful not to reinforce stereotypes of particular generations.

• *Educate the workforce on generational differences.* Provide education on generational differences throughout the organization as part of leadership, ethics, and diversity courses. Engage a diversity champion to speak about the importance of embracing and leveraging generational differences.

• *Use various methods to communicate the change.* A sound communications strategy uses multiple media to deliver a message. This is especially important when the target recipients comprise a multigenerational population. Sending multiple messages using multiple media will help ensure that the message is received and understood.

• *Provide training and other support on the collaborative technology.* In today's fast-paced world, it is unreasonable to expect that people will take the time to learn a new technology unless there is a clearly understood benefit to doing so. Even when the advantage of using the technology is clear, there are still barriers, especially among some age groups, to learning and adopting the technology as a tool. Be sure to provide easily accessible training to assist people in learning how to use a tool and reduce the amount of time needed in this learning. Also, use various delivery methods for the technology training to appeal to the learning styles of the different generations. Some people, especially those who are already comfortable with technology, may prefer an e-learning course, while others may prefer an in-person classroom training. Support should also be provided in the form of pamphlets, desk references, or online support to assist those who are just learning the collaborative technology.

• *Establish and monitor metrics.* Metrics should not simply be about how widely a particular tool is used, but rather should take into account such desired effects as cost avoidance (as a result of the ability to collaborate virtually), percentage of success in achieving project milestones (as opposed to those projects not using virtual collaboration), user satisfaction, and quality of outcomes.

FINAL THOUGHTS

The aging workforce, along with rapid developments in computer and information technologies, provides an imperative for us to consider generational differences in our approach to change management. This chapter has provided an overview of the four generations that make up the employee populations of U.S. corporations and pointed out that each generation is marked by the collaboration technologies its members grew up with, which help define how that generation communicates and collaborates.

An approach to technology deployment planning that takes generational differences into account will be better informed and therefore more useful to technology deployment managers and those supporting virtual collaboration in a generationally diverse workplace. Generations in fact should be used as a proxy for a group to assess, in a systemic way, the opportunity for change.

REMINDERS

• Using the generational makeup of the target organization will inform deployment managers of the scope of change relative to technology adoption readiness and overall change complexity.

• Adoption of technology and differences between the generations is a usable proxy for key change management design requirements.

- To be successful, virtual collaboration initiatives must consider the generations of employees that they support. This consideration should inform the requirements and design of the initiative, particularly in the change management area of the project.

- A well-thought-out deployment project for virtual collaboration should include an assessment of the client base as it relates to the generations it touches.

References

Burke, M. E. (2004, June). *SHRM 2004 benefits survey report.* Alexandria, VA: Society for Human Resource Management.

Cannell, L. (2006, November 13). *Generational differences and resistance to change.* Retrieved February 22, 2007, from http://www.collaborationloop.com.

Czaja, S. (2006) Technological change and the older worker. In J. E. Birren & K. W. Schaie (Eds.), *Handbook of psychology of aging* (5th ed., pp. 547–555). San Diego: Academic Press.

Shelley, M. C., & Thrane, L. (2007). *Generational differences in information technology and political involvement.* Retrieved February 2, 2007, from http://www.igi-pub.com/ articles.

Assessing Training Needs for Virtual Team Collaboration

Marilyn Sawyer Wesner

Participants in virtual collaboration need a multitude of skills, knowledge, and abilities (SKA) to be successful. In many cases, the participants will not possess all of these and will require training and development. Identifying training and development needs for them is complicated because of their methods of working together through the use of technology. Not only must the participants possess subject matter expertise on the actual work content, but they must also be able to use the technology and understand how to collaborate in a virtual workplace.

Training workers can be expensive to the organization in terms of both the costs associated with the development and delivery of instruction and the participants' time away from work. More expensive, though, is the cost of lost business due to poor-quality products and services delivered by unskilled workers. Investing in training to develop competencies in virtual collaboration offers benefits to the organization that go beyond the current work, because these competencies readily transfer from one work group or project to the next, regardless of the content of the collaboration. Because virtual collaboration allows organizations the flexibility to create just-in-time project teams and work groups, the portability of skills and knowledge in the process of working is a significant benefit.

Thorough assessment of training needs for virtual collaboration helps to avoid the costly mistake of creating training interventions that no one needs or ever uses. The process examines, in advance of any training, the situation in the organization to identify possible training needs and solutions and then provides a data-driven response that points instructional designers in the right direction (Rossett, 1995). By carefully assessing these needs upfront, training can be directed toward those who need it most, in the time frame required, and with the methods that are most effective.

This chapter addresses needs assessment for virtual collaboration by first examining two types of analysis: a broad organizational needs analysis to determine if training is the appropriate solution and then a specific training needs analysis or assessment. Questions for each type of analysis are suggested. The chapter presents specific competencies for virtual collaboration with questions designed for collecting data and assessing training needs for each competency. It also makes some fundamental assumptions about workplace learners that may be important to consider and apply in developing training interventions for virtual collaboration.

ORGANIZATIONAL NEEDS ANALYSIS

Many times, organizations and human resource (HR) departments jump to conclusions and decide that the best solution to reaching goals, solving problems, and implementing change is to train the workforce. In 2005 alone, budgets for formal training in U.S. companies were forecast at more than $51 billion (Dolezalek, 2005). The most recent estimate of the American Society for Training and Development for annual expenditures for workplace learning and performance exceeds $109 billion (Ketter, 2006). Unfortunately, this expensive and time-consuming approach does not always yield the anticipated improved performance. To avoid possible costly mistakes associated with unnecessary training, the first step in organizational needs analysis is to clarify exactly what the problem situation is and where it exists to determine the most pressing needs (Rossett, 1995). This step allows the organization to prioritize and allocate resources accordingly.

Organizational needs analysis is a systematic approach to identifying potential areas for performance improvement in organizations. In most cases, an organizational needs analysis should precede training needs assessment (Nadler, 1982). The analysis may be as simple as examining organizational goals and objectives and comparing desired performance to actual performance levels. Or it may be a comprehensive diagnosis of organizational issues that point to specific problem areas. In order for organizational needs analysis to succeed, the requirements related to the performance of the organization must be explored before any solutions, including training, are prescribed.

The outcome of organizational needs analysis is usually a report or briefing to management identifying needs and offering recommended approaches to improving performance. The gaps between desired performance and actual performance are revealed and, once identified, may or may not require formal learning experiences to address them (Stetar, 2005).

General Guidelines for Organizational Needs Analysis

Needs analysis is a common process in most organizations. However, a brief review of the general process is provided here to set the foundation for the more comprehensive and targeted process of assessing training needs:

1. *Clarify the purpose of the analysis.* The needs analyst clarifies the situation or problem related to virtual collaboration and then determines the objectives of the analysis. The objective of the analysis may be as broad as an organizationwide implementation of a virtual workplace or as narrow as the selection of a particular collaborative technology for use with project management.

2. *Identify data sources and collection methods.* Data are necessary to determine the information required to respond effectively to the objectives. Data sources may include existing performance measures, work samples, benchmarking studies, employee surveys, and new sources. In the virtual collaboration setting, some of these data may reside in organizational knowledge management systems including databases and intranet sites. Depending on the data sources identified, a combination of collection methods like surveys, observations, interviews, and focus groups provides different perspectives for identifying needs. On occasion, the needs analyst may develop a new data collection instrument like a survey to collect data. More specific information on data collection methods is offered below.

3. *Collect, summarize, and analyze the data.* Collect data from a variety of sources on the current state of the organization that relate to the objectives of the analysis. Once data collection is complete, review the results to determine if there are trends or patterns. Potential gaps or problems in reaching organizational objectives may emerge.

4. *Share the findings.* Share the findings of the analysis with all stakeholders. This can be accomplished in a formal or informal way. Sharing allows others to validate the initial findings and usually results in a jointly developed series of recommendations for the organization to consider. Some recommendations may not be training related. Those that are related to training are usually broad in scope and may require a comprehensive training needs assessment.

Methods for Collecting Data

Methods for collecting data can be categorized as unobtrusive or obtrusive. Unobtrusive methods are those that do not ordinarily require interaction with others and do not interrupt normal work. They are generally inexpensive and fairly easy to execute. For example, collecting the number of employee users of online chat to resolve problems with their health care benefits may provide some data on the receptivity of employees to virtual collaboration. Obtrusive methods usually involve interaction with various people in the work setting and take time away from regular work. These methods are often a richer source of data but are generally costly and time consuming for the organization.

Table 12.1 lists both types of data collection methods. An important note is that most needs analysts use a combination of both methods to obtain a more robust representation of training needs. However, the context of the needs assessment may dictate one type of method over another. For example, if there is a need for training a work group on a technical skill for using desktop videoconferencing, collecting simple data from individual training histories and asking the group if they have any experience with the technology will probably suffice. The needs analyst will be able to quickly assess if training is needed and determine who needs it.

If there is a need to determine if group members need training on some of the interpersonal skills for effective collaboration, like communication and group

Table 12.1

Unobtrusive and Obtrusive Data Collection Methods

Unobtrusive Data Collection Methods	Obtrusive Data Collection Methods
Document review	Interviews and focus groups of key stakeholders
Organizational publications including:	
Organization personnel charts	Supervisors
Reports from previous needs analysis	Customers
Reports on previous virtual collaborations	Team members
	Technical support
Available training courses	Participants in previous and current virtual collaborations
Job descriptions	
Process flowcharts	Questionnaires and self-evaluations
Training evaluations	Combination of observation and interview
Individual employees	
Performance appraisals	Tests measuring knowledge, skills, and abilities
Educational level	Self-administered checklists
Training history	
Work samples	
Certifications	
Observations	
Physical and virtual spaces	
Group process and meetings	
Individual employee	
Available technology	

leadership, the needs analyst may have to use a combination of both types of methods, for example, reports on previous virtual collaborations, job descriptions, interviews, and focus groups.

Most often the limitations on data collection are the amount of time available to conduct the assessment and the level of disruption allowable in the regular work process. It would be extremely rare for the need analysts to use all of the methods offered.

ASSESSING TRAINING NEEDS FOR VIRTUAL COLLABORATION

Once the organizational needs analysis is complete and training for virtual collaboration is recommended, the next step is training needs assessment (Figure 12.1). In some instances, training needs may already be apparent without an organizational analysis, for example, when new technology for virtual collaboration has been purchased with the expectation that it will enhance performance. Workers will need training on how to use it.

Regardless of how training needs are identified, a key part of successfully addressing specific needs is good data collection and analysis by the training needs analyst. The training needs analyst can be a training specialist in the organization but can also be a manager, supervisor, or team leader. Supervisors and team leaders are in a position to notice the gap between actual and desired performance and often correctly prescribe training as the solution. But when performance issues are complex or major changes are on the horizon, using a training specialist to conduct the assessment is a more systematic and thorough approach.

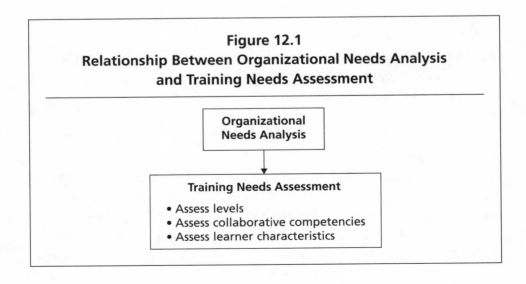

Figure 12.1
Relationship Between Organizational Needs Analysis and Training Needs Assessment

Organizational Needs Analysis

Training Needs Assessment
• Assess levels
• Assess collaborative competencies
• Assess learner characteristics

Training needs analysts usually use a specific framework for their assessments. Frameworks for conducting training needs assessment combine various levels of analysis with specific content areas. Most often these frameworks include an examination of the training needs at the organizational level, work unit or operational level, and individual level (Cascio, 2005).

In most cases, training needs assessment frameworks also put forth a series of questions to guide the data collection process. The relevance of particular questions varies with the situation, so not every question is for the assessment. The needs analyst chooses from the data collection methods to search for answers to the selected questions.

Organizational Level of Analysis

Before training needs can be assessed, there has to be agreement at the organizational level on what work needs to done. In virtual collaboration settings, how the work will be done is also an important step in this process. Once the decision is made to complete work through virtual collaboration, the needs assessment can begin.

These questions help in assessing the organizational needs for training:

1. What is the desired level of performance?

2. What is the existing level of performance?

3. Are there particular problems or causes associated with the current level?

4. Is virtual collaboration a common way of working in this organization?

5. How are projects selected for virtual collaboration efforts?

6. How are participants selected for virtual collaboration efforts?

7. What technical support is available?

8. What other organizational support is available?

Work Group Level of Analysis

The work group analysis begins with identifying the participants in the group. There may be cross-functional members, cross-organizational members, or both. They may be from different functional or professional groups (for example, software developers and human resource managers or engineers and product development). They may have clear boundaries as a team or be loosely coupled.

The collaborative group membership defines the target audience for the training. In every case, knowledge of the characteristics of the participants is important because they may present different kinds of needs and levels of performance.

These questions help assess work group needs:

- Has this group worked together before?
- What are the skills, knowledge, and abilities the group needs to accomplish the tasks?
- Does the group have a designated leader?
- Do all group members work for the same organization or the same boss?
- Are members from the same or different occupational or professional groups (for example, all engineers versus engineers and marketing)?
- Are members from the same or different countries, time zones, or national cultures?

Individual Learner Level of Analysis

Virtual collaboration can occur across all levels in the workplace: individual, work group or team, enterprise, and inter-enterprise (Sumner, 2003). Even when virtual collaboration is the way of working in the enterprise, most training interventions focus on individual learners.

Individuals bring many skills and much knowledge and experience to the collaboration. In most cases, each is a subject matter expert on at least one element of the collaborative work effort. But they may not have the necessary skills to work effectively in a collaborative environment. Conducting a complete analysis of individual learning needs ensures that the training that is developed will be tailored to the target audience (Harris & Castillo, 2002). Learning, especially in virtual settings, relies heavily on individual participants, so extra care must be taken to collect data on the target audience. Some suggested questions for identifying individual learner needs related to participants in virtual collaboration include:

- What computer or teleconferencing technology does the learner use?
- What knowledge, skills, and abilities related to virtual work does the learner possess?

- What types of training, included those delivered virtually, has the learner experienced?

- What is the individual's current level of performance?

TRAINING CONTENT AREAS FOR VIRTUAL COLLABORATION NEEDS

Most training is based on the idea of competencies. A competency is an interrelated set of abilities, behaviors, attitudes, and knowledge that individuals need to be effective in their work (Hellriegel & Slocum, 2006). Effective training addresses the competencies individuals need to develop in order to meet or exceed the expectations of their work. If there already is an existing set of competencies for performing a particular kind of work, the training needs assessment should include data related to those competencies.

Today the boundaries of a particular job or position are much less rigid than in the past, so the needs analyst must think in terms of the work processes and the tasks required to perform successfully. Virtual collaboration, a work process, is completed through the use of a wide variety of telecommunications and computer-assisted technology, so participants in the process must possess skills for using the technology effectively, as well as those necessary for accomplishing specific tasks and group work.

Analyzing training needs for participants in virtual collaboration involves first looking at the broad sets of skills and knowledge required and then getting more specific. Of course, not all participants will require training or education in all of the areas, but they all should be considered to avoid overlooking specific needs that may make or break the collaborative work effort.

Five major areas of competency need attention for successful virtual collaboration:

- Organizational knowledge

- Cross-cultural knowledge

- Work content and subject matter expertise

- Collaborative technology skills and knowledge

- Collaborative work process skills and knowledge

They are described below in somewhat of a chronological order associated with how the virtual collaboration work unfolds. Knowledge and understanding of the organization, its objectives and cross-cultural issues, are usually necessary before most virtual collaborations begin. Next, the work content of the virtual collaboration requires participants with particular subject matter expertise. Then the participants need the ability to use the collaborative technology. And finally, they need the ability to effectively collaborate using virtual methods.

Organizational Knowledge

Virtual collaboration may occur within the same larger organization or across organizations or even industries. Participants need a clear understanding of the goals and objectives for the collaboration. Most often these are set at a higher organizational level. They also need to understand the organizational structure and support in order to know whom to go to for resources and whom to escalate problems and decisions to if needed. In addition, some organizations have knowledge management systems that are available and necessary for the participants to use in order to get their jobs done. Organizational knowledge is a key ingredient for the success of virtual collaboration. Many times the work crosses organizational silos within the same organization, and at other times, the work may cross total organizations and industries. Much of organizational knowledge is tacit, meaning that it is not readily visible to others and is acquired through experience (Hansen, Nohria, & Tierney, 2001). There are simple questions to determine if participants need to know more about the organization before they begin.

The nature of the project, problem, or work that the collaboration will address resides within the organization itself. Thus, initial questions may include:

- What are the goals and objectives of the collaboration?
- What organizational entities are involved? How do these entities interact within the organization?
- What role does the larger organization play in resource allocation and decision making?
- How does the organization recognize and reward collaborative work?
- Is virtual collaboration a new requirement because the organization reorganized and eliminated physical work locations?

- Is virtual collaboration a formal or informal process?
- Are there designated leaders, or will leaders emerge?

Cross-Cultural Skills

The virtual workplace includes a wide diversity of participants, not unlike the face-to-face workplace. Knowing the cross-cultural issues that may be encountered helps the participant be more effective in the collaboration. Differences in languages, time zones, and occupational cultures (for example, engineers and software developers) create a level of complexity that influences effective collaboration. Even if specific differences are not apparent at first, some awareness that they may exist may improves the effectiveness of participants in the collaborative venture.

Thinking of the various cultures that may be present in any virtual collaboration is a key to identifying training needs. Questions to assist in gaining information about potential cross-cultural training needs include:

- What are the national cultures and languages of the participants represented in the virtual collaboration effort?
- Are participants from different regions of the United States?
- What are the functional and occupational cultures of the participants?
- Do any participants require accommodation for disabilities?

Work Content and Subject Matter Expertise

Individuals must possess the subject matter expertise (SME) on the work content of the virtual collaboration. For example, if the purpose of the collaboration is to develop a contract to outsource the staffing function of the HR organization, individual participants need to be well versed in the various areas of the project: employment law, job design, forecasting employment needs, creating contracts, and others. These needs may be met without additional training if the participants are carefully selected primarily for their subject matter expertise. Virtual collaboration occurs both formally and informally in the workplace. Both types rely on SME. Identifying training needs for SMEs may be one of the most straightforward analyses.

Many of these needs may already be met and handled by virtue of careful selection to the virtual team, if formal collaboration is expected. Relevant questions may include:

- What SME is required for successful collaboration?
- Are all areas of SME covered by the participants?
- Is SME current?

Collaborative Technology Skills and Knowledge

Virtual collaboration requires the use of information and telecommunications technology. The technology may be as simple as using standard conference call facilities or as complex as using a piece of collaborative software for project management along with e-mail, standard teleconferencing, and desktop videoconferencing.

The assumption that a participant who is familiar with a particular tool is also expert in using it is not necessarily a sound one. A recent classroom example provides an example of this dilemma. Graduate students who had been using the courseware system Blackboard for over a year to download syllabi, assignments, files, and threaded discussion did not know that they could access and send e-mail to all students in the classroom using the Communications function. E-mail list service is one of the easiest functions on Blackboard, but until the students knew of its existence, they never used it. They learned to use only what they felt they had a need to know (Knowles, 1984). Once they were told about it, they quickly saw the value and became frequent users.

It is important to set assumptions aside with regard to what frequent users of a particular tool know of all its features. Not knowing of the features upfront can create frustration and slow work activity. And although the features may not be needed at first, participants need to know that they exist for potential future needs in the collaborative process.

A necessary part of this analysis is determining what collaborative tools will be used. Once that is determined, appropriate questions may include:

- Do all participants know how to use the tools?
- How much experience do participants have using collaborative technology?
- Do all participants have access to the necessary software, bandwidth, complementary pieces of hardware, server space, and so on?

Collaborative Work Process Skills and Knowledge

Collaborative work processes are the specific methods used to complete tasks through shared work efforts. They are numerous and include communication, leadership, virtual meetings management, project management skills, the ability to sort through and select data (Nemiro, 2004), decision making, problem identification and resolution, and conflict resolution. The list of skills needed for effective virtual collaboration encompasses the laundry list of training often prescribed for teams, virtual teams, managers, and supervisors. Much of this training is generic in nature and may not represent the best financial choice for companies. In addition, some of the collaborative software tools already include the work process skills that participants need. For example, project management software functions include the planning, status, feedback, and evaluation processes to help manage the project. The participant just has to use them.

As a first step, the needs analyst must determine whether the collaboration is a formal collaborative process like work teams, project and task teams, or formal partnerships or informal collaborations like ongoing working relationships, spontaneous work, and informal communities (Beyerlin, McGee, Klein, Nemiro, & Broedling, 2003). Knowing this helps define the range of potential needs. Then one of the first areas to assess is skills in meetings management. Questions may include:

- Are participants experienced in meeting virtually?

- Have participants used collaboration as a major method for accomplishing work assignments before?

- Do any of the participants have experience facilitating or leading virtual collaborations?

Because virtual collaborative skills and knowledge are so important to the success of the work effort and so numerous, it makes sense to determine which ones are priorities. If certain types of training like problem solving have already been completed by the participants, they may only need a refresher on the content or some adjustment to make it applicable to virtual interactions.

Competency Assessment Questions by Level of Analysis

Table 12.2 offers a series of additional questions related to each of the five competency areas, divided by level of analysis: organizational, work group, and individual. These questions ensure that the needs analyst can easily collect data across

Table 12.2
Training Needs Assessment Questions Categorized by Level of Analysis

	Organizational Knowledge and Objectives	Cross-Cultural Knowledge	Work Content or Subject Matter Expertise	Collaborative Technology Skills and Knowledge	Collaborative Work Processes Skills and Knowledge
Organizational level	Is the collaboration organizationwide or a subunit or project level? What are the goals and objectives of the collaboration? How does it fit with the overall goals of the organization? What are the levels of organizational structure and support for the collaboration?	What are the languages, time zones, and regional and national variations in the organization? What are the professional, functional, and occupational groups involved in the collaborations?	Does the organization have all of the SMEs needed?	Will all participants have access to the required information and telecommunications hardware and software? What collaborative technology is available? Is a knowledge management system in place?	What type of collaboration is required? What is the escalation process for the collaborative efforts? How do participants obtain needed resources? Does the organization plan to feed back and evaluate performance on the collaborative effort?

Work group level	What are the objectives of the collaboration? What subunits of the organization are involved? Is a knowledge management system in place?	What are the languages, time zones, regional and or national variations of the participants? Do any participants have disabilities that need accommodation?	Are participants familiar with each other's SME? Do participants know what area of expertise they will add to the collaboration?	What collaborative technologies do participants already use? What technology, including hardware, software, Web-based, and telecommunications technology, will be used? Is there a primary method of collaboration planned?	Have group members worked together before? What experience and training do participants have in group problem solving and decision making? Meetings management? Communication? Feedback and evaluation? Leadership?
Individual level	What are the objectives of the collaboration?	What language(s) does the individual use at work? Does the individual need accommodation for a disability? Has the individual worked effectively with cross-cultural groups before? Does the individual know the relevant cultural characteristics of the group members?	What is the participant's area of subject matter expertise? How competent is the participant in the subject matter area? Does the individual know what SME he or she is to offer to the collaboration?	How much experience does the learner have with the selected technology? What software applications does the learner know? What telecommunications technology does the individual know?	What previous experience does the participant have in virtual collaborations? What training or development has the individual already experienced?

all levels. Once all the data are collected and analyzed, training and other development interventions can be targeted to the appropriate level. These questions serve only as guides for collecting data for training needs assessment. Not every assessment needs to attempt to explore and answer every question; only the questions that fit the current situation should be used.

Every virtual collaborative work setting has unique elements. Some may require more formal training than others. Indeed, some participants' expertise in these areas may result from years of working together in a particular environment or on particular kinds of projects or tasks. The role of the training needs analyst is to identify which areas of competence require additional training.

Following data collection, the needs that the analyst identified serve as the basis for all training development. In many cases, the needs analyst and the training developer are the same person, but in some large organizations, these functions are more specialized and split into different positions. When this is the case, the needs analyst and training developer work closely together to ensure that the training is targeted toward meeting learners' specific needs.

GENERAL ASSUMPTIONS ABOUT INDIVIDUAL LEARNING NEEDS

In the workplace, people cannot always choose those they will work with and what process will be used to complete their work. Because many workers become participants in virtual collaborative work based on assignment rather than choice, preparing them for a different way of thinking and working together requires sound educational processes and creative, engaging approaches to learning.

The workplace, whether virtual or physical, is the setting for the training, education, and development of workers. Because this training and development is expensive, it is important to design and deliver what is needed to achieve optimal levels of performance. In addition to a complete assessment of training needs based on competencies, training needs assessment should include consideration for the needs of the target audience.

Participants in virtual collaboration at work bring a particular set of needs to the learning environment. First, adults prefer as much choice and control over their work lives as possible, including the areas of their personal learning and development (Knowles, Holton, & Swanson, 2005). Second, they have a preferred style of learning and may learn better if conditions match their styles. And finally, today's workforce differs drastically in knowledge and comfort level in using technology, resulting in a wide range of users, from novice to expert.

Assumptions About Adult Learners

Most training interventions are directed toward the individual adult learner. Generally accepted principles of adult learning are fundamental to creating the appropriate content and delivery methods for training interventions, especially in a virtual environment. Knowles et al. (2005) identify the following principles to consider in regard to adult learners:

• *Adults will invest time and effort into learning what they sense they have a need to know.* For this reason, developers of training and facilitators of learning for virtual collaboration must create opportunities for learners to become aware of what they need to know and its importance. Virtual collaboration may be completely new to its participants, and they may not know what they need to know. A checklist for the participants consisting of the skills and knowledge required, along with sources for obtaining training, could be an important tool to offer in advance of the actual work.

• *Adults prefer to make their own choices and decisions.* Some may resist training if they think it is being imposed on them. Facilitators of learning can assist learners in becoming less dependent and more self-directed. By offering participants in virtual collaboration the opportunity to identify their own needs through self-assessment, they may become less resistant to training. Offering an array of learning opportunities, including choices on whether the training needed is new or just a refresher and choices of delivery method (for example, online versus face-to-face), allows participants to make their own decisions.

• *Adults possess a multitude of experiences that can inhibit or facilitate their own learning.* Learners' mental models (Senge, 1990) of training, work, groups, and technology may influence training outcomes. Participants in a virtual collaboration environment may believe that it is exactly like the familiar face-to-face collaboration, just with more technology. Others may think that the project will never succeed unless people meet in person. Facilitators can help participants integrate prior experiences with face-to-face collaboration and virtual collaboration and identify which elements can will transfer in the new situation.

• *Learning for adults is most valued when they think that the training material will help them cope with real-life situations.* Facilitators can assist participants in seeking and using training by ensuring that the training is relevant to the virtual collaboration setting. Case studies may help learners understand the skills they will need in their new roles and tasks.

• *Adults have a task-centered or problem-centered approach to learning.* Training developers can position training content as valuable for solving problems and improving performance issues. The uniqueness of the work situation should be presented, along with some of the issues participants may encounter in virtual collaboration. Training where participants are able to participate by offering their own suggestions for solutions may be especially effective.

• *Adults are interested in learning that will lead to a better quality of life and higher self-esteem,* not just in higher pay or promotion. Facilitators can help participants understand that learning virtual collaboration skills may allow them to exhibit their expertise and creativity to influence more people in more ways and in different projects.

Individual Learning Styles

The second important consideration when developing training for virtual collaboration is that individuals possess different learning styles; as a result, the effectiveness of the training intervention may rest on creating training that supports a variety of styles. Kolb (as cited in Merriam & Caffarella, 1999) identified four major preferences or styles for learning: learning through (1) concrete experience or learning by doing, (2) active experimentation or learning by trying, (3) abstract conceptualization or thinking, and (4) reflective observation or watching.

Training delivered solely by technology presents a significant opportunity to design learning experiences that incorporate learning through all four styles. Interactivity does not have to be ruled out just because the training is technology based. Nor does the facilitator have to be present in real time. For example, the training facilitated by a non-real-time virtual facilitator on the topic of how to use online chat and file sharing might provide opportunities to practice the new skills of online chat and file sharing, experiment with file sharing and receive immediate feedback on mastery, read how to share files and answer reflective questions on the new skills, observe a hypothetical online chat session including file sharing, and then answer reflective questions regarding the session.

A combination of the principles of adult learning that Knowles et al. (2005) proposed and the four learning styles provide a sound foundation for training workers for collaborative work. For example, the training offered may be just-in-time training (principle of need to know) that is offered through practice (trying) and video (watching).

Generational Differences in the Workplace

Recently generational differences in the workplace have been noted as creating a myriad of opportunities and issues for organizations. One of the major characteristics used to differentiate the generations is their knowledge of and experience with technology (Galagan, 2006; Gleeson, 2003). More mature workers may be reluctant to embrace technology, while younger workers are frequently techno-savvy experts. Because virtual collaboration requires the effective use of information and telecommunications technology, the role of the learner's prior experience with technology is a significant element to consider in approaches to training.

Prensky (2001) proposes that there are two distinct types of learners determined by age and experience. The first, *digital natives,* are "native speakers of the digital language" (p. 1). They are aged thirty or under and have essentially spent their entire lives as users of technology. The second, *digital immigrants* (p. 3), are those who began using computer technology later in life and may not necessarily view it a key ingredient for their successful performance. Their approaches to learning are very different.

Natives are the ultimate multitaskers: they use instant messaging while surfing the Web and listening to music, for example. Immigrants are more likely to view technology as a collection of tools to use in specific instances (Prensky, 2001). They also may be reluctant to use the full set of features technology brings. For example, a digital native may be perfectly comfortable using Wikipedia as a source of encyclopedic information, whereas a digital immigrant may use a CD-ROM version of *Encyclopedia Britannica* or perhaps even consult a hard copy if it is available.

These differences present additional challenges in training participants in virtual collaboration. Training experts suggest that younger workers, the digital natives, prefer training that is rapid paced, experiential, and fun (Society for Human Resource Management, 2005). They are quick to learn any new technology and usually learn through experimentation. Games, in particular, are effective methods for teaching them new concepts. More mature workers may first require training on the use of the collaborative technology (Gleeson, 2003). Once they become comfortable using it, training on additional concepts related to virtual collaboration can be offered. One interesting approach to bridging the gaps caused by differing levels of expertise between generations is mutual mentoring, where younger workers tutor less techno-savvy workers in using technology and more senior workers offer lessons from their experiences in the workplace (Maher, 2003).

FINAL THOUGHTS

The bottom line for businesses is that training interventions must improve worker performance. Training can be a significant expense, especially if the outcomes fall short of what were expected. The first step in the process of ensuring the appropriateness and effectiveness of training for virtual collaboration is an organizational needs analysis process. This process clarifies organizational objectives and the desired level of performance. Training may be one or none of the recommendations emerging from this analysis.

When training is one of the recommendations from the initial needs analysis, it is essential to conduct a complete assessment of training needs before designing any training intervention. This assessment begins with collecting data regarding the levels of analysis (organizational, work group, and individual) and the level of competence required for virtual collaboration. In addition, some understanding of the principles of adult learning, differences in learning styles, and the generation of the participants is beneficial.

Training needs generated from this process will provide a complete view of learner needs and assist training professionals in design and delivery decisions. These decisions have the ability to make virtual collaboration an organizational success story.

REMINDERS

- Training is not always the solution to organizational performance problems, including those uniquely associated with virtual collaboration.

- Conduct a brief organizational analysis first to determine if training is a potential solution.

- Use a systemic approach to training needs assessment. Even if all steps are not required, this approach ensures that nothing is overlooked.

- Design the training needs assessment to fit the organization's available time and resources.

- Use a number of data sources, and validate the analysis with key stakeholders.

- A training specialist may be needed to conduct the needs assessment if performance issues are complex or require major changes.

- Understand how the characteristics of the learners affect workplace training to ensure that training recommendations are relevant.

References

Beyerlin, M., McGee, C., Klein, G., Nemiro, J., & Broedling, L. (2003). Introduction and framework for the fieldbook. In M. Beyerlin, C. McGee, G. Klein, J. Nemiro, & L. Broedling (Eds.), *The collaborative work systems fieldbook: Strategies, tools, and techniques* (pp. 1–14). San Francisco: Jossey-Bass/Pfeiffer.

Cascio, W. (2005). *Managing human resources* (6th ed.). New York: McGraw-Hill.

Dolezalek, H. (2005). 2005 industry report. *Training, 42*(12), 13–27.

Galagan, P. (2006). Engaging generation. *T+D, 60*(8), 26–32.

Gleeson, P. (2003). *Managing and motivating the generations: Implications for the student and the employee.* Retrieved September 13, 2006, from http://www.uwsp.edu/education/facets/links_resources/4413.pdf.

Hansen, M., Nohria, N., & Tierney, T. (2001). *Harvard Business review on organizational learning.* Boston: Harvard Business School Press.

Harris, P., & Castillo, O. (2002). Instructional design for WBT. *Info-line 0202.* Alexandria, VA: American Society for Training and Development.

Hellreigel, D., & Slocum, J. (2006). *Organizational behavior* (11th ed.). Mason, OH: Thomson South-Western.

Ketter, P. (2006). Investing in learning: Looking for performance. *T+D, 60*(8), 30–33.

Knowles, M. (1984). *The adult learner: A neglected species* (3rd ed.). Houston: Gulf.

Knowles, M., Holton, E., & Swanson, R. (2005). *The adult learner* (6th ed.). Amsterdam: Elsevier.

Maher, K. (2003). Bridging generations with reverse mentoring. *College journal from The Wall Street Journal.* Retrieved September 23, 2006, from http://www.collegejournal.com/columnists/thejungle/20031119_maher.html.

Merriam, S., & Caffarella, R. (1999). *Learning in adulthood: A comprehensive guide* (2nd ed.). San Francisco: Jossey-Bass.

Nadler, L. (1982). *Designing training programs: The critical events model.* Reading, MA: Addison-Wesley.

Nemiro, J. (2004). *Creativity in virtual teams: Key components for success.* San Francisco: Jossey-Bass/Pfeiffer.

Prensky, M. (2001, September-October). Digital natives, digital immigrants, part 1. *On the Horizon, 9*(5), 3–6.

Rossett, A. (1995). Needs assessment. In G. Anglin (Ed.), *Instructional technology: Past, present and future* (2nd ed., pp. 183–196). Englewood, CO: Libraries Unlimited.

Senge, P. (1990). *The fifth discipline: The art and practice of the learning organization.* New York: Doubleday.

Society for Human Resource Management (2005). *SHRM case study: Generational differences.* Retrieved September 15, 2006, from http://www.shrm.org/hrresources/casestudies_published/CMS_011553.pdf.

Stetar, B. (2005). Training: It's not always the answer. *Quality Progress, 38*(3), 44–49.

Sumner, J. (2003). Finding the value in virtual collaboration. *KM Review, 6*(5), 12–15.

Design Concepts for Virtual Work Systems

Jodi Heintz Obradovich, Philip J. Smith

Because advances in information and communications technologies are creating the ability for collaborative work to be accomplished by team members who are geographically and temporally dispersed, it is important to understand how such virtual work can be most effectively supported.

This chapter presents relevant design best practices and recommendations to be used when constructing virtual work teams and the technology to support those teams. These recommendations are intended to enable effective and efficient interactions among members of virtual work systems.

Case studies are examined from a variety of organizations and disciplines, ranging from health care to aviation to military command and control. The teams may be colocated in space and time, or they may be found in different locations with

This work carried out in part through participation in the Advanced Decision Architectures Collaborative Technology Alliance sponsored by the U.S. Army Research Laboratory under Cooperative Agreement DAA10–01–2–0009.

their interactions mediated by technology. These work domains share the following abstract characteristics:

- High cognitive complexity, characterized by the number and complexity of tasks, the interactions and constraints that need to be considered, how dynamic the work is, the level of uncertainty and risk, and the cognitive demands for information processing that the tasks require (Roth, Patterson, & Mumaw, 2002).
- Distribution of the work (and associated responsibilities) among many people to deal with the high cognitive complexity. This distribution of the work includes planning, monitoring, and execution tasks.
- Distribution of data and knowledge among many people in order to deal with the high cognitive complexity.
- Uncertainty about how scenarios will actually play out.
- Geographical and temporal distribution of the participants.
- A variety of tasks across individuals and organizations that are independent (they can be completed without any need for interaction among the different individuals) or interacting (they require interactions among the different individuals as they perform their own individual tasks).

The analysis of these case studies allows us to develop recommendations to aid in the design of successful virtual work systems. Each case study is first presented and then discussed in terms of the relevant best practices for system design that the case illustrates. As part of each discussion, we present recommendations or questions to be considered when developing or constructing virtual work systems. The case studies generally fit within three themes of best practices: designing work processes, using technology to communicate and coordinate, and building shared perspectives. Table 13.1 illustrates where each case fits within the broader themes. Although some cases span themes, each case is discussed within the major theme it represents.

DESIGNING WORK PROCESSES

Case Study 1: Task Division for a Spatially and Temporally Distributed Virtual Team

Traditionally the way that organizations deal with complexity in work is to divide the task of managing the overall system into subtasks and then assign these subtasks to different individuals. The assumption behind this division of labor is

Table 13.1
Case Studies and Themes of Best Practices
for Virtual Work Systems

Case Studies	Designing Work Process	Using Technology to Communicate and Coordinate	Building Shared Perspectives
Task division for a spatially and temporally distributed team	X		
Nonverbal coordination and communication	X	X	
Coordination during plan adaptation and replanning	X		
Planning contingencies	X	X	
Use of video for coordination and communication		X	
Mediating coordination using auditory technologies		X	
Synchronous and asynchronous problem solving		X	X
Establishing common ground and building shared perspectives		X	X
Sharing data and knowledge to build shared mental models			X

that there is a sufficient degree of independence among the subtasks, so that when each subtask alone is performed well, the combined effects will produce acceptable (rather than optimal) levels of performance for the system as a whole. Because few systems are able to be separated into fully independent subtasks, it is often necessary that individuals responsible for particular subtasks interact with one another when the solutions to these subtasks also interact in significant ways. However, the reality is that these individuals may not know how significantly their subtasks interact, and therefore will not know when collaboration is needed (Smith, McCoy, & Orasanu, 2001).

An illustration of failing to adequately consider the impact of task division on the system as a whole is presented for an incident that occurred in the National Airspace System:

A commercial airliner, flying from Dallas/Fort Worth to Miami, was crossing the Florida Panhandle. A line of thunderstorms was present from Tampa southeastward down to Miami. The airline dispatcher considered these thunderstorms as potentially jeopardizing the airliner's safety and informed the pilot of these concerns. The dispatcher suggested a reroute that would take the flight down the east coast of Florida, and the pilot concurred. The pilot contacted the Jacksonville Traffic Control Center to coordinate this change, and the reroute was approved. The airliner turned east and headed toward Ormond Beach on Florida's east coast.

When the airplane entered the next air traffic control sector, the receiving sector informed the pilot that due to very heavy air traffic along the east coast, they could not accept the pilot's reroute and that the flight needed to return to its original route. The pilot turned the aircraft quickly back to the southwest and returned to its original flight path down Florida's west coast, heading toward Fort Myers. Heavy air traffic caused the pilot to slow the aircraft's flight speed, increasing fuel consumption.

As the aircraft approached the Fort Myers area and prepared to turn east toward Miami, the line of thunderstorms had entered the Miami area and shut down operations at the Miami airport. The aircraft was put into a holding pattern and given "expect further clearance" instructions from air traffic control. The crew was left uncertain as to when the weather would clear and they could proceed into Miami's airport.

At this time, the pilot contacted the airline dispatcher to inform him that their proposed (and initiated) reroute had been refused by the traffic control sector: the flight was back on its original flight plan and was now in airborne holding. (The dispatcher for this flight was also responsible for about thirty other flights simultaneously. Once he believed he had resolved this flight's initial problems with the thunderstorm line, he had turned his attention to other flights' situations and was unaware of the reroute refusal by the air traffic sector.)

As fuel consumption became a serious concern, the situation was further complicated by the fact that all possible alternate airports were unusable due to the weather or were on the opposite side of the line of thunderstorms. Faced with very low fuel, the pilot had no choice but to break through the thunderstorms as the line moved south of Miami and land at Miami airport. The airplane encountered heavy turbulence going through the line of thunderstorms; fortunately, no one was seriously injured. (Figure 13.1 illustrates the weather pattern over Florida and the flight path that the aircraft had to take.)

This case provides an example of one of the ways in which the air traffic management system has been divided into subtasks to reduce the required cognitive complexity for individuals. It also illustrates one potential weakness of such a division of task assignments: if tasks are assigned so that those who have control are not the same as those who have the data or knowledge, interactions between these people will sometimes be required. (In this case, the flight crew should have interacted with their dispatcher to check on the weather.) If such an interaction is not triggered by some system or person, system failure can result. In this case, the locus of control resided with the flight crew and the controller, while the relevant data regarding movement of the storm system were available only to the dispatcher and Federal Aviation Administration (FAA) traffic managers, neither of whom was consulted.

Research supports the view that the interdependent nature of tasks affects the performance of a team in a variety of ways. In addition to requiring interaction among team members, these interdependencies can be viewed as a central

Figure 13.1
A Breakdown in Performance in a Virtual Work System

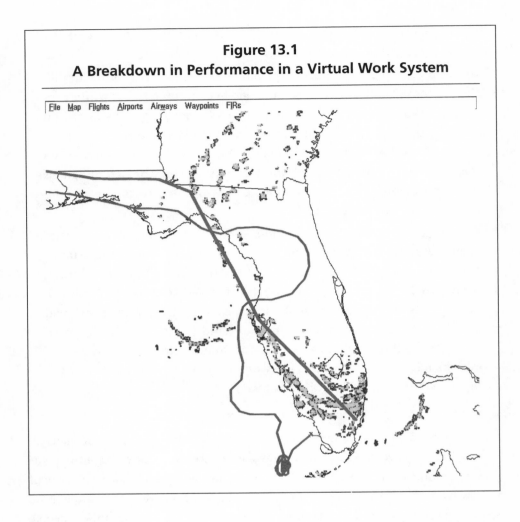

File Map Flights Airports Airways Waypoints FIRs

component of coordination. Coordination theory (Crowston, 1997; Heath & Staudenmayer, 2000; Malone & Crowston, 1994) defines coordination as the management of interdependencies among activities in terms of actors, goals, time, space, quality of products, and so forth. Malone and Crowston (1994) suggest three types of task interdependencies: prerequisite, shared resource, and simultaneity. Prerequisite interdependencies are those that occur when one task must be completed before the next can begin. Therefore, each person's contribution is dependent on the contribution of the person before him or her and affects how the next person will perform his or her task. When a resource such as a person or a database must be shared by more than one task, coordination needs to occur in order to accommodate the dependency that each task has on that resource (data and knowledge). Finally, when two or more tasks occur simultaneously, some coordination is required for the successful completion of those tasks.

In the aviation case study, the interdependency concerned access to a resource. The parties with control at the time of the critical decision to change the route back to the west coast of Florida (the flight crew and air traffic controller) did not have direct access to the relevant data (a bigger view of the weather) as a resource. Malone and Crowston's taxonomy serves to emphasize the need to look at the architecture for distributing work, comparing the match between the allocation of tasks and responsibilities with access to necessary resources.

A characterization of the event solely in terms of this taxonomy is not sufficient to capture critical issues or to guide decisions about how to solve this problem to prevent future occurrences. A second critical contributor was a false assumption by the pilots. This assumption was based on the pilots' incorrect mental model (constructed from past experiences and prior knowledge) that the controller had access to a bigger view of the weather and was asking them to make a reasonable route change. Because of this assumption, the pilots failed to initiate an interaction with their dispatcher, who did have access to the critical resource (weather data). Although a superficial consideration of Malone and Crowston's taxonomy might suggest that we simply give the controller and flight crew direct access to the needed resource (weather data), a more detailed cognitive task analysis leads to the conclusion that other alternative or complementary solutions ought to be considered. One solution may be to develop a critiquing system to alert a team member to critical information, which can then trigger interaction among necessary team members. Another solution may be to provide better training to team members so that they are aware of when an interaction with others is necessary to ensure optimum system performance.

Saavedra, Earley, and Van Dyne (1993) propose team interdependence as another type of interdependency when "group members jointly diagnose, problem solve, and collaborate to complete a task" (p. 63). As the complexity of interdependence among tasks increases, so do the cognitive requirements for coordination, communication, and collaboration among group members (Argote & McGrath, 1993; Gailbraith, 1987; Rico & Cohen, 2005). In part this might be recast as describing a way to distribute resources among team members or the tasks assigned to those members so that an interdependency is created because these resources are distributed.

In summary, this case study and the associated discussion of the relevant literature suggests several design recommendations:

• *Recommendation 1: Decompose the overall task into independent subtasks.* To cope with cognitive complexity and the associated workload for individuals, look for ways to divide the task into nearly independent subtasks so that acceptably good performance is achieved when each individual (or computer agent) completes his or her task independently.

• *Recommendation 2: Design the system to foster detection of situations where interaction is necessary.* In general, real-world systems are at best nearly divisible into independent subtasks: acceptably good performance is usually, but not always, achieved if each subtask is completed independently. It is therefore necessary to design the system so that the independent team members detect those situations where interaction with another team member is required to achieve acceptably good performance and to ensure that those interactions occur and are effective (that is, interaction by exception).

• *Recommendation 3: Use technology to create systems that will ensure needed interaction.* When a system has been designed so that subtasks can normally be completed independently, one common cause of problems is a false assumption by one person about what the other person knows or has done. Such an incorrect mental model can lead that person to assume that no interaction is necessary when an exception may need to be made to trigger an interaction. Technology (critiquing or alerting systems) can sometimes be used to help ensure that when an exception arises, a needed interaction will occur. Training (to correct an incorrect mental model or assumption) may also be useful, but the human factors literature cautions about overreliance on training because it is not always effective.

• *Recommendation 4: Design into the system subtasks that have prerequisite dependencies.* An alternative or complementary solution to designing a system by dividing work into independent subtasks is to explicitly design in dependencies that require the individuals assigned to different tasks to interact with one another. With this design, cognitive complexity is reduced for individuals because each person still focuses on only his or her own subtasks, except that the person with the dependent task knows that he or she must wait for input based on the completion of the prerequisite subtask by another person. This can be thought of as a routine interaction, as contrasted with interaction by exception as outlined in recommendation 2. The potential disadvantage of a task division that requires routine interactions is that interactions can cause increased time or workload for the individuals to perform their tasks. The advantage is that routine interactions are expected and more likely to be practiced and become habitual. These interactions may be less likely to be skipped or completed ineffectively or inefficiently than are interactions where one of the individuals must recognize that she or he is dealing with an exceptional case and needs to initiate an interaction (as might occur in interaction by exception as described earlier).

• *Recommendation 5: Match the locus of control and the distribution of resources.* In evaluating the design of a virtual system, look for mismatches between the locus of control for various subtasks and the distribution of resources such as data, knowledge, and processing capacities (as well as relevant physical resources). Also consider the distribution of goals and priorities among the team members and subtasks.

There are some subtle or seductive traps to implementing this recommendation. For example, in this aviation scenario, one tempting solution is to increase the situation awareness of the air traffic controller by giving him access to the additional data (a more global view of the weather). The need to monitor this additional resource, however, might tax his mental workload, thus negating the original motivation for the task division. In highly complex organizations composed of virtual teams, this concept is particularly important. As more data are available to more people, it is tempting to expect individuals with different task responsibilities to monitor this additional resource. What is at risk is the potential to undesirably negate the original motivation for the task division.

Case Study 2: Nonverbal Coordination and Communication

In case study 1, the focus was on a setting where the people performing various tasks are separated by time and space. In other settings, responsibilities for different subtasks are still distributed, but the individuals are physically colocated and the performance of these subtasks is much more closely interwoven. In this type of setting, face-to-face verbal communication has often been cited as the primary means by which team members accomplish this (Kanki, Lozito, & Foushee, 1989).

However, explicit verbal communication is often not the sole medium for coordinating activities. Other nonverbal media that teams use to coordinate their actions include gestures and activity monitoring and are in part made possible by sharing events and work spaces (Hutchins, 1995; Hollan, Hutchins, & Kirsh, 1998).

The next case study presents an example of a coordination breakdown in a dynamic medical environment involving team performance during trauma patient resuscitation and anesthesia when an unexpected event occurred, requiring team members to respond rapidly to find an alternative solution (Xiao & LOTAS Group, 2001). This example serves to highlight issues associated with reliance on nonverbal communication:

When attempting to revive a trauma patient, medical response teams perform a variety of physical tasks. Some of these tasks have to be coordinated among team members because the tasks require synchronized effort from many people (for example, lifting a patient), because the tasks rely on preconditions (for example, suctioning equipment must be staged and ready to use), or because multiple tasks must be performed simultaneously (for example, establishing an airway and restoring blood circulation).

To facilitate such coordination, team members use a variety of primarily nonverbal tactics. These tactics include following established protocols that specify the distribution of tasks, priorities, immediate goals, and problems to be treated. Furthermore, during attempts to revive and stabilize a patient, team members often determine what they should do by monitoring the actions of the trauma team leader. In moments when team members are not occupied with a task, they often follow the attentional focus of the team leader. By focusing on the leader's actions, other team members are often able to provide materials or assistance before the leader needs to verbally ask for a tool or help.

In this example, a patient had a gunshot wound to the lower abdomen. The patient's condition called for quick insertion of a tracheal breathing tube, which required paralyzing the patient. Normally anesthesia team members wait for surgical team members to insert an intravenous line into the patient, because these lines are the usual route for administering the paralyzing drugs. In this instance, however, difficulty in installing the line and the patient's rapidly declining condition forced the two anesthesia team members to consider abandoning established procedures. Both worked independently of one another to arrive at alternate solutions. However, neither attempted to verbally communicate problems or discuss plans of action. Therefore, each implemented a line of action that conflicted with the other's action. Furthermore, the lack of verbal communication impaired the ability of support team members to provide needed assistance. For example, one member of the anesthesia team decided to use a nonroutine nasal intubation in order to achieve airway access but did not announce the adoption of this nonroutine method. Furthermore, this method required special materials that supporting members of the team had not anticipated. Due to the lack of announcement of this method, support team members' ability to provide assistance was diminished, preparation of necessary materials was delayed, and the procedure included many pauses and delays in implementation.

In this situation, the change in plan during a crisis disrupted the routine distribution of task responsibility. Rather than being able to adjust their responsibilities to account for the new situation and anticipate what resources might be needed for this new course of action, the team members assumed the role of observers while the anesthesia crew member with the unshared plan worked furiously to achieve his new objectives. Because of this situation, "critical steps were left out (e.g., applying cricoid pressure to prevent regurgitation of stomach contents into the lungs after the ET tube was removed)" (Xiao et al., 2001, p. 253).

• *Recommendation 6: Provide support for coordination of distributed, highly interdependent tasks with the ability for nonverbal communication.* When tasks are distributed among team members but are highly interdependent, coordination using nonverbal forms of communication (gestures and activity monitoring in a shared event space) needs to be supported. Being able to interpret and understand the actions of other team members in such a setting may be dependent on the assumption that there is a shared script or mental model among the team that allows an understanding of what actions to expect and how to interpret them. If an abnormal situation arises and that script no longer applies, reliance on the usual nonverbal communications may no longer be adequate, and verbal interactions may need to be triggered and supported.

This concept is particularly relevant as many organizations digitize all aspects of their operations, with each person placed in front of an individual display rather than having team members gathered around a common colocated display as they do their joint work, especially when that work is dynamic and changes rapidly.

Case Study 3: Coordination During Plan Adaptation and Replanning

Planners today need to continually incorporate new information and knowledge into their models of the world and change their plans accordingly. When this planning activity uses collaborative teams, coordination among the members is critical. When the team is distributed in space or time (or both), this coordination becomes more difficult. As each team member considers whether and how the plan must change, a variety of information and knowledge must be exchanged, including events that might change how the plan unfolds, what changes must be made, and at what point activities in the plan need to be synchronized. In addition, what each team member knows, what data are available, and what their assessment of the situation is need to be shared. It is also important to understand each team member's understanding of the changing events and what each thinks are the expected next steps. It may be critical for team members to communicate what contingencies are in place, as well as the goals and priorities that motivate the plan (Woods, 2001).

Using simulated military command-and-control scenarios, Shattuck and Woods (1997) designed situations where actual events deviated from the published plan in order to investigate how team members adapted when events did not go as planned. The investigators were interested in understanding how the team members dealt with the changing circumstances given their understanding of their leader's intent and how they used their leader's intent in adapting to unexpected events. At one extreme, the investigators found that team members would follow the original plans by rote as described by the leader with no regard for the local complicating factors. At the other extreme, team members would act completely autonomously, leaving their leaders out of the loop and failing to coordinate with other relevant team members. The results demonstrated the need to strike a balance in the degree of communication and coordination among leaders who were not physically present and team members who were physically colocated, where those team members need to respond to unanticipated local situations in ways that support achieving higher-level goals.

In the U.S. Army, plan evolution may take various forms. It may be that within the initial plan, there are contingencies in the form of alternative actions and follow-on actions that take into account a thinking, uncooperative, and adaptive adversary. There may also be an adjustment that can be made to the plan that is very local in its execution and impact and thus does not require significant coordination with other participants. In contrast, events may occur that were unanticipated in the original plan and require a significant change in the responsibilities or actions of the various team members. These significant changes require replanning. The following case looks at such an event observed during an army simulated battle activity:

The army corps developed a plan in which a regiment, one of its lower echelons (refer to Figure 13.2 for a model of the levels of command), was required to secure a river-crossing site so that division forces would be able to cross the river unimpeded by enemy forces. In order to do this, the division forces would need to pass between the regiment troops, a complicated military maneuver.

The regiment was not successful in securing the river crossing, which meant the mission could not proceed as planned. However, the division planners had neglected to consider contingencies if any part of the plan failed because they were busy planning further into the future.

Because of the failure of the regiment's part of the plan, the division's plan was no longer viable. As a result, a brigade commander, seeing an opportunity for his troops to secure the river crossing, took the initiative and had his team develop an alternate plan. He synchronized that plan with adjacent brigade commanders, informed the division commander of the plan, and executed the plan. The division then crossed the river, which had been the ultimate goal of this part of the corps mission.

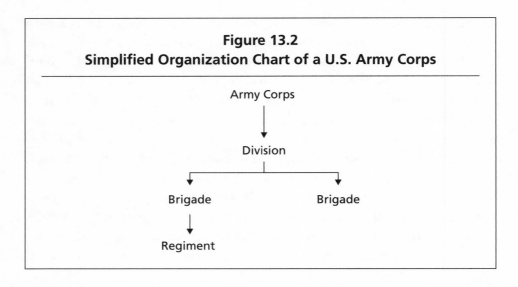

Figure 13.2
Simplified Organization Chart of a U.S. Army Corps

Army Corps

Division

Brigade   Brigade

Regiment

This change in the plan during a dynamically evolving situation disrupted the routine distribution of task responsibility. Because of the robustness of command and the initiative of the brigade commander, the team members were able to modify their roles while remaining consistent with the intent of the original plan. However, the two brigades now had to achieve objectives that were not in their original execution plan. They were able to maintain efficient communication with each other using the tactical radio network while keeping the division commander informed, and this enabled the division to get all of its troops and equipment across the river.

• *Recommendation 7: Support coordination and synchronization among team members.* If an unanticipated situation arises for which an appropriate contingency has not been developed, the organizational structure needs to enable effective responses while ensuring that team members are able to reestablish coordination and resynchronize their activities based on the outcomes of these responses.

USING TECHNOLOGY TO COMMUNICATE AND COORDINATE
Case Study 4: Planning Contingencies
Another aspect to consider in evaluating this army replanning episode is to look at the factors that contributed to the failure of the original plan. One such event was the assumption made by division planners that the regiment would

be successful in the mission to secure the area, clearing the way for the division to get across the river. Because of this assumption, they failed to consider a contingency that could have resulted in a more robust plan.

• *Recommendation 8: Use technology to ensure critical assumptions are assessed and evaluated.* A critical part of planning is the development of appropriate contingencies. The planning process needs to ensure that potential failures of critical plan elements are considered and that appropriate contingencies are developed. Technology (for example, critiquing and alerting systems) can sometimes be used to help ensure that critical assumptions are assessed and evaluated. It can also monitor events during the execution of a plan to help detect situations where assumptions have been violated.

Overall, the example illustrates a success story involving virtual work. However, in addition to improved contingency planning, there was another aspect that could have been improved: ensuring timely replanning, resynchronization, and coordination after the division troops successfully crossed the river. Because the plan and its execution were planned at the brigade echelon, the brigades were "ahead" of the division planners, who were involved in developing plans for activities that were to occur twenty-four to forty-eight hours in the future; thus, once across the river, the brigades had to wait for the division commander to issue a new order for how to proceed. The brigade commanders appropriately decided that they should not proceed beyond this point and act independent of the division, as this would risk desynchronizing the rest of the division plan.

• *Recommendation 9: Support coordination of work across several media.* Support coordination of virtual work across several communication channels—for example, across verbal channels to support auditory coordination, activity monitoring in a shared event space and visual aids to support awareness of the activities of others, and more robust scripts or contingency plans to support prescribed actions.

• *Recommendation 10: Ensure procedures and processes allow virtual teams to quickly resynchronize.* To deal with cases where one subgroup acts opportunistically to achieve an objective, ensure that procedures are in place that specify how each subgroup should perform while a revised plan is developed. Also develop a process that ensures that the overall plan is revised and communicated in a timely manner so that everyone is in sync.

Case Study 5: Use of Video for Coordination and Communication

Most research on video has focused on capturing the images of remote participants as they perform some task together, for example, conducting a problem-solving meeting using videoconferencing (Chapanis, 1981; Dourish & Bly, 1992; Fish, Kraut, Root, & Rice, 1992; Tang & Isaacs, 1993). A number of these studies suggest that adding a medium that allows the presentation of visual information has no effect on either the quality of the interaction or the outcome of the task (Anderson et al., 1997; Hiltz, Johnson, & Turoff, 1986). However, most of the studies reporting these results focus on the use of video to communicate visual aspects of interaction, such as eye gaze, physical gestures, and facial expressions (Chapanis, Ochsman, Parrish, & Weeks, 1972; O'Conaill, Whittaker, & Wilber, 1993; Sellen, 1992; Tang & Isaacs, 1993).

Research results have been more promising in situations where the visual communication of important content was intended to improve coordination and collaboration. For example, Nardi, Kuchinsky, Whittaker, Leichner, and Schwarz (1996) provide an account of such results, using video as data rather than as simply "talking heads," an extension of the concept of a shared event space as discussed in case study 2 of the colocated surgical team involving nonverbal coordination and communication. The context in which Nardi et al. examine this use of technology is the operating room during a neurosurgical procedure. The central role of the video was to provide images of the work pace and work objects, or the data. Following is their account:

During many neurosurgeries, the neurosurgeon views his or her work through a microscope while performing the operation. The rest of the surgical team often relies on a live video feed of the surgery site, and this feed provides the information that allows the team to coordinate their activities with that of the surgeon's needs.

Usually the scrub nurse is most reliant on the video information, which helps the nurse anticipate the materials and surgical tools the surgeon will need. In fact, the TV monitor is usually on a movable cart, and the cart may be repositioned several times during a surgery by a circulating nurse, oriented so that the scrub nurse has a continuing and unimpeded view of the TV monitor. Especially during critical parts of the surgery, the surgeon often works quickly, rapidly changing instruments and requesting supplies. The scrub nurse must be able to quickly select from hundreds of potential instruments and supplies arranged on nearby tables, and the information from the video feed is crucial for anticipating the surgeon's needs and thus not slowing the surgeon's work rate. Such anticipatory teamwork is critical for the success of most neurosurgeries.

Thus, by using video as data rather than simply as an indication of who is present in an activity, the video image allows the coordination of fast-paced activities between collaborative members of a team. It also provides a means of maintaining the attention and focus for members who may not have an active role at any given time but must be ready to act at a moment's notice:

> Rather than facilitating direct interpersonal communication . . . , the video in the operating room permits individuals to work independently . . . [and] supplies enough information so that the need for interpersonal communication is reduced . . . and individuals can figure out what they need to know based on the video itself, circumventing the need to talk to or gesture at someone. . . . The provision of visual information at key moments provides a different channel of communication than that which would be provided through verbal, gestural, or written communication. . . . Collaboration and co-ordination are enabled as each member of the neurosurgery team interprets the visual information, and proceeds to do his or her job based upon an interpretation of that information. The video data, plus individual knowledge and understanding, combine to produce an interpretation that leads to the desired collaboration, with little or no interpersonal interaction [Nardi et al., 1996, p. 84].

• *Recommendation 11: Use video when an accurate and informative picture is needed.* Although mixed results are reported in the literature regarding the value of videoconferencing, the concept of using video as data has strong face validity in case studies like the one reported here. The design implications are clear: if video can be used to provide a sufficiently accurate and informative picture of some event, then it can be a potentially effective means of providing remote access to that event.

A caution is in order, however, regarding the limits for generalizing from this case study. In this illustration, the remote viewers of the video were physically present, so they had the benefit of all of the contextual cues present in the operating room in addition to the data from the video. This context could be lost if the team members are not colocated and are provided with the video but no other means for maintaining situation awareness about the broader context. Thus, understanding the limitations of video systems in providing a shared visual space (for example, what visual cues are enabled, what the field view is of each participant, and what level of detail is needed about the work area) is a necessary consideration (Fussell, Setlock, & Kraut, 2003; Hills, Hauber, & Regenbrecht, 2005).

Case Study 6: Mediating Coordination Using Auditory Technologies

Another category of teamwork is communication and coordination in settings where a primary group of problem solvers needs to converse and a secondary group would benefit from knowing what the primary group is thinking and doing. One example is the use of hot lines at FAA traffic management facilities that allow airline dispatchers to listen in on the conversations of traffic managers, but do not allow them to interject comments into the traffic managers' conversations. A second example is the coordination of activities through voice loops, "an auditory groupware technology . . . that support[s] synchronous communication on multiple channels among groups of people who are spatially distributed" (Patterson, Watts-Perotti, & Woods, 1999, p. 353). Patterson et al. (1999) provide the following discussion that space shuttle ground controllers with different scopes of responsibilities used during an unexpected event:

During a fuel pump problem that occurred on a space shuttle mission, audio voice loops were used by ground-based National Aeronautical and Space Administration personnel to facilitate the identification, diagnosis, and resolution of the problem. At least four groups (systems controllers and support staff, flight directors, communications directors, and astronauts) took part in the problem's resolution and used these voice loops. The voice loops were important for aiding the coordination among the various groups. For instance, the groups could work collaboratively to diagnose the fuel pump difficulties without having to move to the same location. Furthermore, the communications over the public voice loops were less error prone because any member of any of the groups could intervene or ask for clarification. In addition, staff could anticipate questions that would be asked by listening in on such communications. Updates targeted to the flight director were automatically heard by other groups. Even unexpected subsystem changes were more quickly recognized by all groups accessing the voice loops.

The primary point of this case study is that it may be effective to allow secondary participants (for whom knowledge about some situation is relevant for their own tasks) to monitor an interaction among primary participants who are dealing directly with the situation. Because the secondary participants can monitor this interaction in real time (in this case, using a voice loop), they have immediate situation awareness regarding the perceptions and intentions of the primary participants. It may also be unnecessary to provide a later briefing to the secondary participants, thus reducing workload. A corollary point is that the shuttle ground control voice loop allowed a secondary participant to immediately interrupt and interject relevant knowledge that could prevent the primary participants from making a mistake because they lacked certain knowledge or data available only to a secondary participant. This latter feature, which exists for the shuttle ground control example but not for the FAA traffic management hot lines, blurs some of the distinctions between a voice loop and a normal teleconference.

However, this case raises some cautionary points about the use of voice loop technologies. One unanswered question prompted by this example is whether the primary participants conversed as though there were no "lurkers" listening in on their interactions or whether they altered their conversations (or should have done so) because they knew they had an audience who needed additional explanation or data in order to understand the conversation or its implications. (If not, some important information that might normally be provided in a prepared briefing for the secondary participants might never be communicated.) A related question is whether the secondary participants felt they could interject not only to add insight but also to clarify their own understanding of what was being said, something that is not possible with the FAA hot lines. Patterson et al. (1999) did provide an example where a secondary participant interjected additional information in a conversation:

> When the booster controller reports that the performance was nominal, the other controllers can stop focusing their attention on updates from the booster controller and can divert their attention away from how to implement contingency plans in the event of booster engine problems. Note that the booster controller's update is judged to be a lower priority than the discussion about the hydraulic leak. Rather than interrupting their ongoing communications, the booster controller *waits* for those discussions to pause *before updating* the flight director [Patterson et al., 1999, p. 362].

Given these points, it may be that the better characterization is that this is a team discussion where some members are fully focused on the problem-solving part of the conversation (the primary participants), while others (the secondary participants) are expected to be time sharing between this listening task and other tasks of their own.

This perspective raises the question of whether such monitoring could have a negative impact on the completion of other tasks assigned to the secondary participants. Conversely, there is a potential concern for how to ensure that if the secondary participants are time sharing between the listening task and some other primary tasks of their own, they do not miss important information discussed over the voice loop.

• *Recommendation 12: Use one-way communication and "listening-in" technology to enable situation awareness.* This discussion suggests that voice loops or one-way hot lines can be an efficient way to allow spatially distributed teams with primary and secondary roles on some task under discussion to maintain common situation awareness in a timely fashion. A virtual work system with voice loops requires ensuring that the actors have access to all channels required for efficient and effective performance. In this way, all channels (not only those of the voice loop or one-way hot line, but also those within the colocated work space) must be taken into consideration so that the actors do not miss critical information from their primary tasks.

Case Study 7: Synchronous and Asynchronous Problem Solving Using Shared Virtual Work Spaces

People naturally communicate using the multiple modalities available to them. For example, when two people are physically colocated, they can use spoken language, gestures, facial expressions, and nonlinguistic sounds such as laughing or coughing to communicate with one another. Given that physical presence provides the greatest opportunity for the establishment of mutual understanding and mutual knowledge (Clark & Marshall, 1992), providing an environment where collaborators are able to be physically colocated appears to be optimal for establishing common ground. However, it is not practical, or feasible, for members of virtual teams to be physically located together when the need to interact arises. Therefore, providing an environment where the objects, or representations of objects, being referred to are physically present with each of the partners at their distributed locations and where each can interact with the object being referred to (the referent) and with one another through the referent may be an effective alternative to physical colocation.

Recent research on shared work spaces (Obradovich, 2001; Whittaker, 2003; Whittaker, Geelhoed, & Robinson, 1993) has provided support for the effectiveness of shared virtual work spaces. Whittaker et al.'s work examines two-person telephone communication with and without the presence of a shared work space (such as a computer display) and two-person asynchronous communication (that is, not at the same time) using shared drawing surfaces and documents for editing and design tasks. The work space provided a record of the team members' progress during the tasks so that each participant could directly observe the modifications and annotations that the other member made. Viewing this asynchronous, dynamic display of activities often reduced or even eliminated the need for verbal communication between the team members.

• *Recommendation 13: Design the system to allow teams that must interact asynchronously to view the sequence of events and reasoning behind decisions.* Often distributed teams need to work together to solve a problem. If those teams are not only physically separated but also are distributed across multiple time zones, their work must usually occur asynchronously. If the product of one team member or group is the starting point for the work to be accomplished by a second team member or group, the intermediate steps taken by the first team member or group can be displayed visually, such as showing intermediate steps as a design is created and refined by others. This shared virtual work space allows the second person or group to view this sequence of visuals later and may be more effective in helping that person or group to understand both the current state of the product and the reasons or steps that led to the current state rather than simply showing the second person or group the end product produced by the first person or group.

BUILDING SHARED PERSPECTIVES

Within complex organizations, there is often only partial overlap of knowledge and data among decision makers. The decision making is distributed over many practitioners and teams of practitioners who must coordinate the sharing of uniquely held data and knowledge among members of the team in order to achieve both the individual and common goals of these practitioners. Research indicates that the more data and knowledge shared among team members, the more effective and productive the team will be (Cannon-Bowers, Salas, & Converse, 1993; de Vries, van den Hooff, & de Ridder, 2006; Rentsch & Hall, 1994; Rentsch & Klimoski, 2001). Virtual work brings with it the possibility that those who have a decision-making role may not have sufficient knowledge to support their decisions. Also, because members of a team are individuals with different backgrounds, beliefs, and attitudes, as well as different interpretations of events, plans, and goals, the team must work to achieve a shared perspective or common ground (Clark, 1996; Whittaker, 2003).

Case Study 8: Establishing Common Ground and Building Shared Perspectives

Obradovich (2001) similarly demonstrated the value of a shared work space in her study of synchronous but geographically separate communication and problem solving involving airline dispatchers and FAA traffic managers. This investigation focused on how team members from two distinct yet interdependent organizations, each having unique knowledge and expertise, collaborate to solve a shared concern: the inefficiencies occurring within the national airspace.

These team members were spatially distributed and had a shared work space available to them.

This study found that the shared work space, consisting of a visual display, annotation tools, and an auditory channel, can enable interactions and serve as an aid to the collaborators in establishing common ground. An environment that provides a shared visual display with a capability for telepointing (for example, using a computer mouse to point at a particular part of a display) and two-way audio communication may reduce the effort that a virtual team, engaged in a spatially distributed, collaborative problem-solving task, must expend to establish common ground. Through the use of a shared display and audio communication, the team members have the opportunity to establish a virtual copresence with each member (enabled by the physical presence of the display and the ability to point to information on that display and the linguistic copresence established through use of the telephone) that can facilitate the collaborative interaction (Figure 13.3 illustrates the shared display and the telepointer, indicated by the arrow). A culture of collaborative teamwork is enabled through the sharing of perspectives, and a free flow of task- and team-relevant knowledge among the members.

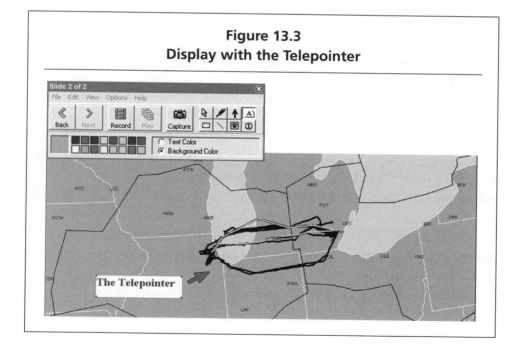

Figure 13.3
Display with the Telepointer

This ability for joint reference (that is, attending and focusing on the same object) aided the team members in effectively coordinating their conversations, establishing mutual understanding, and enabling a "shared mind-set across the cooperating agents about the background field against which the agents can all recognize interesting conditions or behaviors" (Woods, 1991, p. 7).

The shared display also provides contextual cues to help reduce "understanding costs" (Clark, 1996) that could be incurred if only voice communication existed. The persistence of the information on the shared display helps to reduce the cognitive load of the participants by maintaining the context of the interaction in their visual field.

In addition to examining the building of shared knowledge between the dyad partners and their use of that knowledge in their problem-solving task, this study looked at other important aspects of communication that contribute to successful collaboration. Of particular interest was the role of the shared display in enabling the dyad to build common ground as they shared their perspectives and knowledge.

In this study, the participants were geographically distributed and thus did not have available to them all of the modalities present in face-to-face interactions. For example, without the ability to see one's partner, one cannot know at any particular instance in time where the partner is focusing his or her attention. However, with the modalities of speech (by telephone) and gesturing (by telepointer within the shared display) available, partners were able to establish, repair, and maintain common ground.

Because the partners in this study were provided with a telephone and a shared display (the slideshow via NetMeeting, a videoconferencing tool from Microsoft that allows the users to conduct a meeting using the computer with the ability to share audio, video, computer data, and applications), they were looking at the same thing while referring to features of the surrounding context. The shared display provided a common frame of reference and allowed the partners to be informed about where the other was looking or where to direct attention. One interesting aspect of the interaction between the partners as it involved the shared display was how they used reference as a means of establishing a sense of copresence. Also observed was how reference allowed the conversational partners to minimize the necessary effort for grounding their interactions.

The use of the slide show (via NetMeeting) allowed the participants in this study to reduce their effort for grounding. It did this by framing the relevant conversation and thus becoming a lens through which the conversational partners could focus discussion. The traffic manager and dispatcher of each team were better able to track each other's focus of attention, retain their conversational context, and achieve joint reference (Tapie, Terrier, Perron, & Cellier, 2006).

One type of reference that the team members used was deictic expressions (for example, *here* and *there*), usually accompanied by deictic gestures (the physical act of pointing). The telepointer provided by NetMeeting eased the cognitive load in grounding by facilitating the ability of each partner to track the other's attention and aid in focusing attention on a specific part of the visual context (Bangerter, 2004; Suthers, Girardeau, & Hundhausen, 2003). When one partner would say, "Look there," while moving the telepointer to some point in the shared display, the second partner could associate "there" with the referenced location because the first partner produced the utterance and gesture almost simultaneously. The second partner could then simultaneously hear the utterance and look at the location in the display where the pointer had been placed. Figure 13.3 is one of the scenario slides illustrating the use of the telepointer.

- *Recommendation 14: Use shared visual displays combined with synchronized voice and pointing technology to support grounding and focusing of attention.* Whether the communication is synchronous or asynchronous, for tasks where some of the information content is highly visual in nature, providing a shared visual display supported with synchronized voice and pointing technology can be effective in establishing common ground and focusing on specific information during the interaction.

Case Study 9: Sharing Knowledge and Data to Build Shared Mental Models

Research teams suggests that teams can generate representations of a problem that differ from those developed by an individual working alone, potentially providing richer or more effective insights into the problem (Dunbar, 1998). This is possible because teams may bring to the task multiple sources of knowledge and experience, a wider variety of perspectives, and the potential synergy associated with collaborative activity (Bass & Ryterband, 1979; Morgan & Lassiter, 1992; Ogot & Okudan, 2006).

Teams also add complexities to the decision-making process not seen at the individual level. For example, within a team, individual members may have unique information or perceptions about different task elements or cues, but those members may not share their unique information in group discussion (Griffith, Sawyer, & Neale, 2003; Grigone & Hastie, 1993; Stasser & Titus, 1987). Also, different areas of expertise are distributed among the team members so that even when they have access to the same information, they may evaluate it much differently and from different perspectives. Finally, the cognitive burden can become greater for the members of a team performing a decision-making task than it is for an individual decision maker. They must engage in three activities simultaneously. They must recall information (from their memories or notes), exchange that information, by receiving or giving it to others in the group, and process that information, which involves the social and cognitive implications of that information and storing it in memory. Thus, it is possible that engaging in one of the activities interferes with a person's ability to engage fully in the other two (Ball & Zuckerman, 1992; Buckhalt & Oates, 2002; Lamm & Trommsdorff, 1973).

Furthermore, other psychological and emotional issues (such as trust in others, cooperation, coordination, team adaptability, and power or status differences among members) arise within teams (Fiore, Salas, Cuevas, & Bowers, 2003; Guzzo, 1995; Stasser, Vaughan, & Stewart, 2000; Wittenbaum & Stasser, 1996). Thus, understanding the process and means by which teams arrive at decisions requires going beyond a simple extension of individual decision-making practices. One needs to consider a number of factors unique to team decision making, including group dynamics, interpersonal communication skills, conflict, competition, and hidden agendas.

One way of dealing with some of these issues is to design tasks that help to ensure that individuals share their information and knowledge in an appropriate and efficient way. The following example illustrates a process that helps to achieve this objective in a goal-directed way:

In one army brigade, the officers have incorporated into their standard planning procedures an additional step that they refer to as the "red hat wargame." The purpose of this step is to refine and improve the scenarios of enemy actions that are developed to use during their simulated battle exercises and ensure that the entire planning team understands these scenarios.

The red hat wargame is incorporated in the first step of the military decision-making process that is taught to all officers. The participants in the war game include expert representatives from all staff sections and units. These experts bring their specialized knowledge to the game as they take on the role of their enemy counterparts (the "red hats") and discuss how and when they would employ the available red assets to defeat the "generic" friendly course of action that has been developed for the particular scenario being planned.

The end state of the war game is defined as having two fully developed adversary plans for action that will be used in the simulated war-gaming exercise. In addition, all of the team members have built a common understanding of these different plans.

This red hat wargame process allows the team to share different representations of and insights into the problem. These insights might not occur when implementing the standard military decision-making process in which a single individual is responsible for developing the scenarios of potential enemy actions used in the simulated war-gaming exercise. Thus, by bringing together the various team members who have the necessary specialized knowledge and giving them a task that necessitates the application of that knowledge to the planning process, the potential exists for developing comprehensive enemy scenarios incorporating knowledge that might otherwise be left uncommunicated.

This war game step also represents an indirect method for introducing needed cognitive conflict (that is, controversy over the best way to achieve the team's goal), as the enemy scenarios may bring into question aspects of the plan that have been developed for the friendly forces. This is something the literature suggests can improve decision-making effectiveness (Amason, 1996; Jehn, 1995). More specifically, "cognitive conflict stems from the existence of multiple plans or scenarios for achieving group goals" (DeVine, 1999, p. 612). The sharing of these multiple plans among team members increases the members' motivation to describe and justify their positions. The goal of using this method is to encourage team members to question the underlying assumptions and promote the consideration of alternatives.

• *Recommendation 15: Assign tasks to ensure critical information and knowledge is shared.* To deal with issues arising within decision-making teams, such as trust in others, cooperation, coordination, and power or status differences among members, assign tasks that help to ensure that individuals share their information and knowledge in appropriate and efficient ways. Structuring a group's task in a way that encourages the members to discuss alternatives often results in more thoroughly shared information (Wittenbaum, Hollingshead, & Botero, 2004).

• *Recommendation 16: Design tasks to enable team members to engage in behaviors that will aid effective decision making.* Design and assign tasks that induce or influence the team members to engage in desirable behaviors and interactions, such as cognitive conflict, that are likely to improve decision-making effectiveness by encouraging the examination of underlying assumptions and the consideration of alternatives.

FINAL THOUGHTS

Because modern organizations are becoming virtual work systems composed of complex, highly distributed collaborative teams, concepts that support the design of effective virtual work systems are particularly relevant. As virtual work becomes the norm, organizations will require a greater amount of collaboration among a greater number of individuals and groups distributed spatially and temporally. Particular attention needs to be paid to the design of these virtual work systems in both the structure and process of the teams and the technologies used to support them so that effective and efficient interactions occur among all participants.

By investigating successes and failures in a variety of complex, dynamic domains that rely on virtual teams to do the work, a number of design best practices have been identified within the broader themes that could help guide plans for distributing work within virtual work systems. Table 13.2 provides a summary of these best practices and associated recommendations.

REMINDERS

• Advances in technology are creating the ability for collaborative work to be accomplished by teams whose members are distributed across the world.

• These virtual teams must be supported by effective technologies that allow collaboration and coordination among members.

Table 13.2

Virtual Work Systems Best Practices and Recommendations

Theme	Best Practice	Virtual Work System Recommendations
Designing work processes	Division of tasks	Divide overall tasks into independent subtasks.
		Design the system to foster detection of situations where interaction is necessary.
		Use technology to create systems that will ensure needed interaction.
		Design into the system subtasks that have prerequisite dependencies.
		Match the locus of control with the distribution of resources, considering the distribution of goals and priorities.
	Modes of communication	Support nonverbal forms of communication.
		Support coordination and synchronization.
Using technology to communicate and coordinate	Contingency planning	Use technology to ensure assumptions are assessed and evaluated.
	Coordination and synchronization	Support coordination of work across several media.
		Ensure procedures and processes allow teams to resynchronize their activities.
	Use of video	Use video when accurate and informative pictures are needed.
		Support activity monitoring using a shared display.
	Use of auditory technologies	Use one-way communication to enable greater situation awareness.
		Ensure actors have access to all channels that are required for efficient and effective performance.
	Synchronous and asynchronous interaction	Allow asynchronous teams to view the sequence of events and reasoning behind decisions made.
		Use shared visual displays supported with synchronized voice and pointing.
Building shared perspectives	Establish common ground and shared knowledge	Use shared displays combined with voice and pointing technology to focus attention and build common ground.
	Build shared mental models	Assign tasks to ensure sharing of critical information and knowledge.
		Design tasks to enable the team to engage in effective decision making.

- Team tasks must be appropriately divided in order to provide as much task independence as possible; allow team members to know when interaction needs to occur; take into consideration the distribution of resources, such as knowledge and data; and match the locus of control (that is, the authority and responsibility) with those resources.

- The ability to use a variety of modes of communication (for example, nonverbal and verbal) provides team members with the opportunity to do their virtual collaborative work effectively and efficiently.

- The use of technology to communicate and coordinate with team members is important whether the work requires synchronous or asynchronous interaction.

- Assign tasks in such a way that ensures that team members will share essential information and knowledge.

References

Amason, A. C. (1996). Distinguishing the effects of functional and dysfunctional conflict on strategic decision-making: Resolving a paradox for top management teams. *Academy of Management Journal, 39*, 123–148.

Anderson, A. H., O'Malley, C., Doherty-Sneddon, G., Langton, S., Newlands, A., Mullin, J., et al. (1997). The impact of VMC on collaborative problem solving: An analysis of task performance, communicative process and user satisfaction. In K. Fin, A. Sellen, & S. Wilber (Eds.), *Video-mediated communication* (pp. 133–155). Mahwah, NJ: Erlbaum.

Argote, L., & McGrath, J. E. (1993). Group processes in organizations: Continuity and change. In C. L. Cooper & I. T. Robertson (Eds.), *International review of organization and industrial psychology* (pp. 333–389). Hoboken, NJ: Wiley.

Ball, S. A., & Zuckerman, M. (1992). Sensation seeking and selective attention: Focused and divided attention on a dichotic listening task. *Journal of Personality and Social Psychology, 63*, 825–831.

Bangerter, A. (2004). Using pointing and describing to achieve joint focus of attention in dialog. *Psychological Science, 15*(6), 415–419.

Bass, B. M., & Ryterband, E. (1979). *Organizational psychology* (2nd ed.). Needham Heights, MA: Allyn & Bacon.

Buckhalt, J. A., & Oates, D. F. (2002). Sensation seeking and performance on divided attention tasks varying in cognitive complexity. *Personality and Individual Differences, 32*(1), 67–78.

Cannon-Bowers, J., Salas, E., & Converse, S. (1993). Shared mental models in expert team decision making. In N. J. Castellan (Ed.), *Individual and group decision making: Current issues* (pp. 221–246). Hillsdale, NJ: Erlbaum.

Chapanis, A. (1981). Interactive human communication: Some lessons learned from laboratory experiments. In B. Shackel (Ed.), *Man-computer interaction: Human factors aspects of computers and people* (pp. 65–114). Alphen aan den Rijn: Sijthoff & Noordhoff.

Chapanis, A., Ochsman, R. B., Parrish, R. B., & Weeks, G. D. (1972). Studies in interactive communication II: The effects of four communication modes on linguistic performance of teams during cooperative problem solving. *Human Factors, 19,* 101–129.

Clark, H. H. (1996). *Using language.* Cambridge: Cambridge University Press.

Clark, H. H., & Marshall, C. R. (1992). Definite reference and mutual knowledge. In H. H. Clark (Ed.), *Arenas of language use* (pp. 9–59). Chicago: University of Chicago Press.

Crowston, K. (1997). A coordination theory approach to organizational process design. *Organization Science, 8*(2), 157–175.

DeVine, D. J. (1999). Effects of cognitive ability, task knowledge, information sharing, and conflict on group decision-making effectiveness. *Small Group Research, 30*(5), 608–634.

De Vries, R. E., van den Hooff, B., & de Ridder, J. A. (2006). Explaining knowledge sharing: The role of team communication styles, job satisfaction, and performance beliefs. *Communication Research, 33*(2), 115–135.

Dourish, P., & Bly, S. (1992). Portholes: Supporting awareness in a distributed work group. In *Proceedings of the SIGCHI Conference on Human Factors in Computing Systems* (pp. 541–547). New York: ACM Press.

Dunbar, K. (1998). Problem solving. In W. Bechtel & G. Graham (Eds.), *A companion to cognitive science* (pp. 289–298). Malden, MA: Blackwell.

Fiore, S. M., Salas, E., Cuevas, H. M., & Bowers, C. A. (2003). Distributed coordination space: Toward a theory of distributed team process and performance. *Theoretical Issues in Ergonomics Science, 4*(3–4), 340–364.

Fish, R., Kraut, R., Root, R., & Rice, R. (1992). Evaluating video as technology for informal communication. In *Proceedings of the SIGCHI Conference on Human Factors in Computing Systems* (pp. 37–48). New York: ACM Press.

Fussell, S. R., Setlock, L. D., & Kraut, R. E. (2003). Effects of head-mounted and scene-oriented video systems on remote collaboration on physical tasks. In *Proceedings of the SIGCHI Conference on Human Factors in Computing Systems* (pp. 513–520). New York: ACM Press.

Gailbraith, J. R. (1987). Organization design. In J. Lorsch (Ed.), *Handbook of organizational behavior* (pp. 343–357). Upper Saddle River, NJ: Prentice Hall.

Griffith, T. L., Sawyer, J. E., & Neale, M. A. (2003). Virtualness and knowledge in teams: Managing the love triangle of organizations, individuals and information technology. *MIS Quarterly, 27,* 265–237.

Grigone, D., & Hastie, R. (1993). The common knowledge effect: Information sharing and group judgment. *Journal of Personality and Social Psychology, 65,* 959–974.

Guzzo, R. A. (1995). Introduction: At the intersection of team effectiveness and decision making. In R. A. Guzzo, E. Salas, & Associates (Eds.), *Team effectiveness and decision making in organizations* (pp. 1–8). San Francisco: Jossey-Bass.

Heath, C., & Staudenmayer, N. (2000). Coordination neglect: How lay theories of organizing complicate coordination in organizations. *Research in Organizational Behavior, 22,* 153–191.

Hills, A., Hauber, J., & Regenbrecht, H. (2005). Videos in space: A study on presence in video mediating communication systems. In *Proceedings of ICAT2005 (International Conference on Artificial Reality and Telexistence)*. Retrieved October 15, 2006, from http://www.hci.otago.ac.nz/downloads/HillsHauberRegenbrecht_ICAT2005_ShortPaper.pdf.

Hiltz, S. R., Johnson, K., & Turoff, M. (1986). Experiments in group decision making: Communication process and outcome in face-to-face versus computerized conferences. *Human Communication Research, 13*(2), 225–252.

Hollan, J. D., Hutchins, E. L., & Kirsh, D. (1998). *KDI: A distributed cognition approach to designing digital work materials for collaborative workplaces.* Retrieved September 22, 2006, from http://www.nsf.gov/cgi-bin/showaward?award=9873156.

Hutchins, E. (1995). *Cognition in the wild.* Cambridge, MA: MIT Press.

Jehn, K. A. (1995). A multimethod examination of the benefits and detriments of intragroup conflict. *Administrative Science Quarterly, 40,* 256–282.

Kanki, B. G., Lozito, S., & Foushee, H. C. (1989). Communication indices of crew coordination. *Aviation, Space, and Environmental Medicine, 60*(1), 56–60.

Lamm, H., & Trommsdorff, G. (1973). Group versus individual performance on tasks requiring ideational proficiency (brainstorming): A review. *European Journal of Social Psychology, 3,* 367–387.

Malone, T. W., & Crowston, K. (1994). The interdisciplinary study of coordination. *Computing Surveys, 26*(1), 87–119.

Morgan, B. B., & Lassiter, D. L. (1992). Team composition and staffing. In R. W. Swezey & E. Salas (Eds.), *Teams: Their training and performance* (pp. 75–100). Norwood, NJ: Ablex.

Nardi, B. A., Kuchinsky, A., Whittaker, S., Leichner, R., & Schwarz, H. (1996). Video-as-data: Technical and social aspects of a collaborative multimedia application. *Computer Supported Cooperative Work, 4,* 73–100.

Obradovich, J. H. (2001). *Facilitating synchronous collaboration among distributed agents in the air traffic management system: A descriptive study.* Unpublished doctoral dissertation, The Ohio State University, Columbus.

O'Conaill, B., Whittaker, S., & Wilber, S. (1993). Conversations over video-conferences: An evaluation of the spoken aspects of video-mediated interaction. *Human Computer Interaction, 8,* 389–428.

Ogot, M., & Okudan, G. E. (2006). The Five-Factor Model personality assessment for improved student design team performance. *European Journal of Engineering Education, 31*(5), 517–529.

Patterson, E. S., Watts-Perotti, J., & Woods, D. D. (1999). Voice loops as coordination aids in space shuttle mission control. *Computer Supported Cooperative Work, 8,* 353–371.

Rentsch, J. R., & Hall, R. J. (1994). Members of great teams think alike: A model of team effectiveness and schema similarity among team members. In M. M. Beyerlein & D. A. Johnson (Eds.), *Advances in interdisciplinary studies of work teams, Vol. 1: Theories of self-managing work teams* (pp. 223–261). Greenwich, CT: JAI Press.

Rentsch J. R., & Klimoski, R. J. 2001. Why do "great minds" think alike? Antecedents of team member schema agreement. *Journal of Organizational Behavior, 11,* 107–120.

Rico, R., & Cohen, S. (2005). Effects of task interdependence and type of communication on performance in virtual teams. *Journal of Managerial Psychology, 20*(3/4), 261–274.

Roth, E. M., Patterson, E. S., & Mumaw, R. J. (2002). Cognitive engineering: Issues in user-centered system design. In J. J. Marciniak (Ed.), *Encyclopedia of software engineering* (2nd ed., pp. 163–179). New York: Wiley.

Saavedra, R., Earley, P. C., & Van Dyne, L. (1993). Complex interdependence in task-performing groups. *Journal of Applied Psychology, 78*(1), 61–72.

Sellen, A. (1992, May 7). Speech patterns in video-mediated conversations. In *Proceedings of the SIGCHI Conference on Human Factors in Computing Systems* (pp. 49–50). New York: ACM Press.

Shattuck, L., & Woods, D. D. (1997, September). Communication of intent in distributed supervisory control systems. In *Proceedings of the 41st Annual Meeting of the Human Factors and Ergonomics Society,* Santa Monica, CA: Human Factors Society.

Smith, P. J., McCoy, C. E., & Orasanu, J. (2001). Distributed cooperative problem-solving in the air traffic management system. In E. Salas & G. Klein (Eds.), *Linking expertise and naturalistic decision making* (pp. 367–382). Mahwah, NJ: Erlbaum.

Stasser, G., & Titus, W. (1987). Effects of information load and percentage of shared information during group discussion. *Journal of Personality and Social Psychology, 53,* 81–93.

Stasser, G., Vaughan, S. I., & Stewart, D. D. (2000). Pooling unshared information: The benefits of knowing how access to information is distributed among group members, *Organizational Behavior and Human Decision Processes, 82*(1), 102–116.

Suthers, D., Girardeau, L., & Hundhausen, C. (2003). Deitic roles of external representations in face-to-face and online collaboration. In *Designing for change in networked learning environments: Proceedings of the International Conference on Computer Support for Collaborative Learning* (pp. 173–182). Dordrecht: Kluwer.

Tang, J., & Isaacs, E. (1993). Why do users like video: Studies of multimedia-supported collaboration. Technical Report: TR-92–5 (pp. 1–31). Mountain View, CA: Sun Microsystems, Inc.

Tapie, J., Terrier, P., Perron, L., & Cellier, J-M. (2006). Should remote collaborators be represented by avatars? A matter of common ground for collective medical decision-making. *AI and Society, 20,* 331–350.

Whittaker, S. (2003). Things to talk about when talking about things. *Human-Computer Interaction, 18,* 149–170.

Whittaker, S., Geelhoed, E., & Robinson, E. (1993). Shared workspaces: How do they work and when are they useful? *International Journal of Man-Machine Studies, 39*, 813–342.

Wittenbaum, G. M., Hollingshead, A. B., & Botero, I. C. (2004). From cooperative to motivated information sharing in groups: Moving beyond the hidden profile paradigm. *Communication Monographs, 71*(3), 286–310.

Wittenbaum, G. M., & Stasser, G. (1996). Management of information in small groups. In J. L. Nye & A. M. Brower (Eds.), *What's social about social cognition? Research on socially shared cognition in small groups* (pp. 3–28). Thousand Oaks, CA: Sage.

Woods, D. D. (1991). The cognitive engineering of problem representations. In G.R.S. Wier & J. L. Alty (Eds.), *Human-computer interactions and complex systems*. Orlando, FL: Academic Press.

Woods, D. D. (2001). *Building common ground as distributed teams modify plans in progress.* Working document.

Xiao, Y., & LOTAS Group (2001). Understanding coordination in a dynamic medical environment: Methods and results. In M. McNeese, E. Salas, & M. Endsley (Eds.), *Trends in cooperative activities: Understanding system dynamics in complex environments* (pp. 242–258). Santa Monica, CA: Human Factors Society.

PART FIVE

Working on a Collaborative Team

The variety of methods for strengthening team performance and the importance of this topic are reflected in the fact that more chapters in this handbook address this subject than any other. Chapter Fourteen suggests a number of ways to ensure that the technology actually does support the team's functioning. Selecting the most appropriate technology for the team is a matching process that depends on how the members' social presence is promoted or inhibited by the technology and by the media richness the tools provide. As technology improves, a new challenge emerges: how to filter out excess information or set boundaries around available time, so members are not overwhelmed. Team effectiveness depends on decisions framed by an understanding of team processes, organizational culture, and meeting effectiveness, as well as collaborative technologies.

Technology is not enough. The proper use of the technology requires both technical and social skills. Chapter Fifteen points out that the complexity of the situation and the restriction of using technology-mediated communication can result in a vicious downward spiral of team process. Training team members so they can achieve shared understanding, trust, and effective communication enables them to create a virtuous cycle that climbs toward excellent performance.

The challenges for the virtual team begin with the limitations of technology-mediated communication. Differences in team member cultures create important barriers to smooth communication. Chapter Sixteen suggests that an awareness of those differences represents the first step in dealing with them. It takes knowledge, observation, interpretation, skill, and patience for leaders to intervene effectively when cultural differences prevent the members from melding into an effective team. A positive outlook and support and encouragement seem to be valued by the members of all cultures.

A number of key processes within the team deserve attention, such as communicating, learning, adapting, and supporting each other. The outcomes of the processes include effective decision making and problem solving and innovation and creativity. Chapter Seventeen presents a systematic process for problem solving. The quality of the solution depends on drawing ideas from all members of the team. A disciplined process makes that possible. Cultural differences make such a process essential.

Chapter Eighteen provides guidelines for effective decision making. Effective decisions depend on a team approach. Self-serving and politically motivated behaviors prevent good decisions and solutions from emerging for the team. The key is for each member to accept all good ideas, opinions, and decisions as if they were his or her own, which requires a high level of listening to and accepting other members' contributions.

The Technology That Supports Virtual Team Collaboration

Lori Bradley

Virtual collaboration enables distributed expertise to focus on shared problems with a necessary interfacing through technology. Quality of interaction is critical for establishing the framework for successful collaboration on any team, virtual or not; however, the usual hurdles of any group of people coming together to tackle difficult problems is exacerbated in virtual groups by having to rely on technology. For this reason, virtual collaboration should be planned for and supported by the development of specific interaction skills and the technological proficiency that will help ensure project success.

There continues to be a need to understand how technology changes the nature of work and collaboration. The utility of collaborative technology can be restricted because of the limited understanding of human-media interfaces and organizational interaction. Creighton and Adams (1998) warned that hundreds of millions of dollars may be wasted chasing fads and installing technology that people will either ignore or use to work in the same way they worked before they had access to the technology. Thus, an assessment of the utility of collaborative technology and potential impact on individuals, groups, and organizations is needed, given technology's rapid proliferation, as a way to complement or replace face-to-face meetings among geographically dispersed groups (Castella, Abad, Alonso, & Silla, 2000).

This chapter provides an overview of some of the most common types of collaborative technology used in organizations today. It sets out a conceptual framework on which the utility of collaborative technology can be assessed. The framework includes whether the collaborative technological tool offers asynchronous or synchronous interaction, and the degree of social presence and media richness each may possess. The chapter then describes and provides examples of three major types of collaborative technology available today: electronic message systems, audio-video systems, and collaboration support systems. It closes with recommendations for how, in the absence of rich face-to-face interaction, technology can be used to enable collaboration.

A FRAMEWORK FOR ASSESSING COLLABORATIVE TECHNOLOGY

Collaborative technology can be segmented and classified in various ways. The most common classification categories include to what degree a collaborative technological tool offers asynchronous or synchronous interaction, social presence, and media richness.

Asynchronous or Synchronous Interaction

Collaborative technology may be classified according to the capabilities a specific technology enables in relation to the location and time frame of the users. For example, virtual collaboration technology can be segmented into synchronous and asynchronous time-anchored categories (Duarte & Snyder, 2001). Synchronous technology is that which supports same-time interaction, such as audio- or videoconferencing, and Web chatrooms. Asynchronous technology is that which allows different-time interaction, such as e-mail and Web-based bulletin boards. Some recently emerging technologies, such as Weblogs (blogs) and video logs (vlogs) can provide both synchronous and asynchronous capabilities, depending on the desires of the user or the communities that coalesce around them.

Group collaboration and collaborative technology can also be segmented into quadrants (same time–same place, same time–different place, different time–same place, and different time–different place) that add a place component to the categories (Straus, 2002; Gorelick, 2000). Though not commonly referred to as a technology, face-to-face meetings, an increasingly rare working arrangement, fall into the upper left (same time–same place) quadrant.

Social Presence

The concept of social presence refers to the degree of realness or salience that the technology provides to those in the interaction. Social presence is described as a subjective quality that a particular technology medium possesses. It primarily depends on the medium's capacity to convey visual and nonvisual cues. Social presence theorists arrange different communication media on a continuum of social presence, with written correspondence being low on the scale and face-to-face communication being high. The key to effective collaboration is to match the task to the technology that offers the best level of social presence. Technology with a low social presence value generally is acceptable for tasks that require little or no interaction (Piccoli, 2001).

Media Richness

Media richness focuses on the level of information richness that a certain technology provides. One might conceive social presence as focusing on the human factors, while media richness focuses on the technology factors. A communication tool is deemed rich when it facilitates "immediate feedback, transmission of multiple cues, multiplicity of channels, personalization of the message, language variety," and the ability to synthesize divergent views and allows diversity of input (Piccoli, 2001, p. 37). A tool is deemed lean when it does not provide these characteristics. Richer media are more appropriate for conveying complex messages because the lack of contextual cues and immediate feedback of leaner media could cause confusion and inhibit progress toward solutions or decisions. Leaner media are acceptable, sometimes preferable, for less complex messages when contextual cues are not as important as a means to avoid misunderstanding. A list, from richer to leaner, based on the principles of media richness, might look like this: face-to-face interactions, videoconferences, telephone conversations, audioconferences, e-mail, personal written documents, and numerical documents (Piccoli, 2001).

A Tool for Assessing Collaborative Technology

Collaborative technology has been segmented into three major types of systems for the support of interpersonal communication: electronic message systems, audio and video systems, and cooperation supporting systems (Andriessen & van der Velden, 1993). It is now possible to assess each of these three types of systems on the framework presented above. Table 14.1 provides a general overview of the types of collaborative technology and how each fares in terms of asynchronous and synchronous interaction, social presence (low to high), and media richness (lean to rich). Each type of collaborative technology is described in more detail in the next section.

Table 14.1
A Tool for Assessing Collaborative Technology

Type of System	Type of Technology	Synchronous or Asynchronous	Social Presence	Media Richness
Electronic messaging systems	E-mail	Asynchronous	Low	Lean
	Voice mail	Asynchronous	Medium	Lean
Audio and video systems	Teleconferencing	Synchronous	Medium	Lean
	Videoconferencing	Synchronous	High	Moderate to rich
Collaboration supporting systems	Group decision support systems	Synchronous	Medium	Moderate to rich
	Web conferencing	Can be both if sessions are archived	Medium	Rich
	Blogs	Can be both	Varies with the use	Varies with the use

TYPES OF COLLABORATIVE TECHNOLOGY

Electronic Message Systems

Electronic messaging systems include the now common e-mail, voice mail, and paging devices and also other systems that are gaining in popularity such as text messaging and devices that allow both graphics and text to be transmitted. They are asynchronous methods of communication and fit into the different time–different place category. The introduction of electronic message systems usually results in the creation of new communication channels and an increase in the frequency of information exchange (Andriessen & van der Velden, 1993).

These message systems do not drastically reduce travel or meetings but are used in addition to existing communication means. Especially with the ever broadening availability of wireless devices and networks, electronic messaging systems enable information to move quickly between individuals and among teams. Where once the challenge was how to stay connected, now the pervasive use of the BlackBerry and wireless-enabled laptop computers allow one to be connected around the clock and around the world. The new challenge may be learning how to filter out too much information or how to set boundaries around available time. Effective virtual collaborators will learn to establish team norms that ensure that no one is being overwhelmed with too much information and that are respectful of teammates' work/life balance.

Audio and Video Systems

Audio and video systems include the telephone, videophone (sometimes referred to as desktop videoconferencing), and audio- and videoconferencing systems (conference room videoconferencing). They are synchronous methods of communication, and participation usually falls in the same time–different place category.

Audio and video systems offer greater media richness and social presence than electronic messaging systems but less than face-to-face interaction. Unlike e-mail and other messaging systems, theses systems enable linguistic (verbal), paralinguistic (verbal, but with traits of the linguistic signal, such as tone of voice or emphasis on particular words), and, in the case of video, nonverbal information (signals that include facial expressions, posture, and hand gestures) to be transmitted. Audio systems support linguistic and paralinguistic communication but are not helpful for nonverbal communication. Audio channels can support task and group maintenance processes, but situational awareness—signals about the context in which the interaction takes place—is limited, as is the transfer of nonverbal signals and visual object information. Also, if groups have more than three people, careful structuring of the interaction is necessary to effective collaboration.

Video systems overcome some of the limitations of audio-only systems. They allow participants to see some nonverbal signals, support visual object information, and convey situational awareness. However, the low quality of video resolution in some videoconferencing systems and the lack of user knowledge of best practices for structuring a videoconference may result in a marginal gain in social presence, since participants still cannot see nonverbal signals well. Video is effective when assessing the attention of the group, however. This can be important if there is not a great deal of trust among the participants in a meeting. Sometimes the mere knowledge that the other site can see the activity in the room will encourage more attentive and respectful behavior. If attention is the key to performance, then sustained attention on the process of achieving the shared goal results in the highest-quality outcomes.

A high-quality videoconferencing system can allow large groups to work together; however, there are other video applications that are less expensive and easily connect small numbers of people. As opposed to conference room videoconferencing, these systems allow desktop videoconferencing, which is basically a telephone call with the addition of video. The main benefit of desktop videoconferencing seems to be in the greater social presence of the meeting participants. However, rather than being able to see each other, what tends to facilitate collaboration at a higher level is the ability to see the object (which could be a document or a design) that the group's efforts are focused upon. Trust levels are developed by time spent face-to-face. The visual aspect of the desktop video mimics (though admittedly a poor substitute) being in person. Face-to-face interactions create the chance to understand the context of the person one is working with and hence to interpret virtual messages within a specific context. This reduces the chance of misinterpretation, always a risk with asynchronous technology such as e-mail (Meyerson, Weick, & Kramer, 1996).

Collaboration Supporting Systems

A group of professionals doing creative work cannot achieve high-quality solutions if they are working only at the cooperation level. They must achieve some level of collaboration: listening, hearing, integrating others' ideas into their own, cycling through consecutive iterations of possible solutions, and co-evolving a shared perspective on the problem definition, criteria, and solution. That is why I have changed the term from *cooperation* to *collaboration*-supporting systems.

Most of the tools discussed here are computer based and are designed to enable groups to collaborate better. These tools can be synchronous (for example, a Web conference) or asynchronous (for example, electronic message board) and various combinations on the time-place spectrum. The collaboration tools encompass simple instant-messaging utilities, complex systems that enable interactive presentation capabilities, and full-featured Internet-based groupware that offers virtual shared work spaces, such as Team Wave Software's Workplace, and project management capabilities, such as Instinctive Technology's eRoom (Mitchell, 1999) and Macromedia's Breeze.

Computer, video, and audio channels support information exchange in differing ways. Chatrooms and instant messages allow same-time (synchronous) information exchange on the computer, but in synchronous information exchange using a computer is generally more difficult than with teleconference or videoconference. The interactivity is lower on computers, which means that a fluid interaction is more challenging (Andriessen & van der Velden, 1993).

Web-conferencing software allows the user to show presentations, review documents, field questions, and poll audiences with only a standard Web browser. Web conferences are typically used with streaming audio over the Internet or in conjunction with conventional teleconferences. Some groups prefer to use teleconferencing with the Web-conferencing software due to the inconsistent audio quality of many Web-conferencing systems. It is important to remember the distinction between mere communication and collaboration, a disciplined and interactive process that allows a variety of ideas, opinions, and insights to be brought to bear on an issue or challenge.

Many companies are beginning to make more extensive use of sophisticated systems that allow large numbers of people to participate in meetings simultaneously and to brainstorm or comment at the same time through the use of networked computer terminals (Straus, 2002). These technologies are often referred to as electronic meeting systems (EMS). EMS include software programs that, in conjunction with a Web connection, allow participants around the world to share documents and presentations in real time. With the support of EMS, large numbers of people can view or participate in presentations and training sessions complete with graphics and sound, and global companies can communicate with all employees at once (Straus, 2002). In addition to large-scale, well-planned events, EMS technology offers corporations a means to conduct quickly called meetings on the fly, thus helping them to respond quickly to problems or opportunities. Mitchell (1999) sees the advantages as threefold: reducing time to market for enterprises, making the training of long-distance colleagues easier, and enhancing customer relationships online. Achieving the highest levels of creativity should be listed as an additional advantage. The utility of EMS software will increase as subsequent editions offer greater capability and become more cost-effective.

More and more, Web-based tools are being designed and used by organizations to support virtual collaboration. Some specific types of these tools, discussed in detail in sections that follow, are electronic whiteboards, softboards, team Web templates, discussion databases, and group decision support systems.

Electronic Whiteboarding   Electronic whiteboarding technology can contribute to collaborative efforts by digitizing information and saving it in an electronic format that can be printed out and used for future reference and e-mails. The e-whiteboard can also be used for remote meetings by incorporating a modem, which enables transmission of the images as drawn on the board to appear on the monitor of a remotely located computer. When supplemented with teleconferencing, audio exchanges may accompany the whiteboard images. This technology is beneficial for sharing real-time sketches and for brainstorming sessions and eliminates the need for hand-recording ideas illustrated on a traditional whiteboard.

Softboard   A softboard is an electronic writing surface that offers features beyond those offered by standard and electronic whiteboards. The electronic screen has graphics and word processing programs loaded that allow the user to write or draw (using a special stylus or marker) on the actual screen, and then to cut and paste text or drawings or to rearrange items on the writing surface, and print out the results or e-mail them to someone else.

Team Web Template   A team Web template can be used as a base to set up an interactive Web site that allows a group to share information and promote collaboration. The site can be tailored to fit how the team wants to work together. This Web template might provide a set of tabs to provide easy access to a team's most in-demand topics—for example, scheduling, contact information, technology assistance, important documents, or standardized forms. It can also provide links to other important Web sites. Relevant stakeholders may access the team's work through the team's Web template. In addition, the team can use its Web template to communicate with extended communities. A message board can be used to post relevant or urgent news items and to conduct online discussions.

Discussion Database Discussion databases provide electronic forums in which users can exchange information or ideas on topics of common interest. A discussion database is shared among those in a work group or team and is usually focused on a single topic, such as a new product line, a particular project, or even a problem that the team is experiencing and seeking solutions. Discussion databases are effective for activities such as brainstorming, feedback, gathering opinions, discussions on best practices, and daily reporting of information. Any group that has information to share among its members can use a discussion database. Perhaps the greatest benefit is that databases support different time–different place interaction by facilitating communication and collaboration among team members who may work different shifts and are located at different sites. Another important feature is that through the use of the database, a record is created that preserves history and can be referenced in order to orient new team members or to document how a particular decision was made. A new member can be directed to browse the archives of the database as part of his or her orientation.

Group Decision Support Systems Group decision support systems (GDSS) comprise a large subcategory of EMSs. According to Bannon (2003), the increased interest in GDSSs stems from awareness that decision making is often a group event, and thus computer support for communication and the integration of multiple inputs and opinions is valuable.

GDSSs range widely in complexity. They may be as simple as ordinary meeting rooms, where portable PCs can be quickly set up on a local area network. They can also be as complex as the "pod" rooms set up at the London School of Economics, which cost thousands of dollars and are equipped with unique work stations, group display systems, modifiable lighting, and other features (Bannon, 2003). At a minimum, GDSSs usually include features to support various phases of decision making and group activity, such as brainstorming and polling. Some well-known systems are the University of Minnesota's SAMM system, the University of Arizona's Electronic Meeting Systems (marketed as GroupSystems V by Ventana Corporation), Xerox Parc's CoLab, IBM's TeamFocus, and VisionQuest marketed by Collaborative Technologies Corporation (Bannon, 2003).

In the majority of cases, GDSSs require a meeting facilitator and technical support to helps the group in the use of the software tools and processes. GDSSs were originally designed to support colocated real-time collaboration in face-to-face settings, but have been adapted for use in distributed, virtual settings. Ideally each site has a facilitator present. The systems typically include a number of tools designed to assist in the group decision-making process, such as processes for brainstorming activities and for ranking and voting on items.

A major benefit of GDSSs is that they allow anonymity, even in face-to-face meetings. Typically users sit at computer terminals and use a keyboard to enter information. The information can then be compiled and displayed anonymously, which helps skirt potential personality clashes and reduces inhibitions that may result from status differentials among meeting attendees. However, this feature of GDSS should not be used to avoid needed and productive confrontations and effective conflict resolution. GDSS can be particularly useful for helping groups that are high in conflict work together, generating and prioritizing options (brainstorming), dealing with controversial issues, defining problems, and reaching consensus. Again, it is important for the meeting to have a facilitator who can help the group generate dialogue and avoid having the technology become simply a polling or voting device.

An important element of collaboration is the dialogue and discussion about the background of an issue, the definition of the issue, and the group's work to decide how to decide on a possible solution. Once the group is at that point, use of GDSS technology may speed up the process and support the collaboration.

ENABLING COLLABORATION IN THE ABSENCE OF FACE-TO-FACE INTERACTION

Face-to-face meetings offer synchronous and rich communication that is high in social presence. However, for virtual collaborative efforts, face-to-face meetings are a luxury that many teams cannot afford. Table 14.2 lists a series of virtual collaborative options for a variety of tasks (document review, consensus building, and brainstorming) and situations (number of people involved).

Table 14.2
Virtual Collaborative Options in the Absence of a Face-to-Face Meeting

Task	Number of People	Virtual Collaborative Options
Review a document	Two	Option 1: Document is shared by e-mail, then reviewed by telephone call.
		Option 2: Software (for example, Lotus Sametime, NetMeeting) allows both participants to view and edit the document in real time online while on a telephone call. Participants can pass control of the document back and forth.
	Three or more	Option 1: Document is shared by e-mail, then reviewed by conference call.
		Option 2: Software (for example, Lotus Sametime, NeMeeting) allows all participants to view and edit the document in real time online while on a conference call. Participants can pass control of the document around to all participants.
Reach consensus on a pressing issue	Two	Option 1: Telephone call.
		Option 2: Desktop videoconferencing.
	Three or more	Option 1: Conference call.
		Option 2: Conference room videoconferencing.
		Option 3: Desktop videoconferencing.
Group brainstorm session with some members remote (for example, capturing ideas on sticky notes to be integrated in later)	Three or more	*If anonymity is not an issue:*
		Option 1: Conference call or videoconference with one person playing the role of facilitator (to ensure that remote participants are able to participate) and one person as scribe (to write down the remote member's contributions).
		If anonymity is desired:
		Option 1: Remote participants can e-mail their comments to the facilitator, who can write them on sticky notes and add to the local group's work.
		Option 2: Each remote participant can be assigned a "buddy" in the local room and can call, e-mail, or send an instant message with comments. The buddy writes down the remote person's input, adds it to his or her own, and posts it with the rest of the group's.
		Option 3: Software program can be used with all participants at computer workstations. Input is captured and compiled but not attributed.

FINAL THOUGHTS

Advances in technology are creating exciting opportunities for virtual collaboration. An understanding of collaborative technology, team processes, organizational culture, and meeting effectiveness will enable sound processes to be created to guide effective collaboration. It can be challenging to keep up with technology, but those who are willing to invest the time will be rewarded with the knowledge that they are building the foundation for a new way of working. High-quality human interaction through technology brings together diverse approaches to create innovative solutions and designs that are greater than the sum of the minds that created them.

REMINDERS

- The concept of social presence refers to the degree of realness or salience that the technology provides to those involved in the interaction.

- The key to effective collaboration is to match the task to the technology that offers the best level of social presence.

- Media richness focuses on the level of information richness that a certain technology provides. One might conceive social presence as focusing on the human factors and media richness focusing on the technology factors.

- The new challenge may be learning how to filter out too much information or how to set boundaries around available time.

- Effective virtual collaborators will learn to establish team norms that ensure that no one is being overwhelmed with too much information and that are respectful of teammates' work/life balance.

- Video systems allow the user to see some nonverbal signals, support visual object information, and convey situational awareness. However, the low quality of video resolution in some videoconferencing systems and the lack of user knowledge of best practices for structuring a videoconference may result in a marginal gain in social presence, since participants still cannot see nonverbal signals well.

- With the support of electronic meeting systems, large numbers of people can view or participate in presentations and training sessions complete with graphics and sound; and global companies can communicate with all employees at once.

- An understanding of collaborative technology, team processes, organizational culture, and meeting effectiveness will enable sound processes to be created to guide effective collaboration.

References

Andriessen, J., & van der Velden, J. (1993). Teamwork supported by interaction technology: The beginning of an integrated theory. *European Work and Organizational Psychologist, 3*(2), 129–143.

Bannon, L. (2003). *Group decision support systems: An analysis and critique.* Retrieved January 2, 2004, from http://www.ul.ie/~idc/library/papersreports/LiamBannon/32/ECIS.htm.

Castella, V., Abad, A., Alonso, F., & Silla, J. (2000). The influence of familiarity among group members, group atmosphere and assertiveness on uninhibited behavior through three different communication media. *Computers in Human Behavior, 16*(2), 141–159.

Creighton, J. L., & Adams, J. W. (1998). *Cyber meeting: How to link people and technology in your organization.* New York: AMACOM.

Duarte, D., & Snyder, N. (2001). *Mastering virtual teams: Strategies, tools, and techniques that succeed* (2nd ed.). San Francisco: Jossey-Bass.

Gorelick, C. K. (2000). Toward an understanding of organizational learning and collaborative technology: A case study of structuration and sensemaking in a virtual project team. *Dissertation Abstracts International, 61*(05), 1806A. (UMI No. 9973090)

Meyerson, D., Weick, K. E., & Kramer, R. M. (1996). Swift trust and temporary groups. In R. M. Kramer & T. R. Tyer (Eds.), *Trust in organizations: Frontiers of theory and research.* Thousand Oaks, CA: Sage.

Mitchell, L. (1999, August 23). Test center analysis: Make virtual meetings a reality. *InfoWorld.* Retrieved September 13, 2007, from http://www.webex.com/pdf/webex_article29.pdf.

Piccoli, G. (2001). Virtual teams: An investigation of the determinants of team effectiveness and the contribution of managerial behavior control. *Dissertation Abstracts International, 61*(08), 3240A. (UMI No. 9984359)

Straus, D. (2002). *How to make collaboration work.* San Francisco: Berrett-Koehler.

Training for Virtual Collaboration

Beyond Technology Competencies

Arie Baan, Martha Maznevski

Virtual teams are not simply regular teams that work together over technology. Virtual teams share some additional characteristics that raise challenges for smooth functioning and high performance. Moreover, because they are typically created to address tasks that are strategic, a team's performance is usually very important to the organization. Most virtual teams require assistance in developing an effective set of norms and routines to achieve such performance. Learning the technology is not enough: a valuable training and development program also addresses the issues around communication and trust through an action-learning sequence customized to a team's needs.

This chapter describes the three most important challenges of working virtually: complexity, invisibility, and restricted communication. Then these three challenges are related to critical success factors for virtual teams: shared understanding, communication, and trust. Next, the structure and content of a modularized training program for helping teams develop these characteristics are outlined. Finally, the organizational context for effective support of virtual team development and performance is identified. We argue that teams that build shared understanding through effective communication, with continuous awareness of the importance of building trust, can initiate and maintain virtuous cycles of high performance. Training can and should play a critical role in this virtuous cycle.

We developed the insights we set out in this chapter during our design and implementation of learning and competency development programs for a large multinational oil company. The first author designed, delivered, and evaluated learning programs for intact virtual teams at this company. The second author was part of a team of professors delivering general leadership development programs for leaders of this company at an executive education institute. Leading virtual teams was considered to be a core competence for all general managers in this organization, and the topic was integrated into a larger program. The frameworks, tools, and techniques presented in this chapter have been used with many teams and organizations and have been found to be robust and widely generalizable across contexts.

THE CHALLENGES AND KEY SUCCESS FACTORS OF WORKING VIRTUALLY

Typical definitions of virtual teams and virtual collaboration refer to people working across boundaries of place, time, organization, and culture and to the critical role of information and communication technology (for example, Duarte & Snyder, 2006). From these definitions, however, it is difficult to derive what it really takes to work together effectively and successfully as a team across these boundaries. In this section, the three greatest challenges that virtual teams face, and the key success factors for overcoming them, are identified. These insights form the foundation of an effective training and development program.

The Challenges

Three key aspects make day-to-day virtual collaboration critically different from its traditional colocated version:

- *Complexity:* Virtual teams and work groups typically face a greater degree of complexity in their working environment than face-to-face groups do.

- *Invisibility:* The greater complexity is not highly visible, which easily leads to incomplete understanding and incorrect conclusions.

- *Restricted communication:* Communication using electronic media (telephone, e-mail, instant messaging, and others) is significantly less effective in articulating viewpoints and nuances than direct face-to-face communication; however, this apparent deficiency can create some counterintuitive advantages in the right context.

Complexity   Virtual teams are typically created to achieve tasks necessary to the functioning of the organization that cannot be accomplished by colocated teams because the necessary resources are distributed. These tasks almost always include coordination and aligned action across business units. For example, a virtual team may be created to coordinate matrix functions like human resources or global accounts across product business units, or to use specialized R&D and market-related expertise from different parts of the organization to design and implement a new product for a new multinational market segment. By the nature of their task, virtual teams are often more complex than colocated teams. Furthermore, because of the purposes of virtual teams, they are almost inevitably composed of team members who vary widely in terms of:

- National cultures
- Native languages spoken
- Fluency in the common language adopted by the team
- Professional backgrounds
- Organizational cultures (even though the members of the team may be part of the same multinational organization, different units of the organization will have developed different subcultures)

Virtual team composition is also more fluid over time (compared with colocated teams), enabled by the ease with which part-time members can be added to or removed from the team, without significant staff relocation cost or effort. This has a considerable, and negative, impact on the effectiveness of team-building activities. Therefore, diverse composition and fluidity in composition add complexity to the team.

Appreciation of the complexity of the organizational and working environment, understanding its impact, and the ability to work effectively with it are key supporting competencies for successful virtual collaboration and leadership and must be targets of training and learning programs.

Invisibility   In the virtual environment, many events and activities are happening without the individual team members initially becoming aware of them, particularly those related to the group process and how members are engaging in the group task. For example, in the early stages, team members may agree to gather information about customer requirements in their locations; however, they may not realize that they are making different assumptions about which information to collect and why. The effects of these differences often come to team members' attention only at a later stage, when differences create clear discrepancies or even overt conflict. But even at that point, the available contextual information is limited, and team members often jump to the wrong conclusions because of what they do not know.

Argyris's ladder-of-inference concept helps illustrate cognitive steps of how individuals pay attention to information, process it, make decisions, and take action (Argyris, 1982; Senge, Kleiner, Roberts, Ross, & Smith, 1994). People select data and experience from the world around them, attach meaning to this information, apply assumptions, draw conclusions, develop beliefs, and then take action. Each step is influenced by the individual's personality, background, and context. When these characteristics differ among people—for example, because they come from different cultures or different organizational functions—then those people will have different ways of interpreting the world around them: they will select and process different information and take different actions. In diverse colocated teams, these differences are hard enough to detect. In virtual teams, not only are differences more likely due to higher diversity, but they are often impossible to detect. The different physical locations of team members cause different data and experiences to be observed and selected, and the greater variety in cultural backgrounds in the widest sense has an impact on conclusions, beliefs, and action. It is no surprise then that in virtual teams, the same events and information can (justifiably!) lead to different actions by team members. Moreover, others in the larger organization will not appreciate what the team is doing and accomplishing unless the work is visible. As a consequence, resources may be withheld, and team members pulled off the virtual team to work on other projects, hampering the efforts of the team.

Improved awareness of the limitations of available information and compensation for the invisibility through better advocacy and inquiry are key components of virtual teamworking competency and therefore training and development.

Restricted Communication Aggravating the effects of greater complexity of the environment and limited visibility of events and activities on virtual team operation is the use of information and communication technology (ICT) tools for most of the communication and collaboration activities within the team. Compared with face-to-face communication, the ICT media have restricted capacity to deliver information within context (referred to as media information richness by Daft & Lengel, 1984) or to provide the capability for expression and perception of personal aspects (referred to as social presence by Short, Williams, & Christie, 1976). When new ICT media become available, new behaviors have to be adopted to compensate for these deficiencies, and the initial lack of consistency and commonality of these behaviors can hamper their usefulness in the virtual team's ICT media toolkit. Short message service and instant messaging are cases in point: whereas in the private sphere these media have found wide and rapid acceptance, with new varieties of shorthand language springing up spontaneously, a more fragmented and limited use within the organizational environment is seen. Where agreement on rules, language, and codes of conduct is fairly straightforward, such as among professionals in a financial services firm, these technologies are adopted more quickly than elsewhere, but in environments with a larger degree of diversity, the efforts and lead times for development of effective new "languages" for use with the new technology tools should not be underestimated.

While ICT without question restricts communication, this can be turned to the team's advantage under certain circumstances. Teams that overcome differences to create trust and structure complexity with disciplined processes can use the technology to provide focus and efficient progress for the group. More specifically, when team members know each other well enough to understand the context behind messages and trust each other's motivations and commitment to the team, the restriction on communication can be used to filter out all the noise, letting the meaningful information through. For example, asynchronous communication provides people with different language abilities and different personalities or cultural backgrounds with the time and space to reflect before responding, reducing the dominance of native language speakers or individual personalities. As another example, some of the highest-performing virtual teams we have worked with always handled their most difficult conflicts over telephone. These teams first built strong relationships of trust and commitment and had team cultures of disciplined structure and response. But even then, they found that addressing difficult conflicts face-to-face tended to escalate the conflicts from task-related to personal conflicts. Team members reacted to the body language of red and angry faces and defiant postures rather than to the content of the disagreement. Over the telephone, in contrast, team members could focus on the words and content and control their own responses better. Importantly, these teams also debriefed all remote conflicts once they were face-to-face again, after the negative emotions had decreased. At this point, they rebuilt relationships and commitment so they could face the next conflicts. Although some teams use this tactic in a more extreme way than others, most effective virtual teams report that given trust and discipline, ICT can be used to help the team.

Effective use of the new media requires insight into their richness and presence limitations, the ability to compensate for these, and the ability to agree on and adopt rules for their use. When teams are able to overcome the complexity and invisibility dynamics and build norms to use technology well, the new media can be used to support highly focused, effective processes. Working productively in this new environment, and particularly working together, requires new or improved competencies and behaviors, which have to be learned.

Critical Success Factors for Effective Virtual Collaboration

The positive and dynamic interaction of three factors (see Figure 15.1) forms the foundation of effective team collaboration in the virtual mode, and therefore also the foundation of learning programs for virtual working competency:

- *Shared understanding:* To make sense of and structure complexity
- *Trust:* To move ahead together under conditions of invisibility
- *Communication:* To overcome and leverage the effects of restricted communication

These three factors are strongly interrelated (hence the double-headed arrows in Figure 15.1), but in our experience they are also components of a cyclical process for improving virtual team effectiveness, indicated by the larger arrows in the figure. This process is founded on these critical success factors.

Shared Understanding   Shared understanding of key aspects of the group task and context is necessary for the team's performance. According to the ladder of inference, shared understanding within a team or work group can be described

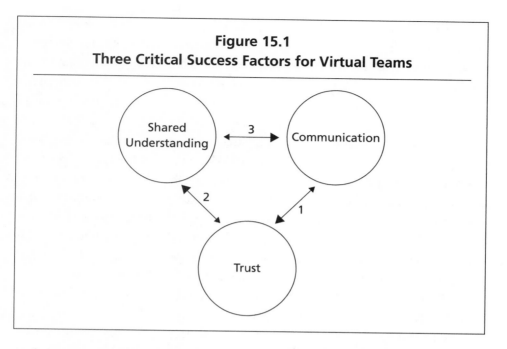

Figure 15.1
Three Critical Success Factors for Virtual Teams

Shared Understanding

3

Communication

2

1

Trust

as the presence of active, mutual knowledge about data and experiences, meanings, assumptions, conclusions, and beliefs that can lead to effective actions by that team or group. Although all team members start with different knowledge, shared understanding can be built from individual understanding through dialogue among team members about the nature and impact of differences. The primary purpose of this sort of dialogue is to reach shared understanding rather than to be a battle of wits or to get individual points of view accepted by the others. This mode of conversation can be created when team members realize that the differences in individual points of view stand in the way of achieving the team's purpose. Through this iterative process of reviewing those attached meanings, shifting assumptions, revising conclusions, and so on, the team can build shared meaning about key aspects of the task, including objectives, stakeholders, and timeline. This process requires changes in individual team members' positions, perceptions, and understanding, which is critically dependent on the presence of trust within the team (arrow 2 in Figure 15.1).

Trust More so than in colocated teams, two types of trust play a role in the dynamics of virtual teams, referred to here as heart trust and head trust. Heart trust is the deeper, feeling-based trust that is mainly created through social interaction of the members of a group over a longer period of time. Someone who has heart trust in another person is comfortable letting that person make important decisions on her or his behalf because of the strong underlying belief that the other person has a genuine interest in the best outcome for all concerned.

Head trust is more task related and is based on the assumptions that members are competent, committed, and capable to work on the team's common purpose. It is based more on thinking than on feeling and can therefore develop faster than heart trust. It has a more limited reach: when a situation develops where the three assumptions of competence, commitment, and capability are no longer valid, head trust disappears quickly. Head trust is similar to the swift trust described for temporary teams with a short lifetime (Meyerson, Weick, & Kramer, 1996), but we see this also as an initial strong component of trust in more permanent virtual teams. Both types of trust are built through communication, whether this is with words or actions (arrow 1 in Figure 15.1).

When a team is working together under conditions of invisibility—each person in the team may come to different conclusions and actions without members really knowing how or why. Trust is the glue that holds them together. It provides the willingness to move past blaming each other for conclusions not understood and begin to ask the kinds of questions that lead to high performance: "I trust that you are motivated and capable and have the team's best interests at heart. So if you've done something I wouldn't have done, it must be because you thought it was the right thing. Help me understand."

Effective Communication   Effective communication is most simply the transfer of meaning from a sender to a receiver and in the way the sender intends (Maznevski, 1994). Effective communication requires active participation by the receiver, for example, with questioning to ensure that implications and insights are well understood. It requires at least some level of shared understanding by the parties involved to be effective; otherwise the receiver's input will be something different from that intended by the sender's output (arrow 3 in Figure 15.1). Although ICT restricts communication, teams that focus on effectiveness of communication through active dialogue (rather than focusing on technology itself) use multiple media to enhance each other and create high-quality communication.

Virtuous and Vicious Cycles

The relationship among these three factors leads to the cycle indicated in Figure 15.1. In the best case, this can be a virtuous cycle where shared understanding is improved by changing individual viewpoints, which requires trust, which is created through effective communication, which is based on good shared understanding. Or it can turn into a vicious cycle, where, for example, a breakdown in trust leads to a decline in shared understanding, which reduces communication effectiveness, which further erodes trust, and so on. Awareness of this process can help to reduce its impact, particularly when the team has agreed on an effective way of signaling when things do not appear to be going well. This awareness must develop over time, but signaling protocols can be agreed to in the team's buildup phase.

The challenge in developing effective virtual collaboration within teams is to take the status quo of these three factors and work on their simultaneous improvement, such that they reinforce each other. Trust is the most difficult to build directly: a trainer cannot simply pull out a worksheet or process and say "trust." If a team focuses on building shared understanding through effective communication, with continuous awareness of the importance of building trust, then a virtuous cycle can be initiated and maintained. Shared understanding (the what) and effective communication (the how) therefore are the most effective starting points for improving team performance.

CHARACTERISTICS OF EFFECTIVE COMPETENCY DEVELOPMENT PROGRAMS FOR VIRTUAL COLLABORATION

To help teams face the key challenges and develop the success factors of virtual teams identified above, learning and development programs for virtual collaboration competency must have several characteristics. The first three characteristics we present are specific to training and development for virtual teams. The fourth articulates best practices for action learning in organizations.

First, they must work with intact, complete teams. The entire team is part of and is affected by complexity, invisibility, and restricted communication and must develop shared understanding, trust, and effective communication. Individual competency development for virtual working can bring improvements for individual learners; the challenge then is to synchronize these among the individual members in the team, where the greatest challenges are faced. Learning as a team and then implementing the output of learning immediately leads to tangible improvements much more quickly and is therefore much more stimulating.

Second, the training must use blended learning techniques: a combination of remote and face-to-face learning, complemented by individual learning activities. This is true partly for pragmatic reasons: the team is unlikely to be able to engage in training together face-to-face much because of the expenses of time and travel. More important, though, blended learning parallels the group's own processes. Most virtual teams work together using some combination of remote, face-to-face, and individual activity. To the extent that learning is conducted in the same context as the actual work, the transfer from learning context to actual is smoother. Moreover, a mixture of learning options accommodates the complexity of different learning styles of team members, for example, due to differences in personality or cultural background.

Third, the training should reflect the fact that virtual teams are complex and that each virtual team is different from others on important dimensions. A modular approach with related yet self-contained learning modules helps to address this complexity. Furthermore, with a modularized approach, teams must identify which modules they need and which they do not early in the team process, thereby providing an initial opportunity for creating shared knowledge about the team and its process and a first step in the virtuous team process cycle.

Finally, an action-learning design is clearly warranted for training and development of virtual teams. In action-learning mode, teams work together with facilitated learning processes on real-life problems, identifying practical solutions and implementing them while paying attention to skill development and learning. When this learning mode is then adopted by intact (virtual) teams that apply it to the actual problem situations they are facing, a highly effective learning environment will be created. With this mode, team members are given sustained exposure to the need to change behavior within the team (Revans, 1980). They share responsibility for the tangible results of action-learning activities, and this focuses their efforts.

Action learning requires the use of diagnostics to help identify areas where the team will benefit most from its learning efforts. Results from team-level diagnostic instruments can also complement the modularity aspect: knowing where competency development will have the greatest impact and then providing a combination of those learning modules that will help this development will give fast and effective results. Although action learning does not require the use of external facilitation or intervention, external support is extremely beneficial, especially in the early stages, to provide an ongoing stimulus for maintaining the learning effort. An external facilitator can, apart from coaching the team to continue on its learning journey, bring in best practices from other teams, both inside and outside the organization, and help to retain an appropriate balance between working and learning.

A MODULAR LEARNING PROGRAM FOR VIRTUAL TEAMS

This section describes the framework and implementation of an actual learning program for virtual teamworking competency as designed, developed, and implemented within a large multinational oil company. The design addresses the three key challenges for virtual teams—complexity, invisibility, and restricted communication—and helps teams build the three key success factors of shared understanding, trust, and effective communication. The program is composed of three integrated sets of modules, focusing on the areas of task, team, and technology, respectively, and therefore is called the T^3 training model.

- *Task:* The task set of modules addresses the team's purpose and (management of) organizational environment and stakeholders. The emphasis here is on understanding and managing complexity, leading to shared understanding.

- *Team:* The team set of modules addresses the experiences, preferences, skills, competencies, and expectations brought by the members of the team and the way in which these aspects can be used to make the team work together more effectively. The emphasis is on improving visibility, which leads to trust.

- *Technology:* The technology set of modules addresses the selection and use of ICT tools. The emphasis is on making the most of restricted communication, leading to effective communication

The nine modules that make up the program are shown in Table 15.1.

A team begins its T^3 learning journey by completing a diagnostic instrument on the current status of the team. By analyzing the results of this diagnosis together with the external facilitator, the team decides which modules it will engage in, in which order, and using which modes. The diagnosis can be done

Table 15.1
Modules in the T³ Training Program

Task complexity leading to shared understanding	**Team Purpose:** Makes an inventory of the differences in individual team members' views of the team's purpose and builds a common purpose based on deeper, shared understanding.
	Stakeholder Engagement: Maps the organizational environment of the team in terms of stakeholders (other teams, organizations, individual people) and their relationships with the team and makes a prioritized inventory of the strategy and tactics for improving these relationships.
	Communications Planning: Starting from the stakeholder engagement module's output, this module creates a detailed, prioritized overview of internal and external communications requirements and activities, providing assistance for the usual situation where available resources do not meet requirements.
Team invisibility leading to trust	**Virtual Working Styles and Preferences:** Leads to an inventory of the various working environments and conditions of the team's members, their experiences with and lessons learned from working virtually, and their preferences for communications media. Helps to build a code of conduct that best matches these conditions and preferences.
	Team Processes: Reviews and creates agreement on rules for the various processes that the team must have in place for efficient and effective operation: for having meetings in various forms, making decisions and resolving conflicts, measuring and managing performance, planning and monitoring delivery of the team's objectives.
	Key Roles and Activities: Makes an inventory of the various roles, responsibilities, and activities needed for maintaining the external relationships of the team, as well as for its internal functioning. Ensures shared understanding of the allocation of all relevant roles, responsibilities and activities within the team.
Technology restricted leading to effective communication	**Tools Selection and Code of Conduct:** Helps the team select those ICT tools for communication, information sharing, and collaboration that are needed to operate in virtual mode and deliver its objectives, agree on what activities they will be used for, and set the rules with which they will be used.
	Shared Work Space: Helps the team build an electronic work space for its information storage and management and to create the rules and roles for its effective use.
Task, team, and technology	**Awareness and Use of Differences:** Helps the team understand the cultural diversity present within the team and builds the foundation for making good use of this diversity.

face-to-face or virtually; however, it takes longer virtually and is more difficult to keep the discussion focused because norms often have not yet been established. Diagnostic instruments have been developed for both new and existing virtual teams or work groups that will help in focusing the learning effort and can be used in measuring progress on the competency development journey.

Each of these learning modules has been designed to be initiated in a face-to-face meeting of the team, although once work on one or two of the modules has been started, teams can initiate additional modules in virtual mode. Each module involves all members of the team, although some of the detailed activities, such as working out the results of the face-to-face sessions, may require a few team members to work together in a subgroup.

In addition to creating behavioral changes, most modules create one or more identifiable output documents; for example, in the Key Roles and Activities module, the team creates a document identifying the team roles, role descriptions, and who is responsible for each role. These documents are intended to be used in the team's activities and need to be kept up-to-date, reflecting the highly dynamic environment in which most virtual teams operate. For each of these documents, an "owner" is assigned whose task is to place the topic on the team's meeting agenda from time to time in order to create a shared awareness and understanding of the changes needed. This way of embedding the training program output in the team's operational procedures is an example of the situated cognition referred to in "Stealth Training for Virtual Audiences" (a chapter by Ken Finley that can be found on the www.wiley.com/go/virtualteamshandbook Web site). The following case study illustrates how a typical global virtual team started its T³ journey. It highlights the diagnostic and initial training phases and shows how these actions set the foundation for high performance.

GLOBAL HR SUPPORT TEAM

A leadership team for a human resource (HR) support function had been formed after previous regional organizations were integrated into a single global structure. Following further streamlining of services, the team had grown in size after its initial face-to-face kick-off meeting. All team members worked from different locations with a wide spread of time zones that needed to be bridged.

There was a growing feeling that lack of alignment between the team members was having a negative impact on the team's effectiveness. Based on the positive experiences of one of the team members with the T³ training program, they decided to use this approach to improve their virtual working environment and competency.

Their T³ journey started with the diagnostic instrument that converts the anonymous feedback from the team members into an indication of which T³ program modules will give most benefits to the team. The diagnostic results are presented in the form of a "radar" graph, where the lower scores indicate areas of attention. The HR team's diagnostic results are shown in Figure 15.2.

For this team, the facilitator recommended giving attention to two main areas:

- Improving the shared understanding of the organizational objectives of the team and the roles of the team members in achieving those objectives, through the combination of the Team Purpose, Stakeholder Engagement, Key Roles and Activities, and Communications Planning modules (see Table 15.1 for details).

- Improving the team's efficiency with the selection and use of communication and collaboration tools (modules: Tools Selection and Code of Conduct, and Shared Work Space).

In a one-day face-to-face meeting, the whole team engaged in three main activities. First, they brought the diversity in views on the team's purpose to the surface. For example, one subgroup of team members described the role of the team as "to support," whereas another subgroup used "to promote"—a world of difference in meaning, especially in the HR function. Team members then converged these views into a single, simple purpose statement.

The second activity prompted by the diagnostic results was the collective creation of a stakeholder map: a graphical representation of the main parties with whom the team interacted. This led to a better shared understanding of the complexity of the team's organizational environment. Stakeholder maps help team members appreciate where and how

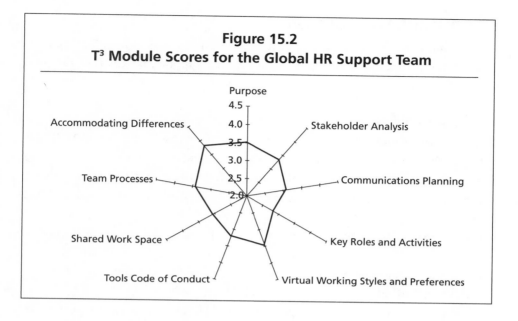

Figure 15.2
T³ Module Scores for the Global HR Support Team

Purpose

Accommodating Differences

Stakeholder Analysis

Team Processes

Communications Planning

Shared Work Space

Key Roles and Activities

Tools Code of Conduct

Virtual Working Styles and Preferences

their own views are different from those of the others. They form a useful starting point for discussing priorities of the team's activities and allocating roles and responsibilities within the team.

A third activity in that same meeting was a discussion about the selection of the tools that the team needed for its day-to-day virtual operation and gaining initial agreement on the set of rules that these tools will be used with. During this discussion, it became apparent which tools required further training.

In this way, by allocating a single day of this face-to-face meeting to the basics of virtual teamwork, the team created a solid foundation for the continuation of this work in virtual mode. According to team members' own views, over time this led to a better alignment of roles, responsibilities, and activities within the team; more effective communication with their stakeholders; and a much improved ability to accommodate organizational changes for the team. Clarifying and fine-tuning the tools and protocols for communication and collaboration helped the team quickly become more productive.

CONDITIONS FOR SUCCESS

The learning programs we have described are more successful in achieving their goals if three conditions are met: organizational support, transparent funding, and ICT support.

Organizational Support

Organizations should support the development of virtual collaboration competency at three levels: team, individual, and organizational. If the organizational climate is supportive of virtual collaboration, then the effects of training will be reinforced and teams are more likely to be successful and sustainable. Most important is support at the team or work group level, that is, providing teams with the materials, resources, best practices, funding policies, and appraisal, reward, and feedback processes that they need to start, execute, and complete a competency development journey. The T^3 program outlined here is an example of how an organization can support teams.

Individual team or work group members should be encouraged and supported to work on improving their skills in virtual collaboration through training and development opportunities as part of, but also in addition to, team learning programs. Given the importance of virtual collaborations to almost all organizations today, concepts and skills for virtual collaboration should be incorporated into general leadership development programs. This provides a good awareness of the complexity, invisibility, and restricted communications that virtual teams face, so that when individuals become part of new virtual teams, they are more likely to begin on the right (virtuous) journey. Individual development should be acknowledged in competency profiles and staff records, such that it can be carried forward from one assignment to another.

At the organizational level, virtual collaboration competency can be incorporated as an element in appraisal and reward procedures like other team and leadership competencies. If virtual collaboration is especially important to an organization's success, centers of expertise (small groups of people with practical experience in the topic area who actively build and maintain a repository of materials and case studies and are able to give advice to new and existing virtual teams) can be formally established and funded; through these, organizational learning, including transfer of best practices, can be achieved more systematically. Last, but not least, the organization's managers should provide visible and tangible management support, for example, leading by example.

Transparent Funding

One of the myths that managers, especially purchasing managers, often hold about virtual teams is that their operation is or should be cost free. Virtual teams are certainly cheaper than face-to-face teams composed of the same people; if those same team members were to meet face-to-face frequently or to move and become colocated, the costs would be enormous. However, virtual teams that are not supported do not have a high success rate. Organizations need to view the funding of virtual teams, starting with their training, as an investment in performance.

Organization-level funding is required for several things. Large organizations should maintain a skill pool of coaches and facilitators who can assist teams and work groups on their development journey. Centers of excellence or competence should also be established: small groups of experienced subject matter experts who can help and advise teams on practical issues and problems with virtual collaboration. Smaller organizations may want to retain the services of external consultants for this purpose.

Funding from the organization or sponsoring business unit is also needed for time, travel, and accommodation costs for at least limited face-to-face interventions such as training. It is extremely difficult for teams to overcome and address complexity, invisibility, and restricted communication without some face-to-face contact. The question should not be, "Should we meet face-to-face?" but instead, "What should we do during the limited face-to-face time we have?" If the team spends its face-to-face time engaging in the types of training activities described here in an action-learning mode, the face-to-face time is an investment that leads to much higher performance, more quickly, than without such interventions or with less effective interventions. Any skepticism about a focus on process rather than content should be countered with the observation that since the team will almost always operate in virtual mode, members must know how to solve problems and respond to emergencies in that mode; precious face-to-face time should be used preparing the team for that.

Support from ICT

The ICT function should provide and support an effective and consistent set of technology tools to facilitate virtual collaboration, and the training should be continually updated to reflect these tools. The organization's response to the many new developments in collaboration tools has to be carefully considered: new tools bring new opportunities, but their new functionality and the best way to use them have to be learned. Comprehensive packages with multiple functionality, such as Net meetings, shared work spaces, calendars, and project management, create opportunities for synergy but often reduce the team's ability to incorporate outsiders or work off-line and require high bandwidth, so communication is not stable for many parts of the world. Simple phone and e-mail solutions are reliable and highly flexible, but create complexity in storing and sharing information. Accommodating the differences in ICT tool portfolios between different organizations, even within the same firm, can pose a challenge. Complications with integration of existing tools are not uncommon. Unfortunately, there is no magic solution here yet, but the best organizations certainly dedicate resources to continually scanning for new solutions and implementing current ones effectively. While standardized training generally advocates a single-technology solution for all teams, modularized training, such as the program described here, can help a team decide for itself which technology it should use and how to use it in order to achieve the performance goals.

CREATING A VIRTUAL TEAM TRAINING AND DEVELOPMENT PROGRAM

Most organizations, especially large ones, have been greatly affected by the drive for globalization and virtualization. In many organizations, though, this has not been a conscious and managed change, particularly with respect to team processes. As a result, most organizations have pockets of good experience and success with virtual collaboration even if the organization has not formally positioned virtual collaboration competency as a skill area. These pockets can form a good starting point for building a modularized action-learning training program and spreading it to other parts of the organization.

One of the first activities is to locate these pockets and learn from the people there about what they have done and what has made them successful. It is important to get their views on how their success could be extended to the organization at large and what the specific critical success factors are. This investigation will also help in setting up a business case for more explicit support of virtual collaboration competency development.

The second stage is to design a provisional virtual collaboration competency development program by creating materials and training facilitators and coaches. The program should combine the organization-specific knowledge identified in the first stage with insights about training virtual teams in general, such as the ideas outlined in this chapter. One or more pilot projects can then be run with volunteer teams that are already collaborating virtually. After review of these pilots and adjustments, the program can be integrated in the organization's portfolio of leadership and staff development programs.

Some of the typical hurdles encountered in setting up a virtual teamworking competency development program are similar to those for any new program; others are specific to virtual teams. Some of the more general hurdles include lack of visible and tangible leadership support and lack of funding for facilitation and support. For example, management teams often ask staff to reduce travel cost but do not lead by example themselves. They also often ask virtual teams to achieve high levels of productivity immediately without recognizing the degree of difficulty of learning the new skills needed.

One challenge more common with virtual teams than other kinds of new programs is associated with workload priorities. The payoff for effective virtual teamwork is neither visible nor quick, and it is easy for managers to assign "real" work as a higher priority than the "virtual" work because the former is more visible. The other challenge related specifically to virtual teams is team fluidity, or frequent changes in team membership and size during the development journey. In the virtual world, it is easy to change the membership of teams and work groups, but the impact on the shared understanding, trust, and effective communication within the teams can be large. A disciplined management team will keep the team workload and composition as stable as possible, at least during training and development.

FINAL THOUGHTS

Most organizations have groups of people who have learned to work well virtually on their own. So why create and implement a comprehensive program, using scarce resources, rather than simply letting everyone learn through experience? First, although there are teams that learn to collaborate well virtually on their own, many of them cannot articulate what they did well in a systematic way. The transfer of learning from a high-performance experience to another is not deliberate and therefore not efficient. Second, the more quickly that teams and entire organizations develop virtual collaboration competencies, the more quickly the virtuous cycle of shared understanding, trust, and communication will be in place to enable performance.

The program we outlined here, which has been well tested in multinational organizations, is based on the most important challenges that virtual teams face: complexity, invisibility, and restricted communication. Using action-learning principles, it builds competencies in creating shared understanding, developing trust, and communicating effectively. The modularized design takes into account the complexities of such teams and allows customization to particular needs.

The business world is quickly becoming more distributed. Virtual collaboration provides a competitive advantage now but in the near future will be a necessity. A good virtual collaboration training program therefore boosts any organization's performance.

REMINDERS

- Virtual teams face three key challenges: complexity of the task and working environment, invisibility of that complexity, and restricted technology-mediated communication.

- Effective virtual collaboration requires integrating three critical success factors: shared understanding, trust, and effective communication.

- Virtual teams can develop vicious or virtuous cycles of the critical success factors; interventions can help teams get on and stay on the virtuous path.

- Competency in virtual teamworking and collaboration is best acquired through a focused, team-based, modular action-learning program based on integration of the task, team, and technology viewpoints.

- When teams guide their own learning through the use of diagnostic tools and selection of appropriate modules, they immediately start on the virtuous path.

- These learning programs can be successful only with appropriate organizational support, transparent funding of the associated facilitation costs, and support from ICT.

- Stealth Training for Virtual Audiences

References

Argyris, C. (1982). The executive mind and double loop learning. *Organizational Dynamics, 11*(2), 5–22.

Daft, R. L., & Lengel, R. H. (1984). Information richness: A new approach to managerial behavior and organizational design. In L. L. Cummings & B. M. Staw (Eds.), *Research in organizational behavior,* 6 (pp. 191–233). Greenwich, CT: JAI Press.

Duarte, D. L., & Snyder, N. T. (2006). *Mastering virtual teams: Strategies, tools, and techniques that succeed* (3rd ed.). San Francisco: Jossey-Bass.

Maznevski, M. L. (1994). Understanding our differences: Performance in decision-making groups with diverse members. *Human Relations, 47*(5), 531–552.

Meyerson, D., Weick, K. E., & Kramer, R. M. (1996). Swift trust and temporary teams. In R. M. Kramer & T. R. Tyler (Eds.), *Trust in organizations* (pp. 166–195). Thousand Oaks, CA: Sage.

Revans, R. (1980). *Action learning: New techniques for action learning.* London: Blond & Briggs.

Senge, P., Kleiner, A., Roberts, C., Ross, R. B., & Smith, B. J. (1994). *The fifth discipline fieldbook.* London: Nicholas Brealey.

Short, J. A., Williams, E., & Christie, B. (1976). *The social psychology of telecommunications.* Hoboken, NJ: Wiley.

Combating Confusion
Virtual Teams That Cross Borders

Sue Freedman

A U.S. executive, concerned about the security of one of his factories in Korea, ordered the installation of a new alarm system. To ensure that those responsible understood exactly how important the system was, he arranged to inspect it personally. Several weeks later, the executive arrived as scheduled. Four of his Koreans subordinates, including the factory manager, met him at the entrance. After appropriate greetings, he walked up and pushed on the door equipped with the new alarm. Nothing happened. No sound at all. The executive was a patient man and understood that sometimes things got confused. He explained very slowly, in precise terms: "When . . . I . . . push . . . on . . . this . . . door, . . . the . . . alarm . . . is . . . to . . . go . . . off." The Koreans apologized profusely, bowing their heads and saying in English, "We fix, we fix." The executive returned the next day, and they went through the whole episode again. The manager explained more vociferously, and with tedious repetition, what he wanted; the Koreans again apologized and promised to correct the problem.

This went on for four days, with the U.S. executive's blood pressure approaching stroke level and his Korean employees continuing to apologize. Finally, the Korean factory manager actually broke with his own norms. He pulled the executive aside and asked in a very quiet voice: "Mr. Boss. It is off?"

This true and not atypical story illustrates the hidden challenges in working with people from different cultures and with different levels of fluency in the language in use. Even when the goals are shared and everyone is both competent and committed, things can go painfully wrong. Unfortunately the way they go wrong usually suggests to both sides that one must clearly be working with idiots. In this case, the American executive clearly thought his Korean subordinates were incompetent, oppositional, or both. One can only imagine what the Koreans thought of their American "big boss."

Virtual team leaders and members are often unaware of the significant differences in values, perspectives, and work habits of their colleagues who were raised in different cultures, speaking different native languages, and with very different ways of working together. Even when it becomes clear that progress is nonexistent and problem solving is frustrating and confusing, many find it difficult to move from blaming their foreign colleagues to making the changes needed to support effective cross-cultural work.

This difficulty is not surprising. The professionals asked to lead international virtual teams are the products of strong national cultures. Their behavior has been refined by years of schooling, followed by careful grooming in successful organizations. Their cultural beliefs and values are expressed in distinctive leadership and communication behaviors refined and perfected by generations of talented people dedicated to finding the best ways to work together. When foreign team members do not respond as expected, their colleagues find them confusing, frustrating, and often not worthy of trust. The problem is that these elegant and efficient processes for establishing priorities, making decisions, and completing work differ with the culture in which one was raised, educated, and has worked.

Successful work with virtual teams that cross borders involves active learning. Successful team leaders and members learn more about themselves, their cultures, and their values by working with people whose ancestors and leaders developed different ways to cope with the challenges and opportunities of life and work. These leaders discover both what is delightfully different and reassuringly common about their colleagues from different cultures.

Sadly, most cross-culture work is not successful. Although most members and leaders adapt in some ways to cultural differences, these teams do not typically perform at levels commensurate with the talent and time involved. Part of the problem is that the learning process for leading a cross-cultural virtual team is typically a discovery process. International virtual team leaders learn on the job through trial and error, making costly mistakes in terms of both time and relationships. During the learning process, these leaders confuse, frustrate, insult, and sometimes even abuse their foreign colleagues. They miss valuable feedback, provide misdirection, and fail to recognize critical needs for confirmation, redirection, and clarification—needs that they respond to with unconscious competence in their home environments. The reason is that they, and their supervisors, simply do not know what they do not know about leading teams composed of people raised in and still residing in very different cultures.

This chapter identifies some the unique risks in virtual, cross-border collaboration and outlines strategies that can mitigate those risks. The discussion first examines common misconceptions, or maybe wishful thinking, about working across borders. It then sets out definitions and examples of cultural dimensions that directly and repeatedly affect cross-cultural team performance, followed by some suggested ways to adapt to those differences. Finally, it looks at the characteristics of successful project teams, the unique challenges cross-border teams face in developing those characteristics, and strategies that can help build those characteristics in teams responsible for specific work outcomes.

HOW HARD CAN IT BE? COMMON MISCONCEPTIONS ABOUT WORKING ACROSS BORDERS

The misconceptions that follow are often heard in American discussions of cross-border work. Each is a compelling combination of truth and misconception that seduces team leaders, their leaders, and more senior management into believing that cross-border work and domestic virtual work is much the same. This "how hard can it be?" mind-set leads to serious mistakes in the initiation, planning, and execution of cross-border projects. It also leads to the selection of team leaders who have neither the perspective nor the skills sets required to manage cross-border teams successfully.

Misconception 1 *They are our subordinates or suppliers. They need to learn our language and our way of work. We do not need to learn theirs.*

There are compelling reasons for foreign team members to learn the language and culture of their supervisors, customers, and partners. Most speak some English and are trying very hard to communicate in language. The problem is in the difficulty of the task. Working across significant differences in language and culture is a complex process with intellectual and emotional challenge. A strong desire to make it work is not enough. Education and repeated exposure are needed in order to accurately interpret the vagaries of communication in language. Deep trust in a relationship is required to ask for clarification and explanation, sometimes repeatedly, when one is unsure of what is meant. Indeed, the more that members of the dominant culture on a team insist that their foreign team members understand and adapt to them, the more they lessen the likelihood that clarity of communication and commonality of goals will take place.

The story at the beginning of this chapter is a powerful example of the fallacies in believing that businesses can simply place the burden for adapting on the less powerful members of the team. Assuming that foreign virtual team partners understand the complex and cue-limited communication of virtual teams because they can speak English in some form is a common, and frequently costly, mistake. All English-speaking countries tend to forget that there are very different versions of English. Microsoft Word's online dictionary provides nineteen versions of English, from Australian to Zimbabwe. Speaking English and speaking American English are entirely different, as are understanding versus speaking a foreign language. Even those who made all A's in French courses usually find it impossible to follow a typical discussion among native French speakers.

A recent research study (Brett, Behfar, & Kern, 2006) found that fluency levels and related problems are one of the four most serious challenges to cross-cultural team success. In addition to the confusion caused by language-related misunderstandings, team members skilled in the dominant language underestimate the abilities of their foreign colleagues, and those less familiar with the language become more cautious and withdrawn. As a result, dominant-language team members do most of the talking, often failing to learn the critical listening and feedback skills needed to communicate with cross-border colleagues.

Misconception 2   *People are pretty much the same everywhere.*

This statement is true at some level. That level, however, argues for, not against, learning the perspectives, preferences, and ways of work of colleagues or customers in other cultures. People perform best when they feel understood, respected, and appreciated. When team members assume that values, ways of interacting, and approaches to decision making are the same or unimportant, they disregard the essence of who their colleagues are and what those colleagues have to contribute. They also tend to interpret and judge the behavior of those colleagues based on their own cultural values and protocols.

A wonderful example of how people from different cultures are both different and alike was discovered by a colleague hosting a group of Vietnamese customers for dinner at her home. As was her practice with new guests to her home, she escorted them through her house, showing treasures she had collected from travels around the world. Her guests commented on the beauty of each piece and then inquired politely, "How much did you pay for this?" They asked the same question for every treasure. The hostess was embarrassed, even offended. She simply could not understand how her sensitive and charming Vietnamese colleagues could be so rude. She remained troubled and confused about what this behavior indicated about her Vietnamese friends. She was not enlightened until she finally visited Vietnam, where prices are never posted and negotiating skills are as valued as golfing skills are in the United States. Her Vietnamese guests were trying to provide their hostess with the opportunity to relive her success in this highly competitive game and to celebrate that success with a group of friends who would applaud it. Appreciating and celebrating another's success is an expression of friendship that crosses borders; it is only the details that produce confusion.

This kind of misunderstanding is typical in cross-border virtual teams. Team members from both cultures offend their colleagues by behaving in ways that are accepted, and often valued, in their home culture. An Israeli team member is likely to be confrontational and emotional when communicating disagreement with a team colleague. A U.S. colleague would be offended, and colleagues from South America, India, or China would likely be so upset by the behavior that it would be difficult for them to continue to participate at all. What is considered acceptable in one culture often communicates a message of disrespect or even disdain in another.

Misconception 3   *I've been working with team members from a variety of cultures for years. It's not a problem for me. I can work with anybody.*

Experience working with local residents from other cultures is extremely valuable. It is important to recognize, however, that foreign-born colleagues are experienced adapters. They have responded well to the dominant culture in which they find themselves not because they agree with it but because have learned to adapt. If they are working in the United States, for instance, they have learned how to thrive in the American workplace by combining elements of their own culture with those valued by the dominant culture. People born and raised in one country with significant experience in another always talk about no longer feeling totally at home in either culture. They have become something unique when it comes to culture and are most comfortable with other immigrants with similar experiences.

Working with people who are living and working in their native country, surrounded by members of their own culture, requires that the team leader adapt. For example, Alan, an American project manager assigned his first Indian team, learned early on that managing an Indian team in India was different from managing Indian-born team members working in America. Eager to start right with his new project members, Alan set up an individual conference call with each of them. He always made these calls with new U.S. members who joined his team, including those born in India, and found the conversations informative, interesting, and conducive to team cohesion.

To his surprise, Alan's calls with his Indian team members, who spoke excellent English, were awkward and frustrating. The team members seemed to avoid answering any direct questions and acted as if they could not wait to end the call. Alan hung up frustrated and a bit insulted. After all, he had taken time out of his busy schedule to talk with each one of them, and they acted as if they did not want to be bothered. His first thought was, "What is wrong with these people?"

If Alan had discussed his plans with his U.S.-based Indian team members, he may have skipped, or at least postponed, his call. He would have learned that

Indians are often more group oriented and deferential to their immediate manager than their U.S. colleagues are. Many of them are uncomfortable offering an individual opinion without talking it over with their fellow team members. A one-on-one telephone call with a new boss, especially one who may outrank their local supervisor, is likely to be a frightening experience for these team members.

The more types of people one works with and enjoys, the easier it is to adapt to a cross-border management role. The maxim, "When in Rome, do as the Romans do," has been around for centuries for a reason: people do things differently in different places, and that rule applies to work as well as to everything else. Learning the work culture and values of international team members or leaders is always time well spent.

Misconception 4 *We have been an international company for over seventy-five years. We know how to work with people in other cultures.*

Companies with a history of international work have a distinct advantage. They typically have a number of employees who have lived and worked in other countries and a number of immigrant employees who have an appreciation of the challenges and rewards of cross-cultural work efforts. When knowledge and understanding of these individuals are adequately disseminated and applied, companies enjoy a significant competitive advantage in cross-border work.

There are two reasons, however, that additional learning about the culture and language of foreign partners is critical even for these companies. The first is that the strategies and perspectives of working across borders, which differ for different cultures, are typically not disseminated. The people with the expertise continue to use it, but rarely is that expertise used to teach others. In addition, much of the knowledge people have is about personal preferences, not about how the people from different cultures can adapt to work together effectively.

A more pressing reason for active learning when working with international virtual teams is that international companies are increasing the complexity of the collaboration required of cross-border teams. Manufacturing and supply arrangements are morphing into the interdependent worlds of lean manufacturing and managed supply chains. They are integrating information technology (IT) systems, developing new markets, and creating new and increasingly complex products in cooperation with their cross-border customers, suppliers, and partners. Each of these activities requires new ways of working together—ways that often differ significantly from those found in any of the participating cultures.

A recent article in PRTM's *Insight* magazine (Peolina, Leu, & Chinn, 2005) on implementing lean manufacturing in China illustrates this point. Peolina and his colleagues list several differences between Chinese and American manufacturing plants that represent barriers to establishing lean manufacturing practices. Examples cited include (1) an acceptance of disorder, or "mess," in the workplace; (2) a "disposable worker" system that does not educate or work to retain a committed workforce; (3) a management system and history that discourages employee empowerment; (4) managers and workers who are uneducated in work process identification and refinement; and (5) a set of relationship values around business partners called *guanxi* that makes it difficult for a plant manager to make American-like demands for accountability to his suppliers.

Imagine the challenge of overcoming these barriers in a virtual team. It is hard to see how an understanding of these challenges could emerge from virtual communication alone. The same is true for integrating IT systems, creating breakthrough products, and the other examples of complex, closely coupled work that are increasingly the purview of cross-cultural teams. Unless planned, funded, and managed correctly, these teams, especially if limited to virtual contact, are likely to fail. A typical scenario involves a great deal of lengthy, boring virtual conversation, accompanied by little or no progress and even less understanding of the reasons that needed changes are not being made.

The difficulty, however, does not mean that the goal is not worthwhile or that the task is impossible. These projects are complex and must be managed in ways that embrace complexity. Decisions about when, how, and with whom to implement this new work are best guided by a sophisticated understanding of the cultures across which the work will take place and with established relationships with those who lead in each participating cultures. Even companies with a long history of international engagement will find their flexibility and adaptability challenged as they depend on colleagues from very different worlds.

WHY AND HOW CULTURE MATTERS

When facing the triple challenge presented by distance, language, and culture, team members and leaders are best armed with a working understanding of critical cultural differences and access to more information as the situation demands. A variety of researchers have developed dimensions or categories to explain how cultures differ. Hofstede (1980, 1993, 1994) developed a groundbreaking model of cultural dimensions that helps explain how and why people from various cultures behave differently. In a study sponsored by IBM, Hofstede found that national culture consists of four key dimensions: power distance, individualism, masculinity, and uncertainty avoidance. In 1993, the Global Leadership Organizational Behavior Effectiveness (GLOBE) Project began an ongoing study of leadership and national culture that served to validate and refine Hofstede's work in terms of accuracy and the longevity of the characteristics. Hofstede and his fellow researchers have continued to expand and validate this initial model (Robbins, 2003).

In developing and delivering training for those who manage projects that cross borders, Freedman and Katz (2005) borrowed from and expanded these dimensions of cultural difference in an effort to identify those most directly related to international project team performance. These dimensions are listed in Figure 16.1, along with the relative positions of selected countries on these dimensions. In the paragraphs that follow, each dimension is explained with examples of how the dimension affects the expectations and behaviors of the team members from different cultures. The final part of the discussion suggests some strategies for managing those differences.

Individual Versus Group Orientation

The United States is the most individualistic culture in the world. Americans and most northern Europeans believe that individuals are primarily responsible for themselves and for making the decisions that affect their own lives. Asian, South American, and Arab cultures are group oriented or collective. They believe that members are responsible primarily to and for the group. An example of the difference is seen in the different ways Indians and Americans approach marriage. Most Indian spouses are recommended by the family, whereas the idea of allowing the family to have significant influence on the selection of one's mate is

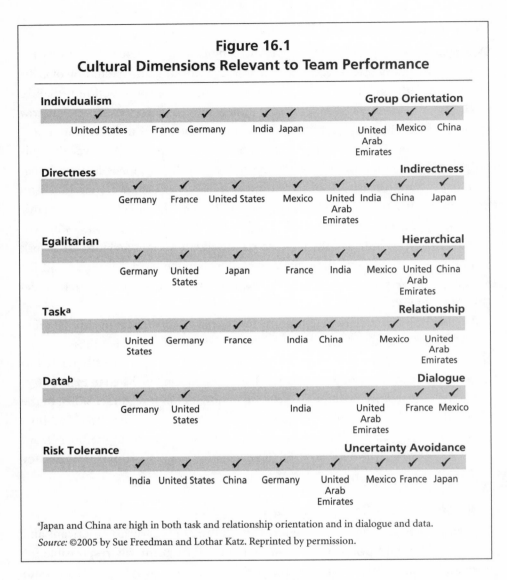

Figure 16.1
Cultural Dimensions Relevant to Team Performance

Individualism / **Group Orientation**

United States France Germany India Japan United Arab Emirates Mexico China

Directness / **Indirectness**

Germany France United States Mexico United Arab Emirates India China Japan

Egalitarian / **Hierarchical**

Germany United States Japan France India Mexico United Arab Emirates China

Task[a] / **Relationship**

United States Germany France India China Mexico United Arab Emirates

Data[b] / **Dialogue**

Germany United States India United Arab Emirates France Mexico

Risk Tolerance / **Uncertainty Avoidance**

India United States China Germany United Arab Emirates Mexico France Japan

[a]Japan and China are high in both task and relationship orientation and in dialogue and data.

Source: ©2005 by Sue Freedman and Lothar Katz. Reprinted by permission.

unthinkable for most Americans. The reasons for approaching marriage in this way are deeply embedded in the cultural values of the two countries and relate specifically to group versus individual orientation.

This difference is important for virtual teams with members from both individualistic and collectivistic cultures, because developing a sense of group is more important to team success for members from group cultures and because violations of group principles will confuse and alienate these members. Members of group cultures typically need more social time to get to know their colleagues and need more information about their colleagues to build the relationships on which trust develops. Individualistic team leaders are likely to be insensitive to and impatient with the needs of their more group-oriented colleagues and then shocked when they find these members are not performing on the team.

It is useful to acknowledge differences in individual and group orientation when a new team forms and to agree that one central task of the team is to find a way to accommodate these differences. A discussion of how each of the member subgroups works best can be useful, as are pleas for patience with the differences among groups. In working with group cultures, it is often more efficient to discuss the need for a decision, discuss key criteria in one meeting, and then adjourn, allowing members to discuss the decisions with their colleagues and return for a second meeting. It is also important to spend some time on non-work-related topics that enable the team to find ways of identifying with each other. Sharing pictures and details about personal life can be valuable.

Directness Versus Indirectness

Directness refers to the degree to which the meaning of communication is found in the words themselves versus in the context in which the words are said, the tone of voice or body language used, or the specific words or sequence of words used (Katz, 2006). Although factors other than words are important in all cultures, the differences are vast. A U.S. team member who is working with Israeli or German colleagues is likely to see these team members as rude and insensitive. If a team leader from a direct culture is working with members who are much less direct, such as those from China or Japan, the impression is often that they are in total agreement with every word that has been said. The truth is that the members from these cultures communicate their disagreement in much subtler ways. In addition, the direct team leader is likely to be perceived as overbearing and rude. He or she may be seen as indicating negative feelings about the person he or she is addressing. The Japanese, for example, use *yes* typically only to acknowledge that you are speaking. Unless one's Japanese colleague is experienced in working with Westerners, *yes* does not mean that one's Japanese colleague understands and certainly not that he or she agrees. Agreement from Japanese colleagues will typically not come quickly and will be accompanied by some form of written confirmation.

Indirect team leaders or members can learn to adapt to their more direct colleagues' differences with some effort. Westerners, especially those in technical fields, are usually quite direct and can become more so should the situation warrant it. The phrase, "What is it about the word *no* that you do not understand?" is designed for people who do not seem able to accept more subtle forms of communication. If the person can get over feeling insulted or insulting, it is possible for indirect team members and leaders to adjust to their more direct team members.

Learning to communicate indirectly is typically more of a challenge. It feels inefficient to communicate less directly than one's culture prescribes. Working with people from indirect cultures requires much more attention to the way in which messages are worded in terms of both sending and receiving. Unless team leaders learn to communicate subtly and listen for the meaning hidden in the often flattering words used, they will not recognize that their indirect colleague is not agreeing, does not understand, or knows that what is being planned will never work and is trying hard to communicate that.

Egalitarian Versus Hierarchical (Power Distance)

Power distance refers to the differences in how people from different cultures relate to those in positions of higher status or authority. People in Canada, Norway, and Switzerland, as examples, tend to be more egalitarian, treating people at all levels in similar ways and frowning on those who act in ways that demonstrate status or class differences. People in Japan, India, Mexico, and China tend to be more hierarchical, behaving differently toward people depending on their status and position and being more formal when communicating across these levels. Hierarchical cultures tend to have clear rules about how the people in various roles relate to each other. Not surprisingly, these differences prescribe the behavior of the ideal leader and the ideal follower.

Clearly, these cultural differences can result in confusion in virtual teams. It is quite possible for a virtual team leader to be seen as a wimp by team members from one culture and a jerk by members of another while behaving in exactly the same way. People from hierarchical cultures rarely do or say anything that could reflect poorly on a superior and are not likely to exert initiative unless specifically directed to do so. If there is a conflict or even a potential conflict between what a team member believes is the right answer and the answer favored by the leader or another high-status member, team members from hierarchical cultures are not likely to voice their ideas. If a team leader or member is interested in feedback or divergent ideas from members from higher-power-distance cultures, he or she must solicit the information in ways that make it safe and expected for hierarchical team members to contribute their ideas and impressions.

It is also important to note that in dealing with hierarchical cultures, diagonal communication is rarely accepted. That is, managers in hierarchical cultures communicate with people at their own management levels. If a team leader needs to resolve a problem with the next level up, he or she will typically need to involve a supervisor. If the team leader and the local supervisor of the members are at the same level in the organization, then the team leader should develop a relationship with that supervisor. It is also important that the team leader's boss develop a relationship with his or her peer in the partnering organization.

Task Versus Relationship Orientation

The United States is among the most task-oriented cultures in the world. Most Americans have no need, and often no interest, in building close relationships with coworkers prior to working together. They develop the relationships as they do the work, building trust as the work gets done and the problems addressed. This is not the way it works in the vast majority of cultures in the world. People from these cultures build relationships first and will not, indeed cannot, work together effectively until they have developed a relationship with the other person.

The importance of this difference became very clear to an IT project leader working for a major telephone equipment company. He spent four years trying to get agreement on the design of a new IT system for a diverse group of foreign partners. The team met virtually every week for three hours for about three years and got nowhere. Finally, management gave in and let the team leader bring the group together for a three-day meeting in Paris to define requirements. He set up the meeting so that he could spend at least one day touring Paris with each of the critical team members. By the time the meeting took place, the members trusted him enough to work through to an agreement. He is convinced that he would never have gotten an agreement without those days spent sightseeing in Paris. Until that time, the various team members could not participate in the complex give-and-take discussions needed to make the trade-offs necessary in deciding what to do.

The power of relationships in relationship-oriented cultures is hard for task-oriented team leaders and members to understand. They continue to discount the importance of relationship building and underestimate the skills of their more relationship-oriented colleagues. The ability to lead teams with members from relationship-oriented cultures requires skills that many task-oriented leaders and members have not developed and may not wish to develop. Many researchers in this area point to the willingness to learn the skills of working collaboratively as a critical prerequisite for all global team leaders.

There are a number of ways to support this critical relationship building in virtual teams. Posting pictures and personal details on Web sites is critical and easy to do. Initial or early meetings that are face-to-face are extremely valuable, with videoconferencing offering the next best alternative. These meetings are essential to build rapport and lay the groundwork for trust. Most important may be a team leader who is willing and able to provide the structure, the support, and the cross-cultural explanations that enable a team to build the relationships needed to navigate complex routes to cross-cultural success (Verma, 1997).

Data Versus Dialogue

Cultures differ in the way their members process information and make decisions. Data-oriented cultures, such as Germany, and to a lesser but significant extent the United States, place a high value on facts and figures, use reports and systems to gather information, enjoy presentations, and prefer e-mail for much of their business communications. Dialogue-oriented cultures place high value on understanding others' thoughts and opinions, use discussions and personal networks to collect and process information, and prefer calls over e-mails and face-to-face meetings over calls. Mexico and France are among the most dialogue-oriented cultures. China and Japan typically use both approaches before making most business decisions.

Team leaders or members from data-oriented cultures find working with members from dialogue cultures difficult, and vice versa. U.S. and German team members often send detailed e-mails summarizing the data and highlighting key decisions to be covered in the team call. When the call begins and they are ready to make good use of their time, they discover that their Mexican or French colleagues have not opened, much less read, their e-mails. These colleagues believe that if their team members had something important they wanted to communicate, they would have called to talk about it.

This is not an uncommon example. Getting clear on how one responds to and handles e-mails is an important step to take early in almost any virtual team process. The problem here is complex. If the team includes members with different ways of collecting and processing information for decision making, the team leader first needs to decide how important both of the perspectives are to a good decision and then to plan and assign work on that basis. It may be advisable to create subteams for much of the work and then manage the integration processes with representatives of those groups only.

Risk Tolerance Versus Uncertainty Avoidance

Uncertainty avoidance is the degree to which members of a culture are comfortable with or seek to avoid uncertainty or risk. This concept is complex because it prescribes both the way in which team members are most comfortable, that is, with clarity around roles, and the kind of project to which they are best suited in terms of low-risk, predictable outcomes or higher-risk, more innovative projects. Most Japanese team members, for example try to avoid uncertainty or minimize risks, while members from the United States are much more comfortable with it. Members from Germany, Austria, and Switzerland tend to avoid uncertainty, while those from India, Mexico, and Singapore are more willing and able to tolerate risk and uncertainty. Evidence of a culture's attitude toward risk can be found in the products they produce and the ways in which they behave. It is not surprising that Japan and other cultures that avoid uncertainty produce the most reliable and resilient cars in the world, while the United States produces the most innovative products.

A team leader for a new technical product learned about Japanese risk avoidance the hard way. His Japanese team members moved much more slowly than the team leader wanted, spending time on detailed planning and analysis that put the project behind schedule. When the team leader objected, the Japanese members became more and more uncomfortable, gently pointing out areas where risk existed and no plan existed to address those risks. The team leader's directives "not to worry about those risks" were impossible for the Japanese team to obey. These team members are educated to find ways to control known risks. To do otherwise would violate them image of themselves as responsible professionals. This characteristic is, of course, extremely valuable when working on products or services where reliability is critical, but it is a problem when time to market is more important. Ultimately the relationship with the Japanese company was severed and the U.S. company moved to find a less risk-averse partner for the project.

As a virtual team leader, it is important know the attitudes or values of the team member around risk and uncertainly. There are Japanese team members who are able to work without accounting for all risk, but they are the exception in Japan. However, it would not be wise to randomly select members of a highly risk-tolerant culture for products in which failure is life threatening. Team leaders and members will do well to expect differences in attitudes about risk and uncertainty tolerance and should talk through those differences early in the project. If work is being done with those from a risk-adverse culture, then the team leader may want to request, or even demand, team members who are better trained in tolerating risk than is typical in that culture. In working with highly risk-tolerant cultures, the team will want to demand more documentation and more testing to ensure that adequate risk mitigation is in fact taking place.

BUILDING EFFECTIVE CROSS-BORDER PROJECT TEAMS

Many, if not most, international or cross-border virtual teams are project teams: they exist to accomplish a specific purpose in a given period of time under the direction of project manager or leader. Much time and money have been spent identifying the characteristics of high-performance project teams and the leadership behaviors necessary to develop those characteristics. One is a critical task of those involved in the education and training of project managers. Gray and Larson (2006) identify eight characteristics of high-performance project teams. These characteristics would seem to be equally predictive of high performance of project teams working across borders:

1. The team shares a common purpose, and each member is willing to work with the others toward achieving project objectives.

2. The team identifies individual talents and expertise and uses them depending on the project's needs at any given time. At these times, the team willingly accepts the influence and leadership of the members whose skills are most relevant to the immediate task.

3. Roles are balanced and shared to facilitate both the accomplishment of tasks and feelings of group cohesion and morale.

4. The team exerts energy toward problem solving rather than allowing themselves to be drained by interpersonal issues or competitive struggles.

5. Differences of opinion are encouraged and freely expressed.

6. To encourage risk taking and creativity, mistakes are treated as opportunities to learn rather than reasons for punishment.

7. Members set high personal standards and encourage each other to realize the objectives of the project.

8. Members identify with the team and consider it an important source of both professional and personal growth.

The advantage of this list, or any other list of this kind, is that it clarifies the need to develop a team with certain characteristics to accomplish the project. All virtual team leaders must find a way to convert a group of people on a conference call to a team of people committed to a common goal. That is never an easy task, but it is one that successful domestic virtual leaders have mastered. Good project managers devote the time and energy necessary to make this happen. Unfortunately, many of them are unconscious of exactly how they do this and the extent to which common values and practice facilitate the process. The list can be used to communicate and discuss the vision for a high-performing team to members and enroll members is developing that vision.

Table 16.1 lists these eight characteristics followed by a description of the special challenges in developing them in international virtual teams. It also lists strategies that have been used to help develop these characteristics in teams that cross borders. Team leaders are encouraged to review the challenges and consider the strategies in building successful international virtual teams.

FINAL THOUGHTS

This is both a critical and exciting stage for cross-border work. Cross-border work projects are dependent on virtual teams and virtual communication for their success. Members and leaders of these teams are the pioneers in establishing new ways to accomplish routine work, develop breakthough innovation, and coordinate complex work activities. These teams are exploring and inspiring new technology and finding new ways to build relationships that bridge the traditional barriers of distance, language, and culture. While cross-border work can be confusing, frustrating, and time consuming, it is also rewarding and exciting. The organizations and individuals who conquer it will dominate much of tomorrow's world.

Table 16.1

Strategies for Developing High-Performing International Project Teams

Characteristic	Additional Challenges for Cross-Border Teams	Strategies to Address Challenges
The team shares a common purpose and each member is willing to work together toward achieving project objectives.	What is important to team members differs across cultures.	Learn and use what is important to team members from different cultures.
	It is easy to marginalize distant members, and much easier still with "foreigners."	Make sure that the purposes of the team are understood and supported by those to whom the members report.
	Even with the best of intentions, it is easy for a culturally unaware team member to send a message that he or she does not respect a foreign colleague.	Communicate your respect for the expertise and the role of your foreign members and their supervisors (e.g., "We want you on the team for your expertise in IT, not in our language").
		Use kickoff meetings, celebrations, and other forms of communication to celebrate progress and build unity.
		Learn and use a few words in the language of your foreign colleagues.
		If the team is too diverse and or too large, consider subdividing it into smaller groups.
The team identifies individual talents and expertise and uses them, depending on the project's needs at any given time. At these times, the team willingly accepts the influence	Behaviors that indicate competence differ across cultures and often are harder to discern in virtual settings.	Train team members on both sides to recognize and discuss cultural differences, especially in terms of leadership, decision making, disagreements, and issues related to competence.
	Native speakers of the in-use language often misinterpret language difficulty as lack of competence.	

and leadership of the members whose skills are most relevant to the immediate task.	The requirements for demonstrating appropriate respect for the leader differ vastly across cultures. Team members with language challenges are often hesitant to speak out. Mistakes made as a result of language issues are often attributed to technical competence.	Explain to everyone that they will get better at understanding what their foreign colleagues' speech and behavior means. Encourage everybody to slow down. Introduce team members to each other, listing each one's achievements or technical competence. Provide abbreviated résumés on the team Web site. Tell foreign members you will be asking them to comment on ideas, in advance if possible, and call on them to do so.
Roles are balanced and shared to facilitate both the accomplishment of tasks and feelings of group cohesion and morale.	Trust is much harder to build across cultures. Competence is harder to access across cultures. Working with those who speak the same language and were trained in the same work behaviors is always easier, so leaders and members often overly depend on those people.	Collect and display photos of team members, team members' families, company sites, local attractions, and key holidays. Provide translations of the organization's mission and other key information about the team. Find ways to assess the feeling of involvement and appreciation and frustration: "What are we doing right?" and "What can do better?" usually generate interesting responses (this can be done with e-mail as well).
The team members exert energy toward problem solving rather than allowing themselves to be drained by interpersonal issues or competitive struggles.	It is much harder to recognize interpersonal or competitive struggles when working across cultures. What looks like cooperation in one culture may be an expression of extreme frustration or even anger in another. The reverse is also true.	Build and maintain strong relationships with and among team members and with their supervisors. Provide structure through responsibility charts, clear escalation paths, and formal reviews.

Table 16.1 (Continued)

Characteristic	Additional Challenges for Cross-Border Teams	Strategies to Address Challenges
	It is much harder to resolve conflict in cross-cultural situations because beliefs about acceptable behavior differ and because resolving conflict requires some element of trust. It also is much easier to resolve these conflicts in a face-to-face situation (and to know when they are not resolved).	Use people who are familiar with both cultures to clarify messages and check for problems and misunderstandings.
		If you are in a conflict, use a face-to-face meeting and the appropriate level of authority to deal with it. In many cultures, communication is accepted only from individuals at the same level.
		Be very careful in communicating concerns in indirect and group-oriented cultures. They are trained to pick up subtle messages.
		Pay careful attention to anything being said when working with people from an indirect culture. They will communicate concerns and issues in subtle ways.
Differences of opinion are encouraged and freely expressed.	What is appropriate, even supportive feedback for one culture, is seen as criticism or lack of respect in another.	Discuss the differences in ways in which cultures disagree or express concerns and the challenges those differences present.
	Attitudes toward leadership and group harmony affect how team members deal with differences of opinion.	Ask for clarification on feedback that can be misinterpreted and encourage team members to do the same. Examples are: "Are you saying you agree with everything John proposed?" or "Are you saying you think none of what John proposed is worthwhile?"

Recognizing when a team member from an indirect culture is disagreeing requires close attention.	Use someone who is familiar with both cultures to interpret.
	Ask for feedback in ways that allow team members to respond without sounding critical, for example, "Please give me the three things you believe are the most significant risks with this approach."
To encourage risk taking and creativity, mistakes are treated as opportunities to learn rather than reasons for punishment.	Discuss your own attitude toward mistakes and learning opportunities. Communicate how team members build and lose trust with you.
Attitudes toward mistakes differ across cultures.	Use indirect and group versus individual communication when exploring mistakes with team members whose cultures support those values.
Publicly mentioning any mistake is seen as punishment in many cultures.	Deal formally with risk. and discuss differences across cultures in terms of dealing with risk.
Attitudes toward risk differ drastically across cultures.	Create frequent check points to ensure everyone is on the same page.
Members set high personal standards and encourage each other to realize the objectives of the project.	Actively work to forestall discouragement in foreign team members.
The definition of high personal standards differs greatly across cultures.	Do not try to change the way foreign team members work within their own groups unless there are strong reasons to do so.
Cross-cultural realities simply add to the challenges that already exist in virtual teams.	Provide frequent reviews and other systems to ensure alignment and check understanding.
	Never accept yes for an answer because it means different things in different cultures. Ask: "What do you like about it?" "What is the date when you are sure it will be finished?"

(Continued)

Table 16.1 (Continued)

Characteristic	Additional Challenges for Cross-Border Teams	Strategies to Address Challenges
Members identify with the team and consider it an important source of professional and personal growth.	What are seen as rewards can differ across cultures and organizations. Working in cross-cultural teams requires patience and more adaptation.	Sympathize with the frustration but not with the blaming involved in working across distance, language, and culture. Make sure everyone knows that it is always harder for people from the non-dominant culture to thrive in these settings.
		Reinforce the marketability of the ability to work successfully across cultures.
		Check with all members on assignments and levels of challenges. Ensure people have the opportunity to give feedback on the issue of growth.
		Communicate your excitement about the team's project, what you are learning, and the importance of learning to work across borders.
		Search and attend to people who are not actively participating.

The current challenge is to capture, organize, and disseminate findings of the multitude of experiments underway. There seems to an emerging consensus around the special challenges of cross-border virtual teams and the additional time and energy investment needed to make them successful. Social scientists and computer tool developers alike recognize that trust and shared understanding are prerequisite to the success in these teams and that the needed trust and shared understanding are difficult, if not impossible, to develop without face-to-face time (Norhayati, Amelinckx, & Wilman, 2004). There is also a growing consensus on the special attitudes and skills that characterize successful cross-border team leaders and members (Brett et al., 2006; Norhayati et al., 2004; Verma, 1997). There is a great deal of valuable knowledge on cultural differences, and the strategies and tactics that result in creative and efficient work across borders are beginning to emerge.

REMINDERS

- Leading international virtual teams requires creating new ways to work together. A first step is ensuring that all team members are aware of cultural differences and prepared to try to understand and adapt.

- Successful cross-border team leaders have the knowledge to recognize cultural phenomena, the ability to observe and interpret subtle behavioral cues, and the skills to adapt their behavior to the needs and expectations of people from different cultures.

- There are often characteristics or work practices of other cultures that will have to change if the team is to reach its goals. A team leader needs patience and persistence to effect these changes.

- Leaders of international virtual teams must adapt the way they manage as well as the way they lead. Dividing the work up to minimize the need for collaboration and create a sense of local ownership is critical. Also critical is providing multiple communication channels, translating complex directions, using as much visual explanation as possible, and using frequent progress checks and reviews to make sure all teams' outcomes are on schedule, compatible with the shared goal, and done in a way that supports integration.

- Educating team sponsors and the team leader's supervisors on the challenges and skills of cross-border virtual work is often critical to the team leader's survival.

- Building relationships with the supervisors of foreign team members is a precursor to success in high-power-distance cultures.

- Leaders who have a positive outlook and provide support and encouragement are valued by the members of all cultures.

References

Bell, M. (2002, January). Leading an international virtual team: Tips for success. *Gartner Research Note 11.*

Brett, J., Behfar, K., & Kern, M. (2006, November). Managing multicultural teams. *Harvard Business Review,* 1–7.

Freedman, S., & Katz, L. (2005, November). *Managing projects across borders.* Participant Guides. The University of Texas at Dallas, Executive Education Program.

Gray, C. E., & Larson, E. W. (2006). *Project management: The managerial process* (3rd ed.). New York: McGraw-Hill.

Hofstede, G. (1980). *Culture's consequence: International differences in work related values.* Thousand Oaks, CA: Sage.

Hofstede, G. (1993). *Cultures and organizations: Software of the mind.* New York: McGraw-Hill.

Hofstede, G. (1994, February). Cultural constraints in management theories. *Academy of Management Executive, 7*(1), 81–93.

Katz, L. (2006). *Negotiating international business: The negotiator's reference guide to 50 countries around the world.* Charleston, SC: Booksurge.

Norhayati, Z., Amelinckx, A., & Wilman, D. (2004). Working together apart? Build a knowledge-sharing culture for global virtual teams. *Creativity and Innovation Management, 13*(1), 15–29.

Peolina, A., Leu, B., & Chinn, A. (2005). Exporting lean to China: Know before you go. *Insight, 17*(2) 1–6.

Robbins, S. P. (2003). *Organizational behavior.* Upper Saddle River, NJ: Prentice Hall.

Verma, V. K. (1997). *Managing the project team* (pp. 102–103). New Town Square, PA: Project Management Institute.

Problem Solving in Virtual Teams

David Braga, Steve Jones, Dennis Bowyer

In order to survive and prosper, organizations have always needed to find solutions to difficult problems. However, current forces are affecting organizations and their management in ways unmatched in history. Higgins (1994) notes:

> Change is occurring at an accelerating rate. The number of competitors is increasing dramatically. Business is globalizing. New technology is being introduced at a rapid pace. The workforce is increasingly diverse. There is a scarcity of certain resources, including highly skilled workers. There is a transformation occurring from an industrial to a knowledge-based society. Economic and market conditions are increasingly unstable, especially on a global basis. Constituents are more demanding. And finally, the entire business environment is becoming more complex [p. v].

As a result, organizations must find creative solutions to an array of organizational problems and in a multitude of organizational environments. With people of diverse backgrounds, knowledge bases, and skill sets dispersed throughout the world, along with advances in collaborative technologies, the understanding of how individuals can come together virtually as a team to solve problems is necessary.

Collaboration is one of the most productive and fundamental forces in human nature. Yet despite the recognition of collaboration as a creative and problem-solving tool, few individuals or organizations use its full potential. In the rush to solve problems, there is a dangerous attractiveness to seeking an immediate fix. Management or customer pressures to come up with a solution, any solution, can lead to a false diagnosis. The consequence of this approach is often a solution that creates more problems.

The growing complexity of organizational and technical problems can exceed an individual's area of expertise and thus necessitate a team approach to solving problems. Often in problem-solving situations, those closest to the problem are charged with the responsibility of forming a team to address the problem. The danger here is that individuals who have direct involvement with the problem may in fact be too close to it. Problem-solving solutions often necessitate the need for individuals from other organizations or groups to participate. The lack of a team approach to problem solving will suppress the emergence of novel ideas and innovative approaches. Albert Einstein noted that problems cannot be solved at the same level of awareness that created them.

Although it is generally accepted that groups of individuals, all involved in the process and all having various perspectives of a problem, increase the quality of the decision, organizations generally place much of their effort in applying programmed approaches to problem solving. Reliance on techniques at the expense of processes often results in working on the wrong problem or ineffective problem solutions or, worse, both. For example, brainstorming a problem is a good technique to generate ideas but does not lend itself to a systematic process in which problems are solved. Although some research indicates that creative problem solving is rooted in human traits, a preponderance of the evidence indicates that it can be taught and developed. How should the problem be defined? How should the team or group proceed? And should the perspectives of the stakeholders be incorporated into an understanding of the system and the problem?

Virtual teams are composed of members who may not know each other well. In addition, individual team members may have an understanding of only one small part of the team's problem or focus and lack an understanding of the overall challenges, forces, and requirements that need to be considered. Also, team members may lack an appreciation for each other's work environment or culture. For these reasons, effective communication among team members is a critical success factor in problem solving on virtual teams.

Communication enablers can help virtual teams in being more productive. This chapter presents an overview of some potentially useful processes and enablers for increasing the effectiveness of virtual teams. Problem solving can be difficult for any team, and dealing with these issues in a virtual environment can be much more arduous. Processes should be defined to address the communication issues in virtual team problem solving more effectively. A common understanding of the problem is essential to effective collaboration. When a common understanding of the problem is not possible, an appreciation of others' positions and views is helpful. Consider an engineering team whose members are part of a virtual team working to develop a new nanotechnology that the other team members—a project manager, business operations, and marketing—do not understand technically. The team nevertheless can work together to understand the engineering point of view that coming up with a new technology is not always predictable. The engineering team representative should be open to understanding the project manager and business operations point of view that budgets and schedule need to be maintained. In addition, virtual team members should be sensitive to the market conditions as defined by the marketing representative. Members of this team can be quickly derailed when a subgroup of the team works long and dedicated hours only to discover that its definition of the problem is not shared and its work is neither appreciated nor supported.

PREPARATION FOR PROBLEM SOLVING

It is essential that virtual problem solvers have the ability to garner information from diverse individuals and in diverse locations. Virtual team members must work together to define the core problems accurately. It is important for the team to develop and understand a variety of options to the solution, as opposed to a quick or a single solution. They must seek to understand the impact of their solution on the larger organization as a whole and how it can affect the organization's long-term outlook. If virtual groups are to work together to solve problems, they need an effective method to help structure their efforts. When there are difficult or complex problems to solve, there are often barriers to overcome, many of them psychological in nature. Altshuller (2000) defined these barriers to problem solving as "psychological inertia." Psychological inertia is often verbalized or unconsciously internalized as "that's the way we've always done it" or "this is the way it has to done." Overcoming these barriers can lead to more creative and alternative solutions.

In order to overcome these psychological barriers virtually, teams should establish certain ground rules or micropractices before starting to solve the problem. The following list can be used to help them get started in defining how they will operate and collectively agree on what the problem is:

- Will the team work to solve the problem synchronously or asynchronously, or some combination?

- List the methods of virtual communications that team members will use: e-mails, blog, videoconferencing, instant messaging, real-time chat, and so forth.

- Describe the process through which the team will document how the problem was resolved: action items list, brainstorming, or dialogue-mapping software or tools.

- Define and clarify virtual team member roles and responsibilities. Create a statement of work. Define shared individual and shared responsibilities. Learn and understand each other's roles.

- Ignoring or not responding to a conflict within a team can disrupt its ability to solve problems. From the initial formation of the team, agree on a set of guidelines that will be followed if and when a conflict arises—for example, acknowledge that a conflict exists, seek a common understanding and invite different viewpoints from members of the virtual team, attack the issue and not each other, and develop an action plan to resolve the dispute.

- State a general narrative description of the problem.

- State the problem in one sentence.

- Describe the activities or processes the team has previously used in trying to resolve this problem.

- List all alternative or potential solutions the team or organization has identified for this problem.

- Assess each of the alternatives listed and select those that the team views as best. Rate how satisfied the team is with the solution it has identified for this problem, using a scale where 1 = least satisfied and 10 = most satisfied.

PROBLEM TYPES

The concept of the term *problem* has been defined in several ways. Perhaps the most common definition of a problem is "the gap between a level of performance desired and the actual level of performance" (Gibson, Ivancevich, & Donnelly, 1988, p. 4). Dewey (1910) delineated three steps in problem solving by asking, "What is the problem?" "What are the alternatives?" and "Which alternative is best?" These steps highlight the emphasis he placed on determining or defining the problem. Although there are many kinds of problems that are likely to be encountered by collaborative problem solvers in business, they can generally be collapsed into two major types: simple problems and complex problems.

Simple Problems

A simple problem has the following characteristics:

- The current state and desired state are readily known and agreed on.
- The possible root causes are straightforward, allowing the collaborators to move quickly toward designing a solution.
- Constraints are well known.
- Solving the problem involves moving in a series of steps from current state to desired state in a linear fashion, although analysis of initial results may result in a refinement of the solution.
- Emphasis is on a structured action to avoid blaming and move efficiently toward a solution.

Here is an example of a simple problem:

An international cargo carrier's airplane veered off the runway to avoid an obstruction. The airplane ended up in the dirt between two parallel runways and suffered substantial damage to its landing gear. The incident occurred at midnight, and this normally busy airport was temporarily closed to other traffic. The airport authorities called the U.S.-based company immediately because they wanted the airplane moved as soon as possible so as to open the airport for the early-morning rush. Because the cargo company operated twenty-four hours a day, seven days a week on a global basis, it had in place a crisis management team (CMT) to handle situations such as this.

The CMT, which consisted of seasoned employees from management, engineering, operations, and maintenance, operated as a truly virtual team. Permanent members of the team had at their disposal a list of company subject matter experts who could be called to participate as an extension of the CMT. In this case, within a half-hour of the incident, the team leader called permanent members of the team as well as subject matter experts in aircraft structures, airplane recovery, parts logistics, and landing gear. Photographs of the airplane were taken and placed on the company server. Within an hour of the incident, members of the CMT from various parts of the world dialed into a teleconference. Each CMT member had been trained by the company in the use of a six-step problem-solving process for simple problems.

By morning, the airplane was towed from the dirt to a hangar, and the airport opened. At the same time, a new set of landing gear was being sent by the supplier to the location. Within a week, the airplane was fixed and returned to service.

The six-step problem-solving method (see Figure 17.1), used by organizations such as Xerox (Jones & Schilling, 2000), is appropriate for simple problems where the emphasis is on disciplined action to achieve rapid results:

Step 1: Identify the Problem

- Be specific in stating the problem; use data rather than opinions.
- Break down general problems into smaller problems.
- Review, combine, eliminate, and rank problem statements.
- Do not imply a cause or solution in the problem statement.

Step 2: Analyze the Problem

- List possible causes of the problem; do not evaluate suggestions.
- Reduce the list to the most likely or probable causes.

Figure 17.1
Six-Step Problem-Solving Process for Simple Problems

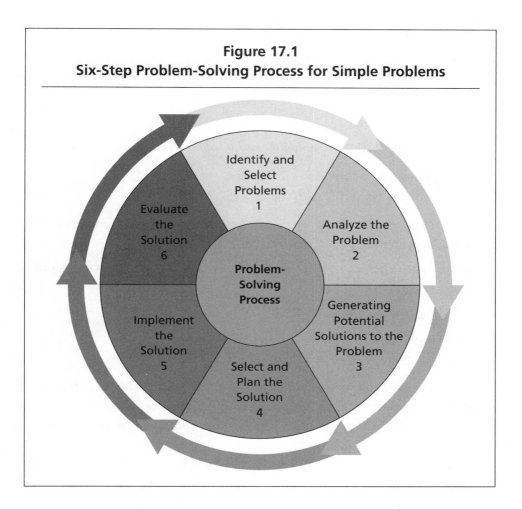

- Identify and prioritize root causes based on the data.
- After analyzing the problem, revise the problem statement.

Step 3: Generate Potential Solutions to the Problem

- Review the problem statement and root causes.
- Generate, but do not evaluate, a list of potential solutions.
- Clarify how potential solutions address the causes of the problem.

Step 4: Select and Plan the Solution

- Determine selection criteria, that is, how potential solutions address the desired state. Select and agree on solutions to implement.

- Develop a written plan specifying who will implement the solution, how, and when.

- Develop a written plan, including measures to monitor and evaluate solution.

Step 5: Implement the Solution

- Follow the written implementation plan.

- Monitor and evaluate the progress or effectiveness of the solution, using the plan developed in step 4.

- As necessary, meet as a team to make midstream corrections or implement contingency plans.

Step 6: Evaluate the Solution

- Based on measures, the team learns how effectively the solution solved the selected problem.

The six-step method is often modified to fit the work and culture of the organization. For example, at Saturn, a seventh step is added between steps 2 and 3. Saturn's seventh step is a temporary solution that will enable work to continue while a long-term solution is being crafted.

Whether the method has six or seven steps is not as important as the common language and structure the team to uses to solve problems rapidly. A virtual team requires this common language and structure to keep all members on the same page and to keep the process moving forward.

The CMT members using the six-step method of problem solving first determined that the most immediate problem was to get the airplane off the runway so that the airport could be opened. During the first meeting, the team agreed that more information was needed to determine if the airplane could be moved without further damage. They agreed to meet back on the conference call in two hours.

During the second meeting, the subject matter experts on the CMT in aircraft structures and landing gear team members determined by on-site inspection and photographs uploaded to the team's shared server that the aircraft could be towed from the runway without further damaging the airplane. The next problem was to determine how to get the airplane repaired and back into service. Potential solutions were developed ranging from fixing the landing gear to replacing the gear. A plan was developed to inspect the landing gear and x-ray the landing for cracks. The team agreed that in any case, new landing gear should be sent to the site because new landing gear was more cost-effective than having the plane down and not producing revenue. The airplane was repaired and back in service within a week.

Complex Problems

Two distinguishing characteristics of complex problems are that the problem is alive and can mutate in reaction to attempts at a solution and that constituents or stakeholders have conflicting views of the problem. According to Rittel and Webber (1973), a complex (or wicked) problem has the following characteristics:

- There is no definitive formulation of a complex problem; the definition depends on who or what group is asked to address it.

- Complex problems have a "no-stopping rule." Since there is no definitive problem, there can be no definitive solution. The problem-solving process ends when resources run out, that is, when the company decides that enough money has been spent on the issues or other issues have taken a higher priority.

- Solutions to complex problems are not true or false; they are evaluated in terms of which one is better, not which one is right.

- The problem changes in reaction to each attempted solution, so a solution can make the problem worse.

- Every complex problem is unique. There are always unique characteristics to each wicked or complex problem so that the solutions to other problems cannot be directly used.

An example of a complex problem is whether to route a highway through or around a city. In this problem, there is no definitive problem definition. Each stakeholder defines the problem and acceptable solution differently, depending on his or her values, economic interests, and political perspectives. In addition, there are no stop rules or a clearly understood time to conclude the problem-solving activity. The location of the proposed highway can be studied from many perspectives. Also, there is no one best or true solution on which all stakeholders can agree. There is usually general agreement that some solutions are better than others. For examples, a route through the city hall would be worse than a route over an old filled-in canal. Finally, each city has unique characteristics requiring consideration.

The method used to address complex problems needs to consider several issues. First, it must be able to facilitate an understanding of each stakeholder's perspective and work to resolve as many of the conflicts as possible. Second, it needs to gain a consensus among the stakeholders for the process to be used, thus building trust and reducing anxiety and ambiguity concerning future steps to be taken. Third, the problem-solving process needs a mechanism for gathering information and data and differentiating facts, opinions, and hearsay. Fourth, a feedback process is needed where learning is encouraged, transferred, and imputed into the process to allow definitions and constraints to change as new information is discovered. Finally, a method for solving complex problems needs to include developing an awareness of potential solutions on other systems, that they have both positive and negative affects, as well as to understand the potential solution's long-term effect on the system itself. For example, a flood control channel will reduce flooding in a particular area; however, it could potentially endanger federally protected plants and animals.

Conklin (2006) created guidelines for what he refers to as "taming the problem." Instead of dealing with the full complexities of a problem, a virtual team should work toward breaking down and trying to simplify it—in other words, make the problem solvable:

The city decided to take a unique approach to its highway problem and create a public forum blog with real-time chat features to address this complex problem. The mayor held a real-time session every Monday for two hours. Those without access to a computer could go to city hall, where computers were made available to the general public. The topics were posted by the mayor on the blog between real-time sessions. The facilitator ensured that everyone stayed on topic and that the discussions were kept informative. The weekly blog threads and real-time discussion could be accessed on the blog. Due to the complexities surrounding the issues, the blog would remain open for approximately six months.

Here is how Conklin's "taming the problem" guidelines (2006) pertain to the city's highway problem:

- *Hold discussions to determine the stakeholders.* Over the course of the next six months by using the city's threaded blog discussions and real-time chats with the mayor, the stakeholders were narrowed to the city council, the property owners along the proposed routes, and citizens.

- *Narrow the problem to a specific problem or subproblem that can be solved. Do not change or expand the problem or its scope.* The problem was narrowed to economic benefit versus traffic and noise associated with the highway.

- *At some point, consider the problem "solved."* The highway was routed around the city, but the main thoroughfare of the city was connected to the highway and widened to accommodate more traffic. The citizen stakeholders and the local business community were satisfied.

- *Consider the parameters that measure the success of the problem.* A balance between an increase in economic benefits and avoiding a marked increase in traffic and noise that a highway would bring the city was achieved.

- *Avoid the tendency to complicate the problem. Keep the solution simple.* A highway running through the middle of the city would create increased traffic and noise. By routing the highway around local businesses, the city would lose out on increased business and tax revenue.

- *Realize the solution may not be the optimum one for the problem.* Connecting the highway with an exit to the city's thoroughfare would bring some economic gain to businesses and the city but would not generate as much noise and traffic routing the highway through the city.

- *Declare that there may be more than one possible solution. Spend the time to consider the many possible options.* The potential options include not only building the highway around or through the city, but building the highway under the city, building an elevated highway through the city, or choosing an entirely different route for the highway.

FINAL THOUGHTS

As the importance of teams has grown, so have the studies investigating them and their role in problem solving. Berkshire (1995) identified the following behaviors that encourage creativity in problem solving: speculative thinking, openness, empowerment, involvement, attentiveness, organization, collaboration, cohesiveness, a willingness to change, acknowledgment, clarifying, commitment, and a sense of history. Berkshire found that the following behaviors hindered creativity: controlling, being noncommittal, competitiveness, blaming, disagreeing, discounting, being unorganized, being unattentive, defensiveness, fearing reprisal, a poor sense of history, rationalizing, routine thinking, and no cohesiveness. Specific attention in addressing a virtual team's structure, group size, cognitive relationships, and issues concerning cohesion, as well as the behavior of individuals in group settings, will add to potential success of the group's problem solving.

REMINDERS

- Developing a common understanding of the problem is essential to effective collaboration.
- Identify what information is present, how reliable the information is, and what information still needs to be acquired.
- Strive to obtain as many thoughtful ideas as possible from every team member.
- Generate a greater understanding among team members of each other's views and perspectives.

References

Altshuller, G. (2000). *The innovation algorithm: TRIZ systematic innovation and technical creativity* (L. Shulyak & S. Rodman, Trans.). Worcester, MA: Technical Innovation Center. (Original work published in 1973)

Berkshire, S. D. (1995). Critical behaviors in innovative and creative decision-making and problem solving work groups. *Dissertation Abstracts International, 56*, 1427.

Conklin, J. (2006). *Dialogue mapping*. Hoboken, NJ: Wiley.

Dewey, J. (1910). *How we think*. New York: Heath.

Gibson, J. W., Ivancevich, J. M., & Donnelly, J. H. (1988). *Organizations: Behavior, structure, processes*. Plano, TX: Business Publishing.

Higgins, J. (1994). *101 creative problem solving techniques*. Winter Park, FL: New Management.

Jones, S., & Schilling, D. (2000). *Measuring team performance: A step-by-step, customizable approach for managers, facilitators, and team leaders*. San Francisco: Jossey-Bass.

Rittel, H., & Webber, M. (1973). Dilemmas in a general theory of planning. *Policy Sciences, 4*, 155–169.

Correcting Chronic Decision-Making Problems Through Effective Collaboration

Mehran Ferdowsian

The intent or endgoal of effective collaboration is to do something together, cohesively (united purpose, vision, and action). Whether done face-to-face or in a virtual way, effective collaboration inevitably results in making a good decision, addressing a complex problem, creating something new, or planning and executing a highly distributed and virtual task or project—all good results. In essence, virtual collaboration and effective decision making and problem solving are inherently linked and require good planning, execution, and wholehearted individual commitment and responsibility for it to succeed (Neilson & Pasternack, 2005). What people often tend to miss in organizations is that collaboration and decision making have an impact on many other things, such as creativity and innovation, efficiency and productivity, and employee well-being and satisfaction, which ultimately translate into organizational health and competitiveness (O'Toole & Lawler, 2006). Strong evidence suggests that a good collaboration and decision-making system is one of the core ingredients for good leadership and effective organizational governance (Bass & Stogdill, 1990).

Today many existing collaboration and decision-making processes are not equipped to handle the diverse, often complex, rapidly changing, and global nature of work environments. This chapter examines the silent, unspoken, or hidden dimension of effective collaboration and decision making and presents a solution that lends itself to virtual collaboration by enabling organizations to tap into and leverage the power of collective intelligence—the diversity of thought, understanding, and different temperaments that exists in the global community to address complex corporate problems.

This chapter examines, explains, and addresses many of the chronic problems associated with effective decision making, problem solving, and virtual collaboration that organizations experience. The driving question for this chapter is what it will take to have an individual go that extra mile, use every available resource at his or her disposal, stand behind a decision in a united manner, and leverage his or her own discretionary time and effort to succeed. This effort was part of a more comprehensive study that examined what it would take to develop a "principled organization" as it develops the capability to deliver sustained superior business results. A principled organization is one that is governed by a specific set of unmovable and unshakable principles such as Trust and Justice. As a result, a principled organization is capable of delivering sustained, superior, and cohesive business results by enabling its employees to achieve meaning and purpose as they make the greatest possible contributions to the society and their work.

The answer to the driving question is that a good decision-making and collaboration system was a major determining factor for developing a competitive edge in high-involvement organizations (O'Toole & Lawler, 2006). Specifically, strong evidence suggested that an effective collaboration and decision-making process had a direct impact on many aspects of organizational governance, such as problem solving, creativity and innovation, work relationships, the development of mutual trust, respect, and understanding, and on how effectively group members were able to transform conjecture into confidence and certainty (Mauzy & Harriman, 2003). In essence, it was concluded that a good collaboration and decision-making process was a key factor in nurturing a healthy and productive work environment since it played a key role in how individuals took initiative and ownership to make decisions or solve problems.

Good collaboration and decision-making process is a core ingredient of organizational governance and an important building block for the development of a principled organization. A CEO of a top-ranking Fortune 100 company said, "Decision making has an impact on our ability to innovate, communicate, manage, and excel. It affects everything we do. How those basics are executed can vary widely in different business units and individuals." A vice president and general manager in charge of organizational effectiveness and productivity at a top-ranking Fortune 100 company noted, "We face aggressive competitiveness in our core business. For us it is all about making the right decisions and then executing flawlessly."

With this new finding, the organization placed a special focus on the art and science of effective consultation as a means to develop a spark of consensus, a process for effective collaboration, and a systematic process to leverage the collective intelligence and make good decisions as well as solve complex problems. This research concluded that a strengthened consultative collaboration and decision-making process is necessary to address many of the complex, diverse, global problems encountered in and out of organizations. As Table 18.1 shows, an effective consultative process enables an organization to tap into and leverage group intelligence, make sound decisions, and have everyone own and champion the final decision. This approach develops greater awareness, creates unity of thought and action, and transforms conjecture into certainty. This same process enables an organization to nurture a meaningful foundation of trust required for effective face-to-face and virtual collaboration, which enables individuals to rapidly resolve differences, address complex problem, and make the best possible decisions (Covey, 2006).

The central message of this chapter is that effective decision making, problem solving, and collaboration are tightly coupled and intertwined and require a solid, comprehensive, and meaningful consultative decision-making process for it to be successful. Corporations need to strengthen their decision-making and collaboration processes by taking these capabilities to the next level of maturity and effectiveness and by infusing good consultative decision-making processes into every aspect of their culture (O'Toole & Lawler, 2006). Any serious attempt to

Table 18.1
Consultation: Benefits, Impact, and Application

Application and Areas Affected	Example
Develops greater consensus and stronger bonds between individuals, groups, and teams	Builds solid work relationships
Guides individual, group, and organizational initiatives by developing greater understanding and transforming conjecture into certainty	Develops true understanding Builds confidence and certainty
Enables people to get to the bottom of each problem, explore root cause issues, and unravel the underlying motives behind a given situation	Results in quality decision making Results in better problem solving
Transforms conjecture into certitude by allowing an idea to grow through frankness, open-mindedness, and freedom of thought	Results in quality decision making Develops individual ownership
Maintains order, directs one's personal affairs, and helps to settle complex human and social differences in groups and organizations	Provides guidance and direction Addresses differences
Eliminates the need to exercise force and power and asks for the subjugation of individual egotism, unruly passions, and partisanship	Reduces unwarranted fears Reduces excessive power
Releases creative energies and ripens and matures one's understanding, with true understanding turned into wisdom (the next step after knowledge)	Develops greater wisdom Produces sound and high-quality decisions
Enables people to leverage the diversity of thought, understanding, knowledge, experiences, teachings, hopes, and temperaments	Maximizes human potential Leverages diversity
If done with the right spirit, develops employee well-being, tranquility, and felicity	Establishes healthier work environments Produces better-satisfied employees

correct chronic decision-making problems requires the wholehearted support of the management team and employees at all levels of the organization. To accomplish this, organizations need to make consultation and consultative decision making one of their core corporate values. Specifically, this chapter:

1. Identifies and briefly discusses a set of silent, unspoken, and often ignored deterrents to effective decision making. Collectively, these deterrents constitute a set of chronic problems that interfere with good decision making.

2. Introduces a core set of principles and prime requisites for effective decision making and virtual collaboration. These essential conditions and prerequisites define the standard for good behavior, which enables virtual collaboration and good decision making to occur at "the speed of trust." These prerequisites are meant to develop a foundation of trust and counteract the negative affects of the silent deterrents that prevent good decision making (Covey, 2006).

3. Proposes a model and process for good decision making that enables corporations to cultivate an open and frank environment where people can freely express their opinions in an unfettered way, where one can clash into the diverse ideas and opinions (not the people), and work to generate a spark of consensus that will get everyone behind a decision. This process becomes especially valuable when dealing with a virtual collaborative environment, where tasks and projects are distributed globally and individuals from different cultures and backgrounds must closely work together in order to make good decisions that stick.

PROBLEM STATEMENT AND VALUE PROPOSITION

As a global community, people have learned to do such complex tasks such as send humans to the moon and bring them back safely, build the world's fastest supercomputers with hundreds of brains, connect to and control home or office from the beach, and fly from one corner of the globe to the another corner at supersonic speeds while relaxing in a lounge chair, sipping apple cider, watching a movie, and sending digital pictures to their children telling them how much they have missed them. But sometimes people still cannot make or execute a good decision even if their lives depended on it. Why is that? Is it because they lack a good decision-making process, or because they are not aware of, understand, or cannot follow their own decision-making processes? A few examples illustrate how bad decisions—those defined as inaccurate, ineffective, unethical, or immoral—that deliberately or mistakenly overlooked one critical idea ended up costing billions in missed opportunities, property damage, and loss of lives:

- "They were laughing at me when I was presenting the eminent dangers of a category 4 or 5 hurricane on the city of New Orleans, the breach of the levees, and the flooding of the entire city" (an engineer).
- "My warnings and cries were unanswered when I predicted and communicated the O-ring problem that resulted in the space shuttle disaster" (an engineer).
- Examine the actions of countless CEOs who refused to admit wrongdoing, listen to the voice of reason, or recall their faulty products already on the shelves and ended up bankrupting their company, devastating their company stock, or resulting in loss of lives.

These and other similar examples point out that an individual may sometimes come to the table with a hidden agenda, with his or her mind already made up or with a self-centered thought that tends to severely limit anyone's ability to collaborate, make effective decisions, or solve a complex problem. This phenomenon develops what is often referred to in the corporate community as "turfs" or "chimneys" that separate people and prevent effective collaboration. What happens is that people tend to shut down, do not listen, pull rank, or use position power, education, or experience to make a decision without consultation. This hidden, silent, or unspoken dimension of effective collaboration develops an emotional attachment to one's own ideas and prevents others from listening, engaging, or getting wholeheartedly behind the final decision as if it were their own. This approach shuts down any kind of effective collaboration and prevents people from making the best possible decisions.

Generally the issues around effective collaboration, decision making, and problem solving are near and dear to most people and widespread, and the impact can be felt across the industry in large and small companies around the world. Imagine as an example what would happen if a bunch of people were put in the same room and asked to make a decision on something that is a bit complex or a subject that requires heavy thinking and brainstorming or something that the participants have a big stake in and is a bit controversial or politically charged (such as subjects dealing with turf, power, or complex social issues). Think of the amount of off-line political maneuvering, wheeling and dealing, negotiating, synchronizing, and a host of other things one has to go through just to be able to come to the table and make a decision. Off-line alignment is a natural part of effective decision making. The problem is that even after all of this excruciating off-line work, one often ends up making a bad decision because members of the organization:

- Did not listen to one another and leverage the collective intelligence
- Did not consider all of the good ideas and ended up missing a key point
- Compromised far too much for the sake of keeping everyone happy
- Tiptoed around the real issue altogether and missed the main point
- Made a decision "for" an individual as if that person were a child
- Made a shortsighted decision that everyone ends up paying for dearly later

The other predicament people often find themselves in is that many of their decisions simply do not stick because others will not wholeheartedly get behind a decision as if it were their own decision. One of the reasons for this lack of commitment and ownership is that people often do not differentiate the process of decision making "for" a child versus how they need to partner and collaborate to make a decision with an adult. Therefore, the end result is one or more of the following:

- Individuals do not get behind the solution wholeheartedly.
- Individuals do not want to accept or execute the resultant changes.
- Individuals intentionally or unintentionally sabotage the end result.
- Individuals do not listen and refuse to accept the final decision.
- Individuals refuse to help address the problems.
- Individuals end up saying, "See, you didn't listen to me, and we failed. I told you so."

Problems are compounded when people have to deal with additional complications associated with globalizations and virtual collaboration, such as problems that deal with:

- National and cross-cultural differences and issues
- Lack of a common language that all involved can understand
- Lack of a global communication etiquette all can use
- Lack of consistent training and right skills
- Lack of unity in thought and actions

One of the major conclusions reached in this study is that in many cases, the reason that people cannot make good decisions, solve complex problems, or carry out a task is that they often overlook, ignore, or tend to dismiss many of the behavioral and relational elements that go into effective collaboration, such as:

- Addressing the silent, hidden, or unspoken aspects of collaboration and decision making (for example, power, position, biases, or egotism)
- Understanding the prime requisites of effective collaboration and decision making (for example, being truthful about the intent or purpose of the decision—the spirit and approach of good decision making)
- Setting the right behavioral expectation and mind-set for good decision making

IMPACT OF BAD AND EFFECTIVE DECISION MAKING AND COLLABORATION

The capability to deliver sustained superior business results and performance requires an effective decision-making, problem-solving, and collaboration process (Kouzes & Posner, 2002). The impact of a bad, ineffective, or unethical or immoral decision-making and collaborative processes can be exhibited on individuals and organizations in a number of ways:

- Prevents people from tapping into the full spectrum of individual ideas and the collective intelligence
- Prevents developing an idea through frankness, open-mindedness, and freedom of thought

- Prevents the genesis or growth of creative new ideas using the collective intelligence and through frank and unfettered thought
- Prevents the maturation of individual understanding that is so critical to the effective transformation of conjecture into certitude
- Prevents releasing creative energies required to transform understandings into wisdom
- Prevents making a decision or solving a problem through a spark of consensus
- Increases the possibility of missing an important idea or opportunity
- Prevents getting to the depth of a problem, exploring the underlying root-cause issues, and unraveling the unspoken or silent motives behind a given situation that prevents people from addressing a specific problem (for example, position power and egotism)

In response, this chapter develops a decision-making process that allows people to:

- Get everyone behind a given solution by separating the ideas from the individuals, clashing into the ideas (not the people), merging all the good ideas into a pool of solutions, and enabling individuals to accept all good ideas as if they were their own (good ideas are separated from individual preferences)
- Leverage the diversity of thought, understanding, knowledge, experiences, teachings, hopes, and temperaments to address complex problems by enabling employees to wholeheartedly participate in the decision-making and problem-solving process
- Enable employees to get to the depth of each problem, explore the root-cause issues, and unravel the underlying motives behind a given situation by transforming conjecture into certitude and allowing an idea to grow through frankness, open-mindedness, and freedom of thought
- Release creative energies, develop and mature human understanding, and transform understanding into wisdom by reducing the exercise of power and subjugating individual egotism and partisanship
- Strengthen individual commitment to the solution by using a two-pass approach to leverage new and nonbiased members to either develop a spark of consensus or accept a majority vote

- Maintain order, settle complex differences, and prevent any possible dilution of the solution by stopping all further discussions on the solution once a consensus has been reached or majority decision has been made
- Set expectations that the final decision will be wholeheartedly executed by all the people involved and that each individual role-models the change and becomes a change agent or champion of change

KEY APPROACHES TO DECISION MAKING AND COLLABORATION

A good, sound, or effective decision is defined as one that is made the first time around and the decision-making group is fully united to stand behind it. Specifically, a good or sound decision possesses the following criteria:

- It addresses the immediate problem or need.
- The decision is made in a timely manner.
- The decision is made with foresight and the end goal in mind.
- The final decision is based on consensus or majority vote.
- The decision is crafted and developed out of the group intelligence.
- The decision is backed up and supported by most or all.
- The decision is rarely reopened (only based on exceptions).

Table 18.2 provides a complete list of decision-making methods used today and outlines the pros and cons of each method.

CURRENT COLLABORATION AND DECISION-MAKING PRINCIPLES

A close examination of the existing collaboration, decision-making, planning, and idea generation processes used by a number of Fortune 100 companies reveals that many have a set of principles to help employees make good and effective decisions. These principles are often integrated into the corporate culture by a variety of means, such as employee training, integration, mentoring, and development programs. For the most part, the workforce is well aware of these principles, knows why they were instituted, understands what is expected of them, and

Table 18.2

Pros and Cons of Collaboration and Decision-Making Methods

Method	Description	Benefits	Problems
Democratic (also referred to as *voting*)	In this approach, each participant gets a single vote and the final decision is made by the majority vote (Tannenbaum & Schmidt, 1958).	Usually a very quick and easy approach to making a decision. It can also be used as a backup process when a group or team cannot reach a consensus through consultation.	This approach may split the group into "winners" and "losers." Also individual responsibility or accountability may be lost or individuals may blame the "winners" when a bad/ineffective decision is made.
Authoritative (decide and announce)	In this approach, the group leader makes the final decision and then the decision or solution is announced to the participants or stakeholders (Tannenbaum & Schmidt, 1958).	This approach is very expeditious because the desired end goal, state, or business results are typically dictated from higher levels. This method should be used in situations in which only one decision is expected or possible.	This method does not allow people to leverage the group intelligence. Further, this method has the lowest level of employee commitment and ownership to the final decision.
Consensus (also referred to as *joint decisions*)	In this method the expectation is that ideas, feedback, and discussion continues until everyone's concerns, interests, and ideas are dispositioned, addressed, and incorporated. This method enables the group or team to make the decision and all members will have to fully agree with the final outcome (Heller & Yukl, 1969).	It can result in or yield the highest level of employee commitment and ownership to the final decision.	This method is probably the most tedious and time-consuming decision-making method. One of the underlying motivations for using this method may be to protect the decision maker from having to be accountable or responsible for the final outcome. If misused or overused, this approach may be controlled by the most rigid or resistant members. This is commonly referred to as the *group think syndrome*, which may lock the members in a common frame of reference and fail to question the underlying motives or assumptions.

(Continued)

Table 18.2 (Continued)

Method	Description	Benefits	Problems
Semiconsultative (commonly referred to as *consultative*)	In this approach, the team members are encouraged to contribute and discuss ideas, suggestions, and opinions in a very open and free manner. However, at the end of the day it is the decision maker that makes the final decision (Bass & Valenzi, 1974).	Group intelligence is leveraged. It is consistent with the cultural practices of encouraging an open environment and constructively confronting issues. It balances involvement with speed.	Need to monitor discipline of "disagree and commit" or the possibility of it breaking down. (Disagreeing and then committing means that one agrees to align efforts with the decision and to explain the rationale behind it, whether or not one agrees.)
Full consultative decision making and collaboration (also referred to simply as *consultation*)	In this approach, the team or group members are expected to provide feedback, ideas, and opinions in an unfettered way, separate themselves from the ideas being presented, and look at the merit of each idea independently. In this approach, the final decision is made based on consensus or majority vote (Kolstoe, 1985).	Group intelligence is fully leveraged, different ideas and options are fully explored, ideas are separated from individuals, and the process will either yield a spark of consensus or generate a majority vote. This decision-making process develops the greatest ownership.	Initially, this process may seem to be frustrating, time consuming, and emotionally draining to the participants.

Source: Tannenbaum and Schmidt (1958).

strives to adhere to them. The following principles seem to be dominant among the corporate community:

- All managers need to identify the key decisions that they and their organizations own, who will make those decisions, when the decision will be made, and how each will be made.

- For the most part, each decision is owned by the person accountable for the results.

- Each decision has one major decision maker who is responsible for it.

- The individual accountable for the results is also empowered to make the decision.

- The decision maker is responsible for defining the process, tools, and roles.

- The expectation is that each decision maker must balance data with timeliness and judgment to maximize the business impact of the decision.

- Once made, the decision will have to be supported by everyone.

- Once made, the decision needs to be communicated clearly to those affected.

At first glance, these and similar other principles seem to be reasonable, logical, and applicable for good collaboration and decision making. However, the reality is that people often see many unwritten, unspoken, or silent micromessages, prejudices, biases, and expectations that sometimes make collaboration, decision making, and problem solving complex and ineffective. Whether malicious or not, these intentional or unintentional micromessages are continuously internalized and interpreted by individuals and will greatly limit the process of collaboration if they are not addressed.

The world has changed, but collaboration and decision-making processes, principles, and expectations have not kept up with the times. In fact, the rapid globalization of the planet has created a challenging, complex, and rapidly changing global work environment. Most of the large and international organizations are now dealing with virtual, highly matrixed, widely distributed, and cross-functional programs and tasks. Digging deeper reveals an unspoken, silent, or hidden dimension to effective collaboration and decision making that is often left out of the equation. For example, when divulged, a number of these unspoken or silent micromessages would get interpreted as follows:

"I know better because I'm wiser [or more educated, more experienced, or older] than the other people."

"Men are more logical, more mathematically oriented, and less emotional. Therefore, men tend to make better decision makers."

"I'm the boss around here, I'm responsible, and therefore I'm making the final decision at the end of the day."

"American workers are more creative and visionary, and Chinese workers work harder and have better work ethics."

"Why should I give my opinion if someone else will end up making the decision?"

"Why should I share anything good if someone else will take the credit for it"?

"Why should I do the work and have my manager end up looking good?"

"Why should I give my opinion if no one is willing to listen to my voice?"

Unfortunately, these silent, unspoken elements of decision making prevent wholeheartedly participating in the decision-making process and accepting the final decision as if it were one's own decision.

CURRENT DECISION-MAKING ROLES, RESPONSIBILITIES, AND PROCESS STEPS

An examination of the roles, responsibilities, and expectations set during a typical collaboration and decision-making session may identify some of the following expectations set for each designated decision maker and the ratifier of the final decision:

- Know or fully understand every aspect of the decision-making process.
- Clarify the scope and boundaries of the issue being addressed with the ratifier.
- Seek to understand the exact preferences of the ratifier of the decision.

- Be regularly in touch with the ratifier, and bounce ideas off this individual.

- Be open and flexible, and allow changes and necessary course correction.

- Recommend decisions to the ratifier, presenting options and the reasons for the decision.

The decision-making ratifier is the individual who needs to:

- Clearly define the scope, the boundary conditions, and assumptions

- Avoid changing his or her mind or make any unnecessary changes

- Clarify who the stakeholders are and why decision makers should worry about them

- Formally approve or veto a specific decision

- Ask questions and strive to understand the reason for the decision

- Enable decision makers to understand the dynamic of the environment

- Support the decisions made, and address any possible pocket vetoes

In summary, a close examination of a number of corporate collaboration and decision-making systems reveals four major and distinguishable phases. The first phase of this process typically consists of some kind of brainstorming, idea generation, benchmarking, or data-gathering process that is expected to help the participants make a decision, address a specific problem, or plan and execute a task. The second phase of most collaboration and decision-making systems is the decision-making step: the participants make a decision, address a problem, or plan and execute a task. The third phase often deals with a halfhearted effort to gain support and commitment from participants, team members, and other stakeholders to execute the decision or address the problem. The fourth and final phase of the collaboration and decision-making system deals with a contingency plan that may have to be carried through in case a course correction or change of direction has to be taken based on incoming new data or information.

Phase 1: Data Gathering and Brainstorming

Employees are expected to provide their feedback, give ideas, and articulate what they expect the outcome to be. This phase of the process is intended to provide an open, nonevaluative, and nonhierarchical atmosphere where employees can submit ideas and relevant data and also gain an understanding about what other members of their team believe. Most employers understand that this phase may get quite heated and emotions may run high. Nevertheless, employees are expected to address the issues in an effective and respectful manner. Issues, not individuals, need to be discussed and dissected. Furthermore, employees are encouraged to provide their point of view and openly discuss difficult matters.

Phase 2: Collaboration and Decision Making

The group or the team is expected to make a recommendation on the decision based on the facts they obtained during the previous phase:

- What decision needs to be made, and why
- When the decision should be made
- Who should make the decision and who is responsible for the final outcome of the decision
- What groups or individuals have to be consulted before the decision is finalized
- Who ultimately will have to ratify the final decision
- Who will have the power to veto the decision
- Who must be informed when the decision is finally ratified and accepted by the ratifier and the stakeholders

Phase 3: Commitment and Support

All participants are expected to provide their full support and execute a decision that the group or team made. It must be noted that most employers understand and anticipate that not everyone will fully agree to the final decision or solution. Nevertheless, the expectation is that everyone commits to it and executes the results even if they disagree with the final outcome. Most employers offer their employees the opportunity to voice their disagreement and clarify the nature of it for the record. Employers then expect that everyone will commit to the final decision.

Phase 4: Execution and Course Correction

This phase provides an avenue for the decision makers to assess and evaluate the decision that was made in the light of new data or information. Most employers point out that the intent of this phase is not to reopen old wounds, rehash old data, or analyze data and information to a point where the team or group is paralyzed. Rather, the objective is to enable the decision makers to revisit a subject in case something of significance was missed.

UNSPOKEN OR SILENT MICROMESSAGES

A number of silent or unspoken pitfalls associated with effective collaboration and decision making were identified as common to most companies. These silent or unspoken micromessages were symptoms of a much bigger problem. That is, most corporate cultures and environments prevent collaboration, decision making, and problem solving from being done with the right spirit and a pure intention. Most environments lack a true spirit of unity, cooperation, and fellowship and prohibit or limit any earnest endeavors to seek out the truth. These silent and chronic issues nurture an environment where people stop presenting ideas or do not wholeheartedly commit to a decision. The net effect is missed opportunities and loss of group intelligence. The examples, micromessages, and scenarios that I describe next are applicable to all corporations and any industry.

Impact of Personal Preferences Versus Individual Ideas

When making decisions, people often do not differentiate between presenting a good idea as opposed to voicing a personal preference. As it turns out, there is a major difference between the two, and this difference has been at the root of many decision-making problems. An idea is just that: a concept or a formulated thought that can add value (or not) to the existing pool of ideas. A personal preference, especially when it resides with an individual in a position of power, can, and often does, completely derail the process and shut down people. The net effect of this simple, silent, but important difference is a loss of one or more good ideas and the loss of group intelligence.

Impact of Emotional Attachment to One's Own Ideas

As a culture, people in the United States are taught to be aggressive and forceful, express their opinions, and attack problems in an open and direct way. Although all of these ideas sound good on the surface, people often run into the problem of not separating themselves from the ideas they present, become emotionally attached to their own ideas, and become close-minded to others' good ideas. Thus, any kind of attack on their ideas is interpreted as a direct assault on their character. In fact, when used in the context of decision making, words such as *confront* or *attack* convey the wrong message. One may argue that people should be passionate about their work and believe in what they say. Nevertheless, the real intent behind using these words is to find an effective way to "clash" the diverse ideas instead of "attacking" the ideas. One way to do this would be to look at the merit of each idea or opinion being presented relative to all the other ideas or opinions. This nonbiased evaluation must be independent of the person who presented the idea—the concept of detachment. Unfortunately, because of people's attachment to their ideas, they presume that others are attacking personally.

Impact of Risk Aversion and the Loss of Ideas

The intent of the brainstorming or free discussion phase of decision making is to have open, nonevaluative, and nonhierarchical discussions. In essence, the real objective of this phase of decision making is to unveil the facts, identify the root cause (or causes) of a problem, and enable a decision maker to leverage group intelligence to make a sound decision. But the fact of the matter is that an employee may become overly concerned about taking any risks and pressing on and as a consequence may stop presenting ideas altogether. Unfortunately, the likelihood that this will happen is very high, especially if the employee has had a bad prior experience or senses the slightest trace of position power, intimidation, or even peer pressure. For example, an employee may hesitate to correct a superior if she believes she will be labeled a troublemaker or will be reprimanded at the time of the focal review. Thus, in this case, the espoused value of risk taking and the actual value being experienced by the employee are not aligned. As a result, the impact of this issue could be the loss of a good idea that could have saved the company millions or prevented great future pain.

Impact of Premature and Silent Messages

The reasoning behind terms such as *constructive confrontation* is a well-recognized and well-intended process by which employees can address problems in an open, honest, and direct way. However, what can easily be observed and what often ends up happening in many cases is that an individual in a position of power can and often does send unspoken signals to stop pressing, such as, "This is not a priority," "I don't have time to listen to this anymore," "I'm tired," "I don't want to hear it again," and "I'm going to do what I want anyway." These silent or unspoken messages nurture an environment that prevent an employee from taking risks, pressing on, and presenting ideas. Thus, a good idea may never get presented and considered by the team, and group intelligence will be undermined.

Impact of Superficial and Halfhearted Commitment to a Decision

The term *disagree and commit* is another well-intended concept that is at times wishful thinking at best. In many situations, people often disagree on something because they believe they do not have any other choice, do not want to take any risks, will be embarrassed, do not feel responsible or feel ownership, or think someone else will ultimately make the decision. In some cases, the employee may simply give up or disengage altogether because he or she was not heard: his or her ideas were not considered and interests were not effectively weighed and prioritized against other ideas and interests. Thus, on the surface, the person will pretend to disagree and commit, while deep down inside may be thinking, "Why should I commit and make others look good?" Even if he or she does commit, it is quite superficial, artificial, or forced on the individual (not done very wholeheartedly). As a consequence, this cavalier attitude will prevent employees from wholeheartedly standing behind a decision or spending any discretionary effort to make the decision successful as if it were their own decision (as a champion of change). This stance often shuts down effective decision making and torpedoes any chance of making good decisions in the future.

Potential Misuse of a Well-Intended Tool as a Weapon of Power and Control

As with any other corporate principle, process, or management tool, a well-intended tool that is misused or placed in the hands of an inexperienced, immature, or unethical individual can be quickly turned into a silent but effective weapon of control and power, which results in a bad decision. For example, a good decision-making principle, management feedback system, or even a watertight 360-degree feedback process can turn into a silent and powerful weapon of control and power by becoming the cause of risk aversion and indecision, resulting in a bad or ineffective decision. Keep in mind that the potential for misuse can be equally from the management side or the employee side and that the abuse of power may occur without any malicious intent or individual awareness. Nonetheless, a well-intended tool or process may serve as a weapon of control and power on both sides and it often does.

Who Is Really Making the Decisions Around Here Anyway?

When people limit and expect the final decision to be made by one individual, then the decision-making group may not be making any type of decision. In reality, the way the process works is that one or more individuals come together to analyze, investigate, and make a solid recommendation. However, the final decision is left to the sole discretion of one individual and not placed in the hands of the team that was assembled to make the decision. Thus, the individuals and team that are directly engaged in the decision-making process should be referred to as the analysis team, not the decision-making team. This distinction should be made at the beginning of the project to prevent frustration later. Furthermore, people often end up informing the affected parties and not really including them or engaging them in the decision-making process. Thus, people may totally bypass one or more good ideas or solutions that could have presented itself.

Nagging Issues Associated with the Roles and Responsibilities of the Decision Maker

Many current decision-making processes have differentiated the roles of stakeholder, decision ratifier, consultants or content experts, analysis team, and final decision maker who is accountable for the outcome. Although this role clarification is good and absolutely necessary, the reality of the matter is that a good part of the workforce may not have fully bought into this division of roles and responsibilities (good or bad). Yes, they may disagree and commit. However, they retain a nagging silent or unspoken resistance to this separation of roles and responsibilities. For example, in this scenario, the decision-making team is not really making a decision since the final decision is often deferred to one decision maker or can be easily vetoed or overturned by either the major stakeholder or the ratifier. Unfortunately, in the midst of this role confusion or conflict, the right or best decision may be lost or never present itself.

Impact of a Competitive Environment and the Erosion of Confidence and Trust

Participants provide ideas and feedback, but the actual power of decision making is placed in the hands of one individual. Thus, an environment is nurtured in which people may say, "Why should I present a good idea and have it be rejected or turned down by the final decision maker?" "Why should I present any ideas if I'm not listened to at the end?" "Why should I give my best ideas if the decision maker will be taking the credit for the final decision?" or "Why should I share any good ideas with the same people I'm competing with during the focal process?" Thus, in many circumstances, diverse points of view and different aspects of a subject may not be debated because of environmental factors such as risk taking, power, politics, loss of trust, perceived inequity or injustice in the overall system, and lack of a good process to get the ideas out and consolidate the results. One of the reasons that this happens is that good and trustworthy work relationships are not built. A second reason this phenomenon occurs is that an environment has been nurtured where competition is the game. As a result, these silent or unspoken perceptions may result in the loss of one or more good ideas that were intentionally or unintentionally left out and could have benefited the company immeasurably.

The Culture of Results Orientation and Its Impact on Shortsighted Decisions

The culture of results orientation, the expectation set to make decisions very rapidly, and the need to demonstrate short-term gains, return on investment, and tangible benefits have collectively contributed to ineffective decision making. Simply recount the number of times you were rushed into making a decision and were never given the chance to consult on the merits of an idea and develop even a spark of consensus. Thus, the drive to come up with a quick answer or the expectation of making a quick decision sometimes pushes the team into the space of making a bad decision, which it ends up paying for later.

The Impact of Not Representing and Aligning Key Stakeholder Interest

In many situations, decisions are made without effectively identifying and aligning the interests of dependent or linked stakeholders. Many of the problems associated with reopening or rehashing a given solution or the problems with addressing latecomers are symptoms of this issue. This does not mean people need to have all those who will be affected present at the decision-making session. However, members of the decision-making group often do not effectively represent the interests (and good ideas) of those who will be affected by the decision and so lose their support in implementing the decision. (The underlying issues and solutions associated with this problem are not within the scope of this chapter.)

The Frequency of Overturned Decisions and the Impact on Low Morale

Having the power to disapprove or veto a team decision can sometimes undermine the concept of effective decision making and empowering individuals to make decisions. The reasoning here is that the employee will argue, "Why should I give it my all, take a risk, look bad or stupid, and at the end have someone overturn a decision or take credit for the ideas I present?" The central concept of this chapter is that the group intelligence can be attained only through the spirit of consultation and not by the final preference or opinion of one individual. Once again, the impact of this unspoken action is loss of group intelligence and missed opportunity.

Potential Problems Associated with the Dilution of the Solution or Decision

Sometimes a decision or a solution has to be reopened or revisited because of unforeseen circumstances, environmental changes, or significant new information. However, aside from a few exceptional circumstances, one needs to still question the underlying reasons that there is a tendency to miss information or a failure to achieve enough unity to stand firm behind a decision and make it work (even if it is not the best decision). People have to ask themselves why they were unable to gather the right information to make a good decision in the first place. Was it because they did not have the right decision makers? Did they not effectively solicit and consider all the ideas? Was it a timing issue?

Two points are being raised here. First, people often end up diluting the final decision if they open it up for discussion after consensus has been reached. Second, if the decision was made with the right spirit, even a bad or wrong decision could have been worked out by the group. Granted, a course correction may have to be made somewhere down the road. However, if the group is fully united through consensus and individuals are wholeheartedly behind the decision, any further discussion can dilute the solution.

The Impact of Lies, Deception, Jealousy, and Other Inappropriate Behavior

At the outset, it is imperative that the collaboration team discuss and set expectations to address the most serious category of silent or unspoken messages that deals with inappropriate, immoral, or malicious intentions. The issues being highlighted deal with such things as ego, lies, deception, jealousy, and the desire for power, position, and leadership. These inappropriate individual behaviors can, and often do, seriously undermine effective collaboration and decision making. Each of these behaviors creates an environment of distrust and disunity. In essence, these unspoken issues can, and often do, hide the underlying truth of a situation and seriously jeopardize effective collaboration and decision making. Currently, most decision-making processes are ill equipped to handle such situations. Nevertheless, these types of problems are very real and need to be quickly identified and addressed before the group begins to collaborate.

LEVERAGING COLLECTIVE INTELLIGENCE THROUGH EFFECTIVE COLLABORATION

Many existing decision-making processes nurture an environment that prevents people from approaching decision making with the right spirit, intention, and motive. The chapter so far has reviewed a set of silent, unspoken, and often ignored deterrents that inhibit people from developing true understanding, transform conjecture into certainty, and prevent people from making the best possible decision. To alleviate these problems, corporations are asked to take a number of actions and seek the full support of their leadership to accomplish the following tasks:

- Provide a decision-making model and process that helps to develop an environment conducive to good teamwork, collaboration, and consultation.

- Provide a clear and consistent set of behavioral expectations that can be used as prerequisites for effective decision making.

- Adopt consultation and the consultative decision-making process as a new corporate value to incorporate into the corporate culture (Mourkogiannis, 2006):
  - Develop and deliver a comprehensive training and communication program that incorporates the new changes.
  - Revamp corporate management and leadership programs to reflect the changes in effective decision making and problem solving.
  - Modify employee assessment processes to expect employees to role-model good decision making. For best results, directly link career advancement opportunities to how well an employee is able to make good decisions or address complex problems.
  - Modify the corporate reward and recognition programs in a way to place the greatest emphasis on teamwork, collaboration, and the consultative decision making (as opposed to the focus on individual results).

NEW PRINCIPLES FOR VIRTUAL COLLABORATION AND EFFECTIVE DECISION MAKING

Virtual collaboration and effective decision making require the use of a number of prime requisites, core decision-making principles, and a set of behavioral expectations that clarify the roles and responsibilities of each participant during the collaboration process. Individual roles and responsibilities are also referred to here as the rules of engagement and procedure. Collectively, these three different but necessary collaboration tools (prime requisites, core decision-making principles, and behavioral expectations) develop an atmosphere of unity of thought and action that is so essential for effective collaboration and decision making.

They will also serve as a guidepost or internal compass to support and develop good behavior, enable individuals to approach collaboration with the right attitude, and nurture an environment of mutual trust and respect, which are the foundation of virtual collaboration and effective decision making (Universal House of Justice, 1980). In essence, effective collaboration requires more than just the mere voicing of personal views and opinions. It demands a foundation of mutual trust and respect and united effort that can only be developed in an atmosphere of a "spiritual conference." These essential attributes combat egotism, biases, and prejudices that can often result from lack of true understanding and appreciation of different cultural, racial, and religious ideologies.

The principles selected and being recommended here help close the chronic problems identified in organizations by nurturing an environment of mutual trust and respect and a spirit of fellowship and unity. Table 18.3 provides a list of these principles. Table 18.4 translates these principles into individual actions, behaviors, and new attitudes toward virtual collaboration. These actions are

---

Table 18.3
Virtual Collaboration and Decision-Making Principles

Wholeheartedly acquiescence to the prime requisites of decision making (Table 18.5).

Wholeheartedly acquiescence to the rules of procedure and engagement (Table 18.4).

Wholeheartedly own, drive, and champion the final decision, solution, or conclusion.

The final decision or solution is owned and is made by the decision-making group.

The decision-making group must take counsel together and consult in all matters.

As the primary goal, the group is obligated to investigate the truth of the matter.

Be united in your thoughts and actions (common purpose, vision, and direction).

Bend every nerve to achieve consensus but accept a majority decision.

Seek a solution that will benefit and serve the collective.

Once the conclusion is reached it belongs to the whole group.

All must obey and submit to the majority decision, conclusion, or solution.

Avoid confrontation and feelings of coolness, alienation, and estrangement.

Actively listen to each other (enter imaginatively into the others' situation).

Enthusiastically take part in the process and the final solutions or decision.

Do not imagine yourself to be right and others wrong (all contribute to consensus).

Avoid stubbornness, persistence of your views, and criticism of the final decision.

Endeavor to fulfill these principles with a spirit of love, fellowship, and respect.

Table 18.4
Rules of Engagement and Procedure: Individual Roles, Responsibilities, and Mutual Expectations

Roles and Responsibilities	Chair Person	Individual or Member	Group or Team
Be open-minded.	X	X	X
Search for the truth.	X	X	X
Listen with patience and restraint.	X	X	X
Make all good ideas and opinions your own.	X	X	
Understand the merits of each idea and opinion.	X	X	X
Strive to improve each idea regardless of its origin.	X	X	
Avoid mentioning your personal preferences.	X	X	
Do not insist on your own views, ideas, and opinions.	X	X	
Separate yourself from your ideas and opinions.	X	X	X
Carefully consider others' views before speaking.	X	X	X
Cultivate frankness, openness, and freedom of thought.	X	X	X
Express thoughts with absolute freedom.	X	X	
Express thoughts as a contribution to consensus, not truth.	X	X	
Express yourself calmly, without passion and rancor.	X	X	
Express your views and feelings with devotion.	X	X	
Express your views and feelings with courtesy.	X	X	

Express your views and feelings with dignity.	X	X	
Express your views and feelings with care.	X	X	
Express your views and feelings with moderation.	X	X	
Consult in a way that prevents discord or ill feeling.	X	X	X
Avoid belittling another person's thoughts.	X	X	
Avoid feeling hurt if others disagree with you.	X	X	
Accept and execute the final decision wholeheartedly.	X	X	X
Do not criticize and object to the final decision, solution, or conclusion.	X	X	
Avoid fruitless and hair-splitting discussions.	X	X	X

individual roles and responsibilities, as well as the specific expectations that should be set by management (rules of engagement and procedure). Table 18.5 provides a list of prime requisites that each individual needs to willingly accept in order to meet the conditions necessary for virtual collaboration and effective decision making. Combined, these prime requisites and core principles, along with a clear set of individual roles, responsibilities, and cultural expectations, help to develop a meaningful process by which individuals can effectively collaborate, make decisions, and address complex problems.

EFFECTIVE COLLABORATION USING THE CONSULTATIVE DECISION-MAKING PROCESS

The previous sections provided a list of core principles and prime requisites for virtual collaboration, effective decision making, and problem solving (Table 18.3 and Table 18.5). It also pointed out how those prime requisites and principles need to be translated into individual actions and clear roles, responsibilities, and

Table 18.5
Essential Prime Requisites for Effective Consultation

Purity of motives	Have genuine and good intentions.
	Set aside all ulterior motives.
	Set aside any personal agendas.
	Be truthful to yourself and others.
	Give up your notions, prejudices, and biases.
Active engagement	Be optimistic, enthusiastic, and fully engaged.
	Show genuine interest in resolving the problem.
	Show genuine concern about the welfare of others.
	Strive to establish new bases for well-being/happiness.
Objectivity and detachment	Strive to be impartial, objective, and nonbiased.
	Do not become emotionally involved with your own opinion. Set aside personal preferences, and be objective.
	Think in terms of consensus and collective good.
Doing the right thing	Be sensitive to the ideas and opinion of others.
	Give your wholehearted support and engagement.
	Strive to address the underlying causal issue.
	Strive to do the right thing regardless of consequences.
Valuing each idea equally and making each voice count	Free yourself from estrangement and separation.
	Do not pull rank and exercise unwarranted power.
	Do not be proud and boastful about your position.
	Show humility and demonstrate equality of opinion.
	Be sincere and genuinely seek help from the group.
Exercising patience	Exercise perseverance, and self-control.
	Be calm, graceful, and patient under stress.
	Be responsible to all, and stop complaining.
Focusing on service and collective good	Work toward a decision that will benefit the collective.
	Strive to provide service and benefits to all.
	Suppress greed, egotism, and selfishness.

behavioral expectations (Table 18.4). This section completes the entire process by leveraging those principles and individual actions to develop a decision-making process that will lend itself to virtual collaboration. This process has been summarized using Figure 18.1 and these process steps:

1. Identify the affected groups and key stakeholders, and ensure each group and their content experts are properly represented.

2. Review, discuss, and obtain buy-in of the prime requisites, core decision-making principles, and the essential behavioral expectations necessary for effective decision making and collaboration.

3. Nurture an environment where people are willing to present their ideas and feedback:

   - Cultivate an open and frank environment so everyone can express their opinions.
   - Support freedom of thought and unfettered individual opinions and ideas (Universal House of Justice, 1980).
   - Make all good ideas and opinions your own. This is a key point.
   - Exercise patience, courtesy, respect, and moderation in all things.
   - Be guarded in your speech. Think about what to say to whom, how, when, and where.
   - Work toward consensus, but accept and support a majority decision.
   - Set aside personal differences, and do not insist on your own opinion.
   - Do not belittle or criticize others or their opinion, and do not censure information.
   - Subjugate all egotism and self-centered passions for the service and good of the team.

4. Identify the current state or situation by seeking to understand the underlying problems, concerns, and the unspoken or silent motives behind the problem (seek out the truth). In this way, you build mutual trust and respect.

   - Get all the details, facts, and assumptions.
   - Discuss the problem background and history.
   - Reflect on the details of the problem.

Figure 18.1
Proposed Decision-Making Model

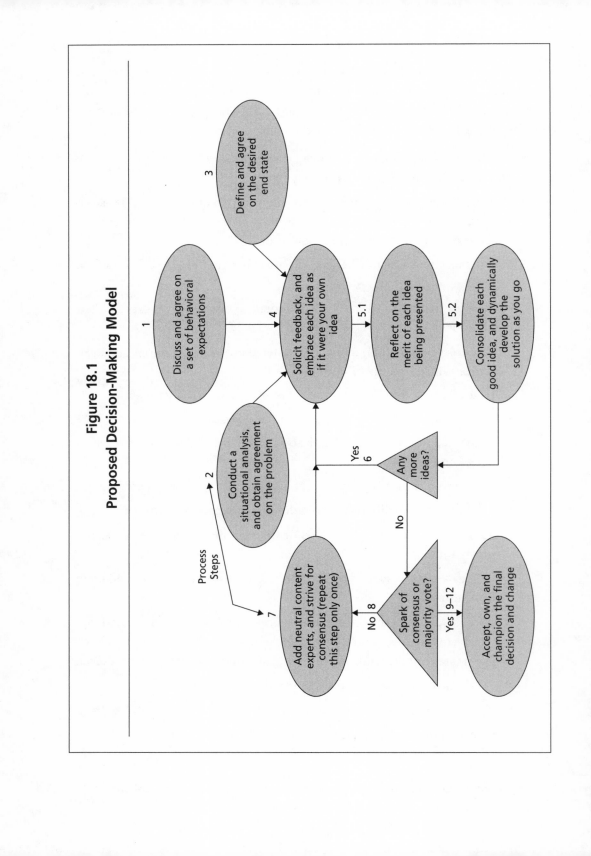

- Look at different perspectives or views.
- Synthesize the information gathered.
- Document the underlying problem.

5. Visualize, define, and document a desired future state that individuals can relate to and agree on (typically this is applicable to more complex problems and situations):
- Ideal end state desired
- Goal or target to achieve
- Best-case situation or scenario
- Practical and measurable solution

6. Solicit feedback to address the issue, close the gap agreed to by all, and embrace each idea as if it were your own:
- Provide your ideas and opinions in an unfettered way. This is a key point.
- Separate yourself from your own ideas or opinions, and do not insist on them. This is a key point.
- Accept all good ideas or opinions as if they were your own ideas. This is a key point.

7. Reflect on and consolidate the good ideas agreed on by the group:
- Clash the diverse ideas presented without any emotions and attachment to the idea, with pure intention to find the underlying truth, and the aim to develop or grow a new idea that did not exist before.
- See whether the group is in agreement with the merits of the idea.
- Strive to consolidate and merge all the good ideas agreed on by the majority.
- Strive to develop or create a new idea from the collective good ideas. If that is not possible, then add each acceptable idea to the existing list of ideas.

8. Continue steps 3 to 6 until a spark of consensus has been reached.

9. If consensus cannot be reached, add several unbiased or neutral members, discuss the issue one more time, and try to achieve consensus.

10. If consensus still cannot be achieved, go with the majority vote.

11. Clearly document the decision, the solution, or the conclusion arrived at by the collaboration group (the underlying truth).

12. Ask how people would like to continuously improve the decision that was made today (for example, if necessary, adjust the decision in the future).

13. Stop further discussions to prevent any possible dilution of the solution.

14. Accept the final decision or result as if it were your own. This is a key point.

15. Take the initiative to execute the final decision wholeheartedly, accept and role-model any resulting changes, and communicate the decision to all affected parties. This is a key point.

FINAL THOUGHTS

Work environments have become so difficult and complex that members cannot even make a decision on how to make a good decision. Existing decision-making and problem-solving processes are simply not equipped to handle the complex, rapidly changing, and global nature of the work environment. Many unspoken factors prevent decision makers from getting to the good ideas, clashing into the ideas (not the people), leveraging the collective intelligence to develop innovative new ideas, reaching a spark of consensus, making the best possible decision, and in the end standing behind the decision as if it were their own.

A new process and model is required that lends itself to close collaboration and enables groups to tap into and leverage the power of collective intelligence and the diversity of thought, understanding, knowledge, experience, educational background, and different temperaments to address complex problems.

This chapter has focused on the impact of the transformational forces on collaboration and decision-making processes, the metamorphosis of decision making itself, and how decision-making processes need to evolve to deal with a highly diverse and complex, and rapidly changing world to make the best possible decision and have people rally around it and make it successful even if it was not the best decision.

REMINDERS

- Virtual collaboration and effective decision making and problem solving require purity of motives and underlying intentions. The prime requisites of decision making address this issue upfront.

- Self-serving tactics and political maneuvering severely limit or even prevent virtual collaboration, good decision making, and effective problem solving.

- Make the investigation of truth the primary objective of collaboration and consultation.

- Give up your trivial notions, prejudices, and biases that prevent you from seeing the truth.

- Seek a solution that will benefit the collective and not just your own needs and requirements.

- Immediately and without any reservation, accept all good ideas, opinions, and decisions as if they were your own ideas, opinions, and decisions.

- Avoid confrontation and adversarial approaches, and provide your ideas and opinion in an unfettered way.

- Nurture a spirit of fellowship and mutual respect, and separate yourself from your own ideas or opinions. Do not insist on them.

- Once a decision is made it belongs to the whole group and not just the majority. The execution of the decision, making it work, and the obedience to the will of the majority must be part of the decision-making and problem-solving processes. Collaboration is not fully consummated until the decision is wholeheartedly owned, championed, and is carried through successfully.

- Take the initiative to execute the final decision wholeheartedly, accept and role-model any resulting changes, and communicate the decision to all affected parties.

References

Bass, B. M., & Stogdill, R. M. (1990). *Handbook of leadership: Theory, research, and managerial applications.* New York: Free Press.

Bass, B. M., & Valenzi, E. R (1974). Contingent aspects of effective management styles. In J. G. Hunt & L. L. Larson (Eds.), *Contingency approaches to leadership.* Carbondale: Southern Illinois University Press.

Covey, S.M.R. (2006). *The speed of trust: The one thing that changes everything.* New York: Free Press.

Heller, F. A., & Yukl, G. (1969). Participation, managerial decision-making, and situational variables. *Organizational Behavior and Human Performance, 4,* 227–241.

Kolstoe, J. E. (1985). *Consultation: A universal lamp of guidance.* Kidlington, Oxford: George Arnold Publisher.

Kouzes, J. M., & Posner, B. Z. (2002). *The leadership challenge.* San Francisco: Jossey-Bass.

Mauzy, J., & Harriman, R. (2003). *Creativity, Inc.: Building an inventive organization.* Boston: Harvard Business School Press.

Mourkogiannis, N. (2006). *Purpose: The starting point of great companies.* New York: Palgrave Macmillan.

Neilson, G. L., & Pasternack, B. A. (2005). *Results: Keep what's good, fix what's wrong, and unlock great performance.* New York: Crown Business.

O'Toole, J., & Lawler, E. E. (2006). *The new American workforce.* New York: Palgrave Macmillan.

Tannenbaum, R., & Schmidt, W. H. (1958). How to choose a leadership pattern. *Harvard Business Review, 36*(2), 95–101.

Universal House of Justice. (1980). *Consultation: A compilation.* Wilmette, IL: Baha'i Publishing Trust.

PART SIX

Tools and Assessments for Collaboration

The chapters that present a variety of tools and assessments for the virtual team begin with a framework for launching new teams in Chapter Nineteen. Virtual teams can equal the effectiveness levels that colocated teams achieve by taking into account the social, technical, environmental, and personal factors that enable members to be fully engaged. The launch of the team needs to address the cultural differences of members that result from geographical, educational, functional, religious, and experiential differences. The best way to get the team off to a good start is a face-to-face meeting using team charters, role clarification processes, operating guidelines, and communication technology-use protocols.

Virtual teams work in multiple modes: solo, colocated subgroups, asynchronous communication, and meetings. The key decisions often emerge from meetings, and the quality of the process of the meetings determines the quality of the decision and their implementation. The authors of Chapter Twenty agree with the point in the prior chapter: the first meeting ought to be face-to-face so trust and personal connection can develop. Good meetings benefit from the chartering process, especially establishing norms around conduct during and between meetings. However, expertise with meeting process takes time to develop. A high-quality process emerges much more quickly with the use of process facilitators who are independent of the issues the team is struggling with.

Since most of the team's meetings are online and a great deal of electronic communication takes place between the meetings, a code of conduct that goes beyond meeting norms can help. Netiquette has developed for nonteam virtual communications around the world, but in Chapter Twenty-One, the authors take it one step further to VEtiquette: the virtual etiquette of virtual teams. VEtiquette begins by establishing a shared understanding around expectations, goals, roles, and responsibilities. Team leaders need to develop skills in facilitation and coaching, virtual meeting, cultural sensitivity, communication, and decision making. Methods for actively engaging distant members build the quality of the process and the decisions. A variety of simple practical steps help members work together toward shared goals.

For virtual teams to achieve high-performance results, creativity is essential. But the process of creativity may be more difficult to achieve through technology-mediated communication. Chapter Twenty-Two provides readers with a variety of techniques for boosting the creativity of both individual virtual team members and the virtual team. The typical virtual team consists of professionals with expert knowledge in a variety of areas who are communicating from distant locations in varied cultures. How can such a diverse group ever come together to share knowledge and synthesize it into original solutions? Chapter Twenty-Two presents a wide array of tools specifically aimed at tapping the creative potential of the team's members, including those that tap different ways of thinking and different ways of sharing.

For years, the goal of motivated team leaders has been to predict what will lead to high performance. In a globally competitive marketplace, this ability to predict successful performance is even more urgent. Contemporary business leaders seek out efficient and reliable methods for predicting successful performance. Chapter Twenty-Three provides valuable insight into the process of identifying individual qualities necessary for virtual collaborators through traits and abilities assessment.

The success of every project, program, and initiative in an organization depends on having adequate resources, and that usually means adequate support from top management. Managers at the top are responsible for the decisions on how to best use resources to generate valued outcomes. One proven method for garnering top management support is the business case. Chapter Twenty-Four presents a step-by-step procedure for building and making the business case to company executives for virtual teams. In the simplest case, that means using people, time, money, and materials to provide service or products to customers in a way that generates a profit. More complex examples are described as well and include varied time frames, alternate methods, and intangible outcomes.

Tools for Effective Virtual Team Start-Ups

Kimball Fisher

There is little disagreement about whether virtual teams are more difficult to manage than colocated ones. Sharing all of the challenges of teams that see each other regularly, virtual teams share few of the advantages. It is not unusual, for example, for members of a virtual team to go long periods without the powerful informal networking that normally occurs when people casually run into each other in the shared hallways and lunchrooms of a brick-and-mortar workplace (Fisher & Fisher, 1998). Without as many opportunities to pass along the tacit knowledge that often differentiates more effective teams from less effective ones, virtual teams must work harder to achieve their success (Fisher & Fisher, 2001). Furthermore, these teams often lack critical cultural elements that can lead to higher performance, including a feeling of trust, identification with, and commitment to the team that can be created by regular face-to-face team-building interactions (Dyer, 1987).

These challenges clearly extend to a number of teams that managers may not consider virtual, including ones where team members might be colocated but still interact only infrequently with each other; examples are temporary project or cross-functional teams, teams with part-time or temporary membership, teams with members who are seldom onsite, and teams that cover multiple shifts. For purposes of this chapter, virtual teams are defined as any team whose participants are normally separated by space, time, or culture (Fisher & Fisher, 2001).

This chapter proposes perspectives and tools that can be useful in considering how to start up or repurpose these virtual teams. I suggest a conceptual framework for designing effective virtual teams and offer practical tools for purposing the team and establishing a culture of effective self-governance, including processes for chartering, developing operating guidelines, and creating and implementing what I call communication technology-use protocols (Fisher & Fisher, 2001).

DESIGNING NEW VIRTUAL TEAMS

Many people consider Eric Trist, Fred Emery, and their colleagues at the Tavistock Institute in the post–World War II United Kingdom as the fathers of the modern team concept. Among their many contributions to the field, Trist and Emery suggested that the design of teams should consider both the social and the technical aspects of work. Justifiably criticizing several early organization design efforts as emphasizing either the social system ("We'll pipe nice music into the factory, and people will be more productive even if we don't have good tools for them to use") or the technical system ("As long as we have the most modern equipment, we'll be more competitive, even if we don't go to the time and expense of training people how to use it"), they posited that both the people structures and processes (social system) and the tools and business systems operated by them (technical system) needed to be "jointly optimized" (Emery & Trist, 1960). They thereby created the sociotechnical systems (STS) perspective that still influences much of the current paradigm of team design and is represented by the Venn diagram shown in Figure 19.1.

Subsequent action research convinced STS practitioners that an essential part of the design equation was the business environment surrounding the team. Thus, the design process evolved to include what Emery and Trist called the environmental scan, which was an essential way to incorporate the customer voice and competitive realities of the external marketplace place into team design (Trist, 1981). Now teams were designed to jointly optimize the social and technical

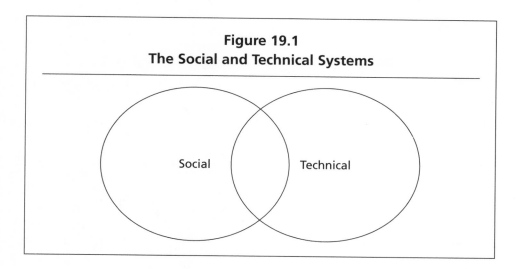

Figure 19.1
The Social and Technical Systems

Social

Technical

systems in a way that responded to real business pressures and often resulted in real business gains (Appelbaum, Bailey, Berg, & Kalleberg, 2000; Fisher, 2006; and Huselid, 1995). This is represented by Figure 19.2.

With the rapid growth of virtual teams, however, the design process needs to incorporate one additional system: the personal system. Although past design processes have often acknowledged that work design affects home life, virtual team design makes the boundary between work and personal life more permeable. Virtual team members often work at least part of their time from home. Furthermore, members of virtual global teams are frequently required to participate in team teleconferences or Web conferences from home because they are conducted outside normal working hours to accommodate team members who live in different time zones. Perhaps most important, we live in a time blessed and cursed by new communication technologies: blessed because the work of virtual teams would be almost impossible without these new technologies, but cursed because virtual team members are forever tethered to work regardless of time or space. For many team members, a certain amount of work, such as checking e-mail or voice mail, is normally done at home. Gone, for virtual team members, is the day when coming home meant a healthy separation from the workplace.

The Technology Tether

When your workplace is cyberspace, it follows you wherever you go. "Modern technologies allow us to work around the clock, and we do" (Stahl, 2006). When

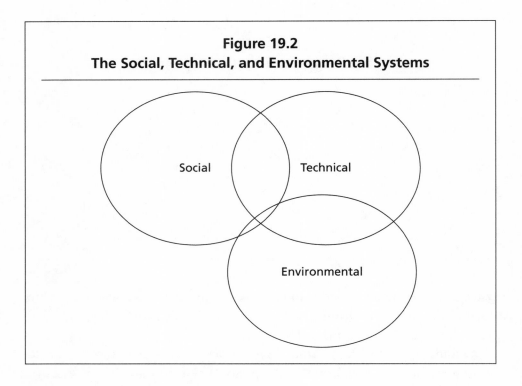

Figure 19.2
The Social, Technical, and Environmental Systems

Social

Technical

Environmental

recently asked what his primary concern was for members of the virtual teams in his organization, the president of Cummins Power Generation declared, "Home and work life balance!" instead of the plethora of motivation and coordination concerns often associated with the senior executives of these organizations. There are good reasons for this. Many people average three hours of e-mail a day, much of it read at home to allow office time to be maximized (Stahl, 2006). An even more startling statistic was found in another study in which members of a virtual sales team spent an average of six hours a day doing e-mail—most of it from home to allow as much face-to-face time with customers as possible.

The Personal System

Organizational designers have been understandably reluctant to intrude into the previously off-limits territory of team members' personal lives when engaging in redesign or start-up activities. This justifiable concern acknowledges the importance of people's ability to maintain private lives and to ensure the protection of their personal rights and security. Ironically, the lack of these discussions in new virtual

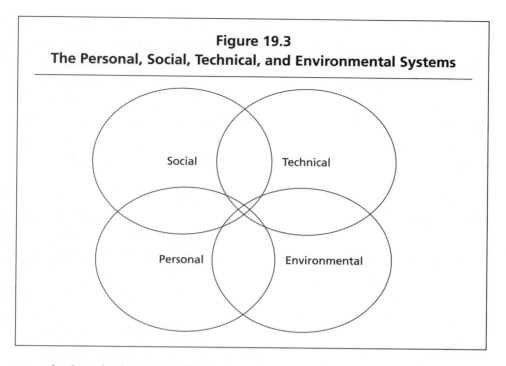

Figure 19.3
The Personal, Social, Technical, and Environmental Systems

Social

Technical

Personal

Environmental

teams leads to further encroachment into the personal space by unrestrained work demands. The use of some of the tools mentioned later in the chapter allows people to reestablish the appropriate boundaries between work and personal life that have been eroded by pervasive technologies. When this is done effectively, many clients report that this improves organizational productivity while reducing personal stress and health problems. By jointly optimizing all four systems (see Figure 19.3 for a representation of the personal, social, technical, and environmental systems), we can now design for the whole human organizational system, a goal referenced by, but unachievable to, many of the organization systems design methodologies of the past (Galbraith, 2000; Hanna, 1988; and Mohrman, Cohen, & Mohrman, 1995).

FOCUSING NEW VIRTUAL TEAMS

Like colocated team members, virtual team members need to understand their goals, roles, and assignments to be effective. Furthermore, creating a team culture that is supportive and productive is especially helpful in teams with only minimal face contact (Fisher & Fisher, 2001). Virtual teams often report that their members suffer from a series of challenges, including the effective use of collaboration technologies, overcoming feelings of isolation, and misalignment around tasks, purpose, and operating procedures. In order to overcome these challenges as efficiently and effectively as possible, most virtual teams find that some sort of face-to-face start-up activity that includes purposing and culture development is essential. At a minimum, this addresses four related but separate tasks: chartering, clarifying roles, establishing productive team norms, and agreeing to technology-use protocols that affect not only the social, technical, and environmental systems but the personal one as well.

Unique Challenges for Virtual Team Start-Ups

Start-up activities are especially difficult for virtual teams for a number of reasons, not the least of which is the time and travel expense of getting people together who may live all over the world. But there are more subtle issues too. The start-up conversations that are relatively straightforward in a synchronous environment, for example, can become a nightmare in an asynchronous one. Some teams have been known to erupt into near-violent disagreement over something as mundane as the timing of meetings. In operations with membership that spans multiple time zones, for example, team members want to know who has to get up in the middle of the night or lose precious weekend time for an international teleconference. "Must the Europeans [or Australians, or Asians, or Africans, or any other group] always be the ones to accommodate their American partners?" they might complain.

To make matters worse, different geographical locations are not the only cause of distance between people on virtual teams. Issues associated with differing cultures may be even more difficult. If we adapt a definition of culture from Schein (1997), anything that falls into the category of a "learned behavior about how to work together" is culture. This covers a broad spectrum ranging from organizational to language and ethnic norms. Gaps in these areas can make it difficult even to understand the potential problems that need to be addressed in the start-up or refocusing activity. Resolving these issues is even more challenging.

Bridging Cultural Distances

Teams that cross countries often find important communication challenges caused by very distinct geographical cultures. At the risk of perpetuating stereotypes, consider what some people have reported about working on global teams. South Americans on the team may see timelines as approximate, while Germans may view them as precise, even though both sit through the same discussion in the same language at the same time. Asians may smile and nod their heads when asked if they agree to something that they know they cannot later support because the rudeness of public disagreement is culturally intolerable for them. North Americans may run roughshod over respected but, in their view, time-consuming practices of other cultures. This short-term efficiency focus may backfire in the long term, as it erodes trust and employee commitment.

Moreover the people on these teams may display differing cultural perspectives that are every bit as distinct as geographical cultures but completely unrelated to their countries of residence or upbringing. If we use Schein's definition (1997), we can see cultural differences that arise from educational, lifestyle, religious, or even functional experience. For example, when I worked at Procter & Gamble, the marketing part of the company had a very different type of culture than the manufacturing part of the company did. Inside the manufacturing part of the company were subcultures. Organized operations were different than in nonunion plants. Maintenance organizations within a plant were distinct from operations. Night-shift culture was different from day-shift culture. Office workers were different from people on the floor. In each of these cases, the cultures had different languages and priorities, as well as distinctive and sometimes contradictory norms when compared to the others.

Creating a Team Charter

How then do individuals overcome the challenges caused by different types of distance and create an effective virtual team? A good place to start is with a chartering activity. A team charter is a statement of joint purpose created by and agreed to by all team members. The charter discussion allows each team member to express his or her views on what the team's core purpose and objectives are, thus clarifying early on where time and energy will be focused and where the key disagreements are.

Team members often have their own ideas of what the team is supposed to do, and those ideas are often not aligned because team members do not have much opportunity to rub shoulders with one another in a series of work activities that may create a common focus. One virtual product development team struggled because many of the engineers had different ideas about the team's purpose. Some people thought their purpose was to produce leading-edge products, others thought they needed to meet customer expectations even if it did not require leading-edge technologies, and still other team members felt that the purpose of the team was to create products that could be easily manufactured. Such differences of opinion caused confusion and inefficiencies until they were resolved several months later. If team purpose, roles, culture, and technology-use protocols are not clarified at the onset, team performance will be suboptimal. Here are two examples of team charters for virtual teams:

Product Development Team Charter

The Autocom Design Team provides state-of-the-art, standardized electronic radio components for automobiles that meet the standards of the countries in which the components will be manufactured and sold (Sweden, France, China, Japan, United States).

Our primary customers are the automobile companies that install the components in their cars and will serve as our development partners.

Our top priority is to meet or exceed the expectations of those customers for reliability (no more than 1 percent D. O. A.'s), ease of implementation, and on-time delivery.

Our first beta test is scheduled for November 22 at the Volvo Truck plant in Sweden, and our release date is April 30.

Accounting Software Implementation Team Charter

Team Purpose: The purpose of the Accounting Software Implementation Team is to plan and oversee the implementation of the new Enterprise Resource Planning software at company headquarters (Detroit) and each of the company's ten locations (Amsterdam, London, Guadalajara, Sacramento, Omaha, Albany, Houston, Redmond, Tokyo, Hong Kong).

Key Customers: Our primary customers are the company accountants at each site and outside customers and vendors whose money will be processed using the new software.

Key Results: The key results expected from the Accounting Software Implementation Team are:

1. Have the program installed and fully operational at all locations by June 30 of next year.

2. Keep all payable and receivable personnel fully informed and up to date on the software implementation.

3. Ensure all government regulations are met at each site.

4. Submit a complete project proposal and timeline within four months.

The written team charter document is less important than the discussion it represents, and what may seem simplistic or trivial to an outsider may reflect a significant insight or carefully worded resolution of conflicting views to people who participated in the process. It is useful to develop a format for these charters that represents the unique requirements of a particular team, but it is not unusual to include something like an overall purpose statement, clarification of customer requirements, and an inclusion of key deliverables.

The charter need not be long. A more common mistake than too much brevity is a document that is too long to be remembered by its creators. If people cannot remember it, they probably will not use it. Much can be learned from the value proposition literature about the most effective way to construct and use these statements of purpose (Anderson & Narus, 1998; Lanning, 1998). The best statements, for example, clearly describe the desired customer experience and therefore keep the team focused on adding value from the perspective of the person who pays for the product or service the team members provide.

PRACTICAL TIPS FOR CHARTERING

Virtual teams provide these tips for chartering:

• *Make sure you involve the key people outside the team as you develop the charter.* These people might include customers, managers, or staff and technical support people. In many cases, some of these people will need to provide approval. It is a good idea to involve them early in the process. Project teams, for example, need clarity from the beginning regarding their assignment and the outcomes their leadership expects. A common problem many virtual team members face is "multiplexing" (Fisher & Fisher, 1998). Multiplexing is the pervasive practice of having multiple concurrent assignments. Because they often serve on several different teams simultaneously, it is difficult for virtual team members to plan their time appropriately unless they know the relative priorities of the projects competing for their attention. This issue can be addressed in chartering if the right people are present.

• *Agree on a tight timeline for completing the chartering process.* This is especially important if you cannot meet face-to-face and are creating the charter from a distance using technology. Establishing clear timelines for when team members need to respond to each step of the process is critical. If creating the charter face-to-face, do not let the process drag on. Getting bogged down here can drain energy and result in discouragement. Get the charter to a point that everyone can live with it and then revise it later if necessary.

• *Strive for practicality, not perfection.* No charter is perfect. Do not expect it to describe everything about your team perfectly. Work to make a practical statement that guides the team and provides clarity about what is expected of it. Keep in mind that the charter can always be revised if necessary.

• *Live by your charter.* Creating a charter needs to be more than just an exercise. The result should be a useful tool for keeping the team focused and on track. For this reason, it is often a good idea to ask each team member to state his or her commitment to following it. Absent a face-to-face venue, a teleconference where each person vocally affirms the charter can suffice.

Role Clarification

The second activity recommended for the virtual team start-up is the use of a role clarification tool. Because much has been written about these kinds of tools, this chapter will not elaborate other than to say that it is important for virtual team members to have a visual indicator that helps them understand the distinct assignments and responsibilities of each member of the team (Liff & Posey, 2004). Already handicapped by their lack of easy access to their peers, virtual team members are less likely to collaborate with people with whom they have unclear responsibilities than with those with whom they have clear, shared responsibilities. Many teams we have worked with use something like the RACI diagram

(Responsible, Accountable, Consulted, or Informed) or CAIRO diagram (same as RACI with the O for Omitted) and post it on their team Web site. These types of common project management tools list each person on the team with corresponding information about his or her role on particular project parameters. The team's Web site is also a good place to post a shared calendar that has key project mileposts and the charter, operating guidelines, and technology protocols discussed in this chapter.

Operating Guidelines

The third start-up tool is operating guidelines: agreements for group interaction that are created and supported by all team members. They identify acceptable and unacceptable behavior for that particular team. For virtual teams, these become a statement of the shared culture that supersedes the differing functional, geographical, or other subcultures that may be divisive to the team.

If a team does not deliberately set operating guidelines, then existing norms or habits become the guidelines by default (Fisher, 2000). Virtual teams may therefore suboptimize their team by incorporating as cultural norms unstated but predictable behavior such as, "We'll have the conference calls when they are best for the team members in the main office locations even if they are not convenient for those in the remote locations," or "Preferential treatment will be given to those who have the best English-speaking skills," or "It's okay to display rude behavior online," or "Team members who live closest to the manager will get the best assignments." Most virtual team members would be horrified to see norms like this written down, but they can become common team behavior if they are not challenged and corrected.

One company discovered a strong statistical correlation between performance review results and distance from management, with the virtual team members getting the lowest scores in most virtual teams being those who lived farthest from the location of the manager. Apparently management trusted those they saw most regularly and tended to reward them with the most important elements of the projects, which then resulted in higher performance rankings for nearby employees. It was not until the trend was identified and discussed that it could be replaced with more appropriate operating guidelines. The problem might have been avoided if a start-up discussion about operating guidelines had allowed employee concerns about the proper functioning of the virtual teams to be addressed.

Ideally, operating guidelines are established while the team is still forming and then continually revised and updated as the team progresses. But it is never too late to create them. A virtual team can be improved by using any of the tools mentioned in this chapter even if the ideal time to use the tool has passed.

Operating guidelines should relate to all aspects of the team's work (day-to-day interactions, responsibilities and assumptions, for example) not just meeting behavior. All team members should be involved in setting the operating guidelines. This allows everyone to hold each other accountable for conformance to the agreements. Here is an example of one virtual team's operating guidelines:

- We follow through on everything we commit to do.
- We keep the team up-to-date.
- We always assume good intentions on the part of other team members.
- If we have an issue with another team member, we will contact him or her personally to discuss the matter.
- We follow the technology protocols we have established.
- Customers are our number one priority. We always make decisions based on what is best for the customer.
- We use agendas for all meetings, virtual and face-to-face, and send out minutes within two days.
- We will have a face-to-face meeting at least quarterly.

Setting Technology Protocols

The final recommended start-up tool is communication technology protocols. One factor that allows virtual teams to function effectively is the availability of numerous and varied communication technologies. However, although these technologies provide the opportunity to transfer increased amounts of information, they do not necessarily improve communication effectiveness (Fisher & Fisher, 2001). In order to facilitate two-way communication and make the most effective use of technology, many virtual teams establish communication protocols. When using e-mail, for example, they may agree to a no-scrolling rule (the message should be short enough to fit on one computer screen so that they do not require scrolling) or to check e-mail at certain intervals during the work-day. Here are examples of e-mail and voice mail protocols:

E-Mail Protocol

- We will clearly identify the subject of the message in the subject line.
- All e-mail messages will be short (no scrolling required) and to the point.
- E-mail will not be used for philosophical debates.
- All distribution lists will be kept current.
- E-mail will not be used for urgent messages.
- We accept responsibility for a personal delivery (face-to-face or voice-to-voice) of any urgent message.
- To enable message prioritization, we will code the top of each message with either "requires action" or "for your information (FYI)."
- We will sign all messages.
- We agree that e-mail is a supplement to, not a substitute for, personal interaction.
- We will not spam.
- We will treat people electronically the same way we would in person.
- Instead of copying long quotes from others, we will briefly summarize them and add attachments, if necessary.

Voice Mail Protocol

- We do not leave messages longer than ten seconds.
- We check our voice mail at least once a day.
- We use the "urgent" code only when a message is truly urgent.
- We limit the use of the "group send" option. We use it only when a message is relevant to all members.

- When forwarding messages, we will leave an explanatory message so the individual knows why the message is being sent.

- We take accountability to follow up voice mail messages with written documentation when necessary.

- We never use voice mail to leave emotionally charged messages. We wait to talk with the person directly (phone or in person) so the problem or issue can be jointly resolved.

Protocols are also useful for instant messaging, Web-, video- and teleconferencing, and any other technology that requires the social system to work effectively with the technical system. These protocols can easily be incorporated into the team's operating guidelines or, if preferred, can become a separate activity and product.

The use of technology protocols also allows team members to acknowledge and incorporate technology preferences into the way they work (for example, Priya prefers e-mails, while Jordan prefers instant messaging). Teams can align expectations around potentially disruptive communication concerns (Why do some people reply more quickly to e-mails than others do?) and help mange technology intrusion into personal lives (Why do some people answer e-mails on weekends while others will not?). With a technology-enabled social system, these agreements may also help people avoid stress-related illnesses and productivity problems by ensuring more effective work/home life balance.

WORK AND HOME LIFE BALANCE

Effective virtual team start-ups can improve not only the social, technical, and environmental systems but the personal one as well. Because of rigorous demands on virtual team members, including the frequent requirement of collaborating with colleagues in different time zones, work hours can be longer in these organizations than in colocated ones. In one *60 Minutes* television segment, a case in point was highlighted. Stahl examined some virtual teams at Best Buy corporate headquarters and discovered that these team members normally worked longer hours than their nonvirtual counterparts. But where the company found ways to make certain accommodations, the stress level and burnout actually decreased when compared with people who worked fewer hours.

Other evidence validates this situation. In the Cummins Power Generation business, many of the best-adjusted and most effective virtual team members and leaders had discovered that they needed to put some personal interaction boundaries in place to maintain their private lives and stay healthy. But these boundaries often required support from other members of the virtual team and therefore required discussion with them. One leader, for example, contracted with his team to reply to evening e-mails quickly, but requested that on the days he was in town he have two hours each evening to have dinner with his wife and put his children to bed. The team members readily agreed. He probably now works later into the night than he would have otherwise but says he is happier and healthier as a result.

Many teams have discussions during the start-up—especially during the development of operating guidelines and technology protocols—that create cultural expectations about matters like whether projects require people to respond to work communications during vacation time and weekends, whether accommodations will be made for religious holidays that affect only a few team members, or whether participating in important family milestone activities or emergencies can be allowed during critical work periods. The way these discussions are handled can affect the trust of the team and either promote or diminish virtual team effectiveness.

FINAL THOUGHTS

Virtual teams are difficult to manage effectively because they lack many of the communication and coordination advantages of a colocated team. But when they are started up effectively, virtual teams may quickly overcome these disadvantages and perform as well as colocated teams. This chapter suggests that four tools in particular are important to put virtual teams on track. Chartering, role clarification, operating guidelines, and technology protocols can help virtual teams address some of the challenges of isolation and misalignment that are common in this type of organization. They help these teams communicate more effectively and provide an opportunity to develop teams where the social, technical, environmental, and personal systems are all jointly optimized.

REMINDERS

- Virtual teams are more difficult to manage than colocated ones but can be just as effective.
- Effective virtual team design considers not only the social, technical, and environmental systems but the personal one as well.

- Home and work life balance is a challenge for virtual team members.

- Technologies such as e-mail, Web conferencing, and instant messaging facilitate virtual team communication, but they can cause impediments to both team and individual effectiveness.

- Virtual teams have unique start-up challenges, many of which stem from the various cultural backgrounds of team members. These cultural differences are not limited to geographical ones, but can also include educational, functional, religious, and a variety of life experiences.

- Four tools are especially helpful for starting up virtual teams: team charters, role clarification processes, operating guidelines, and communication technology-use protocols. Although it is preferable to use these tools at start-up, they can also help to refocus an existing team.

- A start-up process is best done face-to-face.

- The four tools can help virtual teams create a shared work culture that bridges differences and increases clarity and productivity.

- The discussion that creates the charter, roles, and agreements is probably more important than the final product. The participation of all team members is important.

- It is important to include the right people in the chartering process, including people outside the team who have a major impact on the team's ability to be successful, such as key customers or partners and senior management sponsors.

- If operating guidelines are not set and agreed to properly, dysfunctional team norms can take their place as a key predictor of team behavior.

- Operating guidelines and technology use protocols can increase productivity and reduce unhealthy tension among team members.

References

Anderson, J., & Narus, J. (1998). Business marketing: Understand what customers value. *Harvard Business Review, 76*(6), 53–67.

Appelbaum, E., Bailey, T., Berg, P., & Kalleberg, A. (2000). *Manufacturing advantage: Why high performance work systems pay off.* Ithaca, NY: Cornell University Press.

Dyer, W. (1987). *Team building: Issues and alternatives* (2nd ed.). Reading, MA: Addison-Wesley.

Emery, F., & Trist, E. (1960). Socio-technical systems. In C. Churchman & M. Verhuist (Eds.), *Management sciences models and techniques.* London: Pergamon Press.

Fisher, K. (2000). *Leading self-directed work teams: A guide to developing new team leadership skills* (2nd ed.). New York: McGraw-Hill.

Fisher, K. (2006). *Teams and the bottom line: Do good results guarantee the sustainability of teams?* Retrieved June 21, 2006, from www.thefishergroup.com.

Fisher, K., & Fisher, M. (1998). *The distributed mind: Achieving high performance through the collective intelligence of knowledge work teams.* New York: Amacom.

Fisher, K., & Fisher, M. (2001). *The distance manager: A hands-on guide to managing off-site employees and virtual teams.* New York: McGraw-Hill.

Galbraith, J. (2000). *Designing the global corporation.* San Francisco: Jossey-Bass.

Hanna, D. (1988). *Designing organizations for high performance.* Reading, MA: Addison-Wesley.

Huselid, M. (1995). The impact of human resource management practices on turnover, productivity, and corporate financial performance. *Academy of Management Journal, 38,* 635–672.

Lanning, M. (1998). *Delivering profitable value: A revolutionary framework to accelerate growth, generate wealth, and rediscover the heart of business.* Cambridge, MA: Perseus.

Liff, S., & Posey, P. (2004). *Seeing is believing.* New York: Amacom.

Mohrman, S., Cohen, S., & Mohrman, A. (1995). *Designing team-based organizations: New forms for knowledge work.* San Francisco: Jossey-Bass.

Schein, E. (1997). *Organizational culture and leadership* (2nd ed.). San Francisco: Jossey-Bass.

Stahl, L. (2006, April 2). Working 24/7. *60 minutes* [Television broadcast]. New York: CBS News.

Trist, E. (1981). *The evolution of socio-technical systems: A conceptual framework and an action research program.* Toronto: Ontario Quality of Working Life Centre.

Tools for Effective Virtual Team Meetings

Dipti Gupta, Lori Bradley, Terence Yeoh

At one point or another, we have all participated in dysfunctional and ineffective team meetings. Ineffective team meetings can reduce employee productivity and increase frustration. Virtual team meetings are no exception. Although virtual team meetings potentially save time and money and draw on talent and expertise, they also heighten the challenges of communication and interaction due to technological and cross-cultural issues. Virtual team meetings can quickly become ineffective if (Austin, Drakos, & Mann, 2006):

- The objective of the meeting is not clearly outlined.
- The agenda is not circulated before the meeting.
- The meeting does not start or end on time.
- Virtual team members are not given a chance to express their views.
- The meeting is dominated by a few vocal members.

We are thankful to Ambika Prasad for her contribution to the research on which this chapter was based.

- Technological problems occur, such as a time lag or no picture while videoconferencing.

- There is no follow-up (for example, meeting minutes are not sent promptly after the meeting).

When team meetings are effective and efficiently run, team members can accomplish meeting objectives and generate a list of action items to work on following the meeting. Virtual meetings can be effective and efficient with proper planning.

This chapter provides guidelines and tools to assist in making virtual team meetings more effective and efficient. It begins with a description of the situations in which virtual team meetings may not be the optimal choice and face-to-face meetings should be pursued instead. It discusses specific benefits and challenges of virtual team meetings, reviews the areas of education and training necessary for virtual team members, and discusses the special roles of virtual team facilitators and cofacilitators. The remainder of the chapter outlines a series of actions that can and should be taken by virtual team meeting facilitators or team leaders during the team's initial face-to-face meeting and before, during, and after a team's virtual meetings, to ensure meeting effectiveness and success.

WHEN TO USE AND NOT TO USE VIRTUAL MEETINGS

Although virtual teams conduct business through virtual meetings, there are times when meeting virtually may not be effective or recommended. Table 20.1 presents a list of factors for determining when virtual meetings are and are not recommended for collaborative work. As the table indicates, different factors and situations dictate whether a team should meet virtually or face-to-face. In order to ensure an effective outcome, team leaders should evaluate the situation and determine whether a virtual meeting is desirable.

BENEFITS AND CHALLENGES OF VIRTUAL TEAM MEETINGS

Remote team members benefit greatly from virtual team meetings. A list of the most often cited benefits of virtual team meetings are as follows:

- *They save time and money related to travel.* As companies are reducing travel budgets and teams are becoming more global, remote team members now have the option to conduct their day-to-day business virtually.

Table 20.1
Guidelines for When to Hold Virtual Team Meetings

When Virtual Teams Are Recommended	When Virtual Teams Are Not Recommended
Team participants are dispersed or not colocated.	Team participants are colocated.
A face-to-face meeting is not possible.	A face-to-face meeting is possible.
It is not the team's first meeting.	It is the team's first meeting (first meetings should be conducted in person to build trust and develop familiarization).
Team members are already familiar with each other and have built trust.	Team members have not established trust.
The topic of discussion is not likely to generate large amounts of conflict.	Meeting objectives and outcomes are likely to have a major impact on the team members.
Team members have equal access to collaborative technology.	The topic of discussion is likely to generate large amounts of conflict.
Team members do not have to meet for extended periods of time.	Team members do not have equal access to collaborative technology.
	Team members have to meet for extended periods of time.

Source: Bradley, Gupta, Prasad, and Yeoh (2004).

- *They are more convenient than face-to-face meetings.* Time saved translates to team members' convenience. Team members find virtual meetings convenient because they can meet virtually from their office or home location instead of waiting around airports to board flights to attend face-to-face meetings. Thus, they can check and reply to e-mails and spend more time working than commuting to meetings at various locations.

- *They connect geographically distributed team members.* Geographically separated team members can connect and collaborate with each other using technology. Team members can remain in touch at all times during office hours by e-mail, telephone, videophone, or instant messaging.

- *They yield diverse perspectives on problems leading to innovative solutions.* Virtual technology has assisted in bringing together team members located all over the globe to generate innovative solutions and products.

Although virtual meetings provide many advantages, they often present challenges as well—for example:

- *Friction due to cultural differences.* Virtual teams may be made up of individuals from around the world. Although virtual meetings allow these diverse individuals to come together, this does not ensure that these varied participants are accustomed to working together. Friction may occur due to differences in individuals' work ethic, organizational norms, personal philosophy or style, status in the organization, managerial styles, and customs. People's behaviors, customs, and values are a result of their language, religion, and the history of their country. People from different countries have unique customs, traditions, and ways of doing business. Team members working on international projects must understand and appreciate their teammates' culture and customs. Organizations should provide cultural sensitivity training to employees who work on international projects.

- *Fatigue and stress due to time differences.* Team members on international projects may be spread across time zones. For example, a software development team may have the team leader working in the company's headquarters in Dallas, some members are situated in San Jose, California, and other members may be working in Bangalore, India. There may not be a common window of time to have meetings during normal work hours for everyone. A meeting scheduled to start in Dallas at 9:00 A.M. Central Time, is likely too early in the morning for team members in California and too late at night for Indian team members. In this example, some team members will be rested and fresh, while others will be tired at the end of their workday or lose sleep to attend the early meeting. If team meetings are always held at the same time based on the convenience of a team leader, team members who always are inconvenienced by having to get up early or stay late will become frustrated and disengaged. Frequent meetings outside scheduled work hours disrupt employees' work/life balance. An optimal strategy is to rotate among members who must attend meetings outside regular work hours to minimize resentment and disruption.

- *Productivity loss due to technology challenges.* Technology is the foundation that makes virtual meetings possible. However, technology challenges may lead to ineffective and unproductive meetings and frustrated team members. Some of the more prominent technology challenges include these:

  - *Discomfort with technology.* Team members new to virtual work may be intimidated by technology and find it hard to make the transition from face-to-face to virtual meetings. Training or a virtual meeting facilitator can be especially useful for those new to the virtual world.

  - *Equipment malfunction.* Setting up virtual meeting equipment can be time consuming. Despite best efforts, technology sometimes malfunctions and causes delays. Help desk support and other backup plans must be carefully outlined and implemented when technology fails.

  - *Task-technology mismatch.* Organizations spend large amounts of money purchasing and upgrading technology. It is important that team members understand the most effective type of collaboration for a particular task and the technology that supports it. Virtual collaboration training for leaders and meeting facilitators can be especially helpful for gaining the knowledge to select appropriate technology. (See Table 20.1 for suggestions on how to match task to technology.)

- *Frustration due to communication challenges and lack of meeting skills.* There are important communication differences between virtual and face-to-face meetings. Examples include the need to allow for a lag time on some video systems and the need to identify oneself before speaking in teleconferences. Also, team members and facilitators are not able to observe and interpret nonverbal communication. Training in virtual meeting skills can be valuable for helping team members get accustomed to the different requirements that being virtual brings.

EDUCATING FOR VIRTUAL TEAM MEETINGS

Education and training are necessary to avoid many of the frustrations and challenges that accompany virtual team meetings. The purpose of the education and training should be to develop virtual meeting skills and individual comfort with meeting technology. Organizations should provide team members who will be required to meet and work virtually education and training focusing on these topics:

- Basics of operating available virtual collaboration technology such as video-conferencing equipment
- Vendor training for software being used, such as collaborative software or online meeting space
- Effective virtual meeting skills such as preparing and setting a meeting agenda, group dynamics, collaborative problem solving, and cultural sensitivity

The goal should be to develop skills to the extent that the participants' focus is on the meeting objective, not the technical aspects of using the equipment.

USING VIRTUAL MEETING FACILITATORS AND COFACILITATORS

Using a meeting facilitator or cofacilitators can increase a virtual team meeting's effectiveness. The facilitator could be an outside person or a team leader trained in facilitation and meeting processes. Virtual facilitators can help in these ways:

- Free team members to concentrate on meeting objectives rather than on the processes of a virtual meeting
- Improve the quality of a virtual meeting by focusing on the group processes
- Make observations and use interventions to do the following:
  - Keep team members on task and following the agenda
  - Summarize salient points throughout the meeting and tie them back to the objective of the meeting
  - Encourage quiet members to share
  - Operate technology
  - Recognize hidden agendas and resolve any conflicts as they arise
  - Listen carefully for energy drop, halfhearted responses, delays in responding, and silence when conversation is called for

Cofacilitation involves the presence of a facilitator at each site in a virtual meeting. Each site's facilitator serves as an advocate for that site and ensures that the site is getting adequate opportunity to participate. Each cofacilitator can make sure that his or her members fully participate. It is important for cofacilitators to:

- Work well together
- Discuss their facilitation styles and how they will handle differences between them
- Discuss the roles they will play in meetings. Will one lead and the other assist? How will they get the other's attention or indicate that their room is having a problem with technology or would like input?

It is important that cofacilitators discuss their styles and roles prior to the virtual team meeting, so that they are prepared and can help facilitate the virtual meeting smoothly.

Effective process facilitation and coordination by the cofacilitators at each site increases meeting efficiency. Facilitators and team leaders well trained in process facilitation, group dynamics, and technology can manage virtual meetings effectively. This positive experience leaves meeting attendees with a sense of accomplishment.

Future virtual meetings can be more effective if the first team meeting is face-to-face. Team members build relationships and trust that set the stage for a successful working relationship. The face-to-face meeting must be well planned and last for at least one full day, if not more.

The Initial Virtual Meeting

The process of relationship and trust building begins at the initial, or kickoff, face-to-face meeting. Some specific actions that virtual facilitators or team leaders may use to lead the team through this initial face-to-face encounter include:

- Introductions
- Trust-building exercises
- Crafting the team's mission and vision
- Establishing team norms or ground rules

- Determining the next meeting date, times, and agenda, which will most likely be virtual
- Formulating a design for the team's Web site

Begin the meeting with introductions. Have each member state his or her name, tenure with the company, last project worked on, and anything else relevant. An ice-breaking activity can also be included to help the members get more comfortable and familiar with each other; examples are to share a unique hobby or the names of their pets.

Next, have the team discuss the mission and vision of the team. This helps team members develop a common understanding of the objectives of the team. This activity also provides the team with a sense of ownership, belonging, and pride.

After setting the team's objective, have the team generate a list of agreed-on team norms or ground rules of conduct that will serve as a guide for the behavior of the team members. Participation in developing team norms creates a sense of ownership among the team members and increases the likelihood of adherence to them. Team members can begin by establishing some general norms around time, decision making, and accountability. To start the process, it may be useful to provide a general list of team norms—for example (Bradley, Gupta, Prasad, & Yeoh, 2004):

- Begin and end meetings on time.
- Be respectful.
- Do not talk over each other; wait for your turn.
- Appoint a scribe and timekeeper at the beginning of each meeting.
- Develop an agenda, and send it to the team at least three days before the meeting.
- Elicit comments on the agenda.
- Send all documents to be reviewed in a meeting at least twenty-four hours in advance.
- Send all documents to all members.
- Upload all team documents on the team Web site.
- Send meeting minutes within twenty-four hours after the meeting.
- Check and reply to e-mails daily.

- Reply to voice mail within four hours.
- Everyone present in the meeting has an equal vote in the decision.
- Decision will be by consensus.
- If teleconferencing, state your name before speaking.
- Mute the phone if you are typing notes.
- Do not multitask while meeting.
- If joining the meeting late, wait for a pause before identifying yourself.

Team leaders, facilitators, or team members may use this list as a starting point from which to build the team's own list of norms. It is recommended that the list of team norms be posted on the team's Web site.

Before bringing the team's initial face-to-face meeting to a close, make sure team members have decided when the next meeting will be (this next meeting will probably be virtual) and its agenda. A face-to-face meeting also gives the team an opportunity to take pictures of all team members to post on the team's Web site. The team's Web site will be an important "virtual watercooler," where team members can post and share their photographs, talk about hobbies, or share personal achievements.

Virtual teams are recommended to meet face-to-face at least once a year. These meetings will help members reconnect with each other and establish relationships with new team members. They also serve as a platform for team members to recognize good performance and celebrate together.

Stages of Virtual Team Meetings

A successful virtual meeting brings a virtual team together and enables them to accomplish their meeting objectives using collaborative technology. Facilitators and team leaders should understand the actions that are required before, during, and after a virtual meeting to ensure its success.

Virtual meetings, like face-to-face meetings, have three stages: premeeting, meeting, and postmeeting. In premeeting activities, the facilitator or team leader sets up and plans the meeting. The postmeeting activities help the team account for decisions taken during the meeting and resulting action items. Effective facilitator or team leader actions throughout the meeting stages help increase the effectiveness and efficiency of the virtual meeting. The facilitator or team leader actions in each of the three stages of the virtual meeting are discussed in detail in the next section.

Premeeting   The most crucial task of the premeeting stage is to develop a meeting plan, which should include a clear statement of the meeting's objectives and agenda, the roles of those who will attend, the work to be completed prior to the meeting, and the norms that will guide the meeting process. Unfortunately, many meetings (virtual or not) occur without such detailed plans. According to Julia Young of Facilitate.com, team members spend 10 percent of meeting-related time in planning, 80 percent in the actual meeting itself, and 10 percent in follow-up actions after the meeting. Instead, Young suggests 50 percent of meeting-related time should be used for planning a meeting, 20 percent in the actual meeting, and 30 percent on follow-up activities.

Creating a clear meeting plan helps to define the type and purpose of a meeting. The goal of the premeeting stage is to make meeting arrangements so that the meeting will be structured enough to be productive yet flexible enough to encourage creativity and a free flow of information and ideas. Premeeting plans involve communicating the purpose of the meeting and sending all team members a meeting notice, agenda, and all documents that need to be reviewed before the meeting. Exhibit 20.1 provides a sample meeting notice and agenda.

Meetings may be called for a variety of purposes, including sharing of information, viewpoints, and ideas; resolving conflict and building consensus; solving problems and making decisions; planning activities and evaluating options; brainstorming; developing products; socializing; and congratulating and recognizing the efforts of others. Once the purpose of a meeting is determined, the type of technology that will best suit that purpose can be selected.

Care should be taken in selecting the appropriate technology for a virtual team's meeting. The wrong choice of technology can lead to meetings that are not just challenging but frustrating as well. Obvious considerations in selecting meeting technology include how many members will participate in the meeting, how long the meeting will last, and what technology is available to all meeting participants ("Virtual Meetings and Virtual Teams," 2005). Another important consideration in choosing meeting technology, and one that perhaps is not so obvious, is the degree of collaboration needed among the meeting participants. An example

Exhibit 20.1
Sample Meeting Notice and Agenda

XY Virtual Team

Date of meeting: 1/1/08

Time: 10:00 A.M.–12:00 P.M.

Venue: AOB, First Floor, Room 11 (Dallas); Conference Room (New Delhi)

Conference Bridge Line: 1–888–123–4567

Meeting Code Number: 1001

Meeting Purpose: To brainstorm solutions for the ABCD problem

Preparation for the Meeting: Review previous meeting minutes. Read attached documents, and be prepared to share ideas in the brainstorming session.

Attendees: Gupta, Peters, Ramaswamy, and Sharma (New Delhi)

Smith, Turner, Johnson, White, and Small (Dallas)

Agenda

Items	Time (in minutes)
1. Introductions	2
2. Determine the timekeeper and scribe	2
3. Brainstorm session	45
4. Break	10
5. Resume brainstorming	40
6. Summarize and conclusion	5
7. Review Action list	5
8. Set agenda and schedule next meeting	5

of a virtual team meeting that requires a low level of collaboration is an information-sharing meeting or a meeting to review a document. In those situations, a simple form of technology such as e-mail, shared database, or a team bulletin board would be an appropriate choice. A virtual team meeting that requires a high degree of collaboration among its members may involve brainstorming,

Table 20.2
Matching Technology to Degree of Collaboration

Type of Technology	Degree of Collaboration	
	Low	High
SIMPLE	E-mail	Instant messaging
	Team bulletin boards	Teleconference
COMPLEX		Videoconference
		Collaborative software

consensus building around a topic of conflict, or drafting shared documents. In those situations, more complex forms of collaborative technology (such as Net-Meeting, WebEx, Wiki, or Raindance) may be more suitable. Table 20.2 provides a chart with recommendations for matching technology with the degree of collaboration required in a task. Table 20.3 provides a chart to help match technology to meeting purposes and tasks.

The optimal strategy is to choose the simplest technology to meet the needs of the virtual meeting ("Virtual Meetings and Virtual Teams," 2005) and let the required tasks determine the choice of technology. The technology chosen should not interfere with the content or flow of the meeting. Short virtual meetings can be more effective than meetings that last more than two hours (Settle-Murphy & Young, 2006). Also, the number of team members present may influence the choice of technology. For a large group with members at various locations, videoconferencing may be appropriate. Instant messaging may be used for smaller teams. In sum, the choice of technology should be based on the meeting purpose, degree of collaboration needed, number of team members in attendance, and the meeting length. Exhibit 20.2 provides a checklist of actions for virtual meeting facilitators and/or team leaders to consider during the premeeting stage.

During the Meeting   Meticulous and careful premeeting planning help the actual meeting get off to a good start. However, facilitators and team leaders

Table 20.3
Matching Technology to Tasks

Type of Technology	Degree of Collaboration	
	Low Collaborative Tasks	High Collaborative Tasks
SIMPLE	Sharing information	Evaluating options
	Sharing viewpoints and ideas	
	Planning activities	
	Brainstorming	
	Recognizing efforts of others	
	Socializing	
COMPLEX		Building consensus
		Product development
		Solving problems
		Making decisions
FACE-TO-FACE		Resolving conflicts
		Familiarizing
		Socializing

should also understand the unique characteristics of a virtual meeting. The following actions or processes can set the stage for an effective meeting:

• *Opening the meeting.* Start by asking all team members present to introduce themselves. Some virtual team meetings are hybrids (for example, some members are colocated at a site and participating by videoconference, while others join in from other sites by telephone). Introductions help team members know who is attending the meeting. It is easy to forget team members who are attending by telephone if they are quiet listeners. Hence, it is also useful to check in with telephone participants throughout the meeting.

• *Appointing meeting roles.* Meeting roles are especially helpful if there is no designated facilitator. This process helps to organize the meeting by making some team members responsible for various aspects of the meeting. Roles should be

Exhibit 20.2
Checklist of Actions to Take During the
Premeeting Stage

As Soon as Meeting Is Scheduled

☐ Determine the purpose and type of meeting.

☐ Identify meeting participants and check their availability.

☐ Schedule and meet with the cofacilitator(s) if needed.

☐ Reserve room and equipment.

☐ Create and circulate the agenda among all team members for their comments.

☐ Set a deadline for receiving documents needed during the meeting.

Two Days Prior to the Meeting

☐ Distribute agenda and documents.

☐ Verify room and equipment (conference lines, videophone) reservation.

☐ Verify technical support availability and contact information.

Day Before the Meeting

☐ Load documents and set up and test the equipment.

☐ Ensure you have phone numbers of critical contacts.

Day of the Meeting

☐ Arrive at least one hour before the meeting (if possible).

☐ Ensure optimal room and equipment configuration.

☐ Establish contact with other sites (if using videophone).

☐ Discuss last-minute details with cofacilitator(s).

Source: Bradley, Gupta, Prasad, and Yeoh (2004).

clearly defined and assigned so that there is no confusion. Some examples of meeting roles include:

- Timekeeper: Ensures the meeting stays on schedule

- Note taker or scribe: Captures meeting minutes and records important decisions and action plans; distributes meeting minutes and action plans after the meeting

- Process observer: Intervenes if the team drifts from the process it agreed to follow; offers the team feedback on the meeting's process and team dynamics; suggests ways to improve meeting effectiveness

- Devil's advocate: Takes opposing position to prod the team to generate alternative responses and avoid groupthink

- Facilitator: Keeps the team focused on the task; intervenes when the team drifts from the agenda or conflicts arise; reminds the team of its norms when necessary

Exhibit 20.3 lists actions that team leaders or facilitators may find useful to start and guide a virtual team meeting in progress.

Postmeeting   Decisions and action plans made during a virtual team meeting must be appropriately documented and subsequently performed and evaluated. Following a virtual team meeting, the team leader or meeting facilitator, or both, must ensure that the meeting notes or minutes are typed up and sent to all members within the established time frame. All agreed-on decisions and action items should be listed in the notes or minutes. Each action item should also include the person responsible for completing those items and the time frame in which the items must be completed. The meeting facilitator or team leader should follow up with all team members to answer any questions.

Exhibit 20.4 offers a checklist of actions that virtual team leaders or meeting facilitators may find useful once the meeting has ended.

FINAL THOUGHTS

A virtual collaboration effort cannot be successful without efficient virtual meetings. Meetings are the building blocks of collaborating virtually and are crucial for remote team members to conduct their day-to-day business. Effective virtual

Exhibit 20.3
Checklist of Actions to Take During
a Virtual Team Meeting

Starting the Meeting

☐ Define or clarify the meeting purpose.

☐ Review the agenda.

☐ Lead introductions.

☐ Define and appoint meeting roles of scribe, timekeeper, and facilitator.

☐ Review and clarify ground rules.

During the Meeting

☐ Follow the agenda.

☐ Start and finish on time.

☐ Monitor and manage conflict.

☐ Enforce the ground rules.

☐ Stay focused on process.

☐ Do not get involved in content.

☐ Monitor the technology.

☐ In case of teleconference, ask remote members to speak by specifically asking them for comments.

☐ In case of instant messaging, consider using identifiable buddy names and different colors and fonts for different team members.

Source: Bradley, Gupta, Prasad, and Yeoh (2004).

collaboration is dependent on the organization's support of its virtual teams. Organizations should be sensitive to the needs of their virtual teams and provide them with appropriate collaborative technology, training and education, and facilitators. Virtual meeting processes including careful meeting planning, execution, and follow-up to reduce team members' frustration and increase their

---

Exhibit 20.4
Checklist of Postmeeting Actions

☐ Review decisions and action plans.

☐ Ensure that follow-up actions are reviewed and explicit.

☐ Answer any questions.

☐ Schedule the next meeting.

☐ Determine the agenda.

☐ Conduct a critique of the meeting by asking questions:

- Was the meeting successful?

- If not, what would help members feel that the meeting was a success?

- How well did the team follow ground rules and norms?

- How well did the team accomplish the meeting goals?

☐ Send meeting minutes out to team members in the time established in the norms.

Source: Bradley, Gupta, Prasad, and Yeoh (2004).

---

efficiency. Conducting effective virtual meetings is instrumental to the success of virtual teams and their organizations in terms of developing innovative solutions and products.

REMINDERS

- Conduct the first team meeting face-to-face to begin to build trust and personal connection.

- Establish the mission and vision of the team.

- Establish a set of team norms that will guide the team's conduct during and outside meetings.

- Ask for organizational support in providing the proper education and training for virtual team members, leaders, and facilitators.
- Make use of virtual team meeting facilitators and cofacilitators.
- Determine the purpose of the meeting, and then select the appropriate collaborative technology to serve that purpose.
- Spend time on planning the meeting: meeting objectives, agenda, technology, and setup.
- Facilitators and team leaders who serve as facilitators must focus on the process, not the content, of the meeting.
- Conduct follow-up after a meeting has ended with meeting minutes, a list of decisions taken during the meeting, and the resulting action items.
- Have at least one face-to-face meeting yearly to reconnect with team members.
- Create a virtual watercooler.
- Celebrate successes virtually.
- Recognize team members in face-to-face meetings.

References

Austin, T., Drakos, N., & Mann, J. (2006). *Web conferencing amplifies dysfunctional meeting practices*. Retrieved July 24, 2006, from http://www.groupsystems.com/resources/custom/PDFs/Gartner-web_conferencing_amplifies_d_138101.pdf.

Bradley, L., Gupta, D., Prasad, A., & Yeoh, T. (2004). *Brief guide: Effective virtual meetings*. Denton: Center for Collaborative Organizations, University of North Texas.

Settle-Murphy, N., & Young, J. (2006). *Getting great results out of virtual meetings*. Retrieved July 24, 2006, from http://www.guidedinsights.com/chrysalis-ezine-communique.asp.

Virtual meetings and virtual teams: Using technology to work smarter. (2005). *Innovation Insights, 9*. The Pennsylvania State University. Retrieved February 8, 2005, from http://www.psu.edu/president/pia/innovation/Virtual_Meetings_and%20Virtual_Teams2.pdf.

VEtiquette
What Is the Etiquette of Virtual Teams?

Mal Conway, Jack Jennings, Curt Raschke, Mary B. Witort, Michael Beyerlein

The effectiveness of virtual teams depends as much as that of face-to-face teams on the quality of the work process, which includes the process of team member interaction. Habits of interaction that display trust and respect are critical to effective sharing of information. The norms of behavior are more complicated than face-to-face teams because of the mix of cultures that is sometimes present, but the behaviors remain fundamentally alike. Courteous, respectful, thoughtful behavior everywhere is referred to as etiquette. Etiquette is defined as generally recognized and accepted or required norms of behavior in society or a profession. In this chapter, a new word, *VEtiquette,* is coined to represent the special subset of behaviors required in a virtual team and to explore the difference in context that virtual work creates that makes special attention to such behavior particularly important.

WHAT IS VETIQUETTE?

Etiquette represents a set of appropriate behaviors that occur in a real-time, synchronous environment such as face-to-face. It represents conventional requirements for social behavior that can be summarized as, "Be nice; consider others." Since the development of the Internet as a business tool, a subset of behaviors in etiquette has emerged called *netiquette,* which represents asynchronous interaction, such as e-mail exchanges where etiquette is practiced or advocated in electronic communication over a computer network. Netiquette can be summarized as, "Write nice, because it's easy to be misinterpreted (and it's a permanent record)." But virtual collaboration is more than asynchronous, so something additional is needed. *VEtiquette,* which stands for "virtual etiquette," is required in work that is typically real time and synchronous. VEtiquette guides team members' behavior as they collaborate virtually either while speaking or writing using Internet, mobile, or video technologies. It can be summarized as, "Be effective, or don't be heard." This extra attention to virtual interaction matters because the effectiveness of the team depends on it.

COMMON FEATURES OF VIRTUAL TEAMS AND COLOCATED TEAMS

Face-to-face and virtual teams have some important features in common. Both types of teams are organized for the same reasons: to improve work process (a continuous improvement team), plan and execute a project (a project team), or solve a specific problem (referred to as a tiger or red team). In addition, face-to-face and virtual teams may use similar types of team structures, such as natural teams (organized around a common product or service), functional teams (organized around a common set of tasks), and cross-functional teams (organized around a common output or project).

Both face-to-face and virtual teams need structure. Both need to develop team charters, determine meeting frequency and purpose, outline team member roles and responsibilities, establish levels of meeting participation and reporting norms, and determine the appropriate type of leadership and facilitation (dependent on the team's maturity).

Team-building activities are important for both face-to-face and virtual teams. These activities are used to ensure team member participation in formulating mission and goals, build shared commitment to team success and each other, ensure team members feel their work is important and valued, build communication channels between team members, and provide appropriate training for team members.

Finally, both face-to-face and virtual teams need appropriate team member work assignment interactions. Some teams require work assignment coordination, others require work assignment integration, and still others work assignment collaboration.

COLLABORATION AND ORGANIZATIONAL PERFORMANCE: THE IMPORTANCE OF AN OPEN CULTURE

The ability to collaborate is rooted in an organization's fabric, and the impact of collaboration on an organization's performance is mediated by the collection of individuals within an organization that use the collaboration capabilities. Research suggests that having a collaboration technology infrastructure and mandating the use of these tools across an organization is not enough to generate high business performance down the line. An open culture that encourages sharing and open interaction is required. A description of some relevant studies follow.

The firm of Frost and Sullivan conducted a major study for Microsoft and Verizon Business in 2006 entitled, "Meetings Around the World: The Impact of Collaboration on Business Performance." The researchers surveyed 946 decision makers, including company presidents, vice presidents, directors, and managers around the globe in the United States, Europe, and Asia-Pacific. Six kinds of organizations were examined: health care and pharmaceutical, government, financial, manufacturing, professional services, and high tech. The companies tended to be small to midsize, with revenues ranging from $5 million to $10 billion. The overwhelming conclusion from the survey was that collaboration is a key driver of business performance.

The study found that collaboration has a significant impact on profitability, profit growth, and sales growth. The most significant impact of collaboration on a single measure of performance was in customer satisfaction (41 percent). Other factors affect customer satisfaction too, but scoring so high underscores that collaboration is a strong driver of this component of business performance. Companies need to have a solid collaborative capability and leverage it across many aspects of an organization. Each business function studied performed better due to collaborative skills. With so much at stake, it makes sense to pay attention to every facet of the virtual work process, including VEtiquette.

A comparison of top- versus bottom-performing companies by region showed that performance correlates with collaboration. Top-performing companies across all regions demonstrated a significantly higher level of collaborativeness compared to bottom performers. The implication of this information is that regardless of differences in regional business practices, the more collaborative organizations are, the better they perform.

Effective collaboration includes a combination of an open company culture, technology, and processes. Given that collaboration capability is the driver of collaboration quality, tests of this model show that a culture of openness is the most important determinant of collaboration quality. It represents the ease of talking to anyone within the organization, the regularity of cooperation between units within the organization, and the accessibility of persons to those in other departments. Such a culture is difficult for competitors to imitate, which makes it a strategic advantage. Openness depends on trust, so sharing of information is optimized. Trust depends on how people treat each other. VEtiquette provides the guidelines.

DIFFERENCES BETWEEN VIRTUAL AND COLOCATED TEAMS

The constant requirement to improve effectiveness in the global economy has been the impetus for teams to implement roles and responsibilities for virtual collaboration. Functioning within a virtual framework requires a different set of solutions for collaborating. Organizations and researchers have recognized this new environment and are striving to establish direction and build communities of best practice.

Virtual teams have a somewhat different set of practices and procedures. They require a greater emphasis on communication methods and procedures. Virtual team members require training on meeting tools and electronic communications that encompasses an awareness of the increased need for advance preparation and an understanding of time zone differences and virtual team meetings. Virtual teams require establishing and sustaining relationships for success.

The greater emphasis on communications methods and procedures is inherent in teams that may sit across the country or around the world. The composition of the team may range from all but one team member colocated to no team members colocated. A function related to this lack of face-to-face connection is that all team members must be diligent about being visible on online calendars, out-of-office memos, and so on. The team should discuss and agree on specific preferences or expectations for everyday types of communications such as e-mails, voice mail, cell phones, and instant messaging. A virtual team needs a community of practices to document team decisions on agreed-on methods and procedures.

The etiquette of virtual teams is on display in team meetings. The inclusion of electronic tools into team meetings interjects a new set of concerns and actions for team members, especially the team leader. All team members must confirm their ability to use meeting tools, and new members must be provided the opportunity to understand the tools used and become proficient in their use before their first meeting. A periodic confirmation of each team member's knowledge and use of the required meeting tools and electronic communications should be conducted.

In the virtual world, advance preparation for meetings takes on great importance. The meeting coordinator needs to ensure that all participants have the necessary software installed and that it works properly, and allow adequate time to set up the conference call and make the necessary electronic connection. Prior to beginning the meeting, the coordinator should verify volume and ensure all can hear or see the presenter and the presentation material. Time zone differences present both hurdles and opportunities for virtual meetings. Leaders must be aware of the local time for all team members. Adjusting the meeting time for an occasional late-night meeting in the United States to acknowledge the member in China will demonstrate that all team members are valued by sharing the inconvenience of odd hours.

Possibly more so than the traditional team, establishing and sustaining relationships is vital to the success of a virtual team. The team leader should prepare a premeeting team builder, such as: "What town were you born in?" "What is your favorite place to vacation?" or "What was your first job?" This will smooth the occasional technical difficulty in setting up the electronic meeting and identify the points of commonality that bring people together. Team leaders must model behaviors for attendance, preparation, and participation that will guide team members in VEtiquette. The team leader may have to spend more time with virtual members to ensure their inclusion in the team and enhance their team meeting experience. Team members should be trained and given access to materials to gain understanding of the different cultures and countries of other team members.

Virtual teams require a rethinking of team interactions and established norms for meetings. With appropriate training, the roadblocks to virtual teaming can be overcome and VEtiquette interwoven into the workday. A virtual team has the potential to engage all employees to provide a variety of learning opportunities and to be a leader in building collaborative solutions for organizational success.

In summary, virtual teams require:

- A greater emphasis on communication methods and procedures
- Training on meeting tools and electronic communications
- Establishing and sustaining relationships for success
- Advance preparation
- An understanding of the importance of time zone differences to virtual team meetings

VIRTUAL TEAM MEETING PRACTICES THAT MAKE A DIFFERENCE

Given the growing popularity of virtual teams, a number of VEtiquette lessons learned can help newcomers in planning and facilitating virtual team meetings as well as those who are more experienced in working with virtual teams. They include the following lessons applicable to Internet, mobile, and video technology forms of virtual team meetings. By applying these VEtiquette lessons learned, virtual teams will be able to improve the effectiveness of their meetings.

Set Expectations for Working Together

There are three main parts to setting expectations. First is setting goals. While it may sound obvious, setting goals for virtual teams is a critical part of VEtiquette for collaboration toward the accomplishment of those agreed-on goals to happen. Second is defining roles and responsibilities. Various key roles for virtual teams have been identified that mirror roles for traditional face-to-face teams, such as facilitator and leader, participant, and scribe. However, additional roles may also be needed for virtual teams to be successful. The main one is a process monitor or gatekeeper, whose role is to assist the facilitator. This person can pay attention to keeping to the agenda in virtual meetings, documenting issues for an online parking lot for discussion and resolution off-line, keeping track of who is participating and who is not in virtual meetings, and sending private messages to the facilitator so that he or she can attempt to engage any participants who are not actively participating. Third is identifying the team's decision-making method: consensus (majority rule with the understanding that all agree to support and not circumvent the decision even if they did not agree with it), unanimous (everyone must agree), or leader or management decision in which the team has no real decision-making power or authority.

Ensure the Leader or Facilitator Has the Necessary Skills

Leaders must be skillful in these areas:

- *Facilitation and coaching:* Giving specific, constructive, developmental feedback; respecting confidentiality; and giving proper attribution of ideas.

- *Communications:* Paraphrasing; identifying sources on virtual team calls (for example, "Was that Sybil who made the point about coaching? Thank you, Sybil"); and active listening (like, "When I hear you being so passionate about the training option, I sense that it is your strong preference"; "Given the extensive discussion about the pros and cons, it doesn't seem that we are quite ready to make a final decision. Correct?").

- *Cultural sensitivity:* A key leader skill in the light of the growing number of multicultural, global virtual teams. This skill ensures that language in spoken and written form is carefully managed to achieve clarify of meaning. Tips include:

  - Avoid idioms, acronyms, and jargon.

  - Avoid the use of slang expressions because they may confuse and exclude nonnative English-language speakers.

  - Avoid nominalizations, such as making a noun into a verb like, "Google it!"

  - Be careful when using analogies. American sports analogies, for example, may not be understood by team members for whom English is a second language or who have not lived in the United States.

  - Tell stories instead of using humor, as humor can unintentionally be offensive.

  - Check frequently for understanding.

  - Speak slowly and clearly.

  - Use single-syllable words, and try to use Latin root words because they are easier for nonnative English language speakers to comprehend.

- Provide instant messaging or other capability for private feedback if a participant is intimidated by asking questions or expressing lack of understanding publicly.

Practice Virtual Meeting Skills

Virtual teams have their own set of skills:

- Start and end on time.
- Have an activity for participants who sign on to a virtual meeting early.
- Do an audio and video check at the start.
- Tell participants in advance how they can access and download presentation materials.
- Rehearse the set-up process for the meeting to avoid technical and logistical disruption (practice, practice, practice).
- Test connectivity with slow connections.
- Make sure there are sufficient audio lines for the estimated number of participants, plus 15 to 25 percent more in reserve.
- Provide instructions on what to do if there is a technical problem.
- Consider adding the role of a meeting process monitor in addition to a meeting leader or facilitator. The process monitor's responsibility is to send the leader or facilitator private messages with feedback on pace, timing, audience engagement, review points, issues that have not been answered, recorded questions, and follow-up.
- Call attention to a list of participants on the screen if this feature is provided by the tool used. Make it okay to drop out of the meeting when other priorities interfere with participation.
- Have some preview content for early arrivals. Research indicates that the estimated mean length of time Webinars are open prior to start time is eighteen minutes.
- Orient participants on how to send questions to the moderator or all participants and how polling will be conducted if the meeting tool allows polling.
- Allow sufficient time for questions and answers during and at the end of the meeting.

- Keep a frequency count of those who participate so the focus can be shifted to those who have not yet participated.

- Summarize all agreed-on actions, and verify who is responsible for each.

- Introduce presenters to set the stage for the content and the presenters.

- Observe good phone etiquette, such as asking everyone to introduce themselves by name when speaking, try not to talk over others, and put the phone on mute.

- Engage participants. Poll the participants periodically throughout the call, and make sure the meeting tool allows easy interaction. Asking questions is an effective way to encourage engagement and interaction. If the tool has an interactive whiteboard, use it as much as possible to facilitate high interaction and ownership of any renderings developed collaboratively. If the meeting is informational or meant to train, consider recording it and making it available for playback.

- Retain the audience by developing a specific follow-up plan (call to action) and conduct an evaluation survey after the virtual meeting. Sometimes a simple evaluation consisting of two questions (What worked? What needs to be improved?) will suffice. At other times the use of a scale to gauge the intensity of opinions may be appropriate (such as, a statement followed by strongly disagree, disagree somewhat, neutral, agree somewhat, and strongly agree). The tool may limit the options of survey question types, so be sure to check when evaluating tools before using them if this feature is important.

- Manage meeting personality dynamics; for example, acknowledge contributions and suggest to overly talkative participants that it is important to hear the opinions of others. Becoming knowledgeable about personality types can help in managing meeting dynamics effectively. Common tests and exercises that help people identify and analyze their preferred personality type include the Myers-Briggs Personality Type Indicator, the Kolbe Index, the Wilson Learning Styles Inventory, and FIRO-B.

Use Adult Learning Principles

Members of virtual teams are adults. That may seem too obvious to require mentioning, but the assumptions many people bring to adult training and communications do not align with the way most adults function. For example, adults may bring rich experience to the situation and so create complex meaning out of the material presented. They also vary in learning styles, so multiple media need to be used in presenting information. Here are some additional principles and practices that fit adults:

- The KISS principle: Keep it simple and straightforward.
- Make sure that virtual meetings are no longer than a maximum of one hour. Otherwise participants may become fatigued and drop off.
- Use graphics that support the content rather than just for the sake of providing a graphics. Avoid cluttering slides with complex graphics. Simple line drawings usually work best.
- Keep screens uncluttered. Screen text should not look like ransom notes with a hodgepodge of type sizes, types, and colors.
- Be aware of the cultural connotations of certain colors, such as red (danger) and black (death). Avoid the use of red-green color combinations, the most common form of color blindness.
- Group items on the screen to facilitate interpretation and comparison.
- Use a maximum of seven bullets per screen. This is the channel capacity of human short-term memory documented by cognitive psychologist George Miller. Beyond seven discrete bullets, there is little chance of accessing information from one's memory store.

Measure Participant Reactions for Continual Improvement
The quality of the meeting can be assessed with several methods and the resulting data used for improving process:

- Use surveys administered just after the meeting or a follow-up survey given later.
- Collect and analyze reaction data over time. Collecting reaction data may be misleading if used alone since sufficient time may not have elapsed to apply what was discussed and decided on in the meeting. Monitoring meeting reaction data over time is recommended to determine necessary changes.
- If the resources permit, interview a sample of meeting participants and probe to uncover opportunities for improvement.
- Conduct a debriefing session after the meeting in which the leaders debrief with facilitators and process observers (if used).

FINAL THOUGHTS

Creating a world-class team requires building a culture rich in collaboration and teaming. A virtual team has the potential to engage all employees to provide a variety of learning opportunities and to be a leader in building collaborative solutions for organizational success. The quality of interaction for such teams depends on their VEtiquette. The purpose and organization of virtual teams may be the same as for colocated ones, but opportunities for interaction between team members are limited and structured, so the quality of interaction is even more important. Extra attention and effort must be paid to preparing for virtual meetings and other virtual interactions so all participants get the most out of their limited interaction time.

In virtual exchanges, it is important to avoid being a virtual talking head. Seek out ways to engage people to participate. Use tools such as polling and pop questions, and ask action item owners to summarize their new action items before closing the meeting. Make sure microphones are muted when not speaking to avoid unnecessary distractions. When asking or speaking for the first time, team members should introduce themselves. Ask an executive to attend a conference call to acknowledge a recent team milestone or to reignite motivation if it seems to be flagging.

What works for colocated teams is not guaranteed to work for virtual teams. Virtual teams need to change, modify, and tailor their interactions and communications to ensure success. Every opportunity should be explored to allow team members to get better acquainted and connected with the other members of the team.

The more collaborative that enterprises are, the better they perform. Virtual teams are an important new structure for organizations to use to attain a solid collaborative capability and leverage it across many aspects of the organization.

REMINDERS

- Set expectations for working together.
- Define the goals of the virtual team.
- Define members' roles and responsibilities.
- Identify decision-making methods, and teach the tools to all members.

- Ensure leaders have the necessary skills:
  - Facilitation and coaching skills
  - Virtual meeting skills
  - Cultural sensitivity
  - Communications skills
  - Problem-solving and decision-making skills
- Engage participants:
  - Use multiple presenters for online meetings with information purpose.
  - Use on-screen drawing if the tool permits.
  - Retain the audience.
- Use adult learning principles in virtual meetings:
  - KISS: Keep it simple and straightforward—content and process, technology and logistics.
  - Give examples that relate content to participants' prior experience.
- Use color carefully on screens.
- Use graphics to summarize information.
- Provide the opportunity to practice with feedback.
- Measure and improve processes and practices:
  - Measure participants' reactions using a survey after the meeting.
  - Collect and analyze reaction data over time.
  - Interview a sample of participants, and probe to uncover opportunities for improvement.
  - Have leaders debrief with facilitators and buddies, if used, after the meeting
  - Report the results to leaders and facilitators.

Reference

Meeting around the world: The impact of collaboration on business performance. (2006, June). Palo Alto, CA: Frost and Sullivan. Retrieved August 27, 2006, from http://newscenter. verizon.com/kit/collaboration/.

Creativity Techniques for Virtual Teams

Jill Nemiro

Global competition has created a severe need for organizational creativity and innovation. Companies are now expected to get out their creative and innovative efforts, products, or services quickly to potential clients and consumers. Long gone are the days in which a lone scientist or developer worked in a laboratory on creative breakthroughs. Today creative breakthroughs are being performed by teams, with the goal of reducing the time for new ideas and products to reach the marketplace. Teamwork is essential to tap into the best talent to create the highest-quality and fastest response to customer needs. Virtual teams have expanded the ability to connect team members from a single workplace setting to the spanning of the globe.

The ability to be creative is just as important for the members of virtual teams as it was for the lone scientist or developer. Successful virtual teams need members who can be creative by themselves and within the context of their team. This chapter introduces a variety of well-known techniques that individual members of virtual teams and the virtual teams themselves can use to heighten their creativity.

WHAT ARE CREATIVITY TECHNIQUES?

The formal starting point of the scientific study of creativity is often considered to be J. P. Guilford's address to the American Psychological Association in 1950 on creativity. Since then researchers from a variety of disciplines have studied the nature of creativity from a scientific point of view. Others have taken a more pragmatic approach, examining and designing ways to teach creativity with practical creativity techniques, defined as deliberate thinking processes designed to help individuals or teams find ideas and solve problems. Perhaps a useful metaphor for creativity techniques is to view them as tools in a toolbox, in much the same way as one's toolbox for home repairs. The home repair toolbox contains a saw, hammer, wrench, screwdriver, and other useful tools, but it is up to the individual to select the right tool (creativity technique) for the particular situation and task.

Certainly the research on creativity techniques has been around for some time. Three of the best-known creativity techniques are Osborn's brainstorming technique (1963), Altshuller's theory of inventive problem solving (TRIZ; 1996, 1998), and de Bono's lateral thinking (1967). In general, creativity techniques have been classified into two major categories: linear and intuitive approaches (Miller, 1987, 1999). With linear techniques, an individual or team consciously decides to creatively attack a problem using one or more techniques to clarify the problem and generate ideas for solving it. Linear approaches for idea generation provide a structure within which to seek and find alternative solutions. Solutions are arrived at using a logical pattern or sequence of steps. Intuitive techniques assist individuals or teams in achieving an inner state of calmness, out of which unpredictable inspirations or insights may appear. There is little or no sense of a structured path through which a solution emerges, as there is in linear approaches. Rather, solutions spring forth, often leaving an individual feeling surprised as to where the creative thoughts came from. In the pursuit of optimal creativity, both linear and intuitive approaches are necessary. A typical pattern is linear thinking preceding and following intuitive insight (Miller, 1987).

This chapter describes a variety of common creativity techniques using the linear and intuitive categories. Each technique is described: what it is, when is it beneficial to use it, how to use the technique, and tips for how virtual teams might use it.

LINEAR CREATIVITY TECHNIQUES

The portfolio of linear techniques available to teams doing creative work is plentiful and includes such popular tools as attribute listing, morphological analysis, force field analysis, mind mapping, and idea checklists. Each of these tools can be adapted for use by virtual teams.

Attribute Listing

Attribute listing is a technique in which team members examine an existing product or process, break the product or process into parts, identify ways of modifying or improving each part, and then bring these modifications or improvements together to create new forms of products or processes (Crawford, 1954; Morgan, 1993). With attribute listing, one can go beyond what is typical.

When to Use Typically this technique is viewed as useful for improving tangible objects, products, services, or processes. It works best when the emphasis is on looking at each part of a specific object. An examination of the parts one by one can lead to a thorough examination of all possible aspects (or parts) in total.

Although the most common way to use attribute listing is in product development or process improvement, attribute listing can also be useful for more complex problems, issues, or challenges as well. In fact, attribute listing has sometimes been referred to as a "smashing" technique because it assists in smashing fixed or rigid perspectives about ideas, problems, issues, or challenges. By focusing on a specific element of a problem rather than the problem as a whole, it allows one to take for granted the overriding issue or problem and then move to more specific, concrete problems that can be solved. The reduction of larger issues or problems allows individuals to recognize that each general or abstract problem is in essence a combination of several interrelated smaller problems. Each smaller problem can then be reviewed for ideas on how to solve it, and as a result, progress is made in resolving the wider problem.

Procedure To use the technique, first list the attributes of the product, service, process, or problem being examined. A typical attribute listing step-by-step process might involve:

Step 1: Identify the product, service, process, or issue to improve.

Step 2: List the attributes: the parts, properties, qualities, or design elements of the product, service, or issue being examined. For example, attributes of a picture frame might be its rectangular shape, glass covering, wooden frame, opening in the back, and hanging wire (Nemiro, 2004).

Step 3: Select the core attributes that are important, relevant, or interesting (probably best to limit to eight or fewer).

Step 4: Look for ways to improve or modify each attribute. To do this, for each attribute, ask, (1) "How else can this be accomplished?" (2) "How could this be changed?" (3) "What else is similar?" and (4) "What could we copy?" Adopting a nonjudgmental stance is crucial to arrive at original thoughts.

Step 5: Combine one or more of these ideas for improved or modified attributes. For example, the rectangular shape of a picture frame could be changed into the shape of a heart, and the hanging wire could be changed to a suction cup attachment, creating a way to fasten photographs on car dashboards, briefcases, or day planner books.

Perhaps the hardest part of attribute listing is discovering and listing the attributes. This can be aided by the use of another linear creativity technique: idea checklists (see the section in this chapter on idea checklists). For example, each of the following can be explored with any product or problem:

- Physical characteristics
- Emotional impact
- Functional uses or applications
- Resources needed (financial, human, technological)

One problem with using attribute listing is the combinatorial explosion that can occur relatively quickly as the number of attributes and alternatives increases. For example, only five attributes, each of those attributes possessing four alternatives, could lead to over a thousand logically different combinations. Because it is unrealistic to explore all of these possible combinations, it may be more feasible to generate and combine alternatives randomly to stimulate further creative thinking.

Attribute listing can be used for complex problems or challenges as well. To accomplish this, the team lists the main attributes (characteristics, dimensions, parts) of a problem, challenge, or issue. Then they generate ideas to solve each of these attributes as in this example adapted from Harris (2002):

Problem: Poverty

Attributes of the problem: People, crime, lack of food, lack of goods, large families, low self-esteem, welfare, lack of jobs, lack of job skills, lack of education, lack of motivation, poor economic judgment, poor-quality housing.

Examine each attribute for further attributes: Each of the attributes is examined through further attribute analysis. For example, some attributes of poor economic judgment might be buying low-quality items, buying smaller packages at a higher price per ounce, wasteful spending habits, a tendency to spend one's money too quickly, lack of market competition, lack of ability to budget, or tendency to use money for nonfood items that are unnecessary.

Select core attributes: These are the most important and pressing items.

Brainstorm ways to solve core attributes: Generate ideas for how to solve each selected attribute, and combine these ideas in a workable, step-by-step action plan.

Tips for Virtual Teams Attribute listing can be done privately by individual team members; however, the building on ideas that comes from group brainstorming is probably best encouraged when the entire team engages in the technique synchronously or asynchronously. If individuals use this technique, their generated ideas can later be shared with the entire team, perhaps generating a follow-up attribute listing session.

This technique can be accomplished without sophisticated software technology. If feasible, face-to-face meetings with a few resources like a flip chart or whiteboard can be used to perform this technique. However, it is certainly not necessary to get together face-to-face to generate ideas in an attribute listing session. Virtual teams may construct their lists electronically in synchronous computer meetings, using interactive whiteboards and audioconferencing. Asynchronous threaded discussions can be useful in generating ideas for improving different attributes of a product or service. Some idea-generator software programs offer lists of questions or idea triggers, or a team can tailor its own set of questions to provoke new ideas on product attributes.

Morphological Analysis

Morphological analysis was developed by Fritz Zwicky, a Swiss astrophysicist and aerospace scientist based at the California Institute of Technology, in the 1930s as a method for systematically structuring and investigating the total set of relationships contained in multidimensional, nonquantifiable, problem complexes (Zwicky, 1969; Zwicky & Wilson, 1967). Zwicky applied his method to a variety of areas, including the classification of astrophysical objects, the development of jet and rocket propulsion systems, and the legal aspects of space travel and colonization. He founded the Society for Morphological Research and devoted nearly forty years to advancing this technique.

Morphological analysis is basically an extension of the attribute listing procedure and works through two principles of creativity: decomposition (a complex problem is broken down into component variables) and forced association (the identified variables are listed and then randomly and artificially forced together into multiple combinations with the objective of generating new creative possibilities for solving the problem).

When to Use   Morphological analysis can be used for a much broader set of uses than attribute listing. In fact, it can be applied to virtually any problem, challenge, or issue that can be structured dimensionally. In general, the types of problems that tend to be appropriate for this technique are characterized by multidimensionality (possesses several interrelated aspects), uncertainty (something that is nonquantifiable and continuously evolving), and subjectivity (it has no right or wrong solution, only better or worse solutions). When morphological analysis is used to generate new ideas for businesses, it is sometimes referred to as matrix analysis.

An added benefit of morphological analysis is the audit trail of combinations that are examined. This identifying characteristic makes this technique a good choice when it is necessary to document and archive the decisions used to arrive at a solution to a complex problem.

Procedure   According to traditional morphological analysis researchers (Zwicky, 1969), morphological analysis has five steps. These activities could be sequential or iterative and may be adapted at any point:

Step 1: Formulate a concise description of the problem. In describing the problem, perform the following subactivities:

- Identify all issues or relevant aspects that might relate to, be caused by, or cause the problem.

- Define the dimensions (corresponding properties of an issue) that affect the problem.

- Gather the result of these activities into a problem statement. Other idea-generation methods such as brainstorming, followed by voting, may be useful in performing this step.

Step 2: Identify and analyze all relevant and important dimensions for the solution to the problem under investigation. Once a problem has been described:

- Decompose it into the problem's values, which are possible conditions related to dimensions. Each dimension defined in a problem might consist of one or more values (Ritchey, 2003).

- Decompose the values into more specific, detailed aspects, called parameters (Ritchey, 2003).

Step 3: Construct a morphological box (or multidimensional matrix) that contains all potential solutions to the problem. A morphological box is constructed by setting the parameters against each other in an *n*-dimensional space. More specifically, the morphological box consists of a series of morphological fields or cells. Each cell contains one value from each parameter and thus defines a specific state or configuration of the problem under investigation (Ritchey, 2003).

Step 4: Scrutinize and analyze all the solutions listed in the morphological box for those that are possible, practical, or interesting. In this way, the space that contains all the solutions that satisfy one's specified criteria is carved out.

Step 5: Based on the solution space, select optimal and suitable solutions, and apply them through a set of detailed action steps, provided the resources are available.

For business-related applications, the morphological analysis process can be simplified to these steps:

Step 1: Define the problem. Identify the objective of the creative session, defining the problem in a brief, clear statement.

Step 2: Identify attributes. List the things about the situation that can be varied or changed in some way. Select a subset of variables to investigate further.

Step 3: Identify values. For each of the attributes from step 2, list possible values.

Step 4: Combine items. Find a way of combining items from the lists created. If there are only two lists, a matrix may be used. Another way is to combine randomly.

Step 5: Build many creative solutions. Repeatedly combine selections of ideas generated. Do not worry too much at this time if the ideas are not particularly feasible, as they may be developed later or used to trigger other creative possibilities.

Step 6: Evaluate and select ideas to develop into practical solutions to the problem.

Tips for Virtual Teams   Since morphological analysis may take on more of a graphical, structured, and dimensional matrix form than attribute listing, visual outliner programs, shared work spaces for drawing and sketching such as interactive whiteboards, and specifically designed morphological analysis software programs may be useful.

Force Field Analysis

Force field analysis is a simple but powerful technique for building an understanding of the forces that may drive and resist a proposed change. This technique was developed by social psychologist Kurt Lewin to analyze what he termed *driving* and *restraining* forces influencing situations. Driving forces push for and initiate change in a particular direction. Restraining forces act to restrain or decrease the driving forces. In order for any change to be successful, the driving forces must exceed the restraining forces. Equilibrium or balance is then achieved when the sum of the driving forces once again equals the sum of the restraining forces. Figure 22.1 graphically illustrates the logic underlying force field analysis. The longer the line is, the stronger the force. Arrows pointing toward the left are restraining forces, indicating no need for change. Arrows pointing toward the right are driving forces, indicating change is needed. In Figure 22.1, the driving forces are stronger than the restraining forces, indicating a need for change.

When to Use   In addition to its intended purpose of analyzing driving and restraining forces in a proposed change situation, force field analysis can also be used to:

• List pros and cons.

• List actions and reactions.

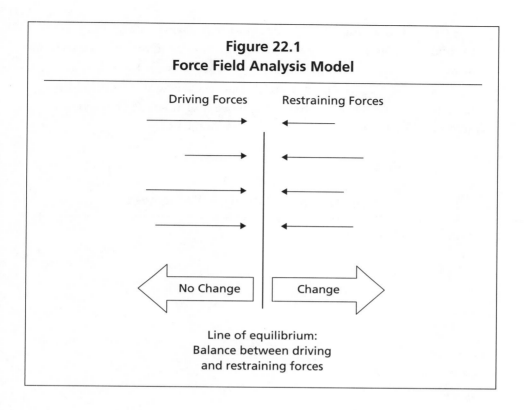

Figure 22.1
Force Field Analysis Model

Driving Forces   Restraining Forces

No Change   Change

Line of equilibrium:
Balance between driving
and restraining forces

- List strengths and weaknesses.

- Compare ideal situations and reality.

- Compare perceptions of opposing parties in negotiating situations.

- List "what we know" and "what we don't know."

Procedure   The typical sequence of steps involved in force field analysis follows:

Step 1. Describe the issue, problem, plan, or proposed change. Draft a brief, objective statement of the problem or challenge the team is facing and put that description in the middle of the worksheet. (See Exhibit 22.1 for a sample worksheet.)

Step 2: List all positive forces for change in one column and all restraining forces against change in another column. Assign a score to each force (for example, 1 = weak to 5 = strong).

Step 3: Review the completed worksheet to decide whether change is viable. If the total of rating scores for driving forces is larger than the total for restraining forces, change is not only feasible but needed to move toward equilibrium and balance. To achieve this indication of needed change, a team could potentially strengthen a listed positive force, weaken or minimize a listed negative force, or add a potentially new positive force to the list.

Exhibit 22.1
Sample Force Field Analysis Worksheet

Problem/Challenge Statement:

Driving/ Positive Forces			Restraining/ Negative Forces		
Force	Score	Action to Increase Strength	Force	Score	Action to Weaken/ Minimize

---

Tips for Virtual Teams One way to begin the force field analysis is to have team members individually create statements describing driving and restraining forces. In this way, all perceptions of the situation can emerge before the team discussion. Individual statements can be posted to a shared database, put into a shared file, or added to a private section of the team's intranet Web page. The team can then schedule a face-to-face meeting or synchronous computer meeting (with access to shared applications such as interactive whiteboards, word processing, and outliner programs) to process the individually created statements and form a joint description of the driving and restraining forces. Adding an audio link (through audioconferencing or desktop audio) may also be useful. From this newly constructed team statement, members can brainstorm actions to reduce restraining forces and increase driving forces toward an ideal change.

Mind Mapping

The credit for originating and developing the mind map as a formal creativity technique is usually given to Tony Buzan, a British brain researcher who in the 1970s developed the mind map as an effective method for note taking and idea generation by association. The rationale underlying a mind map is that the human brain is different from a computer. Memory is naturally associative, not linear, so any idea has potentially numerous links in the mind, attaching it to other ideas and concepts. Mind maps allow these associations and links to be generated and illustrated. They use key words and images that are arranged according to importance and organized in a nonlinear graphical manner into groupings or branches.

Mind maps are useful when there is a central topic, such as a product, market, technology, or process, to build on. The overall picture of a particular problem or challenge is illustrated, as well as the details that make it up. The mind map shows what is known about a particular topic and identifies any critical gaps. When thoughts and perceptions are presented in a graphical form and images, color, and pictures are used, an overview emerges, and new connections can be made visible.

When to Use   Mind maps have a variety of applications in business, educational, and personal situations as aids in problem solving, decision making, and learning. They are most often used for these purposes:

- *Encourage nonlinear, creative thinking.* Mind maps may free individuals or team members from traditional linear thinking and allow new ideas to emerge more readily. They are also a useful way to organize ideas that surface during a brainstorming session.

- *Assist in problem solving.* Mind maps may help individuals or teams to see all the relevant issues in a particular problem and how these issues interrelate. They also offer all stakeholders in a specific problem situation a way to quickly get an overview of all aspects of the situation (not just their own) and the relative importance of each aspect.

- *Aid in project and task management.* All relevant information can be recorded in one place and organized so that team members can view both the entire project work flow and the tasks and activities of the project in one location.

- *Map out strategic planning efforts.* Top management may use this technique to graphically display the overall vision and plan of a particular change initiative and the stages of that initiative as well.

- *Draft out presentations or reports.* Preparing a mind map around the topic and flow of a presentation or report may assist individuals in achieving a coherent organization of the ideas delivered.

- *Organize information for better access and recall.* Mind maps help organize information being delivered into a form that the brain easily assimilates and remembers. They can be used for taking notes on lectures, professional presentations, meeting minutes, interviews, telephone conversations, or books and articles, among others. Whenever information is being retrieved from memory, mind maps allow ideas to be quickly noted as they occur and in an organized manner. They serve as quick and efficient means of review and ensure a high level of recall.

Procedure The mind-mapping procedure begins with writing a central theme and then depicting thoughts and associations, represented by key words, as branches growing in all directions from the central theme. Associations generated are potentially limitless because each association may trigger another. A mind map can reach out in any direction and catch thoughts from any angle. After thoughts and associations are mapped out, users can search for unifying patterns and connections, potentially offering a new idea or creative solution to a problem. Moving and synthesizing concepts into new clusters often provokes new ideas. A mind map may also indicate areas where new information needs to be collected. Through the creation of a mind map, one is able to move from the general (central theme) to the specific (different thoughts and associations), and back again (creative connections and new ideas).

Five steps (and associated guidelines for each step) for using the technique of mind mapping follow (adapted from Buzan, 1991; Buzan & Buzan, 1996; Michalko, 1998; Nemiro, 2004):

Step 1: Start from the center, and work out. The process of mind mapping starts in the center of the page with the main idea (word or image) and works outward in all directions, producing a growing and organized structure composed of key words and images. Put a word or short phase that describes the core of the problem, issue, or challenge on a large sheet of paper (or electronic whiteboard), and draw a circle around it.

Step 2: Record main ideas by writing key words associated with the central theme. Use single, essential words or simple, meaningful phrases or symbols to convey associations around a central theme. Excess or irrelevant words clutter the display. Capture all relevant words or phrases that come to mind (without judgment at this point). Allow ideas to expand outward into branches and subbranches.

Step 3: Look for relationships and cross-linkages between the key words, and graphically represent those connections. Through the links, relationships will emerge that will assist in gathering and later organizing the data into clusters. In this step, connect relationships with lines emanating out from the center. Colors, pictures, symbols, arrows, and other visual aids can be used to highlight important thoughts and illustrate relationships between the ideas generated on the mind map.

Step 4: Cluster words, and organize the clusters into themes. This step moves into an evaluator role of examining associations and noting missing information or areas where alternative or additional ideas are needed.

Step 5: Revise, refine, and elaborate continually on the mind map to move closer to the ultimate answers.

Figure 22.2 presents an example of a mind map (outlining the uses, benefits, and procedures of the mind mapping technique). This mind map was generated through Axon Idea Processor, a creativity software program that assists in graphically representing mind maps.

Figure 22.3 presents another mind map (also generated through Axon Idea Processor). This more powerful mind map shows the degree of complex relationships that can be outlined through creativity software programs. The intent of this map is to "show how the brain works and it illustrates the use of Feedback (upwards) and Feedforward (downwards) loops. In this diagram, an ellipse represents a chunk of gray matter, and its vertical position denotes the abstraction level. Links represent axon (brain) connections" (C. Bok, personal communication, June 6, 2007). However, it is not necessary to use sophisticated technology to create a mind map. Mind maps can be simply produced by hand as well.

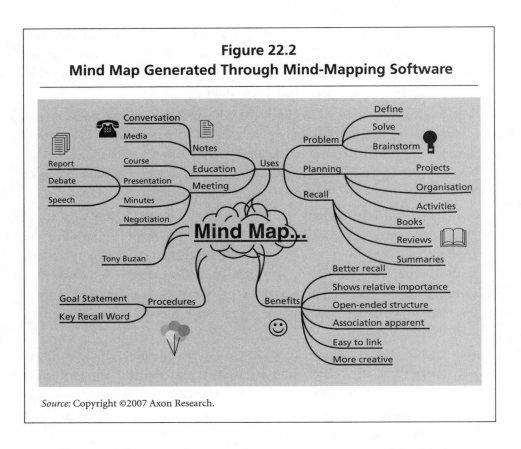

Figure 22.2
Mind Map Generated Through Mind-Mapping Software

Source: Copyright ©2007 Axon Research.

Tips for Virtual Teams   Mind maps can be done individually or by the entire team. All team members may first create their own mind maps and then combine efforts, or work collaboratively as a team to construct a map. Mind maps are easily constructed in a face-to-face meeting with relatively few resources (flip chart, whiteboard). Virtual teams may also construct mind maps electronically using electronic and interactive whiteboards or creativity software programs designed specifically to facilitate mind mapping.

Idea Checklists

Type into any search engine, "What is an idea checklist?" and the result will be a variety of checklists from a variety of disciplines ranging from speech and science to party planning. Checklists have been created to help individuals and teams generate new ways of thinking about an existing product, process, service, or situation.

Figure 22.3

Complex Mind Map Generated Through Mind-Mapping Software

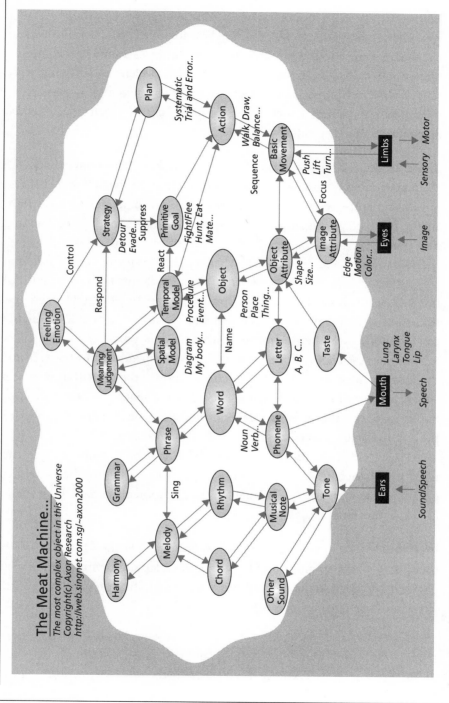

The Meat Machine...
The most complex object in this Universe
Copyright(c) Axon Research
http://lweb.singnet.com.sg/~axon2000

The best-known checklist is Osborn's "73 Idea Spurring Questions" (1963), which contains a series of questions prodding how to put an object to another use; modify, magnify, or minify elements in a product; rearrange the components or sequence in a product or process; or combine and blend other things with a current product or process. By looking at a current product or service and challenging oneself with the series of questions listed in the "checklist," all kinds of possibilities for revised and new products are generated.

When to Use   A variety of traditional idea checklists have been developed. Two of the more commonly used ones are SCAMPER and the five W's and H. These types of idea checklists are useful when the purpose is to come up with ideas for ways to change an existing product, process, or service in order to modify or create an entirely new product, process, or service. The series of questions contained in these idea checklists can be used directly or as starting points for further lateral thinking.

Traditional idea checklists are set up for participants to examine a list of components or attributes for a product one at a time. In situations where the items under examination are interdependent (for example, stages in a production process or service, an administrative procedure, or a problem-solving method), it may not be feasible to alter individual items independent of others. In this case, the idea checklist needs to be adapted to consider the predetermined sequence. An adaptation of the traditional idea checklist, a sequential-attributes matrix, is useful for teams that need to deal with more complex issues or processes. (The procedure for this checklist is described in the next section.)

Although idea checklists are usually thought to be appropriate for generating ideas for physical objects or technical problems, some have been developed to generate new ideas to solve human relations problems as well. One such tool is called dimensional analysis.

Procedure   The procedures for two traditional idea checklists, SCAMPER and the five W's and H, and two idea checklists adapted for more interdependent, complex, or interpersonal situations (sequential-attributes matrix and dimensional analysis) are outlined below:

• *SCAMPER.* The questions in this checklist were taken from Osborn's initial seventy-three idea-spurring questions, and rearranged by Bob Eberle (1996) into the mnemonic of SCAMPER. Each letter in the word SCAMPER stands for a series of changes to consider in the process of revising, adapting, or modifying a product in some fashion. To begin the process, decide on a subject, topic, problem, or challenge the team wants to think about creatively. Then ask and answer the series of questions and see what new ideas and thoughts emerge:

S	Substitute. What or who else can be used instead? Other ingredient? Other process? Other place? Other approach? Other tone of voice?
C	Combine. How about a blend, an alloy, an assortment, an ensemble? Combine units? Combine purposes? Combine appeals? Combine ideas?
A	Adapt. Is there anything else like this? What other idea does this suggest? Does the past offer something parallel or comparable?
M	Modify. New twist or angle? Change meaning, color, motion, sound, odor, form, shape? Other changes? **Magnify?** Can anything be added? More time? Greater frequency? Stronger? Higher? Longer? Thicker? Extra value? Another ingredient? Can it be duplicated? Multiplied? Exaggerated? **Minify?** Can anything be taken away? What can be made smaller? Condensed? Lowered? Shortened? Made lighter? Made slower? Broken up?
P	Put to other uses. New ways to use as is? Other uses if modified?
E	Eliminate. What to subtract? Omit? Streamline? Split up? What could be left unsaid?
R	Reverse. How about opposites? Turn it backward? Turn it upside down? Reverse roles? Change positions or viewpoints? Transpose positive and negative? **Rearrange?** Interchange or swap components? Alter the pattern? Other layout? Other sequence? Transpose cause and effect? Change pace? Change schedule?

• *Five W's and H.* Finding a checklist to stimulate creative thinking can be as easy as opening up the dictionary for several basic question-generating prompts provided in words used daily: Who? Why? What? Where? When? The responses to the questions in the checklist, however, are usually facts rather than actions or problems. For example, the answer to, "Who is responsible for writing this chapter?" could be "Jill Nemiro." Extending this answer into a problem-solving context requires moving to another level—for example, "Okay, if Jill Nemiro is responsible for writing this chapter, what resources might she need to make it easier for her to do so?" This extension of the answers that may be generated from the Five W's and H is the part that may generate some creative new ways of doing things, new action plans, or ideas for implementation.

• *Dimensional analysis.* This is an extension of the five W's and H technique. It takes the words *what, where, when,* and *how* and crafts a set of questions to look at a series of five dimensions to a problem: substantive (What?), spatial (Where?), temporal (When?), quantitative (How much?), and qualitative (How serious?). This technique is most useful as an aid for initial exploration of a problem or evaluating options, particularly those associated with human relations rather than of a technical nature. The five dimensions and set of related idea checklist questions follow (http://www.mycoted.com/Dimensional_Analysis):

Substantive Dimension (What?)

• *Commission/omission?* Doing something wrong or failing to do something?

• *Attitude/deed?* Is it necessary to change attitudes or practices?

• *Ends/means?* Is the irritant we see the actual problem or merely a symptom of it?

• *Active/passive?* Active threat or source of irritation?

• *Visible/invisible?* Is the problem masked (for example, are there covert human relations issues)?

Spatial Dimension (Where?)

• *Local/distant?* Is it merely local, or are there some remote influences?

• *Particular locations within a location?* Recognize the exact area concerned.

• *Isolated/widespread?* Is the problem isolated or linked to several other problem areas?

Temporal (When?)

• *Long-standing/recent?* Which parts are new and which are old?

• *Present/impending?* Is the problem happening or looks as though it may happen?

• *Constant/ebb and flow?* Is the problem always there, irregular, or cyclical?

Quantitative (How much?)

- *Singular/multiple?* Is there a single cause, or are there many?
- *Many/few people?* How many people are affected by the problem?
- *General/specific?* Is the problem applicable to a broad category or specific subarea?
- *Simple/complex?* Are there several elements to the problem with complex interactions?
- *Too much/too little?* Appears as a shortage or surplus?

Qualitative (How serious?)

- *Philosophical/surface?* Is it an issue with deep values or surface practicalities?
- *Survival/enrichment?* Is it a live-or-die issue or one to do with managing quality?
- *Primary/secondary?* What priority does the issue have?
- *What values are being violated?*
- *To what degree are they being violated?* Qualifies the previous answer.
- *Proper/improper values?* Not all values should be honored.
- *Sequential-attributes matrix.* The sequential-attributes matrix (http://www.mycoted.com/Sequential-Attributes_Matrix) applies some of the earlier discussed product modification checklists (Osborn's seventy-three idea-spurring questions, SCAMPER) to items that consist of a sequentially connected element (for instance, a step-by-step process or procedure). It is also useful for physically connected sequences of components. Table 22.1 provides an application of this type of idea checklist to a set of sequentially connected items (things that occur in a predetermined sequence): the making of a peanut butter and jelly sandwich.

To use this technique, create a two-dimensional table as in Table 22.1 and a checklist of generic idea checklist questions or prompts listed across the top. Review each stage in turn, applying the checklist, and think about how it might be adapted, keeping in mind that each stage is dependent on its neighboring elements. Then review the sequence in its entirety and see if it can be altered or changed.

Table 22.1
Example of a Sequential-Attributes Matrix

Stages in Preparing a Peanut Butter and Jelly Sandwich	Idea Checklist Prompts			
	Eliminate	Substitute	Combine	Break Apart
Go to grocery store and purchase food	X (online shopping)			
Put groceries away				
Take out slices of bread				
Take out peanut butter and jelly				
Spread peanut butter on bread			X (product with peanut butter and jelly together)	
Spread jelly on bread			X (product with peanut butter and jelly together)	
Put sandwich together				
Cut in half	X	X (cut in another shape: cookie-cutter heart)		
Put in plastic bag	X (put holder in lunch box)		X	
Put in lunch box	X (create backpack with built-in lunchbox inside)		X	
Put lunch box in child's backpack			X	

Tips for Virtual Teams   Several software programs designed to help individuals and teams generate and process creative ideas have features offering built-in lists to prod team members into new insights. These programs include numerous original prompts or prods to spark ideas and specialized questions to help problem solvers explore alternative solutions.

Brainstorming

Brainstorming is one of the best-known techniques for stimulating creativity and generating ideas, particularly useful for groups. The birth of brainstorming is typically credited to Alex Osborn, a partner in a New York advertising agency, who formalized a set of ground rules for the practice of brainstorming. Osborn (1948, 1963) defined brainstorming as a technique for groups to discover solutions to specific problems by gathering together spontaneously generated ideas by the group members.

Brainstorming is a powerful team technique for creating new ideas, solving problems, and motivating and developing teams. It motivates because it involves team members in larger organizational and management issues and gets a team working together.

When to Use   In general, brainstorming is useful for creating a cross-fertilization of ideas when new ideas are required and there is a need to generate a large list of possibilities. It is also useful for teams working to solve particularly inflexible problems where answers cannot be logically deduced and intense assessment or lateral thinking is needed. Brainstorming is also appropriate when the information about a problem is distributed across several individuals, and it is necessary to gather the information in one place. Finally, brainstorming can be used as a team-building technique: through the creative synergy generated, it can be useful for creating a connection or bond among team members.

Specific uses for brainstorming in business include:

- To assist with developing ideas for new products
- To improve existing products or processes
- To solve marketing, advertising, or personnel problems
- To improve work processes, managerial methods, and company structure and policy

Although brainstorming is a creativity technique in itself, it is also useful in combination with many other creativity techniques such as brainstorming within an idea checklist session and brainstorming while creating a mind map. Brainstorming is not a random activity. It needs to be structured and follow several key rules.

Procedure   In brainstorming, a problem or challenge is defined in neutral terms. Participants then spontaneously share ideas for solving the problem. These ideas are offered under specific conditions. Osborn (1963) set forth these guidelines for a brainstorming session:

- *Postpone criticism of ideas.* Criticism and harsh evaluation will interfere with flexible idea generation. Postponing criticism or judgment of the ideas generated in a brainstorming session encourages a creative atmosphere where new ideas are reinforced rather than punished.

- *Aim for large quantities of ideas.* Creative ideas occur infrequently. The notion underlying brainstorming is that the more ideas that are generated, the higher the probability is that one of the ideas generated will be appropriate and creative. Typically ideas produced later in a brainstorming session (after the easy, quick, automatic or routine responses are out of the way) are more imaginative. The more ideas that are generated, the more likely it is that a team will arrive at the potentially best idea leading to a solution.

- *Build on one another's ideas.* To lengthen the list of ideas, brainstorming participants are encouraged to build on, embellish, and enrich the other ideas generated, spontaneously hitchhiking on the ideas of others.

- *Encourage wild and exaggerated ideas.* Participants are more likely to find a creative and workable idea by being wild first and taming it down rather than criticizing, evaluating, and editing in the process. In a typical brainstorming session, all ideas are accepted; the wilder the ideas, the better. However, most people are not used to pushing for wild ideas. The leader or facilitator of a brainstorming session can assist by modeling how to generate wild ideas or can provide some preliminary practice or warm-up activities to loosen the team up first. When it appears that all ideas have been generated, participants should push for another round of idea generation, allowing themselves to be even more outrageous.

Once participants understand the ground rules, a brainstorming session can begin. It typically has the following steps:

Step 1: Form a brainstorming group with between four and fifteen participants. The optimal size for a brainstorming group is five to seven participants.

Step 2: Select an individual to coordinate and facilitate the brainstorming session. The facilitator guides and monitors the process, making sure all the ground rules are followed.

Step 3: Select a method (and perhaps assign a particular individual to be responsible to do this) to record the ideas generated. Ideas can be recorded on flip charts, sticky notes, overhead projector transparencies, blackboards, whiteboards and electronic whiteboards, or pads of paper. For electronic brainstorming, the computer may function as the memory bank for the ideas generated.

Step 4: Select participants who have a vested interest in solving the problem and specialized knowledge necessary to solve it.

Step 5: Select an appropriate location for the session (for example, a quiet meeting room with a comfortable and informal seating arrangement). Gather other necessary resources as well.

Step 6: To begin the session, the facilitator reviews the ground rules and the purpose and topic for the brainstorming session.

Step 7: During the body of the brainstorming session, facilitators typically take participants through four distinct stages:

1. *Stating the problem:* The facilitator states the problem in neutral terms, so participants begin the brainstorming session with as few preconceived biases with regard to the problem as possible.

2. *Restating the problem:* The facilitator encourages participants to restate the problem in different words. Encouraging restatements helps the team see different perspectives on the problem. The team then selects one or more of the restatements to brainstorm on.

3. *Brainstorming:* The facilitator calls for a free flow of ideas around the problem issue. There may be periods of rapid idea generation and then slow, awkward times when no ideas are being created. During the slow

time, the group should return to the ideas that have been generated and build on them. When sufficient ideas have been generated, the team may benefit from taking a break before moving on to the evaluation stage.

4. *Evaluating generated ideas:* The final list of ideas is subjected to critical judgment and evaluation. A process of elimination is used to weed out the least promising ideas progressively, until the team selects the ideas most likely to solve the problem. Ideas are then developed into specific action plans for implementation.

Tips for Virtual Teams   Traditional brainstorming can be greatly enhanced by using modern technology and software. There are a variety of options for performing electronic brainstorming. Many software programs have been designed to facilitate brainstorming electronically. For example, GroupSystems, an electronic meeting system software package, offers several features (Electronic Brainstorming, Topic Commenter, and Group Outliner) to aid dispersed team members in idea generation.

Other communication tools available to virtual teams, such as videoconferencing, audioconferencing, synchronous computer meetings with video and audio links, and interactive whiteboards, can also be used in electronic brainstorming. The tools are, for the most part, supportive of synchronous brainstorming sessions. Virtual teams may also find asynchronous threaded discussion boards to be valuable tools in allowing for multiple ideas to be generated in parallel sequences.

INTUITIVE TECHNIQUES

Whereas linear techniques structure information and point out where to look for new ideas, intuitive techniques use our ability to perceive whole solutions in sudden leaps of logic. Intuition is more fluent in images, sounds, and symbols than in words. The assumption behind using intuitive approaches is that at some level, we already know the answer. By developing a sense of inner calmness, an individual can access his or her intuition, which makes use of images, sounds, and symbols rather than words. Although intuitive techniques are often viewed skeptically in business settings, intuition is not unreal or untrustworthy. It uses information and data that have been stored away by our linear thought processes. Here we look at four commonly used intuitive techniques: imagery, analogical thinking, drawing, and meditation.

Imagery

Imagery uses symbols, scenes, or images as entry into creative thought and insight. It is defined as "using all the senses to recreate or create an experience in the mind" (Vealey & Walter, 1993, p. 201). Images can be objects, events, or scenes. They can be short-lived or long-lasting and can occur spontaneously or be deliberately generated and manipulated. By focusing on an image, such as a scene from nature or the sound of wind, the solution to a problem may emerge because through this intense focus, the body and mind relax and one's sense of inner calmness emerges.

When to Use   Imagery is useful for solving complex problems or issues where no clear-cut answer previously exists. It has also been used as a stress management and relaxation technique to lead to higher levels of performance under stress or in situations involving high levels of risk. Imagery has been found to have a motivational function as well (Paivio, 1985). It is best used when combined with meditation to relax one's mind and body and create the appropriate condition for the free flow of images.

Procedure   In practicing imagery, participants consider the whole situation and generate images to look for answers. The process can be as short or long as needed; however, participants need to reach the appropriate level of relaxation before images that are deeper and more meaningful than day-to-day random thoughts emerge. Although the process of imagery and the actual images used or generated can be varied, some guidelines for using imagery follow (adapted from Davis, 1999; Michalko, 1998; Miller, 1987, 1997; Nemiro, 2004):

Step 1: Select a problem or challenge that has no clear-cut answer.

Step 2: Relax and free the mind and body through focused breathing, meditation, and listening to soothing sounds or music. Strive to reach a state of relaxation, and block out distracting internal thoughts. Then focus your internal attention on the problem or challenge.

Step 3: Call forth images that symbolically represent the problem or challenge or some aspect of it. Accept whatever images emerge; do not censor or edit some out.

Step 4: Write down or draw the images that come to mind. In describing the images, include all the human senses—hearing, smell, taste, touch, vision, heat, pain, balance, and body awareness—and phrase the descriptions in the present tense (Wenger, 1979).

Step 5: Examine various aspects or qualities of images for how they relate to the problem or challenge under investigation (rather than getting caught up into the literal meaning of the images evoked). Look for analogies or relationships between the images generated and the problem or challenge.

Not all images are positive; in fact, there are times when you will want to stop or defuse negative, compulsive, unexpected, or undesirable images. Useful strategies to deal with unwanted and negative images include switching attention to something more mundane, metaphorically shouting out "stop" to the images, or reversing the images by seeing the positive in the negative.

Tips for Virtual Teams   Imagery is a technique that is best reserved for individual work that is later shared with the rest of the team through synchronous videoconferencing, audioconferencing, or computer conferencing. Threaded discussion boards can be another way to discuss and share images generated. Imagery can also be done by the entire team together. Although it can be performed without any technology, many software programs have been created to assist those participating in an imagery session. Programs that display random images or words, quotations, or affirmations are useful for triggering images and resulting ideas. Virtual meditation tools may also be helpful in practicing imagery.

Analogical Thinking

Analogical thinking involves taking ideas from one context and applying them in a new context. Perhaps 80 percent of creative ideas are grounded in some type of analogical thinking, and examples can be found in every field of human creativity. For example, analogical thinking has been the seed to many new products. The now widely used fastener product Velcro was inspired by the cocklebur, a flowering plant whose stiff, hooked spines stick to fur and clothing and are difficult to remove. Pringles Potato Chips emerged from an analogy of wet leaves, which can be stacked one on top of the other without being damaged.

One powerful example of the use of analogical thinking is Gareth Morgan's book, *Images of Organization* (1997). Morgan compares an organization to a variety of other things: a machine, a natural organism, a human brain, a culture, a political system, a "psychic" prison, a process of flux and transformation, and finally an instrument of domination. Through each metaphor, Morgan helps readers better understand the processes and characteristics of organizations that undermine or enhance their own effectiveness.

When to Use   Analogies are useful for understanding complex phenomena. An analogy works best when the concept being taught is new and hard to grasp. Teachers regularly use analogies as instructional mechanisms in math, science, and language arts to teach new concepts and procedures (Richland, Holyoak, & Stigler, 2004). Analogies help to familiarize participants with concepts that are abstract and outside their previous experience. Using analogies results in conceptual understanding by enabling participants to compare something familiar to something unfamiliar. For example, a teacher might use the analogy of a hamburger to teach the concept of paragraph structure. The top bun is like the topic sentence, the meat and other ingredients are like the descriptive sentences, and the bottom bun is like the closing sentence. A hamburger, like a paragraph, does not taste right and is not complete without all these elements.

Procedure   Although analogous connections may appear to emerge quite spontaneously, this type of technique involves the conscious use of forced analogies and a series of probing questions. To practice analogical thinking, follow this series of steps:

Step 1: Identify the problematic situation or concept for which further understanding or insight is needed. Phrase that problem or concept into a core verb phrase starting with "how to." In the example of teaching paragraph structure, the phrase might be "how to construct a paragraph."

Step 2: For each verb phrase, generate a list of items that is similar in some way (people, situations, objects, processes, actions, places, and so on). So perhaps "how to construct a paragraph" is like baking a cake, building a pyramid, or making a hamburger.

Step 3: Pick one of the generated analogies that is most interesting. Preferably the verb phrase and the analogy are from different domains. For example, constructing a paragraph is from the domain of writing, and making a hamburger sandwich is from the domain of eating.

Step 4: Force the relationship between the verb phrase and the analogy. Describe how the analogy might be relevant to the problematic situation or concept. Does the analogy have features that can be applied directly? Does the comparison suggest other ways of looking at the problem?

Analogical thinking can be augmented by using different types of analogies. William J. J. Gordon developed the synectics problem-solving method, which has four types of analogies: direct analogy, personal analogy, fantasy analogy, and symbolic analogy (Gordon, 1961; Gordon & Poze, 1972, 1980).

A *direct analogy* may be constructed when an individual thinks of ways related problems have been solved. Then a comparison is made to see if how a problem was solved in one setting can assist in solving a related problem in another setting.

With a *personal analogy,* an individual can achieve new perspectives on a problem by imaginatively becoming part of the problem. He or she identifies with an object or process in order to get a new perspective on the problem. Imagining oneself to be an object or process in the problem may stimulate an insider view of the situation and thus inspire some new ideas and insights about the problem. Here, the participant becomes a component of the problematic situation.

With the *fantasy analogy* technique, an individual thinks of fantastic, far-fetched, and ideal solutions. Out of these fantasies, creative yet often practical ideas emerge. This involves thinking of what one ideally wants and then crafting out ideas for how to reach those goals. Ideas are generated without considering the real-world plausibility of those ideas (that can be later). In sum, the process involves capturing the images that come to mind if one were to solve the problem or challenge in one's wildest fantasy world.

The strategy behind a *symbolic analogy* is the creation of two-word phrases that seem self-contradictory but could relate to a particular problem and stimulate ideas. For example, to come up with an affordable vacation plan, one might use the phrase "cheap luxury" to come up with inexpensive but fun ways to pamper oneself.

Tips for Virtual Teams   Analogical thinking can be done individually or in a team session. In either case, it is sometimes helpful to construct some questions that may prod individuals into making an analogical connection. These questions can be created by the team and posted on its intranet Web page, or prepackaged sets of stimulator questions can be found in idea checklist software programs.

Analogies can also be generated with the use of imagery, choosing random objects, cards, or images and forcing relationships between them and the problematic situation. Archiving the analogies created in shared files or databases or in threaded discussion boards may be useful to stimulate analogical thinking in later sessions.

Drawing

In the technique of drawing, the basic idea is to draw a sketch of one's understanding of a particular problem and how it might be solved. The drawings may be symbolic, abstract, or realistic. Drawings assist in bringing out creativity and encouraging individuals to develop new insights and dialogue about problems.

The underlying philosophy of the drawing technique is that much of creative expression is birthed in the unconscious mind. To use this creative expression in everyday life, it is necessary to dip into one's unconscious at will. Drawing allows the unconscious to emerge in symbolic expression. Because intuition may emerge better out of images and symbols rather than words, drawing is an effective way to pull out intuitive creativity. Freehand expressive drawing often liberates spontaneous thoughts that cannot yet be put into words. Rapid response to an idea with an immediate sketch creates momentum, preventing any critical thought processes to intervene.

When to Use   When traditional, linear methods of creative thinking yield little insight on a problem or challenge, intuitive techniques such as drawing may be used to tap into meanings that are not consciously realized yet but feel right. In addition, drawing can be used for more specific applications. For example, it has been used to generate evocative themes and purposes for team meetings. It can be used to create pictorial outlines of action plans. For example, I was facing difficulty getting my two daughters ready for school in a timely manner. An evening of generating drawings to solve the problem produced a visual step-by-step aid that outlined the procedure for getting ready for school, which culminated with a "treat surprise" bag on the way out the door if the girls were ready to leave by 7:50 A.M. (Both daughters have been on time to school every day this year.)

Drawing can also be used as a conflict resolution strategy. Putting one's side of a conflict situation into images rather than words may make it easier to describe concerns to others. Similarly, one may be able to view the conflicting side with more compassion and understanding through expressed images.

Drawing has also been useful in product name generation. Many powerful product names are rooted in metaphors that evoke various emotions and images associated with the product. In sum, drawing can be used for a myriad of applications, from the examination of a complex issue (like creating a company or team vision statement) to the simpler task of setting a theme for weekly team meetings.

Procedure   Some may be intimidated by this technique, feeling they do not have artistic ability. But there are no technical skill requirements to use the drawing technique effectively to generate creative thinking. Stick figure drawings or amateur renderings are just fine. In fact, the more "poorly" one draws, the more metaphorical and less realistic the drawing becomes. The goal is not to produce an objective pictorial description of the actual situation. On the contrary, one is encouraged to be entirely subjective.

Here is a general procedure for using drawing to evoke personal insights about a problematic situation.

Step 1: Set aside some quiet time in a relaxing environment to contemplate the problem, issue, or challenge you are facing.

Step 2: Look for symbols, scenes, or images representing the current situation, and draw a picture that represents it. Allow the images to flow in no set direction, as if the images were directing you to how they want to be seen. As with brainstorming, defer judgment at this time. Use whatever images come to mind to describe the situation.

Step 3: Search for symbols, scenes, or images representing the ideal state (what you would like to happen). Draw a picture that represents this ideal—what you feel the future holds or what you would like to see. Use whatever images come to mind to describe your future or ideal situation.

Step 4: Evaluate and examine the two sets of drawings for what you have learned about the current and ideal reality. You can do this evaluation privately or with someone else. When working with others, show them the picture you have created, tell them about it, let them ask questions, and have them share what they find striking. Work jointly to dislodge and examine beliefs, expectations, feelings, judgments, anxieties, reactions, and so on.

Step 5: Consider what actions might be needed to move in the direction of making that second drawing more of a reality in the future. What ideas emerge as action plans for change?

In creating drawings, sometimes you may need initial points of departure to begin. These can be words or images that have previously been associated with the problem, issue or challenge. For example, to assist two team members in resolving a conflict about the joint use of common resources, consider using the initial point-of-departure words *fun sharing* to get both individuals to generate drawings on how to resolve the conflict.

Drawing may be combined with brainstorming, a technique called *visual brainstorming*. The goal of visual brainstorming is for a team to generate as many sketches as it can on a specific problem. The team begins with individual members privately producing their own sketches and then coming together to share the sketches. With numerous idea sketches now pooled together, the team examines them to generate ideas for even more idea sketches (for example, rotate the sketches, place images on top of other images, cover portions of the images, and so on to inspire further idea sketches). Next, compare and cluster similar idea sketches. Throughout the visual brainstorming session, all ideas are recorded (initial, continuing, and final ideas that emerge through this clustering process).

Tips for Virtual Teams The drawing technique can be used by individual team members with graphic functions in word processing programs or by using specific drawing and graphic programs. For an interactive session, where team members construct drawings jointly, interactive whiteboards and drawing programs that link team members are useful (such as SMART Board). All team members can see what is being drawn and can add to it as well. In addition, many groupware software packages have electronic whiteboard features. During or after the construction of the drawings, the team members discuss and record insights. Combining the use of interactive whiteboards with video and audio links in synchronous computer meetings can assist in processing the drawings and sharing results.

Meditation

Meditation has been described as the process of bringing one's attention inward, allowing one's mind to "settle into stillness" (McLaughlin, 2005). In the process, the meditating person withdraws attention from the external and periphery of consciousness to his or her "center." The goal is to still or quiet one's mind, emotions, thoughts, and body. From the internal quietness achieved through meditation, the mind becomes open to perceive responses to questions that may otherwise be puzzling. From this stillness comes an inner peace and inspiration. Meditation allows one to access original ideas that occur in the "space between our thoughts" (Miller, 1999, p. 80).

Many people mistakenly believe that meditation is a losing of awareness. On the contrary, it involves a heightening (not a loss) of awareness, which is useful for tapping into the inner source of creativity. Meditation reduces anxiety and alleviates stress and tension, all of which inhibit creative thinking. Scientific research has indicated that people who practice meditation are able to achieve a high degree of body relaxation, mental calmness, and deeper levels of insight into themselves and their surrounding situations (Walker, 1975).

When to Use Meditation is useful to gain insight into a problem, issue, or challenge when one feels stuck or when the problem or issue is accompanied by such negative emotions as tension, worry, and anxiety. It can help to alleviate these negative feelings and assist in viewing a situation from a new perspective. Meditation helps participants in problematic situations to develop a sense of detachment from the emotional reactions to these situations through what is called the stance of the observer. Most important, meditation strengthens one's alignment and assists in helping one discover one's purpose or meaning in life. As a result, decisions may be made more easily, weighed against this new insight of self-purpose.

Procedure There are many ways to practice meditation. Here is a general procedure (adapted from McLaughlin, 2005; Nemiro, 2004; Walker, 1975):

Step 1: Set aside a period of time (some suggest twenty to thirty minutes is appropriate) in a comfortable, quiet place free from distractions. As practice improves the experience of meditation, ten minutes once or twice a day is more effective than an hour every once in awhile because it creates a regular habit pattern and rhythm.

Step 2: Sit on the floor in a lotus position (cross legs, with the right foot resting on the left thigh, and the left foot resting on the right thigh) or sit upright, but comfortably, in a chair.

Step 3: Relax your body. Move from one part of the body to another tensing and then releasing any tightness or tension you feel. For each part of the body, breathe deeply, and let all tension, worry, anxiety, and tightness float away.

Step 4: Focus on your breath. Establish a pattern of deep, slow breaths. Breathe in stillness and peace, and breathe out any tensions or worry that remain.

Step 5: Still your emotions. As if you are an outsider, observe your feelings without reacting or judging. Imagine that any negative emotions you feel are being transformed into positive energy.

Step 6: Calm your mind. The goal is to quiet your rational mind to be able to access and work with the abstract mind. Again, become a detached observer, noticing thoughts without trying to stop, change, or judge them. Focus attention fully in the present, letting go of worries about the past or future. A technique that may assist in stilling your mind is to listen inwardly to a single sound in your thoughts and keep your attention focused on it. For example, on each inhale, say the word *um,* and on each exhale say the word *ah.* Continue to breathe in this fashion for a period of time.

Step 7: When your ready to bring the meditation period to a close, allow time to emerge. Do not come out too abruptly. You may wish to revisit each of the parts of the body, reawakening (but not tensing) them. Open your eyes slowly and experience a state of refreshment and relaxation that will allow you to view a challenge, problem, or issue in a new way.

Meditation can also be combined with imagery. The first step is the same as in this procedure: go to a quiet room with no distractions, and set aside adequate time. Then simply focus on soothing images or sounds or listen to a meditation tape (for examples, visit http://www.learningmeditation.com).

Tips for Virtual Teams   A variety of products support virtual meditation. They range from simple tools such as books and audiotapes, to Internet Web sites offering soothing images and sounds to focus on during a meditation session, to discussion boards where meditators exchange ideas and seek support, to even a PC-based desktop virtual meditation chamber for home and/or office use developed by researchers at the Georgia Institute of Technology (Sanders, 2002).

Virtual teams may choose to design their own virtual meditation Web site, perhaps in a particular location on their team intranet Web page. Team members may post their favorite soothing images or sounds and relaxation exercises for all members to share and be able to take a mental break when needed. The team Web site might also have a discussion board where team members can post their reactions and share intuitive insights from meditation experiences. Although meditation is often practiced as an individual activity, virtual teams may sponsor team meditation sessions using synchronous computer meeting tools. Perhaps virtual teams might benefit from having members begin meetings with a joint meditation session to relax before proceeding to the meeting's agenda and work.

SELECTING APPROPRIATE CREATIVITY TECHNIQUES

The following criteria are offered to assist virtual teams in determining what technique is appropriate for a particular situation. When selecting a creativity technique, consider whether the technique is:

- Useful for improving a physical object or solving a complex problem or issue
- Useful for focusing on specific parts of an issue or focusing on the entire whole
- Useful for generating many ideas quickly or for when a longer time period for idea generation is needed
- Best accomplished when done privately by individual team members (and later shared with team members) versus when completed by the entire team together
- Easily performed without the aid of technology versus best performed with the aid of software technology

Use Table 22.2 to identify which creativity techniques covered in this chapter are most appropriate with respect to each of these criteria.

FINAL THOUGHTS

Although each of the creativity techniques discussed in this chapter can be used by itself, often idea generation will be more effective when two or more creativity techniques are combined or used in conjunction with one another. For example, attribute listing is best performed when brainstorming is used when examining each of the attributes for modification. Team members in a force field analysis session may need to use brainstorming when identifying and listing driving and restraining forces. Mind mapping is another technique that encourages the use of brainstorming and can be used to organize information generated from a brainstorming session as well. Imagery and meditation are particularly helpful when used together.

Table 22.2
Creativity Techniques Categorized by Selection Criteria

Physical object

  Attribute listing

  Idea checklist

  Brainstorming

Complex problem or issue

  Morphological analysis

  Force field analysis

  Mind mapping

  Brainstorming

  Imagery

  Analogical thinking

  Drawing

  Meditation

Focus on parts

  Attribute listing

  Morphological analysis

  Mind mapping

  Idea checklist

  Force field analysis

Focus on whole

  Mind mapping

  Brainstorming

  Force field analysis

  Imagery

  Analogical thinking

  Drawing

  Meditation

Ideas generated quickly

  Attribute listing

  Idea checklist

  Brainstorming

  Analogical thinking

  Drawing

Idea generation may take longer

  Morphological analysis

  Force field analysis

  Mind mapping

  Meditation (may require daily practice)

Best performed by individual, and then insights shared with entire team

  Force field analysis (begin with individuals constructing their own problem statements; then bring team together for rest of process)

Best performed by all team members together

  Attribute listing

  Morphological analysis

  Mind mapping

  Brainstorming

  Idea checklists

(Continued)

Table 22.2 (Continued)

Imagery (begin with individual generation of images, followed by a sharing of all team members' personal insights with the entire team)

Analogical thinking

Drawing (begin with individuals constructing their own personal drawings of current and ideal states, followed by a sharing of all team members' drawings with the entire team)

Meditation

Easily performed without technology	Creativity software necessary for best application
Attribute listing (some voting programs may assist in counting and ranking of ideas generated)	Morphological analysis (the more dimensions and values generated, the more it becomes necessary to use software for analysis; ideally, a morphological analysis with more than four values requires the use of morpho-logical analysis software)
Idea checklist	
Brainstorming	
Analogical thinking	
Imagery	
Drawing	
Meditation	Mind mapping (there is an abundance of software to assist in producing mind maps)
	Brainstorming (many groupware programs that have been developed to assist with electronic brainstorming)

Which creativity techniques a virtual team will find most useful depends largely on the philosophy of the team and style of the individual members in approaching creative work. Linear techniques are beneficial for helping teams to find new areas to look for new innovations. Intuitive techniques complement linear thinking by allowing individuals to tap their inner source of creative insight. It is important that the members of a virtual team be fluent in both intuitive and linear techniques, mixing them together and crafting a creative toolbox to suit the team's needs.

REMINDERS

- To use attribute listing in virtual teams:
  - Use face-to-face meetings (with flip chart, whiteboard), if feasible.
  - Use synchronous computer meetings (with interactive whiteboards and audioconferencing).
  - Use asynchronous threaded discussions.
  - Creativity software programs provide questions and idea triggers and ways to organize and structure ideas.
- To use morphological analysis in virtual teams:
  - For problems with a small number of values, use drawing programs, electronic or interactive whiteboards, visual outliners, or even simple word processing programs (creating a table) for two-dimensional matrices.
  - For problems with more than four values, use more sophisticated morphological analysis software to generate the entire number of possible ideas and solutions.
- To use force field analysis in virtual teams:
  - Have members post individual statements to shared databases, shared files, or the intranet Web page.
  - Schedule meetings (face-to-face, teleconference, or synchronous computer) to form joint problem statements, list restraining and driving forces, and generate actions to move the team toward the ideal.
- To use mind mapping in virtual teams:
  - Create mind maps individually and then combine efforts, or develop mind maps together in a team session.
  - Craft out mind maps by hand or with the aid of interactive whiteboards and specifically designed software tools.

- To use idea checklists in virtual teams:
  - Although idea checklists are primarily used for product development and modification, some have been adapted for redesigning complex processes or services or for examining interpersonal issues.
  - Consider developing an idea checklist specific to the team's needs.
- To use brainstorming in virtual teams:
  - Follow appropriate ground rules.
  - Select a method to record ideas and a facilitator to guide the session.
  - Incorporate the use of specially designed software or other forms of asynchronous or synchronous tools to facilitate the sharing of ideas across boundaries.
- To use imagery in virtual teams:
  - First reach an appropriate level of relaxation of mind and body. Virtual meditation tapes or other online resources may be useful.
  - Make use of computer programs that display random images, words, quotations, or affirmations to trigger images and resulting ideas.
  - Capture insights generated from imagery on the team's Web page or other internal communication method.
- To use analogical thinking in virtual teams:
  - Select complex problems or concepts that require understanding and insight.
  - Force relationships between action verb phrases and analogies.
  - Make sure that action verb phrases and analogies are from different domains.
  - Incorporate different analogical thinking strategies: direct, personal, fantasy, and symbolic.
  - Use prepackaged sets of stimulator questions in software programs, custom-tailored questions (perhaps made available on team intranet Web page), and images (physical objects, photos, or pictures on cards) to prod members into analogical connections.
  - Archive analogies created in shared files, databases, or threaded discussion boards.

- To use drawing in virtual teams:
  - Artistic ability is not necessary to use the drawing technique.
  - Drawings need not be literal or objective representations; on the contrary, participants are encouraged to be subjective and metaphorical.
  - Teams can perform joint drawings, supported by interactive whiteboards, drawing programs, or groupware software with a whiteboard feature.
- To use meditation in virtual teams:
  - Individual team members may choose to meditate with the aid of books, audiotapes, or images and sounds posted to the team's Web site.
  - Individual insights from personal meditation sessions can be shared with other team members with the use of groupware and other synchronous or asynchronous communication tools.
  - Joint team meditation may be useful as lead-ins to synchronous computer meetings.
- Select the appropriate creativity technique for the situation. To do so, use the criteria and recommendations suggested in this chapter (refer back to Table 22.2).

References

Altshuller, G. (1996). *And suddenly the inventor appeared. TRIZ: The theory of inventive problem solving.* Worcester, MA: Technical Innovation Center.

Altshuller, G. (1998). *40 principles extended edition: TRIZ keys to technical innovation.* Worcester, MA: Technical Innovation Center.

Buzan, T. (1991). *Using both sides of your brain* (3rd ed.). New York: Plume.

Buzan, T., & Buzan, B. (1996). *The mind map book: How to use radiant thinking to maximize your brain's untapped potential.* New York: Plume.

Crawford, R. (1954). *The techniques of creative thinking.* Burlington, VT: Fraser.

Davis, G. A. (1999). *Creativity is forever* (4th ed.). Dubuque, IA: Kendall/Hunt.

de Bono, E. (1967). *New think.* New York: Basic Books.

Dimensional analysis. Retrieved September 6, 2007, from http://www.mycoted.com/Dimensional_Analysis.

Eberle, B. (1996). *Scamper: Creative games and activities for imagination development.* Waco, TX: Prufrock Press.

Gordon, W.J.J. (1961). *Synetics.* New York: HarperCollins.

Gordon, W.J.J., & Poze, T. (1972). *Strange and familiar.* Cambridge, MA: SES Associates.

Gordon, W.J.J., & Poze, T. (1980). *The new art of the possible.* Cambridge, MA: Porpoise Books.

Guilford, J. P. (1950). Creativity. *American Psychologist, 5*(9), 444–454.

Harris, R. (2002). *Creative thinking techniques.* Retrieved September 6, 2007, from http://www.virtualsalt.com/crebook2.htm.

McLaughlin, C. (2005). *Creative meditation.* Retrieved September 6, 2007, from http://www.visionarylead.org/articles/creative_meditation.htm.

Michalko, M. (1998). *Cracking creativity: The secrets of creative genius.* Berkeley, CA: Ten Speed Press.

Miller, W. C. (1987). *The creative edge: Fostering innovation where you work.* Reading, MA: Addison-Wesley.

Miller, W. C. (1999). *Flash of brilliance: Inspiring creativity where you work.* Cambridge, MA: Perseus Books.

Morgan, G. (1997). *Images of organizations.* Thousand Oaks, CA: Sage.

Morgan, M. (1993). *Creating workforce innovation: Turning individual creativity into organizational innovation.* Chatswood, New South Wales: Business & Professional Publishing.

Nemiro, J. (2004). *Creativity in virtual teams: Key components for success.* San Francisco: Jossey-Bass/Pfeiffer.

Osborn, A. (1948). *Your creative power: How to use imagination.* New York: Scribner.

Osborn, A. (1963). *Applied imagination: Principles and procedures of creative thinking.* New York: Scribner.

Paivio, A. (1985). Cognitive and motivational functions of imagery in human performance. *Canadian Journal of Applied Sport Sciences, 10*(4), 22S–28S.

Richland, L. E., Holyoak, K. J., & Stigler, K. W. (2004). Analogy generation in eighth grade mathematics classrooms. *Cognition and Instruction, 22*(1), 37–60.

Ritchey, T. (2003, July). *Nuclear facilities and sabotage: Using morphological analysis as a scenario and strategy development laboratory.* Paper presented to the 44th Annual Meeting of the Institute of Nuclear Materials Management, Phoenix, AZ.

Sanders, J. (2002). *Modernizing meditation: Researchers create a virtual environment to teach and enhance meditation.* Research Horizons. Retrieved September 6, 2007, from http://www.gtresearchnews.gatech.edu/reshor/rh-ss02/medit.html.

Sequential-Attributes Matrix. Retrieved September 6, 2007, from http://www.mycoted.com/Sequential-Attributes_Matrix.

Vealey, R. S., & Walter, S. M. (1993). Imagery training for performance enhancement and personal development. In J. M. Williams (Ed.), *Applied sport psychology* (2nd ed., pp. 220–224). Mountain View, CA: Mayfield.

Walker, C. E. (1975). *Learn to relax: Thirteen ways to reduce tension.* Upper Saddle River, NJ: Prentice Hall.

Wenger, W. (1979). *Beyond O.K.: Psychegenic tools relating to health of body and mind.* Gaithersburg, MD: Psychegenics Press.

Zwicky, F. (1969). *Discovery, invention, research—Through the morphological approach.* New York: Macmillan.

Zwicky, F., & Wilson, A. (1967). *New methods of thought and procedure: Contributions to the Symposium on Methodologies.* Berlin: Springer.

Using Assessments to Predict Successful Virtual Collaboration Performance

Scott K. Filgo, Scott Hines, Scott Hamilton

Predicting performance has long been the pursuit of motivated team builders, whether for the selection of soldiers, line staff, or high-tech corporate executives. Since the industrial age began, and even more so now, business leaders have sought efficient and reliable methods for predicting successful performance. This has primarily been achieved through skill, attitude, and personality assessments.

These assessments range from physical tests of agility to less obvious measures of opinion and character. Some assessments identify specific aspects of relevant performance, while others tap into constructs related to behavior, capturing a broader picture of the total person. All are designed to help team builders predict performance potential in their candidate pool. The assessment taps into qualities that separate poor and excellent potential for success, especially in the pursuit of selecting quality performers. For example, the Team Feedback System (found on the www.wiley.com/go/virtualteamshandbook Web site) assesses the effectiveness of a team and its members.

Assessments of personality, ability, and achievement have been used for years but became much more popular in the latter years of the twentieth century, when computer technology, including the Internet, helped to make assessment administration and delivery much more convenient for users. Another development brought about by the computer age included new occupations, job settings, and performance dynamics, along with the topic of virtual team collaboration. A new dynamic for the work environment suggests the need for a fresh look at the selection and assessment process.

Classic assessment practice identified constructs such as skills, opinions, and attitudes. Although this continues to be the foundation of assessment, computer technology allows analysts to observe tendencies in performance and personality to identify the correlates of success in the form of job-matched traits and capabilities. It is much easier now to find valid reasons for observing attitudes and traits as they relate to successful performance. No matter the task involved in a job, certain traits and abilities may be found that are common among those who accomplish the task well.

The crux of modern assessment practice is identifying traits and abilities in job candidates as one part of efficient, fair, and valid selection processes. This chapter discusses that process as it relates to virtual collaboration. We focus less on the specific qualities found among successful collaborators in the virtual world, information covered elsewhere in this book, and more on the process of identifying those qualities through traits and abilities assessment. The goal of this chapter is to acquaint human resource (HR) professionals or hiring managers with the world of assessment, its value to them as selection administrators, and the possible pathway to efficient and valid collaborator identification and performance prediction. For readers well versed in the historical and legal aspects of assessments, we encourage skimming ahead to the "Assessments as a Tool for Predicting Virtual Collaboration Success" section of this chapter.

A BRIEF HISTORY OF TALENT ASSESSMENT

Throughout the first half of the twentieth century, military and therapeutic analysts made comprehensive and applicable leaps for the science of identifying traits and abilities. These achievements led to industrial applications that soon were helping human resource professionals enhance the quality of work, performance, and job satisfaction. Prime examples of this period of assessment history are Holland's Self-Directed Search (Holland, 1970) and the 16PF (Cattell, 1970).

With the arrival of the computer age, not only could assessment delivery and report creation be enhanced, but the analysis of much larger pools of employee data became feasible, which allowed analysts to observe factors that relate to successful performance more efficiently than ever before. Companies producing job-related assessments, including ability, achievement, interest, and behavioral measurements, began to flourish in the 1990s. Many have produced reliable assessments that provide professionals with valid information to improve the selection and development of employees. And many others produced flash-in-the-pan products that rarely predicted performance or even described individuals accurately. Thankfully, there are resources to help users find the best assessment for their needs and avoid costly and unfair mistakes.

GOOD PRACTICES AND THE DEPARTMENT OF LABOR

The U.S. Department of Labor (www.dol.gov) maintains a host of information concerning fair assessment practices and is an essential source for HR professionals involved with assessments. Primary to their guidelines are the Testing and Assessment Guides, including, "An Employer's Guide to Good Practices" (U.S. Department of Labor Employment and Training Administration, 1999). Much of these documents relates to the fair use of assessments, including those responsibilities taken on by an assessment user for ensuring that his or her tools are both reliable and valid for the purposes of selection.

Reliability and Validity

Some tests work and some fail. While from afar it may appear that the predictive power of an assessment is a matter of luck or some other intervening factors, the power resides within the test, not in outside influences. Two primary factors account for the success of an assessment: reliability and validity. It is important for assessment customers to be familiar with both, as well as the implications of lacking either.

Reliability   The reliability of a measure refers to its stability, consistency, and dependability. If a person were to take a test more than once, would he or she obtain a reasonably similar score every time? Reliability is "the extent to which measurements are consistent or repeatable" (Cohen & Swerdlik, 2005, p. I-21). A standard wood, metal, or plastic ruler is considered reliable because for any given object measured for length, the result will always be the same (disregarding human error in measurement). If we were to take a measurement on the beach, on a mountain, in the rain, or even on the moon, the measurement for the object would always be the same. Now imagine measuring the same object as before but using a ruler that was made out of Silly Putty. If ten people were asked to measure the object, it is unlikely that any of the ten would report the same length of measurement. In fact, due to the elasticity of the instrument, it is likely that the results would show a wide disparity of scores. The use of this instrument to compare two objects would be meaningless, because no one could ever be sure of the true length of the object. Therefore, the need for a reliable instrument is evident.

Assessments have helped to bring about positive change in many instances. However, measurement alone does not change anything. Rather, the results are analyzed and plans of action are made based on the results. Nevertheless, without a reliable measure, the results of an assessment cannot be held with any sense of certainty, and therefore acting on the results can be risky. Imagine the high-stakes world of intelligence testing, where a single number can stigmatize the test taker. An unreliable assessment may at one administration assess a person as mentally deficient, on a second administration indicate superior intellect, and on a third merely average intellect. Should the person be placed in remedial classes to help catch up to his or her peers, advanced placement classes to spur his or her intellect, or should nothing be done at all? After three administrations, there is as much known about the test taker as at the beginning: nothing. But when an assessment has demonstrated consistent and reliable results, confidence is justified that the score accurately reflects true mental ability. Thus, any actions that need to take place with regard to the individual's placement can rest on a solid foundation.

Common vernacular connotes reliability as positive. We may say, "She is so reliable; she is always there when I need her." Or "Jim is a reliable worker. He can get the job done right." Unlike the common use of the term reliability, psychometrically speaking, assessment reliability refers only to the consistency of results, not to the veracity. If in the morning you step on your bathroom scale and it says that you are fifteen pounds lighter than yesterday, you would quickly and appropriately realize that the scale was reporting inaccurate results. If you step off the scale and back on and the scale still reports you weigh fifteen pounds less, reliability can be ruled out as a problem. The scale is consistent in its measurement but is not reporting an accurate description of weight. In this case the scale is consistent, albeit consistently wrong. That's a validity issue, which will be discussed later.

To express the reliability of an instrument, an index called the reliability coefficient is used (alpha or r). This statistic estimates an assessment's internal consistency and can range from 0.00 (no reliability) to 1.00 (perfectly consistent). The larger the reliability coefficient, the more consistent the test is, although it is unlikely that any assessment reliability coefficient will ever be as high as 1.00. Guidelines developed by the U.S. Department of Labor advise a lowermost boundary of .70 as the minimum standard for assessment reliability. Although factors such as small sample size, sample homogeneity, and random measurement error may reduce reliability (Statsoft, 2003), specific scales within an assessment that do not obtain the .70 mark may be too unreliable and too inconsistent to use and hence may have limited applicability. Therefore, it is important for developers to strive to exceed this minimum standard. The U.S. Department of Labor's Employer's Guide to Good Practices describes reliability coefficients in the following manner:

.90 and up excellent

.80–.89 good

.70–.79 adequate

below .70 may have limited applicability

Validity   Validity is the less complicated and perhaps more important issue when selecting an assessment. Validity indicates how well and how relevantly the assessment measures what it claims to measure. Without validity, a test has no useful function. While reliability reports how consistently an outcome is likely to happen, validity indicates that the outcome (assessment scores) can be related to a relevant criterion (performance). Therefore, the validity of an assessment is synonymous with its usability. As defined by Cohen and Swerdlik (2005), validity is "a judgment or estimate of how well a test measures what it purports to measure in a particular context." In short, can the test predict what it says it can predict and does that prediction have value for the user? In the example in the prior section, a ruler was found to be highly reliable for measuring length, but it would be invalid for measuring weight, age, or friendliness. The measurement tool must measure what is intended and relevant to the task at hand.

To demonstrate test validity, the developers often strive to show that the results of the assessment are linked to a performance standard. This type of study is known as criterion validation and is an integral part of the assessment development procedure. Test developers gather evidence of criterion validity and report this information in their product's technical manual. To assemble this information, a developer will administer the assessment to a sample of individuals. The score(s) of their assessment will then be correlated against some criterion performance data. The resultant statistic generated, the validity coefficient, ranges from 0 to 1.0. The greater this coefficient is, the greater is the assumed relationship between the assessment and the performance criterion. Thus, when a considerable correlation is found, an assessment can be said to be predictive of performance (in the job or organization that the sample represents) and hence validated for use in that area. The U.S. Department of Labor's Employer's Guide to Good Practices describes validity coefficients in the following manner:

above .35 very beneficial

.21–.35 likely to be useful

.11–.20 depends on circumstances

below .11 unlikely to be useful

Results often vary to some degree from one job or organization to the next, so results are generalized to suggest validity in such studies as described above. To fully demonstrate validity for a particular job or organization, the assessment developer or user should conduct criterion validation with a relevant sample; validity makes inferences about the people studied and rarely can be generalized any further. This due diligence will have much greater value in court than any specific validity coefficient.

It is also important to note that an assessment that is not reliable cannot be validated for use. An assessment that is reliable might not demonstrate validity, but an assessment that is valid must demonstrate reliability.

Validation is necessary because not all tests are predictive of performance or otherwise relevant for selection purposes. Therefore, validity must be demonstrated, not inferred. For example, imagine an assessment is created to predict a dog walker's ability to walk dogs. The test may include questions about techniques to control canine behavior, dog breeds, types of leashes, and any other relevant information. After a validation study, the researchers find no relationship between dog walking ability and test scores. Therefore, the test is deemed not to be predictive and is useless in selecting dog walking applicants. After another validation study of the same dog walking assessment, this time validated against sales representatives, the test may be shown (however unlikely) to be predictive of sales performance and hence a valid, if somewhat odd, selection tool.

In this situation, although the assessment may have predictive validity, it would lack face validity (the assessment's item makeup does not appear to be related to the job). As a result, it cannot be assumed that an assessment will be related to performance until it has been shown to be job relevant. Fortunately, judgment of an assessment's reliability and validity has been facilitated by government guidelines that specify what defines a quality assessment. Look for this information in the technical briefs provided by your assessment vendor of choice.

Evaluating Adverse Impact

Even if sufficient documentation supports an assessment's reliability and validity, issues of adverse impact are nonetheless relevant. Adverse impact refers to the use of an assessment or other selection practice that inappropriately disadvantages any protected group. Protected groups include gender; any group that shares a common race, religion, color, or national origin; people over age forty; and people with physical or mental disabilities. In determining whether adverse impact has occurred, a majority of courts rely on the "safe harbor" provided by the "four-fifths" rule contained in the Equal Employment Opportunity Commission Guidelines. Under this rule, adverse impact is found if the selection rate for members of any protected group is less than 80 percent of the rate for the majority demographic group. However, more restrictive state courts, like California's, may determine disparate impact by applying alternative studies including analyses of variance to determine disparate impact.

Investigating the Options

It is recommended that the assessment user do the necessary homework when selecting an assessment. Include in-house HR leadership in the purchase of an assessment and interpreting the technical jargon that relates to an assessment's purported capabilities, especially the big three: reliability, validity for jobs similar to those for which your organization is selecting, and absence of adverse impact. With this preliminary work completed, an employer may be more confident that an assessment will benefit the organization's selection process rather than hinder it.

Product developers should demonstrate their validity and reliability themselves or hire a consultant or statistical vendor to analyze their data. In many cases, a psychologist has designed an assessment, analyzed and documented the data, and sold that package to an assessment company. Smaller assessment companies find that option most convenient.

In any case, the standards for reliability and validity (and other statistics) are not law. Nothing forces a company to present such data, and no penalties exist for failure to run such data. Of course, the competition to sell a sound product or the necessity to defend that product in court should that ever become necessary, are common motivations to openly disclose reliability, validity, and adverse impact information to potential clients. In those circumstances, not having supporting statistical data can be the death knell for an assessment company, its clients, and its products.

There is no centralized validation organization that conducts statistical analyses of assessment products, although the U.S. Department of Labor creates and publishes the standards of reliability and validity. Most corporate research and development departments, led by doctoral-level psychologists and often including master's-level associates and other consultants, conduct their own statistical analyses, including, but not limited to reliability (and the projects related to strengthening the assessment for improved reliability), validity, and adverse impact analyses.

The findings for any company's assessment products should be available in the technical manuals associated with each product and summarized for the layperson in an executive summary or similar document. A preferred and recommended practice is the updating of all documentation as time passes to maintain the latest information concerning each assessment. Those purchasing assessment products are encouraged to ask about the most current documentation. Executive summaries or users' guides are recommended as a reference for most parties, because most technical manuals encompass information that requires advanced statistical training or the assistance of a psychological consultant for correct interpretation.

The bottom line is to demand the support documentation that establishes the quality of what one purchases. In the end, responsibility for the use of a poor assessment lies in the hands of the user.

ASSESSMENTS AS A TOOL FOR PREDICTING VIRTUAL COLLABORATION SUCCESS

Although the study of virtual collaboration is in its infancy, many studies have been conducted, and some are noted in this handbook. Evidence has been gathered pointing to behaviors and attitudes that successful collaborators share. Other evidence is anecdotal although equally valuable for its perspective from the trenches, based on the observations of professionals who have built virtual teams.

Virtual teams are defined by both the remoteness of their members and the unique responsibilities thrust on them. Virtual collaborators share a few common aspects of their work setting:

- Comfort working in isolated situations
- Proficiency for effective and clear communication
- Appreciation for teamwork
- Responsiveness to minimal direction and supervision

These work qualities logically suggest that there are several traits associated with them. There seems to be growing evidence for those core traits that lead to virtual team collaboration success. Traits that reflect the capability and willingness of virtual team members to apply themselves to the task at hand without direct supervision are therefore logical predictors of success in these situations. Assessments that measure these traits can be valuable for selecting virtual team members. So it is possible to easily search for assessments that claim to measure such traits. It seems evident that an assessment should tap into at least the following qualities:

- Reliability
- Organization
- Self-discipline

- Verbal proficiency

- Independence

- Engagement

- Self-motivation

- Trust

In fact, many assessments measure at least some of these traits. As long as an assessment delivers the results that measure these and other traits related to virtual collaboration in a reliable, unbiased, and valid way, the selection manager should acquire much useful information to help in making decisions about a team member or someone who may be joining the team. As a means to a specific end, using assessments to identify specific traits is good practice. Assuming one assessment can deliver a combination of scales that addresses these traits or an employer is willing to procure a battery of assessments to achieve the same end, assessment for virtual team collaboration success is relatively straightforward.

There are also other ways of discovering the antecedents of success, or at least their correlates. For a prepackaged route, the previous method typically suffices. This chapter merely suggests that a little investigatory action can yield far more valid results—the kind of valid results that mean "success."

USING ASSESSMENTS TO ASSOCIATE TRAITS WITH VIRTUAL COLLABORATION

Many kinds of performance-related criteria are deemed relevant to success for many different kinds of jobs. Often HR professionals and line managers are looking for assessments that identify behaviors they believe lead to better results on the job. Examples are the traits of assertiveness, ambition, creativity, intuitiveness, and decisiveness, among many other leadership qualities. Yet just as often, success in a particular job or organizational culture has nothing to do with those traits.

Therefore, the observation has become that every job is unique and that every company is unique, and that possibly there are few, if any, universal behaviors for success in the world of work. Rather, unique traits are associated with top results for each specific job in each specific company. This means there are likely no cookie cutters in the assessment world that can pinpoint the traits for success associated with excellent virtual team collaboration across all jobs and organizational cultures. It takes a little work to find out what works for each individual company and job involving virtual collaboration as an aspect of the workplace.

BENCHMARKING FOR SUCCESS

Benchmarking offers a rich alternative to the traditional interview. Unlike standard procedures, where the candidate is grilled to extract information that may or may not be useful, benchmarking relies on the past to predict the future. The idea is that some people better perform a job because they are better suited to perform it. They share a quality that bottom performers do not.

If a company surveyed its top-producing virtual team members, it may find a common characteristic between them; say, they all prefer the color purple. After a survey of the poor-performing collaborators, the researchers may find that all of them prefer the color green. For whatever reason (this is obviously hypothetical), it can be concluded that color preference is predicting job-related success. After hiring a few purple-oriented team members, the company finds that almost all have become top virtual team members. In this case, the use of color preference has improved the company's selection of top people. Although the use of color preference is not likely to differentiate top and bottom performers in actual practice, this is basically how benchmarking is designed to work. In reality, it is assessment scores for job-relevant traits and abilities that are tied to performance ratings, not color preference, that predict success.

It is important to understand what constitutes success within one's own organization for benchmarking to work properly. Companies of various sizes operate competitively in different arenas. The plant manager of an oil refinery may not have the same skill set as the manager of the gas station around the corner. Employee success in one may not lead to success in the other. Thus, to be most effective, benchmarking should begin with a self-study to assess the current performance strengths and weaknesses of employees. After a careful analysis, benchmarks can be derived by which future candidates can be compared. The goal is not to create a homogeneous group of copycat employees but rather to improve productivity by identifying individuals who are most likely to succeed. Finally, monitoring performance and organizational needs may best capture the most productive employees.

Benchmarking may seem to be complicated, but it is a fruitful process when conducted vigilantly. Consultants and assessment vendors are often available to assist an organization in its benchmarking endeavors. In any case, the process offers both advantages and disadvantages to employee selection that must be weighed.

Advantages of Benchmarking

When implemented properly, a benchmark system as a means of virtual collaboration selection can be used in an even-handed manner across a variety of settings. While other selection methods such as the standard interview may be more expedient, few are as accurate, valid, or versatile as benchmarking.

Flexibility   Selection specialists may find that a major benefit of benchmarking arises from the variety of uses for which it can be employed. Almost any position in any organization from private to nonprofit to governmental can be benchmarked. Hundreds of open positions can be filled with the help of benchmarks in the largest organizations, or a mom-and-pop operation can benchmark a single part-time position. The uses of benchmarking are literally endless.

For organizations with a national or international presence, the flexibility offered by benchmarking is especially useful. A virtual team member at Profiles International may be very successful at his job; a virtual team member at Harcourt Assessment may be equally as successful. While both may be valued members of their respective teams and most likely share many characteristics, the traits needed to perform well in each of these organizations may be quite different. Profiles may demand a fast-paced, independent, and sales-oriented personality, a strategy that may not work in the other organization despite the similarity of tasks and responsibilities in these two jobs. Likewise, a scientific and methodological approach to research may equal success at one company, while suggesting an unproductive mismatch at the other, despite similarities in the job description. The flexible nature of benchmarking allows regional and organizational differences of organizational culture to be accounted for and adjusted as needed. Therefore, patterns for a sales representative in London and Honolulu may overlap substantially but are likely to be fine-tuned to reflect local culture, organizational vision, and managerial preferences.

Finally, once a position is benchmarked, changes can be made to the assessment score profile (the benchmark) to better reflect the changing workplace. Advancements such as the installation of more advanced technology or changes in organizational structure may necessitate the modification of existing benchmarks. The changes may force employees to exhibit a new skill set or attitude to perform the same job that was not needed previously. Fortunately, this is not a problem. Benchmarking encourages an organization to make these changes and remain in step with current employee capabilities and environmental changes.

Fairness As compared to traditional methods of employee selection, benchmarking represents a fair and even-handed approach. As opposed to relying on subjective evaluations of what may or may not lead to productive work behavior, benchmarking relies on past performance as a guide. The benefit comes from observations of employee abilities and traits that have been shown in a criterion validation study to relate to productivity. By knowing its workers, an organization can predict and manage performance. Without such attention, an organization runs the risk of engaging in selection wanderlust, or subjectively filling voids without any real awareness of what knowledge, skills, abilities, and traits are related to success in each position.

While benchmarking can improve the hit-to-miss ratio of employment selection, it is important that the assessment tools used have been validated for its intended use and are nondiscriminatory. The Equal Employment Opportunity Commission (EEOC) suggests that the use of reliable and validated instruments can significantly reduce the risk of lawsuits and add equity to the benchmarking process (Scholz, 2005).

Disadvantages of Benchmarking

Although the benchmarking process is versatile and can be fair when conducted diligently and professionally, it can also be a lengthy and expensive process to complete properly. Individuals looking to measure and benchmark traits related to successful virtual collaboration for selection purposes may wish to weigh the costs in both time and funding before developing a selection system around benchmarking projects.

Time Investment   Like anything else worthwhile, benchmarking requires time to develop the valid standards by which applicants can be compared. It must begin with organizational and job analysis. Assessment is an important key to benchmarking, but is not enough. A plan must be developed to understand what defines success within the organization, that is, what observable characteristics and performance indicators equal successful virtual team collaboration. Once employees have been assessed and performance criteria are established, the organization must understand what makes the top performers the best at what they do. All of these activities may take considerable initiative and time expense; however, most successful organizations have such performance appraisal processes established.

Fortunately, assessment is largely computer based these days. Therefore, assessment and scoring are provided by the vendor on the Internet, where results can be transmitted to those making the selection decisions almost immediately following completion of the assessment battery. This means that applicants may be assessed and screened before they set foot in the interviewer's door.

After performance data and assessment scores are gathered and analyzed, and a benchmark has been set, the benchmark may need to be refined or adjusted over time. This means reevaluating employees and staying on top of organizational needs. Although this maintenance may consume some time, the benefit to the organization is clear. In general, the key concept to understand is that performance measurement and benchmarking is time consuming.

Cost   Testing can be expensive, and the time needed to develop and maintain a benchmarked position substantial. But stocking a company with the wrong people can be even more costly. Employee dissatisfaction can lead to substandard performance and subsequent turnover. The purported cost that organizations incur as a result of lost productivity is worrisome. Turnover could be much more costly; the cost of replacing a manager could range between one and one-half and ten times the annual salary (Garber, 2005; Harcourt Assessment, 2007). Plainly the cost of choosing the wrong candidate is high. The costs associated with testing and benchmarking are modest by comparison.

Employee selection is more critical today than ever before. Companies literally take million-dollar gambles on candidates. Estimating the fit between job and candidate before actually handing over the keys can be difficult. Without an understanding of what skills and traits are needed to perform a job successfully, one can hardly be expected to fill a vacancy efficiently. The essential lesson here is that without shopping wisely and weighing in the benefits, the assessment process (or opting out of it) can be rather costly.

The Benchmarking Process

Benchmarking often makes the connection between successful performance and the measurement of traits, interests, and abilities, while accounting for cultural differences in an organization. It involves the collection of performance data, related to virtual team collaboration in this case. Comparing scores of successful virtual team members with those of people who are challenged in their performance often reveals measurable traits, interests, and abilities common to each performance group.

These findings can help in selecting new employees for positions that involve virtual collaboration and also help to develop those currently in such a position. The results of a benchmarking procedure are relevant and valid only for those involved with that job at that company. Generalization of the benchmark is possible, but easily superseded by analyses carried out with a modest sample from one's own company and composed of one's own employees.

The typical benchmarking, or job-match, process for assessments that offer such a feature is an effective approach that minimizes the time required to efficiently describe jobs and people and their degree of match. The descriptive process usually starts by examining the score pattern of those who are most successful within a position (successful at the criterion of virtual team collaboration, in this case) and those who seem to be overly challenged by the position. From this information, a pattern of scores across the various dimensions measured by an assessment may be developed to serve as the initial benchmark or job-match pattern on which the job matching is based.

The assessment product or the client services branch of an assessment vendor should facilitate concurrent study of available incumbents, job requirement assessments by those who know the job, and a combination of these. Even with a small sample, this is a good place to start the process and an approach that will allow refinement of the job pattern with ongoing evaluation. This initial success profile should be continuously updated as more empirical information becomes available. This is important as a part of continually maintaining the job relevance of any process used in employee placement. How performance is measured is also important and should typically be as objective and measurable as possible because these data are the criteria that define performance and thereby the benchmark associated with each scale in an assessment. Performance ratings for any criterion, including virtual collaboration, should be objectively and consistently applied to all participants in a study. Otherwise the benchmark will lack the validity required to make relevant predictions. Also, it is better to use only a few critical criteria of performance rather than an abundance of unrelated and poorly measured performance indicators. Relevance and measurability are important factors for developing the performance rating.

Based on this knowledge of what is necessary for success in a position, an employer can build a job-match pattern for each scale measured by an assessment if such a feature is available. This pattern consists of a range along each scale in which the scores of the most effective performers tend to fall. The further outside this range a score falls, the less likely it is that there will be a good fit of that individual to the job in regard to that particular factor. Often job match is reported as a percentage match to a specific set of scale benchmarks. This allows a variation of scoring between persons who generally share a good job fit to a position. In other words, benchmarking allows score distributions among top performers to range anywhere along the total score range for a scale. No longer is there a need to depend on scales for which only high scores are equated to top performance. For some jobs in which virtual collaboration is an important aspect, score ranges on various traits could distribute in the middle of the scale, which presents no problem for the benchmarking technique. On a scale-by-scale basis, higher is not necessarily better.

By using benchmarking, it becomes easy to quickly identify individuals who tend to fit well into positions and in what way they might have adjustments to make. This information is important for job placement and job training.

Scale scores are the measure (the independent variable, for you statistical types) that differentiates top and bottom performers. The scores on each scale of an assessment are often reported on a ten-point scale starting with a 1 at the low end and going to 10 on the high end. The raw scores have been standardized so that the distribution of scores for the typical working population will fall on each scale with a normal distribution. In other words, about two-thirds of the scores will fall between 4 and 7, with the frequency of scores tapering off toward the ends of the scale. Other scoring formats are available, each with its own advantages and disadvantages. Percentile scores for each scale are very common and easily understood by users. The important point is that norming of raw scores occurs, so that the score represents more than just a rating of that person's traits; it also represents that individual's traits relative to a relevant population: working adults in a particular culture, job, or organizational role.

Once a valid benchmark has been established, it may be used to evaluate the match to that job for anyone who has taken the assessment. The benchmark is composed of a range of scores for each scale of the assessment. Because they are not absolute, the pattern should include a range of scores, the point being to be inclusive and reflect the variance of scores shared among top performers. Rarely does even a cohesive group of individuals—for instance, those who collaborate well in the virtual world—score exactly the same on any measure of ability or personality. This range represents the range of scores in which those who are expected to perform best in the job tend to score. The further outside this range a score falls, the less likely there will be a good fit of that individual to the job and the current members on the team.

The range of reported job matches may be expressed as a percentage, but whatever the format, job-match scores are typically used to summarize an individual's overall match to the performance-related benchmark. The higher the match or subsection matches reported, the higher the expectancy is that the individual will perform well in the job under consideration. While this benchmarking approach to matching individuals to a job provides information of great value and should be an important part of the placement decision, the results from any assessment should never make up more than a third of the final decision. Interviews, résumés, portfolios, and much more can round out the pool of information used to select candidates and develop staff.

FINAL THOUGHTS

The most relevant and valid way to use assessments for identifying and predicting success in roles that require virtual team membership and collaboration is through job- and employer-specific studies that account for the organizational culture of a company. This is typically carried out through benchmarking; expert advice concerning the universal traits associated with collaborative success, both virtual and face-to-face, can add to the findings of a benchmarking study. Some assessment products offer such features, some may require work with a consultant to carry out such studies, and some offer straightforward scale measures of traits regarding the prevailing opinion concerning which traits equal success in virtual teams.

The benchmarking process is recommended for selecting successful virtual team members. However, all forms of assessment can add value to the information-gathering process. The advantages, obligations, and return on investment of each style of assessment package should be researched diligently before engaging in the assessment purchasing process. In the end, the ability to predict performance and make better hiring decisions can be enhanced by the use of assessments. Virtual teams will show better performance through proper selection practices.

REMINDERS

- The arrival of the computer age has made testing a viable option for selecting virtual team members, allowing applicants and employees to be quickly and accurately assessed and helping employers effectively screen candidates in a timely manner.

- Reliability, validity, and adverse impact are the key issues to examine when evaluating an assessment for use.

- Reliability refers to the consistency of results, and validity refers to the test's effectiveness when used. These components should be reported by the developer in the assessment's technical manual and executive briefs.

- An assessment that is reliable might not demonstrate validity, but an assessment that is valid must demonstrate reliability.

- A test buyer should be aware of the adverse impact an assessment may pose to its users. Adverse impact refers to the use of an assessment or other selection practice that inappropriately disadvantages groups of test takers, such as groups based on ethnicity or gender.

- Virtual teams are often defined by traits that reflect the capability and willingness to apply oneself to the task at hand without direct supervision; therefore, identification of the presence of these traits can improve team productivity.

- Assessments can be used to benchmark behaviors shared among virtual collaborators and predict success in these positions.

- Benchmarking aids in establishing valid predictors. Once a job is benchmarked, employers can efficiently match candidates that share common traits to the job.

- It is important to understand what constitutes success within one's own organization for benchmarking to work properly. The criteria of success can differ from one job or organization to the next.

- Benchmarking may seem complicated, costly, and expensive at first, but it is a fruitful process when conducted vigilantly. Nonetheless, the process offers both advantages and disadvantages to employee selection that must be considered.

RELATED ITEM ON THE WEB

- Team Feedback System: Development Tool

References

Cattell, R. B., Eber, H. W., & Tatsuoka, M. M. (1970). *Handbook for the 16PF.* Champaign, IL: Institute for Personality and Ability Testing.

Cohen, R. J., & Swerdlik, M. E. (2005). *Psychological testing and assessment: An introduction to tests and measurement* (6th ed.). New York: McGraw-Hill.

Garber, S. (2005). Employee dissatisfaction and turnover: One can't afford to ignore it. *Administrative Eyecare.* Retrieved January 19, 2007, from http://www.asoa.org/services/publications/garberae83.html.

Harcourt Assessment. (2007). *Retain your employees before you hire them: Looking beyond the resume.* Retrieved November 11, 2007, from http://harcourtassessment.com/haiweb/Cultures/en-US/Harcourt/Community/TalentAssessment/Research/WhitePapers/reslist.htm.

Holland, J. L. (1970). *The self-directed search.* Palo Alto, CA: Consulting Psychologists Press.

Profiles International. (2007). *Employee turnover: Reduce the cost of employee turnover and hire top performers with Profiles International.* Retrieved January 19, 2007, from http://www.profilesinternational.com/SYC_empturnover.aspx.

Scholz, R. (2005). *Employee turnover: Good or bad?* Leadership Strategies Associates. Retrieved January 19, 2007, from http://www.lead-strat-assoc.com/EmployeeTurnover.pdf.

Statsoft. (2003). *Basic statistics: Electronic textbook.* Retrieved February 24, 2006, from http://www.statsoft.com/textbook/stbasic.html.

U.S. Department of Labor Employment and Training Administration. (1999). *Testing and assessment: An employer's guide to good practices.* Washington, DC: U.S. Government Printing Office.

Building the Business Case to Executives for Virtual Teams

Michael Beyerlein, Susan Beyerlein

Deliberate change in organizations depends on investing appropriate amounts and types of resources. (Accidental and incidental change also consumes resources.) When a company moves toward introduction and increasing reliance on virtual teams, success depends on investing money, attention, time, and other resources. There may be a dozen initiatives competing for those resources. Underinvestment means mediocrity. So the leaders of the initiative have to convince top management that this is a smart investment: it will pay big dividends to do it right. The business case provides a structure for that argument.

Although work groups have been around much longer than teams, the thinking about team problems and successes is increasingly being recorded in written form (in the early years, much of it was in the form of anecdotes and stories from the factory floor). And it is worth noting that virtual teams that have been in existence in companies in recent history have weathered the same kind of checkered history as face-to-face manufacturing teams, that is, frequent errors in design and implementation accompanied by deficits in support from surrounding systems like information technology and information systems (IT/IS), training and development, and leadership—for example:

- An executive states unequivocally, "You will be in teams on Monday," which means no groundwork was done to launch the team in an effective manner.

- An executive says, "We don't want to spend money on travel because of expense [or security], so you cannot have a face-to-face meeting," which means investment in team development is minimal.

- Team members assume that their teammates operate the same way they do, so no adjustments are made for cultural differences, and potentially valuable contributions are never made when outspoken members fail to draw out those with differing styles.

- Executives invest millions in new computer hardware and software but only a fraction of that amount in team training and development, so the potential offered by the equipment is never achieved because the people processes are poor.

Countless other examples of errors happen daily. Mistakes abound when traversing new territory in any field of study and practice, and teams are no exception. However, enough knowledge has been amassed and codified from the trenches that thoughtful leaders and facilitators can avoid many common errors and provide informed guidance for launches of new teams. It is useful to pay attention to the struggles of the boundary spanners who have come before to make their hard-won lessons available to those who are experiencing some of the same virtual teaming challenges. The following sections provide integrative summary guidelines for building the business case for making the investment.

THE BUSINESS CASE FOR VIRTUAL TEAMS

Executives and senior managers continuously make decisions about the best investments of money, time, equipment, knowledge, human resources, and other tangible and intangible assets that are available in varying amounts to enable the organization to meet strategic targets and achieve competitive advantage. Depending on the mix of dynamic organizational and business conditions at the time and personality tendencies, decisions may be driven by time urgency, emotion, threat of real or imagined crisis situations, personal preference, possibilities of political gain, history, and others. More often than not, daily decisions are fueled by less drama and are instead a reflection of the limited data available, thoughtful reflection, integration of multiple viewpoints, resource constraints, and careful review of alternatives.

The business case outlined in this section takes the second, more tempered approach to executive decision making as its starting point and for purposes of discussion formally examines the value and costs of a particular investment decision. An ideal business case presented to an executive in a bid for resources aims at closing performance gaps with a discussion of methods that link to the mission, vision, objectives, goals, and strategies of the organization. It includes economic analyses of costs and benefits, comparisons with alternatives, narrative arguments, illustrative examples, demonstrations, and others in an attempt to provide a comprehensive view of the possibilities. A good written business case takes ample preparation, and effective presentation can make or break its reception.

WHY MAKE THE EFFORT TO WRITE A BUSINESS CASE?

An effective business case provides a rationale and plan for effectively using the organization's resources necessary for implementing and sustaining a change of course in the organization. Resources include money, time, the latest equipment, human resources, knowledge in the form of data, information, and patented technologies, as well as other forms of support for planning, launching, developing, and sustaining the change in the organization. Any or all of these resources can easily be reserved for other projects; thus, there is always a high-stakes competitive backdrop to resource deployment, especially when resource scarcity is the dominant paradigm. From the executive's viewpoint, decisions need to be data driven so that ideally, the most convincing arguments about costs and benefits determine the investment decision. However, it is common lore that decisions are only as good as the data available (GIGO—garbage in/garbage out), so decision makers need to be alert to possible anomalies in the data and their interpretation—in other words, the accuracy and the meanings placed on the numbers by well-meaning associates (see the following for guidelines on assessing teams: Henderson & Green, 1997; Keen & Keen, 1998; Kennedy, 2003; Rupp, 2003; Wohlfarth & Stevens, 2003). It is no secret that ignorance is a show stopper of the greatest magnitude. The example and guidelines that follow provide a conceptual map of some of these pitfalls.

Why should executives invest in virtual teams? Some leading-edge companies such as IBM and Johnson & Johnson are already putting significant resources into virtual collaboration because they recognize that it is a key to their future in competing globally. They understand that undernourished teams fail and that mediocre performance tends to be the rule rather than the exception in this situation. There seems to be an unspoken awareness among knowledgeable executives that an array of resource investments in teams is part of the antidote and an essential factor in achieving high performance (Miles, Coleman, & Creed, 1995). The following problems are often red flags of inadequate investment:

- Poor access to information
- Ambiguous goals and expectations
- Inadequate resources
- Overcontrol by supervisors and managers
- Overload on a project due to understaffing and overload in general as a result of members' overcommitment to multiple projects
- Conflicting demands
- Weak incentives, especially around knowledge sharing

Why use virtual teams at all? The case is obvious. They enable the organization to pull together the most skilled and knowledgeable employees from anywhere in the world and involve local representatives at multiple sites for coordinating global work. This improvement in knowledge management and coordination makes the organization more flexible and responsive to the marketplace. Costs are contained by reducing commuting and travel expense, and working locally frees up workers to be more productive. Astoundingly, the workday on a project can be extended from eight to twenty-four hours by having teams one-third of the way around the world to hand off to at the end of the day. Knowledge can flow and be leveraged through participation of diverse experts from anywhere in the world. The existence of virtual teams makes alliances and mergers between organizations easier to execute and extends resources and markets, thus increasing opportunity and eliminating cost drains. The key is not what you know but your ability to turn what you know into knowledge and intangible assets that contribute to success in the future. Virtual teams are a key to making this happen. "In a world where a slight advantage easily turns into a leading position, think about the profits a company correctly utilizing all its assets might gain over a company that uses only 20 to 30 percent of its assets, that is only the financial ones" (Roos, 1999, p. 14).

THE BUSINESS CASE AS A VEHICLE FOR GARNERING SUPPORT

These points about virtual team value will not matter (and therefore not be realized) unless the individuals responsible for team performance can direct management attention to the issues and make a compelling case for investment in virtual teams. Ultimately the business case represents a process, a written document, a presentation, and a contract that lead to resource acquisition. The process of building the business case clarifies the thinking and strategy of the team leaders and facilitators, enabling them to articulate costs and benefits clearly and a plan for team development. The written document captures the best thinking of the group and makes it public and easily sharable with others, including upper management. The process of sharing with management makes both a case and an impression that can influence decision making. If the presentation is convincing, management commits to providing the resources; thus, the document becomes a contract detailing who will provide what and who will deliver what in order to show that the investment has paid off. Management uses the business case to provide a rationale for the project to its stakeholders, assess its economic pros and cons, analyze the impact on the business, and align the initiative with other factors such as risks, elements in the political environment, board wishes, and other proposals or ongoing projects.

DEMONSTRATING SUCCESS TO KEY STAKEHOLDERS

It is useful to assume that support for the business case will be data driven, but it is also helpful to illustrate the case with relevant real-world success stories that highlight the contrast between success and failure. The metrics of interest will vary somewhat by stakeholder group. Top management, the team members, team leaders and managers, and support system personnel will tend to value differing outcomes that link with their particular performance mandates. However, all will undoubtedly value projects coming in under budget and ahead of schedule with innovative solutions. Be prepared to address variants of the following question many times over during the course of a project sell: "How will improvements in competencies and capabilities resulting from the investment improve cost, speed, and innovation?" In other words, management will expect to be thoroughly convinced that the proposed process and product improvement outcomes are assured and that once realized, they will definitely be worth the investment.

The business case may be long and detailed or brief and to the point. The detail level depends on the composition of the audience and the scope of the project. Typical business cases include background and purpose statement, assessment of the current situation, cost-benefit analysis, comparison of alternative ways of approaching the problem or challenge, a list of deliverables, a time line, and a conclusion. Other categories can be added to build a richer case. In the hypothetical example that follows, the presenters at corporate headquarters for ABC Company in the United States are arguing for funding to launch training for improving the cultural competencies of the team members:

ABC has made the decision to use virtual teams for product development with partners in a variety of cultures. Teams are already underway, and they are generating some results, but not spectacular ones. Evidence for the lack of excellence includes errors, delays, and frustrated members.

Catalogue these factors as qualitative arguments, and present solid examples in story form to convey the context for the data. Focus on the low-quality communications across cultures.

PURPOSE STATEMENT

ABC has a growing number of virtual product development teams spanning the globe. Use of scientists and engineers in partner countries has enabled the company to add a great deal of expertise to its teams at low cost. The teams are productive but do not seem to achieve breakthroughs in new product design very often. Discussion with team members from several partner countries, particularly China, India, and Japan, suggests that the ways members in the United States interact with overseas members is causing problems. This may be a case of limited cultural competence whereby the members in the United States make the assumption that members in the partner countries operate from the same base of assumptions and procedures and thereby ignore the unique qualities of the culture of each of those countries.

Offer training to develop cultural competence in team members as a means of improving skill building, awareness, and understanding that all sites are involved in the same general goals and cross-country (cross-boundary) collaborative team processes. Education on these aspects of cultural competence and others should accelerate the pace for achieving virtual team effectiveness.

SITUATION ASSESSMENT

Thanks to recent computing upgrades, cross-functional virtual team performance at ABC is supported by high-quality, reliable hardware and software and access to Internet and telephone connections. Relationships between members at each site seem to be satisfactory, but relationships across sites have not developed well in most cases. Trainers with bicultural expertise are available from the learning department and have tried to deliver online courses on understanding and managing cultural differences. Coaching of individual team members is available but seldom requested. Negative stereotypes passed on from older family members or coworkers from previous generations, and amply reinforced by current movie and media offerings, appear to exist at each site when members are queried about their distant teammates. Team managers at the various sites also seem to display similar attitudes.

COST/BENEFIT ANALYSIS

A cost/benefit analysis sets up an equation that provides the justification for the investment. The equation basically says that the total of tangible and intangible benefits outweighs the total of tangible and intangible costs to a significant and measurable extent. Thus, the team preparing the case must do a thorough job of identifying potential costs and benefits and making realistic assessments of the amounts involved.

This section of the business case begins with an overview and then moves to specifics.

SAMPLE STATEMENT: COST/BENEFIT ANALYSIS

Overview of Benefits

Training to improve the cultural competencies of all members on the teams is expected to reduce errors, accelerate the work pace, improve learning and the use of existing expertise, and increase buy-in on projects.

Identifying Operational Savings

Errors due to miscommunication and information that is withheld from discussions leads to delays and rework. Notable reduction in these costs should result from improved cultural competencies.

Analysis of Costs

The challenge in this section is to identify relevant costs, including money and time, and put dollar figures on them. Line items include (this is not an exhaustive list):

- One-time expenses such as development costs for a training module— $00,000 for each module in a set of ten (2 individuals, full time for 2 weeks)

- Staff time for assessment: 2 individuals, full time for 1 week—$0,000

- Staff time for training delivery: 4 individuals, full time for 14 weeks — $00,000

- Team member time away from project work to attend training: 126 individuals attending 2 weeks of training—$000,000

- Travel cost of trainers: $0,000 for 2 weeks at corporate

- Vendor costs: $0 for option 1, when internal staff handle all the work on this intervention, but about $00,000 for option 2, when the outside vendors handle as much of the work as possible

- Expense of module development such as use of information technology and information systems staff: $0

- Expense of follow-up assessment: 2 individuals, full time for 1 week — $0,000

- Development of tailored training for special groups, for example, those in overseas partner organizations (built into above costs but tailoring to different countries' needs will add additional expense)

Tangible Benefits

It is argued that training of team members will lead to positive changes in behavior: improved listening; greater contributions from overseas members; more signs of respect and acceptance; direct dollar savings: projects more frequently coming in under budget; indirect dollar savings: reduction in time off task involving rework and increased costs, reduced turnover, reduced new product development cycle time, increased retention of top talent due to improved work climate and conditions (the rule of thumb for turnover cost is that it equals the annual salary of the person being replaced). Line items include (not an exhaustive list):

- Accelerated development for 10 product development teams: an average of 2 weeks per project—$000,000

- 20 percent reduction in errors and rework—$000,000

- Reduced turnover—$000,000

Intangible Benefits

Improved team processes will promote knowledge generation, sharing, and utilization resulting in: *increased intellectual capital*—growing knowledge relevant to current and future projects; *improved concentration*—focusing attention on work rather than being distracted by social errors;

more highly developed and sophisticated human capital as team member skills develop; and *increased collaborative capital* as team members become more effective at working with others from differing cultures and work environments. The supreme challenge here is in finding ways to quantify the intangible benefits. There are a few tools available for estimating the value of intangible assets such as intellectual capital. An Internet search will reveal a number of books and articles on the topic. Line items include (not an exhaustive list):

- Increased intellectual capital within and between teams—$000,000
- Increased collaborative capability for future team projects—$000,000
- Improved team member process skills—$000,000

COMPARISON OF OPTIONS

Every problem has multiple avenues of attack. In preparing the business case, it is useful to identify several possible solutions that differ from the intended course of action as a means of analyzing alternative ways of approaching the problem. Alternatives in a proposed change initiative may include using in-house staff rather than vendors, launching a partial initiative to begin with rather than a full-blown change program, or tabling everything for six month to take a more in-depth look at the issues and needs of the organization.

SAMPLE COMPARISON OF ALTERNATIVES

The proposed solution is development and delivery of ten training modules focused on the basic skills of cultural competence and their use with team members in the four countries involved on the ABC Company heat transfer problem: China, India, Japan, and the United States. This training package would be delivered on-site by our staff members and their associates. Travel of training peers from overseas to our headquarters for two weeks of training will enable them to deliver modules effectively back home rather than flying the project team members here. Alternative approaches include bringing team members here for training, putting training online and inviting participation by team members, hiring a vendor company to deliver training, or tabling the program altogether. Here is a comparison of three alternatives:

	In-House Training	Consulting Firm	No Training
Needs assessment	Thorough	Yes	No
Overview of the countries involved	Yes	Yes	No
Feedback to team members	Extensive	Limited	Read material
Coaching	As needed	Only during training	Limited
Additional services	Trainer as part of team facilitator's team	Limited, adds to cost	No
Experience	Limited	Yes	No
Cost	Employee time, some travel by trainer	Employee time plus substantial fee	Lost team effectiveness
Ongoing training face-to-face	Yes, employee time, some travel	Yes, for fee	No
Ongoing training—virtual	Yes, with IT/IS staff support	Yes, for fee	No
Cost/benefit ratio	$419,500/ 2,700,000	$919,500/ 2,700,000	$0/0

Deliverables

A list of deliverables provides some concrete anchors that are designed to address the expectations of the sponsors. These convey a sense of what the resources are being used for and how the program will pay dividends in visible ways.

SAMPLE DELIVERABLES LIST

The preassessment measurement uses process and survey tools including team member and manager satisfaction surveys, self-assessment questionnaires, and organizational self-assessment checklists of cultural competence variables.

Timeline

The timeline shows when the initiative will be launched, the milestones along the way, and the date of conclusion. Reporting to sponsors may be required at any midpoint but definitely at the conclusion of the project.

Sample timeline: This project is expected to take about 11 months

June 20xx: Assessment of current level of cultural competence and its impact on performance as a baseline measure

July 20xx: Development of training modules

August 20xx: Begin training modules. Modules 1 and 2 presented

September 20xx: Modules 3 and 4 presented

October 20xx: Assess current state of project, and make minor adjustments in direction and content if needed. Modules 5 and 6 presented

November 20xx: Modules 7 and 8 presented

December 20xx: Module 9 and 10 presented. Debriefing of training

March 20xx: Cultural competence reassessed

April 20xx: Final report presented to project sponsor

Summary and Recommendations

Conclude the business case with a summary and set of recommendations. Then respond to questions from the decision makers. Anticipate some difficult questions, and prepare for them. Rehearse answering them when rehearsing the presentation. Exhibit 24.1 provides a checklist of steps for preparing the business case.

SAMPLE SUMMARY AND RECOMMENDATIONS

The initiative described in this proposal is designed to improve cross-cultural working relationships in product development teams in order to improve team effectiveness. Development and delivery of ten modules

Exhibit 24.1
Checklist for Business Case Preparation

- ☐ Is there a focus on the business payoffs of investing in the initiative?

- ☐ Is the case clear and precise?

- ☐ Did the case writers work with the sponsor when writing the business case?

- ☐ Did you rehearse the presentation of the case to the sponsor and executives?

- ☐ Are the problems identified in the business case being addressed by the change effort? Is the vision being achieved?

- ☐ Have you discussed your ideas with others to get a broader view of the overall situation?

- ☐ Does the case include a description of the project?

- ☐ Were the stakeholders affected by the change and their needs identified?

- ☐ Is there a cost/benefits analysis for each alternative?

- ☐ Is the case being adapted and updated to meet the changing needs of the situation?

- ☐ Were possible risks and ways to manage them identified?

- ☐ Did the scope of the business case match the scope of the change initiative being proposed?

Source: Adapted from Beyerlein and Harris (2003).

for building team member cultural competencies was proposed for teams in four countries. The costs and benefits were described and a comparison was made of the pros and cons of using a vendor to do the project or simply tabling the project. The value of building cultural competencies in cross-functional virtual teams will become visible when errors and rework are reduced, top talent is retained, and breakthrough results occur more often under budget and before stated deadlines.

Based on our analysis, we recommend in-house development and delivery of the ten modules beginning in June 20xx.

FINAL THOUGHTS

Companies are relying more and more on virtual teams so expertise can be brought together efficiently from around the world. Doing that well depends on hardware and software but also on the organizational, social, emotional, and cognitive environment that management creates for the team to work in and the competencies of the team members for working together well. This set of conditions requires development and depends on initial and sustaining investment. The business case and its complementary ongoing assessment and feedback about results presented to the top management combine to create a process for winning and sustaining support for the virtual team's initiative. The guidelines and examples in this chapter form a template that can be adapted to each company's context.

REMINDERS

- Different company initiatives typically compete for resources.
- Preparing the business case is a strategic planning process.
- The business case is a communication tool.
- The business case provides a compelling rationale for making the investment.
- Contrasting the desired initiative with alternatives, including no change, highlights the value of the investment.
- The expected payoffs from the initiative become clearer and illustrate the potential cost-to-benefit ratio that drives the decisions about support.
- The quality of the written and verbal presentation of the business case influences the response of top management and therefore is worth the effort.

References

Beyerlein, M., & Harris, C. L. (2003). *Guiding the journey to collaborative work systems: A strategic design workbook.* San Francisco: Jossey-Bass/Pfeiffer.

Henderson, D., & Green, F. (1997). Measuring self-managed work teams. *Journal for Quality and Participation, 20,* 52–58.

Keen, T. R., & Keen, C. N. (1998). Conducting a team audit. *Training and Development, 52*(2), 13–16.

Kennedy, F. (2003). Return on teaming initiative (ROTI): Measuring teaming outcomes to optimize their performance. In M. Beyerlein, C. McGee, G. Klein, J. Nemiro, & L. Broedling (Eds.), *The collaborative work systems fieldbook* (pp. 89–101). San Francisco: Jossey-Bass/Pfeiffer.

Miles, R. E., Coleman, H. J., Jr., & Creed, W. E. (1995). Keys to success in corporate redesign. *California Management Review, 37,* 128–145.

Roos, G. (1999). Intellectual capital services. *London European Management Journal, 17*(4), 391–402.

Rupp, K. (2003). UATTKA performance assessment for fast formed teams. In M. Beyerlein, C. McGee, G. Klein, J. Nemiro, & L. Broedling (Eds.), *The collaborative work systems fieldbook* (pp. 513–542). San Francisco: Jossey-Bass/Pfeiffer.

Wohlfarth, T., & Stevens, M. (2003). Creating and measuring ways to win together. In M. Beyerlein, C. McGee, C. Klein, I. Nemiro, & L. Broedling (Eds.), *The collaborative work systems fieldbook* (pp. 465–477). San Francisco: Jossey-Bass/Pfeiffer.

REAL WORLD EXAMPLES OF HIGH-PERFORMANCE VIRTUAL TEAMS

PART SEVEN

Case Studies

The case study chapters present an inside look at how some companies are implementing and using virtual teams and virtual collaboration to meet a diverse mix of business needs and problems. With examples and case studies from industries as diverse as health care, high tech, and aerospace, the chapters show how virtual collaboration in theory looks in practice. Chapter Twenty-Five describes the unique development and application of virtual teams to meet the challenges threatening the capacity of the United States to successfully address the problems facing its health care system. The authors argue that the challenging and complex demographic, economic, epidemiological, and structural factors and forces that affect health care necessitate alternative strategies to achieve meaningful improvements in health care access, quality, and outcomes. Examples are offered of the varying application of virtual teams in different health care settings with particular emphasis on the virtual integrated practice model, which uses virtual teams to expand and improve chronic disease management in primary care medical offices. Results and lessons learned from the model, as well as implications for the future of virtual teams in health care, are discussed.

Chapter Twenty-Six explores how data of various kinds can be applied using a decision process to determine when and how distributed work can benefit organizations, teams, and individuals. The authors describe the data-driven methods used successfully at Sun Microsystems to make business-focused decisions about distributed work options. The need to understand the decision-making process about distributed work is critical when the potential impact of distributed work on the productivity, cost efficiency, and competitiveness of the organization is considered. The authors detail how data-driven approaches were used to make decisions about the appropriateness of distributed work models, design the supporting system of infrastructure necessary for success, and provide direction to implementation strategies.

In an effort to achieve multiple strategic objectives with the smallest number of resources, many organizations are using matrix reporting relationships as a way to link disparate parts of the organization and encourage collaboration. Chapter Twenty-Seven summarizes what has been learned about designing and implementing a successful matrix with a focus on virtual environments. With a stated intent to demystify this complex organizational form and offering tools to maximize the chance of successful implementation, this chapter addresses how using a matrix structure can promote teamwork in a virtual environment by formalizing the lateral connections among organizational units.

Virtual integrated product teams (VIPTs) are a key coordinating structure for integrative alliances in the aerospace industry. They enable work to be done across distance of disciplines, teams, countries, and even companies who are competitors. Chapter Twenty-Eight describes how the Joint Strike Fighter (JSF) program relied on VIPTs to create collaboration between a disparate group of engineers from three different companies, many of whom had previously been competitors. This chapter discusses the special technical challenges that required an innovative management approach to create a collaborative climate and focus and align a large, distributed, global, virtual integrated product team. The JSF program is a triservice, multinational transformational weapon system with unique requirements, which was won by Lockheed Martin Aeronautics Company in Fort Worth, Texas, in 2001. Recent acquisition reform in the Department of Defense contributed to making this largest aerospace program in history a joint model customized for three of military services—the Navy, the Air Force, and the Marine Corps—as well as foreign customers.

Whether interaction and collaboration needs to happen between team members, within an organization, or across several organizations and countries, virtual collaboration is emerging as a best practice. The case study chapters take us inside some leading companies for a close-up look at how it is being used to drive results.

Virtual Teams in Medical Care Delivery

Steven K. Rothschild, Stan Lapidos

Four factors—demographic, epidemiological, systemic, and economic—represent a converging perfect storm threatening the current and future capacity of the United States to address the challenges and problems facing its health care system. The development and application of virtual teams represent one possible approach to meet these challenges. This chapter describes why the challenging and complex demographic, economic, epidemiological, and structural factors and forces affecting health care necessitate alternative strategies to achieve meaningful improvements in health care access, quality, and outcomes. One of these strategies may be the wider application of virtual teams in health care provision. Examples of the varying application of virtual teams in different health care settings will be cited with particular emphasis on one model, virtual integrated practice (VIP), which uses virtual teams to expand and improve chronic disease management in primary care medical offices. We describe the results and lessons learned from the VIP model and discuss the implications for the future of virtual teams in health care.

The aging of the U.S. population is one of the major demographic factors driving the need for health care transformation and the application of different strategies and models for medical care. The United States, like many other countries, is an aging nation. The 38 million Americans over the age of sixty-five today will increase to 55 million by the year 2020, attributable to the aging of the baby boom generation and increased longevity (U.S. Department of Health and Human Services, 2005). Commensurate with the growth in size and longevity are the increased risks of multiple acute and chronic diseases and disabilities in older populations. Although the incidence of certain diseases is declining, these are offset by the rapid growth in other chronic conditions such as diabetes. As more Americans live longer, their risk of acquiring cognitive impairments such as Alzheimer's disease also rises, especially after age eighty-five. In the population under age sixty-five, the growing epidemic of obesity, the increasing numbers of Americans without health insurance, and the concomitant problems associated with chronic disease and disability and lack of access to health care portend that millions of adults, and increasingly children, will require more intensive treatment for many health-related conditions.

The systemic issues facing U.S. health care also argue strongly for more effective approaches to health care management. Unlike countries that have government-sponsored health care insurance and integrated systems of care such as those in Canada and many European countries, the U.S. health care system is a patchwork of competing insurance plans and health care systems that rarely intersect or collaborate. Such networks and systems range in size and organizational structure from large, integrated managed health care plans with their own clinics, hospitals, and other facilities to more traditional health care insurers that process claims for services provided by consumer- or employer-selected health care providers. For many Americans, the experience of health care is one of episodic health care visits characterized by lack of communication and collaboration among the clinicians they see. This is especially problematic for patients with complex medical and social needs. Team-oriented collaborative care is essential for meeting medically appropriate standards of care for diseases such as diabetes. *Crossing the Quality Chasm,* the Institute of Medicine's (IOM) 2001 report describing the state of health care in the United States, revealed the extent to which the health care system is failing to provide quality standards of medical care for millions of Americans. The IOM attributed much of the failure to lack of sufficient collaboration, coordination, and communication in health care.

The economic issues driving this perfect storm also compel different strategies for health care delivery. The Medicare program, already under severe economic pressure to contain and reduce costs, is projected to nearly triple in spending by the year 2030 (Thorpe & Howard, 2006). Comparable financial pressures also threaten the federal- and state-supported Medicaid program, particularly as the growing problems of the poor and those without needed preventive care will drive increased spending. The aging of the population and the millions of older Americans who will need government-supported long-term care will further burden an already stressed system. Private health care insurers, facing continuous pressures to cut costs, can be expected to push provider networks and groups to increase productivity and achieve savings while capping or decreasing payment to clinicians.

THE NEED FOR VIRTUAL TEAMS IN HEALTH CARE

These issues and challenges underscore the importance of using interdisciplinary teams to manage the complex medical and psychosocial needs of older adults, as well as other demographic groups at increased risk for chronic diseases. Interdisciplinary teams have served as the foundation of geriatric care for many years (Clark, Spence, & Sheehan, 1987) and are used in most geriatric and other health care institutions. Working with multiple other disciplines is an integral and essential component of the caregiving experience. What characterizes teamwork in most of these situations is its interpersonal nature: the face-to-face interaction and communication traditionally viewed as a necessary part of teamwork. The assumption underlying most interdisciplinary health care teams is that members usually work for the same organization and in the same location. The various stages of team organization and development—forming teams, building relationships and trust, developing team goals and objectives, strengthening interpersonal skills, communicating effectively with others, and dealing with conflict—have been major principles used in teaching teamwork. However, these stages imply that maximizing team performance requires members to be in the same place at the same time. These principles have been used in assessing team effectiveness, and they were an integral part of the assessment tools used by the John A. Hartford Foundation–supported Geriatric Interdisciplinary Team Training Program sites in educating student trainees in interdisciplinary care in the mid- to late 1990s.

While it is necessary to teach about interpersonal team behavior, goal setting, team leadership, conflict, and communication, the changes and expectations in health care delivery, particularly in community-based care, will likely require a different set of skills and processes. These skills and processes are less dependent on personal interaction and more driven by the pressures and demands of delivering quality care, meeting revenue requirements, and achieving better results in patient care outcomes.

Transition to New Models of Teams

The introduction of new strategies and complementary technologies for improving communication and collaboration is also beginning to have an impact on health care by increasing collaboration between clinicians and between clinicians and patients. Following the lead and example of other organizations that have been using virtual work teams for many years, some health care organizations have already invested in and attempted to implement new strategies and initiatives for working more virtually.

The managed care industry has been a leader in integrating technology into patient-provider communication and collaboration, with Kaiser Permanente Health Plans and other managed care organizations introducing innovations and processes for working collaboratively and, increasingly, virtually. At Kaiser, patients can go online to schedule appointments, request referrals, receive information about recent tests, and obtain information about health and disease management programs (Lawrence, 2002). At Memorial Clinical Associates, a large group practice in Houston, physicians have been using communications technology and software to organize a medical virtual group enabling physicians to obtain up-to-date information on patients, expedite referrals, and share other clinical information critical to their practice. Since the early 1990s, the VHA Medical Center in Sepulveda, California, has been using a messaging system integrated into its ambulatory care system. Under the Ambulatory Care Information System, clinicians can direct messages, including updated progress notes and other information, to other specialists in anticipation of a future patient visit so that specialties involved in the patient's care are concurrently updated on patient status and medical needs. The messages do not "open" until the next patient visit occurs (Rappaport, 1996). Clinicians at many hospitals, such as Beth Israel Deaconess Medical Center in Boston, have been using systems designed to electronically link interdisciplinary teams in the ambulatory care setting through the use of a shared electronic medical record and e-mail system (Safran et al., 1998). All of these models of communication and care coordination alter the nature of interdisciplinary collaboration and lessen the need for in-person interaction.

Challenges to Virtual Collaboration in Medicine and Primary Care

Although the justification for innovative approaches such as virtual teams to managing chronically ill and frail patients is evident, the difficulties and obstacles to organizing and implementing these kinds of teams are challenging. The prevailing landscape of health delivery today underscores the need for different strategies in primary health care delivery. Over 50 percent of all medical practices in the United States have five or fewer physicians (Wassenar & Thran, 2003), and the majority lack the financial or logistical resources to link other health care disciplines into an integrated coordinated team for their patients.

Lacking the financial resources, willingness, or the time to invest in electronic health records and other tools to organize and improve data management and communication processes, most medical practices are functioning much as they did three or more decades ago, using paper medical files and charts. According to *Health Data Management* magazine ("Survey," 2006), less than 25 percent of physicians currently use an electronic medical record in their practices. A minority of physicians use e-mail or other Web-based tools to communicate with their patients. Many physicians who are accustomed to traditional interpersonal contact with patients may find accommodating new types of interaction difficult.

Another major factor discouraging collaborative interdisciplinary teams in primary care is the fractionated, competitive, and discontinuous nature of the health care system. The vast majority of small group medical practices are paid by multiple insurers, each with different compliance and informational requirements. These burdensome and time-consuming requirements are often compounded by disruptions in physician-patient relationships if employer- or other payer-based systems change or discontinue health care networks for their members, forcing patients to establish new relationships with other doctors.

VIRTUAL INTEGRATED PRACTICE MODEL

At Rush University Medical Center in Chicago, these challenges were the catalyst for Rush clinicians and researchers to develop the idea of using virtual interdisciplinary teams. The results of these efforts—a different approach to interdisciplinary care entitled virtual integrated practice (VIP)—have demonstrated its utility in better coordination of care and improved communication between patients and their health care team.

The VIP model organizes a virtual interdisciplinary collaborative team around a primary care practice. Health care professionals from various disciplines—pharmacy, dietetics, social work, occupational therapy, and others—are recruited as a team and linked to a selected primary care practice or practices. Team members are recruited from a variety of sources, including public and nonprofit agencies (social workers), pharmacy chains (pharmacists), hospitals, and ambulatory clinics (dietitians). Incentives to participate in this system include the potential of adding new patients to their practice and building new revenue and collaborative care opportunities by linking to busy physician practices.

VIP has four types of tools or processes: standardized processes, communication protocols, group visits, and patient self-management. Each tool was designed to support the application of accepted standards of medical care guidelines for treating chronic diseases through a dispersed virtual team. Each offers a variety of options and processes involving some or all members of the virtual team.

Standardized Processes

Standardized processes are the processes, activities, or protocols that a medical practice using VIP employs to improve patient care and make best use of its team assets. With standardized processes, each member of the team is responsible for some part of the caregiving process for patients with multiple medical, and perhaps social, needs. An example is an automatic referral to a VIP team member for a clinical consultation triggered by an abnormal test result, recent hospitalization, or other event.

One of the VIP sites sought to improve performance against benchmarks in diabetes care; in particular, patients made slow progress in achieving targets for diabetes control. The team's analysis indicated that every change in medication, every order for testing, and every referral for specialty services required an action by a physician. Because of overwork, physicians would often delay or defer these time-consuming actions until a later date, hoping the patient would respond to exhortations to "eat better" or "exercise more."

The team decided to implement a standard process for all diabetic patients. Standing orders were prepared that authorized office staff to draw predetermined blood tests every six months whenever a diabetic patient presented to the office. The office nurse reviewed these test results each day; if they were not at predetermined target values, the nurse would contact the patient and inquire about the patient's adherence to medications. Problems with adherence, such as the cost of medications or forgetting to take the medicines, were referred to the team pharmacist who was aware of the process and had identified responses to the common problems. If there were no problems with adherence, the nurse would refer to the team dietitian for intensive nutrition education. Blood tests were also immediately rescheduled in three months to review the patient's progress; if no progress was seen at the repeat blood test, the physician received a report from the nurse highlighting a need to adjust medication therapy. The nurse would then contact the patient and the pharmacist with the new medication plan; the pharmacist would review the change with the patient to ensure that he or she understood the changes.

This approach eliminated the physician as a bottleneck to change, a process sometimes described as clinical inertia. By creating a standardized process for every diabetic patient, team members understood their role in improving patient outcomes against a specific laboratory target. Standing orders empowered front-line team members to initiate interventions and accelerated patient improvements within a few weeks rather than months.

Communication Protocols

Communication protocols serve as the threads or links that define team communication and collaboration and intervention for patient care. Protocols are organized to address which patient care events shall trigger team communication, what tools (such as e-mail, phone, fax) the team will use to communicate and inform other members, and which members of the team will follow up on intervention and treatment.

In the example of standardized processes in diabetes care, the team determined how best to communicate with each other. A large volume of telephone calls, pages, and other real-time contacts could have quickly overwhelmed their system and led to frustration by team members. The group decided at the outset to limit such communications to just two situations: the nurse's contact with patients and in response to certain critical lab values that required urgent physician action. All other contacts could take place asynchronously, not at the same time. Since the pharmacy was already using faxes to contact the physician offices, this became the preferred contact mode, using a form that indicated the patient name, recent test results, and the planned intervention—either medication adherence assistance or adjustment in prescriptions. After the nurse had spoken to the patient, she completed the form and faxed it to the pharmacist, who reviewed it at the start of the next day. Personal preferences also influence communication protocols; in this case, the dietitian preferred e-mail communication to faxes.

Patient Self-Management

Patients are given a variety of educational tools and materials to help them follow through with activities for self-care and to encourage personal health account-ability for. These might include wallet-sized cards (see Exhibit 25.1) to keep track of appointments, test results, and reminders to perform various activities. Information from these cards is then regularly shared with the patient's health care providers during office visits. This low-tech intervention gives team members in different locations access to specific clinical data. As the exhibit shows, the tool also puts specific numerical targets for care into the patient's hands. In place of the traditional interaction where a physician interprets data and indicates whether the patient is healthy, this intervention changes the process to one in which patients can evaluate their own progress. With this approach, patients actively engage VIP team members (listed on the card) to get needed help in improving their own care.

Group Visits

Group visits are included in the VIP toolbox as a means of easing and supporting the challenges of patient compliance. Based on a group visit model successfully used in other health care systems, group visits allow patients with the same diag-nosis to meet with their physician in small group appointments or settings of perhaps ten to twelve patients, allowing them to share issues and problems, receive consultation from their physician or other team clinicians, and helping them address their personal health care issues.

For a practice with large numbers of arthritis patients, a group visit model reg-ularly brought together patients limited by joint pains, following this agenda:

Exhibit 25.1
Personal Diabetes Record

HOW AM I DOING??   The American Diabetes Associate recommends the following standards of care:

Have your doctor check these tests every 3 months!

TEST	GOAL
Hemoglobin A1c	
Blood Pressure	

DATE	DATE	DATE	DATE

DATE	DATE	DATE	DATE

Have these exams or services at least once a year!

TEST	GOAL
Cholesterol Total	
HDL Cholesterol	
LDL Cholesterol	
Triglycerides	

My doctor is _____

Telephone Number:

Rush Nutrition Clinic

Pharmacy _____

DATE	DATE	DATE	DATE

Podiatrist _____

TEST	GOAL
Creatine	
Urine Microalbumen	

Social Worker _____

Rush Eye Center

DATE	DATE	DATE	DATE

Rush University Internal Medicine VIP Project

Dentist _____

I AM TAKING THE FOLLOWING MEDICINES:

PERSONAL DIABETES RECORD

Better care of your diabetes means fewer complications and healthier life! Use this cared to take charge of your health care. Carry it with you at all times and have your doctor or nurse practitioner update it all each visit. Show it to your pharmacist, your eye doctor, your dietician, and other team members who help you with your health.

Incase of Emergency, please call:

Their Telephone Number:

_____

_____

_____

_____

_____

_____

_____

_____

MY OTHER MEDICAL PROBLEMS:

Services	DATE	DATE	DATE
Flu Shot			
Foot Examination			
Ophthalmologist			
Dentist			

Quitting Smoking			

...and don't forget your regular medical care!

WOMEN: Pap Tests, Mammograms

MEN: Prostate Exam, PSA Test

EVERYONE: Colon Cancer Screening

I have talked to my diabetes team about the following issues, and I understand them:

	Dates of discussion & Provider initials		
My diet plan			
Exercise Program			
How to test my sugar			
How to handle high and low sugars			
Caring for my feet			
Handling sick days			
Stress Management			

8:45 A.M.	Patients arrive; nurse records weight, blood pressure.
9:00 A.M.	Welcome; introductions.
9:05 A.M.	Assessments. Physician goes around the room, asking each patient about joint pain and swelling and examines affected joints. Patient questions are answered for the group.
9:45 A.M.	Group discussion. Physical therapist leads conversation about how patients handle common everyday challenges. During this period, physician conducts individual visits in an examination room with patients who wish to have private time with the doctor.
10:20 A.M.	Wrap-up. Topics for next month's visit are determined.

The approach allowed the physician to conduct an effective evaluation of ten or more patients in the time previously used for only four to six patients. Patients found that by seeing a range of other people with problems similar to their own, they gained a better understanding of their disease and different ways it could affect them. During the assessment part of the visit, the physician answered questions and provided education about new medications or treatments of interest to all of the patients. Later, when the physician was examining individual patients, the group continued to meet with a physical therapist to discuss how they were coping with pain and managing everyday activities. Patients highly valued this peer-to-peer interaction. In addition, the group began to identify services they wanted to include in the group visit, such as nutrition education to help them lose weight. Both the doctor and the patients looked forward to this monthly group visit, feeling it provided more time for productive interaction. The group visit also provided an opportunity for previously virtual team members to have periodic real-time contacts with each other, strengthening the bond among team members.

AN APPLICATION OF THE VIP MODEL

To implement VIP for integrated, team-coordinated care, a five-year demonstration project, funded by the John A. Hartford Foundation through its Geriatric Interdisciplinary Teams in Practice Initiative, was launched. Eight medical practices were recruited and enrolled in the project. Four medical practices were each assigned a virtual or VIP team consisting of a dietitian, social service specialist, and pharmacist with whom they could consult in managing patients. VIP team members were recruited from Rush University Medical Center and community-based agencies and pharmacies. Four other practices served as control sites for comparative purposes through the two-year implementation phase of the project. Each of the intervention sites, after participating in a brief series of training sessions, developed protocols and strategies with their VIP team. Using e-mail, telephone, and fax, the physicians and nurses in the VIP sites seldom saw their team members in person yet worked together as a seamless group.

Each practice took a different approach to how they would coordinate care for their patients using their virtual team. One practice developed a special form that the physicians and the dietitian used as an ongoing communication and patient tracking tool to expedite referrals for dietetic counseling, monitor patient compliance with dietary recommendations, and determine the need for other types of care. Another practice implemented a protocol in which any patient with an abnormal glucose result was sent a letter recommending that he or she contact the practice's team dietitian for follow-up dietetic counseling. The dietitian was copied on each letter and contacted patients after thirty days if they had not responded. A third practice implemented a variety of patient self-management tools, including a card for patients to use to keep track of appointments, recent test results, and health habits reminders. The card also served as a reminder and reinforcement of patient compliance with treatment goals.

Analysis of data collected over the two-year implementation period from those practices using VIP compared to the control sites yielded some interesting findings regarding the efficacy of using virtual teams: improved patient communication and understanding of health needs, greater provider collaboration, and modest reduction in use of some health care services, including emergency room visits and rehospitalizations. Physicians in VIP sites reported a greater likelihood of knowing the reason for their patients' visits compared to physicians in control sites. The number of referrals to other providers in VIP sites exceeded those in control sites. Patients reported greater understanding of medication use. Low physically functioning patients in VIP sites had a lower rate of emergency room visits and hospitalizations as compared to comparable patients in control sites.

To illustrate the VIP model in practice, the following case example describes how one patient is cared for in a practice using VIP.

A CASE EXAMPLE OF THE VIP MODEL

Dr. Rosen, an internist, has decided to participate in a new program for managing patients with chronic disease: virtual integrated practice (VIP). He had completed a short orientation and training program that helped him decide what practice improvements he wanted to make and some strategies to achieve them. Since he did not have a dietitian, social worker, or pharmacist to collaborate with already, a team was organized for him consisting of a dietitian based in the hospital dietetics department, a social worker from the city department on aging, and a pharmacist based at a retail pharmacy where about 40 percent of Dr. Rosen's patients get their prescriptions.

One of the first patients Dr. Rosen and his team decided to involve in VIP was Evelyn Brown, an eighty-year-old widow who lives alone. Her medical problems included diabetes, hypertension, and osteoarthritis. For the second time in three months, she had been hospitalized for problems related to poor diabetic control. She had gained more than ten pounds, was eating poorly, and had been depressed since the recent death of her husband. Dr. Rosen was concerned that her difficulties in managing her health needs would lead to further, yet preventable, complications.

In evaluating Mrs. Brown's condition, Dr. Rosen and his team members decided on a number of actions, including assistance in managing her diet, arranging grief counseling, and evaluation of her medications by a pharmacist to determine possible drug interactions and side effects.

Before Mrs. Brown was discharged, Dr. Rosen told her that other health care providers on his team would be contacting her to offer assistance. Since he had changed some of her medications, the team's communication protocol was triggered. Dr. Rosen sent an e-mail to the team pharmacist requesting that he explain to Mrs. Brown how to take her new medications and the effects any herbal medicines she uses may have on them. The dietitian was also contacted and asked to discuss dietary changes Mrs. Brown needed to make. As previously determined by the team's standardized process, her new medications were ready when she visited the pharmacy, and the pharmacist counseled her on the medication management issues Dr. Rosen requested.

The social worker, following an e-mail request from Dr. Rosen, called Mrs. Brown to schedule a home visit. During the visit, she found Mrs. Brown depressed and her house unkempt, with little food at home. The social worker encouraged Mrs. Brown to join a grief support group at a nearby senior center and arranged for the local department on aging to send a homemaker once every two weeks to clean Mrs. Brown's home and assist her with grocery shopping and meal preparation. She requested that Mrs. Brown start receiving home-delivered meals three days a week. The social worker informed Dr. Rosen and the dietitian of these actions in a brief e-mail.

The dietitian contacted Mrs. Brown to see how she was managing and reassured her that she would call her monthly to follow up on her progress. In their regular conversations, the dietitian helped Mrs. Brown make better food choices and engage in self-management of her diabetes.

At Mrs. Brown's next appointment, Dr. Rosen was pleased to see that she had lost several pounds, her lab tests were better, and her mood seemed to have improved. Mrs. Brown continued to function well with the support of her team and avoided any further hospitalizations for the following twelve months.

The case illustrates how Dr. Rosen and his virtual team members agreed on patient needs, arranged appropriate services, and communicated as needed to monitor the patient's progress and care plans.

FINAL THOUGHTS

Current research and investigations focusing on the inadequacies and failures in the provision of health care in the United States are both urgent warnings and compelling reasons for trying different approaches to reorganizing our medical care system. Some industries and their advocates believe increased use of electronic health records, disease management programs, telemedicine, and other innovations and interventions may be the answer to narrowing the gaps in what is needed to ensure sufficient health care and the resources available to bridge them. As-yet-unforeseen changes in the health care system and continued advances in technology may offer exciting new possibilities of care.

For clinicians and investigators, continuing to explore innovative ways of coupling advances in information and communication technology with the interdisciplinary team imperative presents exciting challenges and opportunities to ensure a health care system that is humane, more economically efficient, collaborative, and accessible to all. As clinicians, patients, and caregivers increasingly adapt to and integrate the use of technology in their work and personal lives, the nature of the health care relationship will likely change as well. While still recognizing and valuing the importance of the personal relationship between patient and clinician and among clinicians, interdisciplinary models of care, whether virtual or otherwise, must have as a goal improvements in the quality of care patients receive, with more productive and fulfilling work lives for health care providers as a commensurate result.

REMINDERS

- The health care industry, lagging other industries in its adoption of virtual teams to better link disparate work and practice sites, offers exciting potential for future use. The continued gaps and absence of coordination and collaboration in health care delivery invite the expanded use of virtual teams to overcome these barriers.

- Although the models of virtual teams described in this chapter have largely focused on their application in primary care, virtual teams offer promising opportunities and applications in a variety of health care settings and can be designed and deployed for purposes ranging from interdisciplinary team management of chronic diseases to reinforcing and supporting patient self-help and self-management reminders and techniques.

- Successful virtual teams in health care management more often involve creative and logical use of existing sources rather than development of new ones. Health care providers are more likely to be receptive to using virtual teams for reasons of innovation, potential financial incentives, and commitment to improve patient accessibility and care coordination.

- Virtual teams in health care practice generally require minimal investment of financial resources, making them particularly attractive to health care organizations and providers interested in adapting new processes of patient care but economically constrained from doing so. The real investment comes in health care practitioners' willingness to commit time and effort to learning how virtual teams can be a useful tool and organizing the team of providers with whom they can collaborate.

References

Clark, P. G., Spence, D. L., & Sheehan, J. L. (1987). A service/learning model for interdisciplinary teamwork in health and aging. *Gerontology and Geriatrics Education, 6*(4) 1987, 3–17.

Institute of Medicine. (2001). *Crossing the quality chasm: A new health system for the 21st century.* Washington, DC: National Academy Press

Lawrence, D. L. (2002). *From chaos to care.* Cambridge, MA: Perseus.

Rappaport, S. H. (1996). Supporting the "clinic without walls" with an event-directed messaging system integrated into an electronic medical record. In *Proceedings of the American Medical Informatics Association* (pp. 648–652). Washington, DC: Hanley & Belfus.

Safran, C., Jones, P. C., Rind, D., Bush, B., Cytryn, K. N., & Patel, V. L. (1998). Electronic communication and collaboration in a health care practice. *Artificial Intelligence in Medicine, 12,* 137–151.

Survey: Physician EMR use grows. (2006). *Health Data Management, 14,* 7.

Thorpe, E. K., & Howard, D. H. (2006, August 22). The rise in spending among Medicare beneficiaries: The role of chronic disease prevalence and changes in treatment intensity. *Health Affairs Web Exclusive.* Retrieved September 13, 2007, from http://content.healthaffairs.org.cgi/content/full/25/5/w378.

U.S. Department of Health and Human Services. Administration on Aging. (2005). *A profile of older Americans: 2005.* Washington, DC: U.S. Government Printing Office.

Wassenar, J. D., & Thran, S. L. (Eds.). (2003). *Physician socioeconomic statistics, 2003 edition.* Chicago: AMA Press.

Distributed Work

Using Data to Drive Business-Focused Decision Making

Anita Kamouri, Eric Richert

As workforces in global organizations become increasingly more distributed, the need to make decisions that affect the design, implementation, and management of remote work and virtual teams becomes ever more prevalent. The potential impact of distributed work on the productivity, cost efficiency, and competitiveness of the organization, coupled with the risks of failure to implement a successful transition because of poor decisions, make the need to understand the decision-making process about distributed work critical.

Given the relative newness of distributed work in organizations in general, and virtual teams in particular, it is difficult to make informed decisions based on solid evidence or actual experience with implementing distributed work. A solid knowledge base associated with both the why and how of these decisions has yet to be established. Decision makers in organizations are often taxed with making decisions about areas of distributed work with which they have little or no experience. Consequently many organizational decision makers turn to outside experts to make critical decisions, leaving the organization without the underlying knowledge or internal expertise to make future decisions.

As Sun Microsystems embarked on the exploration of distributed work, it wanted to understand how the transition from proximate work (work performed in physical proximity to others, including face-to-face collaboration) to distributed work (some portion of work activity performed across distance, including remote individual work and virtual team work) would affect desired organizational outcomes. It wanted to use this understanding to make sound business decisions. In creating the rationale for these business decisions, the goal was to make the decision-making process explicit (Nonaka & Konno, 1998). To accomplish this, Sun needed to define the data going into the decisions, describe the expected impact of specific actions on desired outcomes, and identify the range of viable decision options. Accordingly, data-driven approaches (Pfeffer & Sutton, 2006) were adopted because they rely on an explicit process guided by the best available logic, evidence, and knowledge to arrive at decisions. These approaches were used to make decisions about the appropriateness of distributed work models, design the supporting system of infrastructure necessary for success, and provide direction to implementation strategies. These approaches also helped to manage risk by drawing on multiple sources of data as the basis for decisions and avoiding potential problem areas. Finally, these approaches helped to turn the distributed work data into knowledge by creating a foundation for empirically evaluating whether the decisions were working as intended over time.

This chapter explores how data of various kinds can be applied using a decision process to determine when and how distributed work can benefit organizations, teams, and individuals and describes the data-driven methods Sun used successfully to make business-focused decisions about distributed work options.

This chapter first reviews the data used to identify the components of an integrated system of supporting infrastructure that is needed for successful distributed work configurations. Next, it describes how to use the data to evaluate the appropriateness and scope of distributed work within the current organization and create effective implementation strategies. Finally, it reflects on the value of using an explicit data-based approach and how evidence of decision effectiveness can be gathered and used to improve future decisions.

BLACK BOX DECISION MAKING

When organizations invest in infrastructure to support their workforces, the current general practice is to move quickly to investment decisions based on insufficient data or analysis and without directly linking those decisions to business objectives or to the work activities needed to achieve those objectives (Pullen, 2005). Generally decisions are made based on rules-of-thumb or personal heuristics rooted in long-held, often private, tacit assumptions about work: how and where individuals and teams accomplish work, how teams interact, how infrastructure affects individuals and groups, and how work relates to other aspects of nonwork life. At Sun, this is referred to as black box decision making because outsiders do not know how the decisions are being made. These black box decision-making practices are depicted in Figure 26.1.

Because long-held assumptions are typically tacit, they receive little or no discussion before infrastructure decisions are made. Thus, new phenomena such as distributed work and virtual teams can be difficult to grasp because they challenge long-held assumptions and practices. Furthermore, because functional support groups such as real estate (RE), information technology (IT), and human

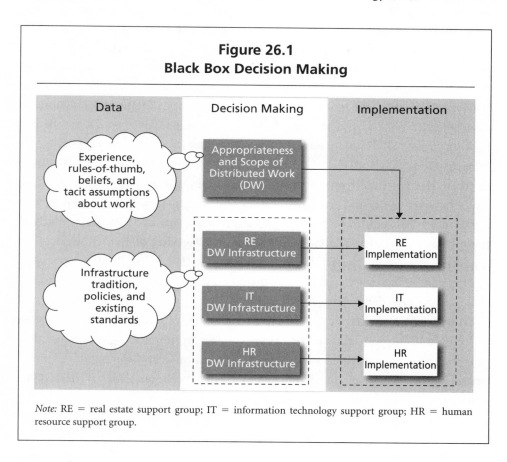

Figure 26.1
Black Box Decision Making

Note: RE = real estate support group; IT = information technology support group; HR = human resource support group.

resources (HR) traditionally have had independent goals and objectives, they typically have engaged in independent planning and implementation (Kaplan & Norton, 2006). While the groups are often aware of what the other is doing, budgets and strategies are typically not developed or changed based on awareness of the needs of other functions. As a result, RE, IT, and HR decisions are not always as integrated as they should be to create an optimal system of support for distributed work.

DATA-DRIVEN DECISION MAKING

In the late 1990s, Sun found that a different approach to making decisions was needed. Initially this need was driven by Sun's first significant shift from desktop to data center products. The change in product strategy required a broad change in how product development and delivery needed to be coordinated across marketing, engineering, and manufacturing teams and in how customers would be engaged and then serviced following purchase of Sun's products. The urgent need to shift product focus, coupled with a long period of rapid growth, caused questions to be asked about how to support key work activities in a way that would be both more effective and more affordable. These questions required discussions of assumptions about work that until then had remained closed to debate. Before making decisions about investment in new places of work and supporting IT infrastructure, Sun's business leaders wanted to understand the options available to them, the potential impacts on their businesses, and the possible effect they could have on teams and employees. Sun's senior management was open to new possibilities but required a strong business case for any changes, particularly if these changes required greater distribution and mobility of the workforce that might put employee effectiveness or loyalty at risk. The ability to develop strong business cases for change ultimately proved essential in garnering the support that would be needed to implement change.

In response, data-driven decision methodologies were introduced to create an objective and business-driven criteria set for determining the right combination of infrastructure components to support the workforce and evaluate the appropriateness and scope of distributed work across the organization. These data-driven decision making practices are depicted in Figure 26.2.

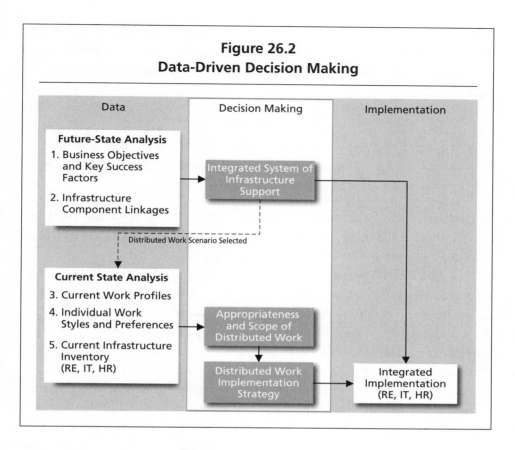

Figure 26.2
Data-Driven Decision Making

As Figure 26.2 suggests, five data perspectives were used to inform distributed work decisions. These five perspectives were selected to represent three levels of analysis: the organization, the work (which includes team activities), and the individual. The first two data perspectives are based on a future-state analysis of the business and provide the guidance necessary to design a viable future system of infrastructure support integrated across infrastructure groups and linked to desired outcomes:

- Business objectives and the key success factors that represent the critical underlying aspects of work needed to accomplish business objectives

- Real estate (RE), information technology (IT), and human resource (HR) infrastructure components needed to support attainment of key success factors

The next three data perspectives are based on a current-state analysis of the business and provide the guidance necessary to determine the appropriateness and scope of distributed work across the current organization and formulate a realistic implementation strategy:

- Current work activity profiles for the workforce involved in the change
- Individual work styles and preferences that can affect behaviors and choices
- Inventory of current infrastructure provided by the RE, IT, and HR groups

Together these data provide an objective foundation on which distributed work decisions can be made. Furthermore, the data provide common criteria for RE, IT, and HR planning and implementation efforts, which has the benefit of fostering an integrated and optimized system of infrastructure support.

In a data-driven approach, information, statistics, and facts need to be critically evaluated to inform each of these data perspectives; otherwise limited personal experience, hype, or unfounded beliefs become the de facto "truths" that drive decisions. To support this approach, some degree of investment in the development of reliable and valid data collection methodologies is recommended (Carmines & Zeller, 1985). In addition to an investment of time and resources, companies often face additional challenges with data-driven decision making, including having too much data, having insufficient good data, and having a management audience that mistrusts the data or is concerned about being misled by data—particularly when the information contradicts their long-held beliefs and assumptions. To overcome these challenges, Sun approached its decisions with a variety of methods that provide a healthy mix of both data and experience, draw on qualitative as well as quantitative information, and involve decision makers so they have a stake in the decision outcome.

FUTURE-STATE ANALYSIS

When considering changes in work distribution or whether distributed work models are appropriate, Sun found it important to first identify the range of viable alternative solutions that should be considered and then systematically examine the extent to which each could be expected to support what the organization was trying to achieve. While distributed work solutions may help some organizations and their teams achieve their future desired outcomes, a more traditional proximate work arrangement may lead to desired outcomes in other organizations and teams. In either case, designing the right integrated system of infrastructure support enables the work activities needed for the accomplishment of desired business outcomes. The following sections describe how the first two data perspectives in Figure 26.2 create an integrated system of infrastructure support based on a systematic evaluation of the explicit linkage between infrastructure components and desired business outcomes.

Data Perspective 1: Business Objectives and Key Success Factors

Business objectives represent what the organization intends to achieve and their desired business outcomes (Hamel & Prahalad, 2005). They may be in the form of goals, strategies, or intents with respect to future business direction. Typical business objectives at Sun have included improving operational efficiencies, increasing customer satisfaction, improving employee satisfaction and retention, and reducing costs. Moving from the current to a desired future business model is another typical business objective, for example, moving from hardware sales to solution-selling models, or moving from reactive customer problem support to proactive, preemptive service delivery.

Business objectives describe how success is defined by the business and define the essential outcomes that any business-driven distributed work solution must support. Although various distributed work alternatives can typically be created, the impacts of distributed work on business objectives are often difficult to establish. This is because the supporting components (the RE, HR, and IT components used to enable distributed work) have an indirect rather than direct impact on business objectives through key practices and behaviors associated with how the work is done by individuals and by teams. For example, increased customer satisfaction (a business objective) can be achieved by delivering on-site twenty-four-hour support using an on-call distributed workforce of customer service technicians. Increased customer satisfaction can also be achieved through knowledge sharing and problem solving among technical experts who are colocated in a centralized operations center. Therefore, additional data that express how the company wants these business objectives to be accomplished become another key input for determining the viability of distributed work models.

Key success factors (KSFs) represent the critical and necessary factors that affect the organization's ability to achieve business objectives (Peffers, Gengler, & Tuunanen,

Table 26.1
Example Key Success Factors

Historically Supported by Distributed Work Models	Historically Supported by Proximate Work Models
Engage with customers anywhere they are located	Solve problems collaboratively with team members
Codevelop solutions with partners in other organizations	Share knowledge informally
Deliver twenty-four-hour support at customer sites	Provide coworker support as needed
Hire and retain talent wherever they are located	Adopt extreme software programming methodologies
Work anywhere, anytime, on any device	Build team affiliation and cohesion
Create, use, and reuse knowledge across the organization	Have immediate, physical access to on-site equipment
Have immediate access to information	Actively mentor and train new employees

2003; Williams & Ramaprasad, 1996). They are the critical mechanism that links infrastructure components to business objectives. They are typically in the form of desired work practices and behaviors reflecting a future state that is often different from current or typical practices in place within the organization. Example KSFs are listed in Table 26.1. As the table suggests, there are some KSFs that distributed work models have historically been designed to support and for which many companies have had success. There are also KSFs that historically have been more effectively supported by proximate work models, and around which many companies have experienced challenges when attempting to implement distributed work. Understanding the types of KSFs that are necessary for accomplishing the organization's unique business objectives becomes critical in evaluating the appropriateness of distributed versus proximate work models.

Since business objectives and KSFs are judgments, and difficult if not impossible to determine empirically, these are defined through interviews or focus groups with the leadership members of an organization who have the appropriate level of influence and perspective. At a basic level, this provides qualitative data to help

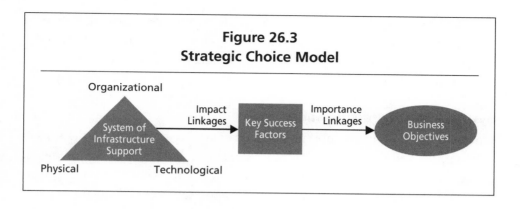

Figure 26.3
Strategic Choice Model

Organizational

System of Infrastructure Support

Impact Linkages

Key Success Factors

Importance Linkages

Business Objectives

Physical

Technological

inform distributed work decisions. To introduce the rigor of data-based decision making, the leaders of the affected organization are asked to make judgments about the importance of KSFs in driving business objectives. These judgments are in the form of numerical ratings that can be aggregated in order to summarize the strength of the perceived linkages. The aggregated linkages reflect the relative importance of KSFs in supporting desired business outcomes and are part of a data-based decision methodology developed for and used extensively at Sun called Strategic Choice. Figure 26.3 provides an overview of the Strategic Choice model.

The value of this decision method is that it makes hypotheses about cause-and-effect relationships explicit within the context of distributed work decision making through the linkage ratings. Many times at Sun, the aggregate rating results challenged the individual assumptions of leaders by showing that distributed work KSFs were perceived to be more important in achieving business objectives than was otherwise assumed. This generated much discussion about traditional assumptions: how historically proximate work practices might be accomplished differently and how distributed work practices could have a more positive impact than proximate practices on desired outcomes such as employee retention (for example by providing more flexibility and work-nonwork balance) and team performance. In addition, the use of the rating data forced decision makers to consider implications across the full range of KSFs rather than focusing on one or two KSFs that might be salient for the business at that particular time. This process shapes decisions that are optimized across all KSFs rather than suboptimized for a limited subset of KSFs.

In summary, the business objectives and KSFs provide a clear depiction of business needs that must be supported by any distributed work solution under consideration and are the key criteria for evaluating the appropriateness and scope of distributed work.

System of Infrastructure Support

Once the KSF-to-business objective linkages have been established, the drivers that support and influence the accomplishment of KSFs need to be identified. These drivers support work activities, which in turn influence KSF achievement. In our work at Sun, an integrated system of support was defined as all the physical (locations, spaces, furniture), technological (voice, data, video, Web), and organizational (structure, policies, norms) components that enable a desired set of KSFs, which in turn underlie attainment of business objectives. This model of influence, introduced in Figure 26.3, represents the three-part nature of the integrated system. Each part of the system—organizational, physical, and technological—is essential, and each area includes a complementary set of infrastructure components. The identification of infrastructure components that will enable KSFs is typically conducted in conjunction with subject matter experts and based on professional knowledge, published research, and practical experience. Table 26.2 illustrates a system of infrastructure support compiled from various Strategic Choice efforts conducted at Sun.

For each infrastructure component, there are choices of how it can be implemented. For example, when considering a component such as work space priority, the workplace design can include the choice of prioritizing group spaces such as conference rooms, team rooms, and informal collaboration spaces that support collaborative work, or prioritizing individual spaces such as private offices that provide individuals with a quiet, distraction-free workplace. When choices from each infrastructure component are made, the configuration of infrastructure choices must be carefully selected to reinforce each other while also avoiding conflict with other choices that could negate their possible positive benefit. In Table 26.2, the middle column presents one set of choices for each infrastructure component that supports distributed work KSFs. For comparison, the far right column presents a second set of alternative choices for each component that is intended to support proximate work KSFs. As the table suggests, the infrastructure choices in each column combine to form a scenario, which can be considered

Table 26.2
Example System of Infrastructure Support

	Infrastructure Components	Example Distributed Work Scenario	Example Proximate Work Scenario
Workplace components	Work space priority	Group	Individual
	Proximity to customer	Proximate	Distant
	Work locations	Distributed	Centralized
	Management work location	Interspersed	Executive row
	Home as a work location	Yes	No
	Workplace office	Unassigned and shared by many	Assigned to individuals
Technology components	Technology access	Portable	Stationary
	Document management	Electronic	Hard copy
	Telephone and voice services	Follow	Fixed
	Collaboration technologies	Robust	Basic
	Technical support	Ubiquitous	Company premises
	Application environment	Portal based	Local
Organization practice components	Group or team processes	Planned	Spontaneous
	Training and skill building	Virtual	In person
	Managing performance	Results based	Process based
	Talent pool hiring	Skill based	Location based
	Accessibility	Protocols	Physical
	Knowledge management	Formal	Informal

a plausible and complete system of integrated infrastructure components to support an organization's work.

Each scenario has different combinations of workplace, technology, and organizational practices choices and therefore requires different commitments on the part of the organization to make them work effectively. Because different choices

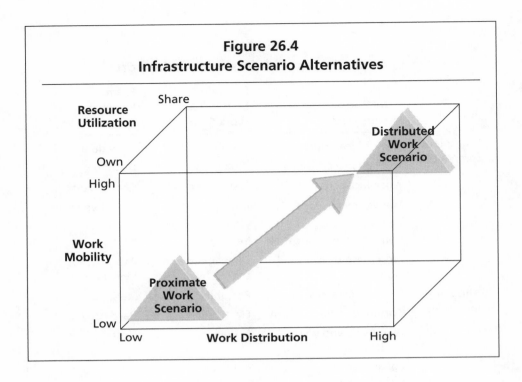

Figure 26.4
Infrastructure Scenario Alternatives

influence KSFs (and ultimately business objectives) differently, some scenarios may be expected to enable attainment of certain goals (such as collaboration or cost reduction) better than others. Consequently, to identify the best system of infrastructure support across a wide range of business objectives and KSFs, several scenarios should be considered as plausible infrastructure design solutions. Figure 26.4 illustrates a cube with three dimensions that provide one way of visualizing a wide range of possible scenarios. Each possibility is illustrative of a feasible alternative design and consists of a unique combination of workplace, technology, and organizational practice infrastructure choices.

Scenarios that fit toward the upper right back corner of the cube in Figure 26.4 provide more support to business objectives and KSFs that imply a more virtual and distributed workforce. However, the KSFs nearly always describe a rich diversity of needed work activities, both proximate and distributed. Confidently selecting the scenario that will best meet an organization's overall needs is best supported by data—data that will suggest which combination of infrastructure components is expected to have the greatest combined positive impact across the range of KSFs.

Data Perspective 2: Infrastructure Component Linkages

While some empirical evidence suggests the potential impact of infrastructure on KSFs, a complete body of knowledge about these impacts is lacking. Strategic choice therefore embeds a methodology to generate infrastructure linkage ratings. This methodology involves collecting data in the form of impact judgments from subject matter experts on the impact that each infrastructure choice will have on each KSF. The judgments are expressed as numerical ratings that representatives from the organization, in conjunction with functional experts, make as a way of expressing their experience-based hypothesized impacts. By quantifying and aggregating the experts' judgments across infrastructure choices, a summary score is created for each alternative scenario that is an expression of what the experts predict will be the impact of the scenarios across all the KSFs and, ultimately, the business objectives. (Refer to the Illustration of Scenario Scoring on the www.wiley.com/go/virtualteamshandbook Web site for an example that illustrates and explains the scoring.) This process produces quantitative data describing the relative predicted effectiveness of alternative scenarios (infrastructure choices) that decision makers can use to make data-driven decisions.

Generating and using expert judgment data in this way is important for several reasons. First, the process and data help ensure that viable scenario choices are appropriately considered. Before deciding on a scenario, decision makers want to know what the other options are and to be convinced why one scenario is better than another. By providing data on the expected impacts of each alternative, this data-based methodology gives decision makers the confidence in the decisions they need to make.

Second, providing judgment data in this manner helps ensure that each KSF will be appropriately considered in the decision-making process. A significant problem with the black box decision approach is that the "KSF of the moment" is often given great weight in decision making, while other KSFs that need support are not acknowledged.

Third, the process and data help mediate between KSFs that are in conflict with each other. The aggregate of expert judgments results in expressions of importance of each infrastructure choice across all KSFs. This helps ensure a reasoned judgment of how much support one KSF that might imply a proximate work model receives versus another KSF that might imply a distributed work model.

Fourth, those who will be most affected by decisions make the expert judgments. This part of the process is of great value if the decisions made indicate the need for substantial change in work activities or in how those activities are supported (infrastructure investments). Those making the judgments are in the end the ones advocating and affected by the changes.

Finally, the data generated and how they are used ensure that decisions about all three of the infrastructure areas are made simultaneously and in an integrated manner. If the decisions move into implementation, the risk that one area, such as HR, will be in conflict with another, such as IT, is greatly reduced. In addition, by focusing on an integrated approach, the tendency for one functional group, such as RE, to implement changes without consideration of HR and IT implications is also reduced.

In summary, data on infrastructure linkages, generated and used as part of the strategic choice process, make explicit any hypotheses about cause-and-effect relationships in the decision process, produce data about predicted scenario effectiveness, and address several concerns associated with black box decision making.

Scenario Selection

A future-state analysis was used to identify business objectives, KSFs, and infrastructure options. This resulted in the identification of one or more scenarios that have the potential to support the organization's desired outcomes effectively. Typically decision makers select one of the higher-scoring scenarios to implement as part of a short- or long-term plan.

Since this approach is not biased toward the selection of either proximate or distributed scenarios, either type could attain a higher score depending on the organization's business objectives and KSFs. If the higher-scoring scenarios better support proximate rather than distributed work and the sponsor of the process believes that distributed work may be effective, further engagement with the organization may be needed to evaluate whether traditional work biases influenced business objectives, KSFs, or the linkage judgments. Although there are situations in which proximate work models can be optimal (for example, centralized delivery of automated or Web-based functions), some degree of change management intervention may be needed before engaging in distributed work decision making to allow consideration of other viable alternatives.

CURRENT-STATE ANALYSIS

When the selected scenario suggests a distributed work arrangement, a current-state analysis provides valuable information to determine the appropriateness and scope of a distributed work initiative across the organization (see Figure 26.2). Understanding existing work profiles and how they vary from the desired work practices embodied in the KSF can help the organization determine the jobs and teams most suitable for distributed work. Understanding individual work styles and preferences can help identify those who are willing and motivated to make a change. Finally, understanding infrastructure components currently in place and how they compare to those in the desired scenario gives insight into the costs, time, and resources required to make the change. The following sections describe how the three current state analysis data perspectives in Figure 26.2 can help evaluate the appropriateness and scope of distributed work within the organization and inform a recommended implementation strategy.

Data Perspective 3: Current Work Profiles

In contrast to KSFs that describe desired future-state practices necessary to accomplish business objectives, existing work profiles describe the work practices currently performed by organizational members. Work profiles represent the current levels of work activities, resources, and context requirements.

Understanding how work is currently accomplished provides an important perspective in determining the applicability of distributed work. In some cases, work practices may be highly consistent with distributed work models, suggesting the appropriateness of maintaining or perhaps expanding the scope and nature of these arrangements. In other cases, current work practices may be more consistent with a proximate work model, and this information can form the foundation for dialogue concerning the desirability of these work activities going forward and what, if anything, may be preventing adoption (or consideration) of distributed work practices.

Assessment of work activities in an organization will probably result in a variety of work profiles. For example, a salesperson's work profile is likely to indicate a high level of work-related mobility, engagement with customers, and a large portion of time spent interacting and communicating. In comparison, a software engineer's work profile is likely to indicate a low level of mobility, engagement with immediate team members doing co-development, and a large portion of time spent doing focused, concentration-intensive work. Work profile variation also often occurs within job types. It is often the case that different people with the same job title engage in different activities and have different work profiles. Working in different product lines, parts or units of an organization, team structures, locations (main office versus satellite), or geographies can create different demands on employees that result in different work profiles even for the same job. For these reasons, it is important that the methodologies used to profile work can accurately represent the inherent complexity and diversity of work.

Table 26.3 summarizes some of the key dimensions that were found to be most useful in profiling existing work practices to evaluate the appropriateness of distributed work models. The example profiles show the pattern of work profile data that would be characteristic of distributed versus proximate work. Again, the distribution and prevalence of different work profiles across the organization can help inform the scope of any distributed work models under consideration.

Multiple methods can be used to generate reliable and valid work profile data for each dimension. Unobtrusive data, one data source, often requires analyzing information accessible in computer systems to draw conclusions about employee work activities. For example, employee badge-swipe data across locations have been used to examine mobility patterns and use of workplace resources. Remote network log-in data have been analyzed to determine remote work frequency, and office keyboard keystrokes have been virtually monitored to analyze office use. Unobtrusive data can yield compelling results. At Sun, the results of a comprehensive analysis of badge-swipe data suggesting high levels of employee mobility generated much attention from senior executives in the company and initiated serious consideration of wide-scale distributed work initiatives.

Despite the compelling nature of unobtrusive data, they typically apply to only a small portion of the work profile dimensions. Therefore, data of this nature typically need to be supplemented with other data-gathering methodologies to provide a sufficiently comprehensive profile of work. Employee surveys are used extensively in documenting work profiles because they can be designed to measure a wide range of work dimensions, efficiently profile a large sample of the employee population, and produce quantifiable results. Results of self-report survey data are sometimes questioned because employees can provide self-serving responses, so it is important to include methods that minimize response

Table 26.3
Example Work Profile Dimensions

	Work Profile Dimensions	Example Distributed Work Profile	Example Proximate Work Profile
Individual work	Work-related mobility	High	Low
	Use of on-site office work space	Low	High
	Independent concentration-intensive work	High	Low
	Need for specialized or fixed work resources	Low	High
Collaborative work	Face-to-face accessibility of team members	Low	High
	Informal team collaboration	Low	High
	Cross-functional interaction	High	Low
	Remote collaboration (e-mail, phone)	High	Low
Work context	Need for privacy and security	Low	High
	Discrete, measurable work outputs	High	Low
	Frequency of urgent or time-sensitive tasks	Low	High
	Frequency of coworker interruptions	Low	High

bias and maximize reliability of results (Fowler, 2002). Supplementing unobtrusive and survey data with observations (such as ethnographic research), interviews, and focus group discussions can help validate quantitative results and lend further credibility to the findings.

All managers, including those involved in deciding on the appropriateness and scope of distributed work models, have preconceived notions about the nature of work activities in their organizations based on their experiences. However, these beliefs do not always coincide with the results of profiling research. For example, because managers often assume that all individuals in a job group engage in similar work activities, the work profile data can be quite valuable in educating them about the realities of work activity diversity. In one project, management was quite surprised to learn that some employees who were believed to be office bound actually spent considerable time working outside their individual offices, a finding that fostered further investigation around their mobility patterns and how they could be better supported when they work outside the office. The profile data also have the advantage of representing the full range of work activities that will be affected by a decision to adopt distributed work models, and this can help prevent decisions based on one salient work activity to the exclusion of other important activities. For example, while a distributed work model may support employees when they work outside their offices, it also needs to address the requirements of face-to-face collaboration and informal interaction these employees may rely on to share knowledge and solve problems.

In summary, work profiles provide a comprehensive description of work practices currently performed in the organization. By accurately representing the complexity and diversity of work activities, these data help ensure that the full range of work patterns is considered as distributed work decisions are made and that any potential negative impacts can be preemptively mitigated. In effect, these profiles are an expression of current demand for distributed work activities and KSFs are an expression of future demand for distributed work activities—what people are doing versus what they will need to be doing to achieve desired objectives. Although the two may not be directly comparable (for example, some KSFs may not exist in the current state), any inconsistencies between *what is* and *what needs to be* provide decision makers and implementers the basis for a road map for modifying workforce skills, management and team processes, goals, and expectations so it can be successful in achieving desired objectives.

Data Perspective 4: Individual Work Styles and Preferences

When distributed work models were first being considered at Sun, a strong business case for change was needed to gain the support of senior management. It was during this time that data about business objectives, key success factors, and current work profiles were introduced to create this business case. Once decisions were made and distributed work programs began to be implemented, it became apparent that other factors, not included in the decision making to date, were having a strong impact on the success of the distributed work initiatives. Even in cases where current work profiles and the organization's desired business objectives were consistent with distributed work, reports of dissatisfaction and reduced work effectiveness associated with the change emerged. What ultimately became apparent was that individual work styles and preferences played a fundamental role in how people work and what motivates individual behaviors that directly affect work performance.

At Sun, some distributed work implementations meant working from home rather than from centralized offices. A portion of knowledge workers who worked at home did not have the self-discipline necessary to work productively in an unstructured work setting like home and as a result were less effective. For others, the central office environment was an important source of social interaction and informal knowledge sharing; without this frequent source of face-to-face interaction, they felt uninformed and detached from the group. These findings led to an examination of individual work style and preference variables that drive success in remote work arrangements. Table 26.4 summarizes some of the key dimensions that were found to significantly predict satisfaction and self-reported

Table 26.4
Example Work Style and Preference Dimensions

Work Style Dimensions	Example Distributed Work Style	Example Proximate Work Style
Proactive expectation setting	High	Low
Autonomous work style	High	Low
Need for self-discipline and self-motivation	High	Low
Personal office preference	Low	High
Need for flexibility	High	Low
Location independence	High	Low
Commute time	High	Low

productivity in remote work arrangements, along with example profiles that are characteristic of distributed and proximate work styles.

These work style and preference dimensions represent psychological constructs, and therefore assessment instruments were determined to be the best method of measurement. Similar to surveys that profile work patterns, these assessments can be designed to measure a range of dimensions, efficiently profile a large sample of the employee population, and produce quantifiable results that can be used to make distributed work decisions at the individual level.

Work style data have provided a unique perspective on the appropriateness of distributed work models compared with the other business and work-related data being considered. Even when a remote work model is desired by the organization and remote work practices are feasible, if the individual cannot be motivated and productive in a remote work arrangement, implementation success can be jeopardized by unintended outcomes such as higher turnover and reduced performance. This knowledge led to a fundamental change in how distributed work decisions were made at Sun. The concept of individuals having a choice in their work arrangement was introduced, as was the option to work remotely at different degrees where feasible (occasional, part time, or full time). In addition, the scope of distributed work decisions changed, and instead of a wide-scale deployment of a remote work model across an organization, decisions were made at the individual and team levels jointly with line management so that business, team, and individual requirements could be considered.

In summary, work style and preference data provide a critical perspective in understanding the appropriateness of distributed work by considering the impact on the individual. Combined with work profile requirements, this additional data-based perspective helps the organization balance the needs of the business and its teams with those of the individual to reach decisions that are more likely to result in implementation success. These data also provide important information about the scope and nature of the change program that will be needed to help individuals be successful in their future work.

Data Perspective 5: Current Infrastructure Inventory

An inventory of current infrastructure in place at the organization is critical to understanding the extent of infrastructure change required to adopt the desired scenario, and is also valuable in planning the implementation effort. An integrated set of infrastructure choices comprises a scenario that is being considered for implementation (see Table 26.2). These same choices can be used to inventory current infrastructure components. The data that comprise the current infrastructure inventory are the judgments of functional experts and reflect which of the infrastructure choices best describes the state of infrastructure currently in place. For example, if the workplace component "work location" has the choices "distributed" and "centralized," the choice that better matches what is currently available would be selected.

By making these judgments for all the choices, a "today state" scenario is created that can be diagrammatically placed in the scenario cube (Figure 26.4) along with other scenarios under consideration. Similar to any other scenario, an aggregated impact rating score is generated using the same impact judgments used to determine the predicted effectiveness of the other scenarios. In this way, the "today state" scenario provides a baseline against which all the other scenarios, and especially the higher-scoring scenarios, can be compared. In some cases, the aggregated impact scores might predict that other scenarios will be more effective than the "today state" scenario in supporting KSFs, but in some cases, the "today state" scenario may be predicted to be as effective as other scenarios.

This comparison between current and possible future infrastructure components provides the basis for understanding the gap between existing and future supply of the enabling components for a distributed work model. By comparing the infrastructure components that will ideally be needed to support KSFs with what is currently in place, decision makers can come to understand the costs and time that will be necessary for implementation. Moreover, changes in RE, IT, and HR infrastructure components cannot be expected to change at the same time, so careful planning is advised. It is also not unusual for the supply gap—the gap between infrastructure in place versus what is needed—to be too large to remedy at one time. Often a phased approach to implementing the new scenario is the route to feasible implementation. At Sun the scenario impact scores resulting from the Strategic Choice analysis allowed a better understanding of what might suffer with less than full implementation of an ideal scenario and allowed decision makers to make informed trade-offs between scope of implementations, costs, and time, always with an eye toward, at minimum, implementing those choices with the highest potential positive impact on KSFs.

In summary, the "today state" data have been particularly useful to decision makers. They have helped determine the scope of change needed in the current system of infrastructure, identify the relative benefits that might be expected from the change (KSF impacts), and highlight components currently lacking that can help ensure a successful implementation.

DISTRIBUTED WORK IMPLEMENTATION SUCCESS

Thus far, this chapter has discussed how the five data perspectives contribute to decisions about the appropriateness and scope of a distributed work model and what should comprise a system of integrated distributed work support. As suggested in Figure 26.2, once decisions have been made about the desired system of distributed work infrastructure support and desired scope of distributed work that is appropriate, implementation considerations become the focus. One of the benefits of the data-based approaches introduced in this chapter is that their value extends well into implementing a model and evolving the system of support over time. In particular, the data have served as the essential basis for creating an effective implementation strategy and for measuring and monitoring the effectiveness of decisions made so that the system of support and quality of future decisions can be improved over time.

Creating an Effective Implementation Strategy

The current-state analysis illustrated how a distributed work scenario can benefit the organization when it is supported by current work profiles, individual work styles, and existing infrastructure components. Sometimes data from all three current-state perspectives are consistent in suggesting a good distributed work fit. However, in many cases the data from all three perspectives do not give consistent results, creating a violation in fit. To illustrate this point, Table 26.5 outlines the nine possible combinations of distributed work fit suggested by the three current-state data perspectives, and implementation strategy considerations that apply to each.

While distributed work may already be a good fit for some organizations, others may need to address possible violations in fit to help ensure implementation success. In many cases, the data suggest that a distributed work model might be successful if appropriate actions are taken by the organization to address the violations in fit. In these situations in particular, it becomes critical to decide on a

Table 26.5
Distributed Work Implementation Considerations

Existing Work Profiles	Individual Work Styles and Preferences	Existing Infrastructure Inventory	Distributed Work Implementation Considerations Based on Data
High	High	High	Distributed work is already in place, along with supporting infrastructure. Use the data to identify how the infrastructure can be improved and extended to provide more support for desired outcomes and KSs.
High	High	Low	Distributed work is in practice and embraced by the workforce, but the infrastructure is not providing the necessary level of support. A concerted investment in time, effort, and resources is needed to create the supporting system of infrastructure enablers. A phased implementation is one way to balance investment needs.
High	Low	High	Distributed work practice and the supporting infrastructure are already in place; however, they conflict with traditional work styles. Organizational change efforts, participation incentives, and individual choice options will be necessary to create and reinforce an employee value proposition for distributed work.
High	Low	Low	Although distributed work practices are in place, employee and organizational support are lacking. Investment in the supporting workplace, technology, and organizational practices is an important first step. These enablers may help overcome employee willingness barriers, but additional organizational change efforts may be needed. Smaller-scale pilot efforts can be beneficial in developing the necessary level of program support.

(Continued)

Table 26.5 (continued)

Existing Work Profiles	Individual Work Styles and Preferences	Existing Infrastructure Inventory	Distributed Work Implementation Considerations Based on Data
Low	High	High	Despite employee willingness and company investment in supporting infrastructure, current work practices are inconsistent with distributed work. Analysis of formal and informal work practice will be needed to identify necessary changes. High-priority areas for change are those practices least consistent with distributed work KSFs.
Low	Low	High	Although the organization can implement a system of distributed work support, it cannot be effective if it is not used. The organization needs to make commensurate changes in work practices (new distributed ways of working) and individual work styles (organizational change) to realize the value of its investment.
Low	High	Low	Employee willingness will not be a barrier to the implementation of distributed work within the organization. Management and leadership barriers may need to be addressed first since they are most likely the underlying reason for a lack of infrastructure investment and work practice change.
Low	Low	Low	Distributed work models will take a significant investment and change effort on the part of the organization in all three areas. Use the data to identify the highest-priority areas for change (the largest infrastructure gaps, for example). Phased implementation or smaller-scale pilot efforts will be important to manage the extent of the change.

Note: Columns 1 to 3 show the distributed fit suggested by the data. The fit is as defined by the match to the example distributed work scenario in Figure 26.4.

system of infrastructure support that will not only enable distributed work success but also help overcome distributed work challenges facing the organization (including support for some KSFs, current work profiles, and individual work styles historically believed to require proximity).

Measuring and Monitoring Decision Effectiveness

Any decision that requires and drives substantial investment in time and resources deserves to have outcomes of the decision monitored and evaluated. Sun made significant investments in new infrastructure to enhance the availability of the workplace, technology, and organizational practice components deemed necessary by the data. As a result Sun wanted to determine whether good decisions were made and the extent to which the implementations were successful. Fortunately, the data-based approach provided an objective basis for monitoring and measuring the impact of decisions that were made.

At a basic level, program data provided insights as to the general effectiveness of the distributed work decisions made. Implementation began with pilots and trial programs and then expanded to include a worldwide program and tens of thousands of participating employees. As a result of this scale, significant cost and space savings objectives were achieved.

Employee satisfaction is typically a desired business objective and was routinely measured as part of implementation efforts at Sun. However, while higher satisfaction levels after implementation compared with before implementation were often found, they could be explained by many factors not directly associated with the specific changes made: the company's stock price was rising, the company's attention to the pilot group members had a Hawthorne effect, and so on. Strategic Choice data offered a more rigorous evaluation of these changes. The linkage judgments collected as part of the process provided specific hypotheses about the expected impact of infrastructure choices on KSFs and became the framework for measurement. The process allowed Sun to empirically examine "if we implement these components, then these key work practices will be in greater evidence than they are today." As infrastructure components were put into place, pre-implementation and post-implementation metrics were used to evaluate the observed impact. These metrics included both documenting the presence of observable KSFs and analyzing self-report data from survey instruments.

In conducting applied research of this nature, a number of practical considerations can affect the results of the measurement efforts. The rate of change across KSFs can vary considerably, so an evaluation three months after implementation might not identify positive impacts, whereas a one-year evaluation could. In addition, it is often not feasible to implement a complete system of infrastructure support at one time. Furthermore, factors such as cost constraints or geographical infrastructure incompatibilities can result in some components being less than fully implemented. These incomplete implementations sometimes constrain the ability to measure predicted KSF impacts. Although it was impossible to control all possible variables, Sun implemented ongoing measurement programs that included pre- as well as multiple (annual) post-implementation data collection to examine trends in impacts across time and across different employee groups.

The implementation of a distributed work initiative is not a project with a beginning and an end. It is an ongoing way of doing business. As such, distributed work needs to be continually adjusted to respond to external conditions and improved in response to internal demands. These responses require ongoing decision making that can benefit greatly from sound data. Annual, ongoing collection of data about infrastructure effectiveness, KSFs in practice, and their respective impacts has created valuable insights that Sun has used to strengthen infrastructure effectiveness, identify new components, and improve ongoing decisions that are made.

FINAL THOUGHTS

This chapter has explored how data of various kinds can be used to make a decision process explicit so that effective business-focused decisions can be made about the appropriateness, scope, and system of support for virtual and distributed work. It discussed how data can enhance successful implementation and evolution of an organization's distributed work capabilities. It also claimed that use of data can help business-focused decision making in ways superior to traditional, tacit methods. This is because we believe, and our experience reinforces, that a healthy hybrid of data and experience, using both quantitative and qualitative methods, provides the ability to address (and constructively debate) tacit assumptions about the work that people do, how they should do it, and how they need to be supported in doing it. In short, the data provide the needed objectivity to drive a business-focused dialogue about where and how to invest to support virtual and distributed work. These approaches have provided the convincing evidence and credibility for acceptance of change in the work environment at Sun and in employees' and managers' behaviors. Furthermore, these approaches create a foundation for gathering empirical evidence about the impacts of infrastructure choices on desired business outcomes and in doing so help create new knowledge of great value to future decisions.

REMINDERS

- Incorporate data-based decision logic that explicitly links infrastructure choices with the business objectives and key success factors (KSFs) that must be supported by any distributed work solution under consideration. These linkages provide clear business-focused criteria for evaluating the appropriateness and scope of distributed work arrangements, convey the possible impact of decisions, and help ensure that decision makers objectively consider all viable alternatives.

- Acknowledge the complexity and diversity of work by considering the full range of KSFs when making distributed work decisions. Focusing on one or two KSFs that might be salient at a particular time can result in solutions that are suboptimized and fail to support other important work activities.

- Involve cross-functional support groups such as real estate, information technology, and human resources in decision making to foster an integrated and optimized system of infrastructure support needed for effective distributed and virtual work.

- An integrated system of distributed work support should include all the physical, technological, and organizational infrastructure components that enable the organization's desired work practices.

- Evaluate data across different perspectives to help balance the needs of the business and its teams with those of the individual and reach distributed work decisions that are likely to result in implementation success.

- Distributed work decisions can be made at the individual or the team level and do not have to include full-scale organizationwide deployment.

- The implementation of a distributed work initiative is not a project with a beginning and an end. It is an ongoing way of doing business that needs to be continually adjusted to respond to external conditions and improved in response to internal demands.

RELATED ITEM ON THE WEB

- Scenario Scoring: Predicted Impacts of Scenarios on Key Success Factors

References

Carmines, E., & Zeller, R. (1985). *Reliability and validity assessment.* Thousand Oaks, CA: Sage.

Fowler, F. (2002). *Survey research methods* (3rd ed.). Thousand Oaks, CA: Sage.

Hamel, G., & Prahalad, C. (2005, July-August). Strategic intent. *Harvard Business Review,* 148–161. (Original work published 1989)

Kaplan, R., & Norton, D. (2006). *Alignment: Using the balanced scorecard to create corporate synergies.* Boston: Harvard Business School Press.

Nonaka, I., & Konno, N. (1998). The concept of "Ba": Building a foundation for knowledge creation. *California Management Review, 40*(3), 40–54.

Pfeffer, J., & Sutton, R. (2006, January). Evidence-based management. *Harvard Business Review,* 63–74.

Peffers, K., Gengler, C., & Tuunanen, T. (2003). Extending critical success factors methodology to facilitate broadly participative information systems planning. *Journal of Management Information Systems, 20*(1), 51–85.

Pullen, W. (2005, October). *Evidence-based reasoning: A new challenge for facility management.* Paper presented at the South African Facilities Management Association, Midrand.

Williams, J., & Ramaprasad, A. (1996). A taxonomy of critical success factors. *European Journal of Information Systems, 5,* 250–260.

Virtual Collaboration in a Matrix Organization

Amy Kates, Paul J. Erickson

The matrix structure is an increasingly common feature on the business landscape. As firms grow more complex and more geographically dispersed, leaders are confronted with the question of how to integrate and align staff who work in remote locations and need to be deployed on several projects simultaneously. The need to integrate resources and reconcile opposing objectives creates the challenge of designing mechanisms that will foster true collaboration instead of simple compromise. In an effort to achieve multiple strategic objectives with the smallest number of resources, many organizations are using matrix reporting relationships as a way to link disparate parts of the organization and encourage collaboration.

Use of a matrix presents a dilemma, however. Three decades of study have shown that the matrix is one of the most powerful ways to force interaction among business units and integrate the diverse parts of an organization. At the same time, experience has demonstrated that it is most successful in organizations that already have a strong foundation of teamwork, joint accountability, and management processes that support collaboration. Therefore, organizations that shift to the matrix in order to get the promised benefits without putting in place the required enabling and support mechanisms quickly find that they have introduced complexity, confusion, and frustration without achieving expected gains. Predictably, they soon revert back to a simpler configuration, adding another example to the many that have abandoned the matrix as simply too hard to do.

The reality is that most businesses today are complex. They need to serve multiple products, markets, and geographies, and, if they are to reap the rewards of growth and scale, they need to integrate laterally and find synergies among all the dimensions of the business. Complex business models result in complex organizations, including matrix relationships. And the organizations that can best manage this complexity without making it burdensome to either customers or frontline employees will gain competitive advantage.

The complexity created by the matrix is usually borne by the middle manager, who provides the connections among all of the various strategic dimensions that the business is trying to achieve. Attention to organization design does not remove complexity for these managers, but it can help ensure that the organization is an enabler instead of a barrier to these managers as they try to achieve the required business results.

Implementing a matrix is a significant leadership decision, and not one to make lightly. This chapter summarizes what has been learned about designing and implementing a successful matrix with a focus on virtual environments. The chapter addresses using a matrix to bridge the barriers of time and space, as well as the challenges of introducing complexity for teams and managers working remotely. The intent is to demystify this much maligned organizational form and offer tools to maximize the chance of successful implementation.

WHAT IS A MATRIX?

A matrix is an organization in which various employees have two or more bosses. It was pioneered in the aerospace and defense sectors in the 1960s and 1970s in response to expansions of scope and complexity represented by initiatives such as the space program (Peters & Waterman, 1982). For example, an engineer at Boeing working on the development of the 747 airliner might have reported to both the manufacturing group and a manager in the commercial aviation product division. The goal of making the engineer accountable to both supervisors was to maintain robust functional expertise while deploying resources where they were most needed.

Soon firms in other sectors experimented with the matrix, with mixed results. In the early 1980s, following Tom Peters and Robert Waterman's claim in *In Search of Excellence* (1982) that no "excellent" companies used a matrix design, it was largely abandoned as overly complex, rigid, and cumbersome.

The mid-1990s saw the matrix return to favor. One driver behind this trend was the need to hold down costs—for example, having a systems analyst report to a local functional manager in New York as well as a product manager in Hong Kong meant that the Hong Kong office would not have to hire a systems analyst. Having the same person working on projects for New York and Hong Kong simultaneously also meant a greater degree of cross-border standardization, which might promote further cost savings. A second driver has been globalization. Outsourcing and offshoring to low-cost manufacturing and processing centers have left North American and European companies with mostly knowledge-based, project-centered work, precisely the conditions that rely on high levels of virtual collaboration and lateral integration.

Despite its reemergence, *matrix* is still a code word among many observers of organizational life for "cumbersome" and "overengineered." The *Economist,* in a major feature on "the new organisation," derides it as the corset from which many companies are still struggling to free themselves (Hindle, 2006). Yet today matrices can be found in most large companies. Rarely is it used as the overall framework of an entire firm, however. More frequently it is used to tie together key roles and ensure that decisions made take multiple business perspectives into consideration. Often the research and development function is configured as a matrix. Researchers belong to specialist groups, but they take part in projects that bring them together in cross-functional teams. Other examples can frequently be found in sales functions. Sales departments are usually structured into regions in order to minimize travel time and draw on local knowledge. However, national accounts, global product lines, and distribution channels (such as resellers and retailers) frequently cut across these regions. In order to coordinate along the customer, product, and channel dimensions as well as the geographic dimension, sales managers may report to two managers in order to ensure a focus on both aspects of the business.

A CASE EXAMPLE

To illustrate the concepts and tools for designing a matrix, we will use a typical example based on a large U.S. bank's information technology (IT) group. Many companies organize their IT groups and other staff functions by both line of business and function, with the goal of gaining scale and consistency while remaining responsive to specific business needs.

The bank has five lines of business, all with different information processing needs. Three are outward facing: wholesale, lending, and retail. "Corporate" refers to all the corporate-level staff functions, and "operations" refers to all the processing functions of the bank. Although these are both internal groups, because of their size they are considered a line of business—that is, a client—by the IT department. Since this bank, like many other large corporations, has grown through mergers and acquisitions, different lines of business are headquartered in different cities.

The business heads want dedicated points of contact and teams that know their business and can develop and implement IT solutions that will drive customer service and revenue growth. The IT relationship managers across the top of Figure 27.1 provide the link to the business from the IT function. They have dedicated teams for that business unit. These managers are measured and rewarded on how well they meet the needs of the business line they support.

At the same time, the bank as an enterprise has objectives that are different from those of its individual lines of business. Some of these objectives are even in opposition. While the business heads want solutions that are customized to their unique needs, the bank wants to hold down IT costs by using common platforms, systems, and applications wherever possible. Such commonality and standardization mean easier transfer of customer and product data across business lines, allowing customers, the sales force, and service center staff to access information centrally. Commonality also means economies of scale in purchasing from vendors and servicing and securing the IT systems themselves. The six functional managers along the side of Figure 27.1 lead dedicated groups focusing on building the long-term, efficient infrastructure for the bank in terms of

Figure 27.1
Example of a Typical Matrix Organization

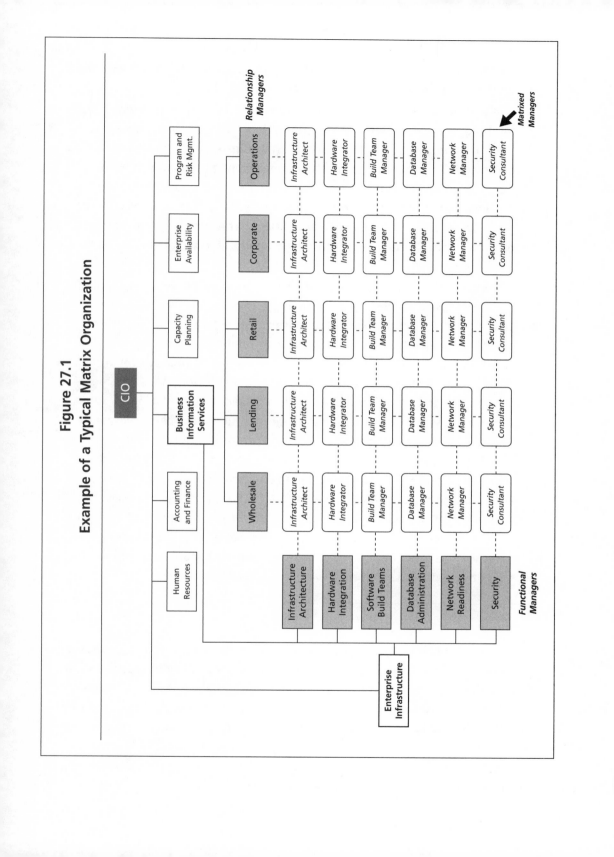

core applications, data centers, networks, and security. They are measured and rewarded for meeting these goals.

These functional managers have IT resources reporting to them from multiple lines of business and in multiple locations. Thus, there are a large number of virtual relationships in a matrix of this type: between dedicated IT resources and the functional manager, between the functional manager and the relationship manager, and between functional specialists who work in the same area but serve different lines of business. By virtue of the dual reporting lines that a matrix creates, almost everything that a manager in a matrix does will involve some form of virtual collaboration.

In Figure 27.1, there are thirty matrixed managers. (They will be called managers because they typically manage projects or processes, even if they do not all directly manage teams of people.) Each of these managers has a line-of-business supervisor, the relationship manager, and a functional manager as a supervisor. They are measured and rewarded against both dimensions. At any time, they may be working on business-specific projects as well as infrastructure projects. As in almost all other organizations, there are never enough resources to meet everyone's needs. Every day trade-offs are made and priorities reset. By setting up a matrix, the organization's leader ensures that these thirty managers make decisions about how they and their teams spend their time based on balancing the priorities of the lines of business and the functions. The matrix forces the underlying tension in the organization about how to allocate scarce resources to the surface. It is intended to compel the relationship and functional managers, called the lead managers, to discuss these trade-offs openly.

This typical example illustrates how introducing the matrix can change the fundamental dynamics of an organization and increase the number of virtual working relationships. The centers of power are purposely aligned against one another. Before using a matrix structure, this IT group had been organized completely functionally. The line-of-business dimension was added to bring more attention to the different needs of specific customers. Six months into the transition to the matrix, one functional manager described the change in this way: "I feel like we've been acquired." The impact on the status quo of introducing a matrix should not be underestimated, nor should the change management aspects of the implementation be given short shrift.

The matrixed manager is also saddled with the additional burden of negotiating among the competing objectives of multiple bosses, some of whom may be rarely seen in person. No wonder the matrix is so difficult to make work. Although it is an elegant solution to the vexing problem of how to have the benefits of both a functional and a customer-oriented structure, the matrix is not easy to implement.

An important caveat to keep in mind is that a matrix itself is not an organizational structure, but rather a set of reporting relationships that tie the organization together laterally. Organizational structures define the hierarchical alignment of people. In the example, the underlying structural framework is aligned according to customer and function. It could just as easily be along the dimensions of geography and product, such as the example of the sales force mentioned earlier. The matrix sits atop the structure as a way to link each side together.

This allows the underlying structure to remain stable. In a matrix configuration, not everyone is in a formally matrixed position, but the goal is to instill in all employees a simultaneous focus on multiple organizational priorities—what is called a matrix mind-set. The IT function in the example has over a thousand employees. The vast majority formally report to just one manager; however, many of these employees may work on virtual project teams and have accountability to other managers. The matrixed reporting relationships at one level reinforce the mind-set and behaviors that are desired at levels below. Once the mind-set becomes part of the culture, the matrix may no longer be necessary. At that point, the complexity it brings in terms of reporting relationships, process, and management coordination can be reduced, leaving the underlying organization structure to remain.

Benefits of a Matrix

When trying to support and promote collaboration across the boundaries of organization, geography, and time, there are a number of reasons that a leader may turn to a matrix.

Flexibility　A matrix is often used to better allocate scarce or expensive talent and flexibly configure and deploy teams around projects, opportunities, customers, problems, and products. It allows the organization to shift resources in response to changing business needs or conditions while preserving a stable framework underneath.

When employees are "locked up" in a unit—whether business, product, or function—they often become invisible and inaccessible to the rest of the company. The unit is always able to generate enough work to keep them busy, but it is hard to determine if they are allocated to the tasks that are most important to the company overall. The matrix creates a mechanism to share these resources and assign them to where their talents and skills are best used. In the example, the thirty matrixed managers are visible to and "owned" by the entire IT function, even though they are dedicated to specific lines of business and functional areas. If a major project arises, such as an acquisition in the retail sector, the IT leadership can reallocate managers and their teams to retail business projects without having to physically or organizationally relocate them. The discussion among the senior team members focuses on how to get the whole portfolio of work accomplished (and what work to delay or drop), avoiding a negotiation among individual managers for resources.

Integration　The matrix builds linkages across organizational boundaries and can help promote integrated solutions and consistent service delivery, which is often particularly challenging for companies that operate in multiple locations. In the example, if the lending business needs a system to support a new product, the matrix forces the lending IT team to consider the need from two perspectives: the state-of-the-art solution for the business and how the team can build or buy a system that fits with existing systems or can even potentially be leveraged by another business line. The result should be one that both meets the needs of the business and can be efficiently built and serviced by the enterprise.

Learning　Another benefit of the matrix is the potential for learning and sharing best practices across groups and locations. There is theoretically more opportunity for transfer of knowledge across the lines of business when employees participate in multiple teams and projects, particularly projects involving colleagues located elsewhere with whom they would rarely interact otherwise. Variations on the matrix are often found in staff functions, and it provides these groups with a unique window onto the enterprise. These staff functions can serve as a vehicle for sharing not only functional information but also business information across units and locations. This potential is beginning to be leveraged in companies that have routinized low-level transactional work and are starting to use staff groups more strategically. For example, a human resource group that is matrixed by business and function can use occasions when the function comes together as an opportunity to identify issues occurring in several businesses and address them systematically. Employees may also have increased learning opportunities as individuals. Working in a matrix can be difficult, but it often results in a greater variety of work, a broader range of contacts across locations within the firm, and an opportunity to develop valuable management skills.

Pitfalls of a Matrix

The potential benefits of a successful matrix are numerous, and an effectively deployed matrix should result in cost savings. Units do not need to duplicate expensive resources, scarce talent can be shared and deployed where most needed, and solutions are developed that are both effective and efficient.

But when not effectively deployed, the matrix used in a virtual environment introduces a significant cost: the diversion of management focus from products and customers to internal negotiation and the time to resolve disputes between groups. Rather than contribute to collaboration, it consumes valuable management attention that must be spent sorting out disagreements. The pitfalls of the matrix are well documented (see Bartlett & Ghoshal, 1990; Peters & Waterman, 1982). The majority of these risks and costs—especially in a virtual environment, where people working together are unable to resolve differences in person—result from confusion and friction about priorities and accountability. We next look at some of the most common pitfalls of a matrix.

Power Struggles   Most managers dislike sharing resources or being told that the results they are accountable for are less important than someone else's. All the power struggles that are inherent in any organization are magnified in a matrix, where managers are often competing for resources with other managers in other locations, whom they may not know personally and whose business they do not see. In every organization there is a tension between the leader who needs all the pieces of the organization to collaborate and the managers at the next level—managers who, despite politically correct talk about teamwork, would prefer to have control over the resources required to deliver the results for which they are held accountable.

The matrix increases the number of interdependencies and reciprocal need among these managers. If the lead managers perceive themselves to be in competition or in a zero-sum game with other managers and allow negotiations over priorities or resources to become personal, the close interactions the matrix forces can become destructive.

Determining "Best Practices"   If the matrix is being used to drive integration and the introduction of more core products and services across locations, regions, or lines of business, someone needs to determine what will be standardized and where differences are legitimate and allowable. This is not easily done and can be a significant source of conflict. Many global companies struggle to come up with a truly global product. For example, in the early 1990s, Ford set the goal of producing a "world car"—a single car sold in essentially the same form in all markets—which would benefit the company by standardizing parts, engineering, and production and capitalizing on Ford's international production and R&D expertise. The design team for the car was divided between Ford's North American and European operations. After a development effort that cost over $6 billion, the car was introduced in Europe as the Mondeo, but by the time regional differences were negotiated, the U.S. version was barely recognizable as the same car. Although the cars were similar under the skin, the only external items the Mondeo shared with the Contour, as it was called in the United States, were the windshield, front windows, front mirrors, and door handles (see "The World Car," 1994; Muller, Welch, Green, Woellert, & St. Pierre, 2000; Mol & Koppius, 2002).

On even mundane levels, the conflict over whose process is best can consume valuable management time and, like most other debates, they are more difficult to have in a virtual environment, where reliance on asynchronous modes of communication results in both a loss of nuance and slower decision making. Whether at the level of product design or setting the performance management calendar, wrangling over regional and line-of-business variations can quickly wear out management patience. Strong leadership is needed to set clear criteria for decisions at lower levels and to quickly arbitrate disputes that are escalated.

Decision Strangulation   The matrix gives equal weight to two or more business dimensions. Ideally, this tension results in better and more creative solutions to problems and opportunities. It certainly means more meetings, telephone calls, and videoconferences and more people participating in decisions. If the organization does not have good meeting practices, clear decision rights, effective technologies and practices for remote communication, and strong conflict resolution processes, the result can be slow decision making or no decisions at all. Managers will put off that which is too hard to deal with, make compromises that benefit no one, or continually elevate disputes up the chain to senior management that should rightfully be settled at their own level. Or they will simply short-circuit the processes of virtual collaboration and make decisions locally for their own groups, without taking the time to work with their colleagues in other locations.

Personal Stress   Most people prefer a work environment of clarity, where they know "what my objectives are, what I am responsible for, and most important, who am I accountable to." A matrix requires a certain amount of personal flexibility and comfort with ambiguity and change. It also requires an ability to understand and adapt to the styles and expectations of two or more supervisors, the fortitude to confront and sort out conflicting directives that may come from above, and the ability to build strong and productive relationships with people who may be located in another city or on another continent.

The organizational flexibility of the matrix also weakens the sense of team identity that is important for many employees and is a challenge in virtual work environments. Staff may find themselves sitting on a number of teams, each with differing subcultures and operating procedures. This is the nature of a project-based environment, and for employees used to a more traditional hierarchy, it can be a major change. The increased dependence on influence and negotiation rather than clear-cut rules and procedures can create stress and job dissatisfaction.

DESIGNING A SUCCESSFUL MATRIX FOR VIRTUAL COLLABORATION

For many organizations, a matrix will be the right solution to the challenge of maintaining close and responsive customer contact in multiple locations while drawing on the resources and platforms of a larger organization. The design of an effective matrix is dependent on the leader's ability to align the organization's components—structure, processes, metrics, and people practices—around a clearly defined strategy (Galbraith, Downey, & Kates, 2002). Those who can do that will find it is worthwhile.

Many leaders find, however, that their experiences with a matrix have not lived up to expectations, and as a result they abandon it out of frustration. Typically this is because the matrix has been "installed" as part of a reorganization rather than carefully designed and implemented. The matrix requires a major shift in the work patterns, relationships, and mind-set of employees in matrixed positions. Thoughtful planning and design of a matrix are essential to achieve its benefits.

The remainder of this chapter provides a set of design principles, actions, and tools for leaders to use in order to maximize this mechanism as a way to foster collaboration (see Table 27.1 for a summary). Most of these suggestions are neither new in the literature nor unique to a matrix. Many will be valuable in any organization, however it is configured, in promoting collaboration. But experience

Table 27.1
Principles and Tools for Designing a Matrix Organization

Principles	Tools
Build social capital	
1. Networks and relationships	Relationship map
2. Collaboration, not compromise	
3. Managers who work well together	
4. A culture of teamwork and joint accountability	
Instill disciplined work and management processes	
5. Clarity around roles and responsibilities	Responsibility chart
6. Governance mechanisms to resolve issues quickly at the right level	Relationship health check
7. Efficient and effective meetings	
8. Minimum management rework	
9. Clear process for objective setting and performance management	

has shown that all are required to make a matrix effective and more so when used in a virtual environment.

Build Social Capital

The first set of enablers addresses the foundation of social capital that must be built in order for any matrix to work. Social capital can be generally thought of as the set of values, norms, and relationships shared among members of a group that permit cooperation among them. The inclusion of the word *capital* also implies investment in these social relations with some expected returns (Lin, 2001). For all the reasons highlighted in the discussion of potential pitfalls, a strong base of trust and interpersonal skills helps managers solve problems jointly and candidly raise and resolve conflicts.

When managers in the matrix work together through virtual relationships, social capital and enabling support systems become even more essential. Just fifteen years ago, many books and articles heralded the end of organizational hierarchy, structure, and the need for traditional offices (see, for example, Wheatley, 1994). Many believed that technology would obviate the need for most face-to-face interaction.

Although technology has allowed separation of much work from a fixed location, businesses find themselves competing more and more on their ability to pull together ideas and knowledge across business lines and geographies to create products and services of greater value. More than ever before, companies need ways to get people from different organizational and national cultures to form quickly into teams and work together efficiently, and they are finding that technology cannot substitute for human interaction. In fact, misunderstandings arising from the use of e-mail, videoconferencing, and conference calls make work harder for those who need to collaborate across time and geographical boundaries. This section provides a set of principles, actions, and tools for building the social capital on which a successful matrix rests.

Design Principle 1: Networks and Relationships   A successful matrix is heavily dependent on good working relationships at every level. A good working relationship can be defined as two people who have had enough positive interactions to establish mutual trust, assume good intent on the part of the other, and are willing to make a personal contribution to the other's success. Matrixed managers may have two or more formal bosses and even other project managers to whom they are accountable. They have to work with peers on at least two formal teams and perhaps on other projects. They may also manage an ongoing team or a set of project teams. In addition, there are clients, vendors, and partners in other parts of the company with whom they need to establish relationships.

Everyone creates some relationships at work. However, if not built deliberately, relationships have the tendency to fall narrowly into two categories. The first are based on day-to-day transactions: Whom do I need to interact with to get my work done? The second are established with people who share some common interest: Whom do I like to spend time with? Although these relationships are important, they are not complete, and they are often restricted to colleagues in the same physical location.

In addition to their formal reporting relationships, managers working in a matrix need a robust set of relationships with people they can call on for advice, resources, political support, and expertise. The flexibility of a matrix depends on the ability to form and reform teams. The more that people on the newly formed team have a prior positive relationship, the more quickly the team can become productive. These connections in what is sometimes called the informal organization must be sought out and cultivated.

One result of a matrix is that few people have full authority over significant decisions. Numerous people must be involved in decisions big and small. If everyone who has an interest in a decision must always be involved (in other words, decision making by committee), the leaders of the organization will soon notice a slowdown in decision making. By building a broad set of relationships based on trust and across multiple locations in an organization, more people can be assured that others understand their perspective and will take it into account when making decisions that affect them. When this is achieved, fewer people need to be involved in each decision, and overall decisions can be made efficiently without compromising quality.

A network is a set of relationships that link people within an organization and beyond it. The power of networks is often underused. Either people fail to see the value of investing in relationships that have no immediate payoff, feel uncomfortable with the whole idea of networking, lack the skills to do it effectively, or focus only on networks that involve people with whom they have face-to-face interaction. But someone who invests only in current interactions or in people they personally like misses out on developing relationships that will pay off down the road. For example, in the IT illustration above (see Figure 27.1), imagine an infrastructure architect who worked on a project a year ago with a peer from database administration in another location. They were in frequent communication during the project but have not had contact since the project ended. The infrastructure architect is now working on a project where advice or an introduction to some expert contacts whom the database administrator knows would be helpful. But since the two have not talked or seen each other in so long, it may feel awkward to ask for a favor seemingly out of the blue.

Most managers understand the value of relationships but do not make the time to invest in them because they seem to offer only personal benefits. In fact, in the example above, both the individual and the organization may benefit from the relationship. Therefore, relationship building is a legitimate activity that can be designed, supported, and even measured. Actively encouraging it is a leadership responsibility.

Here are some ideas on designing relationships and networks:

- *Use relationship maps.* A relationship map is a simple tool that helps people map and evaluate the strength and robustness of their network (see Figure 27.2 and the Relationship Map on the www.wiley.com/go/virtualteamshandbook Web site). A person lists fifteen to twenty people he or she should have a good working relationship with—wherever they may be located—and maps them on a grid based on organizational relationship. Then each relationship is evaluated. The user can quickly see if there are gaps by function (for instance, no one in marketing), level (no one more senior that the current manager), or proximity (no one in another location or outside one's own unit). Anybody can use this tool to think more strategically about developing a healthy network. The real benefit is when it is used as an organizational tool. For example, each matrixed manager in the IT example might sit with both lead managers and identify with whom to actively build a relationship within and beyond the IT function. The lead managers would then make introductions, create opportunities for interactions, encourage the time spent on fostering the relationships, and check in on how well the manager has done. This turns relationship building from an activity left to chance based on personal comfort and style to a strong fabric helping to knit the organization together.

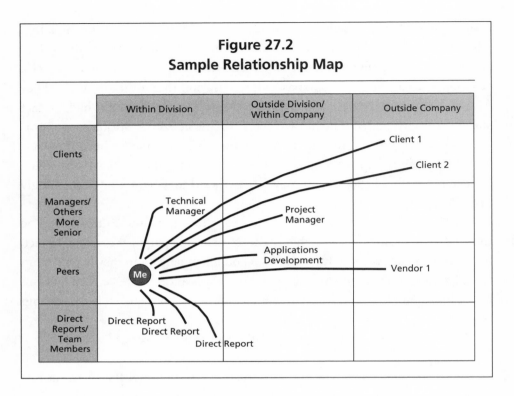

Figure 27.2
Sample Relationship Map

	Within Division	Outside Division/ Within Company	Outside Company
Clients			Client 1 Client 2
Managers/ Others More Senior	Technical Manager	Project Manager	
Peers	Me	Applications Development	Vendor 1
Direct Reports/ Team Members	Direct Report Direct Report Direct Report		

• *Strategically plan face-to-face time.* For geographically dispersed organizations, face-to-face interactions among staff are rare. And when budgets are tight, travel and retreats are often the first expenses to be cut. Yet studies have shown that project teams that meet at least once face-to-face at the beginning of their project have a much higher success rate than teams that initiate projects at the purely virtual level (see Duarte & Snyder, 2001). Teams that come together and create opportunities for members to establish personal connections seem to have many fewer misunderstandings when they then must conduct business on a virtual basis using technology. If the employees within the matrix are not colocated, be sure to bring people together in the beginning, particularly when they are working on expectations and operating procedures. Then use training sessions, retreats, town hall meetings, and forums where people will be brought together physically as a way not just to convey information or solve problems, but to strengthen relationships and networks as well. Assign seating, mix up small groups, create opportunities for communities of interest to meet together, and provide long breaks and lunches and other social time.

• *Make trust tangible.* When describing a good working relationship, most people use the word *trust* as they try to paint a picture of what it looks like. But they will have trouble defining trust: it is one of those things you know when you see it. In fact, the factors that go into trust can be made tangible. When people understand what these factors are, they can actively build trust with others and even rate the quality of relationships. The four major factors of trust, shown in Figure 27.3, are competence, commitment, communication, and consideration (based on Mayer, Davis, & Schoorman, 1995).

Any organization benefits from increased trust levels, but high trust is particularly essential in a matrix and even more important in virtual environments. Encounters that occur in the normal flow of business can be designed to increase

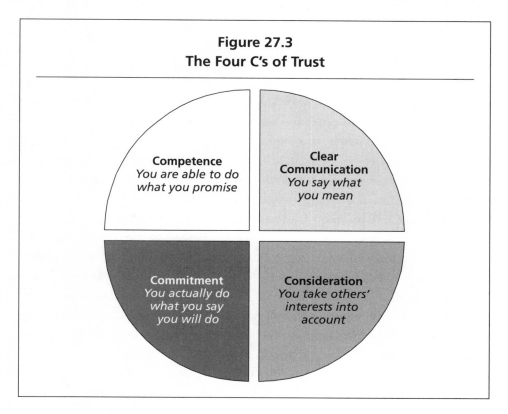

Figure 27.3
The Four C's of Trust

Competence
You are able to do what you promise

Clear Communication
You say what you mean

Commitment
You actually do what you say you will do

Consideration
You take others' interests into account

trust. Consider the weekly conference call between the functional managers and relationship managers in the IT illustration. On the surface, they might be coming together to resolve an agenda of current operating issues. But if these meetings are well designed, the managers will also take time to educate one another about how they view their piece of the world. This allows others to understand their point of view and take it into account back on the job when making decisions (*consideration,* in Figure 27.3). They might also take a few minutes to assess how well they communicate with one another and what can be improved in terms of clarity and response time (*communication*). Highlighting success stories and identifying where unique or sought-after talent and capabilities reside in the organization will make the others more aware of resources they can draw on (*competence*). Finally, shared agreements and follow-through on action plans demonstrate common goals (*commitment*). Out of this meeting comes not only completion of today's agenda but a higher level of trust. This simple model of trust can be used to quickly assess issues within a group, identify the root causes, and address them.

Design Principle 2: Collaboration, Not Compromise   If relationships are the fabric of the organization, then trust strengthens the threads that speed the movement of information and knowledge up, down, and sideways. But good people and goodwill are not enough. People need mechanisms to help resolve the inevitable conflicts that arise in a matrix.

To start, they need an understanding and acceptance that there will be conflicts and that these are not a failing of the organization. In fact, a matrix is designed to bring conflict to the surface; it is intended to bring different points of view into contact. A common frustration in a matrix is that many conflicts are hard to resolve because the two or three opposing views on the issue are all legitimate and no one person can make the call. In the IT example, the lending business that needs a new system truly does need specific functionality and needs it to be delivered within a tight time frame. And the security consultants are being held accountable for ensuring that all new systems conform to enterprise standards. When some of the desired functionality fails to conform to the security standards, a conflict inevitably arises.

The creative tension that comes from trying to reconcile these opposing objectives can yield an outcome that is better for the business overall than for either of the sides. But the risk is that failure to resolve the conflict will result in a delay in decision making, personal acrimony, or escalation of the decision to a more senior level. Worse than these consequences may be compromise: an outcome that sub-optimizes each party's objectives. True collaboration, in which the needs of both parties are met with a different outcome than either party may have had conceived of originally, needs to be designed in. There are several ways to do this:

• *Set criteria for trade-offs.* Senior managers identify and communicate what factors take precedence when trade-offs have to be made. In the IT example, these factors might include time, cost, functionality, and security. These directives are unable to anticipate every situation, but they can provide guidance to lower-level managers when not all objectives can be met.

• *Establish rules for escalation of conflicts.* Frequent escalation of conflicts is a symptom that managers are unclear about the criteria for decision making or lack the managerial maturity to resolve issues at their level. Policy issues should move up the ladder because often it is only the more senior leaders who have a broad enough mandate and perspective to set policy. But when midlevel managers do not get along or are unwilling to collaborate on issues that they can resolve, then the right leadership move is to push the accountability back down for resolution.

• *Define parameters for risk.* In a matrix, both the matrix managers and the lead managers frequently find themselves in situations where they have to take personal risk (such as confronting a manager or colleague) or organizational risk (such as agreeing to a new process or outcome). Conflicts can end in compromise if people perceive compromise as the safe route, one that will do no harm. Many leaders send mixed messages about acceptable risk taking and overlook opportunities to publicly recognize examples of the behaviors they want to encourage. Again, not all situations can be anticipated, but the more often that senior leaders communicate and reward the behaviors that they want to see, the better the matrix will function.

Design Principle 3: Managers Who Work Well Together In a matrix, the most important set of relationships is among the vertical and horizontal lead managers. In the IT example presented in Figure 27.1, these are the relationship and functional managers. Placement of these positions in the hierarchy is important.

Selecting who will be sharing the matrixed resources is just as critical, particularly if these managers will be working virtually. The quality of the working relationships among these managers will set the tone and culture of the whole organization. Here are some design considerations:

• *Set the matrix at the right level.* A matrix works best when the matrixed positions are placed at a fairly high level in the organization. This means that when the matrixed manager has to raise an issue up to the two lead managers, these managers are in a high enough position of authority and knowledge to resolve the issue. If the matrixed manager is placed so low in the organization that the lead managers do not have a broad enough view to make decisions and have to raise them up yet another level or two, then the matrix will become a barrier rather than an enabler of decision making. In general, the goal should be to minimize the levels between the matrixed manager and the person who ultimately has control over both dimensions of the matrix. If possible, try to limit the distance to two levels.

• *Select for management competencies.* For these key positions, selecting people who already demonstrate the ability to work in a complex environment and possess skills in virtual collaboration will be easier than trying to train and develop these skills. Even better would be to have some of these managers come from organizations with experience working laterally and virtually to the degree that the matrix demands. If the lead managers are all in a stretch assignment, the matrix will be much harder to get off the ground. Some of the following interpersonal and management competencies have been shown to be important:

• The ability to manage and resolve conflict

• A level of comfort with ambiguity and change

• Strong project management skills and the ability to manage virtual teams

• The ability to take multiple priorities into account and share decision rights

• The discipline to gather information from multiple sources in order to inform decision making

• Strong communication skills, enabling managers to work with people from other disciplines and backgrounds and communicate effectively through a wide range of communication technologies

- Skills in negotiation, influence, and building networks

- Cultural sensitivity, enabling managers to build relationships with colleagues who are located in other countries and may have different styles of communication and collaboration

- High levels of emotional intelligence: the ability to perceive, assess, and manage the emotions of oneself, of others, and of teams (see Sy & Côté, 2005; Bartlett & Ghoshal, 1990).

Building a cadre of managers who already possess some or all of these competencies will greatly increase the likelihood that a matrix structure will succeed because they will be stronger individual managers and will be able to work together more effectively as a team.

- *Actively build the team through structured meetings.* The importance of occasional face-to-face meetings for the lead managers has been discussed above. The intervening virtual meetings that occur on a regular basis need to be planned as well. A common mistake is to bring these players together only when there is a problem or so rarely that the agenda is overloaded. The lead managers need to establish regular meetings to jointly set overall objectives, review and adjust priorities, educate one another about their work programs, and assess and manage talent. Making decisions and resolving conflicts is more difficult when done remotely, such as by telephone or videoconference, yet this is the work of management teams in a matrix. Therefore, extra attention needs to be given to using the technology effectively and structuring the meetings around outcomes while not harming working relationships. (For a helpful discussion of different communication technologies and how they meet the needs of specific types of virtual meetings, see Chapter Fourteen.)

Design Principle 4: A Culture of Teamwork and Joint Accountability

Teamwork is so overused that it has almost lost its meaning. Few organizations fail to list teamwork as a desired value and behavior. So what is different about teamwork in a matrix? The head of a business moving to a matrix likened it to the difference between football and soccer as a way to help his organization understand how the new organization was different from how they were used to operating. He pointed out that in football, players have well-defined positions, and it is illegal for them to go outside the boundaries of those clearly defined roles. In traditional organizations, job descriptions prescribe the boundaries of one's role. In contrast, soccer positions, although defined, are much more fluid. When one player is in trouble, another will step in and continue moving the ball forward. Sports analogies for business should not be carried too far, but the image can be helpful when trying to convey the culture needed to support a matrix. Since each manager's fate is closely tied to the success of others, the prevailing attitude needs to be, "How can I help?" rather than, "That's not my job."

Too often leaders hold the matrix responsible if they fail to meet their objectives, when the real culprits are a lack of desire, incentive, or ability to work together among the management team. Here are some ways to promote a culture of teamwork:

- *Align rewards.* The matrix cannot be implemented without a realignment of the reward system. It will be quite visible that the matrixed managers will need to be appraised and rewarded for balancing and meeting two sets of objectives. Less obvious, but more important, is to ensure that the lead managers have their compensation linked to the success of the whole organization, not just to meeting their line-of-business, geographical, project, or functional goals. If part of their compensation is tied to the success of their colleagues, the organization will quickly see more "How can I help?" behaviors.

- *Make heroes of those who demonstrate the behaviors.* Look honestly at who the heroes are in the organization. Are they the people who exemplify the behaviors discussed here? Recognition is an inexpensive way to visibly convey the culture and behaviors that are desired. Public thanks, featuring a team on the Web site or newsletter, and selecting individuals for high-profile projects or assignments are all ways to reinforce the message of what personal success in the matrix looks like.

- *Make it easy to share information.* Teamwork and collaboration in a matrix are dependent on strong systems for sharing information about not just the work itself but the people as well. Searchable directories that include information on experience, skills, and interests can help individuals build their networks and speed the assembly of teams for project managers.

Creating a culture in which teamwork and joint accountability are genuine elements of the organization's daily life, and not simply buzzwords, will help staff handle some of the challenges that a matrix presents, particularly around changes in the way that work moves through an organization.

Instill Disciplined Work and Management Processes

The design principles and actions discussed so far build the foundation for the matrix. They will go a long way toward helping employees in a matrix work more effectively together and realize the promise of the matrix. But they are not sufficient. The introduction of a matrix has profound implications on how work gets done. If this is not recognized, an organization will find itself with hard-working, well-intentioned people struggling over where to make hand-offs, who can make decisions, and where roles begin and end, particularly when they have to interact remotely. To extend the soccer analogy a bit, a soccer team is not just a group of athletes willing to help each other out. Rather, the team goes into the game with a well-defined plan, clear roles, and a set of well-practiced plays. For the majority of situations, there is an agreed-on response that allows each person to play out his or her role without worrying about conflicts with team members over who goes after the ball. In the same way, the key managers in a matrix are advised to spend time anticipating—practicing, if you will—the most likely scenarios where hand-offs and decisions will need to be made.

Strong and disciplined management processes are needed in addition to clear work processes. These are the mechanisms that allow leaders in the matrixed organization to manage people, processes, and projects efficiently. Managers need to be selected for either demonstrated experience or a propensity for the behaviors that support virtual collaboration. They need the individual skills to succeed. But neither work flow nor management processes should be left up to the goodwill of individuals. They must be designed and implemented by the top leadership.

Design Principle 5: Clarity Around Roles and Responsibilities   The matrix will change the way work moves through the organization. Process mapping will help test assumptions about who touches the work and what roles are involved at each step. It is not necessary to map every process, just the key ones that cut across the organization and are likely to cause the most confusion.

Once the simplified process map is complete and agreed on, then a responsibility chart (Figure 27.4) can be used to clarify who makes decisions (based on Melcher, 1967; Galbraith, 2002). In a responsibility chart, the key roles are identified across the top (these may be individuals or groups). Key decisions are listed down the left side. For each decision, those involved discuss and agree on:

Responsibility: Who is responsible for making and carrying out the decision? If more than one person is responsible, all have to agree to the decision.

Accountability: Who ultimately will be held accountable? This is not necessarily the person who makes the decision.

Veto: Who can veto the decision because it will significantly affect his or her role or work? This is different from the normal veto a boss has based on positional power.

Consult: Who must be consulted before the decision is made?

Inform: Who needs to be informed about the decision after it is made?

(Fuller instructions for using "Responsibility Charting" can be found on www .wiley.com/go/virtualteamshandbook Web site.)

The purpose of the responsibility chart is to anticipate gray areas and cases where clashes may occur. In a matrix, many interactions are more a series of requests and promises than they are sharply defined tasks and responsibilities. Although job descriptions are important in many companies for setting compensation, they are less useful as a way to describe where one role ends and another begins. They may speak to the activities or outcomes that are expected but are a poor tool for communicating how people are expected to interact with one another (Lawler & Worley, 2006). In addition, the effort to keep them up-to-date is rarely achieved.

Therefore it is more useful in any organization, and especially in one as complex as a matrix, to focus not only on the activities within a role but also on the interfaces between roles. This is especially important in virtual environments, where people may not be aware of what their colleagues are working on from day to day.

Design Principle 6: Governance Mechanisms to Resolve Issues Quickly at the Right Level   A look at any matrixed organization quickly reveals that it does not have a traditionally recognizable leadership structure. The typical group

Figure 27.4
Sample Responsibility Chart

Roles / Decisions	Relationship Manager	Hardware Integrator	Infrastructure Architect	Security Consultant	Build Team Manager	Business Information Services Director	Enterprise Infrastructure Director
1. Staff a server installation team	I	C	C		R		A
2. Determine standards for new system build	C	R	A	V	C	I	I
3. Create pricing for a line of business project	C	C	R		I	C	A

R = Responsible   A = Accountability   V = Veto   C = Consult   I = Inform of five to seven direct reports that an organizational leader usually brings together to set strategy and make decisions that require cross-functional agreement does not exist. In the example of the IT function that has been discussed throughout this chapter (Figure 27.1), who is on the leadership team? Is it the seven direct reports to the CIO? What about the eleven lead managers? How is this important level engaged in leadership decisions?

Rather than focus on the hierarchy, it may be more helpful to identify the range of issues that are likely to require leadership direction and then create councils and committees with the appropriate representation based on the topic. These topics might include standards, pricing, exception processing, resource allocation and staffing, and customer engagement, to name just a few. To make these councils effective, each needs a charter setting out its mandate and scope of authority.

A useful tool for these governing bodies is a relationship health check, shown in Table 27.2. The tool assesses the state of a relationship as perceived by an internal customer or peer group.

The assessment is given to an internal client or peer group and they are asked to indicate what stage of development they perceive the working relationship is at when measured against a set of six dimensions. Follow-up conversations can focus on where there are lower-than-desired ratings and what actions can be taken to build the relationship. The intent of the tool is two-fold. First, it serves as a vehicle to stimulate a structured conversation around what the factors are behind this low rating and how it can be to improved. Second, it creates a baseline to measure results against and a way to communicate relationship expectations to others in the organization. The tool is useful when the nature of the work requires a high degree of collaboration, positive interaction, and trust. A stage 5 rating may be the desired goal, but not all relationships require such a degree of connection, and stage 4 may be sufficient.

Design Principle 7: Efficient and Effective Meetings   Good meeting practice may seem a tired topic. Anyone who has been through a basic management course has learned the value of setting and adhering to an agenda, facilitating group discussions, and capturing and distributing action items after the meeting. And yet the scourge of holding too many meetings, poorly planned and badly run meetings, meetings with the wrong participants in the room, and meetings with no clear outcome continues to plague many organizations. There is no doubt that

Table 27.2
Relationship Health Check

	Stage 1 No Partnership/ Limited Engagement	Stage 2 Coordinating Engagements/ Encountering Frustration	Stage 3 Cooperation	Stage 4 Collaboration	Stage 5 True Partnership
Vision/identity	"Us" and "them," with little or no middle ground; based on negative experiences	"Us" and "them," looking toward a future "we"—building trust	Beginning to think as "we"; some level of personal connection exists	Achieving partnership, based on personal relationship	Us/we, almost transparent—part of the same team
Mind-set/approach	Working together has not come up or is not feasible; sees little or no value in working together	Exploring partnership possibilities; sees other groups as a necessary evil	Work together to achieve our individual goals—quid pro quo	Work together to succeed as a team	Share in both successes and failures
Strategy/purpose	Plans and decisions are made with complete independence	Plans are made behind the scenes and then discussed	Decision making may involve discussion with and consideration of other groups; when asked, groups share objectives or strategy	Decisions and plans are discussed with other groups; input and feedback are requested regarding objectives or strategy	Decisions and plans are discussed and made together—joint strategy development and execution

(Continued)

Table 27.2 (Continued)

	Stage 1	Stage 2	Stage 3	Stage 4	Stage 5
	No Partnership/ Limited Engagement	Coordinating Engagements/ Encountering Frustration	Cooperation	Collaboration	True Partnership
Communication	Little to no communication	Infrequent, but with communication modes being developed	Communication is as needed, to gain understanding of other groups' goals—tactically driven	Communication is the norm; both groups clearly understand the common goals; regular meetings with give-and-take	Communication is frequent, ongoing, honest, and respectful
Trust	Conflicting interests or lack of awareness of common goals or mutual benefits	Aligning interests or are experiencing conflict in current interests	Still a focus on individual interests, but a degree of trust exists	Desire for mutual benefits; seek out help and advice	Desire for a long-term partnership that is mutually beneficial; high level of integrity
Results/value added	Lack of any significant engagement precludes any value added	Value could be added in the future	Value is added for a specific project with a limited time frame	Value added for extended period of time	Continually adding value and creating synergy

the introduction of a matrix means more meetings. Certainly in the planning and transition process, there should be meetings to bring people together around the work processes and interfaces, but on an ongoing basis, there are more meetings as well. Again, the number of meetings, just like the increase in conflicts, is not a failing of the matrix. It should be expected and planned for.

Poorly run meetings, which are even more of a risk in virtual environments, can only sometimes be blamed on the lack of individual skill or knowledge of the leader. Most people know what a good meeting looks like. More often, bad meetings are symptomatic of a lack of overall discipline in the organization. An irony of the matrix is that although it is most often used to drive integration and flexibility, it cannot be run as a loose and informal organization. More thought and care need to be given to creating a common management culture, particularly across multiple locations. The more that operating norms are shared, the easier it will be for people to move between teams and units and focus quickly on the work rather than the mechanics of working together.

If there are no agreed-on and enforced protocols for how meetings are run, information is shared, and decisions are made, the matrix will just exacerbate the usual frustrations of organizational life. People will soon blame the matrix for wasting their time, which can lead to abandoning the intervention prematurely, thereby causing the blame to become a self-fulfilling prophecy. A hard look will likely show that just as much time was being wasted in unproductive meetings before the introduction of the matrix. It only seems that more of it is being wasted now.

Design Principle 8: Minimum Management Rework The reengineering movement of the 1990s brought focus to the cost of badly designed processes, where work and information passed through unnecessary checkpoints and approvals. In the backrooms and operations of most organizations, work now flows efficiently in a streamlined manner. The same cannot be said for most management processes. Organizational assessments and surveys often turn up the complaint that management decisions do not stick—that once made, they are revisited in subsequent meetings, challenged behind closed doors, circumvented through back channels, or renegotiated one-on-one with the leader.

The matrix creates a host of opportunities for management rework. The matrixed managers are clearly in a position to play one lead manager off against another, but clients can do it as well. The problem that clients shop for a better answer is a common complaint of the matrix, one that can be exacerbated by a lack of standard decision criteria across multiple locations. This calls for a well-functioning management team that is clear about the organization's objectives and takes accountability for decisions.

One of the best ways to make visible the problem of management rework is to measure the perceptions of employees in the organization. Regardless of how well the management team believes they are interacting, the perceptions of those they manage are the most important reality. At one company, leaders used a survey to gain focus on these issues and shine a spotlight on where there were gaps in accountability. The survey asked such questions as "How well does the executive team . . ."

- Address the organization's most important issues?
- Follow up on actions and commitments to ensure they were implemented?
- Make decisions that stick?
- Come to closure when there is disagreement or conflict?
- Engage in productive dialogue?
- Differentiate issues that call for a cross-functional approach?
- Lead change as a cohesive group?

The survey was administered before the implementation of an organizational change and then at six-month intervals afterward. Making these issues so visible forced them onto the agenda of the management team.

Design Principle 9: Objective Setting and Performance Management A key management process that must be realigned as part of a matrix design is the practice of objective setting and performance management. The lead managers need to come together and determine jointly what the matrixed managers will be held accountable for and how their performance will be assessed. Here are a few things to consider when modifying the performance management process:

- Although the matrix assumes that some resources are shared, they are not always shared equally, and this should be reflected in the goal-setting and appraisal process. If one manager sets 75 percent of the goals for the year and supervises their attainment, that manager should have 75 percent of the input into the final report or ranking.

• Both lead managers must have explicit input into the process for review and agree to the final result. It cannot be delegated fully to one or the other; although this may feel more efficient and less political, it will drive the wrong behaviors. People cannot help but respond more to those who determine their year-end ratings and compensation.

• Each manager should focus on areas where he or she has direct observation and be responsible for gathering input from other managers and project leaders in other locations as necessary. In this way, the process is less cumbersome. Joint performance discussions can focus on areas of disagreement, ensuring that the collaboration and other values of the organization are met in addition to the business results and identifying development and next job moves.

FINAL THOUGHTS

What has been learned from observing many organizations implement matrix relationships is that the principles and tools for success are neither mysterious nor difficult to employ. The suggestions offered in this chapter are good basic practices that benefit any organization. They just need to be applied fully and consistently in a matrix. Most organizations run into trouble in sustaining the focus and energy during the planning and transition phases to create all the supporting capabilities that will give the matrix a chance of success.

The matrix is complex and can be challenging to implement. Some of these challenges are increased in virtual environments. Conversely, an organization that is already practiced in virtual collaboration may have an easier time adjusting to a matrix because it has built many of the underlying capabilities required.

This chapter has offered a set of tools that can be used in building a matrix, but it is difficult to know what areas to focus on, particularly in a virtual work environment. The accompanying www.wiley.com/go/virtualteamshandbook Web site has a matrix assessment ("Are You Ready for a Matrix?") that can be used to gauge how far your organization is on the road toward building these capabilities. If the assessment indicates that an organization is toward the weak end of the spectrum, especially in the social capital category, we suggest that its leaders spend time strengthening these areas before jumping to changing roles and reporting relationships. If they do so, the organization will be in a much better position to reap the benefits of a matrix and minimize the pain of transition.

REMINDERS

- Using a matrix can promote teamwork in a virtual environment by formalizing the lateral connections among organizational units.

- The matrix is a complex organizational form that works best with mature management teams that have a culture of shared accountability and collaboration.

- Leaders contemplating using a matrix to further foster collaboration in a virtual environment should first build the underlying capability to support success, including:

  - Encouraging the development of social capital, working relationships, and robust interpersonal networks

  - Clarifying roles and responsibilities and streamlining underlying work processes

  - Creating governance mechanisms to set standards and settle conflicts

  - Modeling a culture of disciplined meeting and communication norms

RELATED ITEMS ON THE WEB

- Relationship Map

- Responsibility Charting

- Are You Ready for a Matrix?

References

Bartlett, C. A., & Ghoshal, S. (1990). Matrix management: Not a structure, a frame of mind. *Harvard Business Review, 68*(4), 138–145.

Duarte, D. L., & Snyder, N. T. (2001). *Managing virtual teams.* San Francisco: Jossey-Bass.

Galbraith, J. (2002). *Designing organizations: An executive guide to strategy, structure, and process* (rev. ed.). San Francisco: Jossey-Bass.

Galbraith, J., Downey, D., & Kates, A. (2002). *Designing dynamic organizations.* New York: Amacom.

Hindle, T. (2006, January 21). The new organisation. *Economist.*

Lawler III, E. E., & Worley, C. G. (2006). *Built to change: How to achieve sustained organizational effectiveness.* San Francisco: Jossey-Bass.

Lin, N. (2001). *Social capital: A theory of social structure and action.* Cambridge: Cambridge University Press.

Mayer, R. C., Davis, J. H., & Schoorman, F. D. (1995). An integrative model of organizational trust. *Academy of Management Review, 20*(3), 709–734.

Melcher, R. (1967, May-June). Roles and relationships: Clarifying the manager's job. *Personnel,* 33–41.

Mol, M. J., & Koppius, O. R. (2002). Information technology and the internationalization of the firm. *Journal of Global Information Management, 10*(4), 44–60.

Muller, J., Welch, D., Green, J., Woellert, L., & St. Pierre, N. (2000, September 18). Ford: A crisis of confidence. *Business Week,* pp. 42–43.

Peters, T. J., & Waterman, R. H. Jr. (1982). *In search of excellence.* New York: Warner Books.

Sy, T., & Côté, S. (2005). Emotional intelligence: A key ability to succeed in the matrix organization. *Journal of Management and Development, 235*–6, 437–455.

Wheatley, M. J. (1994). *Leadership and the new science.* San Francisco: Berrett-Koehler.

The world car: Enter the McFord. (1994, July 23). *Economist,* p. 69.

Knowledge Transfer and Learning on Virtual Design Teams

Jude G. Olson

Passing information is very important, like in soccer. If you want to win a game, you've got to learn how to pass to your teammate. Which means you've got to, number one, trust him that he's going to be able to take the ball and keep on going. One of the things I had to teach the kids when they were young was that if they pass the ball, they'll get it back. When they're young, all the action's at the ball, and they think, "I want to keep it." I would say that this collaboration is the same thing, and fits in with this "knowledge is power" sort of thinking. . . . We want to get all the data out there so that everybody is equally successful. One guy scored the goal, but it took the whole team to get it down there.

JSF Design Engineer

Note: Any individual names referenced in this paper are pseudonyms to protect anonymity.

The ability to interact and share knowledge with other companies is becoming a distinctive organizational competence for firms. Many are business alliances that maximize the utilization of complementary assets—where each partner can contribute a distinctive capability or particular value-adding activity. This enables learning alliances, where partners can learn together and acquire from each other technologies and products, as well as skills and knowledge. These alliances also require a complex response internally: the development of new capabilities, skill acquisition, and reconfiguration of resources and processes. Both internal and external change set the stage for complex collaborative dynamics. When multiplied by several partners, all with different perspectives, the challenge to balancing interdependence with selfish interests becomes extraordinary—and much riskier.

Researchers have investigated the structure and processes associated with both cooperation and competition between and among organizations. According to Gray (1989), this struggle can include asymmetrical power distribution among stakeholders distinguishing between those who are more influential and those who are weaker, disparate political cultures with differing values and beliefs about the way the world works, and technical complexity that can hinder collaborative efforts. Fear of loss of important technical expertise and competitive basis are perceived as stronger threats to integrative alliances than are sequential alliances where each partner's contribution lies on a sequential path with clear boundaries between partners (Park & Russo, 1996).

Virtual integrated product teams (VIPTs) are a key coordinating structure for integrative alliances in the aerospace industry. They enable work to be done across distance of disciplines, teams, countries, and even companies that are competitors. This chapter describes how the Joint Strike Fighter (JSF) program relied on these teams to create collaboration between a disparate group of engineers, many of whom had previously been competitors. The special technical challenges also required an innovative management approach, including creating a collaborative climate and focusing and aligning a large, distributed, global, virtual integrated product team.

The JSF program is a triservice, multinational transformational weapon system with unique requirements, awarded in 2001 to the Lockheed Martin Aeronautics Company–led team that covers the globe. Recent acquisition reform in the Department of Defense contributed to making this largest aerospace program in history a joint model customized for three military services—the U.S. Navy, the Air Force, and the Marine Corps—as well as international customers. More than three thousand aircraft are predicted to be designed, built, flown, and supported with export sales alone.

The JSF Program integration manager likens the organizational chart of JSF to a jigsaw puzzle, with many interdependent, sometimes conflicting or competing partnerships. The primary partners are Lockheed Martin, BAE Systems, and Northrop Grumman Company. Other secondary business partnerships were formed as well with multiple key suppliers, emphasizing supply chain management.

JSF was conceived as a world airplane, meaning it would span international boundaries from the development phase throughout its life cycle to its global sustainment phase, after the planes were bought. This project, as it was designed, presented many paradoxical challenges that would strain conventional notions of organizing: having competitor companies work together in a nontraditional partnership, meeting a new standard of interoperability where the United States and its allies would be able to use defense systems that work together, and providing the opportunity for codevelopment where host countries would then become eligible to compete as suppliers.

On the technical side, another unique challenge was the fact that in the United States, the same airplane is expected to fill the needs of three military branches, even building the Marine short takeoff and vertical landing version to lift vertically like a helicopter. The development process also faced unprecedented resource demands, with a great number of engineers and suppliers needed from a variety of backgrounds—all of whom were expected to cooperate—and would be using a novel digital design and logistics process to get the work done. Developing effective team collaboration is essential to sustaining this aerospace program over the next forty years.

JSF Program Integration manager, Tom Burbage, reflected on the challenge: "If one looks at JSF through the legacy management filters we have used in the past, it appears unmanageable. One of our ultimate challenges is to develop a JSF leadership and collaborative culture that will allow us to achieve success."

The risks posed in interfirm collaboration show a record of more alliances failing than succeeding, according to the literature. The relationship across competitors is highly interdependent on information sharing, knowledge transfer, and lateral capabilities across boundaries. Lateral organization capabilities are the coordinating mechanisms that augment the vertical structure of a collaborative organization to enable information sharing. They move information and work through the white space between the boxes on the organization chart and across organizational boundaries (Galbraith, Downey, & Kates, 2002). Lateral capability is the organization's ability to build, manage, and reconfigure these various coordinating mechanisms to achieve its strategic goals.

How innovation actually happens on the job, formally or informally, is still open for exploration. Galbraith (1977) suggested that the least costly forms of integration are the informal interaction that occurs between individuals in the course of performing their work and the specification of procedures that enable work to be integrated without the cost of face-to-face coordination. However, the organizational design may not allow informal integration to occur reliably or quickly enough to meet the performance demands of the organization. Competitive requirements may make it necessary for an organization to perform very quickly or to integrate across multiple complex dimensions, such as products, customers, or countries (Galbraith, 1994). In such situations, he said, the organization needs to specify formal integrating mechanisms responsible for coordinating the different pieces of the process or deliberating complex trade-offs. If the development of coordinating mechanisms is left to chance, he warns that there could be gridlock where there is a lack of collaboration across boundaries, long decision and innovation cycle times, and difficulty in sharing information and leveraging best practices.

BACKGROUND AND DESCRIPTION OF THE CASE

This start-up scenario takes place during the systems design and development (SDD) contract phase of the program that began on October 29, 2001, at program award and was estimated at $19 billion of the contract value. This phase lasts approximately ten years, and JSF was in year 5. The goal of this phase is to build twenty-two test aircraft of the three variants: short takeoff and vertical landing (STOVL), conventional takeoff and landing (CTOL), and carrier variant (CV).

The wing team was an engineering design project with a clear work product whose team collaborates across product teams, partners, suppliers, vendors, and customers. The main task of the team engineers is to design, develop, fabricate, and test the JSF wing module from conceptual design through product delivery. This included fuel tanks, weapons integration, materials selection, gears, and ducts, among others. An alternative method of constructing the wing using composites was being explored, and many tools were being tested. The design process was iterative, with each test providing data to build on lessons learned each step of the way.

The systems engineering integration team (SEIT) was responsible for horizontal integration of processes and standards across the integrated product teams to maintain technical baselines, integration of planning and execution, and a disciplined systems requirement control. Essentially they were to integrate the processes of collaboration while collaborating.

This chapter highlights work done primarily by two teams—the airframe IPT and the wing IPT—during a tumultuous time of preliminary design during program start-up. What made it challenging was that both teams were bringing the three partner companies together to agree on common ground rules for design. Although each company was responsible for building major components of the airplane, which would then be assembled at Lockheed Martin, these common ground rules were critical for ensuring affordability and interchangeable parts. The other challenge was made more complex by trying to design three variants of one airplane simultaneously—something out of the ordinary. The overarching design challenge was the technical challenge itself—no one had ever before invented a supersonic stealthy helicopter that was also long-range and maneuverable, as the engineers like to refer to the STOVL version, which has vertical lift capability. There were few common rules to fall back on, which made the design process iterative and improvisational among partner companies. It was a major paradigm shift that the customer expected the airplane to look as if it was manufactured by the same company. This was a new way of thinking about, designing, and building an airplane for all the partners to consider.

Typical of a company that designs fighter jets, JSF's organizational structure reflects the complexity of information flow and work task that only an engineer could enjoy. The Lockheed Martin concept of using VIPTs within a tier structure was designed to provide three customer interfaces: one is day-to-day interaction from the programs, another is at the strategic level with the executive vice presidents, and the third is at the strategy integration level with the advanced technology function. Most interactions between functions and programs happen at level four of the IPTs, with middle managers and senior engineers.

The IPT matrix structure was chosen because it was considered extremely effective in encouraging collaboration and mutual responsibility with one side of the company focused on executing program performance through IPTs and the other functional side of the company focused on maintaining technical competencies by developing core systems and processes. The employee was encouraged to build relationships with both managers as well as to clarify roles and negotiate tasks.

Each IPT tier consists of an IPT lead, a systems engineering integration team (SEIT) lead, a deployed ever-changing team of full-time, cross-functional members who may have overlapping memberships in other teams, an extended team of part-time members as needed, key suppliers, and customer representation. As a minimum, each lower-level IPT lead sits on the next higher tier IPT lead's staff. Each IPT is provided all the required resources to execute a successful program. The IPT lead may draw on additional resources and expertise from the functional (core) organizations through a disciplined resource management process.

The SEIT teams were a new integration structure introduced to allow program requirements to be channeled so that allocations and resource approvals could be effectively managed on JSF. This was in response to the new affordability requirement for JSF where the IPTs were now fully responsible for managing budget and schedule, as well as the technical capabilities. This required that new basic work processes be defined and agreed on by the partner companies. With each new customer added to the JSF program, it is likely more requirements will surface in requirements creep. SEITs were called the "proactive, integrating bridges" between requirements and design and are considered to be the most complex part of the total organization, yet requiring the most integration.

Complexity increased when each variant of the airplane was at a different phase of design. The SEIT had to sequence their work so that the business practices necessary for one phase of the program would be completed in time to begin another, and then the next one. These business practices might include use of computers, analysis processes, tools, and documentation—moving from the broad view to finer detailed plans for building the parts. Literally thousands of written pages of policy documents and procedures to follow, with accompanying training materials that echo those agreements, were created.

Both IPTs and SEITs were structured to support a fundamental principle with which the program director wanted to guide all program personnel: "A genuine environment for virtual collaborative aircraft design, development, test and support." Another key principle was a team focus, with the hope of maximizing team productivity by integrating a high-performance team environment with an enterprisewide supply chain value stream mind-set—with customers, suppliers, and employees.

STRATEGIES TO MEET CHALLENGES

Two broad categories of coordinating mechanisms are essential conditions for successful virtual collaboration: those that link the organization vertically—shared goals, common vision and a one-team attitude—all reinforced by leadership; and those that linked the organization horizontally—common processes, teams, and knowledge transfer to enable innovation.

Vertical Integration

The vertical integration on JSF relied on a strong foundation of clear business strategy and shared financial rewards with a model designed to leverage a win-win for the primary partners. They reinforced that by selecting best leaders for key positions regardless of their company affiliation. This seemed to engender leadership commitment and was a key strategy for modeling overall team partnership. The sheer size of the program commanded political power as well as resources, including the best engineers who wanted to work on leading-edge technical challenges. Cultural norms were established early in the program on guiding principles, and opportunities for socialization were created to honor cultural differences within the context of being partners. Some pointed to the professionalism and culture of engineers themselves as an aligning force to focus on the task at hand in spite of barriers and differences. These strategies seemed to mirror the recommendations by theorists to create a common collaborative view early on (Gray, 1989; Gulati & Nohria, 1994; Mankin & Cohen, 2004; Vansina, Taillieu, & Schruijer, 1998). Extraordinary goals and shared rewards aligned the partners for mutual success.

George gives his view of the JSF partnership and its benefits:

> Three of the top aircraft companies are the partners, and I believe that the most important reason is to capture the knowledge, and the best practices of each of those companies, and all their experiences from legacy aircraft, and all their manufacturing development, and bring those all together for F-35 so that we could achieve the goals of the aircraft to use the best practices of all three companies.

Glen's perspective adds how having common goals was beneficial to the program:

> The focus is we are in this together, and we are going to succeed together, or we are going to fail together, so we better do everything we can to help each other succeed, and that's the motivation, and I've seen it and I've heard it verbalized. I think having a clearly defined goal and purpose helps keep us focused on this program and is a key to our success.

Cultural norms and team socialization set the tone for a "one-team" mind-set. These norms were communicated from the beginning of the program through leadership messages, briefings to employees, and, most important, how employees were treated and new employees greeted.

The JSF leadership team sponsored a series of strategic off-site meetings every six months to gain agreement among the partners on program design and operating philosophy. They also included inspirational speakers and provided more opportunities for getting to know one another—even their spouses. Lanz remembers:

> The leadership team had quite an extended period of time to sort of get to know each other. That helped with goal alignment, expectations, prioritization of certain things, and allowed trust to be built. Being colocated with a little bit of social time as well as work time is probably key in making things work.

One of the other outcomes of the leadership off-sites was the creation of guiding principles, or norms, for the entire enterprise. These came out of a group discussion involving all partners and customers, to identify what organizational behaviors would be necessary to sustain JSF in the present and future. The top guiding principle is, "JSF First!" meaning that the enterprise was one team: company partners, employees, and suppliers. The intent was to encourage boundaryless trust and pull knowledge from anywhere in the organization. Consequently, internal award programs to recognize these behaviors were created to reinforce them and are still awarded quarterly to employees and leaders across the partner companies.

Horizontal Integration

In terms of horizontal coordinating mechanisms, the examples and stories shared were primarily in the categories of learning transfer and teams. Building trust and relationships between teammates who were previously competitors enabled this knowledge sharing. Lateral processes were referred to in the learning transfer and learning groups and opportunities for design improvisation dependent on sharing best practices from partner and competitors. Teams were described in the partnerships with competitors and wing tiger teams. A tiger team is a temporary, informal team structure to focus on an urgent challenge or task. This iterative design process seemed like a key aspect of many of the examples provided: constant negotiation between individuals, IPT teams, and even partner companies was required to produce breakthroughs in confronting unknown technical challenges.

Lee says it is important to understand the phase or life cycle of an aerospace program to understand its dynamics. For instance, workarounds are normal in the start-up development phase because engineers are focused on building the plane and are creative. She describes the churning environment, which she likens to rapids or white water:

> You are working with an engineering organization that their prime responsibility is to build an aircraft. Engineers by nature are creative beings; that's why they are engineers. To stifle that creativity is a bad thing when you are trying to build a plane. So you have to be tolerant of the ways that they get things done, the creative ways that they go about doing their business when they feel like they've hit a wall and they are under a deadline. You are not going to get the work done by following exact processes down the line, and the more a program is on the cutting edge of trying to do things in innovative ways, the more churn you are going to have in the system. It is the nature of the beast—so you have to be more flexible; you can't be that rigid.

Relationships between competitors were built on demonstrations of individual trust. Perceptions of the quality of partnerships seemed to be built on daily interactions with colleagues. The concept of trust was described in various ways: keeping commitments made, demonstrating technical competence, and being open and honest with one another, especially in sharing best practices. The literature seems to indicate that this needs to be built over time and demonstrated; it cannot be legislated by top management. It is important to lay the foundation for sharing expertise in that knowledge is usually shared in the context of relationships. The strategic benefits of an alliance—that is, innovation and transfer of new knowledge through collaborative practices—may not be realized fully if basic trust is not experienced through relationships.

LEARNING AS KNOWLEDGE TRANSFER

Leveraging knowledge transfer for learning was an informal coordinating mechanism for horizontal integration. A story of hands-on knowledge transfer and learning occurred in 2003. Lead manufacturing engineers from all product teams met at BAE Systems in Salmsbury, England, to review the tests for a new milling machine made in Germany. This machine provided high-precision machining for the inside of the wing's external skins and the surfaces of the understructure. The engineers realized that they could not test the machine's design, tooling, and machining processes at any other site than BAE Systems because the machines on order would not be available in the United States until later that year.

For over six months, teams of F-35 manufacturing engineers traveled to BAE Systems from Lockheed Martin plants in Fort Worth, Texas, and Palmdale, California, and from Northrop Grumman Company in El Segundo, California, to test the new machines' processes on aircraft parts and assemblies. They were replicating the processes that would be used in the United States later. The teams went to BAE Systems for three to four weeks at a time, came back for awhile, and then returned; about twenty engineers were traveling during this exchange. A dedicated operations site was set up in England to support this testing and learning experience, with staffing from BAE Systems experts in the process. George describes the learning challenge:

> We've been bringing teams of manufacturing engineers from Fort Worth, Texas, Palmdale, and El Segundo, California, to BAE Systems to train them how to use some very high-precision machine tools at BAE Systems that won't be available to us here at Lockheed Martin

because there's a delay in shipment. We didn't want to wait until then to get up on the learning curve, so the BAE Systems guys are training the guys on their equipment. We are using the same exact process that we are going to be using on this equipment in-house. It's a real learning transfer.

George reflects on the improvisation and learning process when Lockheed Martin went to BAE Systems to build assemblies on the new precision milling machines:

Information goes along the way; then it changes because when the battle starts, you know, the battle plan goes out the window, and we start improvising from then on. The overall plan was put in place very well. Looking at it on paper, you can get the feel for it to see how the veins run through it, but until you start doing it yourself, you don't realize. You actually have to build something in a new process to understand and transfer knowledge. We just didn't understand the ramifications that come at the final assembly. This was a new process for us.

Later that year, the airframe team hit the ground running in Fort Worth, Texas, when six machines were delivered to different JSF sites. The airframe team completed all of its tests and brought back the hardware from England used for the tests.

LEARNING GROUPS WITH PARTNERS AND SUPPLIERS

The technical team on wing skin fabrication created a fiber placement working group for suppliers and BAE Systems and Lockheed Martin to share information, learn parts, and process what is going to be used on JSF. Fiber placement is an automated manufacturing process for building composite parts. It is a collection point where there is a set of folders on JDL (the JSF data library Web site) for each company to enter data. This data were compiled by engineers into a design guideline that was part of an overall composite design guideline published for everyone on the team. Tim describes the learning challenge of these guidelines:

All three companies are going to use it, and we created a working group to go and make sure that everybody is kind of learning at the same pace. The different companies were at different levels of learning and at different levels of usage, because we're not going to buy the equipment. We're working through suppliers, although Northrop Grumman and BAE Systems have both bought the equipment, and they're going to do it themselves.

The purpose of the group was to coordinate information across partners and suppliers to meet the customer's expectation that all parties would be operating with the same guidelines. Tim describes the coordination required with suppliers:

> I have to coordinate with my suppliers and make sure they're meeting the specs that we need to build to, because it has to be consistent. That's the customer's request. All of that information is being worked and being boiled up into a fiber placement design guide, which will be published as the standard design guide packages that everybody can use. It's been working well.

These experiences seem to reflect what we are starting to discover about how knowledge transfer really works: informally. Often bureaucracies such as large companies seek to improve learning by focusing on outcomes without paying close attention to the processes that lead to these outcomes. These may include organizational initiatives that are outcome based—that is, total quality and reengineering. However, where knowledge transfer is needed, understanding these individual company practices is important in allowing local coherent meaning and not constricting local experiments in the hope of a uniform outcome. This raises issues around how learning really happens in bureaucracies. As Barrett (2005) points out, "Although organizations are primarily hierarchical, the development, dissemination, and use of knowledge is horizontal: knowledge often resists efforts aimed at direct control and manipulation. What is needed are processes that encourage the flow and transfer of knowledge, as well as an infrastructure within which the creation of knowledge can occur" (p. 2).

Knowledge is not absolute but situated dependent on the context and setting of the situation. The conditions for the transfer of knowledge between organizational subunits must acknowledge that this kind of knowledge is more tacit than explicit. The process of acquiring knowledge is itself complex. It often involves multiple parties throughout the process; it can be idiosyncratic, with different parties improvising different solutions to unique challenges; and it is contextual, with different projects and schedules posing different kinds of challenges. The process becomes even riskier when dealing with work like aerospace design in which failure is unacceptable.

Employees reported that this on-site knowledge transfer and learning experience was invaluable for solving problems. Informal communication was encouraged through enabling systems. They could engage in informal, unstructured processes of sensemaking and storytelling.

TIGER TEAMS

Tiger teams are an example of collaborative work when a specific design challenge or task needs to have focused attention in a short period of time, sometimes across different IPTs. These teams are not part of the formal structure of the IPTs. Team members may be pulled from anywhere in the company to focus on the issue until it is resolved. A manager will use discretionary budget and resources for the team.

The delivery VIPT got the task of trying to figure out how to pull the airplane back together after a major change happened in the aircraft mate joints. They shifted from quick tension bolts to an integrated mate joint. This particular tiger team traveled to all the partner companies so one site did not have the burden of doing everything. People who had been talking to each other in teleconferences and Net meetings over nine months finally got to meet one another as they traveled site to site. Often a tiger team room is set up with dedicated space with many computers, which enables the editing capability of a particular design. The network goes much slower when the computer is trying to share one picture at all the locations. Typically the team might have fifteen structural designers together, five from each team, and three to four analysts, one from each team and one local. The designers work on creating five to six options, and the analysts have the luxury of working one option at a time as it becomes concrete.

Chad describes the tiger team workroom and its dynamics of focused concentration on solving a design challenge:

> The tiger team room is a dedicated space with twenty-five computers where we can lock the door, bring meals in and don't let engineers out 'til they're done! This is where we try to come to some agreement on

a design model. We might wind up with twenty designs to choose from and then put them together and create a new design, and then go pursue that. We're relying on things we learned from another company or some pieces of structure embedded deep.

Although engineers reported that most teams work virtually over 50 percent of the time, Chad emphasized the important benefits of getting everyone face-to-face. The program, he said, should have budgeted for even more travel to accommodate these meetings:

> The human brain and especially with four eyeballs looking, or even six or eight, looking at a scope can make decisions in an instant, especially in a collaborative sense, in a room, where, if one guy's having video problems, and two people are having telephone problems, and somebody doesn't hear a key word, and we're just looking at something on a screen, the whole situation can quickly degenerate.

Teams are one of the primary ways people are structured in a collaboration to get work done and provide horizontal integration. They are not new. Their internal organization has been seen as important to product success—especially as it relates to communication and integrating different thought worlds—technical specialties or frames of reference. Their intrinsic disharmony would also reduce the possibility for joint learning, since members of a department may think they already know everything: the not-invented-here (NIH) syndrome where people may cling to their own ideas based on prior experience of success and performance. Dougherty (1992) showed that project teams may be able to overcome these cross-functional or cross-company communication barriers when team members participate in concrete tasks together and violate routines such as usual relationships and divisions of tasks.

Distributed work teams also can improve the capabilities of organizations to introduce new technologies, redefine core organizational processes, and leverage knowledge capabilities. Earley and Gibson (2002) revealed that these teams seem more creative, can generate more and better alternatives including criteria, and perform better on complex, multifaceted tasks. New models of teams are needed to respond to the changing world of alliances and multinational corporations—those that can bridge distributed work and provide a context for more collective work.

INNOVATION AND USE OF IMPROVISATION

One of the primary goals for forming multiparty alliances is the creation of technological innovation. This task of collaborative innovation is enabled and coordinated through knowledge transfer and learning, which has it own unique requirements depending on the nature of the knowledge to be transferred and the social context of relationships between those individuals transferring, receiving, and creating knowledge together.

The creation of the main inlet ducts on the center fuselage is an example of innovation on JSF that could have happened only with all partners involved. It had technologies from all three partner companies. Northrop Grumman had the fiber placement experience that had built one-piece ducts in the past. Lockheed Martin contributed the three-dimensional preforms, a composite technology that gives the pull-off strength to put integral flanges or cobonded flanges onto the duct. Composites are historically two-dimensional. Three-dimensional composites open the possibilities of reduced cost and weight. It was BAE Systems that had the precision milling machine technology, which allowed JSF to face off these flanges after they were cobonded so that the duct would fit in an assembly. This new duct saved having thousands of fasteners on the aircraft, the way it had been done on previous aircraft programs.

Innovation was also enabled by the transfer of knowledge and iterative design. In terms of harvesting the best expertise of each partner company, there was general agreement that Northrop Grumman is known for its low observable (LO), or stealth, experience, and composites; its capability for system integration; and its relationship with the U.S. Navy. Lockheed Martin has the F-16 legacy, knows the U.S. Air Force, and has international relationships in the Netherlands, Denmark, and Norway. BAE Systems brings the international piece for United Kingdom (Royal Navy and Air Force) and STOVL (vertical lift) experience as well as Harrier experience. BAE Systems's expertise in manufacturing experience is also valued, especially now, as JSF heads for the production phase of the program.

Kenny describes the challenge of working in the unknown:

> This is a challenging environment: you try to do something that hasn't been done before, but you are doing it with tools that are brand new and are doing it virtually, so at times it can be frustrating because you can't get the answer right away. Other times when something actually

comes together, you've got a multicompany, multifighter operation agreement, and you can stand back and say, "Wow we've actually learned something, and we've adopted the best practice!"

The complexity of innovation is first seen when trying to collaborate with others in an unknown, iterative design environment. Task interdependence, together with task complexity, is a primary contributor to task uncertainty. This increases the organizational need for adaptation, communication, and integration mechanisms such as learning, knowledge transfer, and improvisation (Galbraith, 1977; Thompson, 1967).

Benefits to partnering that were described include technical learning from each partner company and, in some cases, innovating. BAE Systems has brought the STOVL technology as well as manufacturing best practices to the program. Lockheed Martin excels at best final assembly and delivery of an airplane and is somewhat more experimental in nature. Northrop Grumman contributes expertise in composite manufacturing on the airframe and producing skins.

Mike is excited by the innovation that the collaboration has brought and thinks that the breakthroughs are a result of overcoming blind spots and having disagreements, which seems to illustrate a larger process of iterative design and improvisation:

> It is actually boring when you all agree. When there's violent disagreement, then it is a trigger; there is something in there. Somebody's going to learn something, you know, when there is disagreement. If we can only get in there and find out!

He goes on to describe the process of engineering itself:

> Engineering is not a science. Engineering is an evolutionary incremental iteration of what we did last time for the next time. It is funny how you kind of run down these almost predestined paths based on your company's history, and if you get into a teaming situation, that gives you an opportunity to break out of some ruts on that, ruts that I had no idea we were in at my company until I came here, and participated on this team.

Barrett (1998) built on this idea of improvisation and said new models and metaphors are needed for organizing and interpreting work so that we can empower people at all levels to initiate innovative solutions in an effort to improve processes—a fundamental shift for maximizing learning and creating knowledge in organizations. He took the characteristics of jazz and explored their application to organizational processes: developing a shared orientation toward minimal structures that allow maximum flexibility. He cautioned organizations against trying to avoid change and ambiguity by creating too many standardized operating procedures, rational goals, and forms of centralized control. If improvisation is a loosely structured activity that allows diversity, then only minimal structures are required for minimal consensus and disclosure to balance autonomy and interdependence. Barrett stated:

> What characterizes successful jazz improvisation, perhaps more than any factor, is the ongoing give and take between members. Players are in a continual dialogue and exchange with one another. . . . Jazz improvisation is an emergent, elusive, vital process. At any moment a player can take the music in a new direction, defy expectations, and trigger others to re-interpret what they have just heard [1998, p. 613].

He challenged organizations to consider the trade-offs between developing cultures that service efficiency, relying on routines and pragmatic action, and those that support expression and spontaneous learning. Barrett said new structures and mind-sets are needed to achieve successful organizational performance and support interactive complexity.

USE OF METAPHORS

Other metaphors the engineers shared were especially helpful in providing a context for the experience and design environment of the JSF engineers as they described collaborative tasks. Two broad categories of metaphors emerged. First, the pictures they painted seemed to illustrate the significance of teamwork and partnerships, especially across an international spectrum. The images included an international soccer team, a global village, and the space station, where workers are reaching across distances to work together.

Second, and more often mentioned, was the organizational context and dynamics of working in a seemingly chaotic environment. The environmental scenarios are likened to churning whirlpools, atoms, and molecules with multiple variables and a Venn diagram of overlapping circles that constantly ebb and flow. When the challenges of working in those environments were described, they included images of the floor of the stock exchange, a soccer ball constantly being passed very fast to teammates, and a crew team struggling to have everyone row in the same direction with many voices yelling, "Stroke!"

The descriptions seem to suggest that the environment was exciting and challenging and pointed to the fact that this kind of aerospace program had not been done before. It sounded as if the participants had the pride of being on a new frontier and striving for innovation. These metaphors captured images of chaotic dynamics and environments.

Luke describes his dynamic model of a Venn diagram where three overlapping circles intersect with an area of common interests. He describes how the inside of the diagram ebbs and flows as the tasks do:

> The Venn diagram has three circles intersecting, depicting the inside where all are contributing and the outside where there are different contributors or partners. It is a dynamic process—with ebbs and flows, not hard lines and seamless. Perhaps even with dotted, permeable lines. This is so different from my previous experience at other international firms, which had "hard walls" between functions and partners.

Tim, who has been a soccer coach, plays on a soccer team and has played a lot with his JSF English teammates, especially when they first arrived. He described what happened:

> When they first came over here, we had just kind of a get-together every Wednesday at an indoor soccer rink that was over here, and it was just a pick-up game. Anybody could show up, and it would be about half American and half English, and we'd just go play indoor soccer. Of course, you know, they were always better than we were [laughs]. But it was fun to go do that, and that was one of the things that developed a relationship with the Brits.

His metaphor of a soccer game where passing (information) is important describes his daily challenge of task coordination:

> In soccer, you know, the thing is that passing is very important. If you want to win a game, you've got to learn how to pass to your teammate.

Which means you've got to, number one, trust him that he's going to be able to take the ball and keep on going. One of the things I had to teach the kids when they were young, that if he passes the ball, he'll get it back. When they're young, all the action's at the ball, and "I want to keep it." I would say that this collaboration is the same thing, and fits in with this knowledge-is-power sort of thinking—for instance, "I know all this stuff," and I would much rather have you come to me every single time as opposed to letting you know everything that's going on, so, you know, you're not ever coming back to me, right? I think that's what our working group is, is just that—that the team we've got on fiber placement is, "We want to get all the data out there so that everybody is equally successful. One guy scored the goal, but it took the whole team to get it down there."

Tim thinks this dynamic could have ongoing program benefits as well:

It's just critical to have that face-to-face meeting so they [my partners] are not just a voice on a Net meeting or a telecon, because that's what leads to that trust. From my perspective on the airplane programs, every airplane looks as if it seems to repeat the same problems over and over. The fact is that you've got new people on each program doing things different, and the more that they can reach out to others' experiences, then the better they're going to do their job. There have been a lot of times I've learned a lot from these other folks. That is the way knowledge is transferred: through the people and relationships.

ESSENTIAL CONDITIONS FOR SUCCESSFUL VIRTUAL COLLABORATION

During start-up, it was deemed important by management for leaders and employees of all partner companies to have time to socialize and try to overcome stereotypes or fear of differences. There were English teas hosted in Fort Worth, Texas, to introduce the BAE Systems folks. Soccer games at annual employee picnics put BAE Systems and Lockheed Martin into friendly competition, and soccer teams were formed all year long where all JSF employees could get to know each other more personally and blow off steam together. When folks were visiting in

England, a certain amount of time spent in English pubs seemed to strengthen relationships—and perhaps inspire new ideas.

Leaders reinforced the message of one-team collaboration through modeling and communication during strategic leadership meetings. After the team off-sites, leaders were always encouraged to communicate to the rest of the tiers of employees what was important to focus on in terms of business priorities and expected team behaviors. The concept of collaboration and one team was reinforced by the program leader and his key managers. Each modeled and translated this intent with their own style to set the tone or attitude.

Mike was known for personally reinforcing the partnership by having people identify themselves as JSF team members, and not by their company names:

> On the airframe team, one of the things I enforced rigorously was you had to identify yourself as a member of the center fuselage team, or the forward fuselage team, or the wing team. You didn't come out and say, "I'm Northrop Grumman." You had to reinforce it all the time. It was pretty easy during the CDP phase when there were only a few hundred of us. It has been more challenging as we've grown. The airframe team was 2,300 people when I left.

Some interviewees commented that a strong cultural influence was the professionalism of engineers across the board. This includes a focus on solving tough problems, creating workarounds when needed, searching for best possible designs solutions with innovation, and dedication to getting the job done. Although they can be very competitive, they also seem to be able to overcome cultural differences and security barriers. Arnie says: "When you've got a bunch of engineers together regardless of culture, regardless of background in which country they come from, and you give them a job to do, they just get it done."

Tim, the Lockheed Martin manager, had to reach out and establish new ground rules by asserting, "'This ain't business as usual.' It's going to be a team effort and if you're unwilling to do that, you better tell me right now. It's going to be team information, so if you don't want it shared on the team, then don't introduce it into your parts."

Lee and Keith said the challenges of working with a competitor can be diminished by beginning with the proper attitude of a win-win partnership. They claim that the essential conditions of making this kind of partnership work involve "treating competitors as full partners—giving them full trust—while keeping one's own company's interests protected."

Lee from Lockheed Martin illustrates how his own attitudes and behavior contributed to building a partnership:

> You have to do things for the benefit of the program, and that requires a tremendous amount of trust, and that is primary. If you can't trust your partners to have an open door to bring to the table the best and through your proprietary agreements, and your program perspective to keep sacred what's necessary, then you will never be effective at collaboration. You can't hold back and be an effect collaborator.

FINAL THOUGHTS

Despite the competitor relationship of the partners, the overall commitment to partnering and to getting the job done was reported as strong among the engineers who represented the primary partners—Lockheed Martin, BAE Systems, and Northrop Grumman—during the design phase of the JSF program. People seemed to be motivated, excited, and committed to producing the best they could possibly achieve. They were eager to collaborate, discover areas of interdependence, and innovate and create a new product. This story suggests that the motivating factors of virtual design teams were the presence of a compelling program vision and an equally compelling technical task that challenged their skill levels and the opportunity to contribute to a larger purpose: technological innovation and national defense, for example.

For leaders of alliances that are forming, the stories remind them of the benefits of developing common goals and vision to provide strong vertical integration. Their role as leader is important as a role model, communicator, and sponsor of the new team's common focus and culture. The data reinforce the need for development of effective infrastructure for lateral mechanisms and horizontal integration, especially as it supports information and idea sharing. Here, leaders may need to be prepared to invest more time and money in up-front solutions to making systems more compatible and providing for additional systems training and support.

Broad implications for organizational practice can be drawn from these stories to other multiparty alliances. For organizational designers of collaborative alliances, these stories remind us of both the vulnerabilities of coordinating these partnerships and the practicalities of managing the flow of information across boundaries. Any assessments of organizational culture conducted by the partner companies could help identify historical or current obstacles in employee attitudes and behaviors that might become barriers to assimilating into one team and listening to one another's ideas. There may be opportunities to sponsor both formal and informal forums for knowledge transfer and learning. As the participants reported, these forums can promote the sharing of technical expertise and strengthen partner relationships.

They may also want to revisit their organizational structures, along with their organization designers, to analyze whether there is enough flexibility and resources for employees to create those forums and new processes useful to both the execution of work and innovation. Budget and time are needed to create organizational space for those tiger teams and improvised learning that could be fateful later in any new product program.

Another reflection about these learning experiences is that improvised success at the early design stage of a venture may be fateful. Due to a few established routines, the JSF group was able to improvise solutions when facing challenges early on. These experiences seemed to set the tone and possibility for other collaborative projects later. The lessons learned and relationships built from these early experiences were luminous and became models for future experiments—that is, the tiger teams and inventing new products together. It seemed to legitimize task collaboration, formal and informal, later in the program.

These stories suggest that work relationships cannot be separated from executing the task or learning; they are intertwined and enable one another. If innovation is the goal in an iterative design environment, then the knowledge that would be most useful would be the tacit and complex—not just the explicit, codified knowledge. If this organizational learning is internalized, knowledge can be created, applied, negotiated, and transformed as it moves across process boundaries.

Organizations cannot exploit the virtues of increased information unless they adopt new structures and systems that are compatible with the new setting (Child, 1987; Clark, 1989). These include suppliers linked to designers, manufacturers to retailers, and research and development teams between international partners. Accepting the essential chaos of development and innovation is a particular challenge for large, complex, knowledge-creating organizations due to the challenges inherent in balancing the old and new, the bureaucracy and product development, and strategic determination and emergence. A useful metaphor offered by many researchers to characterize innovation is *tensions* because the term captures the organizing challenges of iterating among diverse activities, working around behaviors, combining insights, and resolving conflicts of seemingly opposing forces (Dougherty, 1996; Jelinek & Schoonhoven, 1990; Pelz & Andrews, 1966). Managing innovation then argues for organizations to be able to combine mechanistic and organic systems.

More organic environments or organizational structures can enable organizational change and learning to support innovation. Brown and Eisenhardt (1998) offered a concept they refer to as "the edge of chaos" for organizations to be able to change continuously. This edge can be described as "a natural state between order and chaos, a grand compromise between structure and surprise." It is the intermediate zone where organizations never quite settle into a stable equilibrium but never quite fall apart either. Here there is enough structure so that change and learning can be organized to happen, but it is not so rigid that it cannot occur, often referred to as self-organization.

New metaphors are also required for the image of product development rather than just a focus as disciplined problem solving. We need to develop new models of organization contexts within which distributed work can occur more naturally, especially forms with a boundaryless nature. Mohrman (1998) said there is a need for an integrative framework for myriad dispersed, multidimensional activities. Following her direction, we see that dispersed teams and networks are a way of organizing work that challenges many of the assumptions and approaches of the traditional hierarchical business model. This may encourage more research into the assumptions of heterarchy versus hierarchy and applications to the management of multinational corporations. Hedlund (1993) suggests we need to explore beyond matrix organizations and learn how to use more of a total systems view to design streamlined organization structures that coordinate along product lines, geographical lines, and functional lines simultaneously. If direct lateral communication is the thread that is needed for heterarchy, then information flow relies on systems and informal mechanisms to encourage shared goals and a strong corporate culture.

Finally, these stories show that alliances can indeed work. Informal collaborative inquiry, whether it occurs on VIPTs or tiger teams, leads to ideas that grow out of conversations, and perhaps it can be more useful than classroom learning. As Barrett (2005) suggests, "Discussion, negotiation, and argument are core to the learning process" (p. 4). Every partnership will bring predictable and unpredictable challenges in executing product development and creating innovation. This case illustrates that even in a very large, globally distributed team in the aerospace industry, people who are motivated by pride of product and program with shared compelling goals will improvise those vertical and horizontal organizational mechanisms needed to get the job done.

REMINDERS

- Innovation requires bridging boundaries. Use cross-company collaboration, on-site visits, and rotational assignments to deepen shared information and strengthen teamwork.

- Sponsor budget and time for new forums and teams to emerge as needed for collaborative design and knowledge transfer. Minimal structures allow maximum flexibility to balance disorder with common purpose.

- Support informal learning opportunities on the job, including dialogue and mentoring. Do not rely solely on formal training programs. Encourage people to start learning by pulling the information they need from anywhere in the organization.

- Integrate teams with representatives of different alliances and partners who bring a variety of experiences and frames of reference. Create a climate for innovation by encouraging diversity of thought and perception.

- Complement virtual communication with social activities like pub time to deepen relationships. Teamwork is critical to innovation success and knowledge transfer.

References

Barrett, F. J. (1998, September–October). Creativity and improvisation in jazz and organizations: Implications for organizational learning. *Organization Science, 9*(5), 605–622.

Barrett, F. J. (2005). *The dynamics of knowledge transfer within communities of practice: Implications for creating a virtual learning community.* Working paper.

Brown, S. L., & Eisenhardt, K. M. (1998). *Competing on the edge: Strategy as structured chaos.* Boston: Harvard Business School Press.

Child, J. (1987). Information technology, organization, and the response to strategic challenges. *California Management Review, 1*, 33–50.

Clark, K. (1989). What strategy can do for technology. *Harvard Business Review, 67,* 94–98.

Dougherty, D. (1992). Interpretive barriers to successful product innovation in large firms. *Organization Science, 3*(2), 179–201.

Dougherty, D. (1996). Organizing for innovation. In S. R. Clegg, C. Hardy, & W. R. Hord (Eds.), *Handbook of organization studies.* Thousand Oaks, CA: Sage.

Earley, P. C., & Gibson, C. B. (2002). *Multinational work teams: A new perspective.* Mahwah, NJ: Erlbaum.

Galbraith, J. R. (1977). *Organization design.* Reading, MA: Addison-Wesley.

Galbraith, J. R. (1994). *Competing with flexible lateral organizations.* Reading, MA: Addison-Wesley.

Galbraith, J., Downey, D., & Kates, A. (2002). *Designing dynamic organizations.* New York: AMACOM.

Gray, B. (1989). *Collaborating: Finding common ground for multi-party problems.* San Francisco: Jossey-Bass.

Gulati, R., & Nohria, N. (1994). Unilateral commitments and the importance of process in alliances. *Sloan Management Review, 35*(3), 61–69.

Hedlund, G. (1993). Assumptions of hierarchy and heterarchy, with applications to the management of the multinational corporation. In S. Ghoshal & D. E. Westney (Eds.), *Organization theory and the multinational corporation.* New York: St. Martin's Press.

Jelinek, M., & Schoonhaven, C. (1990). *The innovation marathon: Lessons from high technology firms.* Oxford: Basil Blackwell.

Mankin, D. A., & Cohen, S. G. (2004). *Business without boundaries: An action framework for collaborating across time, distance, organization and culture.* San Francisco: Jossey-Bass.

Mohrman, S. A. (1998, May). The contexts for geographically dispersed teams and networks. In C.R.D. Cooper (Ed.), *Trends in organizational behavior.* Hoboken, NJ: Wiley.

Park, S., & Russo, M. (1996). When competition eclipses cooperation: An event history analysis of alliance failure. *Management Science, Linthicum, 42*(6), 875–891.

Pelz, D., & Andrews, F. (1966). *Scientists in organizations.* Hoboken, NJ: Wiley.

Thompson, J. D. (1967). *Organizations in action: Social science bases of administration.* New York: McGraw-Hill.

Vansina, L., Taillieu, T., & Schruijer, S. (1998). Managing multi-party issues: Learning from experience. *Research in Organizational Change and Development, 11,* 159–181.

PART EIGHT

Conclusion

There are many facets to virtual team success. This book has presented a large number of principles, tools, and scenarios for guiding creation, development, and sustainability of virtual teams. Chapter Twenty-Nine draws a selection of those principles together. Systematic use of nearly any subset of the principles will have an impact on team success that is often immediate and visible. Making systematic use visible and disciplined will demonstrate an investment in the teams that will also have an impact—generating a greater sense of confidence. Start now. Start simply by choosing five items from the lists. Share the implementation effort with team members. Persist in the application of the principles. Measure your progress. Look for ways to add another principle or two later in the year. Celebrate the successes.

The process of inventing new ways to use collaboration for organizational excellence is far from over. Chapter Thirty ends this handbook with a glimpse into the future from Lipnack and Stamps. The emergence of the technology of social network analysis (SNA) has made it possible to study informal sets of work relationships in ways that can clarify how processes occur within organizations. SNA can produce graphic maps of who talks to whom, how often, what about, and in what way. Maps have been generated to show interaction within small groups, between groups, and between organizations. In the case of the German company described by Lipnack and Stamps, SNA was used to identify important ways for improving and speeding decision-making processes in the company. The map provided a useful profile of collaboration within the company that exceeded the bounds of the formal organization. Collaboration became a better tool across the many parts of the complex organization once the map of interaction processes became clear. Informal collaboration is emerging as a key organizing mechanism in business to complement formal collaborative structures, and tools for understanding and managing that mechanism will make new ways of organizing more effective. Virtual teams take on a new form—virtual groups that emerge, ebb and flow, and fade away as circumstances dictate.

Collaboration in the Real World

Virtual Team Key Take-Away Principles That Work

Michael Beyerlein, Lori Bradley, Jill Nemiro, Susan Beyerlein

O rganizational experiments continue as new forms of organizing bring us closer together around the globe. The Internet, and particularly electronic communication, has made possible new ways of organizing that continue to yield competitive advantage. These are experiments, and while many fail, others take hold, radically improving the human-technology mix and providing new capability for flexible, rapid response in the global marketplace.

The shift from individual task responsibility to teamwork is perhaps the most dramatic and burgeoning trend sweeping U.S. companies in the past two decades, and the advent of teams has also greatly influenced how business is conducted with industry partners around the world. Teams are now found in all organizations across the supply chain as changes have elevated member organization relationships above the traditional sovereignty of nation-state (Friedman, 2005) in search of the holy grail of competitive advantage. Teams make good business sense for a variety of reasons, for example, the logic of partnership agreements with supplier organizations that focus on long-term vendor investment in training and development in securing a continual stream of dedicated, high-quality inputs rather than buyers simply focused on the lowest-cost product.

Collaboration, the hallmark of teams, can be found in many arrangements within and between organizations, including new product development teams (NPDs), consultation teams, project teams, strategic alliances, partnerships, roundtables, networks, and consortia, all dedicated to leveraging knowledge, skills, and resources in solving complex problems (Hardy, Lawrence, & Grant, 2005). In all cases, the effectiveness of the particular collaboration is dependent on local conditions and the general principles that drive a work team's success. Increasingly, virtual teams represent the operational mechanism that makes the collaboration possible.

Technology-based teaming is new enough that the lessons learned and best practices lists continue to evolve. In this handbook, we have gathered together an extensive array of principles, tools, and practices that virtual teams can use in building a solid foundation for moving toward high performance. Some ways of moving toward high performance and excellence in virtual teaming are recapped in the key take-away principles listed next, which have been detailed in various chapters in the book. These principles represent elements of a full program for developing supportive environments that enhance virtual team high performance.

KEY TAKE-AWAY PRINCIPLES

PRINCIPLES OF HIGH-PERFORMANCE VIRTUAL TEAMS

Part One: Working Collaboratively

- Achieving high levels of performance with virtual teams is more difficult than with colocated teams, but with a systematic approach, it can be done.
- Effective virtual collaboration requires integrating three critical success factors: shared understanding, trust, and effective communication.
- Virtual teams are more difficult to manage than colocated ones but can be just as effective.
- The key to effective collaboration is to match the task to the technology that offers the best level of social presence. Media richness focuses on the level of information richness that a certain technology provides.

- Innovation requires bridging boundaries. Use cross-company collaboration, onsite visits, and rotational assignments to deepen shared information and strengthen teamwork.

Part Two: Building a Collaborative Culture

- Trust makes organizations work. It drives performance and business results.
- Charge executive leadership with supporting the design process and removing barriers.
- Teamwork is fundamentally social, so create a cohesive team culture.
- In order for trust to develop, team members need to follow through on commitments and promises to each other.
- Expect that some groups or individuals will have different perceptions of the change.
- Resistance to change is strongest when there are a lot of varied types of negative justice perceptions.
- The goal for all virtual team members at all levels is to embrace change rather than simply cope with it.
- An understanding of collaborative technology, team processes, organizational culture, and meeting effectiveness will enable sound processes to be created to guide effective collaboration.

Part Three: Leading Collaboratively

- Confident people do better work, and people identify more with teams they have confidence in. A virtual team leader who instills confidence reaps both rewards.
- A survey of virtual teams identified the attributes they would like to see in their leader: integrity, a genuine concern for others, and self-confidence.
- Feedback is central to leadership. Not only is it indispensable in setting goals and coordinating team progress, it is a key to personal and team development.
- Virtual team coaches may be best advised to shift from a directive and authoritative standpoint to more of a nondirect role that focuses on defining, facilitating, and encouraging performance.
- Successful cross-border team leaders have the knowledge to recognize cultural phenomena, the ability to observe and interpret subtle behavioral cues, and

the skills to adapt their behavior to the needs and expectations of people from different cultures.

- Leaders of international virtual teams have to adapt the way they manage as well as the way they lead. Methods that aid the team include subdividing the work to minimize the need for collaboration and creating a sense of local ownership, providing multiple communication channels, translating complex directions, using as much visual explanation as possible, and using frequent progress checks and reviews to ensure that everyone has a shared understanding and commitment to the organization's and team's goals.

- Educating team sponsors and the team leader's supervisors on the challenges and skills of cross-border virtual work is often critical to the team leader's survival.

- Leaders who have a positive outlook and provide support and encouragement are valued by the members of all cultures.

- Leaders should strive to obtain more complete and thoughtful input from every team member and generate a greater understanding among team members of other's views and perspectives.

- Ensure that leaders have facilitation and coaching skills, virtual meeting skills, cultural sensitivity, communications skills, and problem-solving and decision-making abilities.

- Leaders should model a culture of disciplined meeting and communication norms.

DESIGNING HIGH-PERFORMANCE VIRTUAL TEAMS

Part Four: Setting Up a Collaborative Team

- Virtual teams can develop vicious or virtuous cycles of the critical success factors. Interventions can help teams get on and stay on the virtuous path.

- Generational differences within the team and between the team and its customers have an impact on effectiveness through diversity of perspective.

- Effective virtual team design considers not only the social, technical, and environmental systems but the personal one as well.

- Align team design with the project so that the right people are involved in the right process.

- Identify key competencies and attributes, and design a comprehensive selection process.

- Identify the most critical measures to track changes in team performance and how they will be maintained and accessed.

- Focus on the intentional design of conversations to build relationships as the foundation of any team, especially when members are not colocated.

- Implementation of virtual teams and their support systems represents change. All change situations have the potential to create feelings of unfairness since roles and rules are renegotiated and expectations may be violated.

- Virtual staffing decisions should focus on finding both the right experts and the experts who are likely to work together well as a team.

- When staffing teams, it is good to analyze the task for requirements at both the individual and team levels.

- Understand how the characteristics of the learners affect workplace training to ensure that training recommendations are relevant.

- Support informal learning opportunities on the job, including dialogue and mentoring. Do not rely solely on formal training programs.

- Important considerations in designing virtual teams include the appropriate division of tasks, use of a variety of modes of communication, and matching members with tasks so essential knowledge is shared.

- Virtual teams have unique start-up challenges, many of them stemming from the varied cultural backgrounds of team members. These cultural differences extend beyond geographical ones to include educational, functional, religious, and a variety of life experiences.

- Four tools are especially helpful for starting up virtual teams: team charters, role clarification processes, operating guidelines, and protocols for the use of communication technology.

- A start-up process is best done face-to-face. The discussion that creates the charter, roles, and agreements is probably more important than the final product. The participation of all team members is important, as is including people outside the team who have a major impact on the team's ability to be successful.

Part Five: Working on a Collaborative Team

- Mission accomplishment is the goal of virtual teams. All else serves this purpose. However, valued outcomes from effective teaming can include development of social capital, working relationships, and robust interpersonal networks across the organization.

- Collaboration is a result of positive synergy that encourages a win-win relationship among team members. It requires trust, shared understanding, and constructive relationships to form among team members and helping members care about the ultimate goal of the team rather than just their own expected contribution.

- The survival of virtual teams depends on active and effective communication despite the location and potential time zone differences among members.

- Celebrate successes virtually, and recognize individual members' contributions.

- Self-serving tactics and political maneuvering severely limit or even prevent virtual collaboration, good decision making, and effective problem solving.

- The lack of human interaction within the virtual team can create substantial obstacles to effective teamwork.

- Dynamic relationships and constructive accountability are needed to make progress on the team project between virtual team meetings.

- Important work is done in virtual meetings. Conduct the first team meeting face-to-face to begin to build trust and personal connection.

- Establish a set of team norms that will guide the team's conduct during and outside meetings.

- Make use of virtual team meeting facilitators and cofacilitators.

- Determine the purpose of the meeting, and then select the appropriate collaborative technology to serve that purpose.

Part Six: Tools and Assessments for Collaboration

- A well-thought-out deployment project for virtual collaboration should include an assessment of the client base as it relates to the generations it touches.

- Conduct a brief organizational analysis first to determine if training *is* a potential solution.

- Use of tools like attribute listing, morphological analysis, and force field analysis can foster creativity on the team.

REAL-WORLD EXAMPLES OF HIGH-PERFORMANCE VIRTUAL TEAMS

Part Seven: Case Studies

- Use and support of virtual teams represent business decisions, so making the business case for resources depends on a structured presentation of the outcomes the teams can achieve when they are properly supported.

- Team members should be trained and motivated to seek a solution that will benefit the collective rather than solely their own needs and requirements.

- The range of applications and the number of successes with virtual teams continues to grow, including a variety of uses in health care where both the sharing of knowledge and the control of cost are essential.

- The implementation of a distributed work initiative is not a project with a beginning and an end. It is an ongoing way of doing business that needs to be continually adjusted to respond to external conditions and improved in response to internal demands.

- Data-based logic can help link infrastructure choices with business objectives and critical success factors that must be supported by any distributed work solution under consideration. The linkage provides clear business-focused criteria for evaluating the appropriateness and scope of distributed work arrangements.

- Integrate teams with representatives of different alliances and partners who bring a variety of experiences and frames of reference. Create a climate for innovation by encouraging diversity of thought and perception.

- Involve cross-functional support groups such as real estate, information technology, and human resources in decision making to foster an integrated and optimized system of infrastructure support needed for effective distributed and virtual work. An integrated system of distributed work support should include all the physical (locations, spaces, furniture), technological (voice, data, video, Web), and organizational (structure, policies, norms) infrastructure components that enable the organization's desired work practices.

BENEFITS OF VIRTUAL COLLABORATION

Virtual teams are here to stay. They allow work to be done no matter where individual team members reside. This handbook has offered a wealth of strategies, tools, techniques, and knowledge to assist readers in achieving high performance in their virtual teams. What distinguishes between a virtual team and a high-performance virtual team is that the latter focuses on collaboration, a requirement in fast-paced business today. Collaboration is often the only way to address the rapid and complex problems that organizations face.

When asked, "What are the benefits of self-managed teams?" a group of work team employees, managers, trainers, consultants, and researchers gave the following responses (Beyerlein, 2002):

- Greater commitment
- Improved organizational viability
- Improved workforce viability
- Higher-skilled workforce
- More responsible workforce
- More employee involvement
- Higher-caliber leaders; improved leadership abilities
- Broader level of individual contribution
- Higher overall quality of work life
- Improved customer satisfaction
- Improved ownership of output and process
- Increased self-worth
- Increased ability to influence
- Increased empowerment
- Better relations between employees and management
- Highly educated workforce with both social and technical skills
- Better long-range planning
- More flexible management styles
- Increased customer loyalty

- Increased revenue and profits
- Fewer management positions
- Long-term security

The benefits of collaboration extend beyond how much or how quickly work can be completed. Collaboration also has benefits in building networks and trust across people and boundaries, as well as building a team esprit de corps. Teams composed of diverse members produce superior and more creative solutions than more homogeneous teams. Although the diverse team may be slower out of the gate, the additional ideas and viewpoints that emerge in the end expand the parameters that would exist within a homogeneous team with similar mental models, and the results are superior. Collaboration can feel slow and cumbersome at first, but effective organizations have learned that superior results justify the time investment in a deliberate and disciplined collaborative process.

An area of concern in our increasingly knowledge-based economy is the need for knowledge transfer. Knowledge transfer has always been a need, but as the baby boomers, who represent a large percentage of our current workforce, age and retire in large numbers, there will be an increased need to retain organizational knowledge in many forms. Because of the shifting demographics of the workforce and the expanding global structures of some organizations, knowledge transfer is more important than ever before. A beneficial by-product of a collaborative approach to work, if planned for effectively, is increased knowledge transfer. By including more junior and senior members on teams, the collaboration can serve as a learning environment (for both the junior and senior members) and help with the transfer of critical knowledge. Having senior members collaborate with junior ones also has the benefit of expanding organizational memory.

In the study referred to above a question was asked about the causes of team failure. Here *failure* means that the team does not meet expectations or goals or achieve full potential. These are some of the responses (Beyerlein, 2002):

- Lack of management support or commitment or understanding
- Failure to involve top management in the change process
- Steering team without line workers as members
- Microperspective instead of a macrofocus on individual teams instead of their context and interrelationships

- Misaligned leadership style: command and control versus empowering and enabling
- Member turnover: too many or too quick, or losing required talent
- Lack of time (for example, for meetings or training)
- Lack of facilities (for example, for meetings and training)
- Lack of money (for example, for rewards or consultants or benchmarking trips)
- Wrong goals—lack of alignment of team goals with business unit goals
- Resistance to change and failure to take the initiative in generating change
- Adopting, not adapting; not tailoring the design to local conditions, and using a cookie-cutter approach instead
- Evaporating instead of deliberately adjourning for closing down project teams
- Teaming selected as a fad, not as a means to world-class performance
- Narrow definition of performance (for example, omitting morale, attendance, innovation, commitment, image with public, customer delight, and internal customers as well as external)
- Time frame to begin too short and too rushed (for example, "Tomorrow you will be in teams")
- Lack of shared vision, mission, values
- Lack of shared mental models within the team, the steering team, or the top management group
- Failing to link change effort to results in strategic planning and accounting
- Wrong choice of team type
- Treating technical professional teams the same as production teams (creative work needs more freedom, language differs, egos intrude)
- Failure to institutionalize the change (for example, when a champion leaves a company, the change initiative dies because a critical mass of support has not been created among remaining members)

Although the Beyerlein survey was investigating self-directed work teams and not specifically virtual teams or teams employing virtual collaboration techniques, many of the issues are relevant and can be used as lessons learned for those seeking to use and support virtual collaboration successfully.

FINAL THOUGHTS

The chapter authors of this handbook have provided a deepening of existing perspectives on the topic of virtual collaboration and teams and, with it, a rich compendium of innovative and useful ideas, tools, and processes for making it a successful and satisfying enterprise. Take the time to digest their ideas and suggestions, and see what resonates with the challenges emerging in your own virtual teams. Capture and share your own challenges and lessons learned within and across your own teams. The dialogue is half the process. Your own thinking on what has been offered here will enrich your own virtual team's journey toward high performance, and together you will participate in shaping a new way of working.

References

Beyerlein, M. M. (2002). *Team survey: What are the benefits of self-managed teams?* Denton: Center for the Study of Work Teams, University of North Texas.

Friedman, T. L. (2005). *The world is flat: A brief history of the twenty-first century.* New York: Farrar, Straus, and Giroux.

Hardy, C., Lawrence, T. B., & Grant, D. (2005). Discourse and collaboration: The role of conversations and collective identity. *Academy of Management Review, 30*(1), 58–77.

The Virtual, Networked Organization

How One Company Became Transparent

Jeffrey Stamps, Jessica Lipnack

Virtual teams live in much larger organizations and, as this handbook indicates, depend on collaboration. Indeed, without working together, the literal meaning of *collaborate*, organizations cannot innovate, produce results, or even conduct a proper teleconference. The previous chapters lay out the fundamental practices by which these new groups carry out their daily work. Here we examine the larger context in which virtual teams exist and bring a different perspective to what can be learned from the formal environments that embed them. The oldest, large-scale organizational structure—the hierarchy—may hold powerful insights that can aid the effectiveness of the newest, the subject of this book—the virtual team. What follows is the case study of one company's experience taking a deep dive into its hierarchical structure, revealing information of immediate use to facilitating virtual working.

Although we have based the story told here on a real company and real people, the identities of both have been disguised in the interest of privacy.

693

THE BIRTH OF THE ORGANIZATION

Mike Riverton had a problem: as the first chief executive of Eleum, a large unit of a major global energy player, he was asked to bring together a new organization. The new regional enterprise would comprise the merger of eight country-based companies owned by one of the oldest, biggest, and most successful global businesses. Once operational, the new organization would generate a significant portion of its parent company's multibillion-dollar income.

It would have been easier for Mike to build an organization that was a legal entity. Instead of incorporating a new company with officers, charters, and other paraphernalia associated with corporate endeavors, Mike's charge was to form a virtual organization. Each country-based company would continue to fulfill local country legal requirements; the debits and credits of business would continue to be carried out as if nothing had changed; people would go on receiving their paychecks from the company located in the country where they went to work.

What would change would be the way people carried out their work. Instead of eight human resource departments, there would be one; instead of eight finance departments, one; instead of eight production departments, the heart of the energy business, there would be one. It sounds like the old central model, which people complained about for decades and ultimately led to decentralization of functions. But Eleum would not be the same as the organizations of old. The functions and the organization's project teams would not colocate. Mike's direct reports, for example, would be in three countries stretching across Europe. And it was the same way down the line. Bosses were no longer sitting down the hall from employees, who were no longer eating in the same cafeterias as their colleagues.

Nevertheless, the new enterprise's design on paper looked a lot like any other traditional organization chart (what Europeans call an *organigram*) with Mike at the top, a senior team of direct reports, and so on down the line. The neatly stacked boxes and vertical lines of authority, however, scarcely reflected the complexity of operating in this new structure.

Eleum is not alone. Many organizations have charts that poorly depict how work is done. And this problem is getting worse as organizations suddenly disperse operations. Many experiments are underway to address the complexity of organizations like Mike's. One popular method is to map people's personal connections, their networks. An organization design approach wildly popular on the Web (think of the FaceBooks and MySpaces), social network analysis is finally getting the attention it deserves. With roots that go back decades, this view of organizations draws the lines of personal relationships: familiarity, influence, charisma. People's inner lives—their interests, passions, desires, and visions—are what make us come to work and what make us want to know one another as human beings. However, the personal connections among people, profound as they are, usually are not the starting points for designing new organizations or reorganizing old ones. An organization comes together to do something. Its structure is typically designed around its purpose and not, for the most part, on the basis of who knows whom.

Mike's challenge is a harbinger of the world to come for organizations regardless of size. Whether a global giant with an instantly recognizable logo like Eleum's or a small one working for a cure for cystic fibrosis, organizations need new maps for the new virtual world and many ways to look at themselves. Eleum's story is about those new maps.

LET'S HEAR IT FOR THE HIERARCHY

In the past few years, the fascination with networks has spread from domain to domain. The word *network* was originally a descriptor just for concrete things like airline routes, road systems, and telecommunication webs. For some time now, it has been used more broadly to describe groups of people with connections that cross boundaries.

In 2002, an unusually provocative book, *Linked: The New Science of Networks* brought new thinking about organizations as networks. A quantum physicist, Albert-László Barabási, and his scientist colleagues in many fields had been studying the similar properties of diverse networks. Until the past few years, the now-classical scientific view was that the nodes—the key connecting points in networks—distribute randomly according to the familiar bell curve. This implies that most nodes have more or less the same number of links.

Starting with a study of the Web, the physicists found something very different: a remarkably consistent, nonrandom structure in networks across multiple domains—from the parlor game, Six Degrees of Kevin Bacon, to how HIV/AIDS spreads to growth of bacteria in a Petri dish, to the distribution of routers (as well as pages) on the Web itself. What they confirmed is that most nodes in a network have very few links, but the hubs, which are about 20 percent, have very many links.

The discovery that real networks have hubs—highly connected nodes—brings both good news and bad. On the upside, such a network is much more robust against accidents than one whose nodes are randomly connected and normally distributed, because there are only a few hubs. The negative side is that a network with hubs is more vulnerable to direct attack on these key points since only a few nodes need to be taken out to collapse the whole network. This explains the great interest in such ideas in a post–9/11 world, where the word *network* variously describes terrorists, energy grids, and the spread of viruses.

Provoked further by a May 2003 *Scientific American* article by Barabási and Eric Bonabeau, we started to wonder whether something else was going on. When people unconsciously use the word *network* to describe their organizations, including those embedded in hierarchies like Mike Riverton's, might they literally be talking about the new organizational structure? Might hierarchies themselves be networks? And if they are, can we make them better and more fit for virtual working? Would organizations reflect the characteristics of scale-free networks?

We had to find out. If we could "see" the networks within the hierarchy, then we would be able to model them. We could apply the tools of the field that has spawned the Barabásis and Bonabeaus of the world the new science of networks—which, as a science, has algorithms, produces findings, and makes it possible to simulate and to optimize. We might be able to design better networks, more suitable organizations that make it easier for people to work across all kinds of virtual boundaries—whether language, time zone, discipline, or corporate border.

MEANWHILE, BACK AT ELEUM . . .

Mike named a program office that engaged hundreds of people in the organization's design. Over nine months, the design team, comprising the best and the brightest, meticulously detailed the requirements of each position, resulting in job descriptions for thousands of slots. Each job was spelled out in detail, even to where the person who occupied it would be situated. Mike also chartered a value-definition exercise to establish the core tenets of the new organization, involving most of those who worked there.

The new organization rolled out in stages, beginning with Mike's filling the first job, CEO, in December 2002. Then Mike and his colleagues defined the next level: approving job descriptions and selecting people to fill those positions. They designed and staffed the following level, and so on. When Eleum officially went live in fall 2003, all but a few of five thousand positions in nine functions were staffed. That was when we went back to Mike with our hypothesis.

The premiere strategic consulting company in the world had recommended the new organizational structure that Mike had just launched. Except for the leadership groups that Mike himself intended to pull together (variations on cross-organizational structures he had been trying out for years in prior postings), his new, distributed, border-crossing, truly virtual organization looked remarkably like every other organization chart he had ever seen. When we pointed him to the *Scientific American* article and suggested that the application of network science might produce some insights, the chief executive gave a green light to explore what this might mean.

Strategy as a Network

Rendering an organization as a network requires two things: data and a network mapping tool. First, we tackled how to define the data. Since a network comprises nodes and links, we had to identify their correlates in the organization. Thus, we shifted our focus from the network of people who staff the organization to the network of positions that comprise the organization's structure. In technical terms, positions are interconnected niches in the organizational landscape, jobs that are either occupied or vacant. Every organizational hierarchy is made up of positions connected through lines of authority to every other position. In network science terms, a position is a node, and the reporting relationship is a link.

Second, we had to find, or make, a tool. This proved a bit more complicated and required some development. Simply speaking, we took a hyperbolic viewer—a network modeling tool invented at the fabled Xerox PARC and commercialized by Inxight—and modified it to visualize the organization chart and generate metrics about it.

With the data defined and a tool for testing it in hand, we were ready to model the hierarchy as a network. We figured we could add less accessible maps of relationships later—leadership groups, locations, nationalities, projects, and even service organizations that cross organizational boundaries—and layer them on top of the base hierarchy map.

To gather our sample data, we worked with Patrick Robertson, Eleum's chief of strategy, who was especially interested because of his responsibility for industrial safety. Although his own organization had barely 250 people, Patrick needed thirty separate organization charts to fully represent it. By entering his data into the network mapping tool, we could click and zoom through his whole organization, interconnected and at once.

The results of the strategy department's mapping exercise circulated quickly among Mike's leadership team. The map itself was illuminating, as it quickly became clear that certain positions were more linked than others. At this point, Robin Christopher, the head of organization development, came forward. He suggested that we take data directly from the company's human resource system, housed in SAP. The enterprisewide database contained exactly the information we needed about positions to allow us to construct a complete map of Eleum. Each position's record included its title, the name of the organizational unit that it belonged to, the name of the person who occupied it, where it was located, and, most critical for our purposes, the position it reported to—a direct link to another position in the data set. From that simple pair-wise relationship, we could construct Eleum's 5,000-position organization chart. What would it look like as a network?

It took us a week to process the data and prepare for display. When we finally ran the model, we saw something we had never seen in our quarter-century of work with networks. Crude as it was, the picture that emerged whole out of the myriad data points seemed to be a glimpse of the true face of an organization. The logic of the hierarchy morphed into spidery strands of nodes and links, tracing now-visible patterns of a giant network that could be viewed from afar yet examined in intimate detail. We dubbed our new network mapper "OrgScope" for its ability to render the obscure visible. (See Figure 30.1 for an example data set similar to Eleum's.) In this example, the nodes represent the positions linked by their direct reporting relationships. Simply stated, this is the organization chart shown in an unusual radial orientation rather than the more conventional top-down view, the same logical hierarchy that makes more efficient use of limited display space, whether on paper or a computer screen.

Once we placed every position in the organization in relationship to all the rest on the map, we could test our hypothesis. Did some of the nodes (that is, positions) have more links than the rest? Or did all the positions have approximately the same number of links (that is, reporting relationships)? In other words, did most people manage about the same number of people? Did most of the managers have an average span of control? We were trying to find out whether there were hubs in the hierarchy, just like Barabási discovered.

Figure 30.1
Hierarchy Network with Hubs

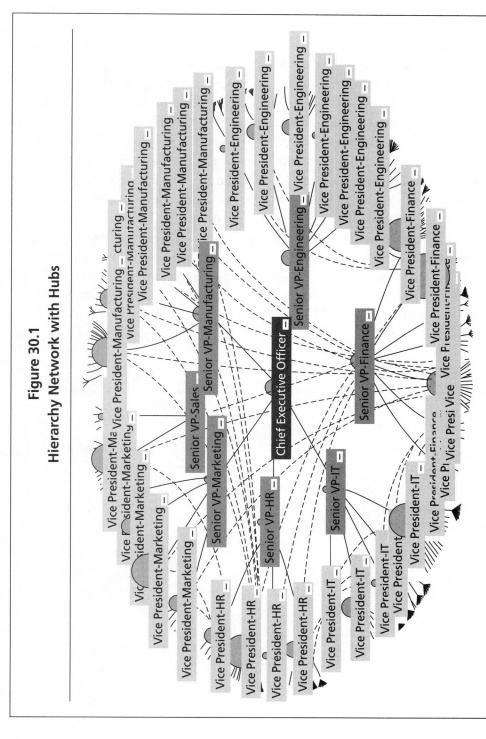

Note: The number of reporting relationships is indicated by the relative size of the wafer next to the hub.

It turned out that in Mike Riverton's organization, roughly 20 percent of the managers had 80 percent of the people reporting to them, and 80 percent of managers had 20 percent of the people reporting to them (see Figure 30.2). In other words, Mike's formal hierarchy had the characteristics of a scale-free network. Certain positions—just by the design of the formal hierarchy—were clearly hubs. Although there is a practical limit to how many people could report to one manager, that number in Mike's organization varied widely, from one to nearly forty. Our guess is, based on our experience at Eleum, that there are seemingly scale-free spans resident in the management of nearly every large organization.

After finding hubs, we took a look at where managers and employees were situated in the organization, that is, how many reporting links away from Mike they were. We thought we would find the classic pyramid, with increasingly more people at each level down the line. Notably, when we asked Patrick how many levels were in the new organization, he said five, by design. According to the numbers? Eight.

Then the next surprise: the organization's shape, according to the number of positions at each reporting level, was a diamond, not a pyramid. We could see the diamond shape by turning the diagram that distributed the positions by level on

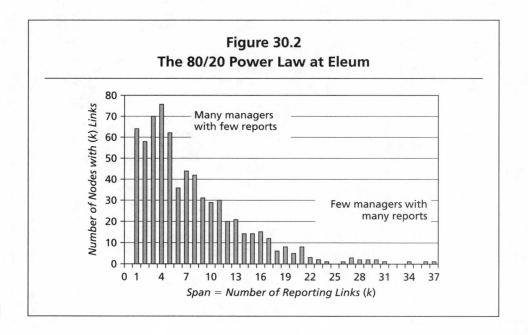

Figure 30.2
The 80/20 Power Law at Eleum

its side. What looks suspiciously like a normal distribution across levels suggests this different shape may be a common one for large organizations. In Figure 30.3, the organization is arrayed by level from top to bottom, with the CEO at level 1 and the lowest-ranking employee at level 8. The width of each bar indicates the total number of employees, the sum of nonmanagement staff (the light bars) and managers (the dark bars).

At Eleum, the management structure was centered at the fifth level, meaning that level 5 has the largest number of managers, while the largest number of employees was situated at level 6. In fact, there were managers at the fifth level with organizations larger than those of some people reporting directly to Mike. Down deep in the organization, below the waterline of what the people at the top

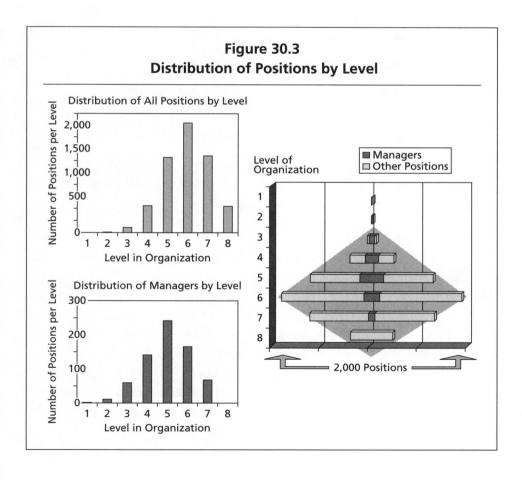

Figure 30.3
Distribution of Positions by Level

could see, a number of people ran very large organizations but were not included in leadership groups.

We presented the first maps at a face-to-face meeting of Mike's entire senior team (with one person calling in by videoconference from northern England). They said they found the pictures both very familiar, like any other organization chart they had seen, and utterly novel. They noticed that some positions had many lines coming into them and others just a few, and the people at the top of the organization (themselves) were not necessarily the ones with the most lines.

At that first meeting, Mike and his leadership team put together a list of questions provoked by the maps:

- What is the distribution of people on the line?
- Where are the hubs? How are they distributed by level?
- What is the impact when matrix reports are added?
- Do we have the right people in the leadership groups?
- Based on results, do we need to change our engagement model?
- How complete is the picture? Do we need to include contractors?
- What is the compelling story about reporting relationships that this has enabled?
- What is the leadership profile at each level?
- What is the shape of our hierarchy? Where is the organizational center of gravity?
- What importance do levels have as an organizing principle?

We continued to explore with them what the maps were telling us. When we looked several levels down, we found additional surprises: the organizational topology was immensely varied, not at all the regular tree structure we typically associate with hierarchies. While some Eleum organizations were relatively flat, others were quite steep. Some were relatively flat for the top few levels and then dropped off into deep crevices at lower depths. Some organizations at the same level were shallow and small, with others relatively large and deeply trenched.

And to our collective great surprise, hubs showed up throughout the organization—at least according to the data from the SAP system. Eleum's executives wondered whether the data were correct. Maybe, they speculated, the maps were generated by faulty data. But as it turned out, the data, even those used in our first trials, were highly accurate: they came from the database used by the human resource system that fed the payroll, which required accuracy. Even so, Eleum's commitment to making certain that the information we were using was accurate was so strong that during our data collection period, they carried out two more companywide efforts to improve it. They also put time into two rounds of identifying the key matrix (dotted-line) relationships. By the time this data washing was complete, we had in hand a benchmark data set to analyze, which would enable us to name and order Eleum's hubs in a context transparent to all.

How Virtual Is Virtual?

Like other organizations working in multiple locations, Mike and his leadership team were considering providing virtual team training across the board. For any company, this is a big undertaking, so we ran the numbers.

Because the location of each position is part of its human resource record, we could tell which managers ran virtual teams. The data revealed that approximately one-third of the formal management teams were in more than one location. This allowed Eleum to target scarce virtual team training at the teams most in need. Even with the bold new cross-border design, people tended to have managers who sat nearby and might be annoyed by a broad-brush campaign that they did not really need.

Our focus on the properties of the management groups led us to the next consideration: the real-world working groups, the true virtual teams that carried out the company's business. Mapping and analyzing all the working groups in the company would have required considerable effort. We started by analyzing one key function that reached across many others: the safety function, Patrick Robertson's original concern. It turned out that this group was very virtual and much larger than the formal organization chart indicated. The safety function, according to the number of employees assigned to that unit, totaled approximately one hundred. When we added in all the nodes in the safety network—including contractors, matrix reporting relationships, and clients—the organization was four times as large. And it was extremely virtual, physically located in "virtually" every Eleum location—dozens in all. Likewise, the matrix reporting relationships were unevenly distributed. Most of the employees—80 percent—had at least two bosses, and 10 percent of those had three or more bosses.

So What?

What did all this mean to Mike? A lot. Mike's company had facts about its organizational design that it could work with, real data to inform their decisions about creating the most effective structure in virtual times. While metrics provided objective information for diagnosing potential trouble spots and for focusing scarce resources, they also could have an impact on corporate communications.

The new analysis explained why Mike's (and everyone else's) cascade theory of communication was not working. When he wanted to send a message down the line, perhaps about new safety precautions or about business performance, Mike brought together the people at the top, either electronically or face-to-face, and passed along the message, which these people were to pass along to their people. By the time the message got to the part of the organization where most of the managers were—and where most of the people were—valuable time would have passed, with the message being degraded with each transmission, time that in the fast pace of their industry could never be recovered.

So they made changes. They revised their approach so that it was no longer "whisper down the line." They turned their communication strategy sideways; Mike started to communicate horizontally to the managers—about 20 percent of the organization. In one click, Mike could reach the entire organization. "That worked," he said. "We were able to get very quick response when we needed it."

They added people who managed the largest organizations, regardless of their level, to their leadership groups. They added other layers of nodes and links to their hierarchy map, like the safety network, which made it easier for organizations considering redesign to see their true job-to-job working relationships. And by recognizing the actual distributed nature of the organization according to the data—not just people's impressions—they were able to decide objectively where to provide precious resources for virtual team training. Mike made his organization chart transparent and thus much more useful to the people in it.

THE AGE OF THE NETWORK

Organizations like Mike's, ones that are virtual and networked, are coming of age, visible in corporate blueprints that link geographies within and between regions while respecting cultural, economic, and legal realities. People thread through the system at all levels in these new organizations, and teams, often global, usually virtual, are everywhere—from senior executives to frontline employees.

To support the many conversations going on across and within levels of organizations and across organizations, we advocate networked hierarchies, drawing new maps that allow people to see where they are and to whom they are connected. These new images are the orienteers needed to make work and home life simpler, not more difficult, no matter where people are located.

As companies cope with increased complexity, with people situated in more locations—bosses here, employees there, and teams in time zones that are so varied that even a teleconference is impossible unless someone gets up in the middle of the night—the structure of the organization becomes more important than ever before. The new science of networks, until now applied only to the scientific domain or to the social one, reveals important data about how to manage—and thrive—in the twenty-first century.

References

Barabási, A. L. (2002). *Linked: The new science of networks.* Cambridge, MA: Perseus Books.

Barabási, A. L., & Bonabeau, E. (2003, May). Scale-free networks. *Scientific American,* 60–69.

Beyerlein, S., 1, 31, 553, 681

Bies, R. J., 197, 199, 210

Blackburn, R., 140, 151, 216, 226, 233, 234, 237

Blaiwes, A. S., 245, 261

Blalock, L., 185, 194

Bly, S., 310, 325

Bok, C., 503

Bommer, W. H., 182, 193

Bonabeau, E., 696, 705

Boon, S. D., 106, 127

Botero, I. C., 322, 328

Bowers, C. A., 252, 258, 320, 325

Bowyer, D., 391

Bradley, L., 1, 263, 331, 461, *463*, 468, *474, 476, 477*, 478, 681

Brady, E., 263

Braga, D., 179, 180, 187, 192, 391

Braksick, L., 76, 83

Brett, J., 370, 389, 390

Briggs, K., 217, 226, 233

Briggs, R. O., 237

Brockner, J., 203, 210

Broedling, L., 2, 23, 285, 293

Brooke, K. A., 83

Brothers, D., 156, 175

Brown, H. G., 112, 127

Brown, S. L., 675, 676

Bryman, A., 181, 190, 192

Buckhalt, J. A., 320, 324

Bunker, B. B., 110, 128

Bunz, U., 224, 238

Burgoon, J. K., 218, 238

Burke, C. S., 245, 262

Burke, M. E., 263, 264, 267, 271

Burns, J. M., 182, 183, 184, 193, 215, 233

Bush, B., 589

Buzan, B., 502, 529

Buzan, T., 501, 502, 529

C

Caffarella, R., 290, 294

Cannell, L., 265, 271

Cannon-Bowers, J. A., 221, 236, 243, 245, 247, 249, 253, 254, 255, *256*, 258, 259, 262, 316, 324

Carayon, P., 229, 237

Carey, M. R., 191, 193

Carmines, E., 596, 618

Cascio, W., 244, 259, 279, 293

Castella, V., 332, 343

Castillo, O., 280, 293

Cattel, R. B., 535, 551

Cellier, J-M., 319, 327

Chamberland, D., 222

Chapanis, A., 310, 325

Charan, R., 215, 237

Chemers, M. M., 220, 238

Chenhall, R. H., 55, 57

Chidambaram, L., 244, 245, 259

Child, J., 674, 676

Chinn, A., 374, 390

Christie, B., 222, 237, 349, 365

Clark, H. H., 315, 316, 318, 325

Clark, K., 674, 677

Clark, P .G., 577, 589

Coad, A. F., 184, 193

Cohen, R. J., 536, 537, 551

Cohen, S., 4, 24, 31, 32, 57, 214, 223, 234, 236, 301, 327, 447, 459, 659, 677

Cole, P., 222, 226, 233

Coleman, H. J., 556, 567

Collison, G., 172, 175

Colquitt, J. A., 197, 199, 204, 210, 211

Confucius, 77

Conger, J. A., 106, 129, 181, 182, 193, 215, 233

Conklin, J., 400, 401, 403

Connaughton, S. L., 214, 218, 222, 233

Connell, J. B., 228, 229, 233

Converse, S., 249, 258, 316, 324

Conway, M., 479

Coovert, M. D., 221, 226, 228, 237

Copper, C., 250, 261

Côté, S., 639, 651

Coulson-Thomas, C. J., 187, 193

Covey, S.M.R., 407, 409, 437

Covey, S. R., 74, 83

Cramton, C. D., 251, 259

Crawford, R., 493, 529

Creed, W. E., 556, 567

Creighton, J. L., 9, 10, 23, 331, 343

Cross, J., 165, 175

Cross, K. P., 193

Crowston, K., 300, 301, 325, 326

Cuevas, H. M., 320, 325

Cummings, T. G., 128

Cytryn, K. N., 589
Czaja, S., 263, 267, 271

D

D'Addario, K. P., 222, 238
Daft, R. L., 215, 234, 250, 259, 349, 365
Daly, B. L., 223, 233
Daly, J. A., 214, 218, 222, 233
Davenport, T. H., 50, 57
Davis, F. D., 225, 234
Davis, G. A., 515, 529
Davis, J. H., 107, 128, 225, 250, 261, 634, 651
de Bono, E., 492, 529
De Cremer, D., 219, 237
de Ridder, J. A., 316, 325
De Vries, R. E., 316, 325
Demarie, S. M., 225, 237
Dennis, A. R., 244, 245, 259
Deutsch, M., 199, 210
DeVine, D. J., 321, 325
Devine, D. S., 250, 259
Dewey, J., 395, 403
Dickson, M. W., 244, 258
Dilts, C., 153
Dineen, B. R., 218, 234
Dion, K. L., 259
Dirksen, V., 50, 57
Dodge, G. E., 214, 233
Doherty-Sneddon, G., 324
Dolezalek, H., 274, 293
Donnelly, J. H., 395, 403
Dorn, R. C., 204
Dougherty, D., 666, 675, 677
Dourish, P., 154, 175, 310, 325

Downey, D., 72, 83, 630, 650, 656, 677
Drakos, N., 461, 478
Driskell, J. E., 214, 234, 261
Duarte, D. L., 4, 24, 154, 175, 332, 343, 346, 365, 634, 650
Dubrovsky, V., 221, 234, 244, 262
Duffy, L. T., 249, 262
Dukerich, J. M., 218, 234
Dunbar, K., 319, 325
Dutton, J. E., 218, 234
Dyer, W., 226, 234, 443, 458

E

Earley, P. C., 301, 327, 666, 677
Eber, H. W., 551
Eberle, B., 506, 529
Eccles, R. G., 250, 261
Einstein, A., 392
Eisenhardt, K. M., 675, 676
Elbaum, B., 172, 175
Elledge, R. L., 226, 236
Ellemers, N., *217*, 218, 219, 234, 237
Ellinger, A. D., 227, 234
Ellinger, A. E., 227, 234
Emery, F., 444, 458
Eraut, M., 175
Erickson, P. J., 619
Evans, C. R., 250, 251, 259

F

Fairholm, G. W., 191, 193
Farmer, S. M., 223, 234
Ferdowsian, M., 405
Fiedler, F. E., 181, 193

Filgo, S. K., 533
Fineman, S., 150, 151
Finley, K., 357
Fiore, S. M., 320, 325
Fish, R., 310, 325
Fisher, K., 11, 24, 443, 444, 445, 447, 452, 453, 454, 459
Fisher, M., 11, 24, 443, 444, 447, 452, 454, 459
Flores, F., 154, 175
Fontenot, R., 185, 194
Foushee, H. C., 303, 326
Fowler, F., 607, 618
Francovich, C., 153
Freedman, S., 367, 375, *376,* 390
Friedman, T. L., 681, 691
Furst, S. A., 140, 148, 151, 216, 226, 227, 233, 234, 237
Fussel, S. R., 312, 325

G

Gabriel, Y., 150, 151
Gailbraith, J. R., 301, 325
Galagan, P., 291, 293
Galbraith, J., 72, 83, 447, 459, 630, 642, 650, 656, 668, 677
Gallupe, R. B., 244, 245, 259
Garber, S., 546, 551
Garton, C., 4, 24
Garud, R., 6, 25
Gay, G., 155, 176
Geelhoed, E., 315, 328
Geister, S., 214, 218, 234
Geller, V., 244, 260
Gengler, C., 597, 618

George, J., 10, 25
George, J. M., 250, 260
Geyer, A.L.J., 182, 193
Ghoshal, S., 627, 639, 650
Gibson, C. B., 4, 24, 107, 116, 128, 214, 226, 227, 234, 236, 666, 677
Gibson, J. W., 393, 395, 403
Gilson, L. L., 207, 211, 214, 236
Girardeau, L., 319, 327
Gleeson, P., 291, 292, 293
Glickman, A. S., 245, 261
Goldsmith, J., 61, 83
Gordon, W.J.J., 518, 530
Gorelick, C. K., 8, 24, 333, 343
Graen, G. B., 106, 129
Granka, L., 221, 238
Grant, D., 682, 691
Gray, B., 654, 659, 677
Gray, C. E., 382, 390
Green, F., 555, 567
Green, J., 628, 651
Greenberg, J., 197, 199, 200, 210
Griffith, T. L., 222, 234, 320, 325
Grigone, D., 320, 325
Guilford, J. P., 492, 530
Gulati, R., 659, 677
Gully, S. M., 250, 259
Gunto, S., 199, 211
Gupta, D., 461, *463*, 468, *474*, *476*, *477*, 478
Guth, W., 199, 210
Guthrie, V. A., 204, 210
Guzzo, R. A., 251, 259, 262, 320, 326

H

Haavind, S., 172, 175
Hackman, J. R., 106, 128, 215, 227, 234, 235, 238, 247, 251, 259
Hagel, J. I., 168, 175
Hall, R. J., 316, 327
Hambley, L. A., 213, 214, 217, 219, 224, 235
Hamel, G., 66, 83, 597, 618
Hamilton, I., 165, 175
Hamilton, S., 533
Handy, C., 250, 259
Hanna, D., 447, 459
Hansen, M., 282, 293
Hardy, C., 682, 691
Harquail, C. V., 218, 234
Harriman, R., 407, 437
Harris, C. L., 1, 23, 45, 51, 54, 57, *565*, 566
Harris, P., 280, 293
Harris, R., 494, 530
Harrison, S., 50, 57
Hartigan, J., 63
Harwood, G. G., 59
Hastie, R., 320, 325
Hater, J. J., 182, 193
Hauber, J., 312, 326
Heath, C., 300, 326
Hedlund, G., 675, 677
Hedlund, J., 228, 235
Heffner, T. S., 249, 262
Heliwell, J. F., 153, 175
Heller, F. A., *415*, 437
Hellreigel, D., 281, 293
Henderson. D., 555, 567
Hendrickson, A. R., 225, 237
Hertel, G., 214, 216, 219, 235, 236
Hibino, S., 133, *135*, 151

Higgins, J., 391, 403
Hills, A., 312, 326
Hiltz, S. R., 244, 245, 260, 310, 326
Hindle, T., 620, 650
Hines, S., 533
Hinkle, S., 218, 235
Hinrichs, G., 131, 132, 139, 148, 151, 152
Hoefling, T., 87
Hoffman, E., 199, 210
Hofstede, G., 375, 390
Hogg, M. A., 218, 219, 235, 237
Hollan, J. D., 304, 326
Holland, J. L., 535, 551
Hollander, E. P., 182, 193
Hollenbeck, J. R., 228, 235
Hollingshead, A. B., 221, 222, 223, 235, 244, 260, 322, 328
Holmes, J. G., 106, 127
Holton, E., 288, 293
Holton, J. A., 112, 118, 128
Holyoak, K. J., 517, 530
Hong, I., 9, 24
Horvath, L., 244, 260
House, R. J., 181, 182, 193, 215, 235
Howard, D. H., 577, 589
Howell, J. M., 182, 185, 193, 194
Huang, H., 153, 175
Huang, W. W., 216, 235
Huizing, A., 50, 57
Hundhausen, C., 319, 327
Huselid, M., 445, 459
Hutchins, E., 304, 326
Hwang, M., 244, 245, 260
Hyatt, C. W., 223, 234

Stasser, G., 320, 327, 328

Staudenmayer, N., 300, 326

Stavros, J., 131, 132, 136, 141, 151, 152

Steidlmeier, P., 190, 192

Stenning, J., 50, 57

Stetar, B., 275, 294

Steuer, J., 222, 237

Stevens, M., 555, 567

Stewart, D. D., 320, 327

Steyrer, J. M., 182, 193

Stigler, K. W., 517, 530

Stogdill, R. M., 406, 437

Straus, D., 333, 337, 338, 343

Straus, S. G., 221, 223, 237, 238

Sumner, J., 280, 294

Suthers, D., 319, 327

Sutton, R., 592, 618

Swanson, R., 288, 293

Swerdlik, M. E., 536, 537, 551

Sy, T., 639, 651

T

Taillieu, T., 659, 677

Tan, B.C.Y., 216, 235

Tang, J., 310, 327

Tannenbaum, R., *415, 416*, 438

Tannenbaum, S. I., 245, 259

Tapie, J., 319, 327

Tatsuoka, M. M., 551

Taylor, R. L., 181, 194

Tennant-Snyder, N., 154, 175

Terrier, P., 319, 327

Tesluck, P. E., 107, 116, 128, 226, 227, 236

Thibaut, J., 199, 211

Thompson, J. D., 668, 677

Thompson, L. F., 221, 226, 228, 237

Thorpe, E. K., 577, 589

Thran, S. L., 579, 589

Thrane, L., 265, 271

Tichy, N., 215, 237

Tierney, T., 282, 293

Tiessen, P., 218, 237

Tinker, R., 172, 175

Titus, W., 320, 327

Tobin, T. J., 244, 260

Torres, C. B., 136, 141, 152

Townsend, A. M., 225, 237

Trice, H. M., 43, 58

Trist, E., 444, 458, 459

Trommsdorff, G., 320, 326

Turner, S., 221

Turoff, M., 244, 260, 310, 326

Tuunanen, T., 597, 618

U

Uhl-Bien, M., 106, 129

V

Valacich, J. S., 110, 129, 245, 261

Valenzi, E. R., *416*, 437

van den Hooff, B., 316, 325

van der Velden, J., 334, 335, 337, 343

Van Dyne, L., 301, 327

Van Knippenberg, B., 219, 237

Van Knippenberg, D., *217*, 219, 237

Vansina, L., 659, 677

Vaughan, S. I., 320, 327

Vealey, R. S., 515, 530

Verma, V. K., 380, 389, 390

Vinokur-Kaplan, D., 250, 262

Vlosky, R., 185, 194

Vogel, D., 214, 236

Volpe, C. E., 245, 249, 259, 262

Vroom, V. H., 181, 194

W

Wageman, R., 216, 219, 227, 228, 229, 235, 238

Waldman, D. A., 182, 194

Walker, C. E., 522, 531

Walker, L., 199, 211

Wallace, D., 50, 58

Wallace, P., 140, 152

Walter, S. M., 515, 530

Walther, J. B., 218, 221, 222, 224, 238

Wang, C., 218, 234

Wang, P., 8, 24

Warshaw, P. R., 225, 234

Wassenar, J. D., 579, 589

Waterman, R. H., Jr., 620, 621, 627, 651

Watson, C. B., 216, 238

Watson, R. T., 220, 235

Watts-Perotti, J., 312, 327

Webber, M., 399, 403

Webber, S. S., 244, 245, 246, 262

Weber, T., 182, 192

Weeks, G. D., 310, 325

Wegryn, K., 4, 24

Wei, K., 216, 235

Weick, K. E., 15, 24, 133, 135, 136, 150, 152, 336, 343, 352, 365

Weisband, S., 221, 222, 228, 238, 245, 251, 262

Welch, D., 628, 651

Welch, J., 215

Wellins, R., 10, 25

Wenger, E., 155, 175, 176

Wenger, W., 516, 531

Wenzel, L. H., 249, 260

Wesner, M. S., 273

Wheatly, M. J., 631, 651

Wheeler, B. C., 245, 261

Whitney, D. J., 250, 259

Whittaker, S., 310, 315, 316, 326, 327, 328

Wiesenfeld, B., 6, 25, 203, 210

Wiig, K., 43, 58

Wilber, S., 310, 326

Wild, E., 204, 211

Williams, E., 218, 222, 237, 349, 365

Williams, E. S., 182, 193

Williams, J., 598, 618

Williams, K. D., 235

Wilman, D., 389, 390

Wilson, A., 496, 531

Wilson, J., 10, 25

Wilson, M. J., 221, 238

Witort, M. B., 479

Wittenbaum, G. M., 320, 322, 328

Wixom, B. H., 244, 245, 259

Woellert, L., 628, 651

Wohlfarth, T., 555, 567

Woods, D. D., 306, 312, 318, 327, 328

Woodard, E. A., 245, 261

Workman, M. D., 7, 25

Worley, C. G., 642, 651

Wren, J. T., 180, 184, 194

Wulf, R., 32, 58

X

Xiao, Y., 304, 305, 328

Y

Yagil, D., 182, 194

Yammarino, F. J., 182, 194

Yen, J., 217, 237

Yeoh, T., 461, *463*, 468, *474, 476, 477*, 478

Yetton, P. W., 181, 194

Young, J., 470, 472, 478

Yuan, Y. C., 155, 176

Yukl, G., 181, 194, 207, 211, *415*, 437

Z

Zaccaro, S. J., 214, 221, 238, 243, 247, 261

Zeller, R., 596, 618

Zubrow, D., 244, 260

Zuckerman, M., 320, 324

Zukin, L., 245, 246, 247, 252, 255, 260

Zwicky, F., 495, 496, 531

SUBJECT INDEX

A

Accenture, 222

Accessible and approachable leaders, 186

Accountability: charting, 642, *643*; for conforming to operating guidelines, 454; constructive, and sensemaking, 132, 136, 138, 139–141, 142, 143, 146; in decision making, 417; establishing roles and, for decision making, 71–73, 81; gaps in, survey for spotlighting, 648; higher levels of, and trust, 154; joint, creating a culture of teamwork and, 639–641; and motivation, 51; negotiating, 113; preferred driver of, 102; traditional, 139

Accounting software team charter, example of an, 450–451

Acquainting team members, agenda including, *97*

Across-unit team structure, 42

Action: committed and coordinated, 133, 147; leadership focusing, 184; learning and, continuous cycle of, 132, 142; translating vision into, 61

Action checklists, for meetings, *474, 476, 477*

Action learning, best practices for, 354–355, 362

Action plans: documenting, importance of, 475; following through on, 636; outlining, using drawing for, 519

Action processes, 247, 249

Action-based trust, emergence of, 10

Actions: protective, 201; trusting, 97–98, 110

Active learning, pressing reasons for, 373

Adaptation, need for, increased, 668

Adapters, experienced, foreign-born colleagues as, 372–373

Administration on Aging, 589

Adult learners, assumptions about, 289–290

Adult learning principles, using, 487–488

Adverse impact, evaluating, of assessments, 539, 540

Advice giving, making additions to, 206

Advocating, 140

Agenda template, 96, *97*

Agenda Tool, 147

Agendas, 470, *471*

Aging population, issue of an, 263–264, 576, 577

Alignment: of design with other corporate systems, 78–79; of key stakeholder interests, lack of, impact of,

Alignment: (*Continued*) 425–426; off-line, and effective decision making, 411; of organizational components, ability of leaders to develop, 630; of people, hierarchical, defining the, 625; of purpose and outcomes, ensuring, 144–145, 149; of rewards, 640; of roles, responsibilities and activities, 359; of support systems, importance of, 54–55

Allocation rules, equity of, 199

Alternatives: predicted effectiveness of, in decision making, 603; purposeful, generating, 134; sample comparison of, 562–563

Ambulatory Care Information System, 578

American Heritage Dictionary, 87

American Psychological Association, 492

American Society for Training and Development, 274

"An Employer's Guide to Good Practices" (U.S. Department of Labor), 535, 537, 538

Analogical thinking, 516–519

Analogy, using, 95

Analysis: cost/benefit, 555, 559–562; current state, *595*, 596, 605–612; dimensional, 506, 508–509, 529; force field, 498–501, 524; future state, 595, 596–604; matrix, 495–498; of organizational needs, 274–278; stakeholder, 77

Analysis levels: competency questions by, 285, *286–287*, 288; types of, described, for training needs assessment, 279–281

Analysis team vs. decision-making team, 424

Anonymity, issue of, 340, *341*, 358

Appraisal procedures, 360

Apprenticeship learning, literature on, 155

"Are You Ready for a Matrix," 649, 650

Assessment: of assumptions, 309; of collaborative technology, 332–334, 335, 336; of meeting management skills, 285; of meetings, 488–489; of relationships, 644, *645, 646*; situation, example of a, 559; of solutions, 40, 394, 400, 402. *See also* Talent assessments; Training needs assessment

Assessment practices, fair, 535–541

Associations, generating and illustrating, technique for, 501–504, *505*

Assumptions: about individual learning needs, 288–292; about training and communication, 487; assessing and evaluating, importance of, 309; of capabilities, 352; of commitment, 352; differing, benefit of, 148; false, and task division, 301, 302; fundamental, 198; of head trust, 352; identifying and challenging, 134, 140; long-held, challenging, 593, 596; opportunities for, 148; in planning, and failing to consider a contingency, 308–309; setting aside, about technology skills and knowledge, 284; testing, about roles and responsibilities, 641; underlying, questioning of, encouraging the, 321, 322

Asynchronous communication/technology, defined, 223, 332

Attack, 422

Attention, placing more, on conversations, 143

Attitude: right, approaching collaboration with the, 428; toward technology, effect of, 224–225

Attitude assessment for predicting performance. *See* Talent assessments

Attribute listing, 493–495, 524

Audience: target, defining the, for training, 280; understanding your, in terms of generational differences, 269

Audio systems: assessing, *334*; described, 335–336

Audit trail, 496

Auditory technologies, mediating coordination using, 312–315. *See also* Technology

Authoritative decision making, *415*, 485

Authority, ability to assert, 11

Autonomy: balancing, and interdependence, 669; control versus, 41; and team coaching, 227

Award programs, internal, 661

Awareness: across-the-board, 154; additional level of, bringing an, 143; of complexity, 360; continuous, of the

importance of building trust, 346; of differences, need for, 283; heightening of, through meditation, 522; and invisibility, 348, 360; optimizing, about trust, 161; situation, 303, 313, 314; of training needs, lack of, 3; of vicious cycles, 353

Axon Idea Processor, 503

Axon Research, *504, 505*

B

Baby boomers: characteristics of, 264, *266*; and retirement, 267, 268; technology approach of, 265

BAE Systems, 655, 662, 663, 664, 667, 668, 671, 673

Balance, work and home life, 446, 456–457

Balancing autonomy and interdependencies, 669

Balancing commitments, 216

Barrier busters, leaders as, 11

Benchmark data set, analyzing, in network mapping, 703

Benchmarking: advantages of, 544–545; described, 543–544; disadvantages of, 545–547; process of, 547–549

Benefits overview, 560

Benefits statement: intangible, 561–562; tangible, 561

Best Buy, 456

Beth Israel Deaconess Medical Center, 578

Biographical information, sharing, 120, 122

Black box decision making, 592–594, 603, 604

BlackBerries, 89

Blended learning techniques, using, 354

Boeing, 620

Boomers. *See* Baby boomers

Boundaries: around time, learning how to set, issue of, 335; cultural, issue of crossing, 9; defining, importance of, 189; establishing, and building trust, 167; identifying the types of, 37–38; managing, 39–40; as a mental imposition, 60; permeability of, 38, 39; tightening, 40; transgressing, 36; virtual meetings connecting teams across, 463; between work and personal life, 445

Boundary conditions, 34–35, 37–38

Boundary crossing: and coordination, 221;

Boundary crossing: (*Continued*) described, 34–40; expecting teams to practice, 90; power of, 91. *See also* Working across boundaries

Boundary, defined, 35

Boundary spanner, defined, 35

Boundary workers, defined, 42

Brainstormed measures, 74, 75

Brainstorming: as a creativity technique, 492, 511–514, 524; in decision making, 419–420; intent of, 422; and problem solving, 392; simultaneously, 337–338; support for, 340; and technology selection, 471–472; visual, 521

Brainstorming alternatives, importance of, 134

Brainstorming issues, 140

Brainstorming sessions: leaders helping with, 206; technology beneficial for, 338; virtual collaborative technology options for, *341*

Bureaucracies, learning in, 664

Burnout, 203, 207, 456

Business analyzers, leaders as, 11

Business case, the: for change, making the, 608; example illustrating, 557–566; final thoughts on, 566; overview of, 553–554; preparing, checklist of steps for, 564, *565*; reason for writing, 555–557; reminders about, 566; as a vehicle for garnering support, 557; for virtual teams, described, 554–555

Business objectives and key success factors, 597–600, 602, 603, 604, 608, 611

Business-focused decision making, using data to drive. *See* Data-driven decision making

C

CAIRO diagram, 453

Calendars, shared, use of, 453

California Institute of Technology, 495

"Call anytime" policy, 7–8

Candor, importance of, for sensemaking, 132, 144, 147–148

Capability assumptions, 352

Cascade theory of communication, problem with the, 704

"Cast the net wider" plan, creating a, 77–78, 82

Celebrations: as confidence-builders, 220; establishing, importance of, 96–97; feedback and, mechanisms for, setting up, 75–77, 82

Center for Creative Leadership, 204

Center for Digital Future, 155, 175

Centralization, 41, 60, 694

Challenges: additional, and strategies to address, for cross-border teams, *384–388*; of coordination, 7, 8, 221–225; of developing potential, 226–230; facing the U.S. health care system, 575, 576–577; hidden, story illustrating, of working with people from different cultures, 367–368; identifying, 346–350; increased, of leading virtual teams, 213, 230; involving collaboration and crossing boundaries, 34–35; issues surrounding the, 5–12; of motivating, 215–220; overview of, 2–4, *5*; providing, to assumptions, reason for, 148; sensemaking properties and accompanying, 136, *137–138*; strategies to meet, in knowledge transfer case study, 659–662; of team meetings, 461, 464–465; unique, for team start-ups, 448; to virtual collaboration in medicine and primary care, 579

Change: accelerating, and sensemaking, 131, 135; blocking, reason for, 198; comfort with, a matrix requiring, 629; communicating, recommendations for, to a multigenerational population, 269; as constant, 78; cultural, 45, 47, 93; and decision making, 417; and generational conflict, 267; improved ability to accommodate, 359; making the business case for, 608; and matrixed managers, 638; pace of, 391; in plans, addressing, 307–308; readiness for, cues to, 197; scope of, data helping to determine, 612; shifting resources in response to, 626; significance of, 195–196; as a support system, 55; systemic view toward, taking a, 204; in the way of thinking about work,

88–90. *See also* Leading change

Change agents, converting leaders to, 184

Change initiatives, managing and aligning, 55

Change management: approaches to, considering generations in, 267–268; and matrix implementation, 625

Change managers, astute, 268

Chartering tips, 451–452

Charters: agenda including, *97*; for councils and committees, 644; creating, 449–451; and dealing with cultural barriers, 45; using, to gain clarity, 145

Check-ins, frequent, establishing, importance of, 97, 124

Checkpoints, periodic, holding, 79

Checks and balances, leadership lending itself to, 190

Chief knowledge officer (CKO): educating, about team needs, importance of, 55; and knowledge management, 50–51

Chief learning officers (CLO), educating, about team needs, importance of, 55

Chimneys, development of, 410

Choice, preference for, 288, 289, 610

Chronic decision-making problems, addressing. *See* Decision-making problems, correcting

Clarity, importance of, for sensemaking, 132, 133, 143, 144–146

Classroom training, providing, 55

Close-mindedness, 422

Closure sessions, leaders helping with, 206

Coaches: leaders as, 11; pool of, maintaining, 361; training, 363

Coaching: ensuring skills in, for facilitators and leaders, 485; providing, 55; team, and developing potential, 227–228

Co-creation: and emotional bandwidth, 91; and sensemaking, 132, 144, 148–149

Coding comments, 201

Coercion, 191

Cognitive conflict, needed, introducing, 321, 322

Cognitive-based trust, 110–111, 112

Cohesion: building, 221; contributor to, 33; and team staffing, 250–251, 255

Cohesive team culture, creating a, *92*, 93–96

Collaboration: active, designing work that requires, 219; approaching, with the right attitude, 428; characteristics of, 32–34; and communication, 93; and the complexity of crossing boundaries, 34–35; culture of, enabling a, 317; and current decision-making principles, 414, 417–418; defined, 1, 32, 107–108; degree of, and technology selection, 470–472, *473*; educating team members on the benefits of, 122; enabling, role of technology in, in the absence of face-to-face interaction, 340, *341*; engaging people through, 93; extending the meaning of, 2; facilitating, with discussion databases, 339; and a framework for working across boundaries, 56; health care system lacking in, 576; and the impact of bad and effective decision making, 412–414; increasing the, required of cross-border teams, 373–374; key approaches to decision making and,

414, *415–416*; leveraging collective intelligence through, 427–428; more effective, setting up the conditions for, 59; new principles for, and effective decision-making, 428–431; and organizational performance, 481–482; patient-provider, integrating technology into, leaders in, 578; as a problem-solving tool, lack of using, 392; protocols linking intervention with communication and, 581–582; seeking, not compromise in a matrix organization, 636–637; strengthened relationships supporting, 116; and trust, 154, 155, 156; using the consultative decision-making process, 431–436; work of, 94. *See also* Decision-making problems, correcting; Real-world collaboration principles; Virtual collaboration

Collaboration-supporting systems: assessing, *334*; described, 336–340

Collaborative leaders, characteristics of, 51–52

Collaborative organizations, defined, 1

Collaborative Technologies Corporation, 340

Collaborative technology: assessing, 332–334, 335, 336; final thoughts on, 342; major types of systems for, *334*; overview of, 331–332; reminders about, 342–343; role of, in enabling collaboration in the absence of face-to-face interaction, 340, *341*; types of, *334*, 335–340. *See also* Technology

Collaborative work structures and processes: leader responsible for, 63; leadership in, 51; mapping out, 41–44. *See also* Work processes

Collaborative work systems (CWS), defined, 2

Collective competency beliefs, 251

Collective efficacy, 251

Collective intelligence, leveraging, 427–428

Collective responsibility. *See* Shared responsibility

Collectivist cultures vs. individualistic cultures, 9, 375–377

Colocated teams: common features of virtual teams and, 480–481; differences between virtual teams and, 482–484; structure of, 42, 155, 480

Comfort level: establishing a, 117–118, 265; of matrixed managers, 638

Commitment: assumptions of, 352; building, 221; to conversations, placing more, 143; and distance, 6; and encouraging positive feedback, 76; and expanding emotional bandwidth, 91; gaining, in decision making, 419, 420; having a clear sense of, importance of, 90; to "I:X by Y," 140, 149; lack of, in decision making, 411; lagging, 94; leadership, engendering, example of, 659; to others' success, 33; and restricted communication, 349, 350; rise in, 63; and sensemaking, 132, 133, 139, 144, 147, 149–150; to shared responsibility, 93; shared, to a task or goal, 250–251; strengthening and deepening, 95; superficial and

halfhearted, to decisions, impact of, 423; sustained, 32; to the team charter, team members stating their, 452; and team coaching, 227

Commitments and promises: competing, balancing, 216; keeping, importance of, for building trust, 10, 110, 118, 124, 159, 167, 635, 636

Committees and councils, creating, 644

Common ground, establishing, 316–319

Common understanding. See Shared/mutual understanding

Common vision, purpose, and destiny, engaging all in a, 66–67, 81

Communication: asking for clarification of, role of trust in, 370; assessing relationships in terms of, 646; barriers to, overcoming, 666; building shared understanding through, benefit of, 346; business case for, 33; cascade theory of, problem with the, 704; challenges of, 7, 461, 465; and collaboration, 93; and coordination, using technology for, best practices and

recommendations for, 308–316, 323; as a critical success factor, 350, 351, 352; culture of responsiveness and, adopting a, 122–123, 221–222; in decision making, 417; and depth of relationships, 115, 117; designing the process of, 77; diagonal, acceptance of, issue of, 379; direct vs. indirect, 376, 377–378; evaluating, surrounding fair change, 204; facilitating, with discussion databases, 339; greater emphasis on, 482; health care system lacking in, 576; horizontal, example of, 704; ignoring, avoiding, 124; importance of, for leaders, 11, 51, 61, 187, 189, 672; improving, 249; increased requirements for, 301; inferior, making do with, 88; informal, encouraging, 665; learning module addressing, 355, 356, 359; lines of, keeping open, 123–124; monitoring, 200–201, 208; need for, increased, 668; nonverbal coordination and, 303–306; patient-provider, integrating technology

Communication:
(*Continued*)
into, leaders in, 578; in premeeting planning, 470; and problem solving, 392–393; protocols for, in the VIP model, 581–582; reducing effectiveness of, 353; relying on technology for, 213, 215; research on, by virtual teams, 244–245; restricted, 347, 349–350, 355, *356*, 359, 360; role of identity in, 9; rules for, enforcing, 222; and shared understanding, 113–114; and team fluidity, issue of, 363; of the team's purpose, 227; that signals justice concerns, indicators of, 201, *202*; timely, importance of, 309; and trust, 10, 112, 155, 156, 250, *635*, 636. *See also* Electronic communication

Communication infra-structure: agreed-on plan for or clear, lack of, problem with, 102; maintaining, 101; planning for, agenda including, *97*

Communication media/ mediums: arranging, on a continuum of

social presence, 333; choice of, importance of, 222–223; genera-tional characteristics in terms of, *266*; and motivation, 215–216, 218; sending multiple messages using multiple, benefit of, 269; supporting coordination of work across, 309. *See also* Technology

Communication program, developing and delivering a, to improve decision making, 428

Communication skills: ensuring, for facilita-tors and leaders, 485; matrixed managers possessing, 638

Communication strategies: development of, that encourage honesty, 147; sound, for a multigenerational population, 269

Communication streams, expanding, 88

Communication tools and technology. *See* Technology

Communication trust: essential behaviors associated with, 157, *158*, 159; virtual, building, illustration of, 168–169

Communicators, leaders as, 186

Communities of practice, literature on, 155

Community building: on the Internet, 88; role of trust in, 171; view of, 91

Competence: assumptions of, 352; core, for all general managers, 346; in the DCOM Model, 80; and trust, *635*, 636

Competence trust: essential behaviors associated with, 157, *158*, 159; virtual, building, illustration of, 169–170

Competencies: identifying, 252–255, *256*; major areas of, assessing training needs for, 281–288; management, selecting for, 638–639; types of, 247, *248*, 253

Competency beliefs, collective, 251

Competency, defined, 281

Competency development programs, effective, characteristics of, 353–354

Competing for the Future (Hamel & Prahalad), 66

Competition, and organi-zational design, 60

Competitive advantage: and building the business case, 557; gaining, new opportunities for, 105,

Coordination theory, 300

Coordinators: use of, 11, 52; when to use, *53*

Core values, generational characteristics in terms of, *266*

Corporate alignment, ensuring, 79

Corporate Leadership Council study, 76, 83

Corporate management, revamping, 428

Cost analysis sample, 560–561

Cost/benefit analysis: determining the investment decision, 555; example of, in building a business case, 559–560; sample statement of, 560–562

Cost-free operation, myth of, 361

Cost-reducing benefit, 244

Costs: of benchmarking, 545, 546–547; and benefits, articulating, 557; containing, means of, 556, 621; of data collection methods, 276; of fad technology, 331; of group decision support systems, 339; of ineffectively deploying a matrix, 627; of lost business, 273; of training, 273, 274, 288; of travel, virtual meetings saving on, 462

Councils and committees, creating, 644

Course correction, 420–421, 426–427

Creativity: behaviors hindering, 402; cultures promoting and inhibiting, 46; enabling, 186; encouraging, 134, 501; enhancing, 108; highest levels of, achieving, meeting systems for, 338; need for, severe, 491; and problem solving, 392; scientific study of and research on, 492; tolerance for, 661

Creativity techniques: described, 492; final thoughts on, 524, 526–527; intuitive, portfolio of, 514–524; linear, portfolio of, 493–514; overview of, 491–492; reminders about, 527–529; selecting appropriate, 524, *525–526*

Criterion validation, 538, 545, 548

Critical success factors, commonly agreed upon, 32. *See also* Success factors

Cross-boundary work, framework for. *See* Working across boundaries

Cross-cultural skills, identifying training needs for, 283, *286–287*

Cross-functional teams, 480

Cultural barriers, dealing with, ways of, 45–46

Cultural boundaries, crossing, issue of, 9. *See also* Boundary crossing

Cultural change, 45, 47, 93

Cultural differences: awareness of, need for, 283; bridging, during team start-ups, 448–449; and establishing team identity, 218–219; fear of, overcoming, 671; friction due to, in meetings, 464; honoring, example of, 659; leadership sensitivity to, 185; misconceptions about, 371–372; recognizing and talking about, benefit of, 45; value of, 47

Cultural dimensions: described, and effects on expectations and behaviors, 375–382; and relative positions of selected countries, *376*

Cultural diversity, potential for, 148

Cultural experience, misconception about having, 372–373

Cultural norms, establishing, example of, 659, 660

Cultural sensitivity, 185, 485, 639

Culture: adapted definition of, 448; addressing, importance of, in order to combat confusion, 375–382; adopting consultation into the, 428; as a challenge, 4, *5*, 8–9, 368; cohesive, creating a, *92*, 93–96; of collaborative teamwork, enabling a, 317; of communication and responsiveness, adopting a, importance of, 122–123, 221–222; defined, 44; improvement in, through trust-building program, 162; learning about, importance of, 373; open, importance of an, 481–482; of overcommunication, promoting a, 222; political, different, effect of, 654; of results orientation, impact of, 425; and shared stories, 98; of silence, 421–427; supportive, crafting a, 43–47, 447; teams creating their own, 45; of teamwork and joint accountability, creating a, 639–641. *See also* Shared culture

Cummins Power Generation, 446, 456–457

Current infrastructure inventory, 610–612

Current state analysis, *595*, 596, 605–612

Current work profiles, 605–608

Customer satisfaction, impact of collaboration on, 481

Cyberbrainstorming, 140

D

Data: analysis of, conducting, in organizational needs analysis, 276; defining, for a networked organization, 697; gathering, in decision making, 419–420, 606, 616; issues associated with, in data-driven decision making, 596; reaction, collecting and analyzing, over time, 488; sharing, to build shared mental models, 319–322; sources of, identifying, 275; taking, from the HR system, 698, 702–703; using video as, concept of, 311–312; on work styles and preferences, using, 608–610

Data collection guides, using questions as, 288

Data collection methods: choosing, for a training needs assessment, 279; investment in, for data-driven decision making, 596; for an organizational needs analysis, 275, 276–278; and problem solving, 400

Data vs. dialogue oriented, *376*, 380–381

Data washing, 703

Database, shared, posting to a, 500

Data-driven decision making: vs. black box decision making, 592–594, 603, 604; current state analysis for, *595*, 596, 605–612; described, 594–596; final thoughts on, 616–617; future state analysis for, 595, 596–604; overview of need for, 591–592; related items on the Web about, 618; reminders about, 617; and successful distributed work implementation, *595*, 612–616

DCOM Model, 79–80

Deadlines, assigning, benefit of, 223–224

Decentralization, 6, 41, 60, 694

Deception, 427

Decide-and-announce method, *415*, 485

Decision making: bad, and bad collaborative processes, impact of, 412–413; black box, 592–594, 603, 604; the business case influencing, 557; consensual, areas for, 100; consensus-based, *415*, 485; consultative, 407, *408*, *416*, 431–436; current, and collaboration, principles of, 414, 417–448; deciding on, 96; distributed, and knowledge overlap, 316; effective, new principles for, and collaboration, 413, 428–431; establishing roles and accountability for, 71–73, 81; good, candor leading to, 147; importance of, 131, 134; key approaches to, and collaboration, 414, *415–416*; likelihood of, 42; in a matrix organization, 632; and matrixed managers, 638; methods of, types of, *415–416*, 485; and morality, 189; within the sensemaking process, 131, 136, 142; shared, encouraging, 51; and sharing

knowledge, 320–321; teams adding complexities to, issue of, 319–320. *See also* Data-driven decision making

Decision strangulation, 629

Decision-making fairness. *See* Procedural justice

Decision-making model, *434*

Decision-making problems, correcting: and awareness of unspoken or silent micromessages, 421–427; and current principles, 417–418; final thoughts on, 436; by knowing the current principles, 414; by leveraging collective intelligence, 427–428; new principles for, 428–431; overview of, 405–409; reminders about, 436–437; with sound decision-making methods, 414, *415–416*; statement and proposition concerning, 409–412; through understanding the impact of bad and effective decision making and collaboration, 412–414; by understanding current roles, responsibilities, and process steps,

418–421; using the consultative decision-making process for, 431–436

Decision-making process steps: current, 418–421; proposed, 433, 435–436

Decision-making sessions, leaders helping with, 206

Decision-making step, 419, 420

Decision-making team vs. analysis team, 424

Decisions: about resource deployment, 555, 556; clarifying roles pertaining to, 642; dilution of, potential problems associated with, 426–427; documenting, importance of, 475, 483; effectiveness of, measuring and monitoring, 615–616; overturned, impact of, 426; quality of, increase in the, 392; reasoning behind, allowing teams to view the, 315–316; rights to, sharing, 638; setting criteria for, in a matrix organization, 628; shortsighted, 425; sound, criteria of, 414; superficial and halfhearted commitment to, impact of, 423

Decisiveness, 185, 189

Decomposition, 496, 497

Degraded messages, 704

Deictic expressions and gestures, 319

Deliverables: described, 563; sample list of, 563–564

Dell, 41

Democratic decision making, *415*

Depth of relationships: actions to promote, 120, *121*, 122, 123–124; successful collaboration and the, 107, *108*, 114–117, 118, 119, 120

Design concepts for work systems. *See* Work systems design concepts

Design principles for successful teams. *See* Team design principles

Designing new virtual teams, 444–447. *See also* Start-up perspectives and tools

Designs, formal vs. informal, 41

Destiny, common, engaging all in a, 66–67, 81

Detachment, 422, 522

Development needs, identifying, issue of, 273. *See also* Training needs assessment

Development of potential: across the team life cycle, *231*; challenges of, addressing the, 226–230; as a leadership function, 213, 214; and transformational leadership, 186, 189

Development process for teams. *See* Team development process

Devil's advocate role, 475

Diagnostic instrument, completing a, 355, 357, 358

Diagonal communication, issue of, 379

Dialogue vs. data oriented, *376*, 380–381

Diamond organizational shape, 700–701

Differences. *See* Cultural differences; Generational differences

Digital immigrants, 291, 292

Digital natives, 291–292

Dilution of the solution/decision, issue with, 426–427

Dimensional analysis, 506, 508–509, 529

Direct analogy, 518

Direction, in the DCOM Model, 80

Directness vs. indirectness, *376*, 377–378

Disciplined work and management processes, instilling, 641–649

Discovery process, learning process as a, 369

Discussion Center, 164–165, 166

Discussion databases, 339

Distance: as a challenge, 4, 5–7, 448; complicating collaboration, 34; separated by time and, identity and, 9

Distance learning designers, difficult issue facing, 165

Distributed decision making, and knowledge overlap, 316

Distributed expertise, issue of, 320

Distributed resources, issue of, 301–302, 303

Distributed team structure, 42

Distributed work, decision-making process about, suggested approach to. *See* Data-driven decision making

Distributed work fit, combinations of, 612, *613–614*

Distributed work models: future desired outcomes from, 596; key success factors of, 598; transition to, 592

Distributive justice, *198*, 199–200, 201, *202*, 203

Distrust. *See* Mistrust

Diversity champion, engaging a, 269

Diversity of thought, ensuring, 269

Diversity potential, 148, 263

Document review, *341*, 471

Document sharing, 472

Documenting decisions and action plans, importance of, 475, 483

Documenting work processes, 70–71, 81, 394

Dominant-language team, issue with the, 370–371

Drafting reports or presentations, 502

Drawing, 519–521

Driving forces, understanding, analysis for, 498–501

Dual reporting, issue of, 54

During-the-meeting stage, 469, 472, 475, *476*

Dynamic, defined, 141

Dynamic design, need for, 78

Dynamic relationships (DR): defined, 141; and sensemaking, 132, 133, 135, 141–142, 143

Dynamics, defined, 141

E

Economist, 621

Educating team members: about teamwork, major principles in, 577; on the benefits of collaboration, 122; designing for, 77; framework for, principles in, 40–56; and organizational leaders on generational differences, 269; setting for, 288; for virtual team meetings, 465–466. *See also* Training; Training needs assessment

Education levels, and information technology literacy, 267

Educational programs, developing. *See* Training programs, developing

Educators, senior executives as, 64, 66–67

Effective implementation strategy, creating an, 612–614

Effective virtual meetings: and awareness of the benefits and challenges, 462–465; ensuring, by beginning with a face-to-face meeting, specific actions for, 467–469; final thoughts on, 475–477; and knowing when to use and not use virtual meetings, 462, *463*; reminders about, 477–478; stages of, 469–475; and understanding ineffective meetings, overview of, 461–462; using facilitators and cofacilitators for, 466–475, *476*, *477*

Effectiveness: of decisions, measuring and monitoring, 615–616; increased, 227; input-process-output model of, 247–249; markers of, emergent states as, 249–251

Efficacy, collective, 251

Efficient organizations: characteristics of, 60; issue with, 67

Egalitarian vs. hierarchical, *376*

Ego, 427

80/20 power law, *700*

E-learning applications, completion rates for, 165

Electronic Brainstorming, 514

Electronic communication: confirming knowledge and use of, 483; and coordination, 224; improper use of, 180; improvements in, relying on, 43; and knowledge sharing, 48; listing methods of, for problem solving, 394; minority of medical practices using, 579; possibilities of, 681; and relationships, 89, 155; for sharing biographical information, use of, 120, 122; training required for, 482; and virtual communities, 88. *See also* Technology

Electronic meeting systems (EMS), 337–338

Electronic Meeting Systems (GroupSystems V), 340, 514

Electronic messaging systems: assessing, *334*; described, 335

Electronic performance monitoring, 229

Electronic whiteboarding, 338

Elitism, issue of, in transformational leadership, 123

E-mail: getting clear on how one responds to and handles, 380–381; setting protocols for, 454–455; time spent on, 446. *See also* Electronic communication

Emergent states: defined, 249; as markers of effectiveness, 249–251

Emoticons, 215, 222

Emotional attachment to one's ideas, impact of, 421–422

Emotional bandwidth, expanding: acceptance of mind shifts for, 88–90; described, 90–93; final thoughts on, 103; overview of, 87–88; related item on the Web, 104; reminders about, 103–104; three-fold path to, *92*, 93–103

Emotional intelligence, of matrixed managers, 639

Emotions: and meditation, 522; regulating, with less rich media, 223; and weekly meetings, 224

Empathy, leaders exhibiting, 11

Employee assessment processes, modifying, 428

Employee satisfaction on the job. *See* Job satisfaction

Employee surveys, using, 79, 606–607

Empowerment of employees, as key, 106, 110, 116, 189, 227–228

Enacting and learning, 135

Enactment, as a property of sensemaking, *138*, 148

Encouraging followers, 186

Endings, leading during, 229, *231*

Energy and understanding, context for, creating the, 67–68, 81, 133

Energy leak, 94

Engagement: selecting assessments that measure, 542; sustained, 155

English-speaking countries, misconceptions held by, 370

Enrolling team members, helping, 101–102

Entry and reentry, addressing, 101–102

Environmental boundaries, 37–38

Environmental systems, incorporating, into team design, 444–445, *446*, *447*

Equal Employment Opportunity Commission (EEOC) Guidelines, 539, 545

Equifinality, leaders believing in, need for, 206

Equipment: adequate, providing, 55; malfunctioning, 465

Equitableness. *See* Fairness

Ethics, and generational conflict, 267. *See also* Morality

Etiquette, defined, 480

Etiquette of virtual teams. *See* VEtiquette

Events, sequence of, allowing teams to view the, 315–316

Execution and course correction, 419, 420–421

Executive leadership: as educators, using, 64, 66–67; leveraging, 63; point of view of, firsthand account reflecting the, 63–64

Expectation setting: clear, importance of, 68; for

leaders, 64–65; by leaders, 187; for working together, 484–485

Expectations: about technology, effect of, 224–225; aligning, in setting technology protocols, 456; for effective decision making, 428, *430–431*, 431; managing, 159, 166–167; in shared leadership, 196; understanding both opportunities and, 201

Expenses. *See* Costs

Expertise: boundary-free access to, 244; centers of, establishing and funding, 360, 361; consideration of, in team staffing, 246–247, 252, 258; distributed, issue of, 320; each team member knowing their, importance of, 124; external, accessibility of, determining, 122; identifying training needs for, 283–284, *286–287*; issue of, 48, 49; outlining each team member's, 219

Expertise scale, 49

Explicit knowledge, 50

External consultants, use of, 361

External facilitators, use of, 355

F

Face validity, 539

Face-to-face coordination techniques, applying, 223–225

Face-to-face cues: capacity to convey, issue of, 333; including, issue of, 215, 222, 228

Face-to-face meetings: beginning with, specific actions for, 467–469; benefits of, 340; cultural preferences for, 380; initial, for start-ups, as essential, 448; learning modules designed to be initiated in, 357, 359; providing opportunities for, 120, 146, 219, 469; strategically planning for, 634–635; and technology selection, *473*

Facilitate.com, 470

Facilitation skills, ensuring, 485

Facilitators: assisting, role of, 484–485; for brainstorming, 513; clarifying the thinking and strategy of, 557; external, use of, 355; leaders as, 207; pool of, maintaining, 361; role of, for meetings, 475; skillful, ensuring, 485–486; systems requiring, for meetings,

340; training, 363; use of, 11, 52, 466–475, *476, 477*; when to use, *53*

Fad technology, 331–332

Fair assessment practices, 535–541

Fairness: of benchmarking, 545; importance of, 189, 198, 199; perceptions of, consideration of, 197, 200, 201, 203, 218

False assumptions and mental models, 301, 302

False transformational leadership, 190–191

Familiarity, relationships developed based on, 115–116, 155

Family structures, generational characteristics in terms of, *266*

Family-work life, issues of. *See* Home life and work

Fantasy analogy, 518

Fatigue, 464

Federal Aviation Administration (FAA) traffic hot lines, 312, 313, 314

Feedback: anonymous, converting, 358; asynchronous, in trust-building program, benefit of, 165–166; and celebration, mechanisms for, setting up, 75–77, 82; in decision making, 419; gathering performance

Feedback: (*Continued*)
information for, 217,
228–229; giving and
receiving, as vital, 169;
lack of agreed-on plan
for or structure for,
problem of, 102; new
form of, 51; private,
encouraging, 201, 486;
and problem solving,
400; providing regular,
216–218; soliciting,
from key stakeholders,
141

Feedback loops, illustrating
use of, 503, *505*

Feedforward loops,
illustrating use of, 503,
505

Financial tracking, issue
with, 54

FIRO-B, 487

Five C model, application
of the, 132, 142–150

Five W's and H's, the, 506,
507–508

Flexibility: of benchmarking, 544–545; in
horizontal integration,
example of, 661; and
improvisation, 669; of
a matrix organization,
626, 632; personal, a
matrix requiring, 629

Focus groups, use of, 607

Focus, lagging, 94

Followers: converting, to
leaders, 184; encourag-
ing, 186; importance
of, shift in emphasis on

the, 181; and morality,
182, 184; taking care of,
focus on, *198*, 201, 203,
205, 206, 207; ways in
which leaders trans-
form, 182. *See also*
Transformational
leadership

Force field analysis,
498–501, 524

Forced analogies, 517–518

Forced association, 496

Ford, 628

Formal integration, spec-
ifying, reason for, 656

Formal leadership role, 54

Formal training, providing,
55

Formal vs. informal
design, 41

Formal work process,
determining if the
collaboration is a,
reason for, 285

Four C's of Trust model,
635, 636

Free-loading, potential for,
149

Frontiers of Management
(Kanter), 60–61

Frost and Sullivan, 481

Functional support
groups: integrated
decision making and
implementation by,
594, *595*, 596, 604; and
key success factors
and business objectives,
597; types of, 593–594.
See also Team support

Functional teams, 480

Funding, issue of, 361

Future state analysis, 595,
596–604

Future, the, visionary of,
187. *See also* Vision

G

Gaps: in accountability,
survey for spotlighting,
648; bridging, in
technology expertise,
between generations,
292; cultural, and team
start-ups, issue of, 448;
revealing, between
desired performance
and actual performance,
275; supply, 611; in
understanding,
attention to, 44

Gatekeepers (process
monitors), 484–485

General Electric, 215

Generation X, characteristics of, 264, *266*

Generation Y. *See* Nexters
(Generation Y/
Millennials)

Generational differences:
in approaches to
technology, 265, 267,
291; assumptions
about, and learning
needs, 291–292;
consideration of, in
change management
approaches, 267–268;
final thoughts on, 270;
generational categories

involved in, 264–265, *266*; and the impact on virtual collaboration, 268; overview of, 263–264; recommendations for dealing with, 269–270; reminders about, 270–271

Generational diversity, potential for, 263

Generations: categories of, 264–265, *266*; mixing of, 263

Generic task work skills, 247, *248*, 253, 255, *256*

Generic teamwork skills, 247, *248*, 253–254, 255, *256*

Geographic boundaries, 37–38

Georgia Institute of Technology, 523

Geriatric Interdisciplinary Teams in Practice Initiative, 584

Geriatric Interdisciplinary Team Training Program, 577

Gestalt tradition, 34

Global Leadership Organizational Behavior Effectiveness (GLOBE) Project, 375

Global Work (O'Hara-Devereaux & Johansen), 4

Globalization, impact of, 41, 154, 213, 362, 412, 417, 621

Goal setting: importance of, 216; relationship between feedback and, 216–217; for working together, 484

Goals: assuming ownership of, 124; clear understanding of the, need for, 282, 447; common, example of, 659, 660; conflicting, managing, 216; focus on, 102; and measures, creating, that are accessible to all, 73–75, 82; open dialogue regarding, creating a forum for, 122; shared, and collaboration, 32–33

Gossip, malicious, 168–169

Governance mechanisms, establishing, in a matrix organization, 642, 644

Great Depression, the, impact of, 264

Ground rules: for brainstorming, 512; clarity of, 145–146; common, partners agreeing on, case study involving, 657; for communication, enforcing, 222; establishing, for commitment, 150; prior to problem solving, establishing, 394; setting, for meetings, 147, 468–469

Group decision support systems (GDSS), 339–340

Group Outliner, 514

Group potency, 251

Group visit model, 582, 584

Group-oriented cultures vs. individualistic cultures, 9, 375–377

GroupSystems V (Electronic Meeting Systems), 340, 514

Groupthink, avoiding, 148

GroupWise, 89

H

Halfhearted commitment, 423

Harcourt Assessment, 546

Hawthorne effect, 615

Head trust, 351, 352

Health care system, U.S., issues facing the, 575, 576–577, 579, 587–588

Health Data Management, 579

Heart trust, 351–352

Helping out, importance of, 98–99

Heroes, recognition for, 640

Hierarchical vs. egalitarian, *376*

Hierarchy: as a barrier, 187; decrease in, 73; examining, 693, 695–696; and generational conflict, 267; mapping of, and

Hierarchy: (*Continued*)
modeling as a network,
697–703; vs. matrix
organization, 625, 629;
networked, advocating
for a, 705; organiza-
tional charts still
reflecting, issue of, 694;
placement of manage-
rial positions in the,
637; shifting focus
from, to creating
councils and
committees, 644

High-performance virtual
teams, path toward, 4, *5*

High-performing teams,
characteristics of,
382–383, *384–388*

High-trust organizations,
working in, conse-
quences of, 153–154

Hiring, consideration of
generational group
when, 269

Hoer, 694–695

Holland's Self-Directed
Search, 535

Home life and work:
balancing, 446,
456–457; boundaries
between, 445; consider-
ing, 216; disrupting
balance in, 464

Honesty: demonstrating,
159, 169; encouraging,
147; establishing, 146;
and leadership, 185, 189

Horizontal communica-
tion, 704

Horizontal integration,
example of, 661–662,
666

How, focusing on just the,
issue with, 67

Hubris/pride, and knowl-
edge sharing, 48–49

Human life cycle stages,
effect of, 265

Human resource (HR)
support team: and
business objectives,
597; and integrated
decision making, 594,
595, 596, 604, 611;
modular learning
program used by, case
study of, 357–359;
traditional decision
making by, 593–594.
See also Support
systems

Human resource (HR)
system, taking data
from, 698, 702–703

Humility, as requisite, 48,
49

Hybrid meetings, 473

Hyperbolic viewer,
modified, 697

I

IBM, 340, 375, 556

IBM Canada, 221

Ice-breaking activity,
including an, 468

Idea checklists, 504–511,
509

Idea generation. *See*
Creativity techniques

Idea-generating software,
495

Ideal Virtual Transforma-
tional Leader Attributes
Tool, 189

Idealized influence, 184

Ideas, loss of, risk aversion
and the, impact of, 422

Identity: assessing
relationships in terms
of, *645*; enhanced, 200;
people measuring their,
170; as a property of
sensemaking, *137*; role
of, in communication,
9; and seeking connec-
tion, 90. *See also* Team
identity

Illustration of Scenario
Scoring: Predicted
Impacts of Scenarios
on Key Success Factors,
603, 618

Imagery, 515–516, 523, 524

Images of Organization
(Morgan), 516–517

Implementation: distrib-
uted work, successful,
and data-driven
decision making, *595*,
612–616; improve-
ments in, likelihood of,
42; integration of
functional support
group decision making
and, 594, *595*, 596, 604,
611; matrix, and
change management,
625; transition from
design to, 77

Implementation strategy, effective, creating an, 612–614

Improvisation, use of, innovation and, 667–669

In Search of Excellence (Peters & Waterman), 621

Inappropriate behaviors, impact of, on decision making, 427

Incompatible technology, problem of, 8

Independence, of team members, selecting assessments that measure, 542

Independent subtasks, dividing overall tasks into, 296, 298, 302

Indirectness vs. directness, *376*, 377–378

Individual boundaries, 37

Individual competency development, improvements from: acknowledging, importance of, 360; synchronizing, 353–354

Individual ideas vs. personal preferences, 421

Individual learner level of analysis, 280–281, *287*

Individual learning needs, assumptions about, 288–292

Individual learning styles, 290–291

Individual task responsibility, shift from, trend of, 681

Individual work styles and preferences, using data on, 608–610

Individualistic cultures vs. collective cultures, 9, 375–377

Individualized consideration, 184, 216

Influence, idealized, 184

Informal communication, encouraging, 665

Informal integration, issue with, 656

Informal leadership role, 54

Informal vs. formal design, 41

Informal work process, determining if the collaboration is an, reason for, 285

Information: access to, issue of, 54; accessing, from other resources, 142; boundary-free access to, 244; equating knowledge with, issue with, 49–50; gathering, and problem solving, 400; good, having access to, 147; organizing, for better access and recall, 502; on performance, gathering and providing, 217, 228–229; relevant,

gathering and applying, 134. *See also* Sharing information

Information and communication technology (ICT). *See* Technology

Information flow: barrier to, 187; complexity of, case study involving, 657; potential for, enhanced, 42

Information loss, at risk for, 180

Information technology (IT) group: and business objectives, 597; and integrated decision making, 594, *595*, 596, 604, 611; matrix organization for, case example of a, 622–625; traditional decision making by, 593–594. *See also* Support systems

Information technology (IT) literacy, impact of generational and socioeconomic differences on, 265, 267

Information technology (IT) systems, integrating, increasing complexity of, 373, 374

Informed person(s), charting the, 642, *643*

Infrastructure: communication, *97*, 101, 102; need for, that enables knowledge creation, 664

Infrastructure component linkages, 603–604
Infrastructure inventory, current, 610–612
Infrastructure support systems, *599*, 600–602, 622, *623*, 624. *See also* Functional support groups
Initiate: Charter for Clarity Tool, 145
Innovation: access to, 148; complexity of, 668; demand for, and decision making, 131; enhancing, 108; exploration of, 656; greater, achieving, 134; need for, severe, 491; and use of improvisation, 667–669
Input, seeking, and building trust, 159, 170
Input-process-outcome model of effectiveness, 247–249
Inside-unit team structure, 42
Inspirational motivation, 184, 215
Instinctive Technology's eRoom, 337
Institute of Medicine (IOM), 576, 589
Institution-based trust, 110, 111
Intangible benefits, statement of, sample of a, 561–562
Integrated product teams (IPT), virtual, case

study involving. *See* Knowledge transfer case study
Integrated support system, *599*, 600
Integration: formal mechanisms for, specifying, reason for, 656; of functional support group decision making and implementation, 594, *595*, 596, 604, 611; horizontal, example of, 661–662, 666; informal, issue with, 656; and the matrix organization, 626; mechanisms for, across teams, 42; need for, increased, 668; of technology into patient-provider communication and collaboration, leaders in, 578; vertical, example of, 659–661
Integration teams, defined, 42
Integres, 63
Integrity: defined, 98; importance of, 189; trust based on, 97
Intellectual capital, 50, 89
Intellectual stimulation, 184
Intention, placing more, on conversations, 143
Intentions, inappropriate, impact of, on decision making, 427
Interaction: challenges of, 461; quality of,

importance of, 331; situations requiring, detection of, designing systems to foster, 302
Interaction capabilities, assessing technology on, 332–333, *334*
Interaction etiquette, 480. *See also* VEtiquette
Interactional justice, *198*, 199, 200, 201, *202*
Interdependencies, task, issue of, 299–301, 668, 669
Interdependent teamwork design, 219
Interdisciplinary health care teams: collaborative, factors discouraging, 579; training, 577. *See also* Virtual integrated practice (VIP) model
Intergenerational workforce, advantages vs. disadvantages, 267
Internal problem solving, promoting, 124
International companies, misconception held by, 373–374
Internet, the: creating and building communities on, 88; generational differences in use of, 265, 267; possibilities of, 681; as transformative, 89
Interpersonal bonding, achieving, 6
Interpersonal cohesion, 250, 251

Knowledge transfer case study: (*Continued*) 676; strategies used to meet challenges in, 659–662; tiger teams in, 665–666; use of metaphors in, 669–671

Knowledgeable employees, accessibility of, 244

Know-what, defined, 50

Kolbe Index, 487

L

Labor market, potential, expansion of, 244

Ladder-of-inference concept, 348

Lagging indicators, 74

Language differences: and establishing team identity, 218–219; misconceptions about dealing with, 370–371

Language fluency, different levels of, issue of, 368, 370

Language, learning about, importance of, 373

Language, universal, creating a, in operating principles, 68–70, 81

Lateral organization capabilities, 656

Lateral reporting relationships. *See* Matrix organization

Lateral thinking, 492

Lead managers, relationships among, 637, 638, 647–648

Leaderless teams: use of, 11, 52; when to use, *53*

Leaders: ability of, to align organizational components, 630; as change agents, 184; clarifying the thinking and strategy of, 557; coaching skills for, importance of, 227; converting followers to, 184; and cultural change, 47; as the decision makers, 485; educating, on generational differences, 269; false or pseudo-transformational, 190–191; focus on, appropriate time and place for, 203; formal and informal, 54; holistic, 184; importance of communication for, 11, 51, 61, 187, 189, 672; key roles and functions of, 213, 214; and morality, 182, 184; new roles for, defining, 51–52, *53*; playing a critical feedback role, 76; playing multiple roles, issue of, 10–11; role of, statement about the, 195; selecting and positioning, for success, 61–66, 80–81; self-sacrifice of, issue with, 203; sending mixed messages, 637; sensemanagers working with, 145, 147; setting team meetings based on the convenience of, problem of, 464; skillful, ensuring, 485–486; survey questions on, 187, *188*; taking care of, focus on, *198*, 203, *205*, 206–207; tension between managers and, 627–628; transformational, characteristics of, 184–187

Leadership: as a challenge, 4, *5*, 10–12; in collaborative work structures and processes, 51; commitment of, engendering, example of, 659; executive, 63–64, 66–67; as a key support system, 54; lack of, effect of, 180; in a matrix organization, 628; overview of, 180–181; and relationship building, 633; shared, 51, 196. *See also* Transformational leadership

Leadership Action Model for Fair Change, 197, *198*, 199

Leadership behaviors, results of, 64–66

Leadership development programs: incorporating virtual collaboration concepts and skills in, 360; revamping, 428

Leadership structures: that leaders depend on, 11–12; when to use, *53*

Leadership style: generational characteristics in terms of, *266*; programs on, popularity of, issue with, 196

Leadership style, going beyond, to lead change. *See* Leading change

Leadership surveys, using, 79

Leading change: action model for fairness in, 197–199; final thoughts on, 207–209; overview of, 195–197; relating the organizational justice types to, 199–200; reminders about, 209–210; suggested actions for, 204–207; triggers for when to engage in, 200–204

Leading indicators, 74

Leading virtual teams: across the team life cycle, 230, *231*; conditions for, example of, 671–672; by coordinating, 213, 214, 221–225, *231*; as a core competence, 346; by developing potential, 213, 214, 226–230, *231*; by example, importance of, 360; final

thoughts on, 230; as a learning process, 369; by motivating, 213, 214, 215–220, *231*; overview of, 213–214; related items on the Web about, 233; reminders about, 232

Leading vs. managing, 197

Lean manufacturing, implementing, issue with, across borders, 374

Leaner media, when to use, 333

Learning: action, best practices for, 354–355, 362; additional, about culture and language, importance of, 373; adult, principles of, using, 487–488; apprenticeship, literature on, 155; in bureaucracies, 664; continuous cycle of, and action, 132, 142; distributing, 89; enacting and, in sensemaking, 135; and information sharing, 94; as knowledge transfer, 662–663; and the matrix organization, 626–627; mutual, quality of, increase in, 219; online, completion rates for, 165; opportunities for, providing, 484

Learning groups, example of, 663–665

Learning modules, training program using, example of, 355–359

Learning needs, individual, assumptions about, 288–292

Learning process, leading cross-cultural virtual teams as a, 369

Learning styles: adults varying in, best approach for, 487–488; different, complexity of, accommodating, 354; individual, 290–291; preferred, 288–289, 290; test for understanding, 487

Learning systems, use of, 55

Learning techniques, blended, using, 354

Liaisons, defined, 42

Lies, 427

Life cycle stages: human, effect of, 265; team, leading across, 223, 230, *231*

Linear creativity techniques: described, 492; portfolio of, 493–514

Linked: The New Science of Networks (Barabasi), 695

Links, silos versus, 41

Listening skills, refocusing, 201

"Listening-in" technology, use of, 313, 314

Lockheed Martin Aeronautics, 655, 657, 662, 663, 667, 668, 671, 673

London School of Economics, 339

Lost-business costs, 273

LOTAS Group, 304, 328

M

Macromedia's Breeze, 337

Maintenance of membership: agenda including, *97*; importance of, 100–101

Managed care industry, 578

Management competencies, selecting for, 638–639

Management processes, disciplined work processes and, instilling, 641–649

Management, revamping, 428

Management rework, opportunities for, matrix organization creating, 647–648

Managers: matrixed, design considerations for, 637–639, 647–648, 658; power struggles among, 627–628; role of, statement about the, 195

Managing partners: use of, 52; when to use, *53*

Managing vs. leading, 197

Mapping: of collaborative work structures and processes, 41–44; of hierarchy, and modeling as a network, 697–703; mind, 501–504, *505*, 512; of people's personal connections or networks, 694–695; process, to test assumptions about roles and responsibilities, 641–642

Matching technology and task, 8

Matrix analysis (morphological analysis), 495–498

Matrix organization: benefits of a, 625–627; case example of a, 622–625; and decision strangulation, 629; and degree of being virtual, 703; described, 620–621; designing a successful, for virtual collaboration, 629–649; and determining best practices, 628; final thoughts on, 649–650; flexibility of a, 626, 632; and integration, 626; and learning, 626–627; overview of, 619–620; pitfalls of, 627; and power struggles, 627–628; reason for choosing, case study example of, 658; related items on the Web about, 650;

reminders about, 650; and stress, 629

Matrixed managers, design considerations for, 637–639, 647–648, 658

Meaning, re-creation of, 148

Measures: goals and, creating, that are accessible to all, 73–75, 82; reliability of, 535–537; types of, considering and defining the, 74; validity of, 53, 537–539

Measuring and monitoring decisions, 615–616

Media richness: assessing technology on, 333, *334*, 335; as a challenge, 349, 350. *See also* Richer media

Medicaid program, 577

Medical care delivery virtual teams: application of the virtual integrated practice model by, 584–587; final thoughts on, 587–588; need for, 577–579; overview of, 575–577; reminders about, 588–589; and the virtual integrated practice model, 579–584

Medicare program, 577

Meditation, 515, 521–524

"Meeting Around the World: The Impact of Collaboration on

Business Performance," 481, 490

Meeting facilitators, systems requiring, 340

Meeting management: assessing skills in, 285; good practices for, establishing, 123, 147

Meeting notices, 470, *471*

Meeting plans, developing, 470

Meeting skills: lack of, 465; practicing, 486–487

Meetings: additional, organizing, 140; amount of time for, establishing, 147; efficient and effective, in a matrix organization, importance of, 644, 647; improving, role of VEtiquette in, 484–488; ineffective, 461–462; providing regular status reports through, 229; quality of, assessing, measures for, 488–489; roles for, appointing, 473, 475; setting ground rules for, 147; structured, establishing, in a matrix organization, 639; weekly, holding, issues surrounding, 224. *See also* Effective virtual meetings; Face-to-face meetings

Member identification, issue of, 6–7

Member orientation, 101–102

Member selection. *See* Team staffing

Memorial Clinical Associates, 578

Mental models: incorrect, and task division, 301, 302; shared, building, 319–322; and team staffing, 249; and training outcomes, 289

Mentoring, 55, 292

Mentors, leaders as, 11

Metaphors: new, need for, 668; using, 94–95, 517, 520, 669–671

Micromanaging, outcomes resulting from, 102

Micromessages, silent or unspoken, issue of, 417, 418, 421–427

Microsoft, 481

Microsoft Word's Online dictionary, 370

Midpoints, leading during, *231*

Millennials. *See* Nexters (Generation Y/ Millennials)

Mind mapping, 501–504, *505*, 512, 524

Mind shifts, acceptance of, for expanding emotional bandwidth, 88–90, *92*

Mindfulness, 148

Mind-sets: assessing relationships in terms of, *645*; new, need for,

669; setting the tone for specific, example, 660

Minutes, 475

Miscommunication, promoting, 122

Misconceptions, common, about working across borders, 369–374

Misinterpretation, chance of, reducing the, 336

Misperceptions, factors leading to, 9

Mission: accomplishing the, as the goal, 102; aligning purpose to, 145; communicating the, importance of, 204; contextual, 247, *248*; conveying the, 215, 216; discussing, at the initial meeting, 468; identifying, and skill requirements, 252–253

Mission parameters, skills based on, need for, example of, *257*

Mistakes, admitting, 168

Mistrust: likelihood of, 9–10; promoting, 122; shifting from, to trust, 111; and silo thinking, 40

Mixed messages, leaders sending, 637

Moderators, leaders as, 224

Modular approach, 43, 354

Modular learning program, example of, 355–359

Mondeo, the, 628

Monitoring performance, electronically, 229

Morale, impact on, of overturned decisions, 426

Morality: basing decisions on, 189; higher levels of, leadership moving followers and leaders to, 182, 184; and motivation, 191

Morphological analysis (matrix analysis), 495–498

Motivation: across the team life cycle, *231*; challenges of, addressing the, 215–220; in the DCOM Model, 80; in distance learning, issue of, 165; fundamental, 198; generational characteristics in terms of, *266*; imagery and, 515; and individual work styles, 609, 610; inspirational, 184, 215; involving rewards and punishment, 182–183; as a leadership function, 213, 214; and morality, 191; new form of, 51; relationship between feedback and, 216–217; and sensemaking, 133; in toxic environments, 207; type of leadership raising levels of, 182

Moving forward: best resources for, 142; conversations for, 146; discussing best way of, 140

Multidimensional problems, 496

Multifactor Leadership Questionnaire, 190

Multifunctional team structure, 42, 54

Multigenerational workforce: permanency of the, 268; recommendations for dealing with, 269–270; research on the, 267; statistics on the, 264

Multiple messages using multiple media, benefits of, 269

Multiple priorities, ability to take into account, 638

Multiple projects and teams, being involved in, balancing, 216

Multiplexing, problem of, 452

Myers-Briggs Type Indicator, 226, 487

Myths, about virtual teams, 361

N

Narcissism/pride, and knowledge sharing, 48–49

National Airspace System, task division in the, 298–303

National differences, issue of, 8–9

Natural teams, 480

Negotiation: of difficult tasks and role activities, 145; and matrixed managers, 639, 658; need for, when ineffectively deploying a matrix, 627; of personal work style differences, importance of, 99–100; of the responsibilities and accountabilities, 113

Netiquette, defined, 480. *See also* VEtiquette

NetMeeting, 472

Network: defining, 632, 695; strategy as a, 697–703

Network development, power of, 91

Network mapping tool, 697, 698

Networkers, leaders as, 186

Networks: accessing team member, 142; age of, 704–705; connecting through, as the process of work, 89; new science of, making use of the, 705; and relationships, developing, for a matrix organization, 631–636; skills in building, matrixed managers and, 639; study of, 695–696; as workplaces, 88–89.

See also Virtual,
networked organization

New market and product
development, increasing complexity of, 373,
374

Nexters (Generation Y/
Millennials): characteristics of, 264, *266*;
technology approach of,
265

Nike, 41

Nonverbal coordination
and communication,
303–306

Northrop Grumman, 655,
662, 664, 667, 668, 673

Note taker role, 475, 484

Not-invented-here (NIH)
syndrome, 666

O

Objective metrics, use of,
compared to subjective
cues, 228

Objective setting and
performance management, 648–649

Objectives, business, and
key success factors,
597–600, 602, 603, 604,
608, 611

Observational data, using,
607

Obtrusive data collection
methods, 276, *277*

Off-line alignment, 411

One-size-fits-all approach,
problem with, 268

"One-team" mind-set, 660

One-way communication,
51, 314

Ongoing events, as a
property of sensemaking, *138*

Online training systems,
providing, 55

Open sharing, importance
of, 50

Openness: establishing,
146, 218, 222; as
requisite, 185

Operating framework,
consideration of, 74

Operating guidelines,
importance of, for
start-ups, 453–454, 457

Operating principles,
universal language in,
creating a, 68–70, 81

Operational savings,
identifying, sample of,
560

Opportunity: conflict as,
being attuned to, 148;
in the DCOM Model,
80; understanding both
expectations and, 201

Options, comparison of,
562, 562–563

Organization: challenge of,
6–7; for efficiency, 60;
new forms of, invention
of, 41; of team members, selecting assessments that measure,
541–542. *See also*
Matrix organization

Organization design
approach, popular, to

address organizational
complexity, 694–695

Organizational boundaries,
38

Organizational care, focus
on, *198*, 201, 204, *205*,
206, 207

Organizational design
options, forms of, 41,
60. *See also* Design
principles

Organizational justice:
leadership action model
based on, 197–199;
types of, relating the, to
team leadership,
199–200

Organizational knowledge,
identifying training
needs for, 282–283,
286–287

Organizational learning,
distributing, 89

Organizational level of
analysis, 279, *286*

Organizational needs
analysis: described,
274–275; general
guidelines for,
275–276; methods
for collecting data for,
276–278; relationship
between training
needs assessment and,
278

Organizational shape,
700–701

Organizational structures:
defining aspect of, 625;
importance of, 705

Organizational support: for developing virtual competency, 360; in system of infrastructure support, *599*, 600, *601*, 602, 615

Organizational topology, varied, 702

Organizational Trust Scale (OTS), 160

Organizational-level funding, as requisite, 361

OrgScope, 698

Osterman Research, 486

Outcome fairness. *See* Distributive justice

Outcomes: alignment of purpose and, ensuring, 144–145, 149; co-creation of, 148; identified, beginning with, 102; successful, producing, *92*, 102–103

Overcommunication, culture of, promoting a, 222

Oversight, controlling, avoiding, 102

Ownership: assuming joint, 108–109, 124; building a sense of, 166, 468; greater, participation leading to, 68; lack of, in decision making, 411; shared, creating, 67

P

Paradigm shift, 181

PARC, 697

PARC's CoLab, 340

Participating and contributing, importance of, 140, 149, 165, 222, 224

Participation: boundary-free, 244; wider, producing, and the multigenerational workforce, 268

Patient self-management tools, 582, *583*

People-centric work, shift from place-centric work to, 88–89

Perception checks, 208

Perceptions: differences in, opportunities for, 148; of fairness, consideration of, 197, 200, 201, 203, 218; silent or unspoken, 425

Performance: breakdown in, example of, 298–299, *300*; framework for team staffing and, 247–251; high, virtuous cycles of, maintaining, 346; identifying potential areas for improvement in, 275; increase in, 227; and individual work styles, 610; information on, gathering and providing, 217, 228–229; interdependent nature of tasks affecting, 299–300; and operating guidelines, 453; organizational, and

collaboration, 481–482; research on, of virtual teams, 244; and trust, 10

Performance and Recognition Tracking Log template, 76

Performance management: components of, aligning, importance of, 54; objective setting, in a matrix organization, 648–649

Performance prediction, using assessments for. *See* Talent assessments

Performance standards, setting, 217–218

Permanent leaders: use of, 11, 52; when to use, *53*

Permanent team structure, 42, 54

Permeability, defined, 38

Personal analogy, 518

Personal development, feedback as key to, 228

Personal flexibility, matrix requiring, 629

Personal identity. *See* Identity

Personal preferences vs. individual ideas, 421

Personal systems, incorporating, into team design, 445, 446–447

Personal work style differences, negotiating, importance of, 99–100

Personalities and habits, talking about, 95

Problem solving:
  (*Continued*)
  synchronous and
  asynchronous,
  315–316, 394; tech-
  nique for assisting in,
  501; and types of
  problems, 395–402.
  See also Creativity
  techniques
Problem-centered
  approach to learning,
  290
Problems: complex, 399,
  400–402; preventing,
  importance of, 100;
  simple, 395–399
Problems with decision
  making, correcting.
  See Decision-making
  problems, correcting
Problem-solving teams, 480
Problem-solving theory,
  inventive, 492
Procedural justice, *198*,
  199, 200, 201, *202*, 204
Process mapping, 641–642
Process monitors
  (gatekeepers), 484–485
Process observer role, 475
Process planning, agenda
  including, *97*
Process steps, decision-
  making: current, 418–
  421; proposed, 433,
  435–436
Procrastination, avoiding,
  223–224
Procter & Gamble, 449

Product development
  team charter, example
  of a, 450
Product name generation,
  520
Profiles International, 551
Project leaders, rotating:
  use of, 52; when to use,
  53
Project management, 502,
  638
Project planning, agenda
  including, *97*
Project team purpose, 480
Project teams, cross-
  border, building
  effective, 382–389
Promises. *See* Commit-
  ments and promises
Promoters, leaders as, 186
Protective actions, 201
Proximate work models:
  and current work
  profiles, 605, *607*;
  future desired out-
  comes from, 597; and
  individual work styles,
  609; and infrastructure
  support, *601*, 602; key
  success factors of, 598;
  transition from,
  understanding the, 592
Proximity, importance of,
  155
PRTM Insight, 374
Pseudo-transformational
  leadership, 190–191
Psychological inertia,
  393–394

Punishment and rewards,
  leadership consisting
  of, 182–183
Purpose: alignment of
  outcomes and,
  ensuring, 144–145, 149;
  assessing relationships
  in terms of, *645*;
  common, engaging all
  in a, 66–67, 81; focus
  on, 133; good, speaking
  with, 159, 168–169; of
  meetings, defining the,
  470; of an organiza-
  tional needs analysis,
  clarifying the, 275;
  setting and communi-
  cating the team's, 227;
  shared, 102, 133;
  ultimate, vividly
  conveying the, 215,
  216; urgency of, and
  collaboration, 32, 33
Purpose statement,
  example of a, in
  building a business
  case, 558–559
Pyramid organizational
  shape, 700

Q

Qualitative dimension, 509
Quality Chasm, The
  (Institute of Medicine),
  576
Quality of life, learning
  that leads to, 290
Quantitative dimension,
  509

Query Space, 161–164, 166
Quick fixes, attraction of, 392

R

RACI diagram, 452–453
Radial orientation, organization chart depicting, 698, *699*
Raindance, 472
Reaction data, 488
Real estate (RE) group: and business objectives, 597; and integrated decision making, 594, *595*, 596, 604, 611; traditional decision making by, 593–594. *See also* Support systems
Real situations: ensuring training is relevant to, 290; using, to assess leader candidates, 62
Real-time collaboration, projects requiring, challenge of, 7
Real-time indicators, 74
Real-world collaboration principles: benefits from following, 688–689; failure to abide by, 689–690; final thoughts on, 691; key take-away, 682–687; overview of, 681–682
Recognition: importance of, 640; and reward programs, modifying, 428

Recommendations for the business case: described, 564; sample of, 564–566, 567
Re-creation of meaning, 148
"Red hat wargame" process, 320–321
Red teams, 480
Reengineering movement, 647
Reentry, addressing, 101–102
Reference List on Leading Virtual Teams—Dan Novak, 230
Reflection, intervention aimed at, providing an, 229
Reina Team Trust Quiz, 161
Reina Trust and Betrayal Model, 156–159, 171, 172
Relationship Health Check tool, 644, *645–646*
Relationship Map, 633, *634*, 642, 650
Relationship vs. task oriented, *376*, 379–380
Relationship-oriented leaders, 187
Relationships: the 5 C's of conversations and, 143–150; among matrixed managers, 637–639, 647–648, 658; assessing the state of, tool for, 644, *645–646*;

building, importance of, 93, 94, 221–222, 467, 633, 661–662; complexity of, increasing, effect of, 154; deeper, creating, 141; developing, trust factor in, 146, 155, 156; dynamic, as the foundation of effective sensemaking, 132, 133, 135, 141–142, 143; and electronic communication, 89, 155; establishing and sustaining, importance of, 483; existing, capitalizing on, 122; giving personal attention to building, 186; good, defined, 631; individualistic vs. collectivist cultures and, 377; networks and, developing, for a matrix organization, 631–636; with a purpose in team settings, definition of, 33; reporting, vs. organizational structures, 625; role, leaders articulating, 11; supporting, 94; trust in, and communication, 370; trusting, seeking, being proactive in, 124; using, as the connecting point, 91. *See also* Depth of relationships

Relevancy of assessments, 539, 540, 548

Relevant information, gathering and applying, 134

Relevant training, importance of, 290

Reliability: consistent, and trust, 98; of data collection methods, investment in, 596; of measures, 535–537, 538, 539, 540, 545; of team members, selecting assessments that measure, 541–542

Reliability coefficients, 537

Replanning, plan adaptation and, coordination during, 306–308

Reporting percentages, 700, 703

Reporting relationships, lateral. See Matrix organization

Reputation: relationships developed based on, 115–116; trust based on, 97

Resilience, 185

Resources: accessing, 142; acquiring, 149; competition for, 627, 628; deployment of, decisions about, 555, 556; investment in, for data-driven decision making, 596; making

the business case for, 555–556; matrixed, sharing, selecting who will be, 638; prioritizing and allocating, 274, 624; providing, 140, 220; shared, and task interdependencies, 300–301, 301–302, 303; shifting of, allowing the, 626; unequal sharing of, and performance appraisal, 648–649; for virtual team training, providing, 704; withholding, 348

Respect: importance of, 200, 479; nurturing an environment of, 428

Responsibilities, roles and. See Roles and responsibilities

Responsibility: charting, 642, 643; collective, quality of, increase in, 219; in decision making, 417; for developing and maintaining relationships, assuming, 123, 633; individual task, shift from, trend of, 681; in shared leadership, 196; for work structures and processes, 63. See also Accountability; Shared responsibility

Responsibility Charting, 642, 643, 650

Restraining forces, understanding, analysis for, 498–501

Restricted communication: awareness of, 360; as a challenge, 347, 349–350; learning module addressing, 355, 356, 359

Results, assessing relationships in terms of, 646

Results catalyst, leaders as, 11

Results orientation, culture of, impact of, 425

Resynchronization, 309

Retirement, 267, 268

Retrospect, as a property of sensemaking, 137

Reward and recognition programs, modifying, 428

Reward procedures, 360

Reward system, realignment of the, 640

Rewards: and punishment, leadership consisting of, 182–183; shared, example of, 659

Richer media: appropriateness of, 333; benefits of, 215–216, 218, 223; promoting use of, 218, 222

Risk aversion and the loss of ideas, impact of, 422

Risk parameters, defining, importance of, 637

Risk taking, sending mixed messages about, 637

Risk tolerance vs. uncertainty avoidance, *376*, 381–382

Role clarity, 146, 452–453

Role confusion or conflict, 424

Role differentiation, 424

Role modeling: as essential to successful collaboration, 672; of good decision making, 428; providing, 55

Role models, leaders as, 11, 186, 672

Role relationships, leaders articulating, 11

Roles and Decision Accountability Matrix, 71–73

Roles and Decision Accountability template, 71

Roles and responsibilities: ability to perform, 159, 169; alignment of, 359; clarifying, for effective team start-ups, 452–453; clarity around, designing, 641–642, 658; decision-making, and process steps, current, 418–421; defining and clarifying, importance of, 394, 428, 431, 484; for effective decision making, 428, *430–431*; establishing accountability for, in decision making, 71–73, 81; exploring, when

positioning leaders, 64; identifying, importance of, 71; issues associated with, in the decision-making process, 424; for meetings, appointing, 473, 475; negotiating the, 113; open dialogue regarding, in relation to goals, creating a forum for, 122; understanding, of every other team member, importance of, 124, 447

Roles, playing multiple, issue of, 10–11

Rotating team leaders: use of, 11, 52; when to use, *53*

Royal Air Force, 667

Royal Navy, 667

Rush University Medical Center, 579, 585

S

Salient cues, as a property of sensemaking, *137*

Sameness, misconception of, 371–372

SAMM system, 340

Sample Review Plan, 75

SAP system, 698, 702

Saturn, 398

Scale scores, 548–549

SCAMPER, 506–507, 509

Scenario selection, 604

Scenarios, predicted effectiveness of, in decision making, 603

Scheduling: challenge of, 7, 8; relationship building and, 94; and virtual communities, 88

Scientific American, 696, 697

Scribe, 475, 484

Selecting leaders, 61–64

Self-assessment, opportunity for, offering, 289

Self-confidence, leaders having, 185, 189, 219

Self-Directed Search, 535

Self-discipline, of team members, selecting assessments that measure, 541–542

Self-esteem: enhanced, fairness and, 200; higher, learning that leads to, 290

Self-image, developing, 94–95

Self-led teams: use of, 52; when to use, *53*

Self-managing teams (SMTs): coaching, 227; as key, 106; and the need for trust, 110

Self-motivation, selecting assessments that measure, 542

Self-perception, 134

Self-sacrifice, issue of, 203, 207

Self-worth, feelings of, 159, 170

Semiconsultative method, *416*

use, problem of, 180; to build shared mental models, 319–322; ensuring, 322; initial opportunity for, providing, 354; and mental models, 249; regarding challenging issues, 140

Shortsighted decisions, 425

Signaling protocols, agreeing to, 353

Silence, interpreting, 201

Silent messages, premature and, impact of, 422–423

Silent micromessages, issue of, 417, 418, 421–427

Silent perceptions, 425

Silo thinking, 39–40, 60

Silos: bypassing, 91; versus links, 41; and pride, 48; teams embedded in, 39, *40*

Simple problems: characteristics of, 395; example of, 395–396; problem-solving methods for, 396–399

Simple technology, 471, 472, *473*

Simplicity, creating, in the foreground, 147

Simultaneity interdependency, 300, 301

Single-function team structure, 42, 54

Single-technology solution, 362

Situation assessment, example of a, in building a business case, 559

Situation awareness, 303, 313, 314

Six-step problem-solving method, 396–399

16PF, 535

60 Minutes, 456

Skills assessment for predicting performance. *See* Talent assessments

Skills, knowledge, and abilities (SKA): multitude of, need for, 273; portability of, 274; requisite, providing a checklist of, 289. *See also specific skills, knowledge, and abilities*

SMART Boards, 521

SMART model, 73–74

Social capital, building, 631–641

Social cohesion, 250, 251

Social context, as a property of sensemaking, *137*

Social information sharing, issue of, 250

Social network analysis, 694–695

Social presence: assessing technology on, 333, *334,* 335, 336; as a challenge, 349, 350

Social processes, quality of, increase in, 219

Social-based trust, fostering, 10

Socialization, 659, 660, 671

Society for Human Resource Management (SHRM), 264, 267, 291, 294

Society for Morphological Research, 496

Sociology, new, 87–88

Sociotechnical systems (STS) perspective: described, 444; illustrated, *445;* incorporating other systems in, *446, 447*

Softboards, 338

Solidarity, factor in, 155

Solutions: alternative or potential, identifying and assessing, 394, 400, 401, 402; dilution of, potential problems associated with, 426–427; quality of, factor in the, 148; and the six-step problem-solving process, 397, 398; testing or piloting, 135. *See also* Problem solving

Spatial boundaries, 37–38

Spatial dimension, 508

Specific task work skills, 247, *248,* 253, 254, 255, *256*

Specific teamwork skills, 247, *248,* 253, 255, *256*

Stakeholder analysis, 77

Stakeholder maps, creation of, benefit of, 359

Stakeholders: contacting, 141; demonstrating success to, example of, 557–566; interests of, not representing and aligning, 425–426; power distribution among, 654; understanding perspectives of and gaining consensus among, for problem solving, 400

Standard operating procedures, setting, 225

Standardization, determining, in a matrix organization, 628

Standardized processes in the VIP model, 580–581

Standardized training, 362

Stand-Up Meetings as Accountability Generating Exchange Tool, 147

Starpoints, defined, 42

Start-up perspectives and tools: and chartering tips, 451–452; and designing new virtual teams, 444–447; final thoughts on, 457; for focusing new virtual teams, 447–456; overview of, 443–444; reminders about, 457–458; for work and

home life balance, 446, 456–457

Start-up stage, leading during the, 215, 216, 223, *231*, 671–672

Statsoft, 537, 551

Status reports, regular, providing, 229

"Stealth Training for Virtual Audiences" (Finley), 357

Stereotyping: overcoming, 671; and trust, 110

Stories, shared, creating, 98

Storytelling, engaging in, 665

Stranded in the Desert survival exercise, 226

Strategic Choice Model, 599, 600, 603, 611, 615

Strategic planning, 502

Strategy: assessing relationships in terms of, *645*; implementation, effective, creating an, 612–614; as a network, 697–703

Stress, 464, 629. *See also* Burnout

Stress management, 515, 522

Stretch assignments, 638

Structure, clear, importance of, 102

Subject matter expertise (SME) on the work content, identifying training needs for, 283–284, *286–287*. *See also* Expertise

Subjective cues, use of objective metrics compared to, 228

Subjective problems, 496

Subordinate satisfaction, enhancing, 182

Substantive dimension, 508

Success: benchmarking for, 543–549; commitment to others', 33; as dependent on collaboration, 34; establishing confidence through, 220; probability of, conditions for the, 59–60

Success factors: business objectives and, 597–600, 602, 603, 604, 608, 611; commonly agreed upon, 32; documenting, to measure decision effectiveness, 615–616; identifying, 346, 350–353

Successful outcomes, producing, *92*, 102–103

Successful virtual collaboration: achieving, 119–124; case example of, 125–126; and the depth of relationships, 107, *108*, 114–117, 118, 119, 120; essential conditions for, case study example of, 671–673; final thoughts on, 126; individual promotion of, *121*, 123–124; key ingredients for, 106–108; mix of ingredients for, 114–119; organizational promotion of, 120, *121*, 122–123; overview of, 105–106; reminders about, 126–127; through shared understanding, 107, *108*, 113–114, 115, 117, 118, 119, 120; trust as essential to, 107, *108*, 110–113, 115, 116, 117, 118, 119, 120; as a win-win effort, 108–109

Summary for the business case: described, 564; sample of, 564–566, 567

Sun Microsystems, 592, 593, 594, 596, 597, 599, 600, 606, 608, 609, 610, 611, 615, 616, 617

Superficial commitment, 423

Supply gap, 611

Support functions, meeting people and, 96

Support systems: aligning and sustaining, 54–55; collaboration, *334*, 336–340; continuous investment in, 56; deficits in, 554; garnering, the business case as a vehicle for, 557; integrated, *599*, 600; organizational, for reinforcing effects of training, 360. *See also*

Infrastructure support systems

Supporting decisions, 419, 420

Supportive culture, crafting a, 43–47, 447

"Survey: Physician EMR Use Grows," 579, 589

Surveys, periodic, conducting, 79–80, 648

Sustainability, designing for, 78–80, 82

Swift trust, 352

Symbolic analogy, 518

Symbols, using, 94–95

Synchronization, 308, 353–354. *See also* Coordination

Synchronous communication/technology, defined, 223, 332

Synectics problem-solving method, 518

Synergy: perpetuating, 101; positive, source of, 109

T

T³training model, 355–359

Tacit knowledge, 50, 282

Tailored organizational responses, creating, 54

Talent assessments: and associating traits with virtual collaboration, 542–543; benchmarking for, 543–549; final thoughts on, 549–550; good practices for, and

the Department of Labor, 535–541; history of, 534–535; investigating options when selecting tools for, 539–541; overview of, 533–534; reminders about, 550–551; selecting, as a tool for predicting virtual collaboration success, 541–542

"Taming the problem," 400, 401–402

Tangible benefits, statement of, sample of a, 561

Tangibles, specific, technique focusing, 493

Task assignments, 223–224, 322

Task cohesion, 250–251

Task complexity, innovation and, 668

Task division, 296, 298–303

Task information sharing, issue of, 250

Task interdependencies, issue of, 299–301, 668, 669

Task management, 502

Task modules, 355, *356*

Task uncertainty, innovation and, 668

Task vs. relationship oriented, *376*, 379–380

Task work requirements, consideration of, 245, 252–253

Task work skills: generic, 247, *248*, 253; specific, 247, *248*, 253, 254
Task-centered approach to learning, 290
Task-related boundaries, 38
Task-technology matching, 471–472, *473*
Task-technology mismatch, 465
Tavistock Institute, 444
Teaching teams. *See* Educating team members
TEAM acronym, meaning of, 33
Team atmosphere, 94
Team building: activities of, importance of, 480–481; and developing potential, 226; effective, in order to combat confusion, 382–383, *384–388*; and networks, 89; using brainstorming for, 511
Team composition: differences in, 482–483; diversity and fluidity of, 347; reflection of, 245; stabilizing, 363; and technology selection for meetings, 472. *See also* Team staffing
Team concept, fathers of the, 444
Team confidence, developing, 219

Team design principles: of creating accessible goals and measures, 73–75; of creating a plan to "cast" the net wider, 77–78; of creating a universal language in operating principles, 68–70; of creating the context of energy and understanding, 67–68; of designing for sustainability, 78–80; of documenting work processes, 70–71; of engaging all in a common vision, purpose, and destiny, 66–67; final thoughts on, 80; overview of, 59–61; and related items on the Web, 82; reminders about, 80–82; of selecting and positioning leaders, 61–66; of setting up feedback and celebration mechanisms, 75–77
Team designs, described, 42
Team development process: factor in, 155; feedback as key to, 228; importance of, 95–96; and maintenance, 100–101; planning for the, 557; sensemanager's role in, 145;

setting for the, 288. *See also* Virtual collaboration training and development programs
Team Development Process Checklist, 96
Team Feedback System, 533
Team formation, 223–224
Team identification, challenge of, 6–7
Team identity: creation of, enabling the, 114; developing, 94–95; emphasizing, during meetings, 224; establishing a, motivation and, 218–220; weakening the sense of, 629
Team interdependency, 301
Team life cycle, leading across the, 223, 230, *231*
Team meetings. *See* Meetings
Team members: assigning tasks and deadlines to, 223–224; believing in your, importance of, 110–113; dissatisfaction of, cues to, 197; performance of, quality of, ensuring, need for, 11
Team member traits, assessing, 541–543
Team modules, 355, *356*
Team planning process, importance of, 95–96
Team processes: appropriate levels of,

promoting, goal of, 252; influence of emergent states on, 249, 250, 251; superordinate categories of, 247, *248*, 249

Team selection, assessing talent for. *See* Talent assessments

Team staffing: final thoughts on, 255–258; overview of, 243–246; reminders about, 258; steps in, 252–255; strategy for, framework for, 246–251

Team states: appropriate levels of, promoting, goal of, 252; influence of, and staffing, 247, *248*, 249–251

Team structures, 42, 155, 480

Team support, *92*, 96–102

Team Wave Software's Workplace, 337

Team Web sites, benefit of, 469

Team Web templates, 338–339

Team-based work, as key, 106

TeamFocus, 340

Teams: failure of, to achieve virtual collaboration, causes of, 689–690; importance of, 243; reasons for, 666; structural dimensions of, 42. *See also specific type of team*

Teamwork: and joint accountability, creating a culture of, 639–641; requirements for, consideration of, 245, 246–247, 252–253; shift to, trend of, 681; teaching, major principles in, 577

Teamwork skills: generic, 247, *248*, 253–254; specific, 247, *248*, 253, 255

Technical boundaries, 37

Technical complexity, 654

Technological support, in system of infrastructure support, *599*, 600, *601*, 602, 615

Technology: access to, generational differences in, issue of, 267; for attribute listing, 495; best practices and recommendations for using, 308–316, *323*; as a challenge, 4, *5*, 8, 349, 465; complex forms of, 472; consideration of the audience for, 269; coordinating, 146–147; and designing for sustainability, 79; effect of, 6; for ensuring needed interaction, 302; generational differences in approaches to, 265, 267, 291; hiding behind, 224; impact of, 154; improvements in, relying on, 43; integrating, into patient-provider communication and collaboration, leaders in, 578; for intuitive techniques, 516, 518–519, 521, 523–524; knowledge of, as necessary, 2; learning new, providing accessible training for, 269–270; for linear techniques, 495, 498, 500–501, 504, 511, 514; measures accessible through, identifying, 73; metrics for, establishing and monitoring, 270; new, issue with, 180; newest, teaching all employees how to use, issue of, 267–268; protocols for, setting, 454–456, 457; rate of developments in, and the aging population, issue of, 263–264; relationship between people and, 89; relying on, 213, 215; selecting, for meetings, 470–472, *473*; simple forms of, 471; and social capital, 631; successful use of, dependent on employee's experience and attitude, 224–225;

needs, 288–292; conducting an organizational needs analysis prior to a, 274–278; final thoughts on, 292; overview of, 273–274; relationship between organizational needs analysis and, *278*; reminders about, 292–293; and training content areas, 281–288; for virtual collaboration, 278–281

Training programs, developing: and consideration of the audience in, 269; for educating team members, 123; for enhancing leaders' transformational behaviors, 190; for learning new technology, recommendations for, 269–270; that consider individual learning needs, 288; unnecessarily, avoiding the mistake of, 274. *See also* Virtual collaboration training and development programs

Training specialist, 278

Transactional leadership models, 181, 182–183, 190

Transactional trust: building, online application of, 166–170;

consistently practicing behaviors that build, result of, 171; facets of, 157, *158*, 159; as the foundation for virtual collaboration, 159–166

Transformational leadership: actual and ideal attributes of, 187–189; characteristics of leaders in, 184–187; final thoughts on, 191; foundation of, 181–184; overview of, 179–180; and an overview of leadership, 180–181; reminders about, 191; shift to, 181; vs. transactional leadership, 182–183; weaknesses in, 190–191

Transformative trust, 171–172

Transition processes, 247

Transparent funding, see

Transparent organization, becoming a. *See* Virtual, networked organization

Travel expenses, virtual meetings saving on, 462

Trust: actions to promote, *121*, 122–123, 124; assessing relationships in terms of, *646*; audio and video systems and, 336; benefits of, 153–154; breakdown in, effect of, 353; as a challenge, 4, *5*, 9–10;

conditions that establish, team building creating, 226; and constructive accountability, 139; as a critical success factor, 350, 351–352; definitions of, 106–107, 250; developing, importance of, 97–98; erosion of, in decision making, 425; as essential to successful collaboration, 107, *108*, 110–113, 115, 116, 117, 118, 119, 120; as a factor in developing relationships, 146, 155, 156; forms of, 110–111; fragility of, 102; giving, to competitors as full partners, 673; and incompatible technology, 8; increase in, result of, 171; individualistic vs. collectivist cultures and, 377; influence between communication and, 159; and information sharing, 159, 479, 482; and knowledge sharing, 48; in leadership, enhancing, 182; learning module addressing, 355, *356*; major factors of, understanding the, importance of, 635–636; member

Trust: (*Continued*)
identification linked to, 6; mutual, 154, 186, 189, 631; nurturing an environment of, 428; and organizational design, 60; and perceived control, 136; persistent breach of, 168; as a prerequisite to the success in teams, 389; principle of, 406; and relationship building, 221; as requisite, 185, 187, 370; and restricted communication, 349, 350; selecting assessments that measure, 542; and team coaching, 227; and team fluidity, issue of, 363; and team staffing, 250; transformative, 171–172

Trust building: application of, using the online program, 166–170; direct, difficulty of, 353; final thoughts on, 172–173; in horizontal integration, example of, 661–662; importance of, continuous awareness of, 346; by keeping commitments and promises, 10, 110, 118, 124, 159, 167, *635*, 636; model for, 156–159; overview of, 153–154; for problem solving, 400; program for, using virtual collaboration, 160–166; related items on the Web about, 174; reminders about, 173–174; and task vs. relationship-oriented cultures, 379, 380; transformative potential in, 171–172; in the virtual environment, 154–156; for virtual team meetings, 467

Trust Building Online: application of, 166–170; development of, 160–161; final thoughts on, 172–173; key features of, 161–165; learning from the initial design of, 165–166

Trustworthiness, importance of, 185, 187, 189, 218

Truth-telling. *See* Honesty

Turfs, development of, 410

Turnover: and employee dissatisfaction, 546; and individual work styles, 610; and trust, 154

Twenty-four-hour workdays, issue of, 7, 8, 34, 335, 445, 556

Two-way communication, 51

2 × 2 Leadership Matrix 64–66

U

Unanimous decision-making method, 485

Uncertainty: and morphological analysis, 496; potential for, creating the, 113; and sensemaking, 131, 135, 136; task, and innovation, 668

Uncertainty avoidance vs. risk tolerance, *376*, 381–382

Understanding: conceptual, creating, technique for, 517; context for, creating the, 67–68, 81; ensuring, 144–145; facilitating, in problem solving, 400; gaps in, attention to, 44; greater, achieving, 134; holistic, adding, 132; need for, in focusing new teams, 447. *See also* Sensemaking; Shared/mutual understanding

United Airlines, 63

U.K. military, 667

U.S. Air Force, 655, 667

U.S. Army Corps, 307–308

U.S. Department of Defense, 655

U.S. Department of Health and Human Services, 576, 589

U.S. Department of Labor Employment and Training Administration, 535, 537, 538, 540, 551

U.S. health care system, issues facing the, 575, 576–577, 579, 587–588

U.S. Marine Corps, 655

U.S. Navy, 655, 667

U.S. workforce, generational composition of the, 264

Unity, atmosphere of, development of an, 428

Universal House of Justice, 433, 438

Universal language, creating a, in operating principles, 68–70, 81

University of Arizona, 340

University of British Columbia, 153

University of Minnesota, 340

Unobtrusive data collection methods, 276, *277*, 606

Unspoken micromessages, issue of, 417, 418, 421–427

Unspoken perceptions, 425

Usability of assessments, 537

User-friendly technology, ensuring, 147

V

Validity: of data collection methods, investment in, 596; of measures, 535, 537–539, 540, 545, 548

Validity coefficient, 538

Value added, assessing relationships in terms of, *646*

Values: agenda including, *97*; core, generational characteristics in terms of, *266*

Velcro, 516

Ventana Corporation, 340

Verbal proficiency, of team members, selecting assessments that measure, 542

Verizon Business, 481

Vertical integration, example of, 659–661

Veterans, characteristics of, 264, *266*

Veterans Health Administration (VHA) Medical Center, 578

VEtiquette: and common features of teams, 480–481; defining and describing, 480; and differences between teams, 482–484; final thoughts on, 489; and openness, 481–482; overview of, 479; practices and lessons of, 484–488; reminders about, 489–490

Veto power: charting, 642, *643*; issue of, 426

VHA Medical Center, 578

Vicious cycles, 352

Video systems: assessing, *334*; described, 335, 336

Video technologies, use of, for coordination and communication, 310–312. *See also* Technology

Virtual collaboration: associating team member traits with, using assessments for, 542–543; benefits of, 688–689; business results of, 3; defined, 2; designing a successful matrix for, 629–649; drivers of, model depicting, *108*; effective, requirements for, 60; failure to achieve, causes of, 689–690; and generational differences, 268; impact of, 412; importance of good design for, 59–60; in medicine and primary care, challenges to, 579; and the path toward high-performance virtual teams, 5; predicting successful, assessment as a tool for, 541–542; skill of, facilitating the, importance of, 154; training needs assessment for, 278–281. *See also* Successful virtual collaboration

Virtual Collaboration Design Worksheet, 80

Virtual collaboration needs, training content areas for, 281–288

Virtual collaboration training and development programs: characteristics of effective, 353–354; conditions for successful, 360–362; creating, 362–363; final thoughts on, 363–364; and identifying the challenges of working virtually, 346–350; and identifying the key success factors of working virtually, 346, 350–353; modular learning program for, 355–359; overview of, 345–346; reminders about, 364

Virtual communication tools. *See* Electronic communication; Technology

Virtual communities, building. *See* Community building

Virtual, defined, 87

Virtual design teams, knowledge transfer and learning on. *See* Knowledge transfer case study

Virtual integrated practice (VIP) model: application of the, 584–587; described, 575, 579–584

Virtual integrated product teams (VIPTs), case study involving. *See* Knowledge transfer case study

"Virtual Meetings and Virtual Teams," 470, 472, 478

Virtual, networked organization: birth of the, 694–695; case study of a, 696–704; and hierarchy, 695–696; increasing visibility of the, 704–705; overview of, 693

Virtual, questioning how virtual is, 703

Virtual reality, meaning of, 87

Virtual team creations, as a challenge, 4, 5. *See also* Culture; Leadership; Trust

Virtual team givens, as a challenge, 4, 5. *See also* Distance; Technology; Time

Virtual teaming, feeling of, 87

Virtual teams: common features of colocated and, 480–481; defined and described, 2–3; differences between colocated teams and, 482–484; myth about, 361; purposes of, 3; research on, 244–245. *See also specific aspects of virtual teams*

Virtual watercooler, 469

Virtual work spaces, shared, using, 315–316, 317

Virtual work systems best practices. *See* Work systems design concepts

Virtual work, way of thinking about, 87, 88. *See also* Emotional bandwidth, expanding

Virtuous cycles: first step in, 354; of high performance, maintaining, 346; and vicious cycles, 352

Vision: of accomplishing a purpose, beginning with a, 102; agenda including, *97*; aligning purpose to, 145; assessing relationships in terms of, *645*; clearly communicating, 187, 189, 204, 215, 216; common, engaging all in a, 66–67, 81; compelling, creating a, 61, 204, 215–216; discussing, at the initial meeting, 468

Vision statements, drafting, 66

VisionQuest, 340

Visual brainstorming, 521

Voice loop technologies, use of, issue of, 312–314

Voice mail protocols, 455–456

Voice over Internet protocol (VOIP), using, to connect and interact, 115

Voting, 340

Voting method, *415*

W

Wal-Mart, 41

War game scenario, 320–321

Watercooler talk, 95

Watson Wyatt Worldwide, 153, 175

Web networks, study of, 695–696

Web templates, team, 338–339

WebEx, 472

Weekly meetings, holding, issues surrounding, 224

What, focusing on just the, issue with, 67

Why, grounding team members in the, benefits of, 67–68

Wiki, 472

Wilson Learning Styles Inventory, 487

Winning, view of, and organizational design, 60

Win-win effort, successful collaboration as a, 108–109

Win-win situation, defined, 107–108

Wisdom of Teams, The (Katzenbach & Smith), 32

Withdrawal, 196, 199

Work and home life: balancing, 446, 456–457; boundaries between, 445; considering, 216; disrupting balance in, 464

Work assignment interactions, appropriate, need for, 481

Work content expertise, identifying training needs for, 283–284, *286–287. See also* Expertise

Work ethic, generational characteristics in terms of, *266*

Work group level of analysis, 279–280, *287*

Work hours, issue of, and balancing home life, 446, 456–457. *See also* Twenty-four-hour workdays

Work plans, agreed-on, importance of, 102

Work processes: collaborative, 41–44, 51; creating, at the heart of design, 70; designing, best practices and recommendations for, 296, 298–307, *323*; disciplined, and management processes, instilling, 641–649; documenting, that are reliable and repeatable, 70–71, 81; formal or informal, determining, 285; improving, teams

for, 480; responsibility for, 63; skills and knowledge in collaborative, identifying training needs for, 285, *286–287*

Work profiles, current, 605–608

Work, redefining, 88–90, *92*

Work requirements, consideration of, 245

Work spaces: adequate, providing, 55; shared virtual, using, 315–316, 317

Work structures, collaborative, 41–44, 51

Work styles: differences in, negotiating, importance of, 99–100; and preferences, using data on, 608–610

Work systems design concepts: on building shared perspectives, 316–322, *323*; on designing work processes, 296, 298–307, *323*; final thoughts on, 322, *323*; overview of, 295–296, *297*; reminders about, 322, 324; on using technology to communicate and coordinate, 308–316, *323*

Workdays, around-the-clock. *See* Twenty-four-hour workdays

Work-family life, issues of.
See Work and home life
Workforce: generational
composition of the,
264; intergenerational,
advantages vs. disad-
vantages of an, 267;
multigenerational, 264,
267, 268, 269–270
Working across boundaries:
and the characteristics
of collaboration, 32–34;
common misconcep-
tions about, 369–374;
and fairness, 198; final

thoughts on, 56;
framework for educat-
ing team members in,
creating a, based on
principles, 40–56; and
organizational design,
60; overview of, 31–32;
reminders about, 56;
and understanding
boundary crossing,
34–40
Workload priorities, 363
Workplace, physical,
supporting the, *599*,
600, 601, 602, 615

Workshops, providing, 55
"World Car, The: Enter the
McFord," 628, 651
World War II, 264, 444
World War II generation
(veterans), characteris-
tics of, 264, *266*

X

Xerox, 340, 396, 697

Z

Zen literature, story from,
48–49
Zero-sum game, 628